58th Annual Meeting of the Association for Computational Linguistics (ACL 2020)

System Demonstrations

Online
5 – 10 July 2020

ISBN: 978-1-7138-1373-6

ACL 2020

**The 58th Annual Meeting of the
Association for Computational Linguistics**

Proceedings of the System Demonstrations

July 5- July 10, 2020

Introduction

Welcome to the proceedings of the system demonstrations session. This volume contains the papers of the system demonstrations presented at the 58th Annual Meeting of the Association for Computational Linguistics on July 5th - July 10th, 2020. This year the ACL 2020 will be an online conference.

The ACL 2020 demonstrations track invites submissions ranging from early research prototypes to mature production-ready systems. We received 122 submissions this year, of which 43 were selected for inclusion in the program (acceptance rate of 35%) after reviewed by three members of the program committee. We would like to thank the members of the program committee for their timely help in reviewing the submissions.

Lastly, we thank the many authors that submitted their work to the demonstrations track. This year, the ACL conference is completely virtual. The demonstrations paper talks are pre-recorded (12 minutes) and will be presented during the two live Q&A video sessions at different times, and a linked RocketChat channel. Each day we will have 2 demonstration track Q&A sessions in different time zones across the world.

Best,
Asli Celikyilmaz and Tsung-Hsien Wen
ACL 2020 Demonstration Track Chairs

Organizers:

Asli Celikyilmaz, Microsoft Research
Tsung-Hsien Wen, Poly-AI

Program Committee:

Malihe Alikhani, University of Pittsburgh
Pepa Atanasova, University of Copenhagen
Awais Athar, European Molecular Biology Laboratory, European Bioinformatics Institute (EMBL-EBI)
Sumit Bhatia, IBM Research
Georgeta Bordea, Université de Bordeaux
Shulin Cao, Tsinghua University
Yun-Nung Chen, National Taiwan University
Lu Chen, Shanghai Jiao Tong University
Xiang Gao, Microsoft Research
Ridong Jiang, Institute for Infocomm Research
Nikita Moghe, University of Edinburgh
Pei-Hao Su, PolyAI
Stergos Afantenos, IRIT and CNRS, University of Toulouse
Chaitanya Ahuja, Carnegie Mellon University
Hassan Alhuzali, The University of Manchester
Cecilia Ovesdotter Alm, Rochester Institute of Technology
Malik H. Altakrori, McGill University /Mila
Prithviraj Ammanabrolu, Georgia Institute of Technology
Mihael Arcan, National Universith of Ireland Galway
Arkady Arkhangorodsky, DiDi Labs
Eleftherios Avramidis, German Research Center for Artificial Intelligence (DFKI)
He Bai, University of Waterloo
Pratyay Banerjee, Arizona State University
Ritwik Banerjee, Stony Brook University
Siqi Bao, Baidu
Mohaddeseh Bastan, Stony Brook University
Timo Baumann, Universität Hamburg
Núria Bel, Universitat Pompeu Fabra
Meriem Beloucif, University of Hamburg
Gábor Berend, University Of Szeged
Leon Bergen, University of California, San Diego
Archna Bhatia, Florida Institute for Human and Machine Cognition
Parminder Bhatia, Amazon
Wei Bi, Tencent AI Lab
Sebastian Bischoff, Technical University of Munich
Rexhina Blloshmi, Sapienza University of Rome
Chris Brockett, Microsoft Research
Jill Burstein, ETS
Andrew Caines, University of Cambridge
Ilias Chalkidis, Athens University of Economics and Business
Guan-Lin Chao, Carnegie Mellon University

Hanjie Chen, University of Virginia
Jun Chen, Baidu Inc
Shizhe Chen, Renmin University of China
Alok Debnath, International Institute of Information Technology, Hyderabad
Louise Deléger, INRAE - Université Paris-Saclay
Shumin Deng, Zhejiang University
Yuntian Deng, Harvard University
Mihail Eric, Amazon Alexa AI
Lucie Flek, Mainz University of Applied Sciences
Varun Gangal, Carnegie Mellon University
Andrew Gargett, Science and Technology Facilities Council
Maram Hasanain, Qatar University
Bjorn Hoffmeister, Apple
Julie Hunter, LINAGORA
Varun Kumar, Amazon Alexa
Jiaqi Li, Harbin Institute of Technology
Pierre Lison, Norwegian Computing Centre
José Lopes, Heriot Watt University
Alex Marin, Microsoft Corporation
Héctor Martínez Alonso, Apple Inc
Mohsen Mesgar, UKP Lab, Technische Universität Darmstadt
Junta Mizuno, NICT
Zheng-Yu Niu, Baidu Inc.
Vasile Rus, The University of Memphis
Ethan Selfridge, Interactions LLC
Igor Shalyminov, Heriot-Watt University
Jun Xu, Harbin Institute of Technology
Xiaohui Yan, Huawei
Yujiu Yang, tsinghua.edu.cn
Semih Yavuz, Salesforce Research
Koichiro Yoshino, Nara Institute of Science and Technology
Erion Çano, Institute of Formal and Applied Linguistics, Charles University in Prague
Abdalghani Abujabal, Amazon Alexa AI
Manoj Acharya, Rochester Institute of Technology
Shubham Agarwal, Heriot Watt University
Rodrigo Agerri, IXA Group, HiTZ Centre, University of the Basque Country UPV/EHU
Željko Agić, Corti
Roee Aharoni, Google
Mohammad Amin Alipour, University of Houston
Miguel A. Alonso, Universidade da Coruña
Rafael Anchiêta, University of São Paulo
Diego Antognini, EPFL
Jun Araki, Bosch Research
Rahul Aralikatte, University of Copenhagen
Hiba Arnaout, Max Planck Institute for Informatics
Akari Asai, University of Washington
Rohit Babbar, Aalto University
Ashutosh Baheti, The Ohio State University
Jorge Balazs, University of Tokyo
Ioana Baldini, IBM Research
Sameer Bansal, Bloomberg LP

James Barry, ADAPT Centre DCU
Valerio Basile, University of Turin
Tilman Beck, UKP Lab, Technische Universität Darmstadt
Ahmad Beirami, Facebook AI
Fernando Benites, Zurich University of Applied Sciences
Eduardo Blanco, University of North Texas
Rishi Bommasani, Cornell University
Laura Ana Maria Bostan, IMS, University of Stuttgart
Florian Boudin, Université de Nantes
Ed Cannon, Expedia Group
Qingqing Cao, Stony Brook University
Spencer Caplan, University of Pennsylvania
Angel Chang, Simon Fraser University
Chung-Chi Chen, Department of Computer Science and Information Engineering National Taiwan
University, Taipei, Taiwan
Guanyi Chen, Utrecht University
Huiyuan Chen, Case Western Reserve University
Fenia Christopoulou, School of Computer Science, The University of Manchester
George Chrysostomou, The University of Sheffield
Yagmur Gizem Cinar, Univ. Grenoble Alpes
Shaobo Cui, Alibaba Group
Xiang Dai, University of Sydney
Forrest Davis, Cornell University
Luciano Del Corro, Max Planck Institute for Informatics
Ning Ding, Tsinghua University
Ondřej Dušek, Charles University
Zhenxin Fu, Peking University
Saadia Gabriel, University of Washington
Matt Gardner, Allen Institute for Artificial Intelligence
Rahul Goel, Google
Sharath Chandra Guntuku, University of Pennsylvania
Mandy Guo, Google
Matthew Henderson, PolyAI
Benjamin Hoover, IBM Research; MIT-IBM Lab
Hen-Hsen Huang, Department of Computer Science, National Chengchi University
Binxuan Huang, CMU
Ali Hürriyetoğlu, Koç University
Jeff Jacobs, Columbia University
Feng Ji, Alibaba Group
Pei Ke, Tsinghua University
Joo-Kyung Kim, Amazon Alexa AI
Gunhee Kim, Seoul National University
Ekaterina Lapshinova-Koltunski, Universität des Saarlandes
Xintong Li, The Ohio State University
Yanran Li, The Hong Kong Polytechnic University
Yang Li, Google
Maolin Li, University of Manchester
Jinchao Li, Microsoft Research
Qian Liu, Beihang University
Andrea Madotto, The Hong Kong University Of Science and Technology
Alexandros Papangelis, Uber AI

Baolin Peng, Microsoft Research
Oleksandr Polozov, Microsoft Research
Stephen Pulman, Apple Inc.
Matthew Purver, Queen Mary University of London
Eugénio Ribeiro, INESC-ID / IST
Lei Shu, Department of Computer Science, University of Illinois at Chicago
Jian Sun, Alibaba Group
Hisami Suzuki, Microsoft Corporation
Ivan Vulić, University of Cambridge
Xianchao Wu, Microsoft
Chien-Sheng Wu, Salesforce
Bowen Wu, Platform and Content Group, Tencent
Caiming Xiong, Salesforce
Zhen Xu, Tencent PCG
Dian Yu, University of California, Davis
Tianyu Zhao, Kyoto University

Table of Contents

Xiaomingbot: A Multilingual Robot News Reporter

Runxin Xu[1]*, Jun Cao[2], Mingxuan Wang[2], Jiaze Chen[2], Hao Zhou[2]
Ying Zeng[2], Yuping Wang[2], Li Chen[2], Xiang Yin[2], Xijin Zhang[2]
Songcheng Jiang[2], Yuxuan Wang[2], and Lei Li[2]†

[1] School of Cyber Science and Engineering, Shanghai Jiao Tong University, Shanghai, China
[2] ByteDance AI Lab, Shanghai, China

`runxinxu@gmail.com`
`{caojun.sh, wangmingxuan.89, chenjiaze, zhouhao.nlp`
`zengying.ss, wangyuping, chenli.cloud,`
`yinxiang.stephen, zhangxijin, jiangsongcheng`
`wangyuxuan.11, lileilab}@bytedance.com`

Abstract

This paper proposes the building of Xiaomingbot, an intelligent, multilingual and multimodal software robot equipped with four integral capabilities: news generation, news translation, news reading and avatar animation. Its system summarizes Chinese news that it automatically generates from data tables. Next, it translates the summary or the full article into multiple languages, and reads the multilingual rendition through synthesized speech. Notably, Xiaomingbot utilizes a voice cloning technology to synthesize the speech trained from a real person's voice data in one input language. The proposed system enjoys several merits: it has an animated avatar, and is able to generate and read multilingual news. Since it was put into practice, Xiaomingbot has written over 600,000 articles, and gained over 150,000 followers on social media platforms.

1 Introduction

The wake of automated news reporting as an emerging research topic has witnessed the development and deployment of several robot news reporters with various capabilities. Technological improvements in modern natural language generation have further enabled automatic news writing in certain areas. For example, GPT-2 is able to create fairly plausible stories (Radford et al., 2019). Bayesian generative methods have been able to create descriptions or advertisement slogans from structured data (Miao et al., 2019; Ye et al., 2020). Summarization technology has been exploited to produce reports on sports news from human commentary text (Zhang et al., 2016).

While very promising, most previous robot reporters and machine writing systems have limited

---

*The work was done while the author was an intern at ByteDance AI Lab.

†Corresponding author.

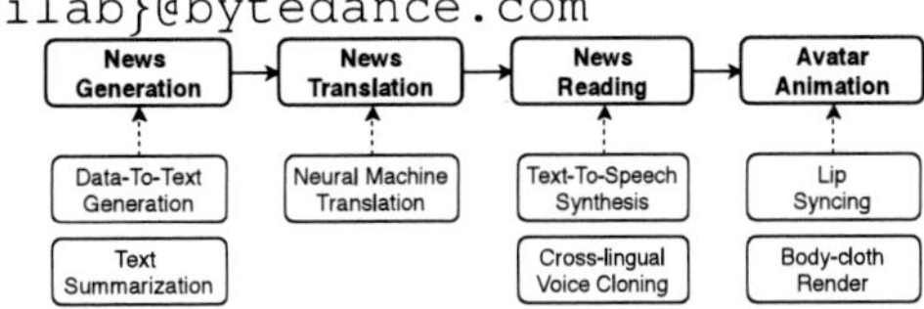

Figure 1: Xiaomingbot System Architecture

capabilities reports on sports news that only focus on text generation. We argue in this paper that an intelligent robot reporter should acquire the following capabilities to be truly user friendly: *a)* it should be able to create news articles from input data; *b)* it should be able to read the articles with lifelike character animation like in TV broadcasting; and *c)* it should be multi-lingual to serve global users. None of the existing robot reporters are able display performance on these tasks that matches that of a human reporter. In this paper, we present Xiaomingbot, a robot news reporter capable of news writing, summarization, translation, reading, and visual character animation. In our knowledge, it is the first multilingual and multimodal AI news agent. Hence, the system shows great potential for large scale industrial applications.

Figure 1 shows the capabilities and components of the proposed Xiaomingbot system. It includes four components: *a)* a news generator, *b)* a news translator, *c)* a cross-lingual news reader, and *d)* an animated avatar. The text generator takes input information from data tables and produces articles in natural languages. Our system is targeted for news area with available structure data, such as sports games and financial events. The fully automated news generation function is able to write and publish a story within mere seconds after the event took place, and is therefore much faster compared with manual writing. Within a few seconds after the events, it can accomplish the writing and publishing of a story. The system also uses a pretrained

1

Proceedings of the 58th Annual Meeting of the Association for Computational Linguistics, pages 1–8
July 5 - July 10, 2020. ©2020 Association for Computational Linguistics

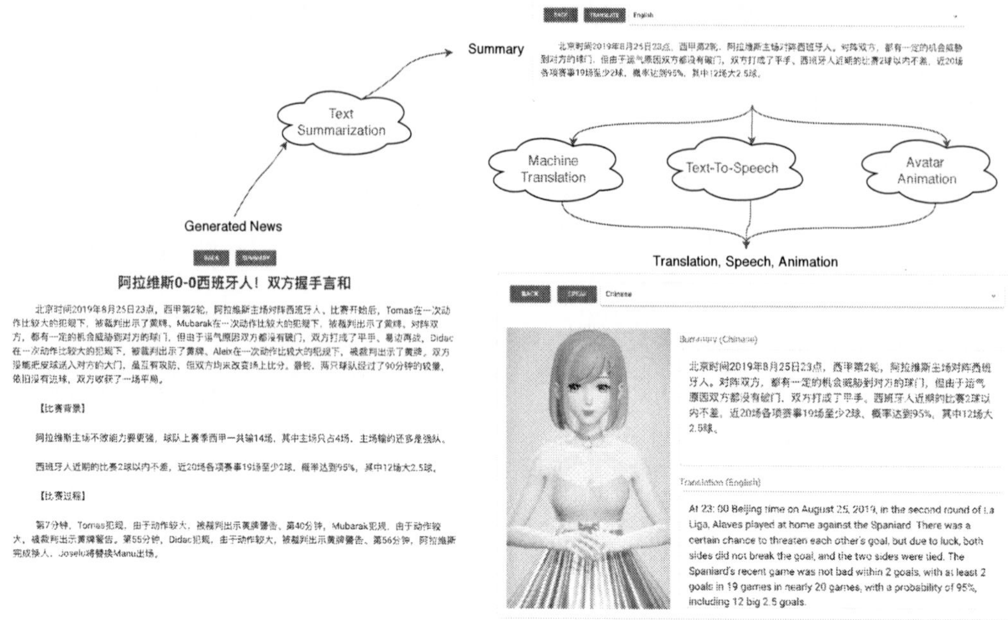

Figure 2: User Interface of Xiaomingbot. On the left is a piece of sports news, which is generated from a Table2Text model. On the top is the text summarization result. On the bottom right corner, Xiaomingbot produces the corresponding speech and visual effects.

text summarization technique to create summaries for users to skim through. Xiaomingbot can also translate news so that people from different countries can promptly understand the general meaning of an article. Xiaomingbot is equipped with a cross lingual voice reader that can read the report in different languages in the same voice. It is worth mentioning that Xiaomingbot excels at voice cloning. It is able to learn a person's voice from audio samples that are as short as only two hours, and maintain precise consistency in using that voice even when reading in different languages. In this work, we recorded 2 hours of Chinese voice data from a female speaker, and Xiaomingbot learnt to speak in English and Japanese with the same voice. Finally, the animation module produces an animated cartoon avatar with lip and facial expression synchronized to the text and voice. It also generates the full body with animated cloth texture. The demo video is available at `https://www.youtube.com/watch?v=zNfaj_DV6-E`. The home page is available at `https://xiaomingbot.github.io`.

The system has the following advantages: *a)* It produces timely news reports for certain areas and is multilingual. *b)* By employing a voice cloning model to Xiaomingbot's neural cross lingual voice reader, we've allowed it to learn a voice in different languages with only a few examples *c)* For better user experience, we also applied cross lingual visual rendering model, which generates synthesis lip syncing in consistent with the generated voice. *d)* Xiaomingbot has been put into practice and produced over $600,000$ articles, and gained over 150k followers in social media platforms.

2 System Architecture

The Xiaomingbot system includes four components working together in an pipeline, as shown in Figure 1. The system receives input from data table containing event records, which, depending on the domain, can be either a sports game with time-line information, or a financial piece such as tracking stock market. The final output is an animated avatar reading the news article with a synthesized voice. Figure 2 illustrates an example of our Xiaomingbot system. First, the text generation model generates a piece of sports news. Then, as is shown on the top of the figure, the text summarization module trims the produced news into a summary, which can be read by users who prefer a condensed abstract instead of the whole news. Next, the machine translation module will translate the summary into the language that the user specifies, as illustrated on the bottom right of the figure. Relying on the text to speech (TTS) module, Xiaomingbot can read both the summary and its translation in different languages using the same voice. Finally, the system can visualize an animated character with synchronized lip motion and facial expression, as well as lifelike body and clothing.

3   News Generation

In this section, we will first describe the automated news generation module, followed by the news summarization component.

3.1   Data-To-Text Generation

Our proposed Xiaomingbot is targeted for writing news for domains with structured input data, such as sports and finance. To generate reasonable text, several methods have been proposed(Miao et al., 2019; Sun et al., 2019; Ye et al., 2020). However, since it is difficult to generate correct and reliable content through most of these methods, we employ a template based on table2text technology to write the articles.

Table 1 illustrates one example of soccer game data and its generated sentences. In the example, Xiaomingbot retrieved the tabled data of a single sports game with time-lines and events, as well as statistics for each player's performance. The data table contains time, event type (scoring, foul, etc.), player, team name, and possible additional attributes. Using these tabulated data, we integrated and normalized the key-value pair from the table. We can also obtain processed key-value pairs such as "Winning team", "Lost team", "Winning Score" , and use template-based method to generate news from the tabulated result. Those templates are written in a custom-designed java-script dialect. For each type of the event, we manually constructed multiple templates and the system will randomly pick one during generation. We also created complex templates with conditional clauses to generate certain sentences based on the game conditions. For example, if the scores of the two teams differ too much, it may generate "Team A overwhelms Team B." Sentence generation strategy are classified into the following categories:

- **Pre-match Analysis.** It mainly includes the historical records of each team.

- **In-match Description.** It describes most important events in the game such as "some-

one score a goal", "someone received yellow card".

- **Post-match Summary.** It's a brief summary of this game , while also including predictions of the progress of the subsequent matches.

3.2   Text Summarization

For users who prefer a condensed summary of the report, Xiaomingbot can provide a short gist version using a pre-trained text summarization model. We choose to use the said model instead of generating the summary directly from the table data because the former can create more general content, and can be employed to process manually written reports as well. There are two approaches to summarize a text: extractive and abstractive summarization. Extractive summarization trains a sentence selection model to pick the important sentences from an input article, while an abstractive summarization will further rephrase the sentences and explore the potential for combining multiple sentences into a simplified one.

We trained two summarization models. One is a general text summarization using a BERT-based sequence labelling network. We use the TTNews dataset, a Chinese single document summarization dataset for training from NLPCC 2017 and 2018 shared tasks (Hua et al., 2017; Li and Wan, 2018). It includes 50,000 Chinese documents with human written summaries. The article is separated into a sequence of sentences. The BERT-based summarization model output 0-1 labels for all sentences.

In addition, for soccer news, we trained a special summarization model based on the commentary-to-summary technique (Zhang et al., 2016). It considers the game structure of soccer and handles important events such as goal kicking and fouls differently. Therefore it is able to better summarize the soccer game reports.

4   News Translation

In order to provide multilingual news to users, we propose using a machine translation system to translate news articles. In our system, we pre-trained several neural machine translation models, and employ state of the art Transformer Big Model as our NMT component. The parameters are exactly the same with (Vaswani et al., 2017). In order to further improve the system and speed up the inference, we implemented a CUDA based NMT system, which is 10x faster than the Tensorflow

Table 1: Examples of Sports News Generation

Time	Category	Player	Team	Generated Text	Translated Text
23'	Score	Didac	Espanyol	第23分钟，西班牙人迪达克打入一球。	In the 23rd minute, Espanyol Didac scored a goal.
35'	Yellow Card	Mubarak	Alavés	第35分钟，阿拉维斯穆巴拉克吃到一张黄牌。	In the 35th minute, Alavés Mubarak received a yellow card.

approach [1]. Furthermore, our machine translation system leverages named-entity (NE) replacement for glossaries including team name, player name and so on to improve the translation accuracy. It can be further improved by recent machine translation techniques (Yang et al., 2020; Zheng et al., 2020).

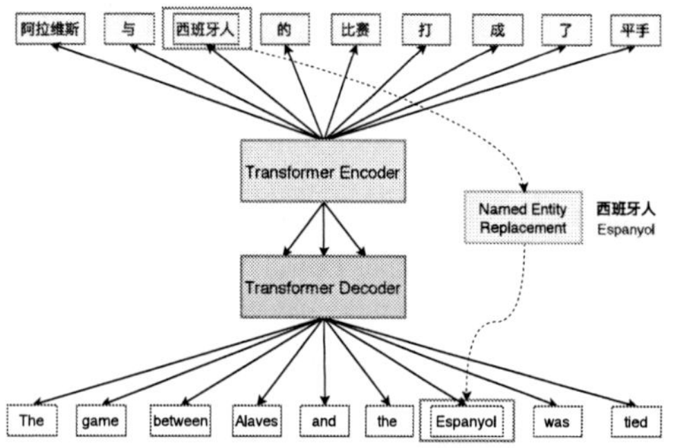

Figure 3: Neural Machine Translation Model.

We use the in-house data to train our machine translation system. For Chinese-to-English, the dataset contains more than 100 million parallel sentence pairs. For Chinese-to-Japanese, the dataset contains more than 60 million parallel sentence pairs.

5 Multilingual News Reading

In order to read the text of the generated and/or translated news article, we developed a text to speech synthesis model with multilingual capability, which only requires a small amount of recorded voice of a speaker in one language. We developed an additional cross-lingual voice cloning technique to clone the pronunciation and intonation. Our cross-lingual voice cloning model is based on Tacotron 2 (J. Shen, 2018), which uses an attention-based sequence-to-sequence model to generate a sequence of log-mel spectrogram frames from an

input text sequence (Wang et al., 2017). The architecture is illustrated in Figure 4, we made the following augmentations on the base Tacotron 2 model:

- We applied an additional speaker as well as language embedding to support multi-speaker and multilingual input.

- We introduced a variational autoencoder-style residual encoder to encode the variational length mel into a fix length latent representation, and then conditioned the representation to the decoder.

- We used Gaussian-mixture-model (GMM) attention rather than location-sensitive attention.

- We used wavenet neural vocoder (Oord et al., 2016).

For Chinese TTS, we used hundreds of speakers from internal automatic audio text processing toolkit, for English, we used libritts dataset (Zen et al., 2019), and for Japanese we used JVS corpus which includes 100 Japanese speakers. As for input representations, we used phoneme with tone for Chinese, phoneme with stress for English, and phoneme with mora accent for Japanese. In our experiment, we recorded 2 hours of Chinese voice data from an internal female speaker who speaks only Chinese for this demo.

6 Synchronized Avatar Animation Synthesis

We believe that lifelike animated avatar will make the news broadcasting more viewer friendly. In this section, we will describe the techniques to render the animated avatar and to synchronize the lip and facial motions.

---

[1] https://github.com/bytedance/byseqlib

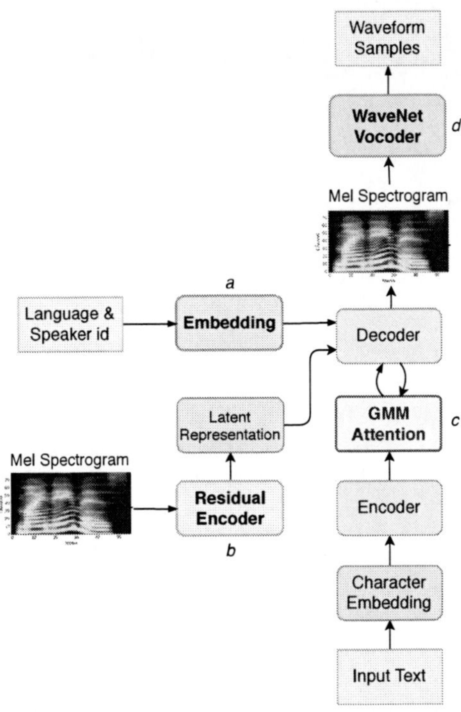

Figure 4: Voice Cloning for Cross-lingual Text-to-Speech Synthesis.

6.1 Lip Syncing

The avatar animation module produces a set of lip motion animation parameters for each video frame, which is synced with the audio synthesized by the TTS module and used to drive the character.

Since the module should be speaker agnostic and TTS-model-independent, no audio signal is required as input. Instead, a sequence of phonemes and their duration is drawn from the TTS module and fed into the lip motion synthesis module. This step can be regarded as tackling a sequence to sequence learning problem. The generated lip motion animation parameters should be able to be re-targeted to any avatar and easy to visualize by animators. To meet this requirement, the lip motion animation parameters are represented as blend weights of facial expression blendshapes. The blendshapes for the rendered character are designed by an animator according to the semantic of the blendshapes. In each rendered frame, the blendshapes are linear blended with the weights predicted by the module to form the final 3D mesh with correct mouth shape for rendering.

Since the module should produce high fidelity

animations and run in real-time, a neural network model that has learned from real-world data is introduced to transform the phoneme and duration sequence to the sequence of blendshape weights. A sliding window neural network similar to Taylor et al. (2017), which is used to capture the local phonetic context and produce smooth animations. The phoneme and duration sequence is converted to fixed length sequence of phoneme frame according to the desired video frame rate before being further converted to one-hot encoding sequence which is taken as input to the neural network in a sliding widow the length of which is 11. Three are 32 mouth related blendshape weights predicted for each frame in a sliding window with length of 5. Following Taylor et al. (2017), the final blendshape weights for each frame is generated by blending every predictions in the overlapping sliding windows using the frame-wise mean.

The model we used is a fully connected feed forward neural network with three hidden layers and 2048 units per hidden layer. The hyperbolic tangent function is used as activation function. Batch normalization is used after each hidden layer (Ioffe and Szegedy, 2015). Dropout with probability of 0.5 is placed between output layer and last hidden layer to prevent over-fitting (Wager et al., 2013). The network is trained with standard mini-batch stochastic gradient descent with mini-batch size of 128 and learning rate of 1e-3 for 8000 steps.

The training data is build from 3 hours of video and audio of a female speaker. Different from Taylor et al. (2017), instead of using AAM to parameterize the face, the faces in the video frames are parameterized by fitting a blinear 3D face morphable model inspired by Cao et al. (2013) built from our private 3D capture data. The poses of the 3D faces, the identity parameters and the weights of the individual-specific blendshapes of each frame and each view angle are joint solved with a cost function built from reconstruction error of the facial landmarks. The identity parameters are shared within all frames and the weights of the blendshapes are shared through view angles which have the same timestamp. The phoneme-duration sequence and the blendshape weights sequence are used to train the sliding window neural network.

6.2 Character Rendering

Unity, the real time 3D rendering engine is used to render the avatar for Xiaomingbot.

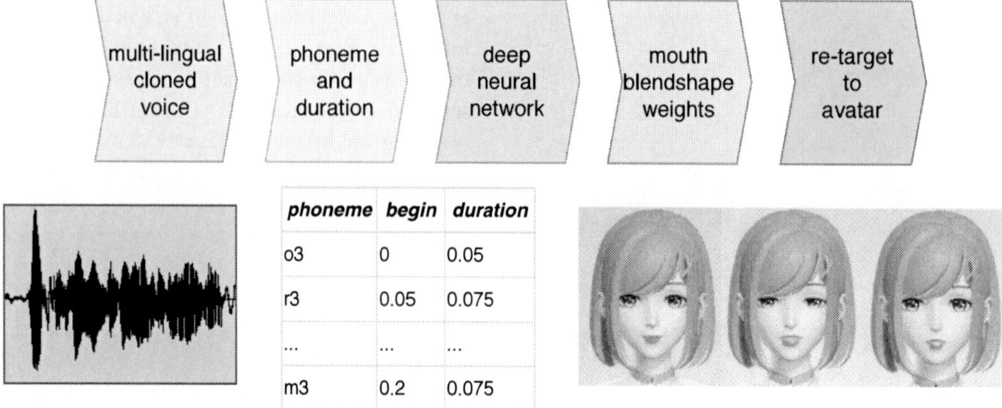

Figure 5: Avatar animation synthesis: a) multi-lingual voices are cloned. b) A sequence of phonemes and their duration is drawn from the voices. c) A sequence of blendshape weights is transformed by a neural network model. d) Lip-motion is synthesized and re-targeted synchronously to avatar animation.

For eye rendering, we used Normal Mapping to simulate the the iris, and Parallax Mapping to simulate the effect of refraction. As for the highlights of the eyes, we used the GGX term in PBR for approximation. In terms of hair rendering, we used the kajiya-kay shading model to simulate the double highlights of the hair (Kajiya and Kay, 1989), and solved the problem of translucency using a mesh-level triangle sorting algorithm. For skin rendering, we used the Separable Subsurface Scattering algorithm to approximate the translucency of the skin (Jimenez et al., 2015). For simple clothing materials, we used the PBR algorithm directly. For fabric and silk, we used Disney's anisotropic BRDF (Burley and Studios, 2012).

Since physical-based cloth simulation algorithm is more expensive for mobile, we used the Spring-Mass System(SMS) for cloth simulation. The specific method is to generate a skeletal system and use SMS to drive the movement of bones (Liu et al., 2013). However, the above approach may cause the clothing to overlap the body. To address this problem, we deployed some new virtual bone points to the skeletal system, and reduced the overlay using the CCD IK method (Wang and Chen, 1991), which displayed great performance in most cases.

7 Conclusion

In this paper, we present Xiaomingbot, a multilingual and multi-modal system for news reporting. The entire process of Xiaomingbot's news reporting can be condensed as follows. First, it learns how to write news articles based on a template based table2text technology, and summarize the news through an extraction based method. Next, its system translates the summarization into multiple languages. Finally, the system produces the video of an animated avatar reading the news with synthesized voice. Owing to the voice cloning model that can learn from a few Chinese audio samples, Xiaomingbot can maintain consistency in intonation and voice projection across different languages. So far, Xiaomingbot has been deployed online and is serving users.

The system is but a first attempt to build a fully functional robot reporter capable of writing, speaking, and expressing with motion. Xiaomingbot is not yet perfect, and has limitations and room for improvement. One such important direction for future improvement is the expansion of areas that it can work in, which can be achieved through a promising approach of adopting model based technologies together with rule/template based ones. Another direction for improvement is to further enhance the ability to interact with users via a conversation interface.

Acknowledgments

We would like to thank Yuzhang Du, Lifeng Hua, Yujie Li, Xiaojun Wan, Yue Wu, Mengshu Yang, Xiyue Yang, Jibin Yang, and Tingting Zhu for helpful discussion and design of the system. The name Xiaomingbot was suggested by Tingting Zhu in 2016. We also wish to thank the reviewers for their insightful comments.

References

Brent Burley and Walt Disney Animation Studios. 2012. Physically-based shading at disney. In *ACM SIGGRAPH*, volume 2012, pages 1–7.

Chen Cao, Yanlin Weng, Shun Zhou, Yiying Tong, and Kun Zhou. 2013. Facewarehouse: A 3d facial expression database for visual computing. *IEEE Transactions on Visualization and Computer Graphics*, 20(3):413–425.

Lifeng Hua, Xiaojun Wan, and Lei Li. 2017. Overview of the NLPCC 2017 shared task: Single document summarization. In *Natural Language Processing and Chinese Computing - 6th CCF International Conference, NLPCC 2017, Dalian, China, November 8-12, 2017, Proceedings*, volume 10619 of *Lecture Notes in Computer Science*, pages 942–947. Springer.

Sergey Ioffe and Christian Szegedy. 2015. Batch normalization: Accelerating deep network training by reducing internal covariate shift. In *Proceedings of the 32nd International Conference on Machine Learning, ICML 2015, Lille, France, 6-11 July 2015*, pages 448–456.

R. J. Weiss M. Schuster N. Jaitly Z. Yang Z. Chen Y. Zhang Y. Wang R. Skerry-Ryan et al. J. Shen, R. Pang. 2018. Natural TTS synthesis by conditioning wavenet on mel spectrogram predictions. *ICASSP*.

Jorge Jimenez, Károly Zsolnai, Adrian Jarabo, Christian Freude, Thomas Auzinger, Xian-Chun Wu, Javier der Pahlen, Michael Wimmer, and Diego Gutierrez. 2015. Separable subsurface scattering. *Comput. Graph. Forum*, 34(6):188–197.

James T Kajiya and Timothy L Kay. 1989. Rendering fur with three dimensional textures. *ACM Siggraph Computer Graphics*, 23(3):271–280.

Lei Li and Xiaojun Wan. 2018. Overview of the NLPCC 2018 shared task: Single document summarization. In *Natural Language Processing and Chinese Computing - 7th CCF International Conference, NLPCC 2018, Hohhot, China, August 26-30, 2018, Proceedings, Part II*, volume 11109 of *Lecture Notes in Computer Science*, pages 457–463. Springer.

Tiantian Liu, Adam W Bargteil, James F O'Brien, and Ladislav Kavan. 2013. Fast simulation of mass-spring systems. *ACM Transactions on Graphics (TOG)*, 32(6):1–7.

Ning Miao, Hao Zhou, Lili Mou, Rui Yan, and Lei Li. 2019. CGMH: Constrained sentence generation by metropolis-hastings sampling. In *the 33rd AAAI Conference on Artificial Intelligence (AAAI)*.

Aaron van den Oord, Sander Dieleman, Heiga Zen, Karen Simonyan, Oriol Vinyals, Alex Graves, Nal Kalchbrenner, Andrew Senior, and Koray Kavukcuoglu. 2016. Wavenet: A generative model for raw audio. *arXiv preprint arXiv:1609.03499*.

Alec Radford, Jeffrey Wu, Rewon Child, David Luan, Dario Amodei, and Ilya Sutskever. 2019. Language models are unsupervised multitask learners. *OpenAI Blog*, 1(8):9.

Zhaoyue Sun, Jiaze Chen, Hao Zhou, Deyu Zhou, Lei Li, and Mingmin Jiang. 2019. GraspSnooker: Automatic Chinese commentary generation for snooker videos. In *the 28th International Joint Conference on Artificial Intelligence (IJCAI)*, pages 6569–6571. Demos.

Sarah Taylor, Taehwan Kim, Yisong Yue, Moshe Mahler, James Krahe, Anastasio Garcia Rodriguez, Jessica Hodgins, and Iain Matthews. 2017. A deep learning approach for generalized speech animation. *ACM Transactions on Graphics (TOG)*, 36(4):1–11.

Ashish Vaswani, Noam Shazeer, Niki Parmar, Jakob Uszkoreit, Llion Jones, Aidan N Gomez, Łukasz Kaiser, and Illia Polosukhin. 2017. Attention is all you need. In *Advances in neural information processing systems*, pages 5998–6008.

Stefan Wager, Sida Wang, and Percy S Liang. 2013. Dropout training as adaptive regularization. In *Advances in neural information processing systems*, pages 351–359.

L-CT Wang and Chih-Cheng Chen. 1991. A combined optimization method for solving the inverse kinematics problems of mechanical manipulators. *IEEE Transactions on Robotics and Automation*, 7(4):489–499.

Yuxuan Wang, R. J. Skerry-Ryan, Daisy Stanton, Yonghui Wu, Ron J. Weiss, Navdeep Jaitly, Zongheng Yang, Ying Xiao, Zhifeng Chen, Samy Bengio, Quoc V. Le, Yannis Agiomyrgiannakis, Rob Clark, and Rif A. Saurous. 2017. Tacotron: Towards end-to-end speech synthesis. In *Interspeech 2017, 18th Annual Conference of the International Speech Communication Association, Stockholm, Sweden, August 20-24, 2017*, pages 4006–4010.

Jiacheng Yang, Mingxuan Wang, Hao Zhou, Chengqi Zhao, Weinan Zhang, Yong Yu, and Lei Li. 2020. Towards making the most of BERT in neural machine translation. In *the 34th AAAI Conference on Artificial Intelligence (AAAI)*.

Rong Ye, Wenxian Shi, Hao Zhou, Zhongyu Wei, and Lei Li. 2020. Variational template machine for data-to-text generation. In *International Conference on Learning Representations (ICLR)*.

Heiga Zen, Viet Dang, Rob Clark, Yu Zhang, Ron J. Weiss, Ye Jia, Zhifeng Chen, and Yonghui Wu. 2019. Libritts: A corpus derived from librispeech for text-to-speech. In *Interspeech 2019, 20th Annual Conference of the International Speech Communication Association, Graz, Austria, 15-19 September 2019*, pages 1526–1530.

Jianmin Zhang, Jin-ge Yao, and Xiaojun Wan. 2016. Towards constructing sports news from live text commentary. In *Proceedings of the 54th Annual Meeting of the Association for Computational Linguistics (Volume 1: Long Papers)*, pages 1361–1371, Berlin, Germany. Association for Computational Linguistics.

Zaixiang Zheng, Hao Zhou, Shujian Huang, Lei Li, Xin-Yu Dai, and Jiajun Chen. 2020. Mirror-generative neural machine translation. In *International Conference on Learning Representations*.

TextBrewer: An Open-Source Knowledge Distillation Toolkit for Natural Language Processing

Ziqing Yang[†], Yiming Cui[‡†], Zhipeng Chen[†],
Wanxiang Che[‡], Ting Liu[‡], Shijin Wang[†§], Guoping Hu[†]
[†]State Key Laboratory of Cognitive Intelligence, iFLYTEK Research, China
[‡]Research Center for Social Computing and Information Retrieval (SCIR),
Harbin Institute of Technology, Harbin, China
[§]iFLYTEK AI Research (Hebei), Langfang, China
[†§]`{zqyang5,ymcui,zpchen,sjwang3,gphu}@iflytek.com`
[‡]`{ymcui,car,tliu}@ir.hit.edu.cn`

Abstract

In this paper, we introduce **TextBrewer**, an open-source knowledge distillation toolkit designed for natural language processing. It works with different neural network models and supports various kinds of supervised learning tasks, such as text classification, reading comprehension, sequence labeling. TextBrewer provides a simple and uniform workflow that enables quick setting up of distillation experiments with highly flexible configurations. It offers a set of predefined distillation methods and can be extended with custom code. As a case study, we use TextBrewer to distill BERT on several typical NLP tasks. With simple configurations, we achieve results that are comparable with or even higher than the public distilled BERT models with similar numbers of parameters. [1]

1 Introduction

Large pre-trained language models, such as GPT (Radford, 2018), BERT (Devlin et al., 2019), RoBERTa (Liu et al., 2019b) and XLNet (Yang et al., 2019) have achieved great success in many NLP tasks and greatly contributed to the progress of NLP research. However, one big issue of these models is the high demand for computing resources — they usually have hundreds of millions of parameters, and take several gigabytes of memory to train and inference — which makes it impractical to deploy them on mobile devices or online systems. From a research point of view, we are tempted to ask: is it necessary to have such a big model that contains hundreds of millions of parameters to achieve a high performance? Motivated by the above considerations, recently, some researchers in the NLP community have tried to design lite models (Lan et al., 2019), or resort to knowledge

distillation (KD) technique to compress large pre-trained models to small models.

KD is a technique of transferring knowledge from a teacher model to a student model, which is usually smaller than the teacher. The student model is trained to mimic the outputs of the teacher model. Before the birth of BERT, KD had been applied to several specific tasks like machine translation (Kim and Rush, 2016; Tan et al., 2019) in NLP. While the recent studies of distilling large pre-trained models focus on finding general distillation methods that work on various tasks and are receiving more and more attention (Sanh et al., 2019; Jiao et al., 2019; Sun et al., 2019a; Tang et al., 2019; Liu et al., 2019a; Clark et al., 2019; Zhao et al., 2019).

Though various distillation methods have been proposed, they usually share a common workflow: firstly, train a teacher model, then optimize the student model by minimizing some losses that are calculated between the outputs of the teacher and the student. Therefore it is desirable to have a reusable distillation workflow framework and treat different distillation strategies and tricks as plugins so that they could be easily and arbitrarily added to the framework. In this way, we could also achieve great flexibility in experimenting with different combinations of distillation strategies and comparing their effects.

In this paper, we introduce **TextBrewer**, a PyTorch-based distillation toolkit for NLP that aims to provide a unified distillation workflow, save the effort of setting up experiments and help users to distill more effective models. TextBrewer provides simple-to-use APIs, a collection of distillation methods, and highly customizable configurations. It has also been proved able to distill BERT models efficiently and reproduce the state-of-the-art results on typical NLP tasks. The main features of TextBrewer are:

---

[1]TextBrewer: `http://textbrewer.hfl-rc.com`

9

Proceedings of the 58th Annual Meeting of the Association for Computational Linguistics, pages 9–16
July 5 - July 10, 2020. ©2020 Association for Computational Linguistics

- **Versatility in tasks and models**. It works with a wide range of models, from the RNN-based model to the transformer-based model, and works on typical natural language understanding tasks. Its usability in tasks like text classification, reading comprehension, and sequence labeling has been fully tested.

- **Flexibility in configurations**. The distillation process is configured by configuration objects, which can be initialized from JSON files and contain many tunable hyperparameters. Users can extend the configurations with new custom losses, schedulers, etc., if the presets do not meet their requirements.

- **Including various distillation methods and strategies**. KD has been studied extensively in computer vision (CV) and has achieved great success. It would be worthwhile to introduce these studies to the NLP community as some of the methods in these studies could also be applied to texts. TextBrewer includes a set of methods from both CV and NLP, such as flow of solution procedure (FSP) matrix loss (Yim et al., 2017), neuron selectivity transfer (NST) (Huang and Wang, 2017), probability shift and dynamic temperature (Wen et al., 2019), attention matrix loss, multi-task distillation (Liu et al., 2019a). In our experiments, we will show the effectiveness of applying methods from CV on NLP tasks.

- **Being non-intrusive and simple to use**. *Non-intrusive* means there is no need to modify the existing code that defines the models. Users can re-use the most parts of their existing training scripts, such as model definition and initialization, data preprocessing and task evaluation. Only some preparatory work (see Section 3.3) are additionally required to use TextBrewer to perform the distillation.

TextBrewer also provides some useful utilities such as model size analysis and data augmentation to help model design and distillation.

2 Related Work

Recently some distilled BERT models have been released, such as DistilBERT (Sanh et al., 2019), TinyBERT (Jiao et al., 2019), and ERNIE Slim[2]. DistilBERT performs distillation on the pre-training task, i.e., masked language modeling.

TinyBERT performs transformer distillation at both the pre-training and task-specific learning stages. ERNIE Slim distills ERNIE (Sun et al., 2019b,c)on a sentiment classification task. Their distillation code is publicly available, and users can replicate their experiments easily. However, it is laborious and error-prone to change the distillation method or adapt the distillation code for some other models and tasks, since the code is not written for general distillation purposes.

There also exist some libraries for general model compression. Distiller (Zmora et al., 2018) and PaddleSlim[3] are two versatile libraries supporting pruning, quantization and knowledge distillation. They focus on models and tasks in computer vision. In comparison, TextBrewer is more focused on knowledge distillation on NLP tasks, more flexible, and offers more functionalities. Based on PyTorch, It provides simple APIs and rich customization for fast and clean implementations of experiments.

3 Architecture and Design

Figure 1 shows an overview of the main functionalities and architecture of TextBrewer. To support different models and different tasks and meanwhile stay flexible and extensible, TextBrewer provides *distillers* to conduct the actual experiments and configuration classes to configure the behaviors of the distillers.

3.1 Distillers

Distillers are the cores of TextBrewer. They automatically train and save models and support custom evaluation functions. Five distillers have been implemented: `BasicDistiller` is used for single-task single-teacher distillation; `GeneralDistiller` in addition supports more advanced intermediate loss functions; `MultiTeacherDistiller` distills an ensemble of teacher models into a single student model; `MultiTaskDistiller` distills multiple teacher models of different tasks into a single multi-task student model (Clark et al., 2019; Liu et al., 2019a). We also have implemented `BasicTrainer` for training teachers on labeled data to unify the workflows of supervised learning and distillation. All the distillers share the same interface and usage. They can be replaced by each other easily.

---

[2]https://github.com/PaddlePaddle/ERNIE

[3]https://github.com/PaddlePaddle/PaddleSlim

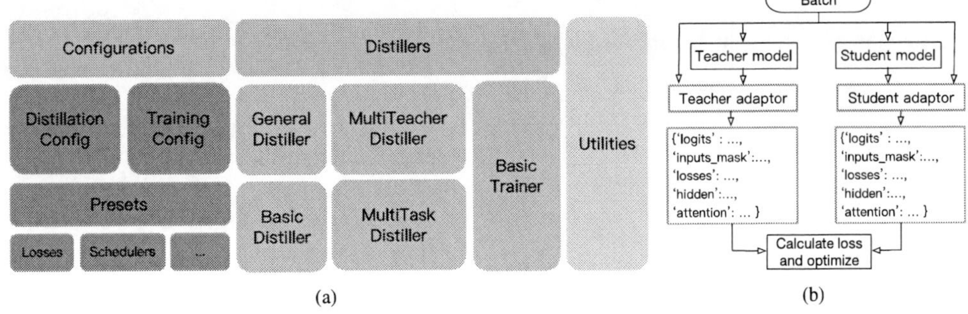

Figure 1: (a) An overview of the main functionalities of TextBrewer. (b) A sketch that shows the function of adaptors inside a distiller.

3.2 Configurations and Presets

The general training settings and the distillation method settings of a distiller are specified by two configurations: `TrainingConfig` and `DistillationConfig`.

TrainingConfig defines the settings that are general to deep learning experiments, including the directory where logs and student model are stored (`log_dir`, `output_dir`), the device to use (`device`), the frequency of storing and evaluating student model (`ckpt_frequencey`), etc.

DistillationConfig defines the settings that are pertinent to distillation, where various distillation methods could be configured or enabled. It includes the type of KD loss (`kd_loss_type`), the temperature and weight of KD loss (`temperature` and `kd_loss_weight`), the weight of hard-label loss (`hard_label_weight`), probability shift switch, schedulers and intermediate losses, etc. Intermediate losses are used for computing the losses between the intermediate states of teacher and student, and they could be freely combined and added to the distillers. Schedulers are used to adjust loss weight or temperature dynamically.

The available values of configuration options such as loss functions and schedulers are defined as dictionaries in presets. For example, the loss function dictionary includes hidden state loss, cosine similarity loss, FSP loss, NST loss, etc.

All the configurations can be initialized from JSON files. In Figure 3 we show an example of `DistillationConfig` for distilling $BERT_{BASE}$ to a 4-layer transformers. See Section 4 for more details.

```python
from textbrewer import GeneralDistiller
from textbrewer import TrainingConfig, DistillationConfig

# We omit the initialization of models, optimizer, and dataloader.
teacher_model : torch.nn.Module = ...
student_model : torch.nn.Module = ...
dataloader : torch.utils.data.DataLoader = ...
optimizer : torch.optim.Optimizer = ...
scheduler : torch.optim.lr_scheduler = ...

def simple_adaptor(batch, model_outputs):
    # We assume that the first element of model_outputs
    # is the logits before softmax
    return {'logits': model_outputs[0]}

train_config = TrainingConfig()
distill_config = DistillationConfig()
distiller = GeneralDistiller(
    train_config=train_config, distill_config = distill_config,
    model_T = teacher_model, model_S = student_model,
    adaptor_T = simple_adaptor, adaptor_S = simple_adaptor)

distiller.train(optimizer, scheduler,
    dataloader, num_epochs, callback=None)
```

Figure 2: A code snippet that demonstrates the minimal TextBrewer workflow.

3.3 Workflow

Before distilling a teacher model using TextBrewer, some preparatory works have to be done:

1. Train a teacher model on a labeled dataset. Users usually train the teacher model with their own training scripts. TextBrewer also provides `BasicTrainer` for supervised training on a labeled dataset.

2. Define and initialize the student model.

3. Build a dataloader of the dataset for distillation and initialize the optimizer and learning rate scheduler.

The above steps are usually common to all deep learning experiments. To perform distillation, take the following additional steps:

1. Initialize training and distillation configurations, and construct a distiller.

2. Define *adaptors* and a *callback* function.

3. Call the `train` method of the distiller.

A code snippet that shows the minimal workflow is presented in Figure 2. The concepts of callback and adaptor will be explained below.

```
{"temperature": 8,
 "temperature_scheduler": 'none'
 "hard_label_weight": 0,
 "hard_label_weight_scheduler": 'none',
 "kd_loss_type": "ce",
 "kd_loss_weight": 1,
 "kd_loss_weight_scheduler": 'none',
 "probability_shift": False,
 "intermediate_matches": [
 {'layer_T':0, 'layer_S':0, 'feature':'hidden',
  'loss': 'hidden_mse', 'weight' : 1,'proj':['linear',312,768]},
 {'layer_T':3, 'layer_S':1, 'feature':'hidden',
  'loss': 'hidden_mse', 'weight' : 1,'proj':['linear',312,768]},
 {'layer_T':6, 'layer_S':2, 'feature':'hidden',
  'loss': 'hidden_mse', 'weight' : 1,'proj':['linear',312,768]},
 {'layer_T':9, 'layer_S':3, 'feature':'hidden',
  'loss': 'hidden_mse', 'weight' : 1,'proj':['linear',312,768]},
 {'layer_T':12, 'layer_S':4, 'feature':'hidden',
  'loss': 'hidden_mse', 'weight' : 1,'proj':['linear',312,768]},
 {'layer_T':[0,0], 'layer_S':[0,0], 'feature':'hidden',
  'loss': 'nst', 'weight': 1}
 {'layer_T':[3,3], 'layer_S':[1,1], 'feature':'hidden',
  'loss': 'nst', 'weight': 1}
 {'layer_T':[6,6], 'layer_S':[2,2], 'feature':'hidden',
  'loss': 'nst', 'weight': 1}
 {'layer_T':[9,9], 'layer_S':[3,3], 'feature':'hidden',
  'loss': 'nst', 'weight': 1}
 {'layer_T':[12,12],'layer_S':[4,4], 'feature':'hidden',
  'loss': 'nst', 'weight': 1}]}
```

Figure 3: An example of distillation configuration. This configuration is used to distill a 12-layer BERT$_{\text{BASE}}$ to a 4-layer T4-tiny.

3.3.1 Callback Function

To monitor the performance of the student model during training, people usually evaluate the student model on a development set at some checkpoints besides logging the loss curve. For example, in the early stopping strategy, users choose the best model weights checkpoint based on the performance of the student model on the development set at the end of each epoch. TextBrewer supports such functionality by providing the callback function argument in the `train` method, as shown in line 24 of Figure 2. The callback function takes two arguments: the student model and the current training step. At each checkpoint step (determined by `num_train_epochs` and `ckpt_frequencey`), the distiller saves the student model and then calls the callback function.

Since it is impractical to implement evaluation metrics and evaluation procedures for all NLP tasks, we encourage users to implement their own evaluation functions as the callbacks for the best practice.

3.3.2 Adaptor

The distiller is model-agnostic. It needs a translator to translate the model outputs into meaningful data. Adaptor plays the role of translator. An Adaptor is an interface and responsible for explaining the inputs and outputs of the teacher and student for the distiller.

Adaptor takes two arguments: the model inputs and the model outputs. It is expected to return a dictionary with some specific keys. Each key explains the meaning of the corresponding value, as shown in Figure 1 (b). For example, `logits` is the logits of final outputs, `hidden` is intermediate hidden states, `attention` is the attention matrices, `inputs_mask` is used to mask padding positions. The distiller only takes necessary elements from the outputs of adaptors according to its distillation configurations. A minimal adaptor only needs to explain logits, as shown in lines 11–14 of Figure 2.

3.4 Extensibility

TextBrewer also works with users' custom modules. New loss functions and schedulers can be easily added to the toolkit. For example, to use a custom loss function, one first implements the loss function with a compatible interface, then adds it to the loss function dictionary in the presets with a custom name, so that the new loss function becomes available as a new option value of the configuration and can be recognized by distillers.

4 Experiments

In this section, we conduct several experiments to show TextBrewer's ability to distill large pre-trained models on different NLP tasks and achieve results are comparable with or even higher than the public distilled BERT models with similar numbers of parameters. [4]

4.1 Settings

Datasets and tasks. We conduct experiments on both English and Chinese datasets. For English datasets, We use MNLI (Wang et al., 2019) for text classification task, SQuAD1.1 (Rajpurkar et al., 2016) for span-extraction machine reading comprehension (MRC) task and CoNLL-2003 (Tjong Kim Sang and De Meulder, 2003) for named entity recognition (NER) task. For Chinese datasets, we use the Chinese part of XNLI

---

[4] More results are presented in the online documentation: `https://textbrewer.readthedocs.io`

Dataset	Task	Metrics	#Train	#Dev
MNLI	Classification	Acc	393K	20K
SQuAD	MRC	EM/F1	88K	11K
CoNLL-2003	NER	F1	23K	6K
XNLI	Classification	Acc	393K	2.5K
LCQMC	Classification	Acc	293K	8.8K
CMRC 2018	MRC	EM/F1	10K	3.4K
DRCD	MRC	EM/F1	27K	3.5K

Table 1: A summary of the datasets used in experiments. The size of CoNLL-2003 is measured in number of entities.

(Conneau et al., 2018), LCQMC (Liu et al., 2018), CMRC 2018 (Cui et al., 2019b) and DRCD (Shao et al., 2018). XNLI is the multilingual version of MNLI. LCQMC is a large-scale Chinese question matching corpus. CMRC 2018 and DRCD are two span-extraction machine reading comprehension datasets similar to SQuAD. The statistics of the datasets are listed in Table 1.

Models. All the teachers are $BERT_{BASE}$-based models. For English tasks, teachers are initialized with the weights released by Google[5] and converted into PyTorch format via Transformers[6]. For Chinese tasks, teacher is initialized with the pre-trained RoBERTa-wwm-ext [7] (Cui et al., 2019a). We test the performance of the following student models:

- T6 and T3 are $BERT_{BASE}$ with fewer layers of transformers. Especially, T6 has the same structure as DistilBERT (Sanh et al., 2019).

- T3-small is a 3-layer BERT with half BERT-base's hidden size and feed-forward size.

- T4-tiny is the same as TinyBERT, a 4-layer model with an even smaller hidden size and feed-forward size.

- BiGRU is a single-layer bidirectional GRU. Its word embeddings are taken from $BERT_{BASE}$.

T3-small and T4-tiny are initialized randomly. The model structures of the teacher and students are summarized in Table 3.

Training settings. To keep experiments simple, we directly distill the teacher model that has been trained on the task, while we do not perform task-irrelevant language modeling distillation in advance. The number of epochs ranges from 30 to 60, and the learning rate of students is 1e-4 for all distillation experiments.

[5]https://github.com/google-research/bert

[6]https://github.com/huggingface/transformers

[7]https://github.com/ymcui/Chinese-BERT-wwm

Model	MNLI		SQuAD		CoNLL-2003
	m	mm	EM	F1	F1
$BERT_{BASE}$	83.7	84.0	81.5	88.6	91.1
Public					
DistilBERT	81.6	81.1	79.1	86.9	-
TinyBERT	80.5	81.0	-	-	-
+DA	82.8	82.9	72.7	82.1	-
TextBrewer					
BiGRU	-	-	-	-	85.3
T6	83.6	84.0	80.8	88.1	90.7
T3	81.6	82.5	76.3	84.8	87.5
T3-small	81.3	81.7	72.3	81.4	78.6
T4-tiny	82.0	82.6	73.7	82.5	77.5
+DA	-	-	75.2	84.0	89.1

Table 2: Performance of $BERT_{BASE}$ (teacher) and various students on the development sets of MNLI and SQuAD, and the test set of CoNLL-2003. *m* and *mm* under MNLI denote the accuracies on matched and mismatched sections respectively.

Distillation settings. Temperature is set to 8 for all experiments. We add intermediate losses uniformly distributed among all the layers between teacher and student (except BiGRU). The loss functions we choose are `hidden_mse` loss which computes the mean square loss between two hidden states, and `NST` loss which is an effective method in CV. In Figure 3 we show an example of distillation configuration for distilling $BERT_{BASE}$ to a T4-tiny. Since their hidden sizes are different, we use `proj` option to add linear layers to match the dimensions. The linear layers will be trained together with the student automatically. We experiment with two kinds of distillers: `GeneralDistiller` and `MultiTeacherDistiller`.

4.2 Results on English Datasets

We list the public results (DistilBERT and Tiny-BERT) and our distillation results obtained by `GeneralDistiller` in Table 2. We have the following observations.

First, teachers can be distilled to T6 models with minor losses in performance. All the T6 models achieve 99% performance of the teachers, higher than the DistilBERT.

Second, T4-tiny outperforms TinyBERT though they share the same structure. This is attributed to the NST losses in the distillation configuration. This result proves the effectiveness of applying KD method developed in CV on NLP tasks.

Third, although T4-tiny has less parameters than T3-small, T4-tiny outperforms T3-small in most

Model	# Layers	Hidden size	Feed-forward size	# Parameters	Relative size
$\text{BERT}_{\text{BASE}}$ (teacher)	12	768	3072	108M	100%
T6	6	768	3072	65M	60%
T3	3	768	3072	44M	41%
T3-small	3	384	1536	17M	16%
T4-tiny	4	312	1200	14M	13%
BiGRU	1	768	-	31M	29%

Table 3: Model sizes of teacher and students. The number of parameters includes embeddings but does not include output layers.

Model	MNLI		SQuAD		CoNLL-2003
	m	mm	EM	F1	F1
Teacher 1	83.6	84.0	81.1	88.6	91.2
Teacher 2	83.6	84.2	81.2	88.5	90.8
Teacher 3	83.7	83.8	81.2	88.7	91.3
Ensemble	84.3	84.7	82.3	89.4	91.5
Student	**84.8**	**85.3**	**83.5**	**90.0**	**91.6**

Table 4: Results of multi-teacher distillation. All the models are $\text{BERT}_{\text{BASE}}$. Different teachers are trained with different random seeds. For each task, the ensemble is the average of three teachers' results.

Model	XNLI	LCQMC	CMRC 2018		DRCD	
	Acc	Acc	EM	F1	EM	F1
RoBERTa-wwm	79.9	89.4	68.8	86.4	86.5	92.5
T3	78.4	89.0	63.4	82.4	76.7	85.2
+DA	-	-	66.4	84.2	78.2	86.4
T3-small	76.0	88.1	46.1	71.0	71.4	82.2
+DA	-	-	58.0	79.3	75.8	84.8
T4-tiny	76.2	88.4	54.3	76.8	75.5	84.9
+DA	-	-	61.8	81.8	77.3	86.1

Table 5: Development set results for the teacher and various students on Chinese tasks.

cases. It may be a hint that narrow-and-deep models are better than wide-and-shallow models.

Finally, data augmentation (DA) is critical. For the experiments in the last line in Table 2, we use additional datasets during distillation: a subset of NewsQA (Trischler et al., 2017) training set is used in SQuAD; passages from the HotpotQA (Yang et al., 2018) training set is used in CoNLL-2003. The augmentation datasets significantly improve the performance, especially when the size of the training set is small, like CoNLL-2003.

We next show the effectiveness of `MultiTeacherDistiller`, which distills an ensemble of teachers to a single student model. For each task, we train three $\text{BERT}_{\text{BASE}}$ teacher models with different seeds. The student is also a $\text{BERT}_{\text{BASE}}$ model. The temperature is set to 8, and intermediate losses are not used. As Table 4 shows, for each task, the student achieves the best performance, even higher than the ensemble result.

5 Results on Chinese Datasets

The results on Chinese datasets are presented in Table 5. We notice that T4-tiny still outperforms T3-small on all tasks, which is consistent with their performance on English tasks. In the experiments with DA, CMRC 2018 and DRCD take each other's dataset as data augmentation. We observe that since

CMRC 2018 has a relatively small training set, DA has a much more significant effect.

6 Conclusion and Future Work

In this paper, we present TextBrewer, a flexible PyTorch-based distillation toolkit for NLP research and applications. TextBrewer provides rich customization options for users to compare different distillation methods and build their strategies. We have conducted a series of experiments. The results show that the distilled models can achieve state-of-the-art results with simple settings.

TextBrewer also has its limitations. For example, its usability in generation tasks such as machine translation has not been tested. We will keep adding more examples and tests to expand TextBrewer's scope of application.

Apart from the distillation strategies, the model structure also affects the performance. In the future, we aim to integrate neural architecture search into the toolkit to automate the searching for model structures.

Acknowledgments

We would like to thank all anonymous reviewers for their valuable comments on our work. This work was supported by the National Natural Science Foundation of China (NSFC) via grant 61976072, 61632011, and 61772153.

References

Kevin Clark, Minh-Thang Luong, Urvashi Khandelwal, Christopher D. Manning, and Quoc V. Le. 2019. BAM! born-again multi-task networks for natural language understanding. In *Proceedings of the 57th Annual Meeting of the Association for Computational Linguistics*, pages 5931–5937, Florence, Italy. Association for Computational Linguistics.

Alexis Conneau, Ruty Rinott, Guillaume Lample, Adina Williams, Samuel Bowman, Holger Schwenk, and Veselin Stoyanov. 2018. XNLI: Evaluating cross-lingual sentence representations. In *Proceedings of the 2018 Conference on Empirical Methods in Natural Language Processing*, pages 2475–2485, Brussels, Belgium. Association for Computational Linguistics.

Yiming Cui, Wanxiang Che, Ting Liu, Bing Qin, Ziqing Yang, Shijin Wang, and Guoping Hu. 2019a. Pre-training with whole word masking for chinese BERT. *CoRR*, abs/1906.08101.

Yiming Cui, Ting Liu, Wanxiang Che, Li Xiao, Zhipeng Chen, Wentao Ma, Shijin Wang, and Guoping Hu. 2019b. A span-extraction dataset for Chinese machine reading comprehension. In *Proceedings of the 2019 Conference on Empirical Methods in Natural Language Processing and the 9th International Joint Conference on Natural Language Processing (EMNLP-IJCNLP)*, pages 5886–5891, Hong Kong, China. Association for Computational Linguistics.

Jacob Devlin, Ming-Wei Chang, Kenton Lee, and Kristina Toutanova. 2019. BERT: Pre-training of deep bidirectional transformers for language understanding. In *Proceedings of the 2019 Conference of the North American Chapter of the Association for Computational Linguistics: Human Language Technologies, Volume 1 (Long and Short Papers)*, pages 4171–4186, Minneapolis, Minnesota. Association for Computational Linguistics.

Zehao Huang and Naiyan Wang. 2017. Like what you like: Knowledge distill via neuron selectivity transfer. *CoRR*, abs/1707.01219.

Xiaoqi Jiao, Yichun Yin, Lifeng Shang, Xin Jiang, Xiao Chen, Linlin Li, Fang Wang, and Qun Liu. 2019. Tinybert: Distilling BERT for natural language understanding. *CoRR*, abs/1909.10351.

Yoon Kim and Alexander M. Rush. 2016. Sequence-level knowledge distillation. In *Proceedings of the 2016 Conference on Empirical Methods in Natural Language Processing*, pages 1317–1327, Austin, Texas. Association for Computational Linguistics.

Zhenzhong Lan, Mingda Chen, Sebastian Goodman, Kevin Gimpel, Piyush Sharma, and Radu Soricut. 2019. ALBERT: A lite BERT for self-supervised learning of language representations. *CoRR*, abs/1909.11942.

Xiaodong Liu, Pengcheng He, Weizhu Chen, and Jianfeng Gao. 2019a. Improving multi-task deep neural networks via knowledge distillation for natural language understanding. *CoRR*, abs/1904.09482.

Xin Liu, Qingcai Chen, Chong Deng, Huajun Zeng, Jing Chen, Dongfang Li, and Buzhou Tang. 2018. LCQMC:a large-scale Chinese question matching corpus. In *Proceedings of the 27th International Conference on Computational Linguistics*, pages 1952–1962, Santa Fe, New Mexico, USA. Association for Computational Linguistics.

Yinhan Liu, Myle Ott, Naman Goyal, Jingfei Du, Mandar Joshi, Danqi Chen, Omer Levy, Mike Lewis, Luke Zettlemoyer, and Veselin Stoyanov. 2019b. Roberta: A robustly optimized BERT pretraining approach. *CoRR*, abs/1907.11692.

Alec Radford. 2018. Improving language understanding by generative pre-training.

Pranav Rajpurkar, Jian Zhang, Konstantin Lopyrev, and Percy Liang. 2016. SQuAD: 100,000+ questions for machine comprehension of text. In *Proceedings of the 2016 Conference on Empirical Methods in Natural Language Processing*, pages 2383–2392, Austin, Texas. Association for Computational Linguistics.

Victor Sanh, Lysandre Debut, Julien Chaumond, and Thomas Wolf. 2019. Distilbert, a distilled version of BERT: smaller, faster, cheaper and lighter. *CoRR*, abs/1910.01108.

Chih-Chieh Shao, Trois Liu, Yuting Lai, Yiying Tseng, and Sam Tsai. 2018. DRCD: a chinese machine reading comprehension dataset. *CoRR*, abs/1806.00920.

Siqi Sun, Yu Cheng, Zhe Gan, and Jingjing Liu. 2019a. Patient knowledge distillation for BERT model compression. In *Proceedings of the 2019 Conference on Empirical Methods in Natural Language Processing and the 9th International Joint Conference on Natural Language Processing (EMNLP-IJCNLP)*, pages 4323–4332, Hong Kong, China. Association for Computational Linguistics.

Yu Sun, Shuohuan Wang, Yu-Kun Li, Shikun Feng, Xuyi Chen, Han Zhang, Xin Tian, Danxiang Zhu, Hao Tian, and Hua Wu. 2019b. ERNIE: enhanced representation through knowledge integration. *CoRR*, abs/1904.09223.

Yu Sun, Shuohuan Wang, Yu-Kun Li, Shikun Feng, Hao Tian, Hua Wu, and Haifeng Wang. 2019c. ERNIE 2.0: A continual pre-training framework for language understanding. *CoRR*, abs/1907.12412.

Xu Tan, Yi Ren, Di He, Tao Qin, Zhou Zhao, and Tie-Yan Liu. 2019. Multilingual neural machine translation with knowledge distillation. In *7th International Conference on Learning Representations, ICLR 2019, New Orleans, LA, USA, May 6-9, 2019*.

Raphael Tang, Yao Lu, and Jimmy Lin. 2019. Natural language generation for effective knowledge distillation. In *Proceedings of the 2nd Workshop on Deep Learning Approaches for Low-Resource NLP (DeepLo 2019)*, pages 202–208, Hong Kong, China. Association for Computational Linguistics.

Erik F. Tjong Kim Sang and Fien De Meulder. 2003. Introduction to the CoNLL-2003 shared task: Language-independent named entity recognition. In *Proceedings of the Seventh Conference on Natural Language Learning at HLT-NAACL 2003*, pages 142–147.

Adam Trischler, Tong Wang, Xingdi Yuan, Justin Harris, Alessandro Sordoni, Philip Bachman, and Kaheer Suleman. 2017. NewsQA: A machine comprehension dataset. In *Proceedings of the 2nd Workshop on Representation Learning for NLP*, pages 191–200, Vancouver, Canada. Association for Computational Linguistics.

Alex Wang, Amanpreet Singh, Julian Michael, Felix Hill, Omer Levy, and Samuel R. Bowman. 2019. GLUE: A multi-task benchmark and analysis platform for natural language understanding. In *7th International Conference on Learning Representations, ICLR 2019, New Orleans, LA, USA, May 6-9, 2019*.

Tiancheng Wen, Shenqi Lai, and Xueming Qian. 2019. Preparing lessons: Improve knowledge distillation with better supervision. *CoRR*, abs/1911.07471.

Zhilin Yang, Zihang Dai, Yiming Yang, Jaime G. Carbonell, Ruslan Salakhutdinov, and Quoc V. Le. 2019. Xlnet: Generalized autoregressive pretraining for language understanding. *CoRR*, abs/1906.08237.

Zhilin Yang, Peng Qi, Saizheng Zhang, Yoshua Bengio, William Cohen, Ruslan Salakhutdinov, and Christopher D. Manning. 2018. HotpotQA: A dataset for diverse, explainable multi-hop question answering. In *Proceedings of the 2018 Conference on Empirical Methods in Natural Language Processing*, pages 2369–2380, Brussels, Belgium. Association for Computational Linguistics.

Junho Yim, Donggyu Joo, Ji-Hoon Bae, and Junmo Kim. 2017. A gift from knowledge distillation: Fast optimization, network minimization and transfer learning. In *2017 IEEE Conference on Computer Vision and Pattern Recognition, CVPR 2017, Honolulu, HI, USA, July 21-26, 2017*, pages 7130–7138.

Sanqiang Zhao, Raghav Gupta, Yang Song, and Denny Zhou. 2019. Extreme language model compression with optimal subwords and shared projections. *CoRR*, abs/1909.11687.

Neta Zmora, Guy Jacob, Lev Zlotnik, Bar Elharar, and Gal Novik. 2018. Neural network distiller.

Syntactic Search by Example

Micah Shlain[1,2]   **Hillel Taub-Tabib**[1]   **Shoval Sadde**[1]   **Yoav Goldberg**[1,2]

[1] Allen Institute for AI, Tel Aviv, Israel
[2] Bar Ilan University, Ramat-Gan, Israel

`{micahs,hillelt,shovals,yoavg}@allenai.org yogo@cs.biu.ac.il`

Abstract

We present a system that allows a user to search a large linguistically annotated corpus using syntactic patterns over dependency graphs. In contrast to previous attempts to this effect, we introduce a light-weight query language that does not require the user to know the details of the underlying syntactic representations, and instead to query the corpus by providing an example sentence coupled with simple markup. Search is performed at an interactive speed due to an efficient linguistic graph-indexing and retrieval engine. This allows for rapid exploration, development and refinement of syntax-based queries. We demonstrate the system using queries over two corpora: the English wikipedia, and a collection of English pubmed abstracts. A demo of the wikipedia system is avilable at: `https://allenai.github.io/spike/`.

1 Introduction

The introduction of neural-network based models into NLP brought with it a substantial increase in syntactic parsing accuracy. We can now produce accurate syntactically annotated corpora at scale. However, the produced representations themselves remain opaque to most users, and require substantial linguistic expertise to use. Patterns over syntactic dependency graphs[1] can be very effective for interacting with linguistically-annotated corpora, either for linguistic retrieval or for information and relation extraction (Fader et al., 2011; Akbik et al., 2014; Valenzuela-Escárcega et al., 2015,

2018). However, their use in mainstream NLP as represented in ACL and affiliated venues remain limited. We argue that this is due to the high barrier of entry associated with the application of such patterns. Our aim is to lower this barrier and allow also linguistically-naïve users to effectively experiment with and develop syntactic patterns. Our proposal rests on two components:

(1) A light-weight query language that does not require in-depth familiarity with the underlying syntactic representation scheme, and instead lets the user specify their intent via a natural language example and lightweight markup.

(2) A fast, near-real-time response time due to efficient indexing, allowing for rapid experimentation.

Figure 1 (next page) shows the interface of our web-based system. The user issued the query:

⟨⟩founder:[e]Paul   was   a   t:[w]founder   of ⟨⟩entity:[e]Microsoft.

The query specifies a sentence (*Paul was a founder of Microsoft*) and three named captures: *founder*, *t* and *entity*. The *founder* and *entity* captures should have the same entity-type as the corresponding sentence words (PERSON for Paul and ORGANIZATION for Microsoft, indicated by [e]), and the *t* capture should have the same word form as the one in the sentence (founder) (indicated by [w]). The syntactic relation between the captures should be the same as the one in the sentence, and the *founder* and *entity* captures should be *expanded* (indicated by ⟨⟩).

The query is translated into a graph-based query, which is shown below the query, each graph-node associated with the query word that triggered it. The system also returned a list of matched sentences. The matched tokens for each capture group (*founder*, *t* and *entity*) are highlighted. The user can then issue another query, browse the results, or download all the results as a tab-separated file.

---

[1]In this paper, we very loosely use the term "syntactic" to refer to a linguistically motivated graph-based annotation over a piece of text, where the graph is directed and there is a path between any two nodes. While this usually implies syntactic dependency trees or graphs (and indeed, our system currently indexes Enhanced English Universal Dependency graphs (Nivre et al., 2016; Schuster and Manning, 2016)) the system can work also with more semantic annotation schemes e.g, (Oepen et al., 2015), given the availability of an accurate enough parser for them.

Proceedings of the 58th Annual Meeting of the Association for Computational Linguistics, pages 17–23
July 5 - July 10, 2020. ©2020 Association for Computational Linguistics

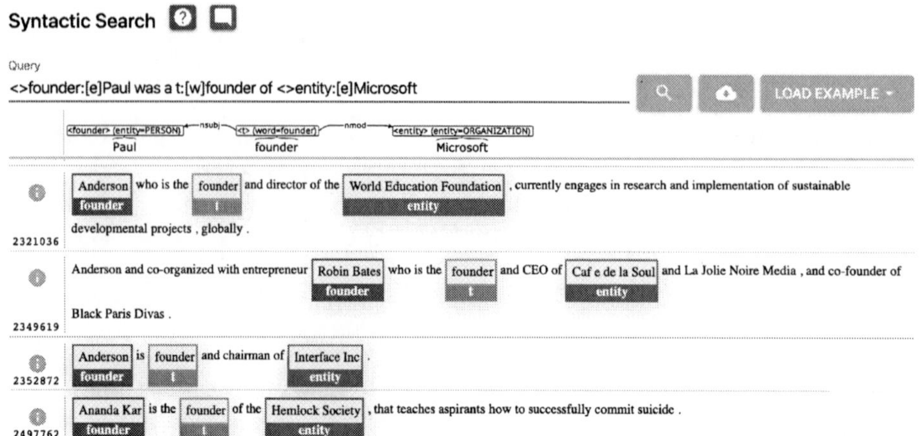

Figure 1: Syntactic Search System

2 Existing syntactic-query languages

While several rich query languages over linguistic tree and graph structure exist, they require a substantial amount of expertise to use.[2] The user needs to be familiar not only with the syntax of the query language itself, but to also be intimately familiar with the specific syntactic scheme used in the underlying linguistic annotations. For example, in Odin (Valenzuela-Escárcega et al., 2015), a dedicated language for pattern-based information extraction, the same rule as above is expressed as:

```
- label: Person
  type: token
  pattern: |
  [entity="PERSON"]+
- label: Organization
  type: token
  pattern: |
  [entity="ORGANIZATION"]+
- label: founded
  type: dependency
  pattern: |
    trigger = [word=founded]
    founder:Person = >nsubj
    entity:Organization = >nmod
```

The Spacy NLP toolkit[3] also includes pattern matcher over dependency trees,using JSON based syntax:

```
[{"PATTERN": {"ORTH": "founder"},
  "SPEC": {"NODE_NAME": "t"}},
 {"PATTERN": {"ENT_TYPE": "PERSON"}},
  "SPEC": {"NODE_NAME": "founder",
        "NBOR_RELOP": ">nsubj",
```

```
        "NBOR_NAME": "t"}},
 {"PATTERN": {"ENT_TYPE": "ORGANIZATION"},
  "SPEC": {"NODE_NAME": "entity",
        "NBOR_RELOP": ">nmod",
        "NBOR_NAME": "t"}}]
```

Stanford's Core-NLP package (Manning et al., 2014) includes a dependency matcher called SEM-GREX,[4] which uses a more concise syntax:

```
{ner:PERSON}=founder
  <nsubj ({word:founder}=t
        >nmod {ner:ORG}=entity)
```

The dep_search system[5] from Turku university (Luotolahti et al., 2017) is designed to provide a rich and expressive syntactic search over large parsebanks. They use a lightweight syntax and support working against pre-indexed data, though they do not support named captures of specific nodes.

```
PERSON <nsubj founder >nmod ORG
```

While the different systems vary in the verboseness and complexity of their own syntax (indeed, the Turku system's syntax is rather minimal), they all require the user to explicitly specify the dependency relations between the tokens, making it challenging and error-prone to write, read or edit. The challenge grows substantially as the complexity of the pattern increases beyond the very simple example we show here.

Closest in spirit to our proposal, the PROP-MINER system of Akbik et al. (2013) which lets the user enter a natural language sentence, mark spans as *subject*, *predicate* and *object*, and have a rule be

---

[2]We focus here on systems that are based on dependency syntax, but note that many systems and query languages exist also for constituency-trees, e.g., TGREP/TGREP2, TigerSearch (Lezius et al., 2002), the linguists search engine (Resnik and Elkiss, 2005), Fangorn (Ghodke and Bird, 2012).

[3]https://spacy.io/

[4]https://nlp.stanford.edu/software/tregex.shtml

[5]http://bionlp-www.utu.fi/dep_search/

generated automatically. However, the system is restricted to ternary subject-predicate-object patterns. Furthermore, the generated pattern is written in a path-expression SQL variant (SerQL, (Broekstra and Kampman, 2003)), which the user then needs to manually edit. For example, our query above will be translated to:

```
SELECT subject, predicate, object
FROM predicate.3 nsubj subject,
     predicate.3 nmod object,
WHERE subject POS NNP
AND predicate.3 POS NN
AND object POS NNP
AND subject TEXT PAUL
AND predicate.3 TEXT founder
AND object TEXT Microsoft
AND subject FULL_ENTITY
AND object FULL_ENTITY
```

All these systems require the user to closely interact with linguistic concepts and explicitly specify graph-structures, posing a high barrier of entry for non-expert users. They also slow down expert users: formulating a complex query may require a few minutes. Furthermore, many of these query languages are designed to match against a provided sentence, and are not indexable. This requires iterating over all sentences in the corpus attempting to match each one, requiring substantial time to obtain matches from large corpora.

Augustinus et al. (2012) describe a system for syntactic search by example, which retrieves tree fragments and which is completely UI based. Our system takes a similar approach, but replaces the UI-only interface with an expressive textual query language, allowing for richer queries. We also return node matches rather than tree fragments.

3   Syntactic Search by Example

We propose a substantially simplified language, that has the minimal syntax and that does not require the user to know the underlying syntactic schema upfront (though it does not completely hide it from the user, allowing for exposure over time, and allowing control for expert users who understand the underlying syntactic annotation scheme).

The query language is designed to be linguistically expressive, simple to use and amenable to efficient indexing and query. The simplicity and indexing requirements do come at a cost, though: we purposefully do not support some of the features available in existing languages. We expect these features to correlate with expertise.[6] At the same time, we also seamlessly support expressing arbitrary sub-graphs, a task which is either challenging or impossible with many of the other systems.

The language is based on the following principles: **(1)** The core of the query is a natural language sentence.
(2) A user can specify the tokens of interest and constraints on them via lightweight markup.
(3) While expert users can specify complex token constraints, effective constraints can be specified by pulling values from the query words.

The required syntactic knowledge from the user, both in terms of the syntax of the query language itself and in terms of the underlying linguistic formalism, remains minimal.

4   Graph Query Formalism

The language is structured around between-token relations and within-token constraints, where tokens can be *captured*.

Formally, our query $G = (V, E)$ is a labeled directed graph, where each node $v_i \in V$ corresponds to a token, and a labeled edge $e = (v_i, v_j, \ell) \in E$ between the nodes corresponds to a between-token syntactic constraint. This query graph is then matched against parsed target sentences, looking for a correspondence between query nodes and target-sentence nodes that adhere to the token and edge constraints.

For example, the following graph specifies three tokens, where the first and second are connected via an 'xcomp' relation, and the second and third via a 'dobj' relation. The first token is unconstrained, while the second token must have the POS-tag of VB, and the third token must be the word home.

Sentences whose syntactic graph has a subgraph that aligns to the query graph and adheres to the constraints will be considered as matches. Example of such matching sentences are:
- John *wanted$_w$ to go$_v$ home$_h$ after lunch.*
- *It was a place she decided$_w$ to call$_v$ her home$_h$.*
The <w>, <v> and <h> marks on the nodes denote *named captures*. When matching a sentence, the sentence tokens corresponding to the graph-nodes will be bound to variables named 'w', 'v' and 'h', in our case {w=wanted, v=go, h=home} for the first sentence and {w=decided, v=call, h=home} for the second. Graph nodes can also be

____
[6]Example of a query feature we do not support is quantifi-

cation, i.e., "nodes a and b should be connected via a path that includes *one or more* 'conj' edges".

unnamed, in which case they must match sentence tokens but will not bind to any variable. The graph structure is not meant to be specified by hand,[7] but rather to be inferred from the example based query language described in the next section (an example query resulting in this graph is "They w:wanted to v:[tag]go h:[word]home").

Between-token constraints correspond to labeled directed edges in the sentence's syntactic graph.

Within-token constraints correspond to properties of individual sentence tokens.[8] For each property we specify a list of possible values (a disjunction) and if lists for several properties are provided, we require all of them to hold (a conjunction). For example, in the constraint tag=VBD|VBZ&lemma=buy we look for tokens with POS-tag of either VBD or VBZ, and the lemma *buy*. The list of possible values for a property can be specified as a pipe-separated list (tag=VBD|VBZ|VBN) or as a regular expression (tag=/VB[DZN]/).

5 Example-based User-friendly Query Language

The graph language described above is expressive enough to support many interesting queries, but it is also very tedious to specify query graphs G, especially for non-expert users. We propose a simple syntax that allows to easily specify a graph query G (constrained nodes connected by labeled edges) using a textual query q that takes the form of an example sentence and lightweight markup.

Let $s = w_1, ..., w_n$ be a proper English sentence. Let D be its dependency graph, with nodes w_i and labeled edges (w_i, w_j, ℓ). A corresponding textual query q takes the form $q = q_1, ..., q_n$, where each q_i is either a word $q_i = w_i$, or a *marked* word $q_i = m(w_i)$. A marking of a word takes the form: :word (unnamed capture) name:word (named capture) or name:[constraints]word , :[constraints]word . Consider the query:

John w:wanted to v:[tag=VB] go h:[word=home] home

corresponding to the above graph query. The marked words are:

q_2 =w:wanted	(unconstrained, name:w)
q_4 =v:[tag=VB]go	(cnstr:tag=VB, name:v)
q_5 =h:[word=home]home	(cnstr:word=home, name:h)

Each of these corresponds to a node v_{qi} in the query graph above.

Let m be the set of marked query words, and m^+ be a minimal connected subgraph of D that includes all the words in m. When translating q to G, each marked word $w_i \in m$ is translated to a named query graph node v_{q_i} with the appropriate restriction. The additional words $w_j \in m^+ \setminus m$ are translated to unrestricted, unnamed nodes v_{q_j}. We add a query graph edge (v_{q_i}, v_{q_j}, ℓ) for each pair in V for which $(w_i, w_j, \ell) \in D$.

Further query simplifications. Consider the marked word h:[word=home] home. The constraint is redundant with the word. In such cases we allow the user to drop the value, which is then taken from the corresponding property of the query word. This allows us to replace the query:

John w:wanted to v:[tag=VB]go h:[word=home]home

with:

John w:wanted to v:[tag]go h:[word]home

This further drives the "by example" agenda, as the user does not need to know what the lemma, entity-type or POS-tag of a word are in order to specify them as a constraint. Full property names can be replaced with their shorthands w,l,t,e:

John w:wanted to v:[t]go h:[w]home

Finally, capture names can be omitted, in which case an automatic name is generated based on the corresponding word:

John :wanted to :[t]go :[w]home

Anchors. In some cases we want to add a node to the graph, without an explicit capture. In such cases we can use the anchor $ ($John). These are interpreted as having a default constraint of [w], which can be overriden by providing an alternative constraint ($[e]John), or an empty one ($[]John).

Expansions When matching a query against a sentence the graph nodes bind to sentence words. Sometimes, we may want the match to be expanded to a larger span of the sentence. For example, when matching a word which is part of a entity, we often wish to capture the entire entity rather than the word. This is achieved by prefixing the term with the "expansion diamond" ◊. The default behavior is to expand the match from the current word to the named entity boundary or NP-chunk that surrounds it, if it exists. We are currently investigating the option of providing additional expansion strategies.

---

[7]Indeed, we currently do not even expose a textual representation of the graph.

[8]Currently supported properties are word-form (**word**), lemma (**lemma**), pos-tag (**tag**) or entity type (**entity**). Additional types can be easily added, provided that we have suitable linguistic annotators for them.

Summary To summarize the query language from the point of view of the user: the user starts with a sentence $w_1, ..., w_n$, and marks some of the words for inclusion in the query graph. For each marked word, the user may specify a name, and optional constraints. The user query is then translated to a graph query as described above. The results list highlights the words corresponding to the marked query words. The user can choose for the results to highlight entire entities rather than single words.

6 Interactive Pattern Authoring

An important aspect of the system is its interactivity. Users enter queries by writing a sentence and adding markup on some words, and can then refine them following feedback from the environment, as we demonstrate with a walk-through example.

A user interested in people who obtained degrees from higher education institutions may issue the following query:

subj:John obtained his d:[w]degree from inst:Harvard

Here, the person in the "subj" capture and the institution in the "inst" capture are placeholders for items to be captured, so the user uses generic names and leaves them unconstrained. The "degree" ("d") capture should match exactly, as the user specified the "w" constraint (exact word match). When pressing Enter, the user is then shown the resulting query-graph and a result list. The user can then refine their queries based on either the query graph, the result list, or both. For the above query, the graph is:

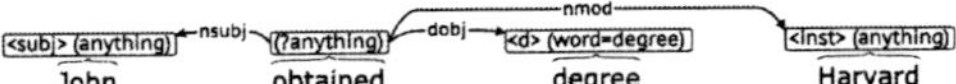

Note that the query graph associates each graph node with the query word that triggered it. The word "obtained" resulted in a graph node even though it was not marked by the user as a capture. The user makes note to themselves to go back to this word later. The user also notices that the word "from" is not part of the query.

Looking at the result list, things look weird:

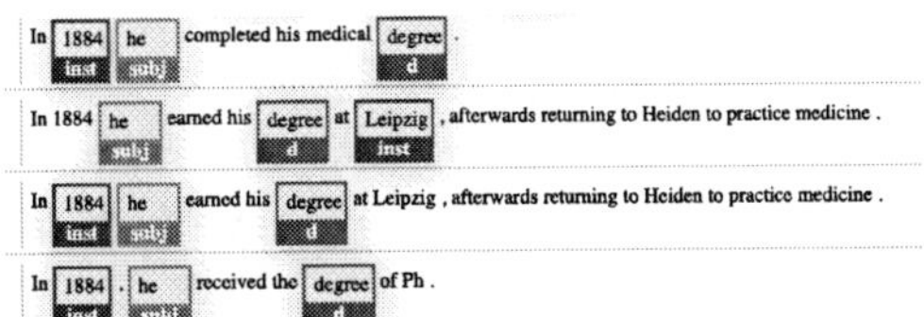

Maybe this is because the word *from* is not in the graph? Indeed, adding a non-capturing exact-word anchor on "from" solves this issue:

subj:John obtained his d:[w]degree $from inst:Harvard

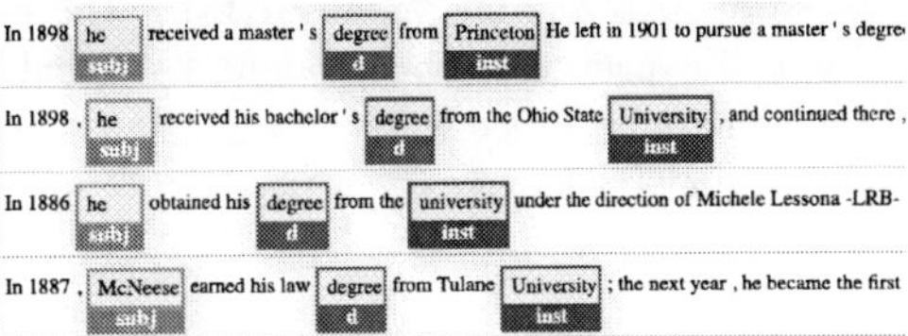

However, the resulting list contains many non-names in the *subj* capture. Trying to resolve this, the user adds an "entity-type" constraint to the *subj* capture:

subj:[e]John   obtained   his   d:[w]degree $from inst:Harvard

Note that the user didn't specify an exact type, yet the query graph correctly resolved PERSON.

The user is interested in the full name of the person and organization, so they change from single-word capture to expanded capture, with the default expansion level (using the diamond prefix ◇):

◇subj:[e]John   obtained   his   d:[w]degree $from ◇inst:Harvard

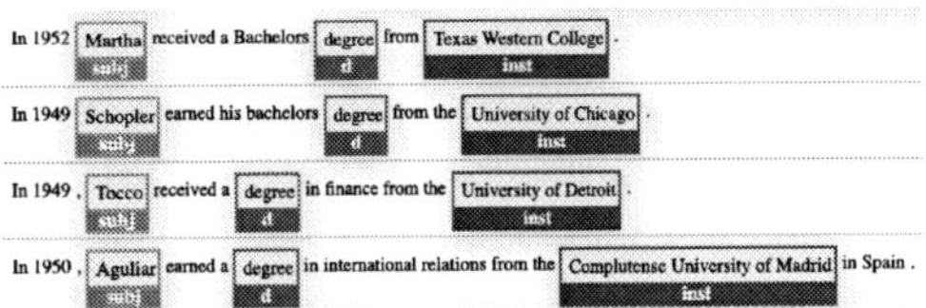

These are the kind of results the user expected, but now they are curious about degrees obtained by females, and their representation in the Wikipedia corpus. Adding the pronoun to the query, the user then issues the following two queries, saving the result-sets from each one as a CSV for further comparative analysis.

◇subj:[e]John   obtained $his   d:[w]degree $from ◇inst:Harvard

◇subj:[e]John   obtained $her   d:[w]degree $from ◇inst:Harvard

Our user now worries that they may be missing some results by focusing on the word *degree*. Maybe other things can be obtained from a university? The user then sets an exact-word constraint on "Harvard", adds a lemma constraint to "obtain" and clears the constraint from "degree":

◇subj:[e]John   :[l]obtained   his   d:degree $from ◇inst:[w]Harvard

Browsing the results, the *d* capture includes words such as "BA, PhD, MBA, certificate". But the result list is rather short, suggesting that either *Harvard* or *obtain* are too restrictive. The user seeks to expand the "obtain" node's vocabulary, adding back the exact word constraint on "degree" while removing the one from "obtain":

⟨⟩subj:[e]John :[]obtained his d:[w]degree $from ⟨⟩inst:[w]Harvard

Looking at the result list in the *o* capture, the user chooses the lemmas "receive, complete, earn, obtain, get", adds them to the *o* constraint, and removes the degree constraint.

⟨⟩subj:[e]John
o:[l=receive|complete|earn|obtain|get]obtained
his d:degree $from ⟨⟩inst:[w]Harvard

The returned result-set is now much longer, and we select additional terms for the degree slot and remove the institution word constraint, resulting in the final query:

⟨⟩subj:[e]John
o:[l=receive|complete|earn|obtain|get]obtained his d:
[w=degree|MA|BA|MBA|doctorate|masters|PhD]degree
$from ⟨⟩inst:Harvard

The result is a list of person names earning degrees from institution, and the entire list can be downloaded as a tab-separated file which includes the named captures as well as the source sentences (over Wikipedia, this list has 6197 rows).[9]

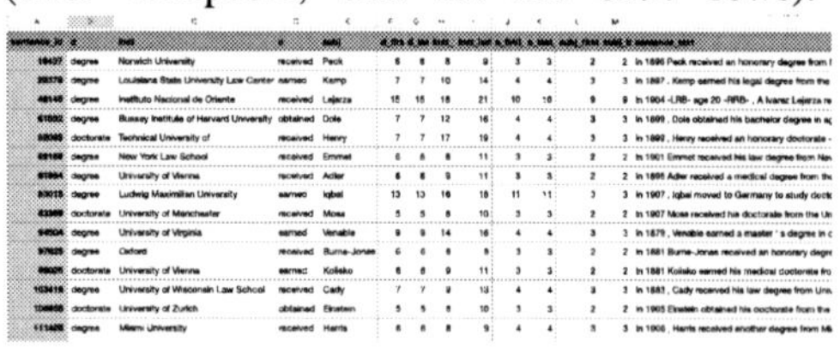

The query can also be further refined to capture *which* degree was obtained, e.g.:

⟨⟩subj:[e]John   o:[l=...]obtained]   his   kind:law d:[w=...]degree $from ⟨⟩inst:Harvard

capturing under *kind* words like *law*, *chemistry*, *engineering* and *DLitt* but also *bachelors*, *masters* and *graduate*.

This concludes our walk-through.

7   Additional Query Examples

To whet the reader's appetite, here are a sample of additional queries, showing different potential use-cases. Over wikipedia:

- p:[e]Sam $[l=win|receive]won an $Oscar.
- ⟨⟩p:[e]Sam $[l=win|receive]won an $Oscar $for
  ⟨⟩thing:something
- $fish $such $as ⟨⟩fish:salmon
- ⟨⟩hero:[t]Spiderman $is a $superhero
- I like kind:coconut $oil
- kind:coconut $oil is $used for purpose:eating

Over a pubmed corpus, annotated with the SciSpacy (Neumann et al., 2019) pipeline:

- ⟨⟩x:[e]aspirin $inhibits ⟨⟩y:thing
- a $combination of ⟨⟩d1:[e]aspirin and
  ⟨⟩d2:[e]alcohol $:[l]causes ⟨⟩t:thing
- ⟨⟩patients:[t]rats were $injected $with ⟨⟩what:drugs

8   Implementation Details

The indexing is handled by Lucene.[10] We currently use Odinson (Valenzuela-Escárcega et al., 2020),[11] an open-source Lucene-based query engine developed at Lum.ai, as a successor of Odin (Valenzuela-Escárcega et al., 2015), that allows to index syntactic graphs and issue efficient path queries on them. We translate our queries into an Odinson path query that corresponds to a longest path in our query graph. We then iterate over the returned Odinson matches and verify the constraints that were not on the path. Conceptually, the Odinson system works by first using Lucene's reverse-index for retrieving sentences for which there is a token matching each of the specified token-constraints, and then verifying the syntactic between-token constraints. To improve the Lucene-query selectivity, tokens are indexed with incoming and outgoing syntactic edge label information, which is incorporated as additional token-constraints to the Lucene engine. The system easily supports millions of sentences, returning results at interactive speeds.

9   Conclusions

We introduce a simple query language that allows to pose complex syntax-based queries, and obtain results in an interactive speed.

A search interface over Wikipedia sentences is available at `https://allenai.github.io/spike/`. We intend to release the code as open source, as well as providing hosted open access to a PubMed-based corpus.

---

[9]The list can be even more comprehensive had we selected additional degree words and obtain words, and considered also additional re-phrasings.

[10]`https://lucene.apache.org`
[11]`https://github.com/lum-ai/odinson/`

Acknowledgments

We thank the team at LUM.ai and the University of Arizona, in particular Mihai Surdeanu, Marco Valenzuela-Escárcega, Gus Hahn-Powell and Dane Bell, for fruitful discussion and their work on the Odinson system.

This project has received funding from the Europoean Research Council (ERC) under the Europoean Union's Horizon 2020 research and innovation programme, grant agreement No. 802774 (iEXTRACT).

References

Alan Akbik, Oresti Konomi, and Michail Melnikov. 2013. Propminer: A workflow for interactive information extraction and exploration using dependency trees. In *Proceedings of the 51st Annual Meeting of the Association for Computational Linguistics: System Demonstrations*, pages 157–162, Sofia, Bulgaria. Association for Computational Linguistics.

Alan Akbik, Thilo Michael, and Christoph Boden. 2014. Exploratory relation extraction in large text corpora. In *Proceedings of COLING 2014, the 25th International Conference on Computational Linguistics: Technical Papers*, pages 2087–2096.

Liesbeth Augustinus, Vincent Vandeghinste, and Frank Van Eynde. 2012. Example-based treebank querying. In *LREC*.

Jeen Broekstra and Arjohn Kampman. 2003. Serql: A second generation rdf query language. In *Proc. SWAD-Europe Workshop on Semantic Web Storage and Retrieval*, pages 13–14.

Anthony Fader, Stephen Soderland, and Oren Etzioni. 2011. Identifying relations for open information extraction. In *Proceedings of the conference on empirical methods in natural language processing*, pages 1535–1545. Association for Computational Linguistics.

Sumukh Ghodke and Steven Bird. 2012. Fangorn: A system for querying very large treebanks. In *Proceedings of COLING 2012: Demonstration Papers*, pages 175–182, Mumbai, India. The COLING 2012 Organizing Committee.

Wolfgang Lezius, Hannes Biesinger, and Ciprian-Virgil Gerstenberger. 2002. Tigersearch manual.

Juhani Luotolahti, Jenna Kanerva, and Filip Ginter. 2017. Dep_search: Efficient search tool for large dependency parsebanks. In *Proceedings of the 21st Nordic Conference on Computational Linguistics*, pages 255–258, Gothenburg, Sweden. Association for Computational Linguistics.

Christopher D. Manning, Mihai Surdeanu, John Bauer, Jenny Finkel, Steven J. Bethard, and David McClosky. 2014. The Stanford CoreNLP natural language processing toolkit. In *Association for Computational Linguistics (ACL) System Demonstrations*, pages 55–60.

Mark Neumann, Daniel King, Iz Beltagy, and Waleed Ammar. 2019. Scispacy: Fast and robust models for biomedical natural language processing.

Joakim Nivre, Marie-Catherine De Marneffe, Filip Ginter, Yoav Goldberg, Jan Hajic, Christopher D Manning, Ryan McDonald, Slav Petrov, Sampo Pyysalo, Natalia Silveira, et al. 2016. Universal dependencies v1: A multilingual treebank collection. In *Proceedings of the Tenth International Conference on Language Resources and Evaluation (LREC'16)*, pages 1659–1666.

Stephan Oepen, Marco Kuhlmann, Yusuke Miyao, Daniel Zeman, Silvie Cinková, Dan Flickinger, Jan Hajič, and Zdeňka Urešová. 2015. SemEval 2015 task 18: Broad-coverage semantic dependency parsing. In *Proceedings of the 9th International Workshop on Semantic Evaluation (SemEval 2015)*, pages 915–926, Denver, Colorado. Association for Computational Linguistics.

Philip Resnik and Aaron Elkiss. 2005. The Linguist's Search Engine: An overview. In *Proceedings of the ACL Interactive Poster and Demonstration Sessions*, pages 33–36, Ann Arbor, Michigan. Association for Computational Linguistics.

Sebastian Schuster and Christopher D Manning. 2016. Enhanced english universal dependencies: An improved representation for natural language understanding tasks. In *Proceedings of the Tenth International Conference on Language Resources and Evaluation (LREC'16)*, pages 2371–2378.

Marco A Valenzuela-Escárcega, Özgün Babur, Gus Hahn-Powell, Dane Bell, Thomas Hicks, Enrique Noriega-Atala, Xia Wang, Mihai Surdeanu, Emek Demir, and Clayton T Morrison. 2018. Large-scale automated machine reading discovers new cancer-driving mechanisms. *Database*, 2018.

Marco A. Valenzuela-Escárcega, Gus Hahn-Powell, and Dane Bell. 2020. Odinson: A fast rule-based information extraction framework. In *Proceedings of the Twelfth International Conference on Language Resources and Evaluation (LREC 2020)*, Marseille, France. European Language Resources Association (ELRA).

Marco A Valenzuela-Escárcega, Gus Hahn-Powell, Mihai Surdeanu, and Thomas Hicks. 2015. A domain-independent rule-based framework for event extraction. In *Proceedings of ACL-IJCNLP 2015 System Demonstrations*, pages 127–132.

Tabouid: a Wikipedia-based word guessing game

Timothée Bernard

National Institute of Advanced Industrial Science and Technology (AIST), Japan

`timothee.bernard@ens-lyon.org`

Abstract

We present Tabouid, a word-guessing game automatically generated from Wikipedia. Tabouid contains 10,000 (virtual) cards in English, and as many in French, covering not only words and linguistic expressions but also a variety of topics including artists, historical events or scientific concepts. Each card corresponds to a Wikipedia article, and conversely, any article could be turned into a card. A range of relatively simple NLP and machine-learning techniques are effectively integrated into a two-stage process. First, a large subset of Wikipedia articles are scored — this score estimates the difficulty, or alternatively, the playability of the page. Then, the best articles are turned into cards by selecting, for each of them, a list of banned words based on its content. We believe that the game we present is more than mere entertainment and that, furthermore, this paper has pedagogical potential.[1]

1 Introduction

Thanks to its considerable size — a total of more than 50 million articles in 300 different languages today — and its availability online, Wikipedia has found many uses other than those of the traditional encyclopaedia. It is indeed frequently used for research in AI and natural language processing (NLP). For example, various large-scale machine-readable knowledge bases have been generated from the online encyclopedia, including YAGO (Suchanek et al., 2007), YAGO2 (Hoffart et al., 2013) or DBpedia (Bizer et al., 2009), in addition to reading comprehension datasets such as SQuAD (Rajpurkar et al., 2016) and TriviaQA (Joshi et al., 2017). The plain text from Wikipedia articles has also been used directly as the only source of knowl-

edge for Question-Answering systems such as the one developed by Chen et al. (2017).

This article presents a system which uses Wikipedia to generate the content of an application that is inspired by Taboo, a word-guessing board game originally published by Parker Brothers in 1989. To play our version of the game, called "Tabouid", all the group (of at least two) players require is a single electronic device (typically a smartphone). The game is divided in turns. During her turn (the length of which is defined by a countdown), the player looks at the *card* displayed on the screen. A card is composed of a *title* and a list of additional *banned words* (the words included in the title are considered banned words). See Figures 1 and 2 for two screenshots of the application (the circle around the title of the card acts as a countdown). The player sets out to make the other players guess the title on the card (in its exact wording). To do so, she has to describe the concept to the other players but without using any of the banned words, nor any words constructed with the same stems (translations of the words into other languages are not allowed either). Once a title has been guessed, the player continues on to the next card. The player has to skip the current card as soon as she mentions a banned word.

The originality of Tabouid lies in the fact that its content has been automatically generated from Wikipedia using a range of NLP and machine learning techniques. This automated process means that Tabouid can benefit from a wealth of 10,000 cards in English, and as many in French, covering not only words and linguistic expressions but also a variety of topics including artists, historical events or scientific concepts. In addition, all cards in Tabouid are associated with a difficulty score. This allows the difficulty level of the game to be set in a straightforward way. With such an adaptable difficulty, the game can accommodate various groups of players,

---

[1] The work presented in this paper is a personal project and is not directly related to my research at AIST.

Proceedings of the 58th Annual Meeting of the Association for Computational Linguistics, pages 24–29
July 5 - July 10, 2020. ©2020 Association for Computational Linguistics

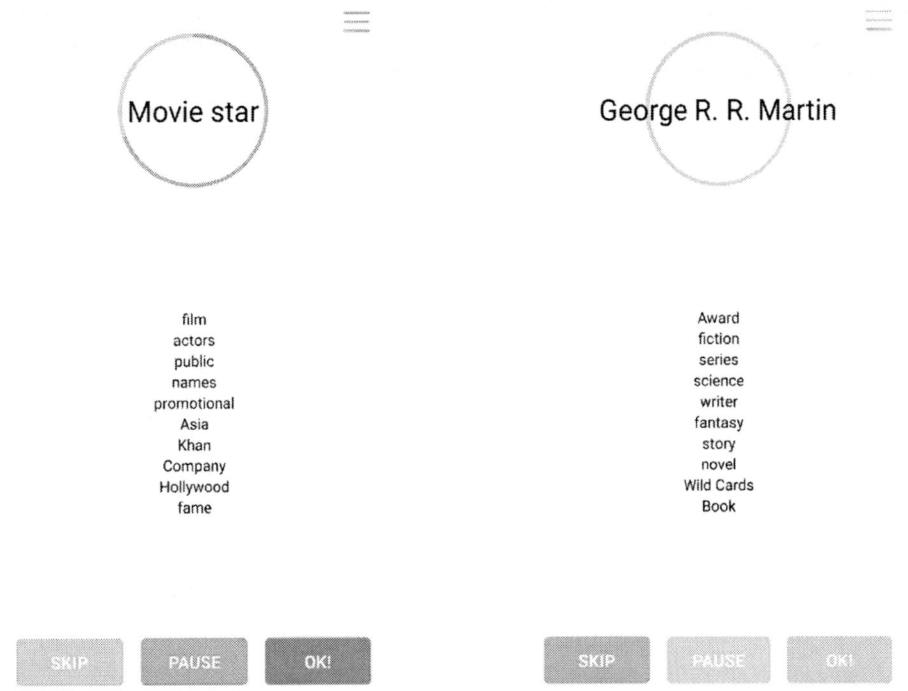

Figure 1: Screenshot of the application with the card `Movie Star`.

Figure 2: Screenshot of the application with the card `George R. R. Martin`.

which could include individuals such as children or foreigners, whose level of proficiency or knowledge of the culture associated with the target language may vary. In addition, we believe that the work presented here can have some pedagogical value by defining an implementation project for students enrolled in NLP or computational linguistic programs.

In this article, we describe how the cards were generated. Each card corresponds to a Wikipedia page. The title of the card is the title of the page, and the additional banned words (or expressions) are extracted from the text (and links) of the page. The automatic process is divided into two parts. First, we compute a difficulty score for each page of (a large subset of) Wikipedia as described in Section 2. Then, for the best pages (i.e., the easiest ones), we select a list of banned words as described in Section 3.

You can currently play Tabouid in English and French. The game is available as an Android[2] and iOS[3] application that is entirely free and does not

contain any advertisement. The cards have been pre-generated and packaged with the application; an internet connection is not required during the game.

2 Page scoring

The computation of difficulty scores is the most complex, and probably also the most crucial, part of the process. Indeed, almost all of the pages in Wikipedia would make for very poor cards, and so represent little to no interest to the game. They broadly fall into two categories. The first category is that of pages referring to entities lying very far from what we can consider *common knowledge*. For example (taken randomly from Wikipedia), `Smrekovec Lodge`, described as "a mountain hostel on the southern slope of the Smrekovec Mountains" (in Slovenia). The other category comprises pages that do refer to relatively familiar concepts, but that are way too specific and technical to be actually guessed in the context of the game. For example, `Taekwondo at the 2016 Summer Olympics - Men's +80 kg.` Wikipedia

[2]`https://play.google.com/store/apps/details?id=com.tot.tabouid`

[3]`https://apps.apple.com/us/app/tabouid/id1477994156`

contains a very large number of pages for sport events of all kinds and in many variations — while some hardcore sport fans might actually enjoy playing such cards, we will assume than most players would quickly get bored after having a good laugh (at best).

By contrast, here are several examples of pages that will make for good cards: `Saturday`, `Feminism`, `Christopher Columbus` and `Bangladesh`. In the middle, pages such as `List of scientists who disagree with the scientific consensus on global warming` and `History of mathematical notation` can be found, which are definitely challenging but still playable and fun for individuals used to the game. We therefore want to compute difficulty scores that reflect this natural gradient.

To do so, we use a neural network that takes as input a vector representation of a page and computes a real-valued score between 0 and 1. The lower the score, the more difficult the page.[4] We first start by describing how the vector representation of each page is computed before turning to the neural network itself before describing the annotation collection.

2.1 Page representation

Each page vector can be divided in two subvectors: a vector of *categories and title features*, containing information about both the categories the page belong to and its title[5], and a vector of *various features*.

There are 10 various features: (1) the number of visits to the page between January 1st 2015 and December 31th 2018, (2) the variance of the monthly distribution of the number of visits between these two dates divided by its squared mean (this is a measure of dispersion of the distribution), (3) the size of the page, (4) the date of creation of the page, (5) the date of last modification of the page, (6) the number of modifications of the page since its creation, (7) the number of translations of the page in other versions of Wikipedia, (8) whether the title contains the name of a month, (9) whether the title is a date (matching some regular expression), and (10) whether the title contains foreign characters. Except for the three last of these, which are binary, each feature is formatted as a real value which is then linearly transformed so that the corresponding distribution over all pages has mean 0 and standard deviation 1.

The *categories and title* vectors are computed as follows. We first build the *title word assignment matrix* W containing one line for each page and where rows represent words, such that $W_{i,j} = 1$ if the title of page i contains word j and 0 otherwise.[6] We also build the *category assignment matrix* C in a similar way, such that $C_{i,j} = 1$ if page i belongs to a category containing word j, and 0 otherwise. Then, we concatenate these two matrices and apply a dimensionality reduction algorithm. More specifically, we use the `TruncatedSVD` algorithm implemented in the Scikit-learn library (Pedregosa et al., 2011) to produce a vector of size 50 for each page.[7]

2.2 Neural network

We use a very simple architecture for the neural network. The reason is that, as explained below, we have very little annotated data to train the system on. Therefore, to prevent overfitting, we define a model with a small number of parameters and such that some of these parameters are (to a certain extent) *interpretable*. One of the advantages of interpretable parameters is that we can manually set them to sensible values at the beginning of the training process. By doing so, we want to encourage the network to leverage actual correlations of the underlying distribution rather than mere artefacts of the training set.

Let u be a page vector (of dimension 60). It is first sent through a square affine layer, $u' = A \cdot u + B$, the result of which is then used to perform an element-wise multiplication, $v = u * u'$. Finally, this vector is sent through a sigmoid layer of height 1 to produce the difficulty score, $s = \sigma(a \cdot v + b)$.

This model contains only 3,844 parameters and

---

[4]Alternatively, the score can be interpreted as a *playability* score: the higher the score, the higher the playability of the page.

[5]In Wikipedia, each page belong to zero, one or more *categories* such as `20th-century women scientists`, `Naturalized citizens of France` or `People from Warsaw`, to name a few of the 58 categories the `Marie Curie` page belongs to. These categories define a hierarchy that is at the heart of knowledge-bases such as (Suchanek et al., 2007) and YAGO2 (Hoffart et al., 2013), in addition to taxonomies, such as WikiTaxonomy (Ponzetto and Strube, 2011) and WikiNet (Nastase et al., 2010).

[6]We ignore stop words and words appearing in less than 0.1% of the page titles. We use a set of one million randomly selected pages.

[7]This algorithm is based on singular value decomposition (SVD; Halko et al., 2011), which is also at the heart of latent semantic analysis (LSA; Dumais et al., 1988).

allows direct multiplicative interaction between each pair of coefficients of the input vector. In addition, if we expand the score as

$$s = \sigma\left(\sum_i (a_i u_i B_i + a_i u_i \sum_j A_{i,j} u_j) + b\right) \quad (1)$$

we can notice the linear $a_i u_i B_i$ terms. We recall that, for $0 \leq i \leq 9$, we know exactly what u_i means.[8] For all of them, we can intuitively guess whether they have a positive or negative impact on the difficulty or playability of the corresponding card, which allows us to initialise the product $a_i B_i$ in a sensible way. For example, we assume that, all other things being equal, the higher the popularity of the page, the lower the difficulty of the card. Similarly, a high dispersion in the visitor distribution might indicate a temporary fame of the page, which would have possibly made an interesting card for a short period after the peak of the distribution, but likely to become obsolete after that. So, we initialise $a_0 B_0$ with a positive value and $a_1 B_1$ with a negative one. More precisely, we initialise $a_i = 1$ for all i and then set $b_0 = 1$, $b_1 = -0.5$, $b_2 = 1$, $b_3 = -1$, $b_4 = 0.5$, $b_5 = 0.5$, $b_6 = 1$, $b_7 = -0.5$, $b_8 = -0.5$, $b_9 = -1$. Note that these weights will be trained with all other parameters, potentially (in)validating our intuitions.

Given a training set $D = (x_i, y_i)_i$ where x_i is a Wikipedia article and y_i is its annotated score, we train the model to minimise the cross-entropy over D, $L = -\sum_i s(x_i) \log(y_i) + (1 - s(x_i)) \log(1 - s(x_i))$. The training is done by stochastic gradient descent with momentum, using L2 regularisation.

2.3 Annotation and results

To train the model described above, we collect annotations for a very small subset of Wikipedia. Pages are annotated with a real-valued score between 0 (hard/unplayable) and 1 (easy). Because, as explained above, Wikipedia is strongly imbalanced towards unplayable pages, manually annotating random pages chosen from a uniform distribution would be a very inefficient process. Instead, we implement an *active learning* process.

In short, we start by scoring the 100 most visited pages, as they contain a high proportion of easy pages. This forms our initial dataset. We train the model on this dataset and use it to score some unlabelled pages among which we select some instances to be scored by a human annotator. We add these 10 instances to the dataset and reiterate.

The query strategy that we adopt is the following: if the average score in the dataset is below 0.5, we select the 10 pages with the highest predicted score, otherwise we select the 10 lowest ones. The rational of this choice was to keep the dataset balanced. In retrospect, more principled techniques such as *expected model change* or *uncertainty sampling* (Settles, 2009; Fu et al., 2013) might have been tried, but this basic strategy yielded satisfying results, so we stuck to it.

After having annotated around 2300 instances in this way, the 500 pages with highest predicted scores were sent to human annotators. Once this process was completed, we trained the model on 70% of the scored pages, dividing the remaining 30% for early stopping and evaluation. One possible way to quantify the performance of this model is to discretise the score space ($[0, 1]$) into two categories ($s \leq 0.5$ and $s > 0.5$) and to compute the accuracy as in a binary classification task. On 10 trained models with the interpretable weights initialised as explained above, the best accuracy is 85.0%, the mean accuracy is 83.5% and the standard deviation is 1.1%. On 10 trained models without the initialisation procedure, the best accuracy is 84.4%, the mean accuracy is 82.9% and the standard deviation is 1.3%. This tends to show that our initialisation procedure is justified and makes the training more effective and reliable.

By manually inspecting the weights of a randomly chosen trained network, we can compute the $a_i B_i$ products for the 10 various features. We will not comment on most values, which are unsurprising but only mention that contrary to our expectations, the product for the size feature is very low ($a_2 B_2 = 0.03$) and the one for the number of translations too ($a_6 B_6 = 0.02$). This does not mean, however, that these features do not have a positive effect on the score of the page, as they are also involved in the multiplicative terms (see 1).[9]

The 10,000 pages with the highest scores (this includes pages annotated by humans) — from Donald Trump (1.0) to Landscape painting (0.59) — have been included as cards in the game. The selection of the banned words for

---

[8]The interpretability of the other coefficients is dependent on the result of the dimensionality reduction, which we will not discuss here.

[9]See for instance the work of Lipton (2018) about the difficulty of interpreting even simple models.

each page is the subject of the next section. The players can set a difficulty setting that determines which cards are shown during the game: if the difficulty is set as $d \in [1, 10000]$, only the d easiest cards are used (in random order). This setting, however, has no effect on each card's list of banned words.

3 Banned words selection

A simplified version of our banned words selection algorithm is as follows. For a given Wikipedia article, its text is first tokenised. Tokens are then stemmed and all stop words are removed. Finally, we select the 10 most frequent stems in the page and use their most frequent tokens (one for each) as banned words. Tokenisation and stemming are performed with the NLTK library (Bird et al., 2009).

There are two main differences between this simplification and the actual algorithm we use. The first is that we add rules to NTLK's stemmer in order to map strongly related words that are stemmed differently to the same class. For example, we send words stemmed as *lawyer* to the *law* class. We send the words stemmed as *pole* or *poland* (but starting with a capital letter) to the *polish* class. For all stems ending in *pean*, we remove the final *ean* (e.g., *European* is sent to *europ*). Around 25 rules have been manually defined during the development of the English version of the game.

Second, we do not ban only single words, but also longer expressions. We detect links pointing to other Wikipedia articles and consider their titles as potential banned expressions. Also, because it appears that entities having a Wikipedia page of their own are usually very informative even when they have comparatively few mentions in the text, we count them with a factor 1.5. Given the name of a Wikipedia article linked in the current page, each of its occurrences counts not only as 1 occurrence for each of the tokens it is composed of but also as 1.5 occurrences of the full name. For example, each occurrence of *Serge Gainsbourg* will count as 1 occurrence of *Serge*, 1 occurrence of *Gainsbourg* and 1.5 occurrences of *Serge Gainsbourg*. An occurrence of a single word entity name, such as *Madonna*, simply counts as 1.5 occurrences of *Madonna*. During the final step of the algorithm, when selecting the banned words or expressions, were two words composing the name of an entity to be selected, we only select this name instead.

This algorithm is not perfect; some important words might be missed because of the way we analyse the page or simply because they do not even appear in the text. In addition, even with our hand-crafted rules supplementing the stemming algorithm, different forms of the same word (or words that, although different, are so strongly related that, according to the rules of the game, banning one is equivalent to banning the other) might be selected as distinct banned words. It is to compensate for such limitations that we build lists of 10 banned words or expressions. Such a relatively high number tends to favour the introduction of false positives, but these are not a major problem. They are only an annoyance in that they unnecessarily slow the player, who has to read them. While we have not performed any quantitative evaluation of this algorithm, it has been, however, extensively tested during various parties, family gatherings, commuting trips and scientific conferences (among others). In addition to the two cards shown in Figures 1 and 2, here are a few other cards present in the game. `World War I` (score 1) with banned words *France, Russia, British Army, forces, Allied Powers, Battle, Britain, Ottoman, Germany,* and *United States*, `Rihanna` (score 1) with banned words *album, music, released, single, Billboard, Girl, song, record, Awards,* and *featured,* and `Artificial intelligence` (score 0.98) with banned words *AI, human, machine, research, learning, computer, problems, systems, networks,* and *algorithms*.

4 Conclusion

In this paper, we have shown how a range of relatively simple NLP and machine-learning techniques can be integrated effectively to automatically generate the content of Tabouid, a word-guessing game freely available on Android and iOS devices. Although easy to understand and implement, these techniques can be developed and improved on in many ways. They also naturally lead to a wide range of practical and theoretical questions relevant to NLP (e.g., data collection and annotation, and model interpretability). In this respect, this work could inspire implementation projects in NLP or computational linguistic programs. Concerning the game itself, we believe that Tabouid is more than just a fun game and can develop and help reinforce general knowledge for players of all backgrounds. It also appears to be an engaging way to practice speaking for language learners.

In addition to improving the banned words selection process, future work on Tabouid includes generating specific lists of cards based on school programs to use the game as an educational tool, using the category system of Wikipedia to let users select more or less specific categories to play with, and adapting the algorithms to leverage the wide variety of languages Wikipedia is available in beyond English and French. Currently, the content of Tabouid aims to reflect the diversity of Wikipedia's encyclopaedic knowledge." As a consequence, some cards include words related to topics that might be deemed inappropriate for children. As suggested by an anonymous reviewer, another possible addition to the game could then be to predict the age appropriateness of a given topic, allowing for cards to be filtered on the basis of an age setting.

Acknowledgements

Many thanks to Élise Dessaux for her work on the graphic design of the application!

References

Steven Bird, Ewan Klein, and Edward Loper. 2009. *Natural language processing with Python: analyzing text with the natural language toolkit.* O'Reilly Media, Inc.

Christian Bizer, Jens Lehmann, Georgi Kobilarov, Sren Auer, Christian Becker, Richard Cyganiak, and Sebastian Hellmann. 2009. DBpedia - A crystallization point for the Web of Data. *Journal of Web Semantics*, 7(3):154–165.

Danqi Chen, Adam Fisch, Jason Weston, and Antoine Bordes. 2017. Reading Wikipedia to Answer Open-Domain Questions. In *Proceedings of the 55th Annual Meeting of the Association for Computational Linguistics (Volume 1: Long Papers)*, pages 1870–1879, Vancouver, Canada. Association for Computational Linguistics.

S. T. Dumais, G. W. Furnas, T. K. Landauer, S. Deerwester, and R. Harshman. 1988. Using latent semantic analysis to improve access to textual information. In *Proceedings of the SIGCHI Conference on Human Factors in Computing Systems*, CHI '88, pages 281–285, Washington, D.C., USA. Association for Computing Machinery.

Yifan Fu, Xingquan Zhu, and Bin Li. 2013. A survey on instance selection for active learning. *Knowledge and Information Systems*, 35(2):249–283.

N. Halko, P. G. Martinsson, and J. A. Tropp. 2011. Finding Structure with Randomness: Probabilistic Algorithms for Constructing Approximate Matrix Decompositions. *SIAM Review*, 53(2):217–288.

Johannes Hoffart, Fabian M. Suchanek, Klaus Berberich, and Gerhard Weikum. 2013. YAGO2: A spatially and temporally enhanced knowledge base from Wikipedia. *Artificial Intelligence*, 194:28–61.

Mandar Joshi, Eunsol Choi, Daniel Weld, and Luke Zettlemoyer. 2017. TriviaQA: A Large Scale Distantly Supervised Challenge Dataset for Reading Comprehension. In *Proceedings of the 55th Annual Meeting of the Association for Computational Linguistics (Volume 1: Long Papers)*, pages 1601–1611, Vancouver, Canada. Association for Computational Linguistics.

Zachary C. Lipton. 2018. The Mythos of Model Interpretability. *ACM Queue*, 16(3):1–27.

Vivi Nastase, Michael Strube, Benjamin Boerschinger, Caecilia Zirn, and Anas Elghafari. 2010. WikiNet: A Very Large Scale Multi-Lingual Concept Network. In *Proceedings of the Seventh International Conference on Language Resources and Evaluation (LREC'10)*, Valletta, Malta. European Language Resources Association (ELRA).

F. Pedregosa, G. Varoquaux, A. Gramfort, V. Michel, B. Thirion, O. Grisel, M. Blondel, P. Prettenhofer, R. Weiss, V. Dubourg, J. Vanderplas, A. Passos, D. Cournapeau, M. Brucher, M. Perrot, and E. Duchesnay. 2011. Scikit-learn: Machine Learning in Python. *Journal of Machine Learning Research*, 12:2825–2830.

Simone Paolo Ponzetto and Michael Strube. 2011. Taxonomy induction based on a collaboratively built knowledge repository. *Artificial Intelligence*, 175(9):1737–1756.

Pranav Rajpurkar, Jian Zhang, Konstantin Lopyrev, and Percy Liang. 2016. SQuAD: 100,000+ Questions for Machine Comprehension of Text. In *Proceedings of the 2016 Conference on Empirical Methods in Natural Language Processing*, pages 2383–2392, Austin, Texas. Association for Computational Linguistics.

Burr Settles. 2009. Active learning literature survey. Computer Sciences Technical Report 1648, University of Wisconsin–Madison.

Fabian M. Suchanek, Gjergji Kasneci, and Gerhard Weikum. 2007. YAGO: A Core of Semantic Knowledge. In *Proceedings of the 16th International Conference on World Wide Web*, WWW '07, pages 697–706, New York, NY, USA. ACM. Event-place: Banff, Alberta, Canada.

Talk to Papers: Bringing Neural Question Answering to Academic Search

Tianchang Zhao and Kyusong Lee *
SOCO AI
{tonyzhao,kyusongl}@soco.ai

Abstract

We introduce Talk to Papers[1], which exploits the recent open-domain question answering (QA) techniques to improve the current experience of academic search. It's designed to enable researchers to use natural language queries to find precise answers and extract insights from a massive amount of academic papers. We present a large improvement over classic search engine baseline on several standard QA datasets, and provide the community a collaborative data collection tool to curate the first natural language processing research QA dataset via a community effort.

1 Introduction

Natural language processing (NLP) is one of the fastest growing field in computational linguistics and artificial intelligence, e.g. ACL has experienced a 140% growth from 2017 (1419 submissions) to 2020 (3429 submissions). Plus, there are more than 4000 pre-prints published at ArXiv in 2019. As a result, it has become increasingly stressful for researchers to keep up with the evolution of new methods. Today, the common way for researchers to find relevant papers is via searching keywords in Google Scholar[2] or Semantic Scholar[3]. Although these search engines are great at curating all the papers, they are limited in the following ways: (1) they are based on classic information retrieval methods, and do not handle natural language queries well, e.g. what effects can we get from label smoothing? (2) they are designed to find relevant documents (title and abstract) instead of direct answers to users' questions. Often researchers are looking for answers on specific research questions, e.g, *how to prevent posterior collapse in VAE?* or

how much is it to label sentences via crowdsourcing? With current search engine, it requires one to read several papers to find these answer. Therefore, it is necessary to create better tools for researchers to find answers from the scientific publications in a more efficient manner.

Meanwhile, machine reading comprehension (MRC), aka question answering (QA) has advanced significantly. Pretrained and then fine-tuned transformer models (Devlin et al., 2018) have surpassed human performance on a number of datasets, e.g. SQuAD (Rajpurkar et al., 2016). Further, Chen et al. (2017) extended single document MRC to machine reading at scale (MRS), combining the challenges of document retrieval with reading comprehension. Their open-domain QA system is able to find precise answers from millions of unstructured documents using natural language queries and has successfully been applied to the entire Wikipedia which contains more than 5 million articles.

The goal of Talk to Papers is to create a new way of finding answers from scientific publications and advance QA research. Concretely, we **first** adapted MRS techniques to create a conversational search portal that enable users to ask natural language questions to find precise answers and extract insights from the last 3 year papers published in top-tier NLP conferences, including ACL, NAACL, EMNLP and etc. **Second**, an initial corpus on these papers is collected and will be released as a publicly available dataset for QA research. We also developed a collaborative annotation toolkit that enable any researcher to contribute to this dataset so that more potential answers from these papers can be annotated. The annotation results will be fed back to the QA corpus after manual validation.

Both authors contributed equally
[1]https://ask.soco.ai
[2]https://scholar.google.com/
[3]https://www.semanticscholar.org/

Proceedings of the 58th Annual Meeting of the Association for Computational Linguistics, pages 30–36
July 5 - July 10, 2020. ©2020 Association for Computational Linguistics

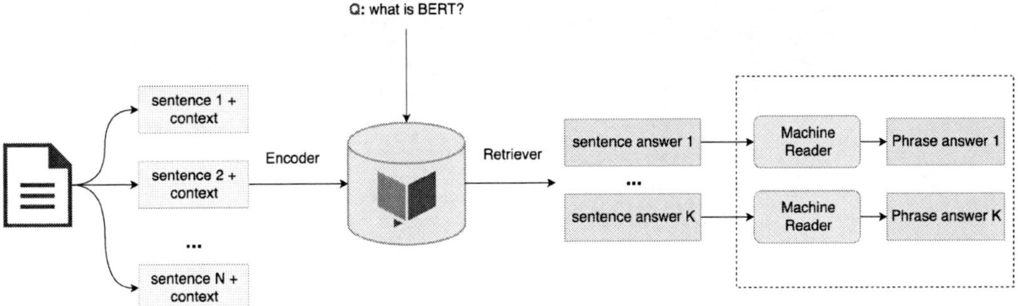

Figure 1: Overall workflow of the proposed SOCO framework. The machine reading step in the dashed box is optional.

2 Related Work

Developing question answering system with text knowledge base has been studied for decades (Voorhees and Tice, 1999). Many of the classic system as well as recent MRC-based open-domain QA systems have relied a pipeline approach (Ferrucci et al., 2010; Chen et al., 2017; Lee et al., 2018; Yang et al., 2019): (1) a information retrieval-based retriever module first finds relevant passages from all the documents and then (2) a reader component (computationally more expensive) extracts precise answer spans from the retrieved passages. Yang et al. (2019) has shown that using paragraphs as the unit of passage outperform sentences or documents. Lee et al. (2019a) proposes a trainable first-stage retriever that improves the recall performance.

Pipeline-based system often suffer from error propagation (Zhao and Eskenazi, 2016). Thus another line of research has been finding an end-to-end approach that enable precise-answer extraction from the entire dataset instead of only the output from the first-stage retriever. Seo et al. (2019) introduced the phrase level representation model that index every potential answer span as vector representation and exploited approximate nearest neighbour (ANN) methods to retrieve the final answer span directly from a large vector index (Slaney and Casey, 2008). Ahmad et al. (2019) argued that phrase-level answer may not always be required or preferred. Instead they proposed to find the right "sentence" as an answer from large body of text, and used universal sentence encoder (Cer et al., 2018) to retrieved the correct sentence given a question.

Our approach follows the sentence-level QA system from (Ahmad et al., 2019) for two reasons: (1) answers to many research questions cannot be cov-ered in a short phrase-level span, and a sentence answer can provide more context to deliver relevant solutions. (2) our preliminary study found that it is important to have a trainable retriever that goes beyond TF-IDF keyword matching to ensure enough recall in the paper domain. Nonetheless, we keep a machine reader as optional post-process to extract phrase-level span from the sentences.

3 The Proposed QA Toolkits: SOCO

We first introduce SOCO (Search Oriented COnversation), which we used to build our Talk to Paper. SOCO [4] is an answer-engine platform that enables developers to easily build universal question answering systems with unstructured documents as its knowledge base. Figure 1 shows the overall architecture of SOCO engine. It's designed to enable users to use natural language queries to find precise answers and extract insights from massive amount of text data. The typical workflow is as following:

1. Split documents into sentences and convert each sentence with its context into semantic index (i.e. a collection of answer embedding, sparse features and other semantic features).

2. Use natural language to query the index, which first converts the query into semantic embedding and then retrieves all the high probable answers.

3. (Optional) Run machine reader to narrow down to phrase-level answers.

3.1 SOCO-Question Answering

We define a frame to be the basic building block of SOCO. Each frame contains $f_i = [a_i, c_i, Q_i] \quad i \in$

---

[4] https://docs.soco.ai/

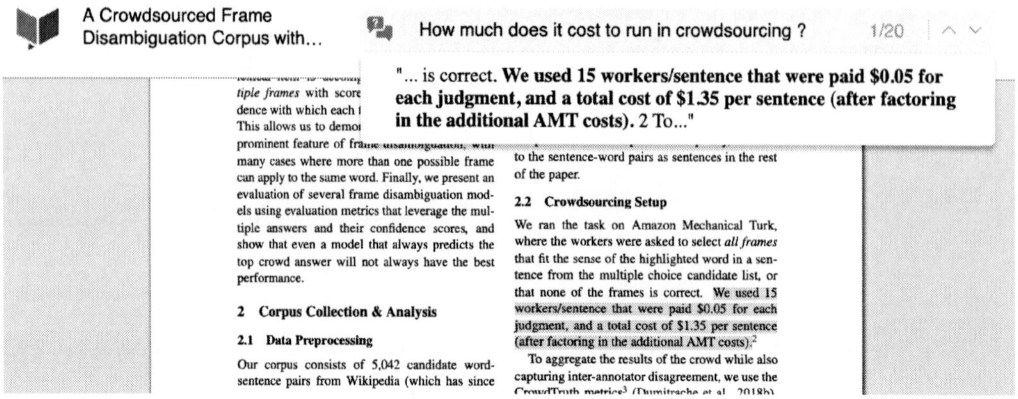

Figure 2: In-paper Search Page of Talk to Paper.

N, where N is the total number of frames, a_i is the potential answer sentence, c_i is surrounding context of a_i, and Q_i is a set of questions that are manually/synthetically associated with the answer a_i. Note that Q_i is optional and often only a small set of frames are manually labelled.

There are two neural network models involve in SOCO QA. The first model $h_a = F_a(a, c)$ is an answer encoder that takes both the answer sentence and its surround context to create a context-sensitive answer embeddings h_a. The second model is a question encoder $h_q = F_q(q)$ that takes a query as input and maps it to a question embedding vector of the same size. Last, we define the relevance between a query and an answer frame to be $s = \cos(h_a, h_q)$.

3.1.1   Training

These two models are trained jointly via supervised learning on existing QA dataset with cross entropy loss, i.e.

$$L = -\sum_{j \in J_{\text{pos}}} \log(s_j) - \sum_{j \in J_{\text{neg}}} \log(1 - s_j) \quad (1)$$

where J_{pos} is the set of ground truth question-answer pairs, and J_{neg} is the set of negative examples with randomly sampled noisy answers.

Given these two models and a set of frames, SOCO creates an index by encoding both the answers and annotated questions using F_a and F_q and save the resulting vectors D for nearest neighbour retrieval. Since F_q and F_a are trained to map the input text into the same embedding space, question-to-answer relevance and question-to-question relevance can be computed and compared in the same scale via cosine similarity.

3.1.2   Inference

At inference stage, SOCO first encodes the input query q' via $h_{q'} = F_q(q')$. Then each answer in the QA-index is scored by the cosine similarity between the query embedding and each answer embedding with a weighted auxiliary score from classic BM25 score (Robertson et al., 2009).

$$y_i = \cos(h_i, h_{q'}) + \alpha \text{BM25}(a_i, q') \quad i \in |D| \quad (2)$$

Note that an answer may have more than one vectors in the index because of the optional annotated question Q set in the frame, i.e. $[h_a, \{h_q\}] \quad q \in Q$. We merge the scores for the same answers via max pooling. Eventually, SOCO outputs the top K answers based on the final score.

3.2   SOCO-Question Generation

One common issue for new users to use question answering system is that they may not know what kind of questions they can ask. Question generation (Du et al., 2017) is one of the solutions to this issue by suggesting users potential questions they may enter. Concretely, we created a question generator by fine-tuning a GPT-2 language model (Radford et al., 2019). We train the model by concatenating question answers pairs $[a, q]$ from QA corpus and fine tune a GPT-2 by maximizing the conditional log likelihood $\log P(q|a)$. The results questions are added to the Q set of each frame and is used to provide auto completion and FAQs in the search interface.

3.3   Implementation Details

The SOCO python package (*soco-core-python*) is publicly available and can be installed as a Python package by running *pip3 install soco-core-python*. Internally, SOCO uses Elastic search (ES) (Gormley and Tong, 2015) as its index backbone. ES has built-in support for vector search, BM25 as well as context filtering. The answer and question encoder are trained on publicly available QA datasets, including SQuAD (Rajpurkar et al., 2016), Natural Questions (Kwiatkowski et al., 2019) and MSMARCO (Nguyen et al., 2016).

4 Talk to Paper

Now we are ready to describe the proposed Talk to Paper application, powered by our SOCO QA framework.

4.1 Data Source

Talk to Paper's data source contains NLP papers published last 3 years in ACL, NAACL, EMNLP and SiGdial in ACL Anthology[5], which attributes to 3897 papers published in the proceedings of these conferences (we will continuously expand the database by adding more papers from previous years as well as new published papers). We first use SOCO's document parser to extract text data from the PDFs and converted them into the frame format defined in the previous section. Then we use soco-core-python to index the frames and query for answers via its RESTful API endpoint. The indexing process takes about 2 hours.

4.2 User Interfaces

Talk to Paper is an web app that can be used on any modern browser. There are three major pages:

- Main search page

- In-paper search page

- Annotation page.

Main Search page: The main search page is similar to the standard Google-like search interface as shown in Figure 3, including input search box and query auto completion (based on generated questions from GPT-2).The responding answers will be highlighted in each returned results.

In-paper Search Page: Previously, people search information in the paper by clicking Control+F, which is a well-known shortcut key often used to find text in the current page using the exact character matching or regular expression. It is often

[5]https://www.aclweb.org/anthology/

Figure 3: Main search page of Talk to Paper.

used to input a keyword and highlight the matched string and allow to navigate the next matching or previous matching. We provide a similar interface to find the answer inside a specific paper as shown in Figure 2. Instead of searching information using a keyword, the proposed method allow to find the information using natural language queries. The retrieved answers are highlighted and it is also allowed to navigate next answer or previous answer. It will be useful to find multiple answers in the paper.

Annotation Page: We allow to annotate the question and answer spans in the in-paper search page as shown in Figure 4. All annotated data are visible in the preview page. If a user wants to annotate the data, the user can simply drag the text and write a question. The data will be automatically saved in the database. Unlike other open-domain QA datasets, we cannot ask to crowd workers, students, or part-time contractors to annotate on academic papers because it is hard to annotate without the domain knowledge. Therefore, we will welcome contributions from the research community to make useful resources together for the further research.

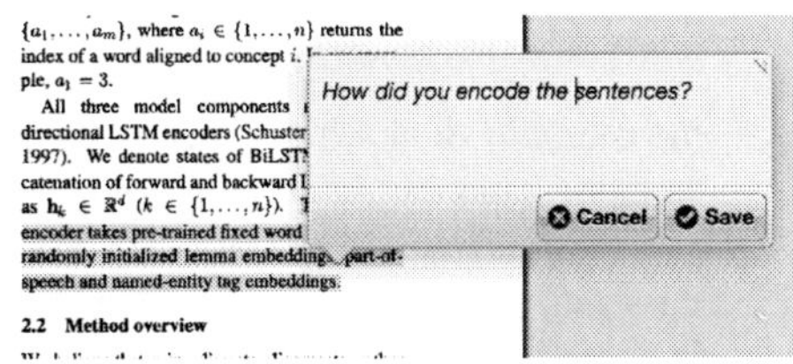

Figure 4: Annotation page of Talk to Paper.

4.3 Use Cases

The typical use cases are as following:

1. A user asks a question or click one of FAQs in the main search page. The N-best results will be presented with the highlighted answer

Examples	Paragraphs
Q: what are pretraining objectives? **A:** that pretraining will improve downstream tasks with fine-tuning on the entire available data **Title:** Pretraining Methods for Dialog Context Representation Learning	... The pretraining objectives are assessed under four different hypotheses: (1) **that pretraining will improve downstream tasks with fine-tuning on the entire available data**, (2) that pretraining will result in better convergence, ...
Q: what is LSTM? **A:** Long Short-Term Memory Network **Title:** Reasoning with Sarcasm by Reading In-between	... The filter width is 3 and number of filters f = 100. LSTM is a vanilla **Long Short-Term Memory Network**. The size of the LSTM cell is set to d = 100. ATT-LSTM (Attention-based LSTM) is a LSTM model with a neural attention mechanism applied to all the...
Q: What is the best system for NLI? **A:** Currently, one of the best performing NLI models (e.g., on the SNLI dataset) for three way classification is (Liu et al., 2019). **Title:** Identification of Tasks, Datasets, Evaluation Metrics, and Numeric Scores for Scientific Leaderboards Construction	... Our work differs in the information extracted and consequently in what context and hypothesis information we model. **Currently, one of the best performing NLI models (e.g., on the SNLI dataset) for three way classification is (Liu et al., 2019).** The authors apply deep neural networks and make use of BERT (Devlin et al., 2019),...

Table 1: Example results from real user queries

with its previous and next context. The related FAQs are also presented with the "You may also want to know" message. The user can also uses filters to narrow down to the answer in one or more specific paper.

2. the user clicks the "view in document" to check the answer with the original paper. The in-paper search page will be shown. The user can either read the paper or uses in-paper search, e.g. *what is the main contribution?* to let Talk to Paper auto scroll and highlight relevant answer spans (Figure 2).

3. the user may think certain span in the paper contains important information and uses the annotation function to add related questions to this span. This new annotations will be saved in to databases and will be added to the public dataset after manual inspection.

4. the user may uses the dataset as way to train and test performance of a question answering system. The Talk to Paper dataset is different from existing corpus because it contains highly technical text data that are substantially different from Wikipedia, which is a major source of most of the existing QA datasets.

5 Experiments and Results

In this section, we first present quantitative preliminary evaluation results the effectiveness of the proposed SOCO-QA framework on a number of standard QA datasets. Then we show results on the data collected from our initial user study.

5.1 Results for SOCO-QA performance

This preliminary studies focuses on comparison between SOCO-QA against classic BM25 (Robertson et al., 2009). BM25-based methods remain to be the mainstream methods for document retrieval in industry. Previous work in open domain question answering has shown that BM25 is a difficult baseline to surpass when questions were written by workers who have prior knowledge of the answer (Lee et al., 2019a). We will leave more comprehensive comparisons against other learning-based methods to future work, since the main goal of this demo paper is to present the system along with its dataset. We use the built-in elastic search (Gormley and Tong, 2015) BM-25 implementation with standard English anazlyer.

Evaluation Methods: we compared performance on four QA datasets, i.e. SQuAD (Rajpurkar et al., 2016), Natural Questions

	Index Size	Num of Queries
SQuAD	10,250	11,426
NQ	7,020	1,772
MARCO	52,933	13,557
Trivia	26,345	8,165

Table 2: Statistics on the evaluation datasets.

	BM25		SOCO	
	MRR	R@5	MRR	R@5
SQuAD	58.0	69.0	**60.9**	**73.2**
Trivia	29.0	38.7	**34.0**	**59.2**
NQ	19.7	25.1	**69.3**	**87.3**
MARCO	20.7	27.0	**73.2**	**92.8**

Table 3: Main evaluation results.

(NQ) (Kwiatkowski et al., 2019), MS MARCO (Nguyen et al., 2016) and Trivia QA (Joshi et al., 2017). We break documents from the development set into sentence-level answer frames, and uses the queries in the development set to compute Mean Reciprocal Rank (MRR) and Recall at 5 (R@5) as the evaluation metrics. The data statics are summarized in Table 2.

Quantitative Results: Table 3 shows the main results. The proposed SOCO-QA model is able to significantly outperform the baseline BM25 on all datasets. The proposed method is particularly powerful on real query data, e.g. NQ and MARCO where the question writer does not the exact answer they are looking for, so that there is often a low word overlapping between the question and the answer. Table 3 shows a striking 251% and 253.6% relative MRR improvement on the NQ and MARCO dataset. On the other hand, SOCO is also able to beat BM25 on SQuAD and Trivia dataset, where there is significant more question-to-answer word lapping.

Qualitative Results: to provide better understanding between BM25-based search versus SOCO-QA, the following are some example side-by-side comparisons:

- **SOCO:** We compare our baselines with a fine-tuned BERT model (Devlin et al., 2018). **BERT is a pre-trained deep bidirectional transformer model that can encode sentences into dense vector representations.** It is trained on large un-annotated corpora such as Wikipedia and the BooksCorpus (Zhu et al., 2015).

- **ES Default (BM25):** for the claim pairs with distance values 2 to 5 as shown in Table 3. We find **that BERT** model **is** consistently the **best** performing model for all distance pairs. As we increase the distance, the models achieve higher prediction performance.

The main observations is that BM25 falls short in understanding the intent of the query. Although it is also able to find sentences that are relevant to the query terms, it does not rank sentences that can "answer" the query higher. On the other hand, SOCO-QA is able to recognize target answer a query is looking for, e.g. a definition, and rank sentences that can directly resolves the questions higher.

5.2 Data Analysis

We asked NLP researchers via social network, e.g. Twitter, to try out Talk to Paper and we are able to collect 3137 queries in roughly two weeks. The logged query data and its annotation will soon be made publicly available). Table 1 shows example queries where the system is able to find relevant answers to real user queries. Analysis shows that the most frequent query type were asking about the objectives or the meaning of terms (e.g., what are pretraining objectives, what is LSTM?). Another popular question type is to ask about the state-of-the-art method to solve a particular problem, e.g. What is the best system for NLI?.

We also found that the generated questions that are presented as auto-completion and FAQs are particularly popular. About 51.7% of queries were from the suggested questions. This results is inline with research work in human-computer interaction that utilizes machine intelligent systems to assist human users to better discover knowledge (Lee et al., 2019b).

6 Conclusion

We present Talk to Paper, a QA system for NLP papers powered by SOCO-QA. Experiments confirm the effectiveness of our proposed approach and show superior search experience compared to traditional search engine. We welcome contributions from the research community to curate useful resources together for the further research. Future work include (1) expanding the database to more papers (2) improving the QA model using the collected data to better handle question answering in the context of research domain.

Acknowledgments

We would like to acknowledge the joint effort from SOCO's development team, including Haolin Wang, Yanran Han and Omer Riaz to make this work possible.

References

Amin Ahmad, Noah Constant, Yinfei Yang, and Daniel Cer. 2019. Reqa: An evaluation for end-to-end answer retrieval models. *arXiv preprint arXiv:1907.04780*.

Daniel Cer, Yinfei Yang, Sheng-yi Kong, Nan Hua, Nicole Limtiaco, Rhomni St John, Noah Constant, Mario Guajardo-Cespedes, Steve Yuan, Chris Tar, et al. 2018. Universal sentence encoder. *arXiv preprint arXiv:1803.11175*.

Danqi Chen, Adam Fisch, Jason Weston, and Antoine Bordes. 2017. Reading Wikipedia to answer open-domain questions. In *Association for Computational Linguistics (ACL)*.

Jacob Devlin, Ming-Wei Chang, Kenton Lee, and Kristina Toutanova. 2018. Bert: Pre-training of deep bidirectional transformers for language understanding. *arXiv preprint arXiv:1810.04805*.

Xinya Du, Junru Shao, and Claire Cardie. 2017. Learning to ask: Neural question generation for reading comprehension. In *Proceedings of the 55th Annual Meeting of the Association for Computational Linguistics (Volume 1: Long Papers)*, pages 1342–1352.

David Ferrucci, Eric Brown, Jennifer Chu-Carroll, James Fan, David Gondek, Aditya A Kalyanpur, Adam Lally, J William Murdock, Eric Nyberg, John Prager, et al. 2010. Building watson: An overview of the deepqa project. *AI magazine*, 31(3):59–79.

Clinton Gormley and Zachary Tong. 2015. *Elasticsearch: the definitive guide: a distributed real-time search and analytics engine.* " O'Reilly Media, Inc.".

Mandar Joshi, Eunsol Choi, Daniel S Weld, and Luke Zettlemoyer. 2017. Triviaqa: A large scale distantly supervised challenge dataset for reading comprehension. *arXiv preprint arXiv:1705.03551*.

Tom Kwiatkowski, Jennimaria Palomaki, Olivia Redfield, Michael Collins, Ankur Parikh, Chris Alberti, Danielle Epstein, Illia Polosukhin, Jacob Devlin, Kenton Lee, et al. 2019. Natural questions: a benchmark for question answering research. *Transactions of the Association for Computational Linguistics*, 7:453–466.

Jinhyuk Lee, Seongjun Yun, Hyunjae Kim, Miyoung Ko, and Jaewoo Kang. 2018. Ranking paragraphs for improving answer recall in open-domain question answering. *arXiv preprint arXiv:1810.00494*.

Kenton Lee, Ming-Wei Chang, and Kristina Toutanova. 2019a. Latent retrieval for weakly supervised open domain question answering. *arXiv preprint arXiv:1906.00300*.

Mina Lee, Tatsunori B Hashimoto, and Percy Liang. 2019b. Learning autocomplete systems as a communication game. *arXiv preprint arXiv:1911.06964*.

Tri Nguyen, Mir Rosenberg, Xia Song, Jianfeng Gao, Saurabh Tiwary, Rangan Majumder, and Li Deng. 2016. Ms marco: a human-generated machine reading comprehension dataset.

Alec Radford, Jeff Wu, Rewon Child, David Luan, Dario Amodei, and Ilya Sutskever. 2019. Language models are unsupervised multitask learners.

Pranav Rajpurkar, Jian Zhang, Konstantin Lopyrev, and Percy Liang. 2016. Squad: 100,000+ questions for machine comprehension of text. *arXiv preprint arXiv:1606.05250*.

Stephen Robertson, Hugo Zaragoza, et al. 2009. The probabilistic relevance framework: Bm25 and beyond. *Foundations and Trends® in Information Retrieval*, 3(4):333–389.

Minjoon Seo, Jinhyuk Lee, Tom Kwiatkowski, Ankur P Parikh, Ali Farhadi, and Hannaneh Hajishirzi. 2019. Real-time open-domain question answering with dense-sparse phrase index. *arXiv preprint arXiv:1906.05807*.

Malcolm Slaney and Michael Casey. 2008. Locality-sensitive hashing for finding nearest neighbors [lecture notes]. *IEEE Signal processing magazine*, 25(2):128–131.

Ellen M Voorhees and Dawn M Tice. 1999. The trec-8 question answering track evaluation. In *TREC*, volume 1999, page 82. Citeseer.

Wei Yang, Yuqing Xie, Aileen Lin, Xingyu Li, Luchen Tan, Kun Xiong, Ming Li, and Jimmy Lin. 2019. End-to-end open-domain question answering with bertserini. *arXiv preprint arXiv:1902.01718*.

Tiancheng Zhao and Maxine Eskenazi. 2016. Towards end-to-end learning for dialog state tracking and management using deep reinforcement learning. In *Proceedings of the 17th Annual Meeting of the Special Interest Group on Discourse and Dialogue*, pages 1–10.

Personalized PageRank with Syntagmatic Information for Multilingual Word Sense Disambiguation

Federico Scozzafava[1,2], Marco Maru[1,2,3], Fabrizio Brignone[4],
Giovanni Torrisi[4], and Roberto Navigli[1,2]

[1]Sapienza NLP Group
[2]Department of Computer Science, Sapienza University of Rome
[3]Department of Literature and Modern Cultures, Sapienza University of Rome
[4]Babelscape, Italy
`firstname.lastname@uniroma1.it`, `lastname@babelscape.com`

Abstract

Exploiting syntagmatic information is an encouraging research focus to be pursued in an effort to close the gap between knowledge-based and supervised Word Sense Disambiguation (WSD) performance. We follow this direction in our next-generation knowledge-based WSD system, SyntagRank, which we make available via a Web interface and a RESTful API. SyntagRank leverages the disambiguated pairs of co-occurring words included in SyntagNet, a lexical-semantic combination resource, to perform state-of-the-art knowledge-based WSD in a multilingual setting. Our service provides both a user-friendly interface, available at `http://syntagnet.org/`, and a RESTful endpoint to query the system programmatically (accessible at `http://api.syntagnet.org/`).

1 Introduction

In Natural Language Processing, Word Sense Disambiguation (WSD) is an open problem concerning lexical ambiguity. It is aimed at determining which sense – among a finite inventory of many – is evoked by a given word in context (Navigli, 2009).

This challenge has been tackled by exploiting huge amounts of hand-annotated data in a supervised fashion (Raganato et al., 2017b; Bevilacqua and Navigli, 2019; Vial et al., 2019; Bevilacqua and Navigli, 2020) or, alternatively, by harnessing structured information (Agirre et al., 2014; Moro et al., 2014; Scarlini et al., 2020), such as that available within existing lexical knowledge bases (LKBs) like WordNet (Fellbaum, 1998). Despite achieving better overall results, supervised systems require tremendous efforts in order to produce data for several languages (Navigli, 2018; Pasini, 2020), whereas knowledge-based approaches can easily be applied in multilingual environments due to the

wide array of languages covered by LKBs like BabelNet[1] (Navigli and Ponzetto, 2012), or the Open Multilingual WordNet (Bond and Foster, 2013). Moreover, it is widely acknowledged that the performance of a knowledge-based WSD system is strongly correlated with the structure of the LKB employed (Boyd-Graber et al., 2006; Lemnitzer et al., 2008; Navigli and Lapata, 2010; Ponzetto and Navigli, 2010). In fact, the knowledge available within LKBs reflects the fact that words can be linked via two types of semantic relations: paradigmatic relations – i.e. the most frequently encountered relations in LKBs – concern the substitution of lexical units, and determine to which level in a hierarchy a language unit belongs by semantic analogy with units similar to it; conversely, syntagmatic relations concern the positioning of such units, by linking elements belonging to the same hierarchical level (e.g., words), which appear in the same context (e.g., a sentence). As a case in point, a paradigmatic relation exists, independently of a given context, between the words $farm_n$ and $workplace_n$ (where a farm is a type of workplace), whereas a syntagmatic relation is entertained between the words $work_v$ and $farm_n$, e.g., in the sentence *'her husband works in a farm as a labourer.'*

In our most recent study (Maru et al., 2019, SyntagNet), we provided further evidence that the nature of LKBs impacts on system performance: the injection of syntagmatic relations – in the form of disambiguated pairs of co-occurring words – into an existing LKB biased towards paradigmatic knowledge enables knowledge-based systems to rival their supervised counterparts.

To make the above results accessible to the research community, in this paper we introduce a Web interface and a RESTful API for SyntagRank, our multilingual WSD system, which applies the

---

[1]`https://babelnet.org/`

Proceedings of the 58th Annual Meeting of the Association for Computational Linguistics, pages 37–46
July 5 - July 10, 2020. ©2020 Association for Computational Linguistics

Personalized PageRank (PPR) algorithm (Haveli-wala, 2002) to an LKB made up of WordNet, the Princeton WordNet Gloss Corpus (PWNG) and the lexical-semantic syntagmatic combinations available in the SyntagNet resource. SyntagRank is the first system to perform multilingual WSD by leveraging an underlying LKB connecting a sizeable amount of syntagmatically-related concepts.

2 Preliminaries

Our disambiguation algorithm relies on an LKB, i.e. a graph in which each node represents a concept, and each connection between nodes represents a semantic relation. In this Section we describe the LKBs whose resulting union we use as our reference graph, and then go on to provide details of the PPR algorithm.

2.1 Lexical Knowledge Bases

WordNet (Fellbaum, 1998) is a lexical-semantic database of English, in which concepts are expressed by means of sets of cognitive synonyms (synsets) that are interlinked to form a semantic network through relation edges.

Relations in WordNet are mainly of a hierarchical, and thus paradigmatic nature, with the most frequently encoded relation being the super-subordinate relation (instantiated in terms of hypernymy and hyponymy; see also Section 1). Other relations linking concepts in WordNet include part-whole relations (meronymy, e.g. between $wheel_n$ and car_n), antonymy relations and cross-part-of-speech relations holding among semantically similar words sharing a stem with the same meaning (e.g. between $speed_n$ and $speedy_a$). As of today, WordNet is the most widely used and *de facto* standard sense inventory for the WSD task (Raganato et al., 2017a).

Princeton WordNet Gloss Corpus (PWNG) is the semantically-annotated gloss corpus made available by WordNet since its 3.0 release.[2] Glosses are short definitions providing proper meanings for synsets, and in PWNG they have been tagged according to the senses in WordNet. Following Agirre et al. (2014), we induce new WordNet relations from PWNG by linking the synset to which the gloss refers to each of the synsets that have been tagged in the gloss itself.

In this way, additional contextual relations are provided, inadvertently covering syntagmatic relations, too.

SyntagNet (Maru et al., 2019) is a database containing almost 90,000 pairs of manually-disambiguated lexical collocations and free word associations. Pairs in SyntagNet link nouns to other nouns or verbs tagged according to the WordNet 3.0 sense inventory and such pairs can therefore be exploited as new relation paths connecting nodes (synsets) in a WordNet-based semantic network. For our purposes, we are especially interested in the fact that SyntagNet is the only high-quality resource to systematically provide syntagmatic information in the form of lexical-semantic combinations. This kind of information becomes particularly valuable when used to enrich semantic networks otherwise biased towards paradigmatic knowledge, by creating direct routes between those concepts whose lexicalizations tend to appear together in the same context more often than by mere chance.

2.2 Personalized PageRank

The original PageRank (Brin and Page, 1998) is an algorithm which uses the connectivity of a graph to assess the probability that each of its nodes has to be reached and visited starting from a random position. As the probability mass (distribution) over the graph nodes is uniform, then, iteratively, the number of ingoing and outgoing connections serves as a means to increase or decrease the relative weight of each node. In order to apply this approach to WSD, following Agirre et al. (2014), SyntagRank uses a variant of the PageRank algorithm, the Personalized PageRank (PPR), in which the initial probability mass is distributed over a restricted set of specific nodes (i.e. the nodes representing the content words to be disambiguated in a given context[3]). Hence, given an initial set of nodes, the outcome of the PPR algorithm is a vector encoding all the information concerning the probability distributions of all the nodes in the graph.

3 Architecture of SyntagRank

SyntagRank is a knowledge-based disambiguation system which uses the PPR algorithm to determine

---

[2] http://wordnetcode.princeton.edu/glosstag.shtml

[3] In SyntagRank, a context is equivalent to a single whole sentence. Therefore, given an input paragraph made up of, say, three sentences, the system will perform the disambiguation task separately for each of these three sentences.

the most appropriate sense of a given word in context. This approach, already discussed by Agirre and Soroa (2009), is here presented in an optimized, rebuilt version, employing the LKBs described in Section 2.1 to achieve state-of-the-art knowledge-based performance across five languages: English, German, French, Spanish, and Italian. Our architecture (Figure 1) is composed of three main modules: (i) multilingual NLP pipeline, (ii) candidate retrieval, and (iii) disambiguator.

3.1 Multilingual NLP Pipeline

In order to allow the user to provide an unprocessed text as input for SyntagRank to disambiguate, our system employs a multilingual NLP pipeline which preliminarily performs the functions of tokenization, sentence splitting, lemmatization and Part of Speech (PoS) tagging. Depending on the input language, SyntagRank utilizes either the Stanford CoreNLP suite[4] (Manning et al., 2014), or the models provided by The Italian NLP Tool (Palmero Aprosio and Moretti, 2016, TINT).

3.2 Candidate Retrieval

English Candidate Retrieval   With each token in the input text already pre-processed, and considering that each node in our graph corresponds to a unique WordNet synset (see Section 2), in this phase we can retrieve, for each content word (target word) in a single sentence, all those candidate concepts (synsets) for which a coincident lexicalization exists. In doing so, in line with the word-to-word heuristics described in (Agirre et al., 2014), we exclude the target word when retrieving the candidate concepts so as to avoid the probability mass being distributed across the most frequent sense of the target word. The resulting set of collected concepts C, which will now include all the possible senses for the non-target words in the input sentence, thus establishes the starting nodes for the PPR algorithm.

In view of the fact that, according to the Linearity Theorem (Jeh and Widom, 2003), the PPR vector computed starting from a set of nodes C is equivalent to the weighted average of the PPR vectors calculated using each of the nodes in C as single starting points, all the PPR vectors in SyntagRank have been preliminarily determined for each

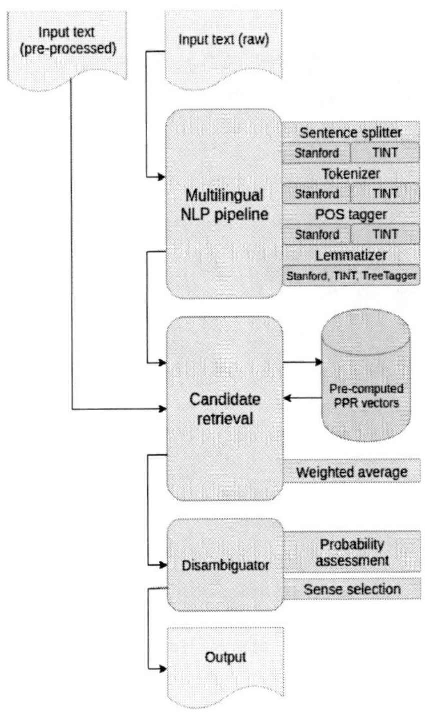

Figure 1: Architecture diagram of SyntagRank.

node in the graph, with the purpose of minimizing execution times[5]. Thus, the PPR vector for a precise context (i.e. an input sentence) is calculated simply by determining the weighted average of the pre-computed PPR vectors for each of its nodes[6]. The weight factor $p(w, s)$, for each candidate s associated with a content word w, is computed as follows:

$$p(w, s) = \frac{1}{N * |senses_w|} freq_{ws} \qquad (1)$$

where N is the number of content words in the input sentence and $senses_w$ is the set of sense candidates associated with w. Moreover, since the graph connectivity gets denser around most frequent senses (MFS) – according to their distribution in SemCor[7] (Miller et al., 1993) –, and in view

---

[4]Except for the English language, for which the Stanford CoreNLP pipeline has full coverage, in order to perform the lemmatization for German, French, and Spanish, we use instead TreeTagger (Schmid, 1995).

[5]All the pre-computed PPR vectors are stored in binary format, and are accessed via a memory-mapped file supported by a Least Recently Used (LRU) cache.

[6]With regard to our PPR implementation details, we opted for a damping factor of 0.85. In addition, the algorithm performs a variable number of iterations (random walks) over the graph until reaching convergence, i.e. when the difference between the scores of any node computed at two successive iterations falls below a threshold of 10^{-4}.

[7]SemCor is the largest, manually sense-annotated corpus of English, and is currently the *de facto* standard reference dataset for several WSD applications.

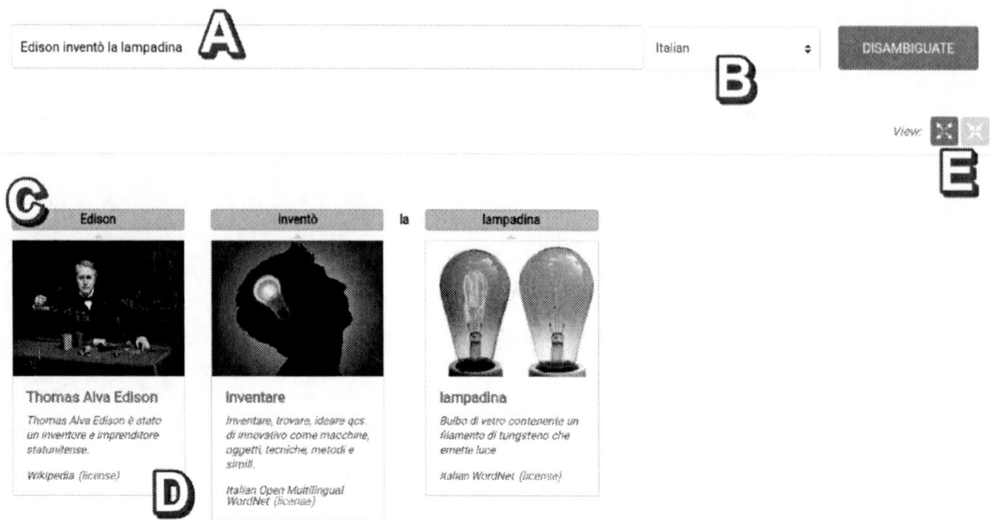

Figure 2: User interface of SyntagRank when the Italian language is selected and the sentence *'Edison inventò la lampadina'* (Edison invented the light bulb) is typed as input query. Disambiguation results are displayed in extended view by default. Overlaying letters over the image are detailed in Section 4.

of the fact that unsupervised systems tend to have a strong bias towards the MFS (Calvo and Gelbukh, 2015; Postma et al., 2016; Pasini et al., 2020), we accounted for potential skew towards MFS by including the parameter $freq_{ws}$, i.e. the normalized value resulting from the number of occurrences for a given word sense in SemCor, divided by the total number of occurrences for all the senses of the same word.

Multilingual Candidate Retrieval Concepts represented in a semantic network are language independent by definition. Still, in order to retrieve sense candidates for words in specific languages, we need the nodes in the graph to be mapped with lexicalizations in those languages. As mentioned in Section 2.1, WordNet provides this information for the English language only, therefore, in order to retrieve the lexicalizations in languages other than English we exploited the BabelNet semantic network, which inherently aligns lexicalizations in 284 distinct languages to the original WordNet 3.0 synsets. Nevertheless, two main flaws lie in this approach: (i) the lexicalizations in BabelNet are induced from automatically-linked resources, hence, their quality might be sub-optimal, and (ii) no SemCor equivalent exists for other languages, which means we do not have any accessible MFS information to exploit when computing the weighted average between vectors. In order to address both these flaws

concurrently, we devised a strategy to mimic the MFS ranking function by associating a confidence score with each of the lexical resources from which BabelNet derives its lexicalizations (e.g. Wikidata, OmegaWiki or Wikipedia, among others). To this end, after conducting an empirical study to assess the quality of random translation samples provided by each individual resource mapped to BabelNet, we assigned a normalized confidence score to them. Consequently, for each unique lexicalization, we have been able to compute its "MFS" score as the average confidence among all the resources providing that lexicalization for a specific concept.

3.3 Disambiguator

After retrieving the PPR vectors for each candidate sense and computing their weighted average (as described in Section 3.2), the last module of SyntagRank serves as a means to finally: (i) extract the probability values for the senses of the target word from the averaged PPR vector, and (ii) select the sense with the highest probability value as the result of the disambiguation for the target word.

4 Web Interface

Figure 2 shows the Web interface of SyntagRank. Its components are explained below.

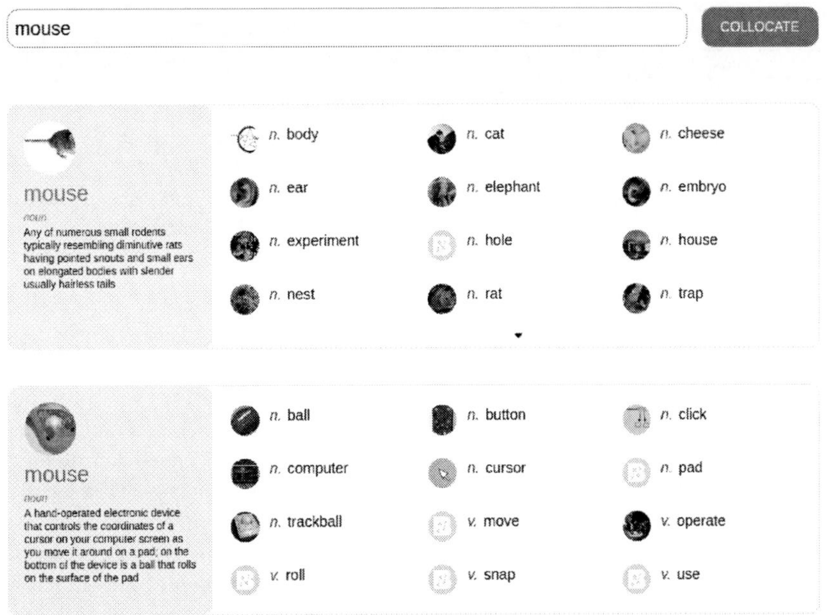

Figure 3: User interface of the SyntagNet Explorer when the English word *mouse* is typed as input query.

A. Query The system takes as input the text to be processed[8]. Users can enter either single words, multiword expressions (MWEs), or full sentences as input queries. In the event that the input text is a sentence, this will be processed by the disambiguator and the system will return a disambiguated sentence (see Paragraph C). Otherwise, if the query matches an entry in the SyntagNet database, the interface will switch to the SyntagNet Explorer (see Section 4.1) to display all the lexical-semantic combinations available for all the senses of the word/MWE provided as input query.

B. Language Selection The drop down menu allows the user to select the language in which the input text is provided. Currently, SyntagRank offers disambiguation in five different languages: English, German, French, Spanish and Italian.

C. Disambiguated Sentence If an input text has been provided, the interface will display the results of the disambiguation here, with tokens highlighted in different colors for *Concepts* (blue) and *Named Entities* (orange).

D. Disambiguated Token Each disambiguated token is accompanied by a tooltip which shows the image, word sense and definition, as retrieved from the corresponding entry in BabelNet 4.0.

E. View Selection The Web interface allows the user to display the disambiguated sentence in extended or compact form. In the extended view, the focus is placed on the tokens: the disambiguated sentence is shown as a horizontal slider, navigable by means of arrows located on the left and right ends of the container, and the user is thereby given a means to quickly leaf through all the disambiguation results at the same time. Instead, when selecting the compact view, the focus is shifted to the sentence. In this mode, the information associated with the disambiguated tokens will be shown only if the user hovers the mouse cursor over a highlighted token.

4.1 SyntagNet Explorer

In addition to the SyntagRank disambiguation system, our Web interface also provides users with full access to the SyntagNet database. By typing into the query bar a word or MWE which is present in SyntagNet[9] (an autocomplete function will provide the user with search suggestions), the interface will switch to the SyntagNet Explorer (Figure 3). The SyntagNet Explorer displays a list of boxes, each containing a sense of the input word/MWE. Senses in the list are ordered according to (i) PoS tag and

---

[8]The Web interface only allows raw text as input.

[9]At the time of writing, the SyntagNet Explorer is available for the English language only.

	English						Multilingual						
							SemEval-13				SemEval-15		
System	Sens2	Sens3	Sem07	Sem13	Sem15	All	IT	ES	DE	FR	IT	ES	All
Babelfy	67.0	63.5	51.6	66.4	70.3	65.5	66.6	69.5	69.4	56.9	-	-	-
UKB	68.8	66.1	53.0	68.8	70.3	67.3	-	-	-	-	-	-	-
SyntagRank	**71.6**	**72.0**	**59.3**	**72.2**	**75.8**	**71.7**	**72.1**	**74.1**	**76.4**	**70.3**	69.0	63.4	71.2

Table 1: F1 scores (%) for English all-words fine-grained WSD (left) and for multilingual all-words fine-grained WSD (right). Statistically-significant differences against our results are underlined according to a χ^2 test, $p < 0.01$. Results under "All" refer to the concatenation of the English (left) and multilingual (right) datasets.

(ii) sense frequency (in line with BabelNet 4.0). On the left side (blue background), the boxes show information for word senses, along with PoS tags, sense definitions and illustrations. By clicking on a sense name, the corresponding BabelNet entry will open in a separate tab. On the right side (white background), all the lexical-semantic items (collocates) linked with the corresponding word senses via SyntagNet are listed. Further information about collocates is provided by hovering the mouse over each item. Finally, clicking on a collocate will start a new query with the selected word.

4.2 Usage of the RESTful API

The RESTful API we provide can be used effectively to query the SyntagRank system programmatically. Unlike the Web interface, our API allows the user to input a pre-processed text in addition to performing standard queries with raw text. For the full documentation of the RESTful API, along with the required parameters description, please refer to Appendix A: API Documentation.

5 Evaluation

In order to assess its performance, we tested SyntagRank on the five English all-words WSD evaluation datasets standardized according to WordNet 3.0 in the framework of Raganato et al. (2017a), namely: Senseval-2 (Edmonds and Cotton, 2001), Senseval-3 (Snyder and Palmer, 2004), SemEval-2007 (Pradhan et al., 2007), SemEval-2013 (Navigli et al., 2013), and SemEval-2015 (Moro and Navigli, 2015). As regards the appraisal of SyntagRank in a multilingual setting, we used the German, Spanish, French and Italian annotations available in the amended version of the SemEval-2013 and SemEval-2015 evaluation datasets[10], which is accordant with the BabelNet API 4.0.1 graph and

enables testing on a larger number of instances than hitherto.

In Table 1, we report F1 scores for SyntagRank in the English (left), and multilingual (right) settings, along with comparisons to the best configurations of two distinct graph-based disambiguation systems: Babelfy (Moro et al., 2014) and UKB (Agirre et al., 2014). As can be seen, SyntagRank outperforms its direct competitors by a considerable margin[11], on both the English and multilingual settings. These results substantiate the idea that applying the PPR algorithm to a graph injected with high-quality syntagmatic knowledge is crucial to enhancing disambiguation performances.

6 Conclusion

In this paper we presented and described the architecture of SyntagRank, our state-of-the-art knowledge-based system for multilingual Word Sense Disambiguation using syntagmatic information. We also provided details concerning the use of SyntagRank's Web interface and RESTful API, accessible at `http://syntagnet.org/` and `http://api.syntagnet.org`, respectively.

Acknowledgments

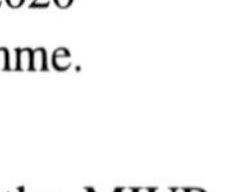The authors gratefully acknowledge the support of the ERC Consolidator Grant MOUSSE No. 726487 and the ELEXIS project No. 731015 under the European Union's Horizon 2020 research and innovation programme.

This work was supported in part by the MIUR under the grant "Dipartimenti di eccellenza 2018-2022" of the Department of Computer Science of Sapienza University.

---

[10]Made available at `https://github.com/SapienzaNLP/mwsd-datasets`.

[11]For the purpose of these experiments, we set a threshold $T = 0.4$ for the PPR values of any given sense; for values failing to reach the threshold, the MFS was chosen instead as the result of the disambiguation.

References

Eneko Agirre, Oier Lopez de Lacalle, and Aitor Soroa. 2014. Random Walks for Knowledge-Based Word Sense Disambiguation. *Computational Linguistics*, 40(1):57–84.

Eneko Agirre and Aitor Soroa. 2009. Personalizing PageRank for Word Sense Disambiguation. In *Proc. of EACL*, pages 33–41, Athens, Greece.

Michele Bevilacqua and Roberto Navigli. 2019. Quasi Bidirectional Encoder Representations from Transformers for Word Sense Disambiguation. In *Proc. of RANLP*, pages 122–131, Varna, Bulgaria.

Michele Bevilacqua and Roberto Navigli. 2020. Breaking the 80% Glass Ceiling: Raising the State of the Art in Word Sense Disambiguation by Incorporating Knowledge Graph Information. In *Proceedings of the 58th Annual Meeting of the Association for Computational Linguistics*, Seattle, WA, USA.

Francis Bond and Ryan Foster. 2013. Linking and extending an open multilingual Wordnet. In *Proceedings of the 51st Annual Meeting of the Association for Computational Linguistics (Volume 1: Long Papers)*, pages 1352–1362, Sofia, Bulgaria. Association for Computational Linguistics.

Jordan Boyd-Graber, Christiane Fellbaum, Daniel Osherson, and Robert Schapire. 2006. Adding Dense, Weighted Connections to WordNet. In *Proceedings of the third international WordNet conference*, pages 29–36, South Jeju Island, Korea.

Sergey Brin and Lawrence Page. 1998. The anatomy of a large-scale hypertextual web search engine. *Computer networks and ISDN systems*, 30(1-7):107–117.

Hiram Calvo and Alexander Gelbukh. 2015. Is the Most Frequent Sense of a Word Better Connected in a Semantic Network? In *Proc. of ICIC*, pages 491–499, Fuzhou, China.

Philip Edmonds and Scott Cotton. 2001. SENSEVAL-2: Overview. In *Proceedings of SENSEVAL-2 Second International Workshop on Evaluating Word Sense Disambiguation Systems*, pages 1–5, Toulouse, France.

Christiane Fellbaum, editor. 1998. *WordNet: an electronic lexical database*. MIT Press, Cambridge, MA, USA.

Taher H. Haveliwala. 2002. Topic-Sensitive PageRank. In *Proceedings of the 11th international conference on World Wide Web*, pages 517–526, Honolulu, HI, USA.

Glen Jeh and Jennifer Widom. 2003. Scaling Personalized Web Search. In *Proceedings of the 12th international conference on World Wide Web*, pages 271–279, Budapest, Hungary.

Lothar Lemnitzer, Holger Wunsch, and Piklu Gupta. 2008. Enriching GermaNet with verb-noun relations - a case study of lexical acquisition. In *Proceedings of the Sixth International Conference on Language Resources and Evaluation, LREC 2008, May 28-30, 2018*, pages 156–160, Marrakech, Morocco.

Christopher Manning, Mihai Surdeanu, John Bauer, Jenny Finkel, Steven Bethard, and David McClosky. 2014. The Stanford CoreNLP natural language processing toolkit. In *Proceedings of 52nd Annual Meeting of the Association for Computational Linguistics: System Demonstrations*, pages 55–60, Baltimore, MD, USA.

Marco Maru, Federico Scozzafava, Federico Martelli, and Roberto Navigli. 2019. SyntagNet: Challenging Supervised Word Sense Disambiguation with Lexical-Semantic Combinations. In *Proceedings of the 2019 Conference on Empirical Methods in Natural Language Processing and the 9th International Joint Conference on Natural Language Processing (EMNLP-IJCNLP)*, pages 3532–3538, Hong Kong, China.

George A. Miller, Claudia Leacock, Randee Tengi, and Ross T. Bunker. 1993. A Semantic Concordance. In *Proc. of HLT*, pages 303–308, Plainsboro, NJ, USA.

Andrea Moro and Roberto Navigli. 2015. SemEval-2015 task 13: Multilingual all-words sense disambiguation and entity linking. In *Proceedings of the 9th International Workshop on Semantic Evaluation (SemEval 2015)*, pages 288–297, Denver, CO, USA.

Andrea Moro, Alessandro Raganato, and Roberto Navigli. 2014. Entity Linking meets Word Sense Disambiguation: a Unified Approach. *TACL*, 2:231–244.

Roberto Navigli. 2009. Word Sense Disambiguation: A Survey. *ACM Computing Surveys*, 41(2):1–69.

Roberto Navigli. 2018. Natural Language Understanding: Instructions for (Present and Future) Use. In *Proc. of IJCAI*, pages 5697–5702, Stockholm, Sweden.

Roberto Navigli, David Jurgens, and Daniele Vannella. 2013. SemEval-2013 Task 12: Multilingual Word Sense Disambiguation. In *Second Joint Conference on Lexical and Computational Semantics (*SEM), Volume 2: Proceedings of the Seventh International Workshop on Semantic Evaluation (SemEval 2013)*, pages 222–231, Atlanta, GA, USA.

Roberto Navigli and Mirella Lapata. 2010. An experimental study of graph connectivity for unsupervised word sense disambiguation. *IEEE Transactions on Pattern Analysis and Machine Intelligence*, 32(4):678–692.

Roberto Navigli and Simone P. Ponzetto. 2012. BabelNet: The Automatic Construction, Evaluation and Application of a Wide-Coverage Multilingual Semantic Network. *Artificial Intelligence Journal*, 193:217–250.

Alessio Palmero Aprosio and Giovanni Moretti. 2016. Italy goes to Stanford: a collection of CoreNLP modules for Italian. *ArXiv e-prints*.

Tommaso Pasini. 2020. The Knowledge Acquisition Bottleneck Problem in Multilingual Word Sense Disambiguation. In *Proceedings of the Twenty-Eighth International Joint Conference on Artificial Intelligence, IJCAI-20*, Yokohama, Japan.

Tommaso Pasini, Federico Scozzafava, and Bianca Scarlini. 2020. CluBERT: a Cluster-Based Approach for Learning Sense Distributions in Multiple Languages. In *Proceedings of the 58th Annual Meeting of the Association for Computational Linguistics*, Seattle, WA, USA.

Simone P. Ponzetto and Roberto Navigli. 2010. Knowledge-Rich Word Sense Disambiguation Rivaling Supervised Systems. In *Proceedings of the 48th Annual Meeting of the Association for Computational Linguistics*, pages 1522–1531, Uppsala, Sweden.

Marten Postma, Ruben Izquierdo, Eneko Agirre, German Rigau, and Piek Vossen. 2016. Addressing the MFS Bias in WSD systems. In *Proc. of LREC*, pages 1695–1700, Portorož, Slovenia.

Sameer S. Pradhan, Edward Loper, Dmitriy Dligach, and Martha Palmer. 2007. SemEval-2007 Task 17: English Lexical Sample, SRL and All Words. In *Proc. of SemEval-2007*, pages 87–92, Stroudsburg, PA, USA.

Alessandro Raganato, Jose Camacho-Collados, and Roberto Navigli. 2017a. Word Sense Disambiguation: A Unified Evaluation Framework and Empirical Comparison. In *Proc. of EACL*, pages 99–110, Valencia, Spain.

Alessandro Raganato, Claudio Delli Bovi, and Roberto Navigli. 2017b. Neural Sequence Learning Models for Word Sense Disambiguation. In *Proc. of EMNLP*, pages 1167–1178, Copenhagen, Denmark.

Bianca Scarlini, Tommaso Pasini, and Roberto Navigli. 2020. SensEmBERT: Context-Enhanced Sense Embeddings for Multilingual Word Sense Disambiguation. In *Proceedings of the 34th AAAI Conference on Artificial Intelligence*, New York, NY, USA.

Helmut Schmid. 1995. Improvements In Part-of-Speech Tagging With an Application To German. In *Proc. of the ACL SIGDAT-Workshop*, pages 47–50, Dublin, Ireland.

Benjamin Snyder and Martha Palmer. 2004. The English all-words task. In *In Proceedings of the 3rd International Workshop on the Evaluation of Systems for the Semantic Analysis of Text (SENSEVAL-3)*, pages 41–43, Barcelona, Spain.

Loïc Vial, Benjamin Lecouteux, and Didier Schwab. 2019. Sense Vocabulary Compression through the Semantic Knowledge of WordNet for Neural Word Sense Disambiguation. In *Proc. of Global Wordnet Conference*, Wroclaw, Poland.

A   API Documentation

In what follows we describe the typical usage of our RESTful API and its parameters. The SyntagRank API allows the user to perform two distinct requests: (i) `Disambiguate Text` and (ii) `Disambiguate Tokens`.

Disambiguate Text With `Disambiguate Text`, SyntagRank will process a raw text provided as input, given a target language among the five currently supported: EN (English), DE (German), FR (French), ES (Spanish), and IT (Italian).

Method type, URL, parameters and response description are specified in detail in Table 2. Figure 4 shows an example of a *success response* for the `Disambiguate Text` query.

```
{
    Code: 200
  - Content: {
        language: "EN"
      - tokens: [
          - {
                senseID: "wn:02604760v"
              - position: {
                    charOffsetBegin: 5
                    charOffsetEnd: 7
                }
            }
          - {
                senseID: "wn:06387980n"
              - position: {
                    charOffsetBegin: 10
                    charOffsetEnd: 14
                }
            }
        ]
    }
}
```

Figure 4: Example of a *success response* for `Disambiguate Text` when the language chosen is English and the input text is "this is a text".

Disambiguate Tokens With `Disambiguate Tokens`, SyntagRank will accept a pre-processed text as input to be disambiguated.

As for `Disambiguate Text`, language specification is required. Each token must show information concerning index (`id`), word form (`word`), lemma form (`lemma`), POS tag (`pos`), and a boolean indicating whether the token is a content word to be disambiguated (`isTargetWord`). In Table 3, we provide exhaustive details concerning method type, URL parameters, token parameters and response description for `Disambiguate Tokens`. Additionally, Figures 5 and 6 show, respectively, an example of a typical request, and its *success response*.

```
{
    lang: "EN"
  - words: [
      - {
            id: "0"
            word: "this"
            lemma: "this"
            pos: "X"
            isTargetWord: false
        }
      - {
            id: "1"
            word: "is"
            lemma: "be"
            pos: "VERB"
            isTargetWord: true
        }
      - {
            id: "2"
            word: "a"
            lemma: "a"
            pos: "X"
            isTargetWord: false
        }
      - {
            id: "3"
            word: "first"
            lemma: "first"
            pos: "ADJ"
            isTargetWord: true
        }
      - {
            id: "4"
            word: "test"
            lemma: "test"
            pos: "NOUN"
            isTargetWord: true
        }
    ]
}
```

Figure 5: A request example in English for `Disambiguate Tokens`.

```
{
    Code: 200
  - Content: {
      - result: [
          - {
                id: "3"
                synset: "wn:06387980n"
            }
          - {
                id: "1"
                synset: "wn:02604760v"
            }
        ]
    }
}
```

Figure 6: *Success response* with `Disambiguate Tokens` for the input shown in Figure 5.

<table>
<tr><td colspan="2"><code>Disambiguate Text</code></td></tr>
<tr><td>Method</td><td>GET/POST</td></tr>
<tr><td>URL</td><td><code>http://api.syntagnet.org/disambiguate?lang=language&text=text</code></td></tr>
<tr><td colspan="2"><code>URL Parameters</code></td></tr>
<tr><td>text (String)</td><td>The text to be disambiguated (max length: 1,500 characters). E.g.: text=this is a text.</td></tr>
<tr><td>lang (String)</td><td>The language of the input text, among the currently supported: EN, DE, FR, ES and IT.</td></tr>
<tr><td colspan="2"><code>Response description</code></td></tr>
<tr><td>language</td><td>The language of the disambiguated tokens.</td></tr>
<tr><td>tokens</td><td>Contains a list of disambiguated tokens.</td></tr>
<tr><td>senseID</td><td>Identifies the WordNet 3.0 offset for the concept assigned to the token.</td></tr>
<tr><td>position</td><td>Contains information concerning the token positioning.</td></tr>
<tr><td>charOffsetBegin</td><td>Highlights the position where a given term instance starts. Expressed as char offset.</td></tr>
<tr><td>charOffsetEnd</td><td>Highlights the position where a given term instance ends. Expressed as char offset.</td></tr>
</table>

Table 2: Details for the `Disambiguate Text` request.

<table>
<tr><td colspan="2"><code>Disambiguate Tokens</code></td></tr>
<tr><td>Method</td><td>POST</td></tr>
<tr><td>URL</td><td><code>http://api.syntagnet.org/disambiguate_tokens</code></td></tr>
<tr><td colspan="2"><code>URL Parameters</code></td></tr>
<tr><td>lang (String)</td><td>The language of the input text, among the currently supported: EN, DE, FR, ES and IT.</td></tr>
<tr><td>words (List<Token>)</td><td>Contains a list of words, each representing a single token of the input text.</td></tr>
<tr><td colspan="2"><code>Token Parameters</code></td></tr>
<tr><td>id (String)</td><td>Identifies the position of the token in the input text.</td></tr>
<tr><td>word (String)</td><td>Identifies the token, as it appears in the input text.</td></tr>
<tr><td>lemma (String)</td><td>The lemmatized form of the token.</td></tr>
<tr><td>pos (String)</td><td>The Part of Speech (PoS) of the token.</td></tr>
<tr><td>isTargetWord (boolean)</td><td>If true, identifies a token (for a content word) to be disambiguated.</td></tr>
<tr><td colspan="2"><code>Response description</code></td></tr>
<tr><td>result</td><td>Contains a list of disambiguated tokens.</td></tr>
<tr><td>id</td><td>Identifies the position of the disambiguated token according to the input text.</td></tr>
<tr><td>synset</td><td>Identifies the WordNet 3.0 offset for the concept assigned to the token.</td></tr>
</table>

Table 3: Details for the `Disambiguate Tokens` request.

pyBART: Evidence-based Syntactic Transformations for IE

Aryeh Tiktinsky   **Yoav Goldberg**   **Reut Tsarfaty**
Allen Institute for AI, Tel Aviv, Israel
Bar Ilan University, Ramat-Gan, Israel
{aryeht,yoavg,reutt}@allenai.org

Abstract

Syntactic dependencies can be predicted with high accuracy, and are useful for both machine-learned and pattern-based information extraction tasks. However, their utility can be improved. These syntactic dependencies are designed to accurately reflect syntactic relations, and they do not make semantic relations explicit. Therefore, these representations lack many explicit connections between content words, that would be useful for downstream applications. Proposals like English Enhanced UD improve the situation by extending universal dependency trees with additional explicit arcs. However, they are not available to Python users, and are also limited in coverage. We introduce a broad-coverage, data-driven and linguistically sound set of transformations, that makes event-structure and many lexical relations explicit. We present pyBART, an easy-to-use open-source Python library for converting English UD trees either to Enhanced UD graphs or to our representation. The library can work as a standalone package or be integrated within a spaCy NLP pipeline. When evaluated in a pattern-based relation extraction scenario, our representation results in higher extraction scores than Enhanced UD, while requiring fewer patterns.

1 Introduction

Owing to neural-based advances in parsing technology, NLP researchers and practitioners can now accurately produce syntactically-annotated corpora at scale. However, the use and empirical benefits of the dependency structures themselves remain limited. Basic syntactic dependencies encode the functional connections between words but lack many functional and semantic relations that exist between the content words in the sentence. Moreover, the use of strictly-syntactic relations results in structural diversity, undermining the efforts to effectively extract coherent semantic information from the resulting structures.

Thus, human practitioners and applications that "consume" these syntactic trees are required to devote substantial efforts to processing the trees in order to identify and extract the information needed for downstream applications, such as information and relation extraction (IE). Meanwhile, semantic representations (Banarescu et al., 2013; Palmer et al., 2010; Abend and Rappoport, 2013; Oepen et al., 2014) are harder to predict with sufficient accuracy, calling for a middle ground.

Indeed, De Marneffe and Manning (2008) introduced *collapsed* and *propagated* dependencies, in an attempt to make some semantic-like relations more apparent. The Universal Dependencies (UD) project[1] similarly embraces the concept of *Enhanced Dependencies* (Nivre et al., 2018)), adding explicit relations that are otherwise left implicit. Schuster and Manning (2016) provide further enhancements targeted specifically at English (Enhanced UD).[2] Candito et al. (2017) suggest further enhancements to address diathesis alternations.[3]

In this work we continue this line of thought, and take it a step further. We present pyBART, an

---

[1]universaldepdenencies.org

[2]In this paper we do not distinguish between the Universal Enhanced UD and Schuster and Manning (2016)'s Enhanced++ English UD. We refer to their union on English as Enhanced UD.

[3]Efforts such as PropS (Stanovsky et al., 2016) and PredPatt (White et al., 2016), share our motivation of extracting predicate-argument structures from treebank-trainable trees, though outside of the UD framework. Efforts such as KNext (Durme and Schubert, 2008) automatically extract logic-based forms by converting treebank-trainable trees, for consumption by further processing. HLF (Rudinger and Van Durme, 2014), DepLambda (Reddy et al., 2016) and UDepLambda (Reddy et al., 2017) attempt to provide a formal semantic representation by converting dependency structures to logical forms. While they share a high-level goal with ours — exposing functional relations in a sentence in a unified way — their end result, logical forms, is substantially different from pyBART structures. While providing substantial benefits for semantic parsing applications, logical forms are less readable for non-experts than labeled relations between content words. As these efforts rely on dependency trees as a backbone, they could potentially benefit from pyBART's focus on syntactic enhancements on top of (E)UD.

Proceedings of the 58th Annual Meeting of the Association for Computational Linguistics, pages 47–55
July 5 - July 10, 2020. ©2020 Association for Computational Linguistics

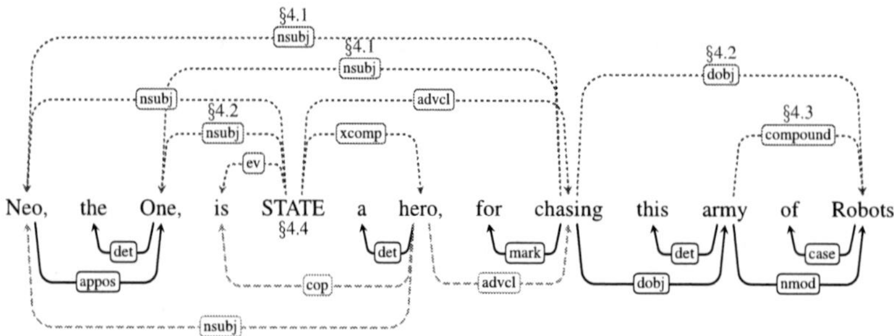

Figure 1: Representation of *Neo, the One, is a hero, for chasing this army of Robots*. The arcs above the sentence are BART additions. The ones below are EUD. Red arcs are removed in BART while black are retained.

easy-to-use Python library which converts English UD trees to a new representation that subsumes the English Enhanced UD representation and substantially extends it. We designed the representation to be linguistically sound and automatically recoverable from the syntactic structure, while exposing the kinds of relations required by IE applications. Some of these modifications are illustrated in Figure 1.[4] We aim to make event structure explicit, and cover as many linguistically plausible phenomena as possible. We term our representation BART (The BIU-AI2 Representation Transformation).

To assess the benefits of BART with respect to UD and other enhancements, we compare them in the context of a pattern-based relation extraction task, and demonstrate that BART achieves higher F_1 scores while requiring fewer patterns.

The python conversion library, pyBART, integrates with the spaCy[5] library, and is available under an open-source Apache license. A web-based demo for experimenting with the converter is also available. `https://allenai.github.io/pybart/`.

2 The BART Representation

We aim to provide a representation that will be useful for downstream NLP tasks, while retaining the following key properties. The proposal has to be **(i) based on syntactic structure** and **(ii) useful for information seeking applications**. As a consequence of (ii), we also want it to **(iii) make event structure explicit** and **(iv) allow favoring recall over precision**.

Being **based on syntax** as the backbone would allow us to capitalize on independent advances in

syntactic parsing, and on its relative domain independence. We want our representation to be not only accurate but also **useful for information seeking applications**. This suggests a concrete methodology (§2.1) and evaluation criteria (§5): we choose which relations to focus on based on concrete cases attested in relation extraction and QA-corpora, and evaluate the proposal based on the usefulness in a relation extraction task.

In general, information-seeking applications favor **making events explicit**. Current syntactic representations prefer to assign syntactic heads as root predicates, rather than actual eventive verb. In contrast, we aim to center our representation around the main event predicate in the sentence, while indicating event properties such as aspectuality (*Sam started walking*) or evidentiality (*Sam seems to like them*) as modifiers of rather than heads. To do this in a consistent manner, we introduce a new node of type STATE for copular sentences, making their event structure parallel to those containing finite eventive verbs (§4.4)

Finally, downstream users may prefer to **favor recall over precision** in some cases. To allow for this, we depart from previous efforts that refrain from providing any uncertain information. We chose to explicitly expose some relations which we believe to be useful but judge to be uncertain, while clearly marking their uncertainty in the output. This allows users to experiment with the different cases and assess the reliability of the specific constructions in their own application domain. We introduce two uncertainty marking mechanisms, discussed in §2.3.

2.1 Data-driven Methodology

Our departure point is the English EUD representation (Schuster and Manning, 2016) and related

---

[4] Some preserved UD relations are omitted for readability.
[5] `https://spacy.io`

efforts discussed above, which we seek to extend in a way which is useful to information seeking applications. To identify relevant constructions that are not covered by current representations, we use a data-driven process. We consider concrete relations that are expressed in annotated task-based corpora: a relation extraction dataset (ACE05, (Walker et al., 2006)), which annotates relations and events, and a QA-SRL dataset (He et al., 2015) which connects predicates to sentence segments that are perceived by people as their (possibly implied) arguments. For each of these corpora, we consider the dependency paths between the annotated elements, looking for cases where a direct relation in the corpus corresponds to an indirect dependency path in the syntactic graph. We identify recurring cases that we think can be shortened, and which can be justified linguistically and empirically. We then come up with proposed enhancements and modifications, and verify them empirically against a larger corpus by extracting cases that match the corresponding patterns and browsing the results.

2.2 Formal Structure

As is common in dependency-based representations, BART structures are labeled, directed multi-graphs whose nodes are the words of a sentence, and the labeled edges indicate the relations between them. Some constructions add additional nodes, such as copy-nodes (Schuster and Manning, 2016) and STATE nodes (§4.4).

An innovative aspect of our approach is that each edge is associated with additional information beyond its dependency label. This information is structured as follows:

SRC: a field indicating the origin of this edge—either "UD" for the original dependency edges, or a pair indicating the type and sub-type of the construction that resulted in the BART edge (e.g., {SRC=(conj,and)} or {SRC=(adv,while)}).

UNC, ALT: optional fields indicating uncertainty, described below.

2.3 Embracing uncertainty

Some syntactic constructions are ambiguous with respect to the ability to propagate information through them. Rather than giving up on all ambiguous constructions, we opted to generate the edges and mark them with an UNC=TRUE flag, deferring the decision regarding the validity of the edge to the user:

```
1  # Load a UD-based english model
2  nlp = spacy.load("en_ud_model")
3
4  # Add BART converter to spaCy's pipeline
5  from pybart.api import converter
6  converter = converter( ... )
7  nlp.add_pipe(converter, name="BART")
8
9  # Test the new converter component
10 doc = nlp("He saw me while driving")
11 me_token = doc[2]
12 for par_tok in me_token._.parent_list:
13     print(par_tok)
14
15 # Output:
16 {'head': 2, 'rel':'dobj', 'src':'UD'}
17 {'head': 5, 'rel': 'nsubj',
18    'src':('advcl','while'), 'alt':'0'}
```

Figure 2: Usage example of pyBART's spaCy-pipeline component.

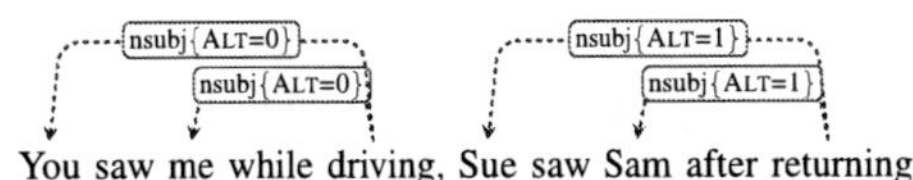

In some cases, we can identify that one of two options is possible, but cannot determine which. In these cases we report both edges, but mark them explicitly as alternatives to each other. This is achieved with an ALT=X field on both edges, with X being a number indicating the pair.

3 Python code and Web-demo

The pyBART library provides a Python converter from English UD trees to BART. pyBART subsumes the enhancements of the EUD Java implementation provided in Stanford Core-NLP,[6] and extends them as described in §4. While pyBART's default performs all enhancements, it can be configured to follow a more selective behavior. pyBART has two modes: (1) a converter from CoNLLU-formatted UD trees to CoNLLU-formatted BART structures;[7] and (2) a spaCy (Honnibal and Montani, 2017) pipeline component.[8] After registering pyBART as a spaCy pipeline, tokens on the analyzed document will have a `._.parent_list` field, containing the

---

[6] https://nlp.stanford.edu/software/stanford-dependencies.html

[7] The extra edge information is linearized into the dependency label after a '@' separator.

[8] This requires a spaCy model trained to produce UD trees, which we provide.

list of parents of the token in the BART structure. Each item is a dictionary specifying—in addition to the parent-token id and dependency label—also the extra information described in §2.2. See Figure 2 for an illustration of the API.

A web-based demo that parses sentences into both EUD and BART graphs, visualizes them, and compares their outputs, is also provided.[9]

4 Coverage of Linguistic Phenomena

BART conversion consists of four conceptual changes from basic UD. The first type propagates shared arguments between predicates in **nested structures**. The second type shares arguments between **parallel structures**. The third type attempts to unify **syntactic alternations** to reduce diversity, making structures that carry similar meaning also similar in structure. Finally, the forth type is designed to make **event structure** explicit in the syntactic representation, allowing finite verbs that indicate event properties to act as event modifiers rather than root predicates. In accordance with that, we further introduce a new STATE node, that acts as the main predicate node for *stative* (copular, verb-less) sentences.

4.1 Nested Structures

Our first type of conversions propagates an external core argument to be explicitly linked as the subject of a subordinate clause.

Complement control: The various EUD representations explicitly indicate the external subjects of *xcomp* clauses containing a *to* marker. We embrace this choice and extend it to cover also clauses without a *to* marker, including imperative clauses and clauses with controlled gerunds.

(1)   Let   my   people   go!
[dobj, nsubj, xcomp]

Noun-modifying clauses: Similarly, EUD links the empty subject of a finite relative clause to the corresponding argument of the external clause. We extend this behavior to also cover **reduced relative clauses** (2a), and we follow Candito et al. (2017) in also including other relative clauses such as **noun-modifying participles** (2b).

(2)   *a.*   *b.*

The neon god they made   A vision softly creeping
[dobj]   *[nsubj]*

Adverbial clauses and "dep": Adverbial modifier clauses that miss a subject, often modify the subject of the main clause. We propagate the external subject to be the subject of the internal clause.[10]

(3)   You shouldn't text while driving
[nsubj]

We observe that many **dep** edges empirically behave like adverbial clauses, and treat them similarly. We mark these edges as "uncertain".

4.2 Parallel structures

The second type of conversions identifies parallel structures in which the latter instance is elliptical, and share the missing core argument contributed by the former instance.

Apposition: Similarly to the PropS proposal (Stanovsky et al., 2016), we share relations across *apposition parts*, making the two, currently hierarchical, phrase, more duplicate-like.

(4)   E.T., the Extraterrestrial, phones home
[appos, nsubj, nsubj]

Modifiers in conjunction: In modified coordinated constructions, we share prepositional (5) and possessive (6) modifiers between the coordinated parts. Since dependency trees are *inherently* ambiguous between conjoined modification and single-conjunct modification, (e.g, compare (5) to "Mogly was lost and raised by wolves", or (6) to "my Father and E.T."), we mark both as UNC.

(5)   I   was   taught   and   raised   by   wolves
[nmod(UNC), nmod]

(6)   My   father   and   mother   met   here
[nmod:poss(UNC), nmod:poss]

Elaboration/Specification Clauses: For noun nominal modifiers that have the form of an *elaboration* or *specification*, we share the head of the modified noun with its dependent modifier. That is, if the modification is marked by *like* or *such as* prepositions, we propagate the head noun to the nominal dependent.

(7)   I   enjoy   fruits   such   as   apples
[dobj, dobj]

---

[9]The dependency graph visualization component uses the TextAnnotationGraphs (TAG) library (Forbes et al., 2018).

[10]In external clauses that include a subject and an object, ambiguity may arise as to which is to be modified. We propagate both and mark the edges as alternates (ALT, (§2.3)).

Indexicals: the interpretation of locative and temporal indexicals such as *here*, *there* and *now* depends on the situation and the speaker, and often modify not only the predicate but the entire situation. We therefore share the adverbial modification from the noun to the main verb. Due to their situation-specific nature, we mark these as UNC.

(8) He wonders in these woods here

Compounds: Shwartz and Waterson (2018) show that in many cases, compounds can be seen as having a multiple-head. Therefore, we share the existing relations across the compound parts.

(9) I used canola oil

As many compounds *do* have a clear head (e.g. *I used baby oil*, where *baby* is clearly not the head), we mark these as uncertain.

4.3 Syntactic Alternations

This type of conversions aim to unify syntactic variability. We identify structures that are syntactically different but share (some) semantic structure, and add arcs or nodes to expose the similarity.

The Passivization Alternation: Following Candito et al. (2017) we relate the *passive* alteration to its *active* variant.

(10) The Sheriff was shot by Bob

Hyphen reconstruction: Noun-verb Hyphen Constructions (HC) which are modifying a nominal can be seen as conveying the same information as a copular sentence wherein the noun is the subject and the verb is the predicate. To explicitly indicate this, we add to all modifying noun-verb HCs a *subject* and a *modifier* relation originating at the verb-part of the HC.

(11) A Miami - based company

Adjectival modifiers: Adjectival modification can be viewed as capturing the same information as a predicative copular sentence conveying the same meaning (so, "a green apple" implies that "an apple is green"). To explicitly capture this productive implication, we add a subject relation from each adjectival modifier to its corresponding modified noun.

(12) I see dead people

Genitive Constructions: Genitive cases can be alternatively expressed as a compound. We add a compound relation to unify the expression of genitives across *X of Y* and *compound* structures.

(13) Army of zombies

4.4 Event-Centered Representations

In many sentences, the finite root predicate does not indicate the main event. Instead, a verb in the subordinated clause expresses the event, and the finite verb acts as its modifier. For example, in sentences like "He started working", "He seems to work there", the main event indicated is "work", while the root predicates ("started", "seemed") modify this event. Here, we present a chain of changes that puts emphasis on *events* by delegating copular and tense auxiliaries (is, was), evidentials (seem, say) and various aspectual verbs (started, continued) to be clausal modifiers, rather than heads of the sentence. This creates a further challenge, since there is a prevalent discrepancy between predicative sentences such as "He works" and copular sentences as "He is smart". The UD structure for the latter lacks a node that clearly indicates a *stative* event (in Vendler (1957)'s terminology). We remedy this by adding a node to represent the STATE and have tense, aspect, modality and evidentiality directly modifying it.[11]

Copular Sentences and Stative Predicates: We added to all copula constructions new node named *STATE*, which represents the *stative* event introduced by the copular clause. This node becomes the root, and we rewire the entire clause around this *STATE*. By doing so we unify it with the structures of clauses with finite predicative. Once we added the *STATE* node, we form a new relation, termed *ev*, to mark event/state modifications. The resulting structure is as follows:

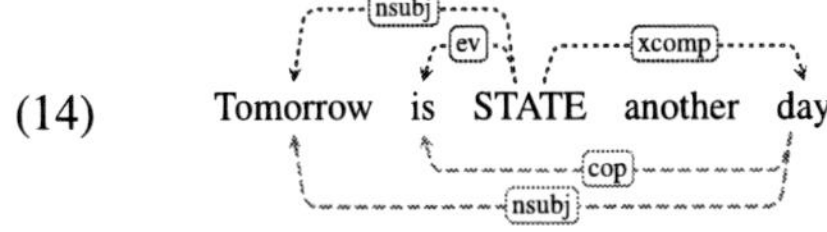

(14) Tomorrow is STATE another day

Evidential reconstructions: We can now explicitly mark properties of events as dependents of the verbal or stative root by means of the label *ev*. We do so, using verbs' white-lists, for verbs marking

---

[11]Pragmatically, some users prefer to not have non-word nodes. pyBART supports this by providing a mode that treats the copula as the head, retaining the other modifications.

evidentiality (15) and for reported-speech (16).

(15)

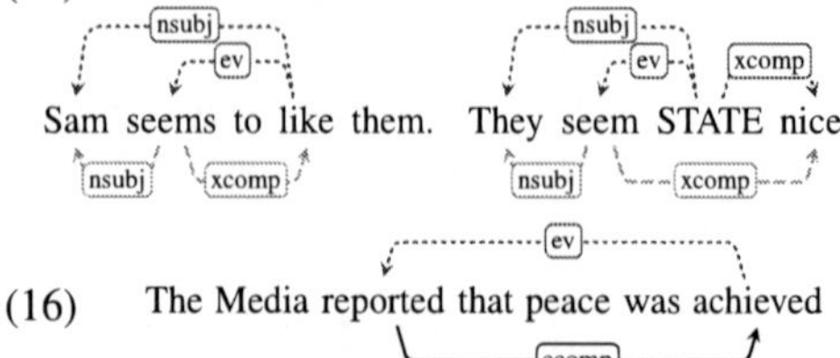

(16)

Aspectual constructions: Finally, we can now also mark aspectual verbs as modifying the complement (matrix) verb denoting the main event. The complement (matrix) verb becomes the root of the dependency structure, and we add the new *ev* relation to mark the aspectual modification of the event.

(17)

5   Evaluation

Our proposed representation attempts to target information-seeking applications, but is it effective? We evaluate the resulting graph structures against the UD and Enhanced UD representations, in the context of a relation-extraction (RE) task. Concretely, we evaluate the representations on their ability to perform pattern-based RE on the TACRED dataset (Zhang et al., 2017).

We use an automated and reproducible methodology: for each of the representations, we use the RE train-set to acquire extraction patterns. We then apply the patterns to the dev-set, compute F1-scores, and, for each relation, filter the patterns that hurt F1-score. We then apply the filtered pattern-set to the test-set, and report F1 scores.

To acquire extraction patterns, we use the following procedure: given a labeled sentence consisting of a relation name and the sentence indices of the two entities participating in the relation, we compute the shortest dependency path between the entities, ignoring edge directions. We then form an extraction pattern from the directed edges on this path. We consult a list of trigger words (Yu et al., 2015) collected for the different relations. If a trigger word or its lemma is found on the path, we form an unlexicalized path except for the trigger word (i.e. E1 <nsubj "founded" >dobj >compound E2). If no trigger-word is found, the path is lexicalized with the word's lemmas (i.e. E1 <nsubj "reduce" >dobj "activity" >compound E2).

Representation	Precision	Recall	F1
UD	76.53	30.65	43.77
Enhanced UD	77.63	32.37	45.69
Ours(w/o-Enhanced)	73.96	33.48	46.09
Ours	74.62	36.65	**49.15**

Table 1: Effectiveness of the different representations on the TACRED relation extraction task.

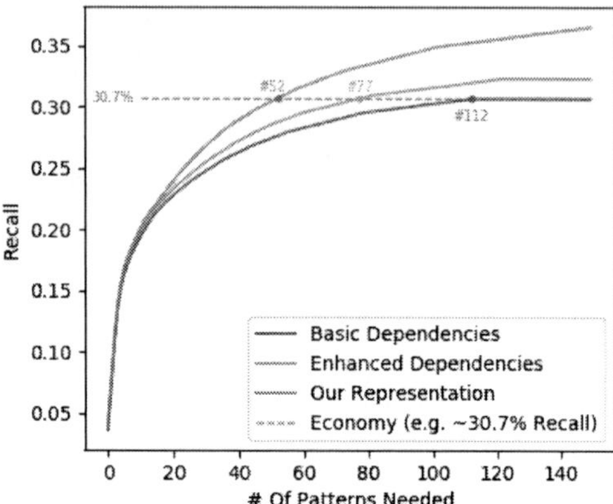

Figure 3: Economy comparison: Recall vs number of patterns, for the different representations.

We use this procedure to compare UD, Enhanced UD (EUD), BART without EUD enhancements, and full BART, which is a superset of Enhanced UD (Table 1). BART achieves a substantially higher F1 score of 49.15%, an increase of 5.5 F1 points over UD, and 3.5 F1 points above Enhanced UD. It does so by substantially improving recall while somewhat decreasing precision.

We also consider *economy*: the number of different patterns needed to achieve a given recall level. Figure 3 plots the achieved recall against the number of patterns. As the curves show, Enhanced UD is more economic than UD, and our representation is substantially more economic than both. To achieve 30.7% recall (the maximal recall of UD), UD requires 112 patterns, EUD requires 77 patterns, while BART needed only 52 patterns.

6   Conclusion

We propose a syntax-based representation that aims to make the event structure and as many lexical relations as possible explicit, for the benefit of downstream information-seeking applications. We provide a Python API that converts UD trees to this representation, and demonstrate its empirical benefits on a relation extraction task.

Acknowledgements

This project has received funding from the European Research Council (ERC) under the European Union's Horizon2020 research and innovation programme, grant agreement 802774 (iEXTRACT) and grant agreement 677352 (NLPRO).

References

Omri Abend and Ari Rappoport. 2013. Universal conceptual cognitive annotation (ucca). In *Proceedings of the 51st Annual Meeting of the Association for Computational Linguistics (Volume 1: Long Papers)*, pages 228–238.

Laura Banarescu, Claire Bonial, Shu Cai, Madalina Georgescu, Kira Griffitt, Ulf Hermjakob, Kevin Knight, Philipp Koehn, Martha Palmer, and Nathan Schneider. 2013. Abstract meaning representation for sembanking. In *Proceedings of the 7th linguistic annotation workshop and interoperability with discourse*, pages 178–186.

Marie Candito, Bruno Guillaume, Guy Perrier, and Djamé Seddah. 2017. Enhanced UD dependencies with neutralized diathesis alternation. In *Proceedings of the Fourth International Conference on Dependency Linguistics (Depling 2017)*, pages 42–53, Pisa,Italy. Linköping University Electronic Press.

Marie-Catherine De Marneffe and Christopher D Manning. 2008. Stanford typed dependencies manual. Technical report, Technical report, Stanford University.

Benjamin Durme and Lenhart Schubert. 2008. Open knowledge extraction through compositional language processing. *Proceedings of the 2008 Conference on Semantics in Text Processing*.

Angus Forbes, Kristine Lee, Gus Hahn-Powell, Marco A. Valenzuela-Escrcega, and Mihai Surdeanu. 2018. Text annotation graphs: Annotating complex natural language phenomena. In *Proceedings of the Eleventh International Conference on Language Resources and Evaluation (LREC'18)*, Miyazaki, Japan. European Language Resources Association (ELRA).

Luheng He, Mike Lewis, and Luke Zettlemoyer. 2015. Question-answer driven semantic role labeling: Using natural language to annotate natural language. In *Proceedings of the 2015 Conference on Empirical Methods in Natural Language Processing*, pages 643–653, Lisbon, Portugal. Association for Computational Linguistics.

Matthew Honnibal and Ines Montani. 2017. spaCy 2: Natural language understanding with Bloom embeddings, convolutional neural networks and incremental parsing. To appear.

Joakim Nivre, Paola Marongiu, Filip Ginter, Jenna Kanerva, Simonetta Montemagni, Sebastian Schuster, and Maria Simi. 2018. Enhancing universal dependency treebanks: A case study. In *Proceedings of the Second Workshop on Universal Dependencies (UDW 2018)*, pages 102–107, Brussels, Belgium. Association for Computational Linguistics.

Stephan Oepen, Marco Kuhlmann, Yusuke Miyao, Daniel Zeman, Dan Flickinger, Jan Hajič, Angelina Ivanova, and Yi Zhang. 2014. SemEval 2014 task 8: Broad-coverage semantic dependency parsing. In *Proceedings of the 8th International Workshop on Semantic Evaluation (SemEval 2014)*, pages 63–72, Dublin, Ireland. Association for Computational Linguistics.

Martha Palmer, Daniel Gildea, and Nianwen Xue. 2010. Semantic role labeling. *Synthesis Lectures on Human Language Technologies*, 3(1):1–103.

Siva Reddy, Oscar Täckström, Michael Collins, Tom Kwiatkowski, Dipanjan Das, Mark Steedman, and Mirella Lapata. 2016. Transforming dependency structures to logical forms for semantic parsing. *Transactions of the Association for Computational Linguistics*, 4:127–140.

Siva Reddy, Oscar Tckstrm, Slav Petrov, Mark Steedman, and Mirella Lapata. 2017. Universal semantic parsing.

Rachel Rudinger and Benjamin Van Durme. 2014. Is the Stanford dependency representation semantic? In *Proceedings of the Second Workshop on EVENTS: Definition, Detection, Coreference, and Representation*, pages 54–58, Baltimore, Maryland, USA. Association for Computational Linguistics.

Sebastian Schuster and Christopher D Manning. 2016. Enhanced english universal dependencies: An improved representation for natural language understanding tasks. In *Proceedings of the Tenth International Conference on Language Resources and Evaluation (LREC'16)*, pages 2371–2378.

Vered Shwartz and Chris Waterson. 2018. Olive oil is made *of* olives, baby oil is made *for* babies: Interpreting noun compounds using paraphrases in a neural model. In *Proceedings of the 2018 Conference of the North American Chapter of the Association for Computational Linguistics: Human Language Technologies, Volume 2 (Short Papers)*, pages 218–224, New Orleans, Louisiana. Association for Computational Linguistics.

Gabriel Stanovsky, Jessica Ficler, Ido Dagan, and Yoav Goldberg. 2016. Getting more out of syntax with props. *arXiv preprint arXiv:1603.01648*.

Zeno Vendler. 1957. Verbs and times. *The Philosophical Review*, 66(2):143–160.

Christopher Walker, Stephanie Strassel, Julie Medero, and Kazuaki Maeda. 2006. Ace 2005 multilingual training corpus. *Linguistic Data Consortium, Philadelphia, LDC2006T06*.

Aaron Steven White, Drew Reisinger, Keisuke Sakaguchi, Tim Vieira, Sheng Zhang, Rachel Rudinger, Kyle Rawlins, and Benjamin Van Durme. 2016. Universal Decompositional Semantics on Universal Dependencies. In *Proceedings of the 2016 Conference on Empirical Methods in Natural Language Processing*, pages 1713–1723, Austin, Texas. Association for Computational Linguistics.

Dian Yu, Heng Ji, Sujian Li, and Chin-Yew Lin. 2015. Why read if you can scan? trigger scoping strategy for biographical fact extraction. In *Proceedings of the 2015 Conference of the North American Chapter of the Association for Computational Linguistics: Human Language Technologies*, pages 1203–1208, Denver, Colorado. Association for Computational Linguistics.

Yuhao Zhang, Victor Zhong, Danqi Chen, Gabor Angeli, and Christopher D. Manning. 2017. Position-aware attention and supervised data improve slot filling. In *Proceedings of the 2017 Conference on Empirical Methods in Natural Language Processing (EMNLP 2017)*, pages 35–45.

A   Appendix

A.1   Additional examples of BART structures

The following are additional examples that we could not fit into the space constraints of the paper.

Complement control   Example (1) shows an example of linking the external subject to a controlled finite verb. The following complementary example shows linking the subject to a controlled gerund:

(18)

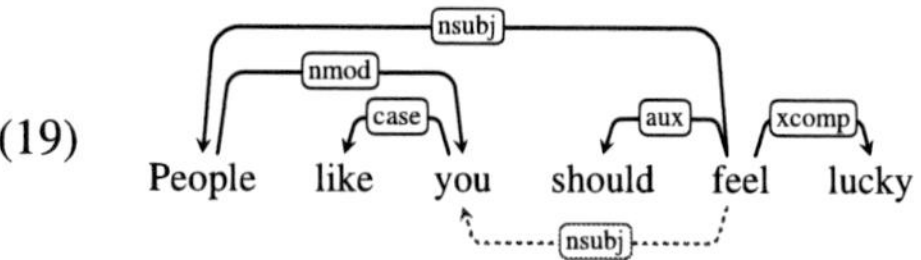

Elaboration/Specification Clauses   Example (7) shows a specification clause connected as an object to the root. The following is a complementary example of using the *like* elaboration-preposition, in which the modifier noun is a *subject* dependant of its head. The modified noun inherits the *subject* relation from its modifier head.

(19)

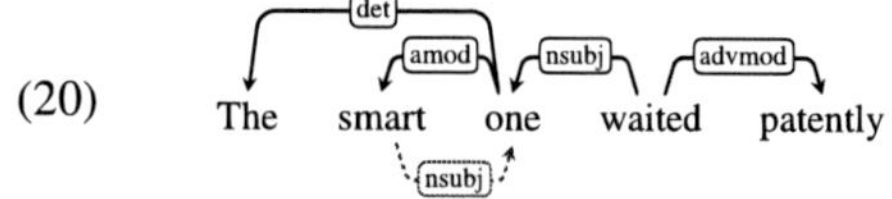

Adjectival modifier

(20)

Copular Sentences and Stative Predicates We show additional examples of these transformations, with explicit comparison to UD.

(21) *UD* :   *BART* :

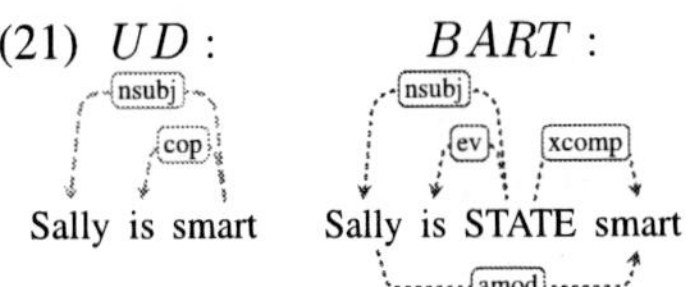

(22) *UD* :   *BART* :

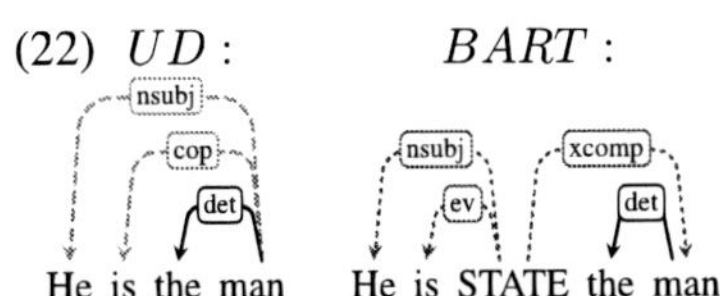

(23) *UD* :   *BART* :

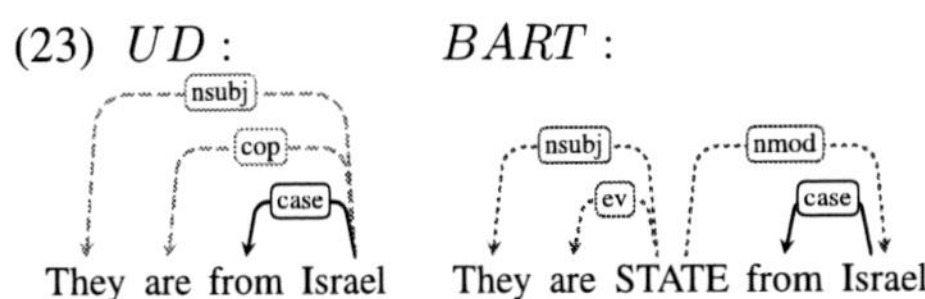

(24) *UD* :   *BART* :

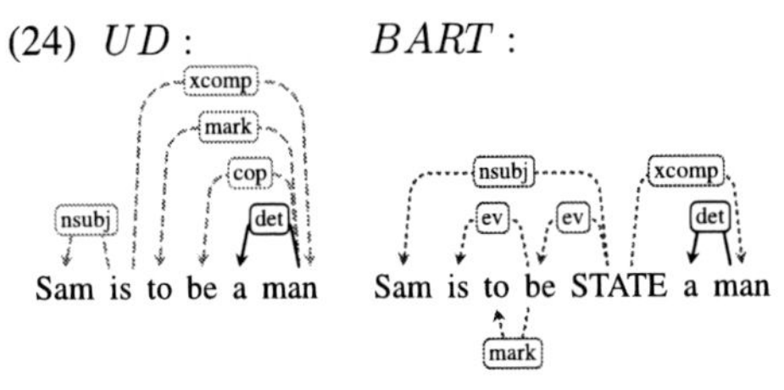

(25) *UD* :   *BART* :

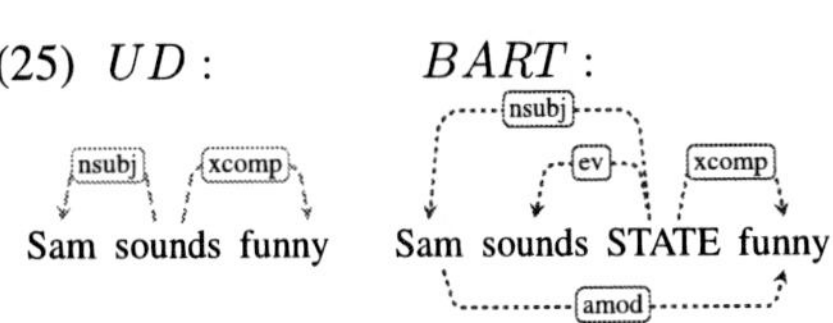

(26) *UD* :   *BART* :

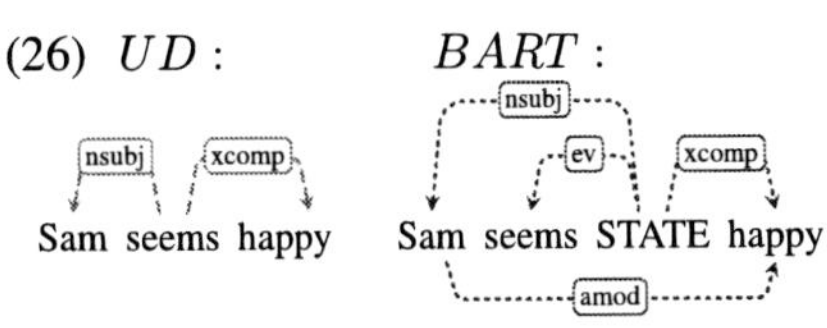

(27) *UD* :   *BART* :

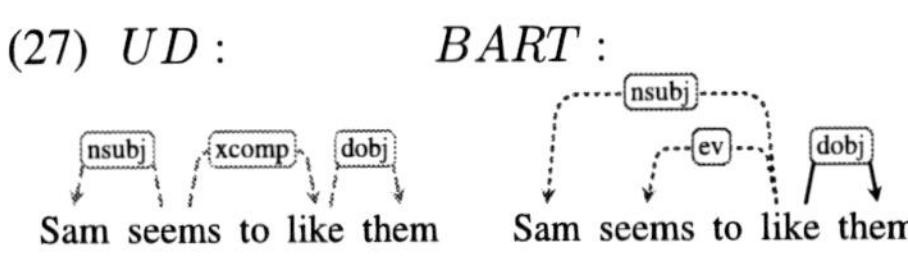

(28) *UD* :   *BART* :

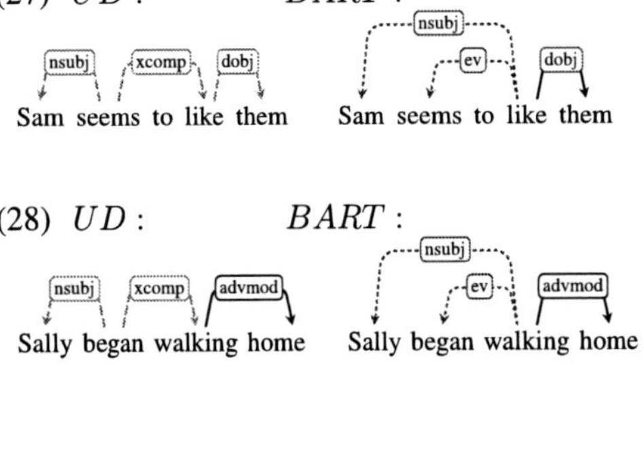

EVIDENCEMINER: Textual Evidence Discovery for Life Sciences

Xuan Wang[1], Yingjun Guan[2], Weili Liu[1], Aabhas Chauhan[1], Enyi Jiang[1], Qi Li[3],
David Liem[4], Dibakar Sigdel[4], J. Harry Caufield[4], Peipei Ping[4], Jiawei Han[1]

[1]Department of Computer Science, University of Illinois at Urbana-Champaign
[2]School of Information Sciences, University of Illinois at Urbana-Champaign
[3]Department of Computer Science, Iowa State University
[4]School of Medicine, University of California, Los Angeles
[1,2]{xwang174,yingjun2,weilil2,aabhasc2,enyij2,hanj}@illinois.edu, [3]qli@iastate.edu,
[4]{dliem,dsigdel,jcaufield,pping}@mednet.ucla.edu

Abstract

Traditional search engines for life sciences
(e.g., PubMed) are designed for document retrieval and do not allow direct retrieval of specific statements. Some of these statements
may serve as textual evidence that is key to
tasks such as hypothesis generation and new
finding validation. We present EVIDENCEM-
INER, a web-based system that lets users query
a natural language statement and automatically
retrieves textual evidence from a background
corpora for life sciences. EVIDENCEMINER
is constructed in a completely automated way
without any human effort for training data annotation. It is supported by novel data-driven
methods for distantly supervised named entity
recognition and open information extraction.
The entities and patterns are pre-computed
and indexed offline to support fast online
evidence retrieval. The annotation results
are also highlighted in the original document
for better visualization. EVIDENCEMINER
also includes analytic functionalities such as
the most frequent entity and relation summarization. EVIDENCEMINER can help scientists uncover essential research issues, leading to more effective research and more in-
depth quantitative analysis. The system of
EVIDENCEMINER is available at `https://
evidenceminer.firebaseapp.com/`[1].

1 Introduction

Search engines on scientific literature have been
widely used by life scientists for discoveries based
on prior knowledge. Each day, millions of users
query PubMed[2] and PubMed Central[3] (PMC) for
their information needs in biomedicine (Allot et al.,
2019). However, traditional search engines for life
sciences (e.g., PubMed) are designed for document

retrieval and do not allow direct retrieval of specific statements (Lu, 2011; Ren et al., 2017; Shen
et al., 2018). With the results from those search
engines, scientists still need to read a large number
of retrieved documents to find specific statements
as textual evidence to validate the input query. This
textual evidence is key to tasks such as developing new hypotheses, designing informative experiments, or comparing and validating new findings
against previous knowledge.

While the last several years have witnessed substantial growth in interests and efforts in evidence
mining (Lippi and Torroni, 2016; Wachsmuth et al.,
2017; Stab et al., 2018; Chen et al., 2019; Majithia
et al., 2019; Chernodub et al., 2019; Allot et al.,
2019), little work has been done for evidence mining system development in the scientific literature.
A significant difference between evidence in the
scientific literature and evidence in other corpora
(e.g., the online debate corpus) is that scientific
evidence usually does not have a strong sentiment
(i.e., positive, negative or neutral) in the opinion
it holds. Most scientific evidence sentences are
objective statements reflecting how strongly they
support a query statement. Therefore, if scientists are interested in finding textual evidence for
"melanoma is treated with nivolumab", they may
expect a ranked list of statements with the top ones
like "bicytopenia in primary lung melanoma treated
with nivolumab" as the textual evidence that supports the input query.

This paper presents EVIDENCEMINER, a web-
based system for textual evidence discovery for
life sciences (Figure 1). Given a query as a natural language statement, EVIDENCEMINER automatically retrieves sentence-level textual evidence
from a background corpora of biomedical literature. EVIDENCEMINER is constructed in a completely automated way without any human effort
for training data annotation. It is supported by

---

[1]A brief demo of EVIDENCEMINER is available at
`https://youtu.be/iYuQ6gsr--I`.
[2]`https://www.ncbi.nlm.nih.gov/pubmed/`
[3]`https://www.ncbi.nlm.nih.gov/pmc/`

Proceedings of the 58th Annual Meeting of the Association for Computational Linguistics, pages 56–62
July 5 - July 10, 2020. ©2020 Association for Computational Linguistics

novel data-driven methods for distantly supervised named entity recognition and open information extraction. EVIDENCEMINER relies on external knowledge bases to provide distant supervision for named entity recognition (NER) (Shang et al., 2018b; Wang et al., 2018b, 2019). Based on the entity annotation results, it automatically extracts informative meta-patterns (textual patterns containing entity types, e.g., CHEMICAL inhibit DISEASE) from sentences in the background corpora. (Jiang et al., 2017; Wang et al., 2018a; Li et al., 2018a,b). Sentences with meta-patterns that better match the query statement is more likely to be textual evidence. The entities and patterns are precomputed and indexed offline to support fast online evidence retrieval. The annotation results are also highlighted in the original document for better visualization. EVIDENCEMINER also includes analytic functionalities such as the most frequent entity and relation summarization. The contributions and features of the EVIDENCEMINER system are summarized as follows.

1. We build EVIDENCEMINER, a web-based system for textual evidence discovery for life sciences. EVIDENCEMINER is supported by novel methods for distantly supervised named entity recognition and pattern-based open information extraction.

2. The retrieved evidence sentences can be easily located in the original text. The entity and relation annotation results are also highlighted in the original document for better visualization.

3. Analytic functionalities are included such as finding the most frequent entities/relations for given entity/relation types and finding the most frequent entities given a relation type with another entity.

2   Related Work

Search engines performing sentence-level retrieval have been developed in the biomedical domain. For example, Textpresso (Müller et al., 2004) highlights the query-related sentences in the retrieved documents. However, the sentence highlighting is only based on query word matching, which does not necessarily find sentences semantically related to the input query. Another example is LitSense (Allot et al., 2019), which retrieves semantically similar sentences in biomedical literature given

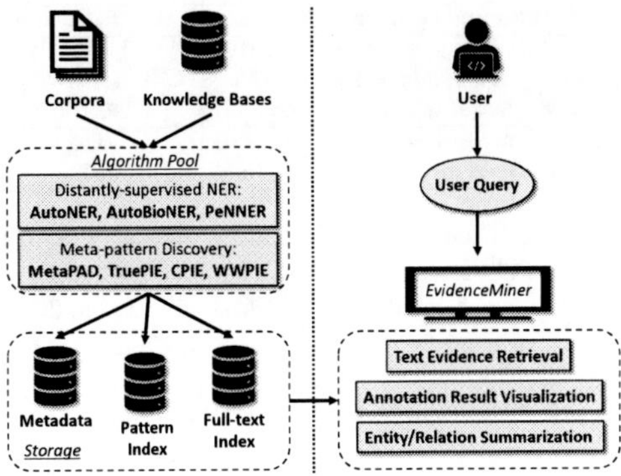

Figure 1: System architecture of EVIDENCEMINER.

a query sentence. It returns best-matching sentences using a combined approach of traditional word matching and neural embedding. However, their neural embeddings are noisy and thus negatively impact the effectiveness in retrieving query-specific evidence sentences. EVIDENCEMINER is more effective compared with LitSense for textual evidence retrieval in biomedical literature.

Similar tools are also developed for other domains, such as claim mining and argument mining tools on Twitter or news articles. PerspectroScope (Chen et al., 2019) allows users to query a natural language claim and extract textual evidence in support or against the claim. ClaimPortal (Majithia et al., 2019) is an integrated infrastructure for searching and checking factual claims on Twitter. TARGER (Chernodub et al., 2019) is an argument mining framework for tagging arguments in the free input text and keyword-based retrieval of arguments from the argument-tagged corpus. Most of these tools rely on fully supervised methods that require human-annotated training data. It is difficult to directly apply these systems to other domains, such as life sciences since it is non-trivial to retrieve the set of human-annotated articles and the annotations are prone to errors (Levy et al., 2017).

3   System Description

EVIDENCEMINER consists of two major components: an open information extraction pipeline and a textual evidence retrieval and analysis pipeline. The open information extraction pipeline includes two functional modules: (1) distantly supervised NER, and (2) meta-pattern-based open information extraction; whereas the textual evidence retrieval and analysis pipeline includes three functional modules: (1) textual evidence search, (2) annotation

Background corpora	Cancers	Heart Diseases
#PubMed abstracts	48,201	11,766
#PMC full-text papers	7,130	1,151
#Sentences in total	1,466,091	246,106
#Entity instances	3,315,092	400,327
#Relation instances	29,160	9,576

Table 1: Basic statistics of background corpora. It includes PubMed abstracts and PMC full-text papers related to cancers and heart diseases published in 2019.

result visualization in the original document, and (3) the most frequent entity and relation summarization. Figure 1 shows the system architecture of EVIDENCEMINER. The functional modules are introduced in the following sections.

3.1 Open Information Extraction

The open information extraction pipeline extracts entities with distant supervision from knowledge bases and relations with automatic meta-pattern discovery methods. In particular, to extract high-quality entities and relations, we design noise-robust neural models for distantly supervised named entity recognition (Shang et al., 2018b; Wang et al., 2019) and wide-window meta-pattern discovery methods to deal with the long and complex sentences in biomedical literature (Wang et al., 2018a; Li et al., 2018b).

Data Collection. To obtain the background corpora for EVIDENCEMINER, we collect the titles and abstracts of 26M papers from the entire PubMed[4] dump, and the full-text contents of 2.2M papers from PubMed Central[5] (PMC). For the demonstration purpose, we select a subset of documents published in 2019 that are specifically related to two important diseases (cancers and heart diseases) to form the background corpora. The subset of documents are selected by concept matching on MeSH[6], a biomedical concept ontology with the concepts related to cancers (Neoplasms) and heart diseases (Cardiovascular Diseases). Table 1 summarizes the statistics of the background corpora.

Distantly Supervised Named Entity Recognition. EVIDENCEMINER relies on UMLS[7], a comprehensive biomedical knowledge base to provide distant supervision for named entity recognition. We select 5 major biomedical entity types (Organism, Fully Formed Anatomical Structure,

Chemical, Physiologic Function, and Pathologic Function) including 17 fine-grained entity types (Archaeon, Bacterium, Eukaryote, Virus, Body Part/Organ/Organ Component, Tissue, Cell, Cell Component, Gene or Genome, Chemical, Organism Function, Organ or Tissue Function, Cell Function, Molecular Function, Disease or Syndrome, Cell or Molecular Dysfunction, Experimental Model of Disease, and Pathological Function) from UMLS as the entity types to be annotated. To tackle the problem of limited coverage of the input dictionary, we first apply a data-driven phrase mining algorithm, AutoPhrase (Shang et al., 2018a), to extract high-quality phrases as additional entity candidates. Then we automatically expand the dictionary with a novel dictionary expansion method (Wang et al., 2019). The expanded dictionary is used to label the input corpora with the 17 fine-grained entity types to train a neural model. We apply AutoNER (Shang et al., 2018b), a state-of-the-art distantly supervised NER method that effectively deals with noisy distant supervision. Comparing with PubTator (Wei et al., 2013), a state-of-the-art BioNER system trained with extensive human annotation on 5 biomedical entity types, EVIDENCEMINER can automatically annotate 17 fine-grained entity types with high quality without any human effort for training data annotation.

Meta-pattern Discovery. Based on the entity annotation results above, meta-patterns can be automatically discovered from the corpora to support textual evidence discovery. Meta-patterns are defined as sub-sequences in an entity-type-replaced corpus with at least one entity type token in it. For example, "PPAR gamma agonist" and "caspase 1 agonist" are two word-sequences in the raw corpus. If we replace all the entities (i.e., "PPAR gamma" and "caspase 1") with their corresponding entity types (i.e., \$GENE) in the raw corpus, "PPAR gamma agonist" and "caspase 1 agonist" are represented as one meta-pattern "\$GENE agonist" in the entity-type-replaced corpus. Meta-patterns containing at least two entity types (e.g., "\$CHEMICAL induce \$DISEASE") are relational meta-patterns. Quality relational meta-patterns can serve as informative textual patterns that guide textual evidence discovery. We apply two state-of-the-art meta-pattern discovery methods, CPIE (Wang et al., 2018a) and WW-PIE (Li et al., 2018b), to extract high-quality meta-patterns from the NER-tagged corpora. Both methods are specifically de-

---

[4] https://pubmed.gov/pubmed
[5] https://pubmed.gov/pmc
[6] https://www.nlm.nih.gov/mesh/
[7] https://www.nlm.nih.gov/research/umls/index.html

signed to better deal with the long and complex sentence structures in the biomedical literature. In EVIDENCEMINER, we combine the meta-pattern extraction results from CPIE and WW-PIE as our informative meta-patterns to guide textual evidence retrieval. We use Elasticsearch[8] to create the index for each sentence for fast online retrieval. In addition to indexing the keywords, we index each sentence with the meta-patterns it matches and the corresponding entities extracted by the meta-patterns in the sentence.

3.2 Textual Evidence Retrieval and Analysis

The textual evidence retrieval and analysis pipeline retrieves textual evidence given a user-input query statement and the indexed corpora. The retrieved evidence sentence can be easily located in the original text. The entity and relation annotation results are also highlighted in the text for better visualization. EVIDENCEMINER also includes analytic functionalities such as finding the most frequent entities and relations as summarization.

Textual Evidence Search. Given a user-input query statement and the indexed corpora, EVIDENCEMINER retrieves and ranks the candidate sentences with a combined approach of keyword weighting and meta-pattern weighting. Sentences with meta-patterns that better match the query statement are ranked higher as textual evidence. This ranking mechanism is more effective compared with existing methods (e.g., LitSense) for textual evidence retrieval in biomedical literature (see Section 4). We use Elasticsearch to support keyword and meta-pattern search over the indexed corpora.

In Figure 2, we show an example of our search interface. For example, if scientists are interested in finding the textual evidence for *"melanoma is treated with nivolumab"*, they can search it in EVIDENCEMINER and see the top results such as "bicytopenia in primary lung melanoma treated with nivolumab" (Figure 2a). If they click one of the top results, the retrieved sentence is highlighted in the original article (Figure 3) on the annotation interface. Moreover, EVIDENCEMINER allows more flexible queries, such as a mixture of keywords and relational patterns. For example, if scientists are interested in finding the diseases that can be treated with the chemical "nivolumab", but are not sure which disease to search, they may input a query like *"nivolumab, DISEASEORSYNDROME treat with*

CHEMICAL". EVIDENCEMINER automatically finds all the textual evidence indicating a "treatment" relationship with the chemical "nivolumab" (Figure 2b).

Annotation Result Visualization. The annotation interface shows all the annotated entities and relations for better visualization. For example, in Figure 3, we color all the annotated entities with different colors for different types. We use five different colors for the five major biomedical entity types and two additional colors for two specific fine-grained types, "Gene or Genome" and "Disease or Syndrome", since those two are the most frequent biomedical entity types. In Figure 3, we see that the "melanoma" is colored as a "Disease or Syndrome" and "nivolumab" is colored as a "Chemical". We also list all the meta-pattern instances and meta-patterns that match the sentences in the article. If the user clicks the meta-pattern instances, the corresponding sentences are also highlighted in the article. In Figure 3, a meta-pattern "DISEASEORSYNDROME patient treat with CHEMICAL" captures the entity pair "melanoma" and "nivolumab" in the article.

Entity and Relation Summarization. To make our system more user-friendly and interesting, we add analytic functionalities for the most frequent entity and relation summarization. For example, in Figure 4, if scientists are interested in finding the most frequent diseases, they can search "entity_type = DISEASEORSYNDROME" in our analytic interface and see the top entities such as *tumor* and *breast cancer*. Similarly, if scientists are interested in finding the most frequent chemical-disease pairs with a treatment relation, they can search "pattern = DISEASEORSYNDROME treat with CHEMICAL" in our analytic interface and see the top entity pairs such as *HCC&sorafenib*. More interestingly, if researchers are interested in finding the most frequent diseases that can be treated by a specific chemical (e.g., nivolumab), they can search "entity = nivolumab & pattern = DISEASEORSYNDROME treat with CHEMICAL" in our analytic interface and see the most frequent diseases, such as *melanoma* and *NSCLC*, that can be treated with nivolumab. With these analytic functionalities, EVIDENCEMINER can help scientists uncover important research issues, leading to more effective research and more in-depth quantitative analysis.

---

[8]https://www.elastic.co/

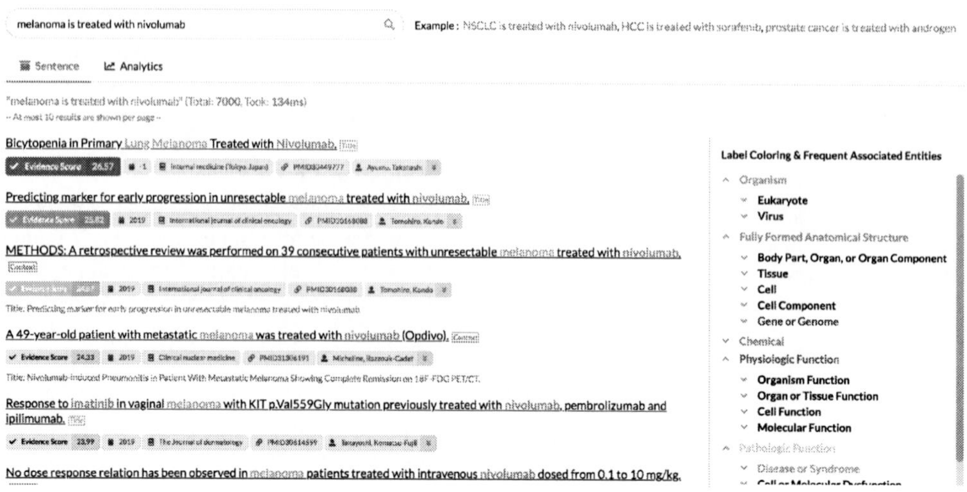

(a) Query: *melanoma is treated with nivolumab*

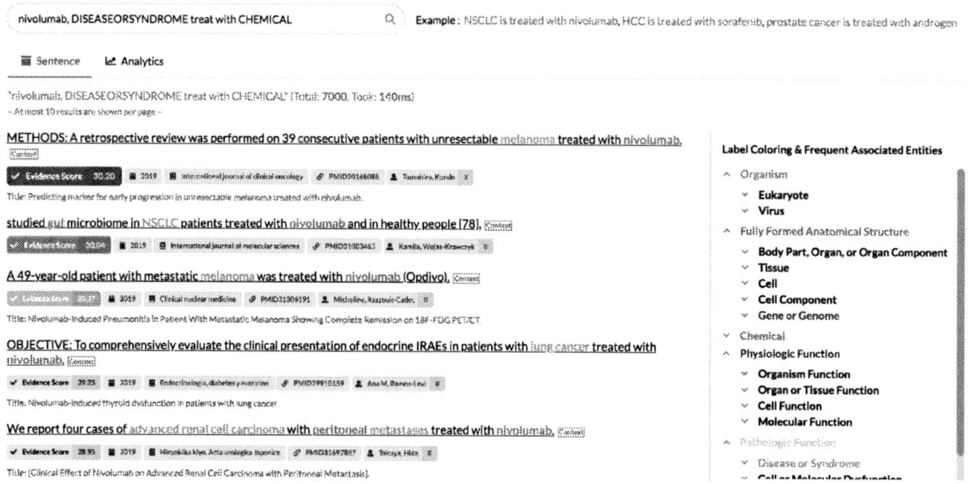

(b) Query: *(nivolumab, DISEASEORSYNDROME treat with CHEMICAL)*

Figure 2: The search interface with the textual evidence retrieved. The evidence score indicates the confidence of each retrieved sentence being a supporting evidence of the input query.

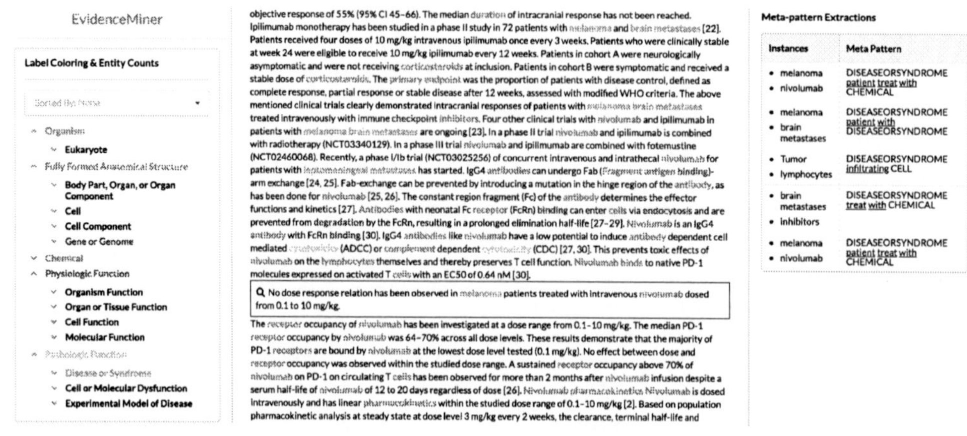

Figure 3: The annotation interface with all the entity and relation annotation results.

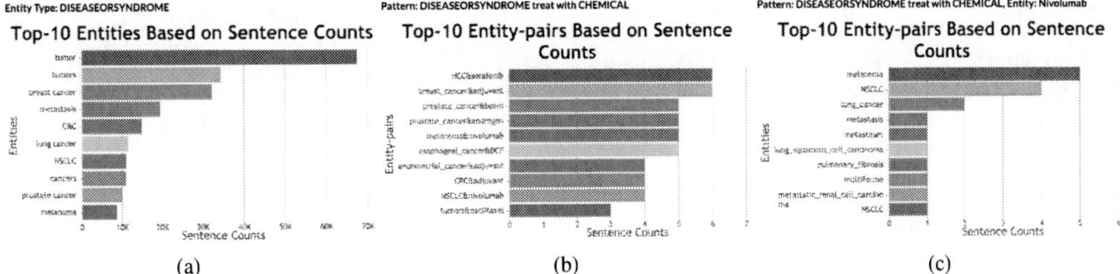

Figure 4: The analytic interface with the entity and relation summarization results. The queries used are (a) entity_type=DISEASEORSYNDROME, (b) pattern=DISEASEORSYNDROME treat with CHEMICAL, and (c) entity=nivolumab&pattern=DISEASEORSYNDROME treat with CHEMICAL.

Method / nDCG	@1	@5	@10
BM25	0.714	0.720	0.746
LitSense	0.599	0.624	0.658
EVIDENCEMINER	**0.855**	**0.861**	**0.889**

Table 2: Performance comparison of the textual evidence retrieval systems with nDCG@1,5,10.

4 Evaluation

To demonstrate the effectiveness of EVIDENCEMINER in textual evidence retrieval, we compare its performance with the traditional BM25 (Robertson et al., 2009) and a recent sentence-level search engine, LitSense (Allot et al., 2019). The background corpus is the same PubMed subset for all the compared methods. We first ask domain experts to generate 50 query statements based on the relationships between three biomedical entity types (gene, chemical, and disease) in the Comparative Toxicogenomics Database[9]. Then we ask domain experts to manually label the top-10 retrieved evidence sentences by each method with three grades indicating the confidence of the evidence. We use the average normalized Discounted Cumulative Gain (nDCG) score to evaluate the textual evidence retrieval performance. In Table 2, we observe that EVIDENCEMINER always achieves the best performance compared with other methods. It demonstrates the effectiveness of using meta-patterns to guide textual evidence discovery in biomedical literature.

5 Further Development

In some cases, a strict query matching may not find sufficiently high-quality answers due to the stringent search requirements or limited available entities that match the search queries. In this case, a smart query processor should automatically kick-in to do an approximate match, such as a graph-based approximate match or an embedding-based semantic match. In other cases, a user may query a set of entities (e.g., genes or diseases) or a timeline. We need to conduct a summary of the major differences among the set of entities or over time by analyzing large text.

6 Conclusion

We build EVIDENCEMINER, a web-based system for textual evidence discovery for life sciences. The retrieved evidence sentences can be easily located in the background corpora for better visualization. EVIDENCEMINER also includes analytic functionalities such as the most frequent entity and relation summarization. We incorporated another corpus on COVID-19 in EVIDENCEMINER to help boost the scientific discoveries (Wang et al., 2020b,a). We are further developing EVIDENCEMINER to be a more intelligent system that can assist in more efficient and in-depth scientific discoveries.

Acknowledgment

Research was sponsored in part by US DARPA KAIROS Program No. FA8750-19-2-1004 and SocialSim Program No. W911NF-17-C-0099, National Science Foundation IIS 16-18481, IIS 17-04532, and IIS-17-41317, and DTRA HD-TRA11810026. Any opinions, findings, and conclusions or recommendations expressed herein are those of the authors and should not be interpreted as necessarily representing the views, either expressed or implied, of DARPA or the U.S. Government. The U.S. Government is authorized to reproduce and distribute reprints for government purposes notwithstanding any copyright annotation hereon.

---

[9] http://ctdbase.org

References

Alexis Allot, Qingyu Chen, Sun Kim, Roberto Vera Alvarez, Donald C Comeau, W John Wilbur, and Zhiyong Lu. 2019. Litsense: making sense of biomedical literature at sentence level. *Nucleic acids research*.

Sihao Chen, Daniel Khashabi, Chris Callison-Burch, and Dan Roth. 2019. Perspectroscope: A window to the world of diverse perspectives. page 129134.

Artem Chernodub, Oleksiy Oliynyk, Philipp Heidenreich, Alexander Bondarenko, Matthias Hagen, Chris Biemann, and Alexander Panchenko. 2019. Targer: Neural argument mining at your fingertips. In *ACL: System Demonstrations*, pages 195–200.

Meng Jiang, Jingbo Shang, Taylor Cassidy, Xiang Ren, Lance M Kaplan, Timothy P Hanratty, and Jiawei Han. 2017. Metapad: Meta pattern discovery from massive text corpora. In *KDD*, pages 877–886. ACM.

Ran Levy, Shai Gretz, Benjamin Sznajder, Shay Hummel, Ranit Aharonov, and Noam Slonim. 2017. Unsupervised corpus–wide claim detection. In *Proc. Work. Arg. Min.*, pages 79–84.

Qi Li, Meng Jiang, Xikun Zhang, Meng Qu, Timothy P Hanratty, Jing Gao, and Jiawei Han. 2018a. Truepie: Discovering reliable patterns in pattern-based information extraction. In *KDD*, pages 1675–1684. ACM.

Qi Li, Xuan Wang, Yu Zhang, Qi Li, Fei Ling, Cathy Wu H, and Jiawei Han. 2018b. Pattern discovery for wide-window open information extraction in biomedical literature. In *BIBM*. IEEE.

Marco Lippi and Paolo Torroni. 2016. Margot: A web server for argumentation mining. *Expert Systems with Applications*, 65:292–303.

Zhiyong Lu. 2011. Pubmed and beyond: a survey of web tools for searching biomedical literature. *Database*, 2011.

Sarthak Majithia, Fatma Arslan, Sumeet Lubal, Damian Jimenez, Priyank Arora, Josue Caraballo, and Chengkai Li. 2019. Claimportal: Integrated monitoring, searching, checking, and analytics of factual claims on twitter. In *ACL: System Demonstrations*, pages 153–158.

Hans-Michael Müller, Eimear E Kenny, and Paul W Sternberg. 2004. Textpresso: an ontology-based information retrieval and extraction system for biological literature. *PLoS Biol.*, 2(11):e309.

Xiang Ren, Jiaming Shen, Meng Qu, Xuan Wang, Zeqiu Wu, Qi Zhu, Meng Jiang, Fangbo Tao, Saurabh Sinha, David Liem, et al. 2017. Life-inet: A structured network-based knowledge exploration and analytics system for life sciences. In *ACL: System Demonstrations*, pages 55–60.

Stephen Robertson, Hugo Zaragoza, et al. 2009. The probabilistic relevance framework: Bm25 and beyond. *FnT Inf. Ret.*, 3(4):333–389.

Jingbo Shang, Jialu Liu, Meng Jiang, Xiang Ren, Clare R Voss, and Jiawei Han. 2018a. Automated phrase mining from massive text corpora. *TKDE*.

Jingbo Shang, Liyuan Liu, Xiang Ren, Xiaotao Gu, Teng Ren, and Jiawei Han. 2018b. Learning named entity tagger using domain-specific dictionary. In *EMNLP*. ACL.

Jiaming Shen, Jinfeng Xiao, Xinwei He, Jingbo Shang, Saurabh Sinha, and Jiawei Han. 2018. Entity set search of scientific literature: An unsupervised ranking approach. In *SIGIR*, pages 565–574. ACM.

Christian Stab, Johannes Daxenberger, Chris Stahlhut, Tristan Miller, Benjamin Schiller, Christopher Tauchmann, Steffen Eger, and Iryna Gurevych. 2018. Argumentext: Searching for arguments in heterogeneous sources. In *Proceedings of the 2018 conference of the North American chapter of the association for computational linguistics: demonstrations*, pages 21–25.

Henning Wachsmuth, Martin Potthast, Khalid Al Khatib, Yamen Ajjour, Jana Puschmann, Jiani Qu, Jonas Dorsch, Viorel Morari, Janek Bevendorff, and Benno Stein. 2017. Building an argument search engine for the web. In *Proceedings of the 4th Workshop on Argument Mining*, pages 49–59.

Xuan Wang, Weili Liu, Aabhas Chauhan, Yingjun Guan, and Jiawei Han. 2020a. Automatic textual evidence mining in covid-19 literature.

Xuan Wang, Xiangchen Song, Yingjun Guan, Bangzheng Li, and Jiawei Han. 2020b. Comprehensive named entity recognition on cord-19 with distant or weak supervision. *arXiv preprint arXiv:2003.12218*.

Xuan Wang, Yu Zhang, Qi Li, Yinyin Chen, and Jiawei Han. 2018a. Open information extraction with meta-pattern discovery in biomedical literature. In *BCB*, pages 291–300. ACM.

Xuan Wang, Yu Zhang, Qi Li, Xiang Ren, Jingbo Shang, and Jiawei Han. 2019. Distantly supervised biomedical named entity recognition with dictionary expansion. In *2019 IEEE International Conference on Bioinformatics and Biomedicine (BIBM)*, pages 496–503. IEEE.

Xuan Wang, Yu Zhang, Qi Li, Cathy H. Wu, and Jiawei Han. 2018b. PENNER: pattern-enhanced nested named entity recognition in biomedical literature. In *BIBM*, pages 540–547.

Chih-Hsuan Wei, Hung-Yu Kao, and Zhiyong Lu. 2013. Pubtator: a web-based text mining tool for assisting biocuration. *Nucleic Acids Res.*, 41(W1):W518–W522.

Trialstreamer: Mapping and Browsing Medical Evidence in Real-Time

Benjamin E. Nye
Northeastern University
`nye.b@husky.neu.edu`

Ani Nenkova
UPenn
`nenkova@seas.upenn.edu`

Iain J. Marshall
King's College London
`iain.marshall@kcl.ac.uk`

Byron C. Wallace
Northeastern University
`b.wallace@northeastern.edu`

Abstract

We introduce *Trialstreamer*, a living database of clinical trial reports. Here we mainly describe the *evidence extraction* component; this extracts from biomedical abstracts key pieces of information that clinicians need when appraising the literature, and also the relations between these. Specifically, the system extracts descriptions of trial participants, the treatments compared in each arm (the *interventions*), and which outcomes were measured. The system then attempts to infer which interventions were reported to work best by determining their relationship with identified trial outcome measures. In addition to summarizing individual trials, these extracted data elements allow automatic synthesis of results across many trials on the same topic. We apply the system at scale to all reports of randomized controlled trials indexed in MEDLINE, powering the automatic generation of *evidence maps*, which provide a global view of the efficacy of different interventions combining data from all relevant clinical trials on a topic. We make all code and models freely available[1] alongside a demonstration of the web interface.[2]

1 Introduction and Motivation

The highest-quality evidence to inform healthcare practice comes from randomized controlled trials (RCTs). The results of the vast majority of these trials are communicated in the form of unstructured text in journal articles. Such results accumulate quickly, with over 100 articles describing RCTs published daily, on average. It is difficult for healthcare providers and patients to make sense of and keep up with this torrent of unstructured literature.

Consider a patient who has been newly diagnosed with diabetes. She would like to con-

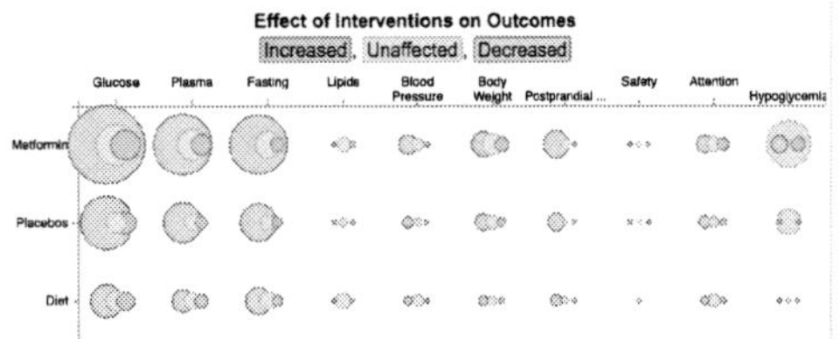

Figure 1: A portion of an example evidence mapping Interventions and their inferred efficacy for Outcomes, given the condition (or Population) of *Type II Diabetes*. These maps are generated automatically using the NLP system we describe in this work.

sult (in collaboration with her healthcare provider) the available evidence regarding her treatment options. But she may not even be aware of what her treatment options are. Further, she may only care about particular outcomes (for instance, managing her blood pressure). Currently, it is not straightforward to retrieve and browse the evidence pertaining to a given condition, and in particular to ascertain which treatments are best supported for a specific outcome of interest.

Trialstreamer is a first attempt to solve this problem, making evidence more browseable via NLP technologies. Figure 1 shows one of the key features of the system: an automatically generated *evidence map* that displays treatments (vertical axis) and outcomes (horizontal) identified for a condition specified by the user (here, migraines). We elaborate on this particular example to illustrate the use of the system in Section 3.

Trialstreamer aims to facilitate efficient evidence mapping with a user friendly method of presenting a search across a broad field (here, being a clinical condition) (Miake-Lye et al., 2016). We use NLP technologies to provide browseable, interactive overviews of large volumes of literature, on-demand. These may then inform subsequent, formal syntheses, or they may simply guide ex-

---

[1] https://github.com/bepnye/evidence_extraction/
[2] http://bit.ly/trialstreamer

Proceedings of the 58th Annual Meeting of the Association for Computational Linguistics, pages 63–69
July 5 - July 10, 2020. ©2020 Association for Computational Linguistics

ploration of the primary literature. In this work we describe an open-source prototype that enables evidence mapping, using NLP to generate interactive overviews and visualizations of all RCT reports indexed by MEDLINE (and accessible via PubMed).

When mapping the evidence one is generally interested in the following basic questions:

- What interventions and outcomes have been studied for a given condition (population)?

- How much evidence exists, both in terms of the number of trials and the number of participants within these?

- Does the evidence seem to support use of a particular intervention for a given condition?

In the remainder of this paper we describe a prototype system that facilitates interactive exploration and mapping of the evidence base, with an emphasis on answering the above questions. The Trialstreamer mapping interface allows structured search over study populations, interventions/comparators, and outcomes — collectively referred to as PICO elements (Huang et al., 2006). It then displays key clinical attributes automatically extracted from the set of retrieved trials. This is made possible via NLP modules trained on recently released corpora (Nye et al., 2018; Lehman et al., 2019), described below.

2 System Overview

The evidence extraction pipeline is composed of four primary phases. First, text snippets that convey information about the trial's treatments (or *interventions*), outcome measures, and results are extracted from abstracts. Relations between these snippets are then inferred to identify which treatments were compared against each other, and which outcomes were measured for these comparisons. The extracted relations and evidence statements are then used to infer an overall conclusion about the comparative efficacy of the trial's interventions. Finally, the clinical concepts expressed in the extracted spans are normalized to a structured vocabulary in order to ground them in an existing knowledge base and allow for aggregations across trials.

A typical RCT report would pertain to a single clinical condition (the *population*), but might report multiple numerical results, each concerning a particular intervention, comparator, and outcome measure (which we describe as an ICO triplet).

Because the end-to-end task combines NLP subtasks that are supported by different datasets, we collected new development and test sets — 160 abstracts in all, exhaustively annotated — in order to evaluate the overall performance of our system. Two medical doctors[3] annotated these documents with the all of the expressed entities, their mentions in the text, the relations between them, the conclusions reported for each ICO triplet and the sentence that contains the supporting evidence for this (Lehman et al., 2019).

We were unable to obtain normalized concept labels for the ICO triplets due to the excessive difficulty of the task for the annotators.

Modeling decisions were informed by the 60 document development set, and we present evaluations of the first four information extraction modules with regard to the 100 documents in the unseen test set.

2.1 Preprocessing

Enabling search over RCT reports requires first compiling and indexing all such studies. This is, perhaps surprisingly, non-trivial. One may rely on "Publication Type" (PT) tags that codify study designs of articles, but these are manually applied by staff at the National Library of Medicine. Consequently, there is a lag between when a new study is published and when a PT tag is applied. Relying on these tags may thus hinder access to the most up-to-date evidence available. Therefore, we instead use an automated tagging system that uses machine learning to classify articles as RCT reports (or not). This model has been validated extensively in prior work (Marshall et al., 2018), and we do not describe it further here.

Next, we replace all abbreviations with their long forms using the Ab3P algorithm (Sohn et al., 2008). Using long forms has the complementary advantages of improving PICO labeling accuracy while also reducing the amount of context needed for prediction by downstream model components.

2.2 Study Descriptor Recognition

PICO Elements

In order to identify the spans of text corresponding to the PICO elements of the trial, we use the *EBM-NLP* corpus (Nye et al., 2018). This is a dataset

---

[3]Hired via Upwork (`http://www.upwork.com`).

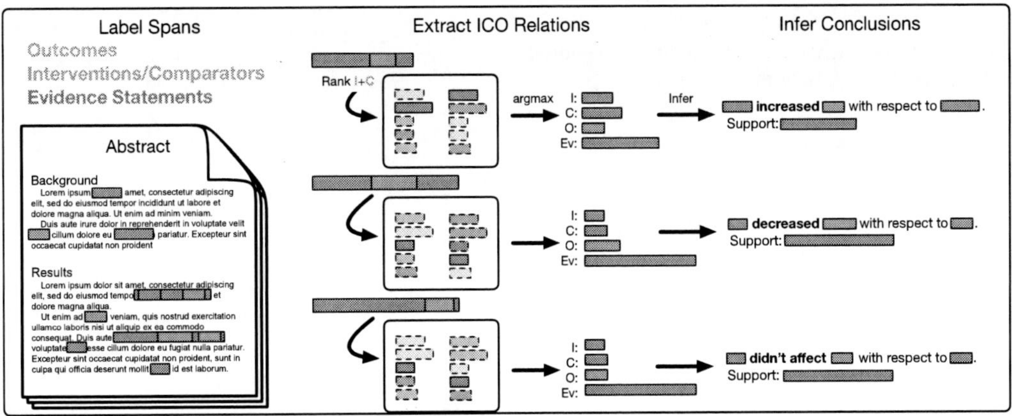

Figure 2: Overview of the evidence extraction pipeline, applied to all RCT article abstracts automatically identified. Text spans are first extracted from these abstracts, then assembled into relations that reflect the structure of the trials, and finally used to infer the effect interventions were reported to have on measured outcomes, as compared to the control treatment.

	F1	Precision	Recall
Tokens	0.63	0.56	0.72
Clinical Entities	0.67	0.55	0.87

Table 1: Macro-averaged scores for ICO span prediction at both the token and clinical entity level.

	F1	Precision	Recall
Evidence	0.69	0.53	0.97

Table 2: Performance for identifying evidence-bearing sentences.

comprising ∼5,000 abstracts of RCT reports that have been annotated to demarcate textual spans that describe the respective PICO elements. In addition to these spans, it contains more granular annotations on information within spans (e.g., specific Population attributes like age and sex).

We follow our prior work (Nye et al., 2018) in training a BiLSTM-CRF model that learns to jointly predict each PICO element using EBM-NLP. Recent work has shown the efficacy of BERT (Devlin et al., 2018) representations in this space, e.g., Beltagy *et al.* achieved state-of-the-art performance on EBM-NLP using this approach (2019). Therefore, for all text encoding we use BioBERT (Lee et al., 2019), which was pretrained on PubMed documents.[4]

Results for Interventions/Comparators and Outcomes on our test set are reported in Table 1. Since these spans will serve as inputs to downstream models in the pipeline, high recall at the expense of precision is preferable; we will allow subsequent classifiers to discard spurious spans. We achieve 0.87 recall at the clinical concept level.

Evidence Statements

In addition to PICO elements, we extract all sentences in the abstract that are predicted to contain evidence concerning the relative efficacy of an Intervention. Our training data for this model is sourced from the *Evidence-Inference* corpus (Lehman et al., 2019), which comprises ∼10,000 annotated 'prompts' across ∼2,400 unique full-text articles. Each prompt specifies an Intervention, a Comparator, and an Outcome. Doctors have annotated the prompts for each article, supplying an extracted snippet that presents the conclusion for these ICO elements, as well as an inference concerning whether the Outcome increased, decreased, or remained the same in the intervention group (as compared to the comparator group).

We frame evidence identification as a sentence classication task, and train a linear classification layer on top of BioBERT outputs. Our positive training examples are the sentences containing evidence snippets in Evidence-Inference, and we draw an equal number of length-matched negatives randomly from the rest of the document. As shown in Table 2, we achieve extremely high recall on the test set, but only middling precision. On inspection, many of these false positives are sentences from the conclusion that provide a high-

---

[4]For PICO tagging on EBM-NLP we found that BioBERT performed comparably to SciBERT (Beltagy et al., 2019).

level summary of the evidence, but aren't the best evidence statement — as provided by the annotator — for any given ICO prompt.

2.3 Relation Extraction

To transform the extracted spans into a semantic representation of the trial that can be used to construct an evidence map, we must identify all instances of an outcome being reported, and infer which two treatments were being directly compared as the intervention and comparator with respect to said outcome. Finally, given each assembled ICO prompt, we can then predict the trial's findings regarding whether the outcome increased, decreased, or was not statistically different under the intervention versus the comparator. In effect, we are aiming to jointly extract ICO prompts *and* infer the directionality of the results reported concerning these, whereas prior work (Nye et al., 2018; Lehman et al., 2019) has considered these problems only in isolation.

Our strategy for assembling ICO prompts is informed by the style in which results are commonly described in abstracts.When results are described in an article the outcome is typically referenced explicitly, while the intervention and especially the comparator are often referenced either indirectly ("Mean headache duration was similar between groups"), or not at all ("No significant difference was observed for recovery time"). In the fully annotated dev set collected for this work, 87% of outcomes were described explicitly in an evidence span, while only 28% of treatments were explicit.

Motivated by this observation, we use the (explicit) outcomes extracted from an evidence snippet as a starting point; for each of these outcomes, the associated intervention and comparator are then inferred. This has the significant advantage of explicitly linking each outcome to the evidence that will be used to infer the directionality of the reported finding. This also provides the end-user with an interpretable rationale for the inference concerning treatment efficacy.

To link candidate extracted treatments to specific outcome mentions, we train a model that takes in a candidate treatment, an evidence statement containing the outcome, and the surrounding context from the document, and predicts if the treatment is the participating intervention, the participating comparator, or if it is not involved in

	F1	Precision	Recall
No Difference	0.91	0.94	0.89
Increased	0.73	0.69	0.77
Decreased	0.76	0.75	0.78

Table 3: Per-class prediction scores for each outcome in the test set.

this particular evaluation. We use the evidence-inference corpus to provide training examples for the first two classes, and manually generate negative samples for the final class. The negatives are constructed to mimic common errors that the treatment extraction module made on the dev set, including: mislabeling an outcome as a treatment; extracting compound phrases containing multiple individual treatments; and, finally, extracting spurious spans that don't represent a study descriptor.

The model is a linear classifier on top of BioBERT. Inputs are constructed as: [CLS] TREATMENT [SEP] EVIDENCE. CONTEXT. [SEP]. We experimented with different slices of the document as the context, and achieved the highest dev performance using the first four sentences of the article. The class probabilities from this model are used to rank the possible interventions and comparators for each outcome, and when sufficiently probable candidates are identified we generate a complete ICO prompt.

After assembling all ICO prompts in a document, we feed them to a final classifier to predict the directionality of findings for each outcome, with respect to the given intervention and comparator. This model is trained over the evidence-inference corpus using the provided I, C, and O spans coupled with the sentences that contain the corresponding evidence statement. Empirically, we found that signal for the classifier is dominated by the outcome text and evidence span, with almost no contribution from the intervention and comparator. This is unsurprising given the regularity of the language used to describe conclusions. The reported directionality of the result is almost exclusively framed with respect to the intervention, and only 4.0% of all outcomes ever have different results for another I+C linking within the same document. The best performing model input was simply [CLS] OUTCOME [SEP] EVIDENCE [SEP], and the results on the test set are reported in Table 3.

Strict	Precision	Recall
Extracted spans	0.26	0.24
Expert spans	0.23	0.26
Relaxed	Precision	Recall
Extracted spans	0.32	0.34
Expert spans	0.31	0.34

Table 4: Performance for predicting an article's exact MeSH terms using the rule-base system, run on both the automatically extracted spans and the expert-provided test spans.

False Neg		False Pos	
Name / Count		**Name / Count**	
Humans	185	Patients	115
Middle Aged	93	Aging	42
Adult	84	Therapeutics	42
Aged	62	Weights/Measures	33
Double-Blind Method	50	Placebos	33
Treatment Outcome	42	Time	21
Adolescent	39	Serum	17
Prospective Studies	27	Safety	17
Time Factors	20	Pain	16
Child, Preschool	20	Women	14

Table 5: Ten most common over- and under-predicted MeSH terms for the test set of 191 articles.

2.4 Normalizing PICO Terms

In order to standardize the language used to categorize the articles with respect to their PICO elements, we turn to the structured vocabulary provided by the National Libaray of Medicine (NLM) in the form of Medical Subject Heading (MeSH) terms. This resource codifies a comprehensive set of medical concepts into an ontology that includes their descriptions, properties, and the structured relationships between them. Each article in the MEDLINE database maintained by the NLM is annotated with the relevant MeSH terms by expert library scientists (subject to the same lag that necessitates an RCT classifier instead of relying on annotated Publication Types).

To induce relevant MeSH terms for an extracted text span, we reproduced the method described in the Metamap Lite paper (Demner-Fushman et al., 2017) to extract MeSH terms describing the PICO elements. In short, we generated a large dictionary of synonyms for medical terms algorithmically using data from the UMLS Metathesaurus, with synonyms being matched to unique identifiers pertaining to concepts in the MeSH vocabulary. We used this dictionary to map matching strings in our extracted PICO text to MeSH terms, yielding a set of normalized concepts describing each of the population, intervention, and outcome spans in the documents.

To evaluate the accuracy of this approach, we compare the differences between the MeSH terms produced by our system against those provided by the NLM for the 191 articles that comprise the test set for EBM-NLP.

The test articles are provided with an average of 14.8 MeSH terms per article, while our system induces 14.0 terms on average. The strictest evaluation for this module is to require exact matches between the predicted MeSH terms and the official MEDLINE terms – a daunting task given the $30,000$ possible labels we have to chose from.

However, because the concepts in the ontology exist in varying levels of specificity (for example *Migraine with Aura* is a subset of *Migraine Disorders*), it is often the case that the predicted MeSH term is sufficiently close to the provided MeSH term for practical purposes, but differs in the level of specificity.

To better characterize the performance of our approach, we therefore also consider relaxing the equivalence criteria to include matching immediate parents or children in the MeSH hierarchy. This modification results in a 42% relative increase in recall and a 23% increase in precision, as shown in Table 4.

We observe that while the absolute accuracy is not high, this technique generally captures the key terms for the PICO elements. The most common mistakes, shown in Table 5, mostly involve missing age or publication type terms, and systematic differences between the general MeSH terms commonly applied to articles (for example, we might apply *Patients* rather than *Humans*).

A more sophisticated alignment between the way MeSH terms are applied by experts and the terms produced by our system has the potential to improve the overall effectiveness of the tool; we intend to pursue this in future work.

3 Illustrative Example

To illustrate the envisioned use of our automatic mapping system, we return to the example we began with at the outset of this paper: seeking evidence concerning treatment of Type II Diabetes. To begin, the user specifies a condition (Population) of interest. We rely on Medical Subject Headings (MeSH) terms,[5] which as dis-

---

[5] https://www.ncbi.nlm.nih.gov/mesh

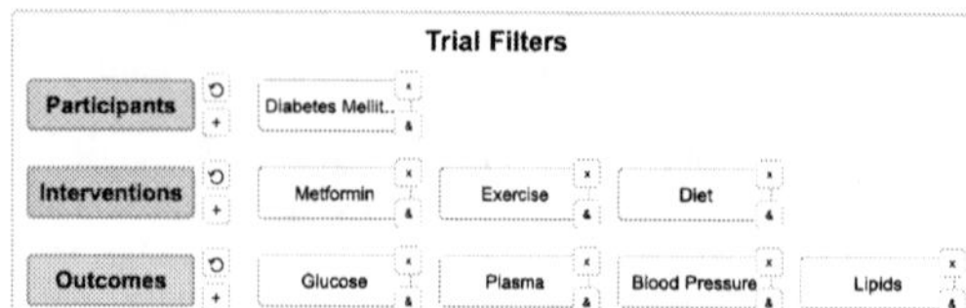

Figure 3: View of a collected set of concepts used to specify trials of interest. The search interface allows concepts to be combined using and/or operators.

Figure 4: Detailed view of selected abstracts that contribute to the evidence map. These are automatically annotated with all extracted information.

cussed above is a structured vocabularly maintained by the NLM. We allow users to enter a search string and provide auto-complete options from the MeSH vocabulary. Users can additionally provide interventions or outcomes of interest to further narrow the search. We show an example of a constructed set of filters in Figure 3.

Once a set of search terms is specified, relevant RCTs are retrieved from the comprehensive and up-to-date database.[6] The interface then displays counts of unique interventions and outcomes covered by the retrieved trials. Each bar in these plots can be clicked to explicitly include that concept in the search terms, allowing for a data-driven approach to building up the search parameters via iterative refinement.

At this point, the evidence map shown in Figure 1 is also displayed, providing a summary of the evidence available for the effectiveness of the selected interventions with respect to their co-occurring outcomes. The user can mouse-over plot elements to view tooltips that include snippets of contributing evidence from the underlying abstracts, or click through to browse these texts annotated with all of the extracted information, as shown in Figure 4.

4   User Study

To evaluate the system's utility for a real-world task, we provided the tool to a team of researchers at Cures Within Reach for Cancer (CWR4C).[7] Domain experts reviewed the extracted ICO conclusions and automatically generated plots for a randomly selected subset of documents pertaining to cancer trials, a domain that is particularly challenging given the prevalence of complex compound interventions that often share individual components between trial arms.

The reviewers were asked to evaluate the types of mistakes made by the system as well as the overall precision and recall of the extracted conclusions for each document. Across 21 documents average precision was 54% and average recall was 75%, and the team expressed excitement about the efficacy of the system for their purposes. CWR4C has continued to work with this tool as a source of information about cancer-related clinical trials.

5   Conclusions

We have presented the evidence extraction component of Trialstreamer, an open-source prototype that performs end-to-end identification of published RCT reports, extracts key elements from the texts (intervention and outcomes descriptions), and performs relation extraction between these, i.e., attempts to determine which intervention was reported to work for which outcomes.

We use this pipeline to provide fast, on-demand overviews of all published evidence pertaining to a condition of interest. Moving forward, we hope to refine the linking of extracted snippets to structured vocabularies to run a more comprehensive user-study to evaluate the use of the system in practice by different types of users. We also hope to develop a joint extraction and inference model, rather than relying on the current pipelined approach.

Acknowledgements

This work was funded in part by the National Institutes of Health (NIH) under the National Library of Medicine (NLM) grant 2R01LM012086, and by the National Science Foundation (NSF) CAREER award 1750978.

---

[6]We update this database nightly by scanning MEDLINE for new RCT reports using our RCT classifier (Marshall et al., 2018).

---

[7]https://www.cwr4c.org/

References

Iz Beltagy, Arman Cohan, and Kyle Lo. 2019. Scibert: Pretrained contextualized embeddings for scientific text. *arXiv preprint arXiv:1903.10676.*

Dina Demner-Fushman, Willie J Rogers, and Alan R Aronson. 2017. Metamap lite: an evaluation of a new java implementation of metamap. *Journal of the American Medical Informatics Association*, 24(4):841–844.

Jacob Devlin, Ming-Wei Chang, Kenton Lee, and Kristina Toutanova. 2018. Bert: Pre-training of deep bidirectional transformers for language understanding. *arXiv preprint arXiv:1810.04805.*

Xiaoli Huang, Jimmy Lin, and Dina Demner-Fushman. 2006. Evaluation of pico as a knowledge representation for clinical questions. In *AMIA annual symposium proceedings*, volume 2006, page 359. American Medical Informatics Association.

Jinhyuk Lee, Wonjin Yoon, Sungdong Kim, Donghyeon Kim, Sunkyu Kim, Chan Ho So, and Jaewoo Kang. 2019. Biobert: a pre-trained biomedical language representation model for biomedical text mining. *CoRR*, abs/1901.08746.

Eric Lehman, Jay DeYoung, Regina Barzilay, and Byron C. Wallace. 2019. Inferring Which Medical Treatments Work from Reports of Clinical Trials. In *Proceedings of the Conference of the North American Chapter of the Association for Computational Linguistics (NAACL)*, pages 3705–3717.

Iain J Marshall, Anna Noel-Storr, Joël Kuiper, James Thomas, and Byron C Wallace. 2018. Machine learning for identifying randomized controlled trials: an evaluation and practitioner's guide. *Research synthesis methods*, 9(4):602–614.

Isomi M Miake-Lye, Susanne Hempel, Roberta Shanman, and Paul G Shekelle. 2016. What is an evidence map? a systematic review of published evidence maps and their definitions, methods, and products. *Syst. Rev.*, 5:28.

Benjamin Nye, Junyi Jessy Li, Roma Patel, Yinfei Yang, Iain J Marshall, Ani Nenkova, and Byron C Wallace. 2018. A corpus with multi-level annotations of patients, interventions and outcomes to support language processing for medical literature. In *Proceedings of the conference. Association for Computational Linguistics. Meeting*, volume 2018, page 197. NIH Public Access.

Sunghwan Sohn, Donald C Comeau, Won Kim, and W John Wilbur. 2008. Abbreviation definition identification based on automatic precision estimates. *BMC bioinformatics*, 9(1):402.

SyntaxGym:
An Online Platform for Targeted Evaluation of Language Models

Jon Gauthier[1]**, Jennifer Hu**[1]**, Ethan Wilcox**[2]**, Peng Qian**[1]**,** and **Roger Levy**[1]

[1] Department of Brain and Cognitive Sciences, Massachusetts Institute of Technology
[2] Department of Linguistics, Harvard University
`jon@gauthiers.net, wilcoxeg@g.harvard.edu`
`{jennhu,pqian,rplevy}@mit.edu`

Abstract

Targeted syntactic evaluations have yielded insights into the generalizations learned by neural network language models. However, this line of research requires an uncommon confluence of skills: both the theoretical knowledge needed to design controlled psycholinguistic experiments, and the technical proficiency needed to train and deploy large-scale language models. We present SyntaxGym, an online platform designed to make targeted evaluations **accessible** to both experts in NLP and linguistics, **reproducible** across computing environments, and **standardized** following the norms of psycholinguistic experimental design. This paper releases two tools of independent value for the computational linguistics community:

1. A website, **`syntaxgym.org`**, which centralizes the process of targeted syntactic evaluation and provides easy tools for analysis and visualization;
2. Two command-line tools, `syntaxgym` and `lm-zoo`, which allow any user to reproduce targeted syntactic evaluations and general language model inference on their own machine.

1 Introduction

Recent work in evaluating neural network language models focuses on investigating models' fine-grained prediction behavior on carefully designed examples. Unlike broad-coverage language modeling metrics such as perplexity, these evaluations are targeted to reveal whether models have learned specific knowledge about the syntactic structure of language (see e.g. Warstadt et al., 2020; Futrell et al., 2019; Marvin and Linzen, 2018).

Research in this line of work requires an uncommon intersection of skills: a) the engineering strength of NLP researchers necessary to train and

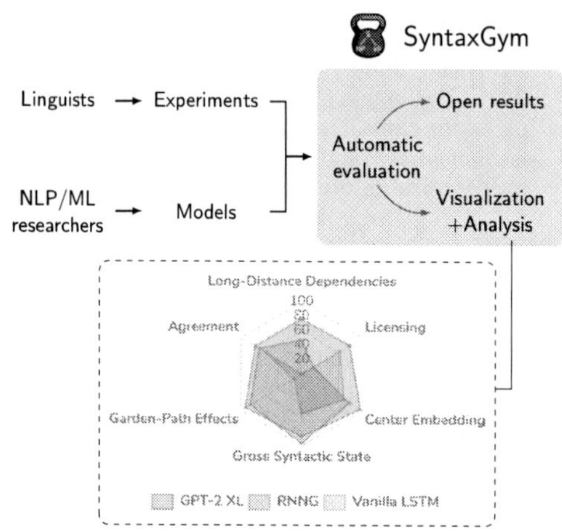

Figure 1: SyntaxGym allows linguists to easily design and run controlled experiments on the syntactic knowledge of language models, and allows NLP experts to test their own models against these standards. Users submit targeted syntactic evaluation experiments to the site, and they are automatically evaluated on language models available in the Gym. SyntaxGym analyzes and visualizes these evaluation results.

deploy large-scale neural network language models, and b) the linguistic knowledge of language scientists necessary to design controlled, theoretically interesting psycholinguistic experiments.

In this paper, we introduce **SyntaxGym**: an online platform and open-source framework that makes targeted syntactic evaluations more accessible to experts in NLP and linguistics (Figure 1). The core of SyntaxGym is a website, **`syntaxgym.org`**, that automates the entire evaluation pipeline: collecting tests and models, running evaluations, and displaying results through interactive visualizations. Language scientists can use the site to design and submit targeted syntactic evaluations, testing whether language models have derived human-like syntactic knowledge. Indepen-

70

Proceedings of the 58th Annual Meeting of the Association for Computational Linguistics, pages 70–76
July 5 - July 10, 2020. ©2020 Association for Computational Linguistics

dently, NLP experts can submit their own language models for evaluation on these assays. By separating the tasks performed by these two user groups, the SyntaxGym site lowers the barrier to entry for the broader community of language researchers.

While SyntaxGym will serve as a centralized repository of syntactic evaluations and language models, we also release a set of command-line tools that allow users to reproduce the site's evaluations offline. The computation underlying the SyntaxGym site is structured around a command-line tool `syntaxgym`, which allows any user to run targeted syntactic evaluations on their own computer. We accomplish this by developing a new standard API for interacting with state-of-the-art neural network language models, operationalized in a second tool `lm-zoo`.

Taken together, these tools create a platform that makes the process of targeted syntactic evaluation more standardized, reproducible, and accessible to the broader communities of NLP experts and language scientists. Our goal is for SyntaxGym to facilitate the advancement of language model evaluation, leading to the development of models with more human-like linguistic knowledge.

2 Background

Before presenting the SyntaxGym framework, we briefly introduce the targeted syntactic evaluation paradigm as a way to assess the quality of neural language models.

2.1 Perplexity

Standard left-to-right language models are trained to predict the next token given a context of previous tokens. Language models are typically assessed by their *perplexity*, the inverse geometric mean of the joint probability of words $w_1, \ldots, w_N$ in a held-out test corpus:

$$\mathrm{PPL}(C) = p(w_1, w_2, \ldots w_N)^{-\frac{1}{N}} \qquad (1)$$

However, a broad-coverage metric such as perplexity may not be ideal for assessing whether a language model has human-like syntactic knowledge. Recent empirical results suggest that models with similar perplexity measures can still exhibit substantial variance in syntactic knowledge (Hu et al., 2020; van Schijndel et al., 2019), according to evaluation paradigms described in the next section.

2.2 Targeted tests for syntactic generalization

Alternatively, a language model can be evaluated on its ability to make human-like generalizations for specific syntactic phenomena. The targeted syntactic evaluation paradigm (Linzen et al., 2016; Lau et al., 2017; Gulordava et al., 2018; Marvin and Linzen, 2018; Futrell et al., 2019; Warstadt et al., 2020) incorporates methods from psycholinguistic experiments, designing sentences which hold most lexical and syntactic features of each sentence constant while minimally varying features that determine grammaticality or surprise characteristics of the sentence. For example, the following minimal-pair sentences differ in subject–verb agreement:

(1)   The farmer near the clerks <u>knows</u> many people.

(2)   *The farmer near the clerks <u>know</u> many people.

A model that has learned the proper subject–verb number agreement rules for English should assign a higher probability to the grammatical plural verb in the first sentence than to the ungrammatical singular verb in the second (Linzen et al., 2016).

3 SyntaxGym

The targeted syntactic evaluation paradigm allows us to focus on highly specific measures of language modeling performance, which more directly distinguish models with human-like representations of syntactic structure. SyntaxGym was designed to serve as a central repository for these evaluations, and to make the evaluations reproducible and accessible for users without the necessary technical skills or computational resources.

Section 3.1 first describes the standards we designed for specifying and executing these targeted syntactic evaluations. Section 3.2 then offers a tour of the SyntaxGym site, which is built around these standards.

3.1 Standardizing targeted syntactic evaluation

We represent targeted syntactic evaluations as *test suites*, visualized in Figure 2. These test suites are the core component of psycholinguistic assessment, and should be familiar to those experienced in psycholinguistic experimental design. We will present the structure of a test suite using the running example of subject–verb agreement, introduced in the previous section. We describe the components of a test suite from bottom-up:

Condition	Regions							
	intro	np_subj	prep	the	prep_np	matrix_verb	continuation	
match_sing	The	farmer	near	the	clerks	knows	many people	Item 1
mismatch_sing	The	farmer	near	the	clerks	know	many people	
mismatch_plural	The	farmers	near	the	clerk	knows	many people	
match_plural	The	farmers	near	the	clerk	know	many people	
match_sing	The	manager	to the side of	the	architects	likes	to gamble	Item 2
mismatch_sing	The	manager	to the side of	the	architects	like	to gamble	
mismatch_plural	The	managers	to the side of	the	architect	likes	to gamble	
match_plural	The	managers	to the side of	the	architect	like	to gamble	

...

Prediction:
$$\left(\text{match\_sing}.\text{matrix\_verb} < \text{mismatch\_sing}.\text{matrix\_verb} \right)$$
$$\&\ \left(\text{match\_plural}.\text{matrix\_verb} < \text{mismatch\_plural}.\text{matrix\_verb} \right)$$

Figure 2: SyntaxGym test suites evaluate predictions about language models' surprisal values (negative log-probabilities) within regions (columns above) across experimental conditions (leftmost column). A prediction can assert the conjunction of multiple inequalities across conditions. Prediction results are aggregated across items (vertical blocks above) to yield overall accuracy estimates.

Regions The atomic unit of a test suite is a region: a (possibly empty) string, such as the `matrix_verb` region in Figure 2. Regions can be concatenated to form full sentences.

Conditions Regions vary systematically across experimental conditions, shown as colored pill shapes in Figure 2. Here the `matrix_verb` and `np_subj` regions vary between their respective singular and plural forms, as described by the condition.

Items Items are groups of related sentences which vary across experimental conditions. An item is characterized by its lexical content and takes different forms across conditions. For example, *The farmer near the clerk knows* and **The farmer near the clerk know* are different sentences under two conditions of the same item.

Predictions Test suites are designed with a hypothesis in mind: if a model has correctly learned some relevant syntactic generalization, then it should assign higher probability to grammatical continuations of sentences. Test suite predictions operationalize these hypotheses as expected inequalities between total model surprisal values in different experimental conditions (i.e., between rows within item blocks in Figure 2). The SyntaxGym standard allows for arbitrarily complex disjunctions and conjunctions of such inequalities. Figure 2 shows a prediction with two inequalities between model surprisals at `matrix_verb` across two pairs of conditions.

We designed a standard JSON schema for describing the structure and content of test suites using the above concepts. Interested readers can find the full schema and documentation on the SyntaxGym site.[1]

3.1.1 A standard API for language models

Reproducing research results with modern neural network architectures can be notoriously difficult, due to variance in computing environments and due to each individual project's tangled web of package dependencies. In addition, inconsistencies in data preprocessing — for example, in tokenization practices and the management of out-of-vocabulary items — often make it difficult to evaluate even the same model on different datasets. In order to address these difficulties, we designed a standardized API for interacting with trained language models, built to solve these reproducibility issues and allow for highly portable computing with state-of-the-art language models. Users can easily connect with this API through the `lm-zoo` command-line tool, described later in Section 4.

The standard is built around the Docker containerization system. We expect each language model to be wrapped in a Docker image, including a thin API exposing a set of standardized binary commands: `tokenize`, which preprocesses natural-language sentences exactly as a language

---

[1] `http://docs.syntaxgym.org`

model expects; `get-surprisals`, which computes per-token language model surprisals on natural language input; and `unkify`, which indicates exactly which tokens in an input text file are in-vocabulary for the language model.

Language model creators or third-party maintainers can produce such Docker images wrapping language model code. At present, this API is designed to mainly serve the needs of the SyntaxGym evaluation process. In the future, however, we plan to extend the API for other common uses of language models: for example, to extract the next-word predictive distributions from the model, and to extract the model's internal word and sentence representations. This standard is documented in full at `cpllab.github.io/lm-zoo`.

3.2 The SyntaxGym website

The SyntaxGym website provides a centralized domain for collecting targeted syntactic evaluations and evaluating them on state-of-the-art language models. It provides intuitive, user-friendly tools for visualizing the behavior of any language model on any syntactic test suite, and also exposes all of the resulting raw data to interested advanced users. This section presents a brief tour through the major features of the SyntaxGym site.

Create test suites Non-technical users can use SyntaxGym's browser-based interface to design and submit their own psycholinguistic test suites (Figure 3). Separately, the site supports uploading pre-made test suites as a JSON-formatted file. This functionality may be useful for advanced users who prefer to automatically generate test suites.[2]

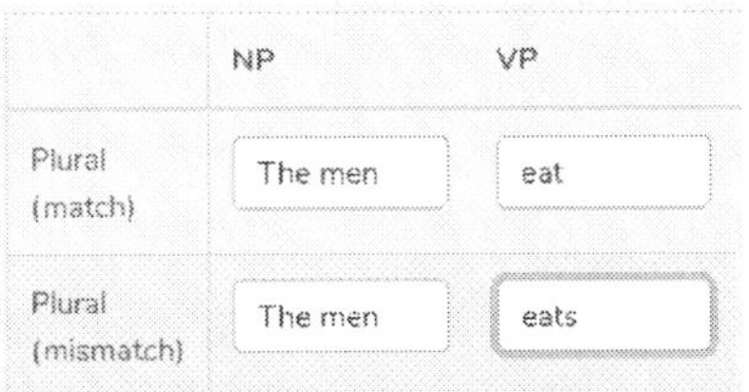

Figure 3: Non-technical users can design their own test suites with a browser-based form.

Submit language models Users interested in evaluating their own language models first create a public Docker image conforming to the API specified by the SyntaxGym standard (Section 3.1.1). After users submit these language models on the SyntaxGym site, the models are automatically validated for conformity to the API by the SyntaxGym backend. Valid models are added to the SyntaxGym collection, and will be evaluated on all past and future available test suites in the Gym.

Automatic evaluation Whenever novel test suites or language models are submitted, SyntaxGym automatically evaluates the relevant suites and models in the cloud. For each test suite and model, the evaluation yields a prediction accuracy — the number of items for which the prediction holds. These prediction accuracies, along with the raw surprisal data, are stored in the SyntaxGym database and made available in visualizations such as Figure 4b.

Visualization and data analysis The site provides a variety of interactive charts that allow users to visualize results at different levels of granularity. On the coarsest level, users can compare aggregate performance across language models and groups of theoretically related test suites called *tags* (see Figure 1). Users can also compare accuracy across models on a single test suite (Figure 4a), across tags for a single model, and across test suites within a single tag. On the finest level, users can view raw region-by-region surprisal values to analyze in-depth performance of a particular language model on a particular test suite (Figure 4b).

3.3 Seed data and results

We have seeded the SyntaxGym website with a collection of test suites and language models by aggregating prior research. These materials and relevant evaluation results are separately presented in Hu et al. (2020). Here we provide only a brief summary in order to illustrate the features of the SyntaxGym website.

1. We wrapped 8 modern neural network language models (summarized in Table 1) to be compatible with the `lm-zoo` standard, using open-source research code or standard Python frameworks such as Hugging Face Transformers (Wolf et al., 2019).

2. We aggregated past research on targeted syntactic evaluation into 33 test suites, each probing language models' performance on distinct grammatical phenomena.

---

[2]In a future release, we will also allow users to import test suites from spreadsheets as CSV-formatted files.

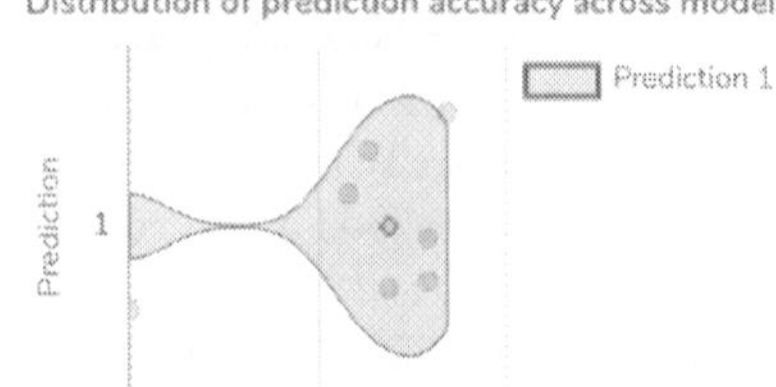

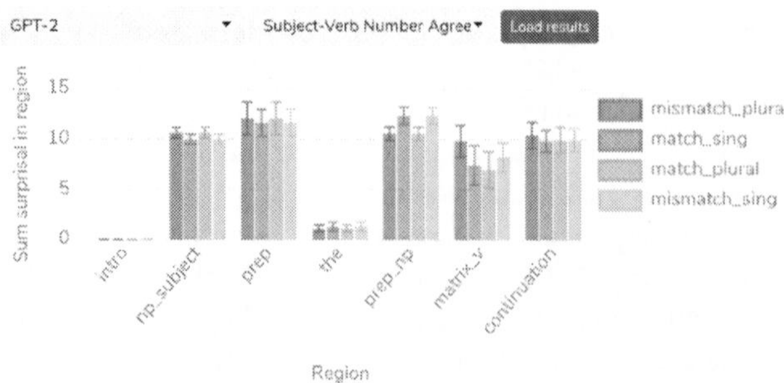

(a) The site automatically evaluates language models on test suites and visualizes summary results (here, for a subject–verb number agreement test). (click to see page)

(b) Users can also view all of the raw language model data behind these analyses (here, average per-region surprisal values of GPT-2 for a subject–verb number agreement test) and download the raw data for further analysis. (click to see page)

Figure 4: Screenshots of example visualizations from the SyntaxGym website.

Model	Reference	Training data (# tokens)
GPT-2	Radford et al. (2019)	WebText (~8B)
GPT-2 XL	Radford et al. (2019)	WebText (~8B)
Transformer XL	Dai et al. (2019)	WikiText-103 (103M)
JRNN	Jozefowicz et al. (2016)	1B Benchmark (1.04B)
GRNN	Gulordava et al. (2018)	Wikipedia (90M)
Ordered Neurons	Shen et al. (2019)	BLLIP (42M)
LSTM	Hochreiter and Schmidhuber (1997)	BLLIP (42M)
RNNG	Dyer et al. (2016)	BLLIP (42M)

Table 1: Language models currently supported in the SyntaxGym framework.

Interested readers can find more details on these test suites and language models, along with the evaluation results and visualizations, on the SyntaxGym site.

4   Command-line tools

While the SyntaxGym website allows for easy centralization of test suites and public access to results, all of its underlying infrastructure is also available independently for researchers to use. We release two command-line tools, available to any user with Python and Docker installed.

4.1   `lm-zoo`: black-box access to SOTA language models

We first designed a general command-line tool for interacting with state-of-the-art neural language models, called `lm-zoo`. Figure 5b demonstrates how this tool can be used to easily extract prediction data from an arbitrary language model. Full documentation and installation instructions are available at `cpllab.github.io/lm-zoo`.

4.2   `syntaxgym`: targeted syntactic evaluation

Users can completely reproduce the targeted syntactic evaluation paradigm of SyntaxGym outside of the website using a second command-line tool, `syntaxgym`, shown in Figure 5a. This tool does the work of converting test suites into actual natural-language sentences appropriately formatted for a particular language model, executing the model, and mapping the results back to a SyntaxGym-friendly format ready for analysis. It deals with the wide variation in tokenization and out-of-vocabulary token handling across models. Full documentation and installation instructions are available at `syntaxgym.org/cli`.

5   Related work

Marvin and Linzen (2018) release a dataset of minimal-pair sentences designed to test language models' syntactic generalization capabilities. However, the syntactic coverage of the dataset is limited to a small set of phenomena: subject-verb agreement, reflexive anaphor licensing, and negative polarity items.

Warstadt et al. (2020) release a large dataset aggregating a broad collection of targeted syntactic evaluations from prior research, known as BLiMP. Like the Marvin and Linzen dataset, BLiMP consists of a collection of minimal-pair sentences which contrast in grammaticality, following the standard shown in Examples (1) and (2). The BLiMP evaluation requires that language models assign a higher total probability to the grammatical (1) than the ungrammatical (2). The authors design abstract templates which specify grammatical–

```
$ syntaxgym list models
gpt-2, gpt-2-xl, transformer-xl, ...

$ syntaxgym list suites
number-orc, number-src, mvrr, ...

# Evaluate model "gpt-2" on suite "mvrr"
$ syntaxgym evaluate gpt-2 mvrr
Accuracy: 0.7857 (22/28 correct)

# Evaluate arbitrary model on custom suite
$ syntaxgym evaluate \
>    docker://me/my-model my-suite.json
Accuracy: 0.575 (23/40 correct)
```

(a) The `syntaxgym` tool allows users to evaluate language models on test suites — both models and suites hosted by SyntaxGym, and models and suites created by the user.

```
$ echo "This is a sentence." > foo.txt

$ lm-zoo list models
gpt-2, gpt-2-xl, transformer-xl, ...

$ lm-zoo tokenize transformer-xl foo.txt
This is a sentence .

$ lm-zoo get-surprisals transformer-xl foo.txt
sentence_id   token_id   token   surprisal
1             1          This    0.0000
1             1          is      4.1239
1             1          a       1.0126
...
```

(b) The `lm-zoo` tool provides lower-level access to SyntaxGym-hosted language models, allowing users to retrieve models' predictions, tokenization choices, and more.

Figure 5: We built SyntaxGym around command-line tools for probing and evaluating neural network language models, which can be used independently of the SyntaxGym site.

ungrammatical pairs for many linguistic phenomena, and then generate example sentences based on these templates.

While BLiMP and SyntaxGym are similarly motivated, they differ slightly in methodology. First, BLiMP requires models to satisfy only a single inequality between sentence probabilities. While the SyntaxGym system can support such predictions, it is designed to support much stricter tests of language models, such as the conjunction of inequalities across multiple conditions (see Figure 2). Second, BLiMP compares model judgments about total sentence probabilities. In contrast, SyntaxGym is designed to compare model judgments only in critical test regions, which allows us to more fairly evaluate language model predictions only in pre-specified spans of interest. Finally, the BLiMP sentences are automatically generated from abstract grammars exemplifying syntactic phenomena of interest. Since automatic methods can easily yield a large number of sentences, they can help us control for other possible sources of noise in test materials. However, many grammatical phenomena of interest are fiendishly difficult to capture in abstract grammars, and require careful design by native speakers.[3] This BLiMP data is thus complementary to the hand-designed test suites currently presented on the SyntaxGym site. We plan to adapt such large-scale test suites on SyntaxGym in the future.

6   Conclusion

This paper presented SyntaxGym, an online platform and open-source framework for targeted syntactic evaluation of neural network language models. SyntaxGym promises to advance the progress of language model evaluation by uniting the theoretical expertise of linguists with the technical skills of NLP researchers. The site is fully functional at `syntaxgym.org`, and the entire framework is available as open-source code.

SyntaxGym is continually evolving: we plan to add new features to the site, and to develop further in response to user feedback. In particular, we plan to incorporate *human performance* as a reference metric, integrating psycholinguistic experimental results and supporting easy experimental design starting from the test suite format.

We also plan to further incorporate language models into the `lm-zoo` tool, allowing broader access to state-of-the-art language models in general. We welcome open-source contributions to the website and to the general framework, and especially encourage the NLP community to contribute their models to the `lm-zoo` repository.

Acknowledgments

J.G. is supported by an Open Philanthropy AI Fellowship. J.H. is supported by the NIH under award number T32NS105587 and an NSF Graduate Research Fellowship. R.L. is supported by a Google Faculty Research Award. This work was also supported by the MIT-IBM Watson AI Lab.

---

[3]For example, one such phenomenon is the garden-path disambiguation effect (Futrell et al., 2019), which is highly sensitive to nuanced lexical and world-knowledge features of sentences.

References

Zihang Dai, Zhilin Yang, Yiming Yang, Jaime G Carbonell, Quoc Le, and Ruslan Salakhutdinov. 2019. Transformer-xl: Attentive language models beyond a fixed-length context. In *Proceedings of the 57th Annual Meeting of the Association for Computational Linguistics*, pages 2978–2988.

Chris Dyer, Adhiguna Kuncoro, Miguel Ballesteros, and Noah A Smith. 2016. Recurrent neural network grammars. In *Proceedings of NAACL-HLT*, pages 199–209.

Richard Futrell, Ethan Wilcox, Takashi Morita, Peng Qian, Miguel Ballesteros, and Roger Levy. 2019. Neural language models as psycholinguistic subjects: Representations of syntactic state. In *Proceedings of the 2019 Conference of the North American Chapter of the Association for Computational Linguistics: Human Language Technologies, Volume 1 (Long and Short Papers)*, pages 32–42, Minneapolis, Minnesota. Association for Computational Linguistics.

Kristina Gulordava, Piotr Bojanowski, Edouard Grave, Tal Linzen, and Marco Baroni. 2018. Colorless green recurrent networks dream hierarchically. In *Proceedings of NAACL-HLT*, pages 1195–1205.

Sepp Hochreiter and Jürgen Schmidhuber. 1997. Long short-term memory. *Neural Computation*, 9(8):1735–1780.

Jennifer Hu, Jon Gauthier, Peng Qian, Ethan Wilcox, and Roger Levy. 2020. A systematic assessment of syntactic generalization in neural language models. In *Proceedings of the Association of Computational Linguistics*.

Rafal Jozefowicz, Oriol Vinyals, Mike Schuster, Noam Shazeer, and Yonghui Wu. 2016. Exploring the limits of language modeling. *arXiv preprint arXiv:1602.02410*.

Jey Han Lau, Alexander Clark, and Shalom Lappin. 2017. Grammaticality, acceptability, and probability: A probabilistic view of linguistic knowledge. *Cognitive Science*, 5:1202–1247.

Tal Linzen, Emmanuel Dupoux, and Yoav Goldberg. 2016. Assessing the ability of LSTMs to learn syntax-sensitive dependencies. In *Transactions of the Association for Computational Linguistics*, volume 4, pages 521–535.

Rebecca Marvin and Tal Linzen. 2018. Targeted syntactic evaluation of language models. In *Proceedings of the 2018 Conference on Empirical Methods in Natural Language Processing*, pages 1192–1202, Brussels, Belgium. Association for Computational Linguistics.

Alec Radford, Jeffrey Wu, Rewon Child, David Luan, Dario Amodei, and Ilya Sutskever. 2019. Language models are unsupervised multitask learners. *OpenAI Blog*, 1(8):9.

Marten van Schijndel, Aaron Mueller, and Tal Linzen. 2019. Quantity doesn't buy quality syntax with neural language models. In *Proceedings of the 2019 Conference on Empirical Methods in Natural Language Processing and the 9th International Joint Conference on Natural Language Processing (EMNLP-IJCNLP)*, pages 5835–5841.

Yikang Shen, Shawn Tan, Alessandro Sordoni, and Aaron Courville. 2019. Ordered neurons: Integrating tree structures into recurrent neural networks. In *International Conference on Learning Representations*.

Alex Warstadt, Alicia Parrish, Haokun Liu, Anhad Mohananey, Wei Peng, Sheng-Fu Wang, and Samuel R Bowman. 2020. BLiMP: A benchmark of linguistic minimal pairs for English. In *Proceedings of the Society for Computation in Linguistics*.

Thomas Wolf, Lysandre Debut, Victor Sanh, Julien Chaumond, Clement Delangue, Anthony Moi, Pierric Cistac, Tim Rault, R'emi Louf, Morgan Funtowicz, and Jamie Brew. 2019. Huggingface's transformers: State-of-the-art natural language processing. *ArXiv*, abs/1910.03771.

GAIA: A Fine-grained Multimedia Knowledge Extraction System

Manling Li[1]*, **Alireza Zareian**[2]*, **Ying Lin**[1], **Xiaoman Pan**[1], **Spencer Whitehead**[1],
Brian Chen[2], **Bo Wu**[2], **Heng Ji**[1], **Shih-Fu Chang**[2]
Clare Voss[3], **Daniel Napierski**[4], **Marjorie Freedman**[4]
[1]University of Illinois at Urbana-Champaign [2]Columbia University
[3]US Army Research Laboratory [4]Information Sciences Institute
{manling2, hengji}@illinois.edu, {az2407, sc250}@columbia.edu

Abstract

We present the first comprehensive, open source multimedia knowledge extraction system that takes a massive stream of unstructured, heterogeneous multimedia data from various sources and languages as input, and creates a coherent, structured knowledge base, indexing entities, relations, and events, following a rich, fine-grained ontology. Our system, GAIA [1], enables seamless search of complex graph queries, and retrieves multimedia evidence including text, images and videos. GAIA achieves top performance at the recent NIST TAC SM-KBP2019 evaluation[2]. The system is publicly available at GitHub[3] and DockerHub[4], with complete documentation[5].

1 Introduction

Knowledge Extraction (KE) aims to find entities, relations and events involving those entities from unstructured data, and link them to existing knowledge bases. Open source KE tools are useful for many real-world applications including disaster monitoring (Zhang et al., 2018a), intelligence analysis (Li et al., 2019a) and scientific knowledge mining (Luan et al., 2017; Wang et al., 2019). Recent years have witnessed the great success and wide usage of open source Natural Language Processing tools (Manning et al., 2014; Fader et al., 2011; Gardner et al., 2018; Daniel Khashabi, 2018; Honnibal and Montani, 2017), but there is no comprehensive open source system for KE. We release

---

*These authors contributed equally to this work.

[1]System page: http://blender.cs.illinois.edu/software/gaia-ie

[2]http://tac.nist.gov/2019/SM-KBP/index.html

[3]GitHub: https://github.com/GAIA-AIDA

[4]DockerHub: text knowledge extraction components are in https://hub.docker.com/orgs/blendernlp/repositories, visual knowledge extraction components are in https://hub.docker.com/u/dannapierskitoptal

[5]Video: http://blender.cs.illinois.edu/aida/gaia.mp4

Figure 1: An example of cross-media knowledge fusion and a look inside the visual knowledge extraction.

a new comprehensive KE system, GAIA, that advances the state of the art in two aspects: (1) it extracts and integrates knowledge across multiple languages and modalities, and (2) it classifies knowledge elements into fine-grained types, as shown in Table 1. We also release the pretrained models[6] and provide a script to retrain it for any ontology.

GAIA has been inherently designed for multimedia, which is rapidly replacing text-only data in many domains. We extract complementary knowledge from text as well as related images or video frames, and integrate the knowledge across modalities. Taking Figure 1 as an example, the text entity extraction system extracts the nominal mention *troops*, but is unable to link or relate that due to a vague textual context. From the image, the entity linking system recognizes the flag as Ukrainian and represents it as a *NationalityCitizen* relation in the knowledge base. It can be deduced, although not for sure, that the detected people are Ukrainian. Meanwhile, our cross-media fusion system grounds the *troops* to the people detected in the image. This establishes a connection between the knowledge

---

[6]Pretrained models: http://blender.cs.illinois.edu/resources/gaia.html

Proceedings of the 58th Annual Meeting of the Association for Computational Linguistics, pages 77–86
July 5 - July 10, 2020. ©2020 Association for Computational Linguistics

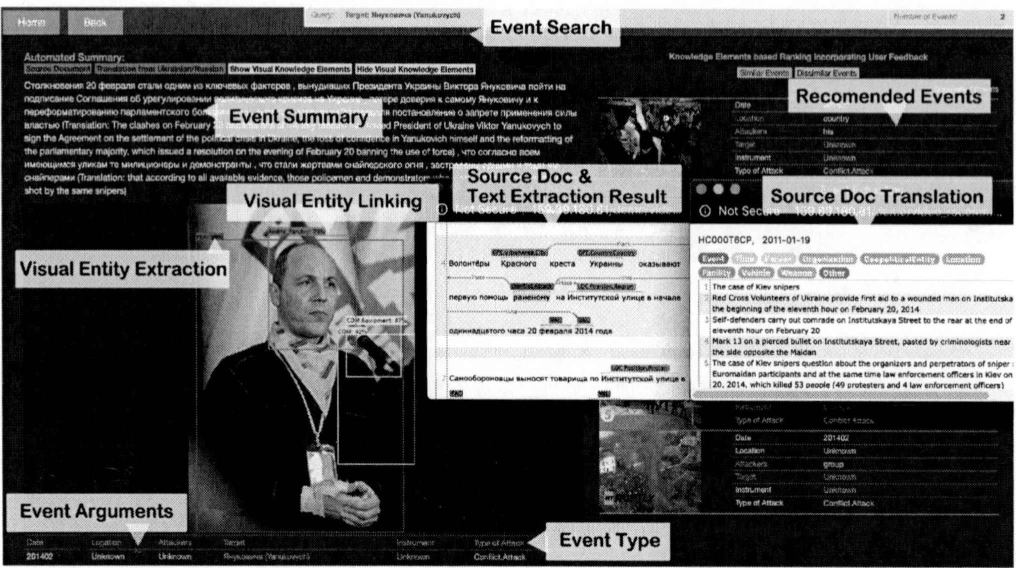

Figure 2: User-facing views of knowledge networks constructed with events automatically extracted from multimedia multilingual news reports. We display the event arguments, type, summary, similar events, as well as visual knowledge extracted from the corresponding image and video.

extracted from the two modalities, allowing to infer that the *troops* are Ukrainian, and *They* refers to the Ukrainian government.

Compared to coarse-grained event types of previous work (Li et al., 2019a), we follow a richer ontology to extract fine-grained types, which are crucial to scenario understanding and event prediction. For example, an event of type *Movement.TransportPerson* involving an entity of type *PER.Politician.HeadOfGovernment* differs in implications from the same event type involving a *PER.Combatant.Sniper* entity (*i.e.*, a political trip versus a military deployment). Similarly, it is far more likely that an event of type *Conflict.Attack.Invade* will lead to a *Contact.Negotiate.Meet* event, while a *Conflict.Attack.Hanging* event is more likely to be followed by an event of type *Contact.FuneralVigil.Meet*.

	Coarse-grained Types	Fine-grained Types
Entity	7	187
Relation	23	61
Event	47	144

Table 1: Compared to the coarse-grained knowledge extraction of previous work, GAIA can support fine-grained entity, relation, and event extraction with types that are a superset of the previous coarse-grained types.

The knowledge base extracted by GAIA can support various applications, such as multimedia news event understanding and recommendation. We use Russia-Ukraine conflicts of 2014-2015 as a case study, and develop a knowledge exploration interface that recommends events related to the user's ongoing search based on previously-selected attribute values and dimensions of events being viewed[7], as shown in Figure 2. Thus, this system automatically provides the user with a more comprehensive exposure to collected events, their importance, and their interconnections. Extensions of this system to real-time applications would be particularly useful for tracking current events, providing alerts, and predicting possible changes, as well as topics related to ongoing incidents.

2 Overview

The architecture of our multimedia knowledge extraction system is illustrated in Figure 3. The system pipeline consists of a Text Knowledge Extraction (TKE) branch and a Visual Knowledge Extraction (VKE) branch (Sections 3 and 4 respectively). Each branch takes the same set of documents as input, and initially creates a separate knowledge base (KB) that encodes the information from its respec-

---

[7]Event recommendation demo: `http://blender.cs.illinois.edu/demo/video_recommendation/index_attack_dark.html`

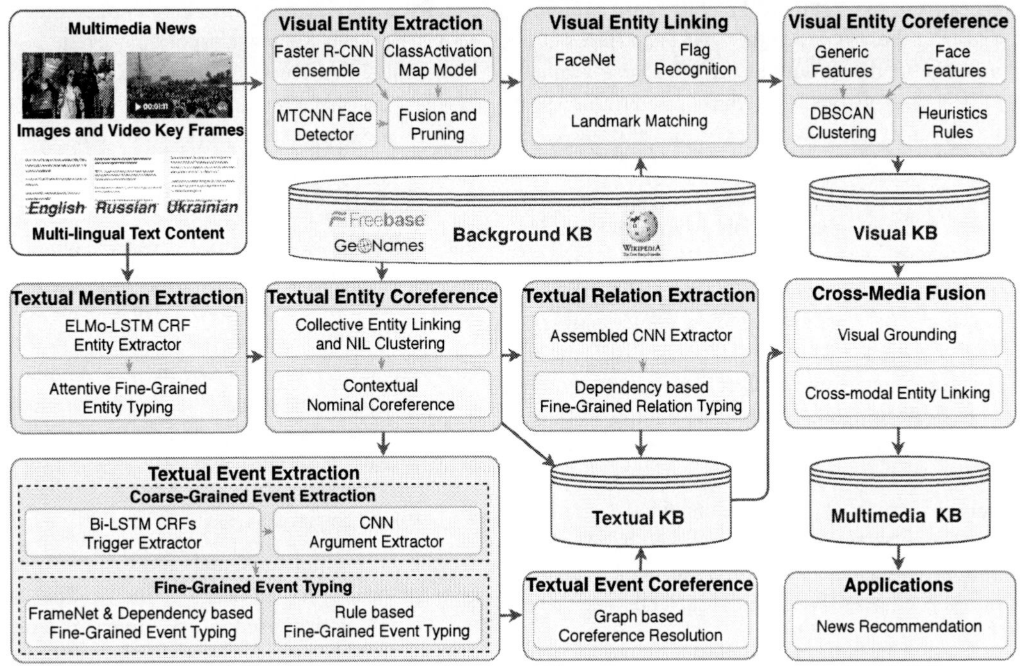

Figure 3: The architecture of GAIA multimedia knowledge extraction.

tive modality. Both output knowledge bases make use of the same types from the DARPA AIDA ontology[8], as referred to in Table 1. Therefore, while the branches both encode their modality-specific extractions into their KBs, they do so with types defined in the same semantic space. This shared space allows us to fuse the two KBs into a single, coherent multimedia KB through the Cross-Media Knowledge Fusion module (Section 5). Our user-facing system demo accesses one such resulting KB, where attack events have been extracted from multi-media documents related to the 2014-2015 Russia-Ukraine conflict scenario. In response to user queries, the system recommends information around a primary event and its connected events from the knowledge graph (screenshot in Figure 2).

3 Text Knowledge Extraction

As shown in Figure 3, the Text Knowledge Extraction (TKE) system extracts entities, relations, and events from input documents. Then it clusters identical entities through entity linking and coreference, and clusters identical events using event coreference.

3.1 Text Entity Extraction and Coreference

Coarse-grained Mention Extraction We extract coarse-grained named and nominal entity mentions using a LSTM-CRF (Lin et al., 2019) model. We use pretrained ELMo (Peters et al., 2018) word embeddings as input features for English, and pre-train Word2Vec (Le and Mikolov, 2014) models on Wikipedia data to generate Russian and Ukrainian word embeddings.

Entity Linking and Coreference We seek to link the entity mentions to pre-existing entities in the background KBs (Pan et al., 2015), including Freebase (LDC2015E42) and GeoNames (LDC2019E43). For mentions that are linkable to the same Freebase entity, coreference information is added. For name mentions that cannot be linked to the KB, we apply heuristic rules (Li et al., 2019b) to same-named mentions within each document to form NIL clusters. A NIL cluster is a cluster of entity mentions referring to the same entity but do not have corresponding KB entries (Ji et al., 2014).

Fine-grained Entity Typing We develop an attentive fine-grained type classification model with latent type representation (Lin and Ji, 2019). It takes as input a mention with its context sentence and predicts the most likely fine-grained type. We obtain the YAGO (Suchanek et al., 2008) fine-grained

[8]https://tac.nist.gov/tracks/SM-KBP/2019/
ontologies/LDCOntology

types from the results of Freebase entity linking, and map these types to the DARPA AIDA ontology. For mentions with identified, coarse-grained GPE and LOC types, we further determine their fine-grained types using GeoNames attributes *feature_class* and *feature_code* from the GeoNames entity linking result. Given that most nominal mentions are descriptions and thus do not link to entries in Freebase or GeoNames, we develop a nominal keyword list (Li et al., 2019b) for each type to incorporate these mentions into the entity analyses.

Entity Salience Ranking To better distill the information, we assign each entity a salience score in each document. We rank the entities in terms of the weighted sum of all mentions, with higher weights for name mentions. If one entity appears only in nominal and pronoun mentions, we reduce its salience score so that it is ranked below other entities with name mentions. The salience score is normalized over all entities in each document.

3.2 Text Relation Extraction

For fine-grained relation extraction, we first apply a language-independent CNN based model (Shi et al., 2018) to extract coarse-grained relations from English, Russian and Ukrainian documents. Then we apply entity type constraints and dependency patterns to these detected relations and re-categorize them into fine-grained types (Li et al., 2019b). To extract dependency paths for these relations in the three languages, we run the corresponding language's Universal Dependency parser (Nivre et al., 2016). For types without coarse-grained type training data in ACE/ERE, we design dependency path-based patterns instead and implement a rule-based system to detect their fine-grained relations directly from the text (Li et al., 2019b).

3.3 Text Event Extraction and Coreference

We start by extracting coarse-grained events and arguments using a Bi-LSTM CRF model and a CNN-based model (Zhang et al., 2018b) for three languages, and then detect the fine-grained event types by applying verb-based rules, context-based rules, and argument-based rules (Li et al., 2019b). We also extract FrameNet frames (Chen et al., 2010) in English corpora to enrich the fine-grained events.

We apply a graph-based algorithm (Al-Badrashiny et al., 2017) for our language-independent event coreference resolution. For each event type, we cast the event mentions as nodes in a graph, so that the undirected, weighted edges between these nodes represent coreference confidence scores between their corresponding events. We then apply hierarchical clustering to obtain event clusters and train a Maximum Entropy binary classifier on the cluster features (Li et al., 2019b).

4 Visual Knowledge Extraction

The Visual Knowledge Extraction (VKE) branch of GAIA takes images and video key frames as input and creates a single, coherent (visual) knowledge base, relying on the same ontology as GAIA's Text Knowledge Extraction (TKE) branch. Similar to TKE, the VKE consists of entity extraction, linking, and coreference modules. Our VKE system also extracts some events and relations.

4.1 Visual Entity Extraction

We use an ensemble of visual object detection and concept localization models to extract entities and some events from a given image. To detect generic objects such as person and vehicle, we employ two off-the-shelf Faster R-CNN models (Ren et al., 2015) trained on the Microsoft Common Objects in COntext (MS COCO) (Lin et al., 2014) and Open Images (Kuznetsova et al., 2018) datasets. To detect scenario-specific entities and events, we train a Class Activation Map (CAM) model (Zhou et al., 2016) in a weakly supervised manner using a combination of Open Images with image-level labels and Google image search.

Given an image, each R-CNN model produces a set of labeled bounding boxes, and the CAM model produces a set of labeled heat maps which are then thresholded to produce bounding boxes. The union of all bounding boxes is then post-processed by a set of heuristic rules to remove duplicates and ensure quality. We separately apply a face detector, MTCNN (Zhang et al., 2016), and add the results to the pool of detected objects as additional *person* entities. Finally, we represent each detected bounding box as an entity in the visual knowledge base. Since the CAM model includes some event types, we create event entries (instead of entity entries) for bounding boxes classified as events.

4.2 Visual Entity Linking

Once entities are added into the (visual) knowledge base, we try to link each entity to the real-world entities from a curated background knowledge base. Due to the complexity of this task, we develop distinct models for each coarse-grained entity type.

Figure 4: Examples of visual entity linking, based on face recognition, landmark recognition and flag recognition.

For the type *person*, we train a FaceNet model (Schroff et al., 2015) that takes each cropped human face (detected by the MTCNN model as mentioned in Section 4.1) and classifies it in one or none of the predetermined identities. We compile a list of recognizable and scenario-relevant identities by automatically searching for each person name in the background KB via Google Image Search, collecting top retrieved results that contain a face, training a binary classifier on half of the results, and evaluating on the other half. If the accuracy is higher than a threshold, we include that person name in our list of recognizable identities. For example, the visual entity in Figure 4 (a) is linked to the Wikipedia entry *Rudy Giuliani* [9].

To recognize *location*, *facility*, and *organization* entities, we use a DELF model (Noh et al., 2017) pre-trained on Google Landmarks, to match each image with detected buildings against a predetermined list. We use a similar approach as mentioned above to create a list of recognizable, scenario-relevant landmarks, such as buildings and other types of structure that identify a specific location, facility, or organization. For example, the visual entity in Figure 4 (b) is linked to the Wikipedia entry *Maidan Square* [10]

Finally, to recognize *geopolitical* entities, we train a CNN to classify flags into a predetermined list of entities, such as all the nations in the world, for detection in our system. Take Figure 4 (c) as an example. The flags of *Ukraine*, *US* and *Russia* are linked to the Wikipedia entries of corresponding countries. Once a flag in an image is recognized, we apply a set of heuristic rules to create a nationality affiliation relationship in the knowledge base between some entities in the scene and the detected country. For instance, a person who is holding a Ukrainian flag would be affiliated with the country

Ukraine.

4.3 Visual Entity Coreference

While we cast each detected bounding box as an entity node in the output knowledge base, we resolve potential coreferential links between them, since one unique real-world entity can be detected multiple times. Cross-image coreference resolution aims to identify the same entity appearing in multiple images, where the entities are in different poses from different angles. Take Figure 5 as an example. The red bounding boxes in these two images refer to the same person, so they are coreferential and are put into the same NIL cluster. Within-image coreference resolution requires the detection of duplicates, such as the duplicates in an collage image. To resolve entity coreference, we train an instance-matching CNN on the Youtube-BB dataset (Real et al., 2017), where we ask the model to match an object bounding box to the same object in a different video frame, rather than to a different object. We use this model to extract features for each detected bounding box and run the DBSCAN (Ester et al., 1996) clustering algorithm on the box features across all images. The entities in the same cluster are coreferential, and are represented using a NIL cluster in the output (visual) KB. Similarly, we use a pretrained FaceNet (Schroff et al., 2015) model followed by DBSCAN to cluster face features.

Figure 5: The two green bounding boxes are coreferential since they are both linked to "Kirstjen Nielsen", and two red bounding boxes are coreferential based on face features. The yellow bounding boxes are unlinkable and also not coreferential to other bounding boxes.

We also define heuristic rules to complement the aforementioned procedure in special cases. For example, if in the entity linking process (Section 4.2), some entities are linked to the same real-world entity based on entity linking result, we consider them coreferential. Besides, since we have both face detection and person detection which result in two entities for each person instance, we use their bounding box intersection to merge them into the same entity.

---

[9] https://en.wikipedia.org/wiki/Rudy_Giuliani

[10] https://en.wikipedia.org/wiki/Maidan_Nezalezhnosti

5 Cross-Media Knowledge Fusion

Given a set of multimedia documents which consist of textual data, such as written articles and transcribed speech, as well as visual data, such as images and video key frames, the TKE and VKE branches of the system take their respective modality data as input, extract knowledge elements, and create separate knowledge bases. These textual and visual knowledge bases rely on the same ontology, but contain complementary information. Some knowledge elements in a document may not be explicitly mentioned in the text, but will appear visually, such as the Ukrainian flag in Figure 1. Even coreferential knowledge elements that exist in both knowledge bases are not completely redundant, since each modality has its own unique granularity. For example, the word *troops* in text could be considered coreferential to the individuals with military uniform detected in the image, but the uniforms being worn may provide additional visual features useful in identifying the military ranks, organizations and nationalities of the individuals.

To exploit the complementary nature of the two modalities, we combine the two modality-specific knowledge bases into a single, coherent, multimedia knowledge base, where each knowledge element could be grounded in either or both modalities. To fuse the two bases, we develop a state-of-the-art visual grounding system (Akbari et al., 2019) to resolve entity coreference across modalities. More specifically, for each entity mention extracted from text, we feed its text along with the whole sentence into an ELMo model (Peters et al., 2018) that extracts contextualized features for the entity mention, and then we compare that with CNN feature maps of surrounding images. This leads to a relevance score for each image, as well as a granular relevance map (heatmap) within each image. For images that are relevant enough, we threshold the heatmap to obtain a bounding box, compare that box content with known visual entities, and assign it to the entity with the most overlapping match. If no overlapping entity is found, we create a new visual entity with the heatmap bounding box. Then we link the matching textual and visual entities using a NIL cluster. Additionally, with visual linking (Section 4.2), we corefer cross-modal entities that are linked to the same background KB node.

Component			Benchmark	Metric	Score
Mention Extraction			CoNLL-2003	F_1	91.8%
Relation Extraction		English	ACE&ERE	F_1	65.6%
		Russian	AIDA	F_1	72.4%
		Ukrainian	AIDA	F_1	68.2%
Event Extraction	En	Trigger	ERE	F_1	65.4%
		Argument	ERE	F_1	85.0%
	Ru	Trigger	AIDA	F_1	56.2%
		Argument	AIDA	F_1	58.2%
	Uk	Trigger	AIDA	F_1	59.0%
		Argument	AIDA	F_1	61.1%
Visual Entity Extraction		Objects	MSCOCO	mAP	43.0%
		Faces	FDDB	Acc	95.4%
Visual Entity Linking		Faces	LFW	Acc	99.6%
		Landmarks	Oxf105k	mAP	88.5%
		Flags	AIDA	F_1	72.0%
Visual Entity Coreference			YoutubeBB	Acc	84.9%
Crossmedia Coreference			Flickr30k	Acc	69.2%

Table 2: Performance of each component. The benchmarks references are: CoNLL-2003 (Sang and De Meulder, 2003), ACE (Walker et al., 2006), ERE (Song et al., 2015), AIDA (LDC2018E01:AIDA Seedling Corpus V2.0), MSCOCO (Lin et al., 2014), FDDB (Jain and Learned-Miller, 2010), LFW (Huang et al., 2008), Oxf105k (Philbin et al., 2007), YoutubeBB (Real et al., 2017), and Flickr30k (Plummer et al., 2015).

6 Evaluation

6.1 Quantitative Performance

The performance of each component is shown in Table 2. To evaluate the end-to-end performance, we participated with our system in the TAC SM-KBP 2019 evaluation[11]. The input corpus contains 1999 documents (756 English, 537 Russian, 703 Ukrainian), 6194 images, and 322 videos. We populated a multimedia, multilingual knowledge base with 457,348 entities, 67,577 relations, 38,517 events. The system performance was evaluated based on its responses to *class queries* and *graph queries*[12], and GAIA was awarded first place.

Class queries evaluated cross-lingual, cross-modal, fine-grained entity extraction and coreference, where the query is an entity type, such as *FAC.Building.GovernmentBuilding*, and the result is a ranked list of entities of the given type. Our entity ranking is generated by the entity salience score in Section 3.1. The evaluation metric was

[11]http://tac.nist.gov/2019/SM-KBP/index.html
[12]http://tac.nist.gov/2019/SM-KBP/guidelines.html

Average Precision (AP), where AP-B was the AP score where ties are broken by ranking all Right responses above all Wrong responses, AP-W was the AP score where ties are broken by ranking all Wrong responses above all Right responses, and AP-T was the AP score where ties are broken as in TREC_Eval[13].

Class Queries			Graph Queries		
AP-B	AP-W	AP-T	Precision	Recall	F_1
48.4%	47.4%	47.7%	47.2%	21.6%	29.7%

Table 3: GAIA achieves top performance on Task 1 at the recent NIST TAC SM-KBP2019 evaluation.

Graph queries evaluated cross-lingual, cross-modal, fine-grained relation extraction, event extraction and coreference, where the query is an argument role type of event (e.g., *Victim* of *Life.Die.DeathCausedByViolentEvents*) or relation (e.g., *Parent* of *PartWhole.Subsidiary*) and the result is a list of entities with that role. The evaluation metrics were Precision, Recall and F_1.

6.2 Qualitative Analysis

To demonstrate the system, we have selected Ukraine-Russia Relations in 2014-2015 for a case study to visualize attack events, as extracted from the topic-related corpus released by LDC[14]. The system displays recommended events related to the user's ongoing search based on their previously-selected attribute values and dimensions of events being viewed, such as the fine-grained type, place, time, attacker, target, and instrument. The demo is publicly available[15] with a user interface as shown in Figure 2, displaying extracted text entities and events across languages, visual entities, visual entity linking and coreference results from face, landmark and flag recognition, and the results of grounding text entities to visual entities.

7 Related Work

Existing knowledge extraction systems mainly focus on text (Manning et al., 2014; Fader et al., 2011; Gardner et al., 2018; Daniel Khashabi, 2018; Honnibal and Montani, 2017; Pan et al., 2017; Li et al., 2019a), and do not readily support fine-grained

knowledge extraction. Visual knowledge extraction is typically limited to atomic concepts that have distinctive visual features of daily life (Ren et al., 2015; Schroff et al., 2015; Fernández et al., 2017; Gu et al., 2018; Lin et al., 2014), and so lacks more complex concepts, making extracted elements challenging to integrate with text. Existing multimedia systems overlook the connections and distinctions between modalities (Yazici et al., 2018). Our system makes use of a multi-modal ontology with concepts from real-world, newsworthy topics, resulting in a rich cross-modal, as well as intra-modal connectivity.

8 Conclusion

We demonstrate a state-of-the-art multimedia multilingual knowledge extraction and event recommendation system. This system enables the user to readily search a knowledge network of extracted, linked, and summarized complex events from multimedia, multilingual sources (e.g., text, images, videos, speech and OCR).

Acknowledgement

This research is based upon work supported in part by U.S. DARPA AIDA Program No. FA8750-18-2-0014 and KAIROS Program No. FA8750-19-2-1004. The views and conclusions contained herein are those of the authors and should not be interpreted as necessarily representing the official policies, either expressed or implied, of DARPA, or the U.S. Government. The U.S. Government is authorized to reproduce and distribute reprints for governmental purposes notwithstanding any copyright annotation therein.

References

Hassan Akbari, Svebor Karaman, Surabhi Bhargava, Brian Chen, Carl Vondrick, and Shih-Fu Chang. 2019. Multi-level multimodal common semantic space for image-phrase grounding. In *Proceedings of the IEEE Conference on Computer Vision and Pattern Recognition*, pages 12476–12486.

Mohamed Al-Badrashiny, Jason Bolton, Arun Tejasvi Chaganty, Kevin Clark, Craig Harman, Lifu Huang, Matthew Lamm, Jinhao Lei, Di Lu, Xiaoman Pan, et al. 2017. Tinkerbell: Cross-lingual cold-start knowledge base construction. In *TAC*.

Desai Chen, Nathan Schneider, Dipanjan Das, and Noah A Smith. 2010. Semafor: Frame argument resolution with log-linear models. In *Proceedings of*

---

[13]https://trec.nist.gov/trec_eval/

[14]LDC2018E01, LDC2018E52, LDC2018E63, LDC2018E76, LDC2019E77

[15]http://blender.cs.illinois.edu/demo/video_recommendation/index_attack_dark.html

the 5th international workshop on semantic evaluation, pages 264–267. Association for Computational Linguistics.

Ben Zhou Tom Redman Christos Christodoulopoulos Vivek Srikumar Nicholas Rizzolo Lev Ratinov Guanheng Luo Quang Do Chen-Tse Tsai Subhro Roy Stephen Mayhew Zhili Feng John Wieting Xiaodong Yu Yangqiu Song Shashank Gupta Shyam Upadhyay Naveen Arivazhagan Qiang Ning Shaoshi Ling Dan Roth Daniel Khashabi, Mark Sammons. 2018. Cogcompnlp: Your swiss army knife for nlp. In *11th Language Resources and Evaluation Conference*.

Martin Ester, Hans-Peter Kriegel, Jörg Sander, Xiaowei Xu, et al. 1996. A density-based algorithm for discovering clusters in large spatial databases with noise. In *Kdd*, volume 96, pages 226–231.

Anthony Fader, Stephen Soderland, and Oren Etzioni. 2011. Identifying relations for open information extraction. In *Proceedings of the Conference of Empirical Methods in Natural Language Processing (EMNLP '11)*, Edinburgh, Scotland, UK.

Delia Fernández, David Varas, Joan Espadaler, Issey Masuda, Jordi Ferreira, Alejandro Woodward, David Rodríguez, Xavier Giró-i Nieto, Juan Carlos Riveiro, and Elisenda Bou. 2017. Vits: video tagging system from massive web multimedia collections. In *Proceedings of the IEEE International Conference on Computer Vision Workshops*, pages 337–346.

Matt Gardner, Joel Grus, Mark Neumann, Oyvind Tafjord, Pradeep Dasigi, Nelson Liu, Matthew Peters, Michael Schmitz, and Luke Zettlemoyer. 2018. Allennlp: A deep semantic natural language processing platform. *arXiv preprint arXiv:1803.07640.*

Chunhui Gu, Chen Sun, David A Ross, Carl Vondrick, Caroline Pantofaru, Yeqing Li, Sudheendra Vijayanarasimhan, George Toderici, Susanna Ricco, Rahul Sukthankar, et al. 2018. Ava: A video dataset of spatio-temporally localized atomic visual actions. In *Proceedings of the IEEE Conference on Computer Vision and Pattern Recognition*, pages 6047–6056.

Matthew Honnibal and Ines Montani. 2017. spacy 2: Natural language understanding with bloom embeddings, convolutional neural networks and incremental parsing. *To appear*, 7(1).

Gary B Huang, Marwan Mattar, Tamara Berg, and Eric Learned-Miller. 2008. Labeled faces in the wild: A database forstudying face recognition in unconstrained environments.

Vidit Jain and Erik Learned-Miller. 2010. Fddb: A benchmark for face detection in unconstrained settings. Technical report, UMass Amherst technical report.

Heng Ji, Joel Nothman, Ben Hachey, et al. 2014. Overview of tac-kbp2014 entity discovery and linking tasks. In *Proc. Text Analysis Conference (TAC2014)*, pages 1333–1339.

Alina Kuznetsova, Hassan Rom, Neil Alldrin, Jasper Uijlings, Ivan Krasin, Jordi Pont-Tuset, Shahab Kamali, Stefan Popov, Matteo Malloci, Tom Duerig, et al. 2018. The open images dataset v4: Unified image classification, object detection, and visual relationship detection at scale. *arXiv preprint arXiv:1811.00982.*

Quoc Le and Tomas Mikolov. 2014. Distributed representations of sentences and documents. In *International conference on machine learning*, pages 1188–1196.

Manling Li, Ying Lin, Joseph Hoover, Spencer Whitehead, Clare Voss, Morteza Dehghani, and Heng Ji. 2019a. Multilingual entity, relation, event and human value extraction. In *Proceedings of the 2019 Conference of the North American Chapter of the Association for Computational Linguistics (Demonstrations)*, pages 110–115.

Manling Li, Ying Lin, Ananya Subburathinam, Spencer Whitehead, Xiaoman Pan, Di Lu, Qingyun Wang, Tongtao Zhang, Lifu Huang, Heng Ji, Alireza Zareian, Hassan Akbari, Brian Chen, Bo Wu, Emily Allaway, Shih-Fu Chang, Kathleen McKeown, Yixiang Yao, Jennifer Chen, Eric Berquist, Kexuan Sun, Xujun Peng, Ryan Gabbard, Marjorie Freedman, Pedro Szekely, T.K. Satish Kumar, Arka Sadhu, Ram Nevatia, Miguel Rodriguez, Yifan Wang, Yang Bai, Ali Sadeghian, and Daisy Zhe Wang. 2019b. Gaia at sm-kbp 2019 - a multi-media multi-lingual knowledge extraction and hypothesis generation system. In *Proceedings of TAC KBP 2019, the 26th International Conference on Computational Linguistics: Technical Papers*.

Tsung-Yi Lin, Michael Maire, Serge Belongie, James Hays, Pietro Perona, Deva Ramanan, Piotr Dollár, and C Lawrence Zitnick. 2014. Microsoft coco: Common objects in context. In *European conference on computer vision*, pages 740–755. Springer.

Ying Lin and Heng Ji. 2019. An attentive fine-grained entity typing model with latent type representation. In *Proceedings of the 2019 Conference on Empirical Methods in Natural Language Processing and the 9th International Joint Conference on Natural Language Processing (EMNLP-IJCNLP)*, pages 6198–6203.

Ying Lin, Liyuan Liu, Heng Ji, Dong Yu, and Jiawei Han. 2019. Reliability-aware dynamic feature composition for name tagging. In *Proceedings of the 57th Annual Meeting of the Association for Computational Linguistics*, pages 165–174.

Yi Luan, Mari Ostendorf, and Hannaneh Hajishirzi. 2017. Scientific information extraction with semi-supervised neural tagging. *arXiv preprint arXiv:1708.06075.*

Christopher D Manning, Mihai Surdeanu, John Bauer, Jenny Rose Finkel, Steven Bethard, and David Mc-Closky. 2014. The stanford corenlp natural language processing toolkit. In *Proceedings of 52nd annual meeting of the association for computational linguistics: system demonstrations*, pages 55–60.

Joakim Nivre, Marie-Catherine De Marneffe, Filip Ginter, Yoav Goldberg, Jan Hajic, Christopher D Manning, Ryan McDonald, Slav Petrov, Sampo Pyysalo, Natalia Silveira, et al. 2016. Universal dependencies v1: A multilingual treebank collection. In *Proceedings of the Tenth International Conference on Language Resources and Evaluation (LREC'16)*, pages 1659–1666.

Hyeonwoo Noh, Andre Araujo, Jack Sim, Tobias Weyand, and Bohyung Han. 2017. Large-scale image retrieval with attentive deep local features. In *Proceedings of the IEEE international conference on computer vision*, pages 3456–3465.

Xiaoman Pan, Taylor Cassidy, Ulf Hermjakob, Heng Ji, and Kevin Knight. 2015. Unsupervised entity linking with abstract meaning representation. In *Proceedings of the 2015 conference of the north american chapter of the association for computational linguistics: Human language technologies*, pages 1130–1139.

Xiaoman Pan, Boliang Zhang, Jonathan May, Joel Nothman, Kevin Knight, and Heng Ji. 2017. Cross-lingual name tagging and linking for 282 languages. In *Proc. the 55th Annual Meeting of the Association for Computational Linguistics*.

Matthew E Peters, Mark Neumann, Mohit Iyyer, Matt Gardner, Christopher Clark, Kenton Lee, and Luke Zettlemoyer. 2018. Deep contextualized word representations. In *Proceedings of NAACL-HLT*, pages 2227–2237.

James Philbin, Ondrej Chum, Michael Isard, Josef Sivic, and Andrew Zisserman. 2007. Object retrieval with large vocabularies and fast spatial matching. In *2007 IEEE conference on computer vision and pattern recognition*, pages 1–8. IEEE.

Bryan A Plummer, Liwei Wang, Chris M Cervantes, Juan C Caicedo, Julia Hockenmaier, and Svetlana Lazebnik. 2015. Flickr30k entities: Collecting region-to-phrase correspondences for richer image-to-sentence models. In *Proceedings of the IEEE international conference on computer vision*, pages 2641–2649.

Esteban Real, Jonathon Shlens, Stefano Mazzocchi, Xin Pan, and Vincent Vanhoucke. 2017. Youtube-boundingboxes: A large high-precision human-annotated data set for object detection in video. In *Proceedings of the IEEE Conference on Computer Vision and Pattern Recognition*, pages 5296–5305.

Shaoqing Ren, Kaiming He, Ross Girshick, and Jian Sun. 2015. Faster r-cnn: Towards real-time object detection with region proposal networks. In

Advances in neural information processing systems, pages 91–99.

Erik F Sang and Fien De Meulder. 2003. Introduction to the conll-2003 shared task: Language-independent named entity recognition. *arXiv preprint cs/0306050*.

Florian Schroff, Dmitry Kalenichenko, and James Philbin. 2015. Facenet: A unified embedding for face recognition and clustering. In *Proceedings of the IEEE conference on computer vision and pattern recognition*, pages 815–823.

Ge Shi, Chong Feng, Lifu Huang, Boliang Zhang, Heng Ji, Lejian Liao, and Heyan Huang. 2018. Genre separation network with adversarial training for cross-genre relation extraction. In *Proceedings of the 2018 Conference on Empirical Methods in Natural Language Processing*, pages 1018–1023.

Zhiyi Song, Ann Bies, Stephanie Strassel, Tom Riese, Justin Mott, Joe Ellis, Jonathan Wright, Seth Kulick, Neville Ryant, and Xiaoyi Ma. 2015. From light to rich ere: annotation of entities, relations, and events. In *Proceedings of the the 3rd Workshop on EVENTS: Definition, Detection, Coreference, and Representation*, pages 89–98.

Fabian M Suchanek, Gjergji Kasneci, and Gerhard Weikum. 2008. Yago: A large ontology from wikipedia and wordnet. *Journal of Web Semantics*, 6(3):203–217.

Christopher Walker, Stephanie Strassel, Julie Medero, and Kazuaki Maeda. 2006. Ace 2005 multilingual training corpus. *Linguistic Data Consortium, Philadelphia*, 57.

Qingyun Wang, Lifu Huang, Zhiying Jiang, Kevin Knight, Heng Ji, Mohit Bansal, and Yi Luan. 2019. Paperrobot: Incremental draft generation of scientific ideas. *arXiv preprint arXiv:1905.07870*.

Adnan Yazici, Murat Koyuncu, Turgay Yilmaz, Saeid Sattari, Mustafa Sert, and Elvan Gulen. 2018. An intelligent multimedia information system for multimodal content extraction and querying. *Multimedia Tools and Applications*, 77(2):2225–2260.

Boliang Zhang, Ying Lin, Xiaoman Pan, Di Lu, Jonathan May, Kevin Knight, and Heng Ji. 2018a. Elisa-edl: A cross-lingual entity extraction, linking and localization system. In *Proceedings of the 2018 Conference of the North American Chapter of the Association for Computational Linguistics: Demonstrations*, pages 41–45.

Kaipeng Zhang, Zhanpeng Zhang, Zhifeng Li, and Yu Qiao. 2016. Joint face detection and alignment using multitask cascaded convolutional networks. *IEEE Signal Processing Letters*, 23(10):1499–1503.

Tongtao Zhang, Ananya Subburathinam, Ge Shi, Lifu Huang, Di Lu, Xiaoman Pan, Manling Li, Boliang Zhang, Qingyun Wang, Spencer Whitehead, Heng

Ji, Alireza Zareian, Hassan Akbari, Brian Chen, Ruiqi Zhong, Steven Shao, Emily Allaway, Shih-Fu Chang, Kathleen McKeown, Dongyu Li, Xin Huang, Kexuan Sun, Xujun Peng, Ryan Gabbard, Marjorie Freedman, Mayank Kejriwal, Ram Nevatia, Pedro Szekely, T.K. Satish Kumar, Ali Sadeghian, Giacomo Bergami, Sourav Dutta, Miguel Rodriguez, and Daisy Zhe Wang. 2018b. Gaia - a multi-media multi-lingual knowledge extraction and hypothesis generation system. In *Proceedings of TAC KBP 2018, the 25th International Conference on Computational Linguistics: Technical Papers*.

Bolei Zhou, Aditya Khosla, Agata Lapedriza, Aude Oliva, and Antonio Torralba. 2016. Learning deep features for discriminative localization. In *Proceedings of the IEEE conference on computer vision and pattern recognition*, pages 2921–2929.

Multilingual Universal Sentence Encoder for Semantic Retrieval

Yinfei Yang[a†], Daniel Cer[a†], Amin Ahmad[a], Mandy Guo[a],
Jax Law[a], Noah Constant[a], Gustavo Hernandez Abrego[a], Steve Yuan[b], Chris Tar[a],
Yun-Hsuan Sung[a], Brian Strope[a], Ray Kurzweil[a]

[a]Google AI
Mountain View, CA

[b]Google
Cambridge, MA

Abstract

We present easy-to-use retrieval focused multilingual sentence embedding models, made available on TensorFlow Hub. The models embed text from *16 languages* into a shared semantic space using a multi-task trained dual-encoder that learns tied cross-lingual representations via translation bridge tasks (Chidambaram et al., 2018). The models achieve *a new state-of-the-art in performance on monolingual and cross-lingual semantic retrieval (SR)*. Competitive performance is obtained on the related tasks of translation pair bitext retrieval (BR) and retrieval question answering (ReQA). On transfer learning tasks, our multilingual embeddings approach, and in some cases exceed, the performance of English only sentence embeddings.

1 Introduction

We introduce three new multilingual members in the *universal sentence encoder* (USE) (Cer et al., 2018) family of sentence embedding models. The models target performance on tasks that involve multilingual semantic similarity and achieve a new state-of-the-art in performance on monolingual and cross-lingual semantic retrieval (SR). One model targets efficient resource usage with a CNN model architecture (Kim, 2014). Another targets accuracy using the Transformer architecture (Vaswani et al., 2017). The third model provides an alternative interface to our multilingual Transformer model for use in retrieval question answering (ReQA). The *16 languages* supported by our multilingual models are given in Table 1.[1]

---

† Corresponding authors:
{yinfeiy, cer}@google.com

[1]Language coverage was selected based, in part, on the ease of obtaining data for the tasks used to train our models. Due to character set differences, we treat Simplified Chinese, zh, and Traditional Chinese, zh-tw, prominently used in Taiwan, as two languages within our model.

Languages	Family
Arabic (ar)	**Semitic**
Chinese (PRC) (zh) Chinese (Taiwan) (zh-tw)	**Sino-Tibetan**
Dutch(nl) English(en) German (de)	**Germanic**
French (fr) Italian (it) Portuguese (pt) Spanish (es)	**Latin**
Japanese (ja)	**Japonic**
Korean (ko)	**Koreanic**
Russian (ru) Polish (pl)	**Slavic**
Thai (th)	**Kra–Dai**
Turkish (tr)	**Turkic**

Table 1: Multilingual universal sentence encoder's supported languages (ISO 639-1). Multilingual sentences are mapped to a shared semantic space.

2 Model Toolkit

Our multilingual models are implemented in TensorFlow (Abadi et al., 2016) and made publicly available on TensorFlow Hub.[2] Listing 1 illustrates the easy-to-use generation of multilingual sentence embeddings. The models conveniently only rely on TensorFlow without requiring additional libraries or packages. Listing 2 demonstrates using the question answering interface. Responses are encoded with additional context information such that the resulting context aware embeddings have a high dot product similarity score with the questions they answer. This allows for retrieval of indexed candidates using efficient nearest neighbor search.[3]

3 Encoder Architecture

3.1 Multi-task Dual Encoder Training

Similar to Cer et al. (2018) and Chidambaram et al. (2018), we target broad coverage using a

---

[2]https://www.tensorflow.org/hub/, Apache 2.0 license, with models available as saved TF graphs.

[3]Popular efficient search tools include FAISS https://github.com/facebookresearch/faiss, Annoy https://github.com/spotify/annoy, or FLANN https://www.cs.ubc.ca/research/flann.

Proceedings of the 58th Annual Meeting of the Association for Computational Linguistics, pages 87–94
July 5 - July 10, 2020. ©2020 Association for Computational Linguistics

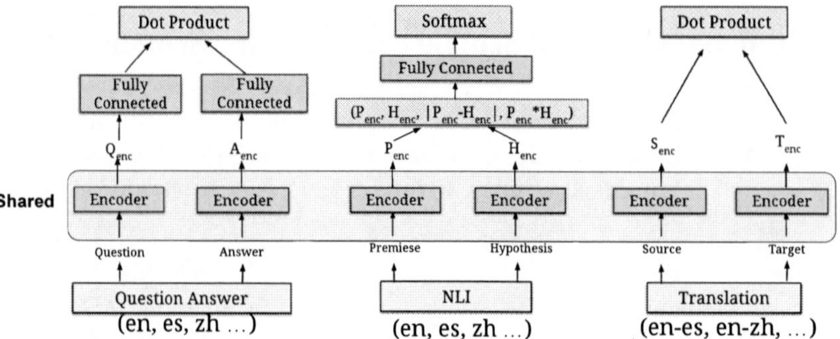

Figure 1: Multilingual universal sentence encoder model training architecture using multi-task training over: (i) retrieval question-answering (ReQA), natural language inference (NLI) and translation ranking. Transformer or CNN based sentence embedding models provide a shared encoder across all tasks.

```
import tensorflow_hub as hub

module = hub.Module("https://tfhub.dev/google/"
    "universal-sentence-encoder-multilingual/1")

multilingual_embeddings = module([
 "Hola Mundo!", "Bonjour le monde!", "Ciao mondo!"
 "Hello World!", "Hallo Welt!", "Hallo Wereld!",
 "你好世界!", "Привет, мир!", "مرحبا بالعالم!"])
```

Listing 1: Python code mapping multilingual sentences into a shared semantic embedding space.

```
module = hub.Module("https://tfhub.dev/google/"
    "universal-sentence-encoder-multilingual-qa/1")

query_embeddings = module(
    dict(text=["What is your age?"]),
    signature="question_encoder", as_dict=True)

candidate_embeddings = module(
    dict(text=["I am 20 years old."],
        context=["I will be 21 next year."]),
    signature="response_encoder", as_dict=True)
```

Listing 2: Python code embedding a question and answer for retrieval Question-Answering (ReQA).

multi-task dual-encoder training framework, with a single shared encoder supporting multiple downstream tasks. The training tasks include: a multi-feature question-answer prediction task,[4] a translation ranking task, and a natural language inference (NLI) task. Additional task specific hidden layers for the question-answering and NLI tasks are added after the shared encoder to provide representational specialization for each type of task. The model training architecture is illustrated at figure 1.

3.2 SentencePiece

SentencePiece tokenization (Kudo and Richardson, 2018) is used for all of the 16 languages supported by our models.[5] A single 128k SentencePiece vocabulary is trained from 8 million sentences sampled from our training corpus and balanced across the 16 languages. For validation, the vocab is used to process a development set, separately sampled from the sentence encoding model training corpus. We find the development set character coverage is higher than 99% for all languages, with less than 1% out-of-vocabulary tokens. Each token in the vocab is mapped to a fixed length embedding vector.[6]

3.3 Shared Encoder

Two distinct architectures for the sentence encoding models are provided: (i) transformer (Vaswani et al., 2017), targeted at higher accuracy at the cost of resource consumption; (ii) convolutional neural network (CNN) (Kim, 2014), designed for efficient inference but obtaining reduced accuracy.

Transformer The transformer encoding model embeds sentences using the *encoder* component of the transformer architecture (Vaswani et al., 2017). Bi-directional self-attention is used to compute context-aware representations of tokens in a sentence, taking into account both the ordering and the identity of the tokens. The context-aware token representations are then averaged together to obtain a sentence-level embedding.

CNN The CNN sentence encoding model feeds the input token sequence embeddings into a con-

---

[4]Question-answer prediction is similar to conversational-response prediction (Yang et al., 2018). We treat the question as the conversational input and the answer as the response. For improved answer selection, we provide a bag-of-words (BoW) context feature as an additional input to the answer encoder. For our models, we use the entire paragraph containing the answer as context. The context feature is encoded using a separate DAN encoder.

[5]`https://github.com/google/sentencepiece`

[6]Out-of-vocabulary characters map to an <UNK> token.

Task Name	Task Type	Data Source	Native or Not
Retrieval Question-Answering (ReQA)	Ranking	Web Crawled	Native + MT
Translation Ranking	Ranking	Web Crawled	Native
Natural Language Inference (NLI)	3 way classification	Human Written	Native (en) + MT

Table 2: Training tasks for the multilingual sentence encoder. For better coverage across languages, we combine native text with machine translated (MT) data. For NLI, native data is only used for English (en).

Lang	QA Native + Translated	Translation Native	NLI Translated
ar	60M	158M	570K
de	75M	517M	570K
en	2.7B	–	570K
es	340M	416M	570K
fr	92M	586M	570K
it	103M	261M	570K
ja	384M	69M	570K
ko	60M	57M	570K
nl	60M	574M	570K
pt	180M	536M	570K
pl	60M	292M	570K
ru	112M	148M	570K
th	60M	70M	570K
tr	69M	415M	570K
zh	1B	112M	570K
zh-t	147M	112M	570K

Table 3: Training examples by task for each of the 16 languages understood by our models.

Model	Quora	AskUbuntu	Average
USE_{Trans}	89.1	**42.3**	**65.7**
USE_{CNN}	**89.2**	39.9	64.6
Gillick et al. (2018)	87.5	37.3	62.4

Table 4: MAP@100 on SR (English). Models are compared with the best models from Gillick et al. (2018) that exclude in-domain training data.

We also translate a portion of question-answer pairs to ensure each language has a minimum of 60M training pairs. For each of our datasets, we use 90% of the data for training, and the remaining 10% for development/validation. Table 2 and 3 lists the details of data used for each task / langauge.

4.2 Model Configuration

Input sentences are truncated to 256 tokens for the CNN model and 100 tokens for transformer. The CNN encoder uses 2 CNN layers with filter width of [1, 2, 3, 5] and 256 filters per width. The Transformer encoder employs 6 transformer layers, with 8 attentions heads, hidden size 512, and filter size 2048. Similar to our prior work (Cer et al., 2018), we configure our models with the intention of making them small and fast enough to be used directly within many downstream applications without the need for model distillation. Model hyperparameters are tuned on development data sampled from the same sources as the training data. We export sentence encoding modules for our two encoder architectures: USE_{Trans} and USE_{CNN}. We also export a larger graph for QA tasks from our Transformer based model that includes QA specific layers and support providing context information from the larger document as $USE_{QA\ Trans+Cxt}$.[10]

volutional neural network (Kim, 2014). Similar to the transformer encoder, average pooling is used to turn the token-level embeddings into a fixed-length representation. Sentence embeddings are then obtained by passing the averaged representation through additional feedforward layers.

4 Training and Configuration

4.1 Training Corpus

Training data consists of mined question-answer pairs,[7] mined translation pairs,[8] and the Stanford Natural Language Inference (SNLI) corpus (Bowman et al., 2015).[9] SNLI only contains English data. The number of mined questions-answer pairs also varies across languages with a bias toward a handful of top tier languages. To balance training across languages, we use Google's translation system to translate SNLI to the other 15 languages.

5 Experiments on Retrieval Tasks

In this section we evaluate our multilingual encoding models on semantic retrieval, bitext and

---

[7]QA pairs are mined from online forums and QA websites, including Reddit, StackOverflow, and YahooAnswers.

[8]The translation pairs are mined using a system similar to the approach described in Uszkoreit et al. (2010).

[9]MultiNLI (Williams et al., 2018), a more extensive corpus, contains examples from multiple sources but with different licences. Employing SNLI avoids navigating the licensing complexity of using MultiNLI to training public models.

[10]While $USE_{QA\ Trans+Cxt}$ uses the same underlying shared encoder as USE_{Trans} but with additional task specific layers, we anticipate that the models could diverge in the future.

Model	en-es	en-fr	en-ru	en-zh
USE$_{\text{Trans}}$	86.1	83.3	88.9	78.8
USE$_{\text{CNN}}$	85.8	82.7	87.4	79.5
Yang et al. (2019)	**89.0**	**86.1**	**89.2**	**87.9**

Table 5: P@1 on UN translation pair bitext retrieval (BR). Yang et al. (2019) is a specialized translation retrieval model and the current state-of-the-art.

retrieval question answer tasks.

5.1 Semantic Retrieval (SR)

Following Gillick et al. (2018), we construct semantic retrieval (SR) tasks from the Quora question-pairs (Hoogeveen et al., 2015) and AskUbuntu (Lei et al., 2016) datasets. The SR task is to identify all sentences in the retrieval corpus that are semantically similar to a query sentence.[11]

For each dataset, we first build a graph connecting each of the positive pairs, and then compute its transitive closure. Each sentence then serves as a test query that should retrieve all of the other sentences it is connected to within the transitive closure. Mean average precision (MAP) is employed to evaluate the models. More details on the constructed datasets can be found in Gillick et al. (2018). Both datasets are English only.

Table 4 shows the MAP@100 on the Quora and AskUbuntu retrieval tasks. We use Gillick et al. (2018) as the baseline model, which is trained using a similar dual encoder architecture. The numbers provided here are for models without focused in-domain training data. [12] Both USE$_{\text{CNN}}$ and USE$_{\text{Trans}}$ outperform the prior state-of-the-art. USE$_{\text{Trans}}$ and USE$_{\text{CNN}}$ perform comparably on Quora. However, USE$_{\text{Trans}}$ performs notably better than USE$_{\text{CNN}}$ on AskUbuntu, suggesting the AskUbuntu data could be more challenging.

5.2 Bitext Retrieval (BR)

Bitext retrieval performance is evaluated on the United Nation (UN) Parallel Corpus (Ziemski et al., 2016), containing 86,000 bilingual document pairs matching English (en) documents with with their translations in five other languages: French (fr),

Spanish (es), Russian (ru), Arabic (ar) and Chinese (zh). Document pairs are aligned at the sentence-level, which results in 11.3 million aligned sentence pairs for each language pair.

Table 5 shows sentence-level retrieval precision@1 (P@1) for the proposed models as well as the current state-of-the-art results from Yang et al. (2019), which uses a specialized translation pair retrieval model. USE$_{\text{Trans}}$ is generally better than USE$_{\text{CNN}}$, performing lower than the SOTA but not by too much with the exception of en-zh.[13]

Model	SQuAD Dev	SQuAD Train
Paragraph Retrieval		
USE$_{\text{QA Trans+Cxt}}$	**63.5**	**53.3**
BM25 (baseline)	61.6	52.4
Sentence Retrieval		
USE$_{\text{QA Trans+Cxt}}$	**53.2**	**43.3**
USE$_{\text{Trans}}$	47.1	37.2

Table 6: P@1 for SQuAD ReQA. Models are *not trained* on SQuAD. Dev and Train only refer to the respective sections of the SQuAD dataset.

5.3 Retrieval Question Answering (ReQA)

Similar to the data set construction used for the SR tasks, the SQuAD v1.0 dataset (Rajpurkar et al., 2016) is transformed into a retrieval question answering (ReQA) task.[14] We first break all documents in the dataset into sentences using the sentence splitter distributed with the ReQA evaluation suite.[15] Each question of the (question, answer spans) tuples in the dataset is treated as a query. The task is to retrieve the sentence designated by the tuple answer span. Search is performed on a retrieval corpus consisting of all of the sentences within the corpus. We contrast sentence and paragraph-level retrieval using our models, with the later allowing for comparison against a BM25 baseline (Jones et al., 2000).[16]

---

[11]The task is related to paraphrase identification (Dolan et al., 2004) and Semantic Textual Similarity (STS) (Cer et al., 2017), but with the identification of meaning similarity being assessed in the context of a retrieval task.

[12]The model for Quora is trained on Paralex (http://knowitall.cs.washington.edu/paralex) and AskUbuntu data. The model for AskUbuntu is trained on Paralex and Quora.

[13]Performance is degraded from Yang et al. (2019) due to using a single sentencepiece vocabulary to cover 16 languages. Languages like Chinese, Korean, Japanese have much more characters. To ensure the vocab coverage, sentencepiece tends to split the text of these languages into single characters, which increases the difficulty of the task.

[14]The retrieval question answering task was suggested by Chen et al. (2017) and then recently explored further by Cakaloglu et al. (2018). However, Cakaloglu et al. (2018)'s use of sampling makes it difficult to directly compare with their results and we provide our own baseline based on BM25.

[15]https://github.com/google/retrieval-qa-eval

[16]BM25 is a strong baseline for text retrieval tasks. Paragraph-level experiments use the BM25 implementa-

Model	en	ar	de	es	fr	it	ja	ko	nl	pt	pl	ru	th	tr	zh / zh-t
Cross-lingual Semantic Retrieval (cl-SR)															
Quora															
USE$_{Trans}$	89.1	**83.1**	**85.5**	**86.3**	**86.7**	**86.8**	**85.1**	**82.5**	**83.8**	**86.5**	82.1	**85.7**	**85.8**	**82.5**	**84.8**
USE$_{CNN}$	**89.2**	79.9	83.7	85.0	85.0	85.5	82.4	77.6	81.3	85.2	78.3	83.8	83.5	79.9	81.9
LASER		79.7	82.2	83.5	83.1	83.7	-	73.4	82.8	83.6	**82.3**	82.6	78.6	79.9	-
AskUbuntu															
USE$_{Trans}$	**42.3**	**38.2**	**40.0**	**39.9**	**39.3**	**40.2**	**40.6**	**40.3**	**39.5**	**39.8**	**38.4**	**39.6**	**40.3**	**37.7**	**40.1**
USE$_{CNN}$	39.9	33.0	35.0	35.6	35.2	36.1	35.5	35.1	34.5	35.6	32.9	35.2	35.2	32.8	34.6
LASER		24.5	26.1	26.4	26.5	27.0	-	22.0	26.2	26.2	25.7	25.6	23.8	25.0	-
Average															
USE$_{Trans}$	**65.7**	**60.7**	**62.8**	**63.1**	**63.0**	**63.5**	**63.8**	**62.4**	**61.7**	**63.2**	**60.7**	**62.7**	**63.1**	**60.1**	**62.5**
USE$_{CNN}$	64.6	56.5	59.4	60.3	60.1	60.8	59.0	56.4	57.9	60.4	55.6	59.5	59.4	56.4	58.3
LASER		52.1	54.2	55.0	54.8	55.4	-	47.7	54.5	54.9	54.0	54.6	51.2	52.5	-
Cross-lingual Retrieval Question Answering (cl-ReQA)															
SQuAD train															
USE$_{QA\ Trans+Cxt}$	43.3	33.2	35.2	37.2	37.0	37.0	32.9	31.1	36.6	37.7	34.5	33.2	36.9	32.3	32.7

Table 7: Cross-lingual performance on Quora/AskUbuntu cl-SR (MAP) and SQuAD cl-ReQA (P@1). Queries/questions are machine translated, while retrieval candidates remain in English.

We evaluated ReQA using the SQuAD dev and train sets and without training on the SQuAD data.[17] The sentence and paragraph retrieval P@1 are shown in table 6. For sentence retrieval, we compare encodings produced using context from the text surrounding the retrieval candidate, USE$_{QA\ Trans+Cxt}$, to sentence encodings produced without contextual cues, USE$_{Trans}$. Paragraph retrieval contrasts USE$_{QA\ Trans+Cxt}$ with BM25.

5.4 Cross-lingual Retrieval

Our English retrieval experiments are extended to explore cross-lingual semantic retrieval (cl-SR) and cross-lingual retrieval question answering (cl-ReQA). SR queries and ReQA questions are machine translated into other languages, while keeping the retrieval candidates in English.[18] Table 7 provides our cross-lingual retrieval results for our transformer and CNN multilingual sentence encoding models. We compare against the state-of-the-art LASER multilingual sentence embedding library (Artetxe and Schwenk, 2019).[19]

On both the Quora and AskUbuntu cl-SR tasks, USE$_{Trans}$ outperforms USE$_{CNN}$ and LASER on all datasets, except the Polish (pl) Quora data where LASER achieves slightly better performance.[20] USE$_{CNN}$ tends to outperform LASER on Quora and always outperforms LASER by a sizable margin on AskUbuntu. We note that our CNN based model not only outperforms LASER, but also relies on simpler model architecture than LASER's LSTM based archtitecture. Given the similar level of performance on Quora between USE$_{CNN}$ and LASER, we suspect the notably better performance on AskUbuntu over LASER is due to differences in the training data provided to encoding models.

6 Experiments on Transfer Tasks

For comparison with prior USE models, English task transfer performance is evaluated on SentEval (Conneau and Kiela, 2018). For sentence classification transfer tasks, the output of the sentence encoders are provided to a task specific DNN. For the pairwise semantic similarity task, the similarity of sentence embeddings u and v is assessed using $- \arccos\left(\frac{uv}{\|u\|\ \|v\|}\right)$, following Yang et al. (2018). In table 8, our multilingual models show competitive transfer performance when compared to state-of-the-art sentence embedding models. USE$_{Trans}$ performs better than USE$_{CNN}$ on all tasks. Our new

---

tion: `https://github.com/nhirakawa/BM25`, with default parameters. We exclude sentence-level BM25, as BM25 generally performs poorly at this granularity.

[17]For sentences, the resulting retrieval task for development set consists of 11,425 questions and 10,248 candidates, and the retrieval task for train set is consists of 87,599 questions and 91,703 candidates. For paragraph retrieval, there are 2,067 retrieval candidates in the development set and 18,896 in the training set. To retrieve paragraphs with our model, we first run sentence retrieval and use the retrieved nearest sentence to select the enclosing paragraph.

[18]Poor translations are detected and rejected when the original English text and English back translation have a cosine similarity < 0.5 according our previously released English USE$_{Trans}$ model (Cer et al., 2018).

[19]`https://github.com/facebookresearch/LASER`

[20]Results are not presented for LASER on ja and zh due unicode errors.

Model	MR	CR	SUBJ	MPQA	TREC	SST	STS Bench (dev / test)
USE mutlilingual models							
USE$_{\text{CNN}}$	73.8	83.2	90.1	87.7	96.4	78.1	0.829 / 0.809
USE$_{\text{Transformer}}$	78.1	**87.0**	92.1	89.9	**96.6**	80.9	**0.837 / 0.825**
The state-of-the-art English embedding models							
InferSent (Conneau et al., 2017)	81.1	86.3	92.4	**90.2**	88.2	84.6	0.801 / 0.758
Skip-Thought LN (Ba et al., 2016)	79.4	83.1	93.7	89.3	–	–	–
Quick-Thought (Logeswaran and Lee, 2018)	**82.4**	86.0	94.8	**90.2**	92.4	**87.6**	–
USE$_{\text{DAN}}$ for English (Cer et al., 2018)	72.2	78.5	92.1	86.9	88.1	77.5	0.760 / 0.717
USE$_{\text{Transformer}}$ for English (Cer et al., 2018)	82.2	84.2	**95.5**	88.1	93.2	83.7	0.802 / 0.766

Table 8: Performance on English transfer tasks from SentEval (Conneau and Kiela, 2018).

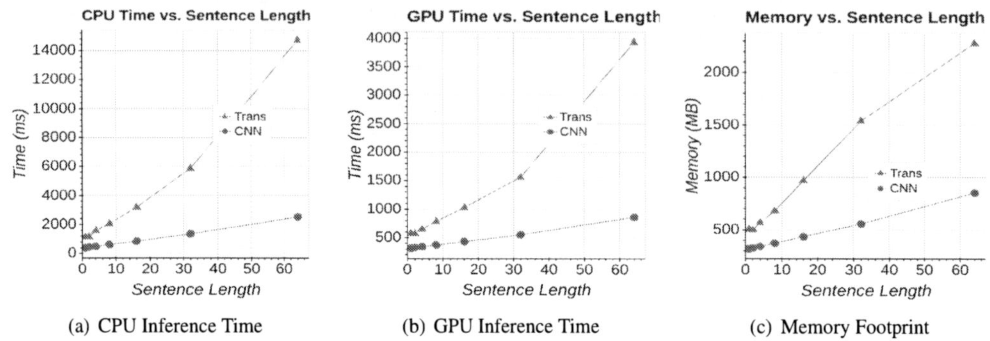

(a) CPU Inference Time   (b) GPU Inference Time   (c) Memory Footprint

Figure 2: Resource usage for the multilingual Transformer and CNN encoding models.

multilingual USE$_{\text{Trans}}$ model outperforms our best previously released English only model, USE$_{\text{Trans}}$ for English (Cer et al., 2018), on some tasks.

7 Resource Usage

Figure 2 provides compute and memory usage benchmarks for our models.[21] Inference times on GPU are 2 to 3 times faster than CPU. Our CNN models have the smallest memory footprint and are the fastest on both CPU and GPU. The memory requirements increase with sentence length, with the Transformer model increasing more than twice as fast as the CNN model.[22] While this makes CNNs an attractive choice for efficiently encoding longer texts, this comes with a corresponding drop in accuracy on many retrieval and transfer tasks.

8 Conclusion

Easy-to-use retrieval focused multilingual models for embedding sentence-length text are made avail-

able on TensorFlow Hub. Our models embed text from 16 languages into a shared semantic embedding space and *achieve a new state-of-the-art in performance on monolingual and cross-lingual semantic retrieval (SR)*. The models achieve good performance on the related tasks of translation pair bitext retrieval (BR) and retrieval question answering (ReQA). Monolingual transfer task performance approaches, and in some cases exceeds, English only sentence embedding models. Our models are freely available under an Apache license with additional documentation and tutorial colaboratory notebooks at:

```
https://tfhub.dev/s?q=universal-
sentence-encoder-multilingual
```

Acknowledgments

We thank our teammates from Descartes and other Google groups for their feedback and suggestions. Special thanks goes to Muthu Chidambaram for his early exploration of multilingual training, Taku Kudo for the SentencePiece model support, Chen Chen for the templates used to perform the transfer learning experiments and Mario Guajardo for an early version of the ReQA tutorial Colab.

---

[21]CPU benchmarks are run on Intel(R) Xeon(R) Platinum 8173M CPU @ 2.00GHz. GPU benchmarks were run on an NVidia v100. Memory footprint was measured on CPU.

[22]Transformer models are ultimately governed by a time and space complexity of $O(n^2)$. The benchmarks show for shorter sequence lengths the time and space requirements are dominated by computations that scale linearly with length and have a larger constant factor than the quadratic terms.

References

Martín Abadi, Paul Barham, Jianmin Chen, Zhifeng Chen, Andy Davis, Jeffrey Dean, Matthieu Devin, Sanjay Ghemawat, Geoffrey Irving, Michael Isard, Manjunath Kudlur, Josh Levenberg, Rajat Monga, Sherry Moore, Derek G. Murray, Benoit Steiner, Paul Tucker, Vijay Vasudevan, Pete Warden, Martin Wicke, Yuan Yu, and Xiaoqiang Zheng. 2016. Tensorflow: A system for large-scale machine learning. In *Proceedings of USENIX OSDI'16*, OSDI'16, pages 265–283.

Mikel Artetxe and Holger Schwenk. 2019. Massively multilingual sentence embeddings for zero-shot cross-lingual transfer and beyond. *Transactions of the Association for Computational Linguistics*, 7:597–610.

Lei Jimmy Ba, Ryan Kiros, and Geoffrey E. Hinton. 2016. Layer normalization. *CoRR*, abs/1607.06450.

Samuel R. Bowman, Gabor Angeli, Christopher Potts, and Christopher D. Manning. 2015. A large annotated corpus for learning natural language inference. In *Proceedings of the 2015 Conference on Empirical Methods in Natural Language Processing*, pages 632–642.

Tolgahan Cakaloglu, Christian Szegedy, and Xiaowei Xu. 2018. Text embeddings for retrieval from a large knowledge base. *CoRR*, abs/1810.10176.

Daniel Cer, Mona Diab, Eneko Agirre, Iñigo Lopez-Gazpio, and Lucia Specia. 2017. SemEval-2017 task 1: Semantic textual similarity multilingual and crosslingual focused evaluation. In *Proceedings of the 11th International Workshop on Semantic Evaluation (SemEval-2017)*, pages 1–14.

Daniel Cer, Yinfei Yang, Sheng-yi Kong, Nan Hua, Nicole Limtiaco, Rhomni St. John, Noah Constant, Mario Guajardo-Cespedes, Steve Yuan, Chris Tar, Brian Strope, and Ray Kurzweil. 2018. Universal sentence encoder for English. In *Proceedings of the 2018 Conference on Empirical Methods in Natural Language Processing: System Demonstrations*, pages 169–174.

Danqi Chen, Adam Fisch, Jason Weston, and Antoine Bordes. 2017. Reading Wikipedia to answer open-domain questions. In *Proceedings of the 55th Annual Meeting of the Association for Computational Linguistics (Volume 1: Long Papers)*, pages 1870–1879.

Muthuraman Chidambaram, Yinfei Yang, Daniel Cer, Steve Yuan, Yun-Hsuan Sung, Brian Strope, and Ray Kurzweil. 2018. Learning cross-lingual sentence representations via a multi-task dual-encoder model. *CoRR*, abs/1810.12836.

Alexis Conneau and Douwe Kiela. 2018. SentEval: An evaluation toolkit for universal sentence representations. In *Proceedings of the Eleventh International Conference on Language Resources and Evaluation (LREC-2018)*.

Alexis Conneau, Douwe Kiela, Holger Schwenk, Loïc Barrault, and Antoine Bordes. 2017. Supervised learning of universal sentence representations from natural language inference data. In *Proceedings of the 2017 Conference on Empirical Methods in Natural Language Processing*, pages 670–680, Copenhagen, Denmark. Association for Computational Linguistics.

Bill Dolan, Chris Quirk, and Chris Brockett. 2004. Unsupervised construction of large paraphrase corpora: Exploiting massively parallel news sources. In *COLING 2004: Proceedings of the 20th International Conference on Computational Linguistics*, pages 350–356.

Daniel Gillick, Alessandro Presta, and Gaurav Singh Tomar. 2018. End-to-end retrieval in continuous space. *CoRR*, abs/1811.08008.

Doris Hoogeveen, Karin M. Verspoor, and Timothy Baldwin. 2015. Cqadupstack: A benchmark data set for community question-answering research. In *Proceedings of the 20th Australasian Document Computing Symposium*, ADCS '15, pages 3:1–3:8.

K. Sparck Jones, S. Walker, and S. E. Robertson. 2000. A probabilistic model of information retrieval: Development and comparative experiments. *Inf. Process. Manage.*, 36(6):779–808.

Yoon Kim. 2014. Convolutional neural networks for sentence classification. In *Proceedings of the 2014 Conference on Empirical Methods in Natural Language Processing (EMNLP)*, pages 1746–1751.

Taku Kudo and John Richardson. 2018. SentencePiece: A simple and language independent subword tokenizer and detokenizer for neural text processing. In *Proceedings of the 2018 Conference on Empirical Methods in Natural Language Processing: System Demonstrations*, pages 66–71.

Tao Lei, Hrishikesh Joshi, Regina Barzilay, Tommi Jaakkola, Kateryna Tymoshenko, Alessandro Moschitti, and Lluís Màrquez. 2016. Semi-supervised question retrieval with gated convolutions. In *Proceedings of the 2016 Conference of the North American Chapter of the Association for Computational Linguistics: Human Language Technologies*, pages 1279–1289.

Lajanugen Logeswaran and Honglak Lee. 2018. An efficient framework for learning sentence representations. In *International Conference on Learning Representations (ICLR)*.

Pranav Rajpurkar, Jian Zhang, Konstantin Lopyrev, and Percy Liang. 2016. SQuAD: 100,000+ questions for machine comprehension of text. In *Proceedings of the 2016 Conference on Empirical Methods in Natural Language Processing*, pages 2383–2392.

Jakob Uszkoreit, Jay Ponte, Ashok Popat, and Moshe Dubiner. 2010. Large scale parallel document mining for machine translation. In *Proceedings of the 23rd International Conference on Computational Linguistics (Coling 2010)*, pages 1101–1109.

Ashish Vaswani, Noam Shazeer, Niki Parmar, Jakob Uszkoreit, Llion Jones, Aidan N Gomez, Ł ukasz Kaiser, and Illia Polosukhin. 2017. Attention is all you need. In *Proceedings of NIPS*, pages 6000–6010.

Adina Williams, Nikita Nangia, and Samuel Bowman. 2018. A broad-coverage challenge corpus for sentence understanding through inference. In *Proceedings of the 2018 Conference of the North American Chapter of the Association for Computational Linguistics: Human Language Technologies, Volume 1 (Long Papers)*, pages 1112–1122.

Yinfei Yang, Gustavo Hernández Ábrego, Steve Yuan, Mandy Guo, Qinlan Shen, Daniel Cer, Yun-Hsuan Sung, Brian Strope, and Ray Kurzweil. 2019. Improving multilingual sentence embedding using bi-directional dual encoder with additive margin softmax. *CoRR*, abs/1902.08564.

Yinfei Yang, Steve Yuan, Daniel Cer, Sheng-yi Kong, Noah Constant, Petr Pilar, Heming Ge, Yun-Hsuan Sung, Brian Strope, and Ray Kurzweil. 2018. Learning semantic textual similarity from conversations. In *Proceedings of The Third Workshop on Representation Learning for NLP*, pages 164–174.

Michał Ziemski, Marcin Junczys-Dowmunt, and Bruno Pouliquen. 2016. The united nations parallel corpus v1.0. In *Proceedings of the Tenth International Conference on Language Resources and Evaluation (LREC 2016)*, pages 3530–3534.

BENTO: A Visual Platform for Building Clinical NLP Pipelines Based on CodaLab

Yonghao Jin, Fei Li and **Hong Yu**

Department of Computer Science, University of Massachusetts
Lowell, MA, USA

Abstract

CodaLab[1] is an open-source web-based platform for collaborative computational research. Although CodaLab has gained popularity in the research community, its interface has limited support for creating reusable tools that can be easily applied to new datasets and composed into pipelines. In clinical domain, natural language processing (NLP) on medical notes generally involves multiple steps, like tokenization, named entity recognition, etc. Since these steps require different tools which are usually scattered in different publications, it is not easy for researchers to use them to process their own datasets. In this paper, we present *BENTO*, a workflow management platform with a graphic user interface (GUI) that is built on top of CodaLab, to facilitate the process of building clinical NLP pipelines. BENTO comes with a number of clinical NLP tools that have been pre-trained using medical notes and expert annotations and can be readily used for various clinical NLP tasks. It also allows researchers and developers to create their custom tools (e.g., pre-trained NLP models) and use them in a controlled and reproducible way. In addition, the GUI interface enables researchers with limited computer background to compose tools into NLP pipelines and then apply the pipelines on their own datasets in a "what you see is what you get" (WYSIWYG) way. Although BENTO is designed for clinical NLP applications, the underlying architecture is flexible to be tailored to any other domains.

1 Introduction

With the machine learning research going deep, computational models are becoming increasingly large with intensive hyper-parameters tuning, making the research difficult to reproduce. To tackle

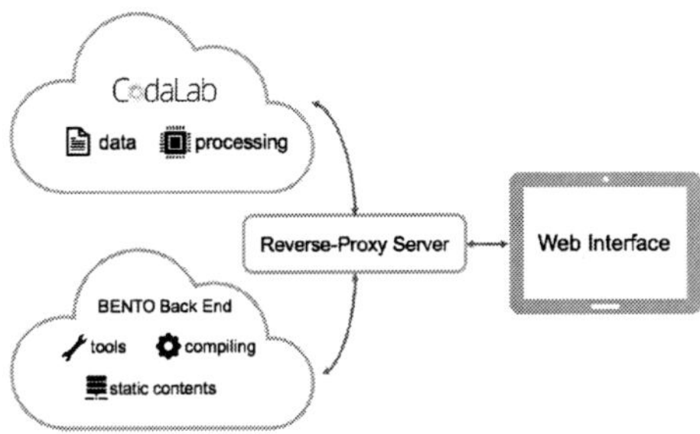

Figure 1: The architecture of BENTO. The BENTO back end stores the description files of various tools (e.g., pre-trained NLP models), processes static contents of the application and handles compilation of the user-defined pipelines. The CodaLab back end stores the datasets (bundles) and executes computational jobs. The two back end servers are brought behind a single domain name using a reverse proxy server.

this problem, researchers have developed CodaLab as an open-source platform for researchers and software developers. However, CodaLab has limited support for reusable tools that can be easily applied to different datasets and be composed into computational pipelines.

Building pipelines is essential for the research of certain domains. Take the medical informatics research as an example, a complete NLP analysis on medical notes often involves multiple steps like tokenization, de-identification (Dernoncourt et al., 2017; Liu et al., 2017), entity recognition (Li et al., 2018; Xu et al., 2017; Jagannatha and Yu, 2016) and normalization (Li et al., 2019, 2017; Cho et al., 2017), relation extraction (Li et al., 2018; He et al., 2019), etc. Since these steps require different tools and these tools are usually scattered in different publications, it is far from trivial to leverage these tools on new datasets even though the authors have released the source code. Therefore, we developed a user-friendly workflow management platform,

---

[1]codalab.org

Proceedings of the 58th Annual Meeting of the Association for Computational Linguistics, pages 95–100
July 5 - July 10, 2020. ©2020 Association for Computational Linguistics

BiomEdical Nlp TOolkits (*BENTO*), to facilitate the process of building and applying of clinical NLP pipelines.

The architecture of BENTO is illustrated in Figure 1. BENTO has three main components. The web interface is supported by two back ends brought together by a reverse-proxy server. The CodaLab back end stores the datasets and executes computational jobs. The BENTO back end serves tool information and transforms user-defined pipelines to CodaLab commands.

The advantages of such architecture are two-fold. First, it is flexible to use CodaLab as the back end for adding custom tools (e.g., pre-trained NLP models) and processing data in a controlled and reproducible way. All the tools are containerized with Docker[2], which makes the platform to keep a unified interface to manage the models and not need to maintain different operating environment for different models. Second, the web interface makes it easier for users to construct NLP pipelines through editing flowcharts and then apply the pipelines to their data. The web-based architecture also makes the platform widely accessible without complex installation and configuration.

In this paper, we also show the examples of using BENTO to integrate several clinical NLP applications such as hypoglycemia detection (Jin et al., 2019) and adverse drug event extraction (Li et al., 2018), and build pipelines based on these tools. BENTO helps build NLP pipelines, which is a promising system to accelerate the medical informatics research.

2   Related Work

Galaxy (Afgan et al., 2018) is a similar computational platform that is focused in bioinformatics and computational biology, whose interface inspires the design of ours. The main restriction of the Galaxy platform is that users can only access the tools managed by administrators and cannot define their own tools. In linguistic research community, other related platforms include lingvis.io (El-Assady et al., 2019), which is focused on integrating NLP operations with visualizations , and Argo (Rak et al., 2012), a web-based text mining workbench based on the UIMA framework. Stanford CoreNLP (Manning et al., 2014) provides a commonly used NLP tool set. On the library level, NLTK (Hardeniya et al., 2016) is a popular Python library that inte-

---

[2]docker.com

grates multiple widely used NLP tools. OpenNLP (Morton et al., 2005) is a Java library that provides machine learning based toolkits for NLP tasks. FudanNLP (Qiu et al., 2013) is a Java based library which integrates the machine learning models and datasets for Chinese NLP.

In the medical domain, NILE (Yu and Cai, 2013) is a Java package which includes rule based NLP methods for information extraction from medical notes. Apache cTAKES (Apache cTAKES, 2018) and CLAMP (Soysal et al., 2018) are two clinical NLP systems with pipeline-based architecture in the UIMA framework. Both systems have a graphical user interface, allowing users to build pipelines from build-in UIMA components. However, the UIMA framework has a steep learning curve. It is also not widely used in the machine-learning-based NLP research. Furthermore, most NLP applications are often released as command line programs. Therefore, it is hard to extend applications that use the UIMA framework with new models. In contrast, tools on our BENTO platform are based on command line programs and users can easily define their own tools with little restriction.

3   System Description

BENTO mainly comprises three parts: a front-end web application, a BENTO back end server and a CodaLab back end. As shown in Figure 1, BENTO has a web-based user interface, from which users can upload data, edit tools, submit jobs and perform various other operations. The BENTO back end is a web server that is mainly used for storing the tools, including the user-defined ones, so they can be accessed in different sessions. The CodaLab back end is used for execution of each computational job. When a tool is being executed, BENTO will generate a series of CodaLab commands based on the tool information and the input bundles. The outputs of the tool are the run bundles generated from those commands which can be passed on to the down-stream tools and inspected by the users on the CodaLab interface.

3.1   Web Interface

As shown in Figure 2, the user interface of our platform is a web application that can be roughly divided into three panels from left to right: tool panel, canvas panel and worksheet panel. The tool panel lists the current available tools on the platform organized in a hierarchical file system struc-

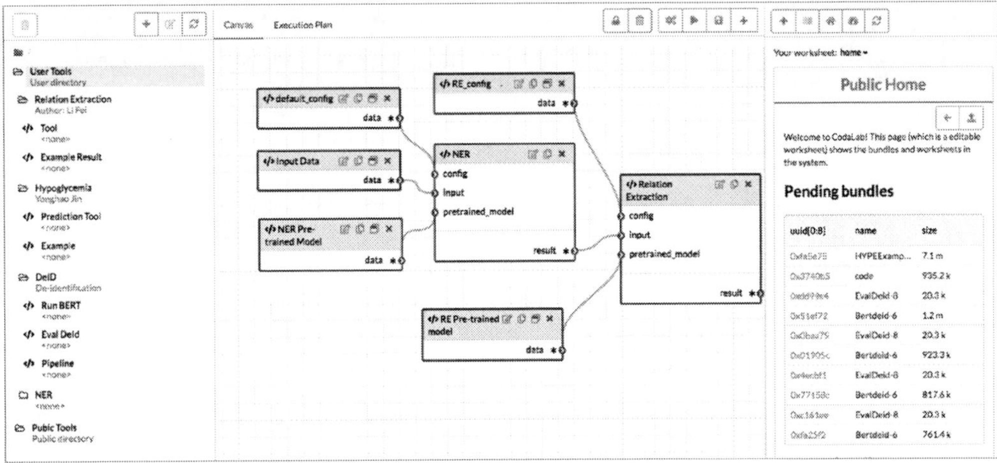

Figure 2: BENTO Web Interface. The interface can be roughly divided into three parts from left to right: tool panel, canvas panel and worksheet panel. The tool panel lists the current available tools organized in a tree view. The canvas panel contains the flowchart of the current pipeline. Every node represents a tool or dataset and each connection indicates the data flow in the pipeline.[3] This figure shows an example of the pipeline for entity and relation extraction. The worksheet panel displays the content of the CodaLab worksheet such as bundles and their UUIDs.

ture along with the meta information. Users can edit the *User Tools* folder using the buttons listed on the top menu bar. To run a tool, users can simply drag it to the canvas panel to the right and a tool node will appear on the canvas. A node, shown in the workflow Figure 2, contains several input and output ports, corresponding to the inputs and outputs of the tool.

Tool nodes can be linked together to form a pipeline and the connections represent the data flow during execution (Figure 2). A connection starts from an output port and ends in an input port. An input port accepts only a single connection while an output port can initiate one or multiple connections. Users can edit the tool by clicking the *Editor button* (✎) on the top right corner and the node will be toggled to an editor interface (Figure 3). The editor contains the expression of the tool (Section 3.3), which can be modified by the users. The rightmost part is the worksheet panel that displays the content of the current selected worksheet. Worksheets are editable markup documents provided by CodaLab. Dragging a bundle entry from the worksheet panel to the canvas will create a data node. A data node is similar to the tool node except that it does not have any input port which naturally represents a data entity in a computational pipeline.

---

[3]For simplicity, pre-processing steps like tokenization is built-in in each tool.

3.2   CodaLab Back End

An important design goal of BENTO is flexibility. Users should be able to easily define their own tools on the BENTO platform and customize existing tools at the command line level. For this reason, we use CodaLab as the back end for tool execution on the BENTO platform. CodaLab is a cloud-based platform designed for running computational experiments in data-oriented research. In CodaLab, researchers can easily set up a reproducible environment and run arbitrary command line by specifying a docker image and bundle dependencies. In CodaLab, bundles are immutable objects that hold the content of datasets. The output files produced by that command will be saved into a new bundle and can be further passed to down-stream experiments.

All datasets in BENTO are stored as CodaLab bundles. The tools and pipelines will be compiled into CodaLab commands. Users could submit commands to the CodaLab back end via the web interface. Such design makes the computational results of the BENTO platform reproducible through CodaLab. Since CodaLab will record dependency information in run bundles, it is also easy to recreate the pipeline on our platform from existing result bundles. Using CodaLab as the back end also mitigates the engineering challenges such as job scheduling and data management.

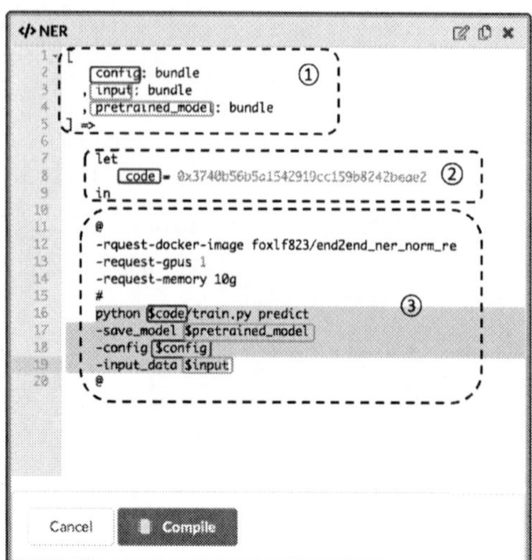

Figure 3: The CodaLang expression for the tool NER in Figure 2. The expression can be roughly split into three sections indicated by the dashed squares. The first section declares the arguments of this tool. As seen, the tool takes three bundles as inputs: *config*, *input* and *pretrained_model*. The second section declares a constant *code* which is initialized with an existing bundle. The third section is a string template for generating the CodaLab command.

3.3 BENTO Back End

The BENTO back end is for storing tools and generating CodaLab commands from the pipeline graphs.

3.3.1 CodaLang: A Tool Configuration Language

The tools in BENTO are described via our custom language called *CodaLang*[4] It acts as an intermediate layer between the web interface and CodaLab. It has a succinct syntax for specifying the interfaces of a tool, i.e. the inputs and outputs. It also provides a string template mechanism for creating CodaLab commands from input arguments. For example, the CodaLang expression for the node NER in Figure 2 is shown in Figure 3.

The configuration is composed of three sections which are highlighted with dotted squares. The first section declares the arguments of the tool, corresponding to the three input ports of the node. The second section creates a constant variable *code* which is assigned an existing bundle. The third section is a string template for generating the CodaLab command.

---

[4]A thorough introduction can be found at https://github.com/jyh1/codalang .

Figure 4: The CodaLab commands generated from the pipeline in Figure 2. Two CodaLab commands are generated based on two steps in the pipeline, namely NER and relation extraction. The bundle dependency information is highlighted in orange and the shell commands are colorized in red. The results in the first step are saved in the variable *bundle_0* (circled in blue squares), which is used as a bundle dependency in the command of the second step.

daLab command. It includes execution options (e.g., *request-docker-image*) and tool bash commands. The template variables are circled by the squares in the same color with their declarations. Once the values of the tool arguments are determined, a CodaLab command can be easily generated based on the command template. The run bundle created by the command will be used as results and can be passed on to down-stream tools in the pipeline. Through CodaLang, users can easily modify existing tools or create their own tools. The tool configuration can also be automatically generated from the dependency information of a bundle.

3.3.2 Pipeline Execution

We have described how BENTO transforms a single tool to a CodaLab command. In this section, we will describe how BENTO transforms a tool pipeline into multiple CodaLab commands. In a tool pipeline, tools are connected together to form a directed acyclic graph. During execution, tools are transformed to CodaLab commands according to their topological order in the graph. Take the pipeline in Figure 2 as an example, its corresponding CodaLab commands shown in Figure 4.

As shown in Figure 4, the bundle dependency information is highlighted in orange and the shell commands are colorized in red. The two CodaLab commands correspond to the two tool nodes in the pipeline of Figure 2. The first command is generated from the tool NER based on its tool configuration in Figure 3. The results of this command are saved in the variable *bundle_0*, which will be employed as a bundle dependency in the command of the tool for relation extraction. The web interface takes the responsibility of submitting the generated commands to CodaLab. When the pipeline begins to run, the worksheet panel will display the information of the newly created run bundles.

4 Tools Integrated in BENTO

In this section, we list the tools that have already been integrated to our platform, including:

- Hypoglycemic Event Detection (Jin et al., 2019): Hypoglycemic events are common and potentially dangerous conditions among patients being treated for diabetes. This tool can be used to automatically detect hypoglycemic events from EHR notes.

- Clinical Entity Recognition (Li et al., 2018): This tool has been built to recognize 9 types of clinical entities such as medications, indications and adverse drug events (ADEs).

- Clinical Relation Extraction (Li et al., 2018): This tool is able to extract 7 types of relations between clinical entities such as medications and their durations, dosages and frequencies.

- Disease Name Normalization (Li et al., 2019): This tool can be used to normalize disease names to some controlled vocabularies such SNOMED[5] and MEDIC (Davis et al., 2012).

- De-identification: This tool is able to recognize 18 types of protected health information that needs to be removed to de-identify patient notes. We employed BERT (Devlin et al., 2019) to build a de-identification model whose performance is comparable with the state-of-the-art system (Dernoncourt et al., 2017).

We provide examples and instructions to use these tools on the demo page of our platform. For convenience, these tools all take plain text files as inputs and have the pre-processing and tokenization components built-in. In the future, we will integrate stand-alone components dedicated for pre-processing and tokenization to BENTO which can be shared by different application tools. We also plan to incorporate more NLP tools developed by our group(Rumeng et al., 2017; Rawat et al., 2019; Lalor et al., 2019; Zheng and Yu, 2018).

[5]https://www.snomed.org

5 Conclusion

In this paper, we have described the design of the workflow management platform BENTO. To the best of our knowledge, BENTO represents the first web-based workflow management platform for NLP research. Using BENTO, researchers can make use of existing tools or define their own tools. Computational pipelines can be configured through a web-based user-interface and then automatically executed on CodaLab. BENTO includes a number of clinical NLP tools to facilitate the process of EHR notes. A demo of our platform is available at bio-nlp.org/bentodemo/.

References

Enis Afgan, Dannon Baker, Bérénice Batut, Marius Van Den Beek, Dave Bouvier, Martin Čech, John Chilton, Dave Clements, Nate Coraor, Björn A Grüning, et al. 2018. The galaxy platform for accessible, reproducible and collaborative biomedical analyses: 2018 update. *Nucleic acids research*, 46(W1):W537–W544.

TM Apache cTAKES. 2018. clinical text analysis knowledge extraction system.

Hyejin Cho, Wonjun Choi, and Hyunju Lee. 2017. A method for named entity normalization in biomedical articles: application to diseases and plants. *BMC bioinformatics*, 18(1):451.

Allan Peter Davis, Thomas C Wiegers, Michael C Rosenstein, and Carolyn J Mattingly. 2012. Medic: a practical disease vocabulary used at the comparative toxicogenomics database. *Database*, 2012.

Franck Dernoncourt, Ji Young Lee, Ozlem Uzuner, and Peter Szolovits. 2017. De-identification of patient notes with recurrent neural networks. *Journal of the American Medical Informatics Association*, 24(3):596–606.

Jacob Devlin, Ming-Wei Chang, Kenton Lee, and Kristina Toutanova. 2019. BERT: Pre-training of deep bidirectional transformers for language understanding. In *Proceedings of the 2019 Conference of the North American Chapter of the Association for Computational Linguistics: Human Language Technologies, Volume 1 (Long and Short Papers)*, pages 4171–4186, Minneapolis, Minnesota. Association for Computational Linguistics.

Mennatallah El-Assady, Wolfgang Jentner, Fabian Sperrle, Rita Sevastjanova, Annette Hautli, Miriam Butt, and Daniel Keim. 2019. lingvis. io-a linguistic visual analytics framework. In *Proceedings of the 57th Annual Meeting of the Association for Computational Linguistics: System Demonstrations*, pages 13–18.

Nitin Hardeniya, Jacob Perkins, Deepti Chopra, Nisheeth Joshi, and Iti Mathur. 2016. *Natural Language Processing: Python and NLTK*. Packt Publishing Ltd.

Bin He, Yi Guan, and Rui Dai. 2019. Classifying medical relations in clinical text via convolutional neural networks. *Artificial intelligence in medicine*, 93:43–49.

Abhyuday N Jagannatha and Hong Yu. 2016. Structured prediction models for rnn based sequence labeling in clinical text. In *Proceedings of the conference on empirical methods in natural language processing. conference on empirical methods in natural language processing*, volume 2016, page 856. NIH Public Access.

Yonghao Jin, Fei Li, Varsha G Vimalananda, and Hong Yu. 2019. Automatic Detection of Hypoglycemic Events From the Electronic Health Record Notes of Diabetes Patients: Empirical Study. *JMIR medical informatics*, 7(4):e14340.

John P Lalor, Beverly Woolf, and Hong Yu. 2019. Improving electronic health record note comprehension with noteaid: Randomized trial of electronic health record note comprehension interventions with crowdsourced workers. *Journal of medical Internet research*, 21(1):e10793.

Fei Li, Yonghao Jin, Weisong Liu, Bhanu Pratap Singh Rawat, Pengshan Cai, and Hong Yu. 2019. Fine-Tuning Bidirectional Encoder Representations From Transformers (BERT)-Based Models on Large-Scale Electronic Health Record Notes: An Empirical Study. *JMIR medical informatics*.

Fei Li, Weisong Liu, and Hong Yu. 2018. Extraction of Information Related to Adverse Drug Events from Electronic Health Record Notes: Design of an End-to-End Model Based on Deep Learning. *JMIR medical informatics*.

Haodi Li, Qingcai Chen, Buzhou Tang, Xiaolong Wang, Hua Xu, Baohua Wang, and Dong Huang. 2017. Cnn-based ranking for biomedical entity normalization. *BMC bioinformatics*, 18(11):79–86.

Zengjian Liu, Buzhou Tang, Xiaolong Wang, and Qingcai Chen. 2017. De-identification of clinical notes via recurrent neural network and conditional random field. *Journal of biomedical informatics*, 75:S34–S42.

Christopher Manning, Mihai Surdeanu, John Bauer, Jenny Finkel, Steven Bethard, and David McClosky. 2014. The stanford corenlp natural language processing toolkit. In *Proceedings of 52nd annual meeting of the association for computational linguistics: system demonstrations*, pages 55–60.

Thomas Morton, Joern Kottmann, Jason Baldridge, and Gann Bierner. 2005. Opennlp: A java-based nlp toolkit. In *Proc. EACL*.

Xipeng Qiu, Qi Zhang, and Xuan-Jing Huang. 2013. Fudannlp: A toolkit for chinese natural language processing. In *Proceedings of the 51st Annual Meeting of the Association for Computational Linguistics: System Demonstrations*, pages 49–54.

Rafal Rak, Andrew Rowley, William Black, and Sophia Ananiadou. 2012. Argo: an integrative, interactive, text mining-based workbench supporting curation. *Database*, 2012.

Bhanu Pratap Singh Rawat, Fei Li, and Hong Yu. 2019. Naranjo question answering using end-to-end multi-task learning model. In *Proceedings of the 25th ACM SIGKDD International Conference on Knowledge Discovery & Data Mining*, pages 2547–2555.

Li Rumeng, N Jagannatha Abhyuday, and Yu Hong. 2017. A hybrid neural network model for joint prediction of presence and period assertions of medical events in clinical notes. In *AMIA Annual Symposium Proceedings*, volume 2017, page 1149. American Medical Informatics Association.

Ergin Soysal, Jingqi Wang, Min Jiang, Yonghui Wu, Serguei Pakhomov, Hongfang Liu, and Hua Xu. 2018. Clamp–a toolkit for efficiently building customized clinical natural language processing pipelines. *Journal of the American Medical Informatics Association*, 25(3):331–336.

Kai Xu, Zhanfan Zhou, Tianyong Hao, and Wenyin Liu. 2017. A bidirectional lstm and conditional random fields approach to medical named entity recognition. In *International Conference on Advanced Intelligent Systems and Informatics*, pages 355–365. Springer.

S Yu and T Cai. 2013. Nile: fast natural language processing for electronic health records. *Preprint at https://arxiv. org/abs/1311.6063*.

Jiaping Zheng and Hong Yu. 2018. Assessing the readability of medical documents: a ranking approach. *JMIR medical informatics*, 6(1):e17.

🖋 Stanza: A Python Natural Language Processing Toolkit for Many Human Languages

Peng Qi*   Yuhao Zhang*   Yuhui Zhang
Jason Bolton   Christopher D. Manning
Stanford University
Stanford, CA 94305
{pengqi, yuhaozhang, yuhuiz}@stanford.edu
{jebolton, manning}@stanford.edu

Abstract

We introduce Stanza, an open-source Python natural language processing toolkit supporting 66 human languages. Compared to existing widely used toolkits, Stanza features a language-agnostic fully neural pipeline for text analysis, including tokenization, multi-word token expansion, lemmatization, part-of-speech and morphological feature tagging, dependency parsing, and named entity recognition. We have trained Stanza on a total of 112 datasets, including the Universal Dependencies treebanks and other multilingual corpora, and show that the same neural architecture generalizes well and achieves competitive performance on all languages tested. Additionally, Stanza includes a native Python interface to the widely used Java Stanford CoreNLP software, which further extends its functionality to cover other tasks such as coreference resolution and relation extraction. Source code, documentation, and pretrained models for 66 languages are available at https://stanfordnlp.github.io/stanza/.

1 Introduction

The growing availability of open-source natural language processing (NLP) toolkits has made it easier for users to build tools with sophisticated linguistic processing. While existing NLP toolkits such as CoreNLP (Manning et al., 2014), FLAIR (Akbik et al., 2019), spaCy[1], and UDPipe (Straka, 2018) have had wide usage, they also suffer from several limitations. First, existing toolkits often support only a few major languages. This has significantly limited the community's ability to process multilingual text. Second, widely used tools are sometimes under-optimized for accuracy either due to a focus on efficiency (*e.g.*, spaCy) or use of less powerful models (*e.g.*, CoreNLP), potentially mislead-

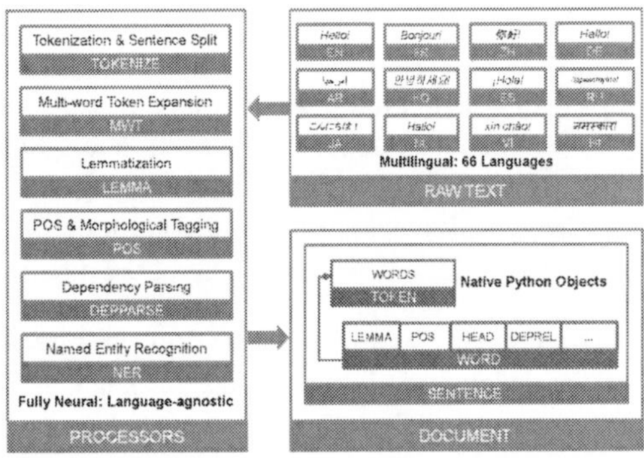

Figure 1: Overview of Stanza's neural NLP pipeline. Stanza takes multilingual text as input, and produces annotations accessible as native Python objects. Besides this neural pipeline, Stanza also features a Python client interface to the Java CoreNLP software.

ing downstream applications and insights obtained from them. Third, some tools assume input text has been tokenized or annotated with other tools, lacking the ability to process raw text within a unified framework. This has limited their wide applicability to text from diverse sources.

We introduce Stanza[2], a Python natural language processing toolkit supporting many human languages. As shown in Table 1, compared to existing widely-used NLP toolkits, Stanza has the following advantages:

- **From raw text to annotations.** Stanza features a fully neural pipeline which takes raw text as input, and produces annotations including tokenization, multi-word token expansion, lemmatization, part-of-speech and morphological feature tagging, dependency parsing, and named entity recognition.

- **Multilinguality.** Stanza's architectural design is language-agnostic and data-driven, which allows us to release models support-

---

*Equal contribution. Order decided by a tossed coin.
[1] https://spacy.io/

[2] The toolkit was called StanfordNLP prior to v1.0.0.

Proceedings of the 58th Annual Meeting of the Association for Computational Linguistics, pages 101–108
July 5 - July 10, 2020. ©2020 Association for Computational Linguistics

System	# Human Languages	Programming Language	Raw Text Processing	Fully Neural	Pretrained Models	State-of-the-art Performance
CoreNLP	6	Java	✓		✓	
FLAIR	12	Python		✓	✓	✓
spaCy	10	Python	✓		✓	
UDPipe	61	C++	✓		✓	✓
Stanza	66	Python	✓	✓	✓	✓

Table 1: Feature comparisons of Stanza against other popular natural language processing toolkits.

ing 66 languages, by training the pipeline on the Universal Dependencies (UD) treebanks and other multilingual corpora.

- **State-of-the-art performance.** We evaluate Stanza on a total of 112 datasets, and find its neural pipeline adapts well to text of different genres, achieving state-of-the-art or competitive performance at each step of the pipeline.

Additionally, Stanza features a Python interface to the widely used Java CoreNLP package, allowing access to additional tools such as coreference resolution and relation extraction.

Stanza is fully open source and we make pretrained models for all supported languages and datasets available for public download. We hope Stanza can facilitate multilingual NLP research and applications, and drive future research that produces insights from human languages.

2 System Design and Architecture

At the top level, Stanza consists of two individual components: (1) a fully neural multilingual NLP pipeline; (2) a Python client interface to the Java Stanford CoreNLP software. In this section we introduce their designs.

2.1 Neural Multilingual NLP Pipeline

Stanza's neural pipeline consists of models that range from tokenizing raw text to performing syntactic analysis on entire sentences (see Figure 1). All components are designed with processing many human languages in mind, with high-level design choices capturing common phenomena in many languages and data-driven models that learn the difference between these languages from data. Moreover, the implementation of Stanza components is highly modular, and reuses basic model architectures when possible for compactness. We highlight the important design choices here, and refer the reader to Qi et al. (2018) for modeling details.

| (fr) L'Association _des_ Hôtels |
| _(en) The Association of Hotels_ |
| (fr) Il y a _des_ hôtels en bas de la rue |
| _(en) There are hotels down the street_ |

Figure 2: An example of multi-word tokens in French. The _des_ in the first sentence corresponds to two syntactic words, _de_ and _les_; the second _des_ is a single word.

Tokenization and Sentence Splitting. When presented raw text, Stanza tokenizes it and groups tokens into sentences as the first step of processing. Unlike most existing toolkits, Stanza combines tokenization and sentence segmentation from raw text into a single module. This is modeled as a tagging problem over character sequences, where the model predicts whether a given character is the end of a token, end of a sentence, or end of a multi-word token (MWT, see Figure 2).[3] We choose to predict MWTs jointly with tokenization because this task is context-sensitive in some languages.

Multi-word Token Expansion. Once MWTs are identified by the tokenizer, they are expanded into the underlying syntactic words as the basis of downstream processing. This is achieved with an ensemble of a frequency lexicon and a neural sequence-to-sequence (seq2seq) model, to ensure that frequently observed expansions in the training set are always robustly expanded while maintaining flexibility to model unseen words statistically.

POS and Morphological Feature Tagging. For each word in a sentence, Stanza assigns it a part-of-speech (POS), and analyzes its universal morphological features (UFeats, _e.g._, singular/plural, $1^{st}/2^{nd}/3^{rd}$ person, etc.). To predict POS and UFeats, we adopt a bidirectional long short-term memory network (Bi-LSTM) as the basic architecture. For consistency among universal POS (UPOS),

---

[3]Following Universal Dependencies (Nivre et al., 2020), we make a distinction between _tokens_ (contiguous spans of characters in the input text) and syntactic _words_. These are interchangeable aside from the cases of MWTs, where one token can correspond to multiple words.

treebank-specific POS (XPOS), and UFeats, we adopt the biaffine scoring mechanism from Dozat and Manning (2017) to condition XPOS and UFeats prediction on that of UPOS.

Lemmatization. Stanza also lemmatizes each word in a sentence to recover its canonical form (*e.g.*, *did→do*). Similar to the multi-word token expander, Stanza's lemmatizer is implemented as an ensemble of a dictionary-based lemmatizer and a neural seq2seq lemmatizer. An additional classifier is built on the encoder output of the seq2seq model, to predict *shortcuts* such as lowercasing and identity copy for robustness on long input sequences such as URLs.

Dependency Parsing. Stanza parses each sentence for its syntactic structure, where each word in the sentence is assigned a syntactic head that is either another word in the sentence, or in the case of the root word, an artificial root symbol. We implement a Bi-LSTM-based deep biaffine neural dependency parser (Dozat and Manning, 2017). We further augment this model with two linguistically motivated features: one that predicts the *linearization* order of two words in a given language, and the other that predicts the typical distance in linear order between them. We have previously shown that these features significantly improve parsing accuracy (Qi et al., 2018).

Named Entity Recognition. For each input sentence, Stanza also recognizes named entities in it (*e.g.*, person names, organizations, etc.). For NER we adopt the contextualized string representation-based sequence tagger from Akbik et al. (2018). We first train a forward and a backward character-level LSTM language model, and at tagging time we concatenate the representations at the end of each word position from both language models with word embeddings, and feed the result into a standard one-layer Bi-LSTM sequence tagger with a conditional random field (CRF)-based decoder.

2.2 CoreNLP Client

Stanford's Java CoreNLP software provides a comprehensive set of NLP tools especially for the English language. However, these tools are not easily accessible with Python, the programming language of choice for many NLP practitioners, due to the lack of official support. To facilitate the use of CoreNLP from Python, we take advantage of the existing server interface in CoreNLP, and implement a robust client as its Python interface.

When the CoreNLP client is instantiated, Stanza will automatically start the CoreNLP server as a local process. The client then communicates with the server through its RESTful APIs, after which annotations are transmitted in Protocol Buffers, and converted back to native Python objects. Users can also specify JSON or XML as annotation format. To ensure robustness, while the client is being used, Stanza periodically checks the health of the server, and restarts it if necessary.

3 System Usage

Stanza's user interface is designed to allow quick out-of-the-box processing of multilingual text. To achieve this, Stanza supports automated model download via Python code and pipeline customization with processors of choice. Annotation results can be accessed as native Python objects to allow for flexible post-processing.

3.1 Neural Pipeline Interface

Stanza's neural NLP pipeline can be initialized with the `Pipeline` class, taking language name as an argument. By default, all processors will be loaded and run over the input text; however, users can also specify the processors to load and run with a list of processor names as an argument. Users can additionally specify other processor-level properties, such as batch sizes used by processors, at initialization time.

The following code snippet shows a minimal usage of Stanza for downloading the Chinese model, annotating a sentence with customized processors, and printing out all annotations:

```python
import stanza
# download Chinese model
stanza.download('zh')
# initialize Chinese neural pipeline
nlp = stanza.Pipeline('zh', processors='tokenize,
    pos,ner')
# run annotation over a sentence
doc = nlp('斯坦福是一所私立研究型大学。')
print(doc)
```

After all processors are run, a `Document` instance will be returned, which stores all annotation results. Within a `Document`, annotations are further stored in `Sentences`, `Tokens` and `Words` in a top-down fashion (Figure 1). The following code snippet demonstrates how to access the text and POS tag of each word in a document and all named entities in the document:

```
# print the text and POS of all words
for sentence in doc.sentences:
    for word in sentence.words:
        print(word.text, word.pos)

# print all entities in the document
print(doc.entities)
```

Stanza is designed to be run on different hardware devices. By default, CUDA devices will be used whenever they are visible by the pipeline, or otherwise CPUs will be used. However, users can force all computation to be run on CPUs by setting `use_gpu=False` at initialization time.

3.2 CoreNLP Client Interface

The CoreNLP client interface is designed in a way that the actual communication with the backend CoreNLP server is transparent to the user. To annotate an input text with the CoreNLP client, a `CoreNLPClient` instance needs to be initialized, with an optional list of CoreNLP annotators. After the annotation is complete, results will be accessible as native Python objects.

This code snippet shows how to establish a CoreNLP client and obtain the NER and coreference annotations of an English sentence:

```
from stanza.server import CoreNLPClient

# start a CoreNLP client
with CoreNLPClient(annotators=['tokenize','ssplit
    ','pos','lemma','ner','parse','coref']) as
    client:
    # run annotation over input
    ann = client.annotate('Emily said that she
    liked the movie.')
    # access all entities
    for sent in ann.sentence:
        print(sent.mentions)
    # access coreference annotations
    print(ann.corefChain)
```

With the client interface, users can annotate text in 6 languages as supported by CoreNLP.

3.3 Interactive Web-based Demo

To help visualize documents and their annotations generated by Stanza, we build an interactive web demo that runs the pipeline interactively. For all languages and all annotations Stanza provides in those languages, we generate predictions from the models trained on the largest treebank/NER dataset, and visualize the result with the Brat rapid annotation tool.[4] This demo runs in a client/server architecture, and annotation is performed on the server side. We make one instance of this demo publicly available at `http://stanza.run/`. It can also be run locally with proper Python libraries installed.

---

[4]`https://brat.nlplab.org/`

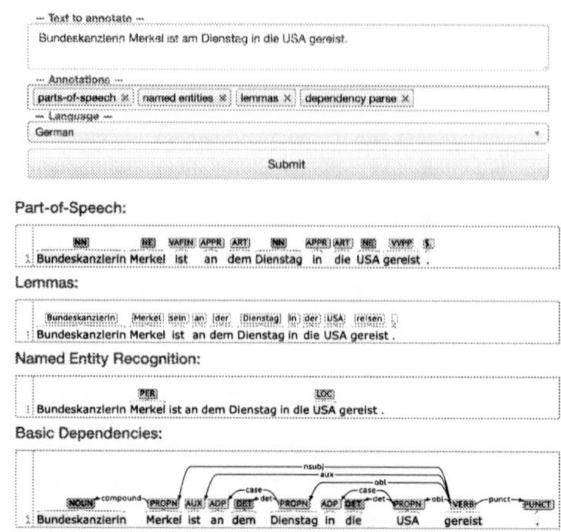

Figure 3: Stanza annotates a German sentence, as visualized by our interactive demo. Note *am* is expanded into syntactic words *an* and *dem* before downstream analyses are performed.

An example of running Stanza on a German sentence can be found in Figure 3.

3.4 Training Pipeline Models

For all neural processors, Stanza provides command-line interfaces for users to train their own customized models. To do this, users need to prepare the training and development data in compatible formats (i.e., CoNLL-U format for the Universal Dependencies pipeline and BIO format column files for the NER model). The following command trains a neural dependency parser with user-specified training and development data:

```
$ python -m stanza.models.parser \
    --train_file train.conllu \
    --eval_file dev.conllu \
    --gold_file dev.conllu \
    --output_file output.conllu
```

4 Performance Evaluation

To establish benchmark results and compare with other popular toolkits, we trained and evaluated Stanza on a total of 112 datasets. All pretrained models are publicly downloadable.

Datasets. We train and evaluate Stanza's tokenizer/sentence splitter, MWT expander, POS/UFeats tagger, lemmatizer, and dependency parser with the Universal Dependencies v2.5 treebanks (Zeman et al., 2019). For training we use 100 treebanks from this release that have non-copyrighted training data, and for treebanks that do not include development data, we randomly split out 20% of

Treebank	System	Tokens	Sents.	Words	UPOS	XPOS	UFeats	Lemmas	UAS	LAS
Overall (100 treebanks)	Stanza	99.09	86.05	98.63	92.49	91.80	89.93	92.78	80.45	75.68
Arabic-PADT	Stanza	**99.98**	80.43	**97.88**	**94.89**	**91.75**	**91.86**	**93.27**	**83.27**	**79.33**
	UDPipe	**99.98**	**82.09**	94.58	90.36	84.00	84.16	88.46	72.67	68.14
Chinese-GSD	Stanza	**92.83**	98.80	**92.83**	**89.12**	**88.93**	**92.11**	**92.83**	**72.88**	**69.82**
	UDPipe	90.27	**99.10**	90.27	84.13	84.04	89.05	90.26	61.60	57.81
English-EWT	Stanza	**99.01**	**81.13**	**99.01**	**95.40**	**95.12**	**96.11**	**97.21**	**86.22**	**83.59**
	UDPipe	98.90	77.40	98.90	93.26	92.75	94.23	95.45	80.22	77.03
	spaCy	97.30	61.19	97.30	86.72	90.83	–	87.05	–	–
French-GSD	Stanza	99.68	**94.92**	**99.48**	**97.30**	–	**96.72**	**97.64**	**91.38**	**89.05**
	UDPipe	99.68	93.59	98.81	95.85	–	95.55	96.61	87.14	84.26
	spaCy	98.34	77.30	94.15	86.82	–	–	87.29	67.46	60.60
Spanish-AnCora	Stanza	**99.98**	**99.07**	**99.98**	**98.78**	**98.67**	**98.59**	**99.19**	**92.21**	**90.01**
	UDPipe	99.97	98.32	99.95	98.32	98.13	98.13	98.48	88.22	85.10
	spaCy	99.47	97.59	98.95	94.04	–	–	79.63	86.63	84.13

Table 2: Neural pipeline performance comparisons on the Universal Dependencies (v2.5) test treebanks. For our system we show macro-averaged results over all 100 treebanks. We also compare our system against UDPipe and spaCy on treebanks of five major languages where the corresponding pretrained models are publicly available. All results are F_1 scores produced by the 2018 UD Shared Task official evaluation script.

the training data as development data. These treebanks represent 66 languages, mostly European languages, but spanning a diversity of language families, including Indo-European, Afro-Asiatic, Uralic, Turkic, Sino-Tibetan, etc. For NER, we train and evaluate Stanza with 12 publicly available datasets covering 8 major languages as shown in Table 3 (Nothman et al., 2013; Tjong Kim Sang and De Meulder, 2003; Tjong Kim Sang, 2002; Benikova et al., 2014; Mohit et al., 2012; Taulé et al., 2008; Weischedel et al., 2013). For the WikiNER corpora, as canonical splits are not available, we randomly split them into 70% training, 15% dev and 15% test splits. For all other corpora we used their canonical splits.

Training. On the Universal Dependencies treebanks, we tuned all hyper-parameters on several large treebanks and applied them to all other treebanks. We used the word2vec embeddings released as part of the 2018 UD Shared Task (Zeman et al., 2018), or the fastText embeddings (Bojanowski et al., 2017) whenever word2vec is not available. For the character-level language models in the NER component, we pretrained them on a mix of the Common Crawl and Wikipedia dumps, and the news corpora released by the WMT19 Shared Task (Barrault et al., 2019), except for English and Chinese, for which we pretrained on the Google One Billion Word (Chelba et al., 2013) and the Chi-

nese Gigaword corpora[5], respectively. We again applied the same hyper-parameters to models for all languages.

Universal Dependencies Results. For performance on UD treebanks, we compared Stanza (v1.0) against UDPipe (v1.2) and spaCy (v2.2) on treebanks of 5 major languages whenever a pretrained model is available. As shown in Table 2, Stanza achieved the best performance on most scores reported. Notably, we find that Stanza's language-agnostic architecture is able to adapt to datasets of different languages and genres. This is also shown by Stanza's high macro-averaged scores over 100 treebanks covering 66 languages.

NER Results. For performance of the NER component, we compared Stanza (v1.0) against FLAIR (v0.4.5) and spaCy (v2.2). For spaCy we reported results from its publicly available pretrained model whenever one trained on the same dataset can be found, otherwise we retrained its model on our datasets with default hyper-parameters, following the publicly available tutorial.[6] For FLAIR, since their downloadable models were pretrained

[5] https://catalog.ldc.upenn.edu/LDC2011T13

[6] https://spacy.io/usage/training#ner
Note that, following this public tutorial, we did not use pretrained word embeddings when training spaCy NER models, although using pretrained word embeddings may potentially improve the NER results.

Language	Corpus	# Types	Stanza	FLAIR	spaCy
Arabic	AQMAR	4	**74.3**	74.0	–
Chinese	OntoNotes	18	**79.2**	–	–
Dutch	CoNLL02	4	89.2	**90.3**	73.8
	WikiNER	4	**94.8**	**94.8**	90.9
English	CoNLL03	4	92.1	**92.7**	81.0
	OntoNotes	18	88.8	**89.0**	85.4*
French	WikiNER	4	**92.9**	92.5	88.8*
German	CoNLL03	4	81.9	**82.5**	63.9
	GermEval14	4	85.2	**85.4**	68.4
Russian	WikiNER	4	**92.9**	–	–
Spanish	CoNLL02	4	**88.1**	87.3	77.5
	AnCora	4	**88.6**	88.4	76.1

Table 3: NER performance across different languages and corpora. All scores reported are entity micro-averaged test F_1. For each corpus we also list the number of entity types. * marks results from publicly available pretrained models on the same dataset, while others are from models retrained on our datasets.

on dataset versions different from canonical ones, we retrained all models on our own dataset splits with their best reported hyper-parameters. All test results are shown in Table 3. We find that on all datasets Stanza achieved either higher or close F_1 scores when compared against FLAIR. When compared to spaCy, Stanza's NER performance is much better. It is worth noting that Stanza's high performance is achieved with much smaller models compared with FLAIR (up to 75% smaller), as we intentionally compressed the models for memory efficiency and ease of distribution.

Speed comparison. We compare Stanza against existing toolkits to evaluate the time it takes to annotate text (see Table 4). For GPU tests we use a single NVIDIA Titan RTX card. Unsurprisingly, Stanza's extensive use of accurate neural models makes it take significantly longer than spaCy to annotate text, but it is still competitive when compared against toolkits of similar accuracy, especially with the help of GPU acceleration.

5 Conclusion and Future Work

We introduced Stanza, a Python natural language processing toolkit supporting many human languages. We have showed that Stanza's neural pipeline not only has wide coverage of human languages, but also is accurate on all tasks, thanks to its language-agnostic, fully neural architectural design. Simultaneously, Stanza's CoreNLP client extends its functionality with additional NLP tools.

Task	Stanza		UDPipe	FLAIR	
	CPU	GPU	CPU	CPU	GPU
UD	10.3×	3.22×	4.30×	–	–
NER	17.7×	1.08×	–	51.8×	1.17×

Table 4: Annotation runtime of various toolkits relative to spaCy (CPU) on the English EWT treebank and OntoNotes NER test sets. For reference, on the compared UD and NER tasks, spaCy is able to process 8140 and 5912 tokens per second, respectively.

For future work, we consider the following areas of improvement in the near term:

- Models downloadable in Stanza are largely trained on a single dataset. To make models robust to many different genres of text, we would like to investigate the possibility of pooling various sources of compatible data to train "default" models for each language;

- The amount of computation and resources available to us is limited. We would therefore like to build an open "model zoo" for Stanza, so that researchers from outside our group can also contribute their models and benefit from models released by others;

- Stanza was designed to optimize for accuracy of its predictions, but this sometimes comes at the cost of computational efficiency and limits the toolkit's use. We would like to further investigate reducing model sizes and speeding up computation in the toolkit, while still maintaining the same level of accuracy.

- We would also like to expand Stanza's functionality by adding other processors such as neural coreference resolution or relation extraction for richer text analytics.

Acknowledgments

The authors would like to thank the anonymous reviewers for their comments, Arun Chaganty for his early contribution to this toolkit, Tim Dozat for his design of the original architectures of the tagger and parser models, Matthew Honnibal and Ines Montani for their help with spaCy integration and helpful comments on the draft, Ranting Guo for the logo design, and John Bauer and the community contributors for their help with maintaining and improving this toolkit. This research is funded in part by Samsung Electronics Co., Ltd. and in part by the SAIL-JD Research Initiative.

References

Alan Akbik, Tanja Bergmann, Duncan Blythe, Kashif Rasul, Stefan Schweter, and Roland Vollgraf. 2019. FLAIR: An easy-to-use framework for state-of-the-art NLP. In *Proceedings of the 2019 Conference of the North American Chapter of the Association for Computational Linguistics (Demonstrations)*. Association for Computational Linguistics.

Alan Akbik, Duncan Blythe, and Roland Vollgraf. 2018. Contextual string embeddings for sequence labeling. In *Proceedings of the 27th International Conference on Computational Linguistics*. Association for Computational Linguistics.

Loïc Barrault, Ondřej Bojar, Marta R. Costa-jussà, Christian Federmann, Mark Fishel, Yvette Graham, Barry Haddow, Matthias Huck, Philipp Koehn, Shervin Malmasi, Christof Monz, Mathias Müller, Santanu Pal, Matt Post, and Marcos Zampieri. 2019. Findings of the 2019 conference on machine translation (WMT19). In *Proceedings of the Fourth Conference on Machine Translation (Volume 2: Shared Task Papers, Day 1)*. Association for Computational Linguistics.

Darina Benikova, Chris Biemann, and Marc Reznicek. 2014. NoSta-D named entity annotation for German: Guidelines and dataset. In *Proceedings of the Ninth International Conference on Language Resources and Evaluation (LREC'14)*.

Piotr Bojanowski, Edouard Grave, Armand Joulin, and Tomas Mikolov. 2017. Enriching word vectors with subword information. *Transactions of the Association for Computational Linguistics*, 5.

Ciprian Chelba, Tomas Mikolov, Mike Schuster, Qi Ge, Thorsten Brants, Phillipp Koehn, and Tony Robinson. 2013. One billion word benchmark for measuring progress in statistical language modeling. Technical report, Google.

Timothy Dozat and Christopher D. Manning. 2017. Deep biaffine attention for neural dependency parsing. In *International Conference on Learning Representations (ICLR)*.

Christopher D. Manning, Mihai Surdeanu, John Bauer, Jenny Finkel, Steven J. Bethard, and David McClosky. 2014. The Stanford CoreNLP natural language processing toolkit. In *Association for Computational Linguistics (ACL) System Demonstrations*.

Behrang Mohit, Nathan Schneider, Rishav Bhowmick, Kemal Oflazer, and Noah A Smith. 2012. Recall-oriented learning of named entities in Arabic Wikipedia. In *Proceedings of the 13th Conference of the European Chapter of the Association for Computational Linguistics*. Association for Computational Linguistics.

Joakim Nivre, Marie-Catherine de Marneffe, Filip Ginter, Jan Hajič, Christopher D. Manning, Sampo Pyysalo, Sebastian Schuster, Francis Tyers, and

Daniel Zeman. 2020. Universal dependencies v2: An evergrowing multilingual treebank collection. In *Proceedings of the Twelfth International Conference on Language Resources and Evaluation (LREC'20)*.

Joel Nothman, Nicky Ringland, Will Radford, Tara Murphy, and James R Curran. 2013. Learning multilingual named entity recognition from Wikipedia. *Artificial Intelligence*, 194:151–175.

Peng Qi, Timothy Dozat, Yuhao Zhang, and Christopher D. Manning. 2018. Universal dependency parsing from scratch. In *Proceedings of the CoNLL 2018 Shared Task: Multilingual Parsing from Raw Text to Universal Dependencies*. Association for Computational Linguistics.

Milan Straka. 2018. UDPipe 2.0 prototype at CoNLL 2018 UD shared task. In *Proceedings of the CoNLL 2018 Shared Task: Multilingual Parsing from Raw Text to Universal Dependencies*. Association for Computational Linguistics.

Mariona Taulé, M. Antònia Martí, and Marta Recasens. 2008. AnCora: Multilevel annotated corpora for Catalan and Spanish. In *Proceedings of the Sixth International Conference on Language Resources and Evaluation (LREC'08)*. European Language Resources Association (ELRA).

Erik F. Tjong Kim Sang. 2002. Introduction to the CoNLL-2002 shared task: Language-independent named entity recognition. In *COLING-02: The 6th Conference on Natural Language Learning 2002 (CoNLL-2002)*.

Erik F. Tjong Kim Sang and Fien De Meulder. 2003. Introduction to the CoNLL-2003 shared task: Language-independent named entity recognition. In *Proceedings of the Seventh Conference on Natural Language Learning at HLT-NAACL 2003*.

Ralph Weischedel, Martha Palmer, Mitchell Marcus, Eduard Hovy, Sameer Pradhan, Lance Ramshaw, Nianwen Xue, Ann Taylor, Jeff Kaufman, Michelle Franchini, et al. 2013. OntoNotes release 5.0. *Linguistic Data Consortium*.

Daniel Zeman, Jan Hajič, Martin Popel, Martin Potthast, Milan Straka, Filip Ginter, Joakim Nivre, and Slav Petrov. 2018. CoNLL 2018 shared task: Multilingual parsing from raw text to universal dependencies. In *Proceedings of the CoNLL 2018 Shared Task: Multilingual Parsing from Raw Text to Universal Dependencies*. Association for Computational Linguistics.

Daniel Zeman, Joakim Nivre, Mitchell Abrams, Noëmi Aepli, Željko Agić, Lars Ahrenberg, Gabrielė Aleksandravičiūtė, Lene Antonsen, Katya Aplonova, Maria Jesus Aranzabe, Gashaw Arutie, Masayuki Asahara, Luma Ateyah, Mohammed Attia, Aitziber Atutxa, Liesbeth Augustinus, Elena Badmaeva, Miguel Ballesteros, Esha Banerjee, Sebastian Bank, Verginica Barbu Mititelu, Victoria Basmov, Colin

Batchelor, John Bauer, Sandra Bellato, Kepa Bengoetxea, Yevgeni Berzak, Irshad Ahmad Bhat, Riyaz Ahmad Bhat, Erica Biagetti, Eckhard Bick, Agnė Bielinskienė, Rogier Blokland, Victoria Bobicev, Loïc Boizou, Emanuel Borges Völker, Carl Börstell, Cristina Bosco, Gosse Bouma, Sam Bowman, Adriane Boyd, Kristina Brokaitė, Aljoscha Burchardt, Marie Candito, Bernard Caron, Gauthier Caron, Tatiana Cavalcanti, Gülşen Cebiroğlu Eryiğit, Flavio Massimiliano Cecchini, Giuseppe G. A. Celano, Slavomír Čéplö, Savas Cetin, Fabricio Chalub, Jinho Choi, Yongseok Cho, Jayeol Chun, Alessandra T. Cignarella, Silvie Cinková, Aurélie Collomb, Çağrı Çöltekin, Miriam Connor, Marine Courtin, Elizabeth Davidson, Marie-Catherine de Marneffe, Valeria de Paiva, Elvis de Souza, Arantza Diaz de Ilarraza, Carly Dickerson, Bamba Dione, Peter Dirix, Kaja Dobrovoljc, Timothy Dozat, Kira Droganova, Puneet Dwivedi, Hanne Eckhoff, Marhaba Eli, Ali Elkahky, Binyam Ephrem, Olga Erina, Tomaž Erjavec, Aline Etienne, Wograine Evelyn, Richárd Farkas, Hector Fernandez Alcalde, Jennifer Foster, Cláudia Freitas, Kazunori Fujita, Katarína Gajdošová, Daniel Galbraith, Marcos Garcia, Moa Gärdenfors, Sebastian Garza, Kim Gerdes, Filip Ginter, Iakes Goenaga, Koldo Gojenola, Memduh Gökırmak, Yoav Goldberg, Xavier Gómez Guinovart, Berta González Saavedra, Bernadeta Griciūtė, Matias Grioni, Normunds Grūzītis, Bruno Guillaume, Céline Guillot-Barbance, Nizar Habash, Jan Hajič, Jan Hajič jr., Mika Hämäläinen, Linh Hà Mỹ, Na-Rae Han, Kim Harris, Dag Haug, Johannes Heinecke, Felix Hennig, Barbora Hladká, Jaroslava Hlaváčová, Florinel Hociung, Petter Hohle, Jena Hwang, Takumi Ikeda, Radu Ion, Elena Irimia, Ọlájídé Ishola, Tomáš Jelínek, Anders Johannsen, Fredrik Jørgensen, Markus Juutinen, Hüner Kaşıkara, Andre Kaasen, Nadezhda Kabaeva, Sylvain Kahane, Hiroshi Kanayama, Jenna Kanerva, Boris Katz, Tolga Kayadelen, Jessica Kenney, Václava Kettnerová, Jesse Kirchner, Elena Klementieva, Arne Köhn, Kamil Kopacewicz, Natalia Kotsyba, Jolanta Kovalevskaitė, Simon Krek, Sookyoung Kwak, Veronika Laippala, Lorenzo Lambertino, Lucia Lam, Tatiana Lando, Septina Dian Larasati, Alexei Lavrentiev, John Lee, Phương Lê Hồng, Alessandro Lenci, Saran Lertpradit, Herman Leung, Cheuk Ying Li, Josie Li, Keying Li, KyungTae Lim, Maria Liovina, Yuan Li, Nikola Ljubešić, Olga Loginova, Olga Lyashevskaya, Teresa Lynn, Vivien Macketanz, Aibek Makazhanov, Michael Mandl, Christopher Manning, Ruli Manurung, Cătălina Mărănduc, David Mareček, Katrin Marheinecke, Héctor Martínez Alonso, André Martins, Jan Mašek, Yuji Matsumoto, Ryan McDonald, Sarah McGuinness, Gustavo Mendonça, Niko Miekka, Margarita Misirpashayeva, Anna Missilä, Cătălin Mititelu, Maria Mitrofan, Yusuke Miyao, Simonetta Montemagni, Amir More, Laura Moreno Romero, Keiko Sophie Mori, Tomohiko Morioka, Shinsuke Mori, Shigeki Moro, Bjartur Mortensen, Bohdan Moskalevskyi, Kadri Muischnek, Robert Munro, Yugo Murawaki, Kaili Müürisep, Pinkey Nainwani, Juan Ignacio Navarro Horñiacek, Anna Nedoluzhko, Gunta Nešpore-Bērzkalne, Lương Nguyễn Thị, Huyền Nguyễn Thị Minh, Yoshihiro Nikaido, Vitaly Nikolaev, Rattima Nitisaroj, Hanna Nurmi, Stina Ojala, Atul Kr. Ojha, Adédayọ Olúòkun, Mai Omura, Petya Osenova, Robert Östling, Lilja Øvrelid, Niko Partanen, Elena Pascual, Marco Passarotti, Agnieszka Patejuk, Guilherme Paulino-Passos, Angelika Peljak-Łapińska, Siyao Peng, Cenel-Augusto Perez, Guy Perrier, Daria Petrova, Slav Petrov, Jason Phelan, Jussi Piitulainen, Tommi A Pirinen, Emily Pitler, Barbara Plank, Thierry Poibeau, Larisa Ponomareva, Martin Popel, Lauma Pretkalniņa, Sophie Prévost, Prokopis Prokopidis, Adam Przepiórkowski, Tiina Puolakainen, Sampo Pyysalo, Peng Qi, Andriela Rääbis, Alexandre Rademaker, Loganathan Ramasamy, Taraka Rama, Carlos Ramisch, Vinit Ravishankar, Livy Real, Siva Reddy, Georg Rehm, Ivan Riabov, Michael Rießler, Erika Rimkutė, Larissa Rinaldi, Laura Rituma, Luisa Rocha, Mykhailo Romanenko, Rudolf Rosa, Davide Rovati, Valentin Rosca, Olga Rudina, Jack Rueter, Shoval Sadde, Benoît Sagot, Shadi Saleh, Alessio Salomoni, Tanja Samardžić, Stephanie Samson, Manuela Sanguinetti, Dage Särg, Baiba Saulīte, Yanin Sawanakunanon, Nathan Schneider, Sebastian Schuster, Djamé Seddah, Wolfgang Seeker, Mojgan Seraji, Mo Shen, Atsuko Shimada, Hiroyuki Shirasu, Muh Shohibussirri, Dmitry Sichinava, Aline Silveira, Natalia Silveira, Maria Simi, Radu Simionescu, Katalin Simkó, Mária Šimková, Kiril Simov, Aaron Smith, Isabela Soares-Bastos, Carolyn Spadine, Antonio Stella, Milan Straka, Jana Strnadová, Alane Suhr, Umut Sulubacak, Shingo Suzuki, Zsolt Szántó, Dima Taji, Yuta Takahashi, Fabio Tamburini, Takaaki Tanaka, Isabelle Tellier, Guillaume Thomas, Liisi Torga, Trond Trosterud, Anna Trukhina, Reut Tsarfaty, Francis Tyers, Sumire Uematsu, Zdeňka Urešová, Larraitz Uria, Hans Uszkoreit, Andrius Utka, Sowmya Vajjala, Daniel van Niekerk, Gertjan van Noord, Viktor Varga, Eric Villemonte de la Clergerie, Veronika Vincze, Lars Wallin, Abigail Walsh, Jing Xian Wang, Jonathan North Washington, Maximilan Wendt, Seyi Williams, Mats Wirén, Christian Wittern, Tsegay Woldemariam, Tak-sum Wong, Alina Wróblewska, Mary Yako, Naoki Yamazaki, Chunxiao Yan, Koichi Yasuoka, Marat M. Yavrumyan, Zhuoran Yu, Zdeněk Žabokrtský, Amir Zeldes, Manying Zhang, and Hanzhi Zhu. 2019. Universal Dependencies 2.5. LINDAT/CLARIAH-CZ digital library at the Institute of Formal and Applied Linguistics (ÚFAL), Faculty of Mathematics and Physics, Charles University.

`jiant`: A Software Toolkit for Research on General-Purpose Text Understanding Models

Yada Pruksachatkun,[1][*] Phil Yeres,[1][*] Haokun Liu,[1] Jason Phang,[1]
Phu Mon Htut,[1] Alex Wang,[1] Ian Tenney,[2] Samuel R. Bowman[1]

[1]New York University, [2]Google Research

{yp913,bowman}@nyu.edu

Abstract

We introduce `jiant`, an open source toolkit for conducting multitask and transfer learning experiments on English NLU tasks. `jiant` enables modular and configuration-driven experimentation with state-of-the-art models and implements a broad set of tasks for probing, transfer learning, and multitask training experiments. `jiant` implements over 50 NLU tasks, including all GLUE and SuperGLUE benchmark tasks. We demonstrate that `jiant` reproduces published performance on a variety of tasks and models, including BERT and RoBERTa. `jiant` is available at `https://jiant.info`.

1 Introduction

This paper introduces `jiant`,[1] an open source toolkit that allows researchers to quickly experiment on a wide array of NLU tasks, using state-of-the-art NLP models, and conduct experiments on probing, transfer learning, and multitask training. `jiant` supports many state-of-the-art Transformer-based models implemented by Huggingface's Transformers package, as well as non-Transformer models such as BiLSTMs.

Packages and libraries like HuggingFace's Transformers (Wolf et al., 2019) and AllenNLP (Gardner et al., 2017) have accelerated the process of experimenting and iterating on NLP models by both abstracting out implementation details, and simplifying the model training pipeline. `jiant` extends the capabilities of both toolkits by presenting a wrapper that implements a variety of complex experimental pipelines in a scalable and easily controllable setting. `jiant` contains a task bank of over 50 tasks, including all the tasks presented in GLUE (Wang et al., 2018), SuperGLUE (Wang

et al., 2019b), the edge-probing suite (Tenney et al., 2019b), and the SentEval probing suite (Conneau and Kiela, 2018), as well as other individual tasks including CCG supertagging (Hockenmaier and Steedman, 2007), SocialIQA (Sap et al., 2019), and CommonsenseQA (Talmor et al., 2019). `jiant` is also the official baseline codebase for the SuperGLUE benchmark.

`jiant`'s core design principles are:

- Ease of use: `jiant` should allow users to run a variety of experiments using state-of-the-art models via an easy to use configuration-driven interface.

- Reproducibility: `jiant` should provide features that support correct and reproducible experiments, including logging and saving and restoring model state.

- Availability of NLU tasks: `jiant` should maintain and continue to grow a collection of tasks useful for NLU research, especially popular evaluation tasks and tasks commonly used in pretraining and transfer learning.

- Availability of cutting-edge models: `jiant` should make implementations of state-of-the-art models available for experimentation.

- Open source: `jiant` should be free to use, and easy to contribute to.

Early versions of `jiant` have already been used in multiple works, including probing analyses (Tenney et al., 2019b,a; Warstadt et al., 2019; Lin et al., 2019; Hewitt and Manning, 2019; Jawahar et al., 2019), transfer learning experiments (Wang et al., 2019a; Phang et al., 2018), and dataset and benchmark construction (Wang et al., 2019b, 2018; Kim et al., 2019).

---

[*]Equal contribution.

[1]The name `jiant` stands for "`jiant` is an NLP toolkit".

Proceedings of the 58th Annual Meeting of the Association for Computational Linguistics, pages 109–117
July 5 - July 10, 2020. ©2020 Association for Computational Linguistics

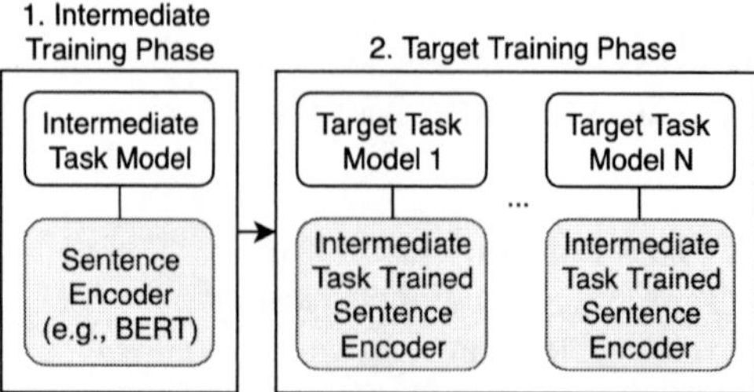

Figure 1: Multi-phase `jiant` experiment configuration used by Wang et al. (2019a): a BERT sentence encoder is trained with an intermediate task model during `jiant`'s intermediate training phase, and fine-tuned with various target task models in `jiant`'s target training phase.

2   Background

Transfer learning is an area of research that uses knowledge from pretrained models to transfer to new tasks. In recent years, Transformer-based models like BERT (Devlin et al., 2019) and T5 (Raffel et al., 2019) have yielded state-of-the-art results on the lion's share of benchmark tasks for language understanding through pretraining and transfer, often paired with some form of multitask learning.

`jiant` enables a variety of complex training pipelines through simple configuration changes, including multi-task training (Caruana, 1993; Liu et al., 2019a) and pretraining, as well as the sequential fine-tuning approach from STILTs (Phang et al., 2018). In STILTs, intermediate task training takes a pretrained model like ELMo or BERT, and applies supplementary training on a set of intermediate tasks, before finally performing single-task training on additional downstream tasks.

3   `jiant` System Overview

3.1   Requirements and Deployment

`jiant` can be cloned and installed from GitHub: `https://github.com/nyu-mll/jiant`. `jiant` v1.3.0 requires Python 3.5 or later, and `jiant`'s core dependencies are PyTorch (Paszke et al., 2019), AllenNLP (Gardner et al., 2017), and HuggingFace's Transformers (Wolf et al., 2019). `jiant` is released under the MIT License (Open Source Initiative, 2020). `jiant` runs on consumer-grade hardware or in cluster environments with or without CUDA GPUs. The `jiant` repository also contains documentation and configuration files demonstrating how to deploy `jiant` in Kubernetes clusters on Google Kubernetes Engine.

3.2   `jiant` Components

- **Tasks**: Tasks have references to task data, methods for processing data, references to classifier heads, and methods for calculating performance metrics, and making predictions.

- **Sentence Encoder**: Sentence encoders map from the indexed examples to a sentence-level representation. Sentence encoders can include an input module (e.g., Transformer models, ELMo, or word embeddings), followed by an optional second layer of encoding (usually a BiLSTM). Examples of possible sentence encoder configurations include BERT, ELMo followed by a BiLSTM, BERT with a variety of pooling and aggregation methods, or a bag of words model.

- **Task-Specific Output Heads**: Task-specific output modules map representations from sentence encoders to outputs specific to a task, e.g. entailment/neutral/contradiction for NLI tasks, or tags for part-of-speech tagging. They also include logic for computing the corresponding loss for training (e.g. cross-entropy).

- **Trainer**: Trainers manage the control flow for the training and validation loop for experiments. They sample batches from one or more tasks, perform forward and backward passes, calculate training metrics, evaluate on a validation set, and save checkpoints. Users can specify experiment-specific parameters such as learning rate, batch size, and more.

- **Config**: Config files or flags are defined in HOCON[2] format. Configs specify parameters for `jiant` experiments including choices of tasks, sentence encoder, and training routine.[3]

Configs are `jiant`'s primary user interface. Tasks and modeling components are designed to be modular, while `jiant`'s pipeline is a monolithic, configuration-driven design intended to facilitate a number of common workflows outlined in 3.3.

3.3   `jiant` Pipeline Overview

`jiant`'s core pipeline consists of the five stages described below and illustrated in Figure 2:

---

[2] Human-Optimized Config Object Notation (lightbend, 2011). `jiant` uses HOCON's logic to consolidate multiple config files and command-line overrides into a single run config.

[3] `jiant` configs support multi-phase training routines as described in section 3.3 and illustrated in Figure 2.

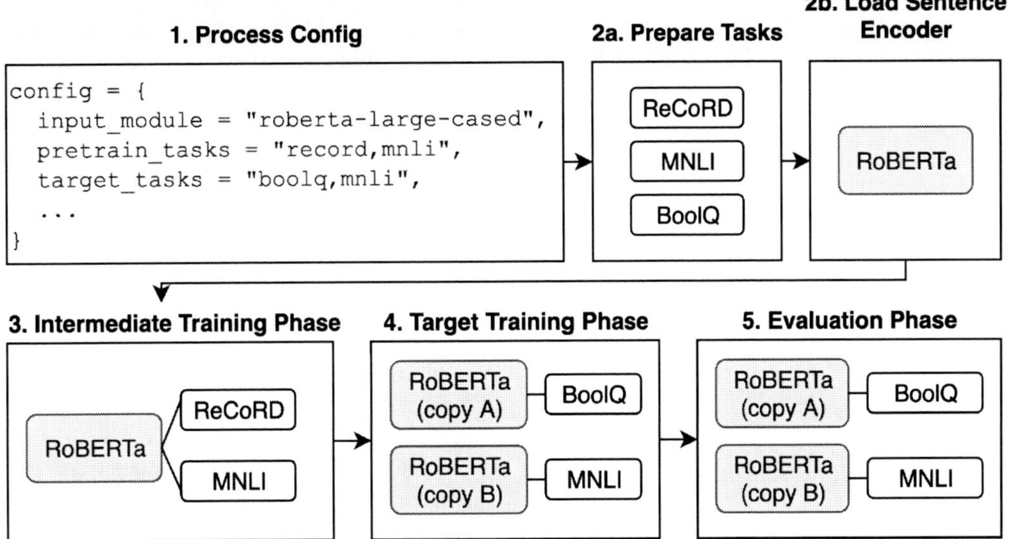

Figure 2: `jiant` pipeline stages using RoBERTa as the sentence encoder, ReCoRD and MNLI tasks as intermediate tasks, and MNLI and BoolQ as tasks for target training and evaluation. The diagram highlights that during target training and evaluation phases, copies are made of the sentence encoder model, and fine tuning and evaluation for each task are conducted on separate copies.

1. A config or multiple configs defining an experiment are interpreted. Users can choose and configure models, tasks, and stages of training and evaluation.

2. The tasks and sentence encoder are prepared:

   (a) The task data is loaded, tokenized, and indexed, and the preprocessed task objects are serialized and cached. In this process, AllenNLP is used to create the vocabulary and index the tokenized data.

   (b) The sentence encoder is constructed and (optionally) pretrained weights are loaded.[4]

   (c) The task-specific output heads are created for each task, and task heads are attached to a common sentence encoder. Optionally, different tasks can share the same output head, as in Liu et al. (2019a).

3. Optionally, in the intermediate phase the trainer samples batches randomly from one or more tasks,[5] and trains the shared model.

4. Optionally, in the target training phase, a copy of the model is configured and trained or fine-tuned for each target task separately.

5. Optionally, the model is evaluated on the validation and/or test sets of the target tasks.

3.4 Task and Model resources in `jiant`

`jiant` supports over 50 tasks. Task types include classification, regression, sequence generation, tagging, masked language modeling, and span prediction. `jiant` focuses on NLU tasks like MNLI (Williams et al., 2018), CommonsenseQA (Talmor et al., 2019), the Winograd Schema Challenge (Levesque et al., 2012), and SQuAD (Rajpurkar et al., 2016). A full inventory of tasks and task variants is available in the `jiant/tasks` module.

`jiant` provides support for cutting-edge sentence encoder models, including support for Huggingface's Transformers. Supported models include: ELMo (Peters et al., 2018), GPT (Radford, 2018), BERT (Devlin et al., 2019), XLM (Conneau and Lample, 2019), GPT-2 (Radford et al., 2019), XLNet (Yang et al., 2019), RoBERTa (Liu et al., 2019b), and ALBERT (Lan et al., 2019). `jiant` also supports the from-scratch training of (bidirectional) LSTMs (Hochreiter and Schmidhuber, 1997) and deep bag of words models (Iyyer et al., 2015), as well as syntax-aware models such

---

[4] The sentence encoder's weights can optionally be left frozen, or be included in the training procedure.

[5] Tasks can be sampled using a variety of sample weighting methods, e.g., uniform or proportional to the tasks' number of training batches or examples.

```
// Config for BERT experiments.

// Get default configs from a file:
include "defaults.conf"
exp_name = "bert-large-cased"

// Data and preprocessing settings
max_seq_len = 256

// Model settings
input_module = "bert-large-cased"
transformers_output_mode = "top"
s2s = {
    attention = none
}
sent_enc = "none"
sep_embs_for_skip = 1
classifier = log_reg
// fine-tune entire BERT model
transfer_paradigm = finetune

// Training settings
dropout = 0.1
optimizer = bert_adam
batch_size = 4
max_epochs = 10
lr = .00001
min_lr = .0000001
lr_patience = 4
patience = 20
max_vals = 10000

// Phase configuration
do_pretrain = 1
do_target_task_training = 1
do_full_eval = 1
write_preds = "val,test"
write_strict_glue_format = 1

// Task specific configuration
commitbank = {
    val_interval = 60
    max_epochs = 40
}
```

Figure 3: Example `jiant` experiment config file.

as PRPN (Shen et al., 2018) and ON-LSTM (Shen et al., 2019). `jiant` also supports word embeddings such as GloVe (Pennington et al., 2014).

3.5 User Interface

`jiant` experiments can be run with a simple CLI:

```
python -m jiant \
  --config_file roberta_with_mnli.conf \
  --overrides "target_tasks = swag, \
            run_name = swag_01"
```

`jiant` provides default config files that allow running many experiments without modifying source code.

`jiant` also provides baseline config files that can serve as a starting point for model development

and evaluation against GLUE (Wang et al., 2018) and SuperGLUE (Wang et al., 2019b) benchmarks.

More advanced configurations can be developed by composing multiple configurations files and overrides. Figure 3 shows a config file that overrides a default config, defining an experiment that uses BERT as the sentence encoder. This config includes an example of a task-specific configuration, which can be overridden in another config file or via a command line override.

Because `jiant` implements the option to provide command line overrides with a flag, it is easy to write scripts that launch `jiant` experiments over a range of parameters, for example while performing grid search across hyperparameters. `jiant` users have successfully run large-scale experiments launching hundreds of runs on both Kubernetes and Slurm.

3.6 Example `jiant` Use Cases and Options

Here we highlight some example use cases and key corresponding `jiant` config options required in these experiments:

- Fine-tune BERT on SWAG (Zellers et al., 2018) and SQUAD (Rajpurkar et al., 2016), then fine-tune on HellaSwag (Zellers et al., 2019):
  ```
  input_module = bert-base-cased
  pretrain_tasks = "swag,squad"
  target_tasks = hellaswag
  ```

- Train a probing classifier over a frozen BERT model, as in Tenney et al. (2019a):
  ```
  input_module = bert-base-cased
  target_tasks = edges-dpr
  transfer_paradigm = frozen
  ```

- Compare performance of GloVe (Pennington et al., 2014) embeddings using a BiLSTM:
  ```
  input_module = glove
  sent_enc = rnn
  ```

- Evaluate ALBERT (Lan et al., 2019) on the MNLI (Williams et al., 2018) task:
  ```
  input_module = albert-large-v2
  target_task = mnli
  ```

3.7 Optimizations and Other Features

`jiant` implements features that improve run stability and efficiency:

- `jiant` implements checkpointing options designed to offer efficient early stopping and to show consistent behavior when restarting after an interruption.

- `jiant` caches preprocessed task data to speed up reuse across experiments which share common data resources and artifacts.

- `jiant` implements gradient accumulation and multi-GPU, which enables training on larger batches than can fit in memory for a single GPU.

- `jiant` supports outputting predictions in a format ready for GLUE and SuperGLUE benchmark submission.

- `jiant` generates custom log files that capture experimental configurations, training and evaluation metrics, and relevant run-time information.

- `jiant` generates TensorBoard event files (Abadi et al., 2015) for training and evaluation metric tracking. TensorBoard event files can be visualized using the TensorBoard Scalars Dashboard.

3.8 Extensibility

`jiant`'s design offers conveniences that reduce the need to modify code when making changes:

- `jiant`'s task registry makes it easy to define a new version of an existing task using different data. Once the new task is defined in the task registry, the task is available as an option in `jiant`'s config.

- `jiant`'s sentence encoder and task output head abstractions allow for easy support of new sentence encoders.

In use cases requiring the introduction of a new task, users can use class inheritance to build on a number of available parent task types including classification, tagging, span prediction, span classification, sequence generation, regression, ranking, and multiple choice task classes. For these task types, corresponding task-specific output heads are already implemented.

More than 30 researchers and developers from more than 5 institutions have contributed code to the `jiant` project.[6] `jiant`'s maintainers welcome pull requests that introduce new tasks or sentence encoder components, and pull request are actively reviewed. The `jiant` repository's continuous integration system requires that all pull requests pass unit and integration tests and meet Black[7] code formatting requirements.

3.9 Limitations and Development Roadmap

While `jiant` is quite flexible in the pipelines that can be specified through configs, and some components are highly modular (e.g., tasks, sentence encoders, and output heads), modification of the pipeline code can be difficult. For example, training in more than two phases would require modifying the trainer code.[8] Making multi-stage training configurations more flexible is on `jiant`'s development roadmap.

`jiant`'s development roadmap prioritizes adding support for new Transformer models, and adding tasks that are commonly used for pretraining and evaluation in NLU. Additionally, there are plans to make `jiant`'s training phase configuration options more flexible to allow training in more than two phases, and to continue to refactor `jiant`'s code to keep `jiant` flexible to track developments in NLU research.

4 Benchmark Experiments

To benchmark `jiant`, we perform a set of experiments that reproduce external results for single fine-tuning and transfer learning experiments. `jiant` has been benchmarked extensively in both published and ongoing work on a majority of the implemented tasks.

We benchmark single-task fine-tuning configurations using CommonsenseQA (Talmor et al., 2019) and SocialIQA (Sap et al., 2019). On CommonsenseQA with RoBERTa$_{\text{LARGE}}$, `jiant` achieves an accuracy of 72.2, comparable to 72.1 reported by Liu et al. (2019b). On SocialIQA with BERT-large, `jiant` achieves a dev set accuracy of 65.8, comparable to 66.0 reported in Sap et al. (2019).

Next, we benchmark `jiant`'s transfer learning regime. We perform transfer experiments from MNLI to BoolQ with BERT-large. In this configuration Clark et al. (2019) demonstrated an accuracy improvement of 78.1 to 82.2 on the dev set, and `jiant` achieves an improvement of 78.1 to 80.3.

---

[7]`https://github.com/psf/black`

[8]While not supported by config options, training in more than two phases is possible by using `jiant`'s checkpointing features to reload models for additional rounds of training.

5   Conclusion

`jiant` provides a configuration-driven interface for defining transfer learning and representation learning experiments using a bank of over 50 NLU tasks, cutting-edge sentence encoder models, and multi-task and multi-stage training procedures. Further, `jiant` is shown to be able to replicate published performance on various NLU tasks.

`jiant`'s modular design of task and sentence encoder components make it possible for users to quickly and easily experiment with a large number of tasks, models, and parameter configurations, without editing source code. `jiant`'s design also makes it easy to add new tasks, and `jiant`'s architecture makes it convenient to extend `jiant` to support new sentence encoders.

`jiant` code is open source, and `jiant` invites contributors to open issues or submit pull request to the `jiant` project repository: `https://github.com/nyu-mll/jiant`.

Acknowledgments

Katherin Yu, Jan Hula, Patrick Xia, Raghu Pappagari, Shuning Jin, R. Thomas McCoy, Roma Patel, Yinghui Huang, Edouard Grave, Najoung Kim, Thibault Févry, Berlin Chen, Nikita Nangia, Anhad Mohananey, Katharina Kann, Shikha Bordia, Nicolas Patry, David Benton, and Ellie Pavlick have contributed substantial engineering assistance to the project.

The early development of `jiant` took at the 2018 Frederick Jelinek Memorial Summer Workshop on Speech and Language Technologies, and was supported by Johns Hopkins University with unrestricted gifts from Amazon, Facebook, Google, Microsoft and Mitsubishi Electric Research Laboratories.

Subsequent development was possible in part by a donation to NYU from Eric and Wendy Schmidt made by recommendation of the Schmidt Futures program, by support from Intuit Inc., and by support from Samsung Research under the project *Improving Deep Learning using Latent Structure*. We gratefully acknowledge the support of NVIDIA Corporation with the donation of a Titan V GPU used at NYU in this work. Alex Wang's work on the project is supported by the National Science Foundation Graduate Research Fellowship Program under Grant No. DGE 1342536. Any opinions, findings, and conclusions or recommendations expressed in this material are those of the author(s) and do not necessarily reflect the views of the National Science Foundation. Yada Pruksachatkun's work on the project is supported in part by the Moore-Sloan Data Science Environment as part of the NYU Data Science Services initiative. Sam Bowman's work on `jiant` during Summer 2019 took place in his capacity as a visiting researcher at Google.

References

Martín Abadi, Ashish Agarwal, Paul Barham, Eugene Brevdo, Zhifeng Chen, Craig Citro, Greg S. Corrado, Andy Davis, Jeffrey Dean, Matthieu Devin, Sanjay Ghemawat, Ian Goodfellow, Andrew Harp, Geoffrey Irving, Michael Isard, Yangqing Jia, Rafal Jozefowicz, Lukasz Kaiser, Manjunath Kudlur, Josh Levenberg, Dandelion Mané, Rajat Monga, Sherry Moore, Derek Murray, Chris Olah, Mike Schuster, Jonathon Shlens, Benoit Steiner, Ilya Sutskever, Kunal Talwar, Paul Tucker, Vincent Vanhoucke, Vijay Vasudevan, Fernanda Viégas, Oriol Vinyals, Pete Warden, Martin Wattenberg, Martin Wicke, Yuan Yu, and Xiaoqiang Zheng. 2015. TensorFlow: Large-scale machine learning on heterogeneous systems. Software available from tensorflow.org.

Rich Caruana. 1993. Multitask learning: A knowledge-based source of inductive bias. In *ICML*.

Christopher Clark, Kenton Lee, Ming-Wei Chang, Tom Kwiatkowski, Michael Collins, and Kristina Toutanova. 2019. BoolQ: Exploring the surprising difficulty of natural yes/no questions. In *Proceedings of the 2019 Conference of the North American Chapter of the Association for Computational Linguistics: Human Language Technologies, Volume 1 (Long and Short Papers)*, pages 2924–2936, Minneapolis, Minnesota. Association for Computational Linguistics.

Alexis Conneau and Douwe Kiela. 2018. SentEval: An evaluation toolkit for universal sentence representations. In *Proceedings of the Eleventh International Conference on Language Resources and Evaluation (LREC-2018)*, Miyazaki, Japan. European Languages Resources Association (ELRA).

Alexis Conneau and Guillaume Lample. 2019. Cross-lingual language model pretraining. In *Advances in Neural Information Processing Systems 32*, pages 7057–7067.

Jacob Devlin, Ming-Wei Chang, Kenton Lee, and Kristina Toutanova. 2019. BERT: Pre-training of deep bidirectional transformers for language understanding. In *Proceedings of the 2019 Conference of the North American Chapter of the Association for Computational Linguistics: Human Language Technologies, Volume 1 (Long and Short Papers)*, pages 4171–4186, Minneapolis, Minnesota. Association for Computational Linguistics.

Matt Gardner, Joel Grus, Mark Neumann, Oyvind Tafjord, Pradeep Dasigi, Nelson F. Liu, Matthew Peters, Michael Schmitz, and Luke S. Zettlemoyer. 2017. AllenNLP: A deep semantic natural language processing platform. Unpublished manuscript available on arXiv.

John Hewitt and Christopher D. Manning. 2019. A structural probe for finding syntax in word representations. In *Proceedings of the 2019 Conference of the North American Chapter of the Association for Computational Linguistics: Human Language Technologies, Volume 1 (Long and Short Papers)*, pages 4129–4138, Minneapolis, Minnesota. Association for Computational Linguistics.

Sepp Hochreiter and Jürgen Schmidhuber. 1997. Long short-term memory. *Neural computation*, 9(8):1735–1780.

Julia Hockenmaier and Mark Steedman. 2007. CCG-bank: A corpus of CCG derivations and dependency structures extracted from the Penn treebank. *Computational Linguistics*, 33(3):355–396.

Mohit Iyyer, Varun Manjunatha, Jordan Boyd-Graber, and Hal Daumé III. 2015. Deep unordered composition rivals syntactic methods for text classification. In *Proceedings of the 53rd Annual Meeting of the Association for Computational Linguistics and the 7th International Joint Conference on Natural Language Processing (Volume 1: Long Papers)*, pages 1681–1691, Beijing, China. Association for Computational Linguistics.

Ganesh Jawahar, Benoît Sagot, and Djamé Seddah. 2019. What does BERT learn about the structure of language? In *Proceedings of the 57th Annual Meeting of the Association for Computational Linguistics*, pages 3651–3657, Florence, Italy. Association for Computational Linguistics.

Najoung Kim, Roma Patel, Adam Poliak, Patrick Xia, Alex Wang, Tom McCoy, Ian Tenney, Alexis Ross, Tal Linzen, Benjamin Van Durme, Samuel R. Bowman, and Ellie Pavlick. 2019. Probing what different NLP tasks teach machines about function word comprehension. In *Proceedings of the Eighth Joint Conference on Lexical and Computational Semantics (*SEM 2019)*, pages 235–249, Minneapolis, Minnesota. Association for Computational Linguistics.

Zhenzhong Lan, Mingda Chen, Sebastian Goodman, Kevin Gimpel, Piyush Sharma, and Radu Soricut. 2019. ALBERT: A lite BERT for self-supervised learning of language representations.

Hector J. Levesque, Ernest Davis, and Leora Morgenstern. 2012. The Winograd schema challenge. In *Proceedings of the Thirteenth International Conference on Principles of Knowledge Representation and Reasoning*, KR'12, pages 552–561. AAAI Press.

lightbend. 2011. HOCON (human-optimized config object notation). `https://github.com/lightbend/config/blob/master/HOCON.md`.

Yongjie Lin, Yi Chern Tan, and Robert Frank. 2019. Open sesame: Getting inside BERT's linguistic knowledge. In *Proceedings of the 2019 ACL Workshop BlackboxNLP: Analyzing and Interpreting Neural Networks for NLP*, pages 241–253, Florence, Italy. Association for Computational Linguistics.

Xiaodong Liu, Pengcheng He, Weizhu Chen, and Jianfeng Gao. 2019a. Multi-task deep neural networks for natural language understanding. In *Proceedings of the 57th Annual Meeting of the Association for Computational Linguistics*, pages 4487–4496, Florence, Italy. Association for Computational Linguistics.

Yinhan Liu, Myle Ott, Naman Goyal, Jingfei Du, Mandar Joshi, Danqi Chen, Omer Levy, Mike Lewis, Luke Zettlemoyer, and Veselin Stoyanov. 2019b. RoBERTa: A robustly optimized BERT pretraining approach.

Open Source Initiative. 2020. The MIT License.

Adam Paszke, Sam Gross, Francisco Massa, Adam Lerer, James Bradbury, Gregory Chanan, Trevor Killeen, Zeming Lin, Natalia Gimelshein, Luca Antiga, Alban Desmaison, Andreas Kopf, Edward Yang, Zachary DeVito, Martin Raison, Alykhan Tejani, Sasank Chilamkurthy, Benoit Steiner, Lu Fang, Junjie Bai, and Soumith Chintala. 2019. PyTorch: An imperative style, high-performance deep learning library. In H. Wallach, H. Larochelle, A. Beygelzimer, F. d' Alché-Buc, E. Fox, and R. Garnett, editors, *Advances in Neural Information Processing Systems 32*, pages 8024–8035. Curran Associates, Inc.

Jeffrey Pennington, Richard Socher, and Christopher Manning. 2014. Glove: Global vectors for word representation. In *Proceedings of the 2014 Conference on Empirical Methods in Natural Language Processing (EMNLP)*, pages 1532–1543, Doha, Qatar. Association for Computational Linguistics.

Matthew Peters, Mark Neumann, Mohit Iyyer, Matt Gardner, Christopher Clark, Kenton Lee, and Luke Zettlemoyer. 2018. Deep contextualized word representations. In *Proceedings of the 2018 Conference of the North American Chapter of the Association for Computational Linguistics: Human Language Technologies, Volume 1 (Long Papers)*, pages 2227–2237, New Orleans, Louisiana. Association for Computational Linguistics.

Jason Phang, Thibault Févry, and Samuel R. Bowman. 2018. Sentence Encoders on STILTs: Supplementary Training on Intermediate Labeled-data Tasks. Unpublished manuscript available on arXiv.

Alec Radford. 2018. Improving language understanding by generative pre-training.

Alec Radford, Jeff Wu, Rewon Child, David Luan, Dario Amodei, and Ilya Sutskever. 2019. Language models are unsupervised multitask learners.

Colin Raffel, Noam Shazeer, Adam Roberts, Katherine Lee, Sharan Narang, Michael Matena, Yanqi Zhou, Wei Li, and Peter J. Liu. 2019. Exploring the limits of transfer learning with a unified text-to-text transformer. Unpublished manuscript available on arXiv.

Pranav Rajpurkar, Jian Zhang, Konstantin Lopyrev, and Percy Liang. 2016. SQuAD: 100,000+ questions for machine comprehension of text. In *Proceedings of the 2016 Conference on Empirical Methods in Natural Language Processing*, pages 2383–2392, Austin, Texas. Association for Computational Linguistics.

Maarten Sap, Hannah Rashkin, Derek Chen, Ronan Le Bras, and Yejin Choi. 2019. Social IQa: Commonsense reasoning about social interactions. In *Proceedings of the 2019 Conference on Empirical Methods in Natural Language Processing and the 9th International Joint Conference on Natural Language Processing (EMNLP-IJCNLP)*, pages 4463–4473, Hong Kong, China. Association for Computational Linguistics.

Yikang Shen, Zhouhan Lin, Chin-Wei Huang, and Aaron C. Courville. 2018. Neural language modeling by jointly learning syntax and lexicon. In *6th International Conference on Learning Representations, ICLR 2018, Vancouver, BC, Canada, April 30 - May 3, 2018, Conference Track Proceedings*.

Yikang Shen, Shawn Tan, Alessandro Sordoni, and Aaron C. Courville. 2019. Ordered neurons: Integrating tree structures into recurrent neural networks. In *7th International Conference on Learning Representations, ICLR 2019, New Orleans, LA, USA, May 6-9, 2019*.

Alon Talmor, Jonathan Herzig, Nicholas Lourie, and Jonathan Berant. 2019. CommonsenseQA: A question answering challenge targeting commonsense knowledge. In *Proceedings of the 2019 Conference of the North American Chapter of the Association for Computational Linguistics: Human Language Technologies, Volume 1 (Long and Short Papers)*, pages 4149–4158, Minneapolis, Minnesota. Association for Computational Linguistics.

Ian Tenney, Dipanjan Das, and Ellie Pavlick. 2019a. BERT rediscovers the classical NLP pipeline. In *Proceedings of the 57th Annual Meeting of the Association for Computational Linguistics*, pages 4593–4601, Florence, Italy. Association for Computational Linguistics.

Ian Tenney, Patrick Xia, Berlin Chen, Alex Wang, Adam Poliak, R. Thomas McCoy, Najoung Kim, Benjamin Van Durme, Samuel R. Bowman, Dipanjan Das, and Ellie Pavlick. 2019b. What do you learn from context? probing for sentence structure in contextualized word representations. In *7th International Conference on Learning Representations, ICLR 2019, New Orleans, LA, USA, May 6-9, 2019*.

Alex Wang, Jan Hula, Patrick Xia, Raghavendra Pappagari, R. Thomas McCoy, Roma Patel, Najoung Kim, Ian Tenney, Yinghui Huang, Katherin Yu, Shuning Jin, Berlin Chen, Benjamin Van Durme, Edouard Grave, Ellie Pavlick, and Samuel R. Bowman. 2019a. Can you tell me how to get past sesame street? sentence-level pretraining beyond language modeling. In *Proceedings of the 57th Annual Meeting of the Association for Computational Linguistics*, pages 4465–4476, Florence, Italy. Association for Computational Linguistics.

Alex Wang, Yada Pruksachatkun, Nikita Nangia, Amanpreet Singh, Julian Michael, Felix Hill, Omer Levy, and Samuel Bowman. 2019b. SuperGLUE: A stickier benchmark for general-purpose language understanding systems. In *Advances in Neural Information Processing Systems 32*, pages 3261–3275.

Alex Wang, Amanpreet Singh, Julian Michael, Felix Hill, Omer Levy, and Samuel Bowman. 2018. GLUE: A multi-task benchmark and analysis platform for natural language understanding. In *Proceedings of the 2018 EMNLP Workshop BlackboxNLP: Analyzing and Interpreting Neural Networks for NLP*, pages 353–355, Brussels, Belgium. Association for Computational Linguistics.

Alex Warstadt, Yu Cao, Ioana Grosu, Wei Peng, Hagen Blix, Yining Nie, Anna Alsop, Shikha Bordia, Haokun Liu, Alicia Parrish, Sheng-Fu Wang, Jason Phang, Anhad Mohananey, Phu Mon Htut, Paloma Jeretic, and Samuel R. Bowman. 2019. Investigating BERT's knowledge of language: Five analysis methods with NPIs. In *Proceedings of the 2019 Conference on Empirical Methods in Natural Language Processing and the 9th International Joint Conference on Natural Language Processing (EMNLP-IJCNLP)*, pages 2870–2880, Hong Kong, China. Association for Computational Linguistics.

Adina Williams, Nikita Nangia, and Samuel Bowman. 2018. A broad-coverage challenge corpus for sentence understanding through inference. In *Proceedings of the 2018 Conference of the North American Chapter of the Association for Computational Linguistics: Human Language Technologies, Volume 1 (Long Papers)*, pages 1112–1122. Association for Computational Linguistics.

Thomas Wolf, Lysandre Debut, Victor Sanh, Julien Chaumond, Clement Delangue, Anthony Moi, Pierric Cistac, Tim Rault, R'emi Louf, Morgan Funtowicz, and Jamie Brew. 2019. Huggingface's transformers: State-of-the-art natural language processing. Unpublished manuscript available on arXiv.

Zhilin Yang, Zihang Dai, Yiming Yang, Jaime Carbonell, Russ R Salakhutdinov, and Quoc V Le. 2019. XLNet: Generalized autoregressive pretraining for language understanding. In *Advances in Neural Information Processing Systems 32*, pages 5754–5764.

Rowan Zellers, Yonatan Bisk, Roy Schwartz, and Yejin Choi. 2018. SWAG: A large-scale adversarial dataset for grounded commonsense inference. In

Proceedings of the 2018 Conference on Empirical Methods in Natural Language Processing, pages 93–104, Brussels, Belgium. Association for Computational Linguistics.

Rowan Zellers, Ari Holtzman, Yonatan Bisk, Ali Farhadi, and Yejin Choi. 2019. HellaSwag: Can a machine really finish your sentence? In *Proceedings of the 57th Annual Meeting of the Association for Computational Linguistics*, pages 4791–4800, Florence, Italy. Association for Computational Linguistics.

The Microsoft Toolkit of Multi-Task Deep Neural Networks for Natural Language Understanding

**Xiaodong Liu*, Yu Wang*, Jianshu Ji, Hao Cheng, Xueyun Zhu, Emmanuel Awa,
Pengcheng He, Weizhu Chen, Hoifung Poon, Guihong Cao and Jianfeng Gao**
Microsoft Corporation
{xiaodl,yuwan,jianshuj,chehao,xuzhu}@microsoft.com

Abstract

We present MT-DNN[1], an open-source natural language understanding (NLU) toolkit that makes it easy for researchers and developers to train customized deep learning models. Built upon PyTorch and Transformers, MT-DNN is designed to facilitate rapid customization for a broad spectrum of NLU tasks, using a variety of objectives (classification, regression, structured prediction) and text encoders (e.g., RNNs, BERT, RoBERTa, UniLM). A unique feature of MT-DNN is its built-in support for robust and transferable learning using the adversarial multi-task learning paradigm. To enable efficient production deployment, MT-DNN supports multi-task knowledge distillation, which can substantially compress a deep neural model without significant performance drop. We demonstrate the effectiveness of MT-DNN on a wide range of NLU applications across general and biomedical domains. The software and pretrained models will be publicly available at https://github.com/namisan/mt-dnn.

1 Introduction

NLP model development has observed a paradigm shift in recent years, due to the success in using pretrained language models to improve a wide range of NLP tasks (Peters et al., 2018; Devlin et al., 2019). Unlike the traditional pipeline approach that conducts annotation in stages using primarily supervised learning, the new paradigm features a universal **pretraining** stage that trains a large neural language model via self-supervision on a large unlabeled text corpus, followed by a **fine-tuning** step that starts from the pretrained contextual representations and conducts supervised learning for individual tasks. The pretrained language models can effectively model textual variations and distributional similarity. Therefore, they can make subsequent task-specific training more sample efficient and often significantly boost performance in downstream tasks. However, these models are quite large and pose significant challenges to production deployment that has stringent memory or speed requirements. As a result, **knowledge distillation** has become another key feature in this new learning paradigm. An effective distillation step can often substantially compress a large model for efficient deployment (Clark et al., 2019; Tang et al., 2019; Liu et al., 2019a).

In the NLP community, there are several well designed frameworks for research and commercial purposes, including toolkits for providing conventional layered linguistic annotations (Manning et al., 2014), platforms for developing novel neural models (Gardner et al., 2018) and systems for neural machine translation (Ott et al., 2019). However, it is hard to find an existing tool that supports all features in the new paradigm and can be easily customized for new tasks. For example, (Wolf et al., 2019) provides a number of popular Transformer-based (Vaswani et al., 2017) text encoders in a nice unified interface, but does not offer multi-task learning or adversarial training, state-of-the-art techniques that have been shown to significantly improve performance. Additionally, most public frameworks do not offer knowledge distillation. A notable exception is DistillBERT (Sanh et al., 2019), but it provides a standalone compressed model and does not support task-specific model compression that can further improve performance.

We introduce MT-DNN, a comprehensive and easily-configurable open-source toolkit for building robust and transferable natural language understanding models. MT-DNN is built upon PyTorch (Paszke et al., 2019) and the popular Transformer-

---

*Equal Contribution.

[1]The complete name of our toolkit is MT^2-DNN (The **M**icrosoft **T**oolkit of **M**ulti-**T**ask **D**eep Neural Networks for Natural Language Understanding), but we use MT-DNN for sake of simplicity.

Proceedings of the 58th Annual Meeting of the Association for Computational Linguistics, pages 118–126
July 5 - July 10, 2020. ©2020 Association for Computational Linguistics

based text-encoder interface (Wolf et al., 2019). It supports a large inventory of pretrained models, neural architectures, and NLU tasks, and can be easily customized for new tasks.

A key distinct feature for MT-DNN is that it provides out-of-box adversarial training, multi-task learning, and knowledge distillation. Users can train a set of related tasks jointly to amplify each other. They can also invoke adversarial training (Miyato et al., 2018; Jiang et al., 2019; Liu et al., 2020), which helps improve model robustness and generalizability. For production deployment where large model size becomes a practical obstacle, users can use MT-DNN to compress the original models into substantially smaller ones, even using a completely different architecture (e.g., compressed BERT or other Transformer-based text encoders into LSTMs (Hochreiter and Schmidhuber, 1997)). The distillation step can similarly leverage multi-task learning and adversarial training. Users can also conduct pretraining from scratch using the masked language model objective in MT-DNN. Moreover, in the fine-tuning step, users can incorporate this as an auxiliary task on the training text, which has been shown to improve performance. MT-DNN provides a comprehensive list of state-of-the-art pre-trained NLU models, together with step-by-step tutorials for using such models in general and biomedical applications.

2 Design

MT-DNN is designed for modularity, flexibility, and ease of use. These modules are built upon PyTorch (Paszke et al., 2019) and Transformers (Wolf et al., 2019), allowing the use of the SOTA pre-trained models, e.g., BERT (Devlin et al., 2019), RoBERTa (Liu et al., 2019c) and UniLM (Dong et al., 2019). The unique attribute of this package is a flexible interface for adversarial multi-task fine-tuning and knowledge distillation, so that researchers and developers can build large SOTA NLU models and then compress them to small ones for online deployment.The overall workflow and system architecture are shown in Figure 1 and Figure 3 respectively.

2.1 Workflow

As shown in Figure 1, starting from the neural language model pre-training, there are three different training configurations by following the directed arrows:

- Single-task configuration: single-task fine-

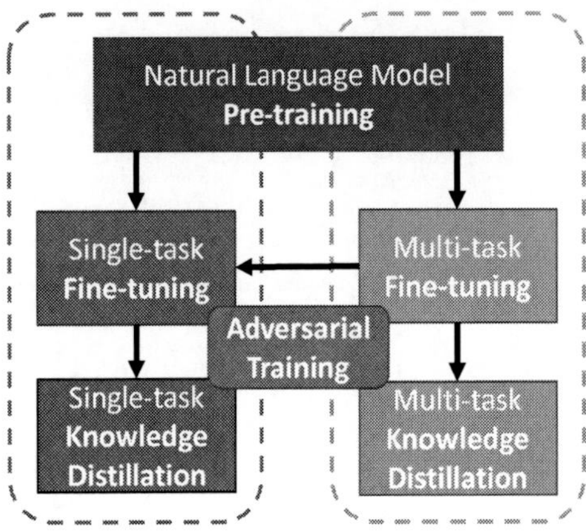

Figure 1: The workflow of MT-DNN: train a neural language model on a large amount of unlabeled raw text to obtain general contextual representations; then fine-tune the learned contextual representation on downstream tasks, e.g. GLUE (Wang et al., 2018); lastly, distill this large model to a lighter one for online deployment. In the later two phrases, we can leverage powerful multi-task learning and adversarial training to further improve performance.

tuning and single-task knowledge distillation;

- Multi-task configuration: multi-task fine-tuning and multi-task knowledge distillation;

- Multi-stage configuration: multi-task fine-tuning, single-task fine tuning and single-task knowledge distillation.

Moreover, all configurations can be additionally equipped with the adversarial training. Each stage of the workflow is described in details as follows.

Neural Language Model Pre-Training Due to the great success of deep contextual representations, such as ELMo (Peters et al., 2018), GPT (Radford et al., 2018) and BERT (Devlin et al., 2019), it is common practice of developing NLU models by first pre-training the underlying neural text representations (text encoders) through massive language modeling which results in superior text representations transferable across multiple NLP tasks. Because of this, there has been an increasing effort to develop better pre-trained text encoders by multiplying either the scale of data (Liu et al., 2019c) or the size of model (Raffel et al., 2019). Similar to existing codebases (Devlin et al., 2019), MT-DNN supports the LM pre-training from scratch with multiple types of objectives, such as masked LM (Devlin et al., 2019) and

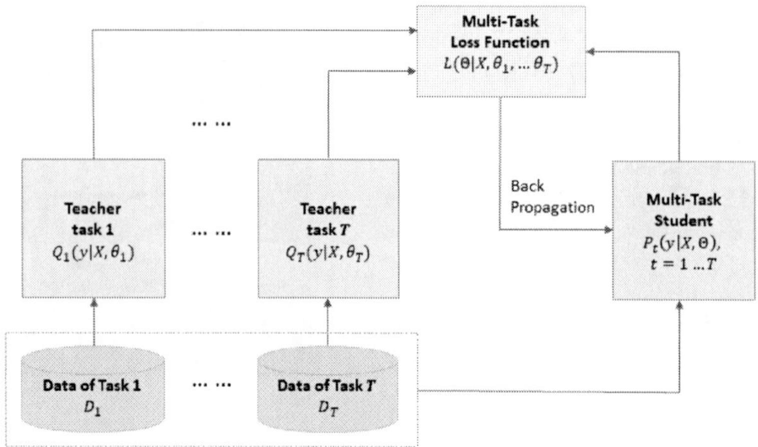

Figure 2: Process of knowledge distillation for MTL. A set of tasks where there is task-specific labeled training data are picked. Then, for each task, an ensemble of different neural nets (teacher) is trained. The teacher is used to generate for each task-specific training sample a set of soft targets. Given the soft targets of the training datasets across multiple tasks, a single MT-DNN (student) shown in Figure 3 is trained using multi-task learning and back propagation, except that if task t has a teacher, the task-specific loss is the average of two objective functions, one for the correct targets and the other for the soft targets assigned by the teacher.

next sentence prediction (Devlin et al., 2019).

Moreover, users can leverage the LM pre-training, such as masked LM used by BERT, as an auxiliary task for fine-tuning under the multi-task learning (MTL) framework (Sun et al., 2019; Liu et al., 2019b).

Fine-tuning Once the text encoder is trained in the pre-training stage, an additional task-specific layer is usually added for fine-tuning based on the down-stream task. Besides the existing typical single-task fine-tuning, MT-DNN facilitates a joint fine-tuning with a configurable list of related tasks in a MTL fashion. By encoding task-relatedness and sharing underlying text representations, MTL is a powerful training paradigm that promotes the model generalization ability and results in improved performance (Caruana, 1997; Liu et al., 2019b; Luong et al., 2015; Liu et al., 2015; Ruder, 2017; Collobert et al., 2011). Additionally, a two-step fine-tuning stage is also supported to utilize datasets from related tasks, i.e. a single-task fine-tuning following a multi-task fine-tuning. It also supports two popular sampling strategies in MTL training: 1) sampling tasks uniformly (Caruana, 1997; Liu et al., 2015); 2) sampling tasks based on the size of the dataset (Liu et al., 2019b). This makes it easy to explore various ways to feed training data to MTL training. Finally, to further improve the model robustness, MT-DNN also offers a recipe to apply adversarial training (Madry et al., 2017; Zhu et al., 2019; Jiang et al., 2019) in the fine-tuning stage.

Knowledge Distillation Although contextual text representation models pre-trained with massive text data have led to remarkable progress in NLP, it is computationally prohibitive and inefficient to deploy such models with millions of parameters for real-world applications (e.g. BERT large model has 344 million parameters). Therefore, in order to expedite the NLU model learned in either a single-task or multi-task fashion for deployment, MT-DNN additionally supports the multi-task knowledge distillation (Clark et al., 2019; Liu et al., 2019a; Tang et al., 2019; Balan et al., 2015; Ba and Caruana, 2014), an extension of (Hinton et al., 2015), to compress cumbersome models into lighter ones. The multi-task knowledge distillation process is illustrated in Figure 2. Similar to the fine-tuning stage, adversarial training is available in the knowledge distillation stage.

2.2 Architecture

Lexicon Encoder (l_1): The input $X = \{x_1, ..., x_m\}$ is a sequence of tokens of length m. The first token x_1 is always a specific token, e.g. [CLS] for BERT Devlin et al. (2019) while <s> for RoBERTa Liu et al. (2019c). If X is a pair of sentences (X_1, X_2), we separate these sentences with special tokens, e.g. [SEP] for BERT and [</s>] for RoBERTa. The lexicon encoder maps X into a sequence of input embedding vectors,

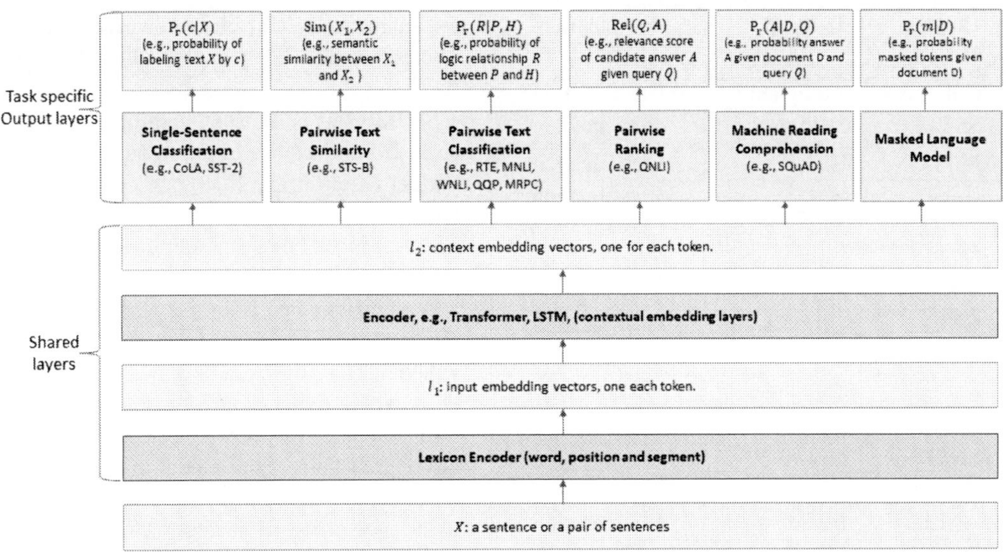

Figure 3: Overall System Architecture: The lower layers are shared across all tasks while the top layers are task-specific. The input X (either a sentence or a set of sentences) is first represented as a sequence of embedding vectors, one for each word, in l_1. Then the encoder, e.g a Transformer or recurrent neural network (LSTM) model, captures the contextual information for each word and generates the shared contextual embedding vectors in l_2. Finally, for each task, additional task-specific layers generate task-specific representations, followed by operations necessary for classification, similarity scoring, or relevance ranking. In case of adversarial training, we perturb embeddings from the lexicon encoder and then add an extra loss term during the training. Note that for the inference phrase, it does not require perturbations.

one for each token, constructed by summing the corresponding word with positional, and optional segment embeddings.

Encoder (l_2): We support a multi-layer bidirectional Transformer (Vaswani et al., 2017) or a LSTM (Hochreiter and Schmidhuber, 1997) encoder to map the input representation vectors (l_1) into a sequence of contextual embedding vectors $C \in R^{d \times m}$. This is the shared representation across different tasks. Note that MT-DNN also allows developers to customize their own encoders. For example, one can design an encoder with few Transformer layers (e.g. 3 layers) to distill knowledge from the BERT large model (24 layers), so that they can deploy this small mode online to meet the latency restriction as shown in Figure 2.

Task-Specific Output Layers: We can incorporate arbitrary natural language tasks, each with its task-specific output layer. For example, we implement the output layers as a neural decoder for a neural ranker for relevance ranking, a logistic regression for text classification, and so on. A multi-step reasoning decoder, SAN (Liu et al., 2018a,b) is also provided. Customers can choose from existing task-specific output layer or implement new

one by themselves.

3 Application

In this section, we present a comprehensive set of examples to illustrate how to customize MT-DNN for new tasks. We use popular benchmarks from general and biomedical domains, including GLUE (Wang et al., 2018), SNLI (Bowman et al., 2015), SciTail (Khot et al., 2018), SQuAD (Rajpurkar et al., 2016), ANLI (Nie et al., 2019), and biomedical named entity recognition (NER), relation extraction (RE) and question answering (QA) (Lee et al., 2019). To make the experiments reproducible, we make all the configuration files publicly available. We also provide a quick guide for customizing a new task in Jupyter notebooks.

3.1 General Domain Natural Language Understanding Benchmarks

• **GLUE.** The General Language Understanding Evaluation (GLUE) benchmark is a collection of nine natural language understanding (NLU) tasks. As shown in Table 1, it includes question answering (Rajpurkar et al., 2016), linguistic acceptability (Warstadt et al., 2018), sentiment analy-

Corpus	Task	Formulation
GLUE		
CoLA	Acceptability	Classification
SST	Sentiment	Classification
MNLI	NLI	Classification
RTE	NLI	Classification
WNLI	NLI	Classification
QQP	Paraphrase	Classification
MRPC	Paraphrase	Classification
QNLI	QA/NLI	Classification
QNLI v1.0	QA/NLI	Pairwise Ranking
STS-B	Similarity	Regression
Others		
SNLI	NLI	Classification
SciTail	NLI	Classification
ANLI	NLI	Classification
SQuAD	MRC	Span Classification

Table 1: Summary of the four benchmarks: GLUE, SNLI, SciTail and ANLI.

Model	MNLI Acc	RTE Acc	QNLI Acc	SST Acc	MRPC F1
BERT	84.5	63.5	91.1	92.9	89.0
BERT + MTL	85.3	79.1	91.5	93.6	89.2
BERT + AdvTrain	85.6	71.2	91.6	93.0	91.3

Table 2: Comparison among single task, multi-Task and adversarial training on MNLI, RTE, QNLI, SST and MPRC in GLUE.

Model	Dev	Test
BERT$_{\text{LARGE}}$ (Nie et al., 2019)	49.3	44.2
RoBERTa$_{\text{LARGE}}$ (Nie et al., 2019)	53.7	49.7
RoBERTa-LARGE + AdvTrain	57.1	57.1

Table 3: Results in terms of accuracy on the ANLI.

sis (Socher et al., 2013), text similarity (Cer et al., 2017), paraphrase detection (Dolan and Brockett, 2005), and natural language inference (NLI) (Dagan et al., 2006; Bar-Haim et al., 2006; Giampiccolo et al., 2007; Bentivogli et al., 2009; Levesque et al., 2012; Williams et al., 2018). The diversity of the tasks makes GLUE very suitable for evaluating the generalization and robustness of NLU models.

• **SNLI**. The Stanford Natural Language Inference (SNLI) dataset contains 570k human annotated sentence pairs, in which the premises are drawn from the captions of the Flickr30 corpus and hypotheses are manually annotated (Bowman et al., 2015). This is the most widely used entailment dataset for NLI.

• **SciTail** This is a textual entailment dataset derived from a science question answering (SciQ) dataset (Khot et al., 2018). In contrast to other entailment datasets mentioned previously, the hypotheses in SciTail are created from science questions while the corresponding answer candidates and premises come from relevant web sentences retrieved from a large corpus.

• **ANLI**. The Adversarial Natural Language Inference (ANLI, Nie et al. (2019)) is a new large-scale NLI benchmark dataset, collected via an iterative, adversarial human-and-model-in-the-loop procedure. Particular, the data is selected to be difficult to the state-of-the-art models, including BERT and RoBERTa.

• **SQuAD**. The Stanford Question Answering Dataset (SQuAD) (Rajpurkar et al., 2016) contains about 23K passages and 100K questions. The passages come from approximately 500 Wikipedia articles and the questions and answers are obtained by crowdsourcing.

Following (Devlin et al., 2019), table 2 compares different training algorithm: 1) BERT denotes a single task fine-tuning; 2) BERT + MTL indicates that it is trained jointly via MTL; at last 3), BERT + AdvTrain represents that a single task fine-tuning with adversarial training. It is obvious that the both MLT and adversarial training helps to obtain a better result. We further test our model on an adversarial natural language inference (ANLI) dataset (Nie et al., 2019). Table 3 summarizes the results on ANLI. As Nie et al. (2019), all the dataset of ANLI (Nie et al., 2019), MNLI (Williams et al., 2018), SNLI (Bowman et al., 2015) and FEVER (Thorne et al., 2018) are combined as training. RoBERTa-LARGE+AdvTrain obtains the best performance compared with all the strong baselines, demonstrating the advantage of adversarial training.

3.2 Biomedical Natural Language Understating Benchmarks

There has been rising interest in exploring natural language understanding tasks in high-value domains other than newswire and the Web. In our release, we provide MT-DNN customization for three representative biomedical natural language understanding tasks:

• Named entity recognition (NER): In biomedical natural language understanding, NER has received greater attention than other tasks and datasets are available for recognizing various biomedical entities such as disease, gene, drug (chemical).

• Relation extraction (RE): Relation extraction is more closely related to end applications, but annotation effort is significantly higher compared to NER. Most existing RE tasks focus on binary relations within a short text span such as a sentence of an abstract. Examples include gene-disease or protein-chemical relations.

• Question answering (QA): Inspired by interest in QA for the general domain, there has been some effort to create question-answering datasets in biomedicine. Annotation requires domain expertise, so it is significantly harder than in general domain, where it is to produce large-scale datasets by crowdsourcing.

The MT-DNN customization can work with standard or biomedicine-specific pretraining models such as BioBERT, and can be directly applied to biomedical benchmarks (Lee et al., 2019).

3.3 Extension

```
 1  snli:
 2    data_format: PremiseAndOneHypothesis
 3    task_layer_type: LinearLayer
 4    labels:
 5      - contradiction
 6      - neutral
 7      - entailment
 8    metric_meta:
 9      - ACC
10    loss: CeCriterion
11    kd_loss: MseCriterion
12    adv_loss: KlCriterion
13    n_class: 3
14    task_type: Classification
```

Figure 4: The configuration of SNLI.

We will go though a typical Natural Language Inference task, e.g. SNLI, which is one of the most popular benchmark, showing how to apply our toolkit to a new task. MT-DNN is driven by configuration and command line arguments. Firstly, the SNLI configuration is shown in Figure 4. The configuration defines tasks, model architecture as well as loss functions. We briefly introduce these attributes as follows:

1. *data_format* is a required attribute and it denotes that each sample includes two sentences (premise and hypothesis). Please refer the tutorial and API for supported formats.

2. *task_layer_type* specifies architecture of the task specific layer. The default is a "linear layer".

3. *labels* Users can list unique values of labels. The configuration helps to convert back and forth between text labels and numbers during training and evaluation. Without it, MT-DNN assumes the label of prediction are numbers.

4. *metric_meta* is the evaluation metric used for validation.

5. *loss* is the loss function for SNLI. It also supports other functions, e.g. MSE for regression.

6. *kd_loss* is the loss function in the knowledge distillation setting.

7. *adv_loss* is the loss function in the adversarial setting.

8. *n_class* denotes the number of categories for SNLI.

9. *task_type* specifies whether it is a classification task or a regression task.

Once the configuration is provided, one can train the customized model for the task, using any supported pre-trained models as starting point.

MT-DNN is also highly extensible, as shown in Figure 4, *loss* and *task_layer_type* point to existing classes in code. Users can write customized classes and plug into MT-DNN. The customized classes could then be used via configuration.

4 Conclusion

Microsoft MT-DNN is an open-source natural language understanding toolkit which facilitates researchers and developers to build customized deep learning models. Its key features are: 1) support for robust and transferable learning using adversarial multi-task learning paradigm; 2) enable knowledge distillation under the multi-task learning setting which can be leveraged to derive lighter models for efficient online deployment. We will extend MT-DNN to support Natural Language Generation tasks, e.g. Question Generation, and incorporate more pre-trained encoders, e.g. T5 (Raffel et al., 2019) in future.

Acknowledgments

We thank Liyuan Liu, Sha Li, Mehrad Moradshahi and other contributors to the package, and the anonymous reviewers for valuable discussions and comments.

References

Jimmy Ba and Rich Caruana. 2014. Do deep nets really need to be deep? In *Advances in neural information processing systems*, pages 2654–2662.

Anoop Korattikara Balan, Vivek Rathod, Kevin P Murphy, and Max Welling. 2015. Bayesian dark knowledge. In *Advances in Neural Information Processing Systems*, pages 3438–3446.

Roy Bar-Haim, Ido Dagan, Bill Dolan, Lisa Ferro, and Danilo Giampiccolo. 2006. The second PASCAL recognising textual entailment challenge. In *Proceedings of the Second PASCAL Challenges Workshop on Recognising Textual Entailment*.

Luisa Bentivogli, Ido Dagan, Hoa Trang Dang, Danilo Giampiccolo, and Bernardo Magnini. 2009. The fifth pascal recognizing textual entailment challenge. In *In Proc Text Analysis Conference (TAC'09*.

Samuel R. Bowman, Gabor Angeli, Christopher Potts, and Christopher D. Manning. 2015. A large annotated corpus for learning natural language inference. In *Proceedings of the 2015 Conference on Empirical Methods in Natural Language Processing (EMNLP)*. Association for Computational Linguistics.

Rich Caruana. 1997. Multitask learning. *Machine learning*, 28(1):41–75.

Daniel Cer, Mona Diab, Eneko Agirre, Inigo Lopez-Gazpio, and Lucia Specia. 2017. Semeval-2017 task 1: Semantic textual similarity-multilingual and cross-lingual focused evaluation. *arXiv preprint arXiv:1708.00055*.

Kevin Clark, Minh-Thang Luong, Urvashi Khandelwal, Christopher D Manning, and Quoc V Le. 2019. Bam! born-again multi-task networks for natural language understanding. *arXiv preprint arXiv:1907.04829*.

Ronan Collobert, Jason Weston, Léon Bottou, Michael Karlen, Koray Kavukcuoglu, and Pavel Kuksa. 2011. Natural language processing (almost) from scratch. *Journal of machine learning research*, 12(Aug):2493–2537.

Ido Dagan, Oren Glickman, and Bernardo Magnini. 2006. The pascal recognising textual entailment challenge. In *Proceedings of the First International Conference on Machine Learning Challenges: Evaluating Predictive Uncertainty Visual Object Classification, and Recognizing Textual Entailment*, MLCW'05, pages 177–190, Berlin, Heidelberg. Springer-Verlag.

Jacob Devlin, Ming-Wei Chang, Kenton Lee, and Kristina Toutanova. 2019. Bert: Pre-training of deep bidirectional transformers for language understanding. In *Proceedings of the 2019 Conference of the North American Chapter of the Association for Computational Linguistics: Human Language Technologies, Volume 1 (Long and Short Papers)*, pages 4171–4186.

William B Dolan and Chris Brockett. 2005. Automatically constructing a corpus of sentential paraphrases. In *Proceedings of the Third International Workshop on Paraphrasing (IWP2005)*.

Li Dong, Nan Yang, Wenhui Wang, Furu Wei, Xiaodong Liu, Yu Wang, Jianfeng Gao, Ming Zhou, and Hsiao-Wuen Hon. 2019. Unified language model pre-training for natural language understanding and generation. In *Advances in Neural Information Processing Systems*, pages 13042–13054.

Matt Gardner, Joel Grus, Mark Neumann, Oyvind Tafjord, Pradeep Dasigi, Nelson Liu, Matthew Peters, Michael Schmitz, and Luke Zettlemoyer. 2018. Allennlp: A deep semantic natural language processing platform. *arXiv preprint arXiv:1803.07640*.

Danilo Giampiccolo, Bernardo Magnini, Ido Dagan, and Bill Dolan. 2007. The third PASCAL recognizing textual entailment challenge. In *Proceedings of the ACL-PASCAL Workshop on Textual Entailment and Paraphrasing*, pages 1–9, Prague. Association for Computational Linguistics.

Geoffrey Hinton, Oriol Vinyals, and Jeff Dean. 2015. Distilling the knowledge in a neural network. *arXiv preprint arXiv:1503.02531*.

Sepp Hochreiter and Jürgen Schmidhuber. 1997. Long short-term memory. *Neural computation*, 9(8):1735–1780.

Haoming Jiang, Pengcheng He, Weizhu Chen, Xiaodong Liu, Jianfeng Gao, and Tuo Zhao. 2019. Smart: Robust and efficient fine-tuning for pretrained natural language models through principled regularized optimization. *arXiv preprint arXiv:1911.03437*.

Tushar Khot, Ashish Sabharwal, and Peter Clark. 2018. SciTail: A textual entailment dataset from science question answering. In *AAAI*.

Jinhyuk Lee, Wonjin Yoon, Sungdong Kim, Donghyeon Kim, Sunkyu Kim, Chan Ho So, and Jaewoo Kang. 2019. Biobert: pre-trained biomedical language representation model for biomedical text mining. *arXiv preprint arXiv:1901.08746*.

Hector Levesque, Ernest Davis, and Leora Morgenstern. 2012. The winograd schema challenge. In *Thirteenth International Conference on the Principles of Knowledge Representation and Reasoning*.

Xiaodong Liu, Hao Cheng, Pengcheng He, Weizhu Chen, Yu Wang, Hoifung Poon, and Jianfeng Gao. 2020. Adversarial training for large neural language models. *arXiv preprint arXiv:2004.08994*.

Xiaodong Liu, Kevin Duh, and Jianfeng Gao. 2018a. Stochastic answer networks for natural language inference. *arXiv preprint arXiv:1804.07888*.

Xiaodong Liu, Jianfeng Gao, Xiaodong He, Li Deng, Kevin Duh, and Ye-Yi Wang. 2015. Representation learning using multi-task deep neural networks for semantic classification and information retrieval. In *Proceedings of the 2015 Conference of the North American Chapter of the Association for Computational Linguistics: Human Language Technologies*, pages 912–921.

Xiaodong Liu, Pengcheng He, Weizhu Chen, and Jianfeng Gao. 2019a. Improving multi-task deep neural networks via knowledge distillation for natural language understanding. *arXiv preprint arXiv:1904.09482*.

Xiaodong Liu, Pengcheng He, Weizhu Chen, and Jianfeng Gao. 2019b. Multi-task deep neural networks for natural language understanding. In *Proceedings of the 57th Annual Meeting of the Association for Computational Linguistics*, pages 4487–4496, Florence, Italy. Association for Computational Linguistics.

Xiaodong Liu, Yelong Shen, Kevin Duh, and Jianfeng Gao. 2018b. Stochastic answer networks for machine reading comprehension. In *Proceedings of the 56th Annual Meeting of the Association for Computational Linguistics (Volume 1: Long Papers)*. Association for Computational Linguistics.

Yinhan Liu, Myle Ott, Naman Goyal, Jingfei Du, Mandar Joshi, Danqi Chen, Omer Levy, Mike Lewis, Luke Zettlemoyer, and Veselin Stoyanov. 2019c. Roberta: A robustly optimized bert pretraining approach. *arXiv preprint arXiv:1907.11692*.

Minh-Thang Luong, Quoc V Le, Ilya Sutskever, Oriol Vinyals, and Lukasz Kaiser. 2015. Multi-task sequence to sequence learning. *arXiv preprint arXiv:1511.06114*.

Aleksander Madry, Aleksandar Makelov, Ludwig Schmidt, Dimitris Tsipras, and Adrian Vladu. 2017. Towards deep learning models resistant to adversarial attacks. *arXiv preprint arXiv:1706.06083*.

Christopher D Manning, Mihai Surdeanu, John Bauer, Jenny Rose Finkel, Steven Bethard, and David McClosky. 2014. The stanford corenlp natural language processing toolkit. In *Proceedings of 52nd annual meeting of the association for computational linguistics: system demonstrations*, pages 55–60.

Takeru Miyato, Shin-ichi Maeda, Masanori Koyama, and Shin Ishii. 2018. Virtual adversarial training: a regularization method for supervised and semi-supervised learning. *IEEE transactions on pattern analysis and machine intelligence*, 41(8):1979–1993.

Yixin Nie, Adina Williams, Emily Dinan, Mohit Bansal, Jason Weston, and Douwe Kiela. 2019. Adversarial nli: A new benchmark for natural language understanding. *arXiv preprint arXiv:1910.14599*.

Myle Ott, Sergey Edunov, Alexei Baevski, Angela Fan, Sam Gross, Nathan Ng, David Grangier, and Michael Auli. 2019. fairseq: A fast, extensible toolkit for sequence modeling. *arXiv preprint arXiv:1904.01038*.

Adam Paszke, Sam Gross, Francisco Massa, Adam Lerer, James Bradbury, Gregory Chanan, Trevor Killeen, Zeming Lin, Natalia Gimelshein, Luca Antiga, et al. 2019. Pytorch: An imperative style, high-performance deep learning library. In *Advances in Neural Information Processing Systems*, pages 8024–8035.

Matthew E Peters, Mark Neumann, Mohit Iyyer, Matt Gardner, Christopher Clark, Kenton Lee, and Luke Zettlemoyer. 2018. Deep contextualized word representations. *arXiv preprint arXiv:1802.05365*.

Alec Radford, Jeffrey Wu, Rewon Child, David Luan, Dario Amodei, and Ilya Sutskever. 2018. Language models are unsupervised multitask learners.

Colin Raffel, Noam Shazeer, Adam Roberts, Katherine Lee, Sharan Narang, Michael Matena, Yanqi Zhou, Wei Li, and Peter J Liu. 2019. Exploring the limits of transfer learning with a unified text-to-text transformer. *arXiv preprint arXiv:1910.10683*.

Pranav Rajpurkar, Jian Zhang, Konstantin Lopyrev, and Percy Liang. 2016. SQuAD: 100,000+ questions for machine comprehension of text. In *Proceedings of the 2016 Conference on Empirical Methods in Natural Language Processing*, pages 2383–2392, Austin, Texas. Association for Computational Linguistics.

Sebastian Ruder. 2017. An overview of multi-task learning in deep neural networks. *arXiv preprint arXiv:1706.05098*.

Victor Sanh, Lysandre Debut, Julien Chaumond, and Thomas Wolf. 2019. Distilbert, a distilled version of bert: smaller, faster, cheaper and lighter. *arXiv preprint arXiv:1910.01108*.

Richard Socher, Alex Perelygin, Jean Wu, Jason Chuang, Christopher D Manning, Andrew Ng, and Christopher Potts. 2013. Recursive deep models for semantic compositionality over a sentiment treebank. In *Proceedings of the 2013 conference on empirical methods in natural language processing*, pages 1631–1642.

Yu Sun, Shuohuan Wang, Yukun Li, Shikun Feng, Hao Tian, Hua Wu, and Haifeng Wang. 2019. Ernie 2.0: A continual pre-training framework for language understanding. *arXiv preprint arXiv:1907.12412*.

Raphael Tang, Yao Lu, Linqing Liu, Lili Mou, Olga Vechtomova, and Jimmy Lin. 2019. Distilling task-specific knowledge from bert into simple neural networks. *arXiv preprint arXiv:1903.12136*.

James Thorne, Andreas Vlachos, Christos Christodoulopoulos, and Arpit Mittal. 2018. Fever: a large-scale dataset for fact extraction and verification. *arXiv preprint arXiv:1803.05355*.

Ashish Vaswani, Noam Shazeer, Niki Parmar, Jakob Uszkoreit, Llion Jones, Aidan N Gomez, Łukasz Kaiser, and Illia Polosukhin. 2017. Attention is all you need. In *Advances in neural information processing systems*, pages 5998–6008.

Alex Wang, Amanpreet Singh, Julian Michael, Felix Hill, Omer Levy, and Samuel R Bowman. 2018. Glue: A multi-task benchmark and analysis platform for natural language understanding. *arXiv preprint arXiv:1804.07461*.

Alex Warstadt, Amanpreet Singh, and Samuel R Bowman. 2018. Neural network acceptability judgments. *arXiv preprint arXiv:1805.12471*.

Adina Williams, Nikita Nangia, and Samuel Bowman. 2018. A broad-coverage challenge corpus for sentence understanding through inference. In *Proceedings of the 2018 Conference of the North American Chapter of the Association for Computational Linguistics: Human Language Technologies, Volume 1 (Long Papers)*, pages 1112–1122. Association for Computational Linguistics.

Thomas Wolf, Lysandre Debut, Victor Sanh, Julien Chaumond, Clement Delangue, Anthony Moi, Pierric Cistac, Tim Rault, R'emi Louf, Morgan Funtowicz, and Jamie Brew. 2019. Huggingface's transformers: State-of-the-art natural language processing. *ArXiv*, abs/1910.03771.

Chen Zhu, Yu Cheng, Zhe Gan, Siqi Sun, Thomas Goldstein, and Jingjing Liu. 2019. Freelb: Enhanced adversarial training for language understanding. *arXiv preprint arXiv:1909.11764*.

LinggleWrite: a Coaching System for Essay Writing

Chung-Ting Tsai[1], Jhih-Jie Chen[2], Ching-Yu Yang[2], Jason S. Chang[2]
[1]Institute of Information Systems and Applications
[2]Department of Computer Science
National Tsing Hua University
{jjc, jason}@nlplab.cc

Abstract

This paper presents *LinggleWrite*, a writing coach that provides writing suggestions, assesses writing proficiency levels, detects grammatical errors, and offers corrective feedback in response to user's essay. The method involves extracting grammar patterns, training models for automated essay scoring (AES) and grammatical error detection (GED), and finally retrieving plausible corrections from a n-gram search engine. Experiments on public test sets indicate that both AES and GED models achieve state-of-the-art performance. These results show that *LinggleWrite* is potentially useful in helping learners improve their writing skills.

1 Introduction

Essay writing has been an essential part of language assessments (e.g., TOEFL, IELTS) but a challenging task for most students. To write a good essay not only requires sustained practice, but also demands instructional feedback from teachers. However, pressed with teaching load, teachers can only provide limited corrective feedback on students' essays. This has encouraged the development of computer-assisted writing systems to meet growing needs of automated feedback as a means of writing coaching. Computer Assisted Language Learning (CALL) has been an active field of computational linguistics and pedagogy. Some existing computer aided writing systems detect and correct grammatical errors, and give an overall score (e.g., *Grammarly* (www.grammarly.com) and *Pigai* (www.pigai.org)).

Instead of directly correcting users' essays, *Write&Improve* (writeandimprove.com) only marks highly-likely incorrect words on the grounds that automated grammatical error correction is still very imprecise. Recently, researchers have begun to apply neural network models to both automated essay scoring (AES) and grammatical error detection (GED), gaining significant improvement (e.g., Dong et al. (2017); Rei and Søgaard (2018)). However, these Web services fall short of providing sufficient "coaching" information (e.g., grammar patterns, collocations, examples) to learners to improve their writing skills.

Provide writing suggestions as a user types away or during editing is another emerging approach to coaching the learner. For example, *WriteAhead* (writeahead.nlpweb.org) provides context-sensitive suggestions, right in the process of writing or self-editing. Google recently released *Smart Compose* that offers users word or phrase completion suggestions while writing an email (Chen et al., 2019).

In line with these systems, we also suggest that feedback on learners' writings could be more effective if a system not only acts as an editor providing direct corrections, but also a coach performing grammatical error detection and offering interactive suggestions (Hearst, 2015). Moreover, illustrating word usage with bilingual examples can better help non-native English learners. This would enhance learners' skills of self-editing and pave the way to lifelong language learning.

With that in mind, we developed a web-based system *LinggleWrite* (f.linggle.com) with many assistive writing functions. With *LinggleWrite* users can write or paste their essays and get informative feedback including just-in-time writing suggestions, essay scoring, error detection, and related word usage information retrieved from Linggle(linggle.com).

2 The *LinggleWrite* System

The system consists of 4 components: (1) Interactive Writing Suggestion, (2) Essay Scoring, (3) Grammatical Error Detection, and (4) Corrective

Proceedings of the 58th Annual Meeting of the Association for Computational Linguistics, pages 127–133
July 5 - July 10, 2020. ©2020 Association for Computational Linguistics

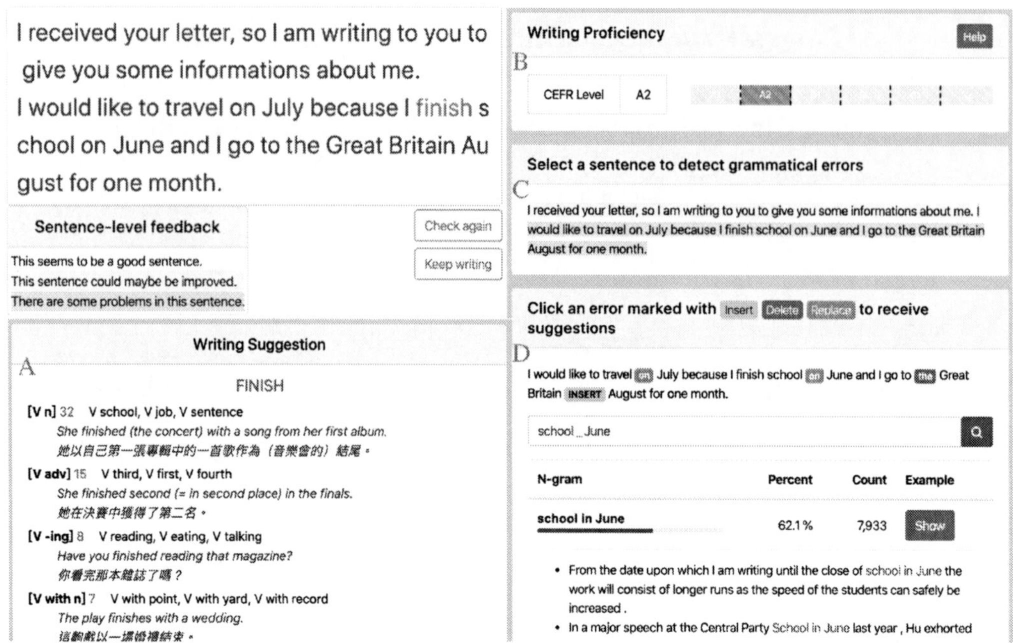

Figure 1: The screenshot of the system *LinggleWrite*

Feedback. The first component, Writing suggestion, will help users with word usage information while writing. The other three components are aimed at providing evaluation and constructive feedback after a user finishes writing. The system is available at f.linggle.com. We'll describe each component as follows.

2.1 Interactive Writing Suggestion

When a user begins to write an essay, the system responds with prompts of related grammar patterns, collocations, and bilingual examples. These continuous writing suggestions are based on the last word or phrase the user has entered. Additionally, the user can get information of a certain word by mousing over it. For example, suggestions for "finish" are shown in Section A of Figure 1 (bottom left). Once finishing the writings, the user can click the *Check* button triggering the following components.

2.2 Essay Scoring

After accepting an essay longer than 30 words, *LinggleWrite* assesses user's writing proficiency. The assessment is provided in the form of CEFR Levels[1] (A1-C2) as shown in Section B of Figure 1 (top right).

[1]https://www.coe.int/en/web/common-european-framework-reference-languages/level-descriptions

2.3 Grammatical Error Detection

LinggleWrite tries to detect potential grammatical errors in each sentence. Sentences with potential errors are marked with yellow (1 possible error) or orange (2 or more possible errors) background, as shown in Section C of Figure 1 (center right). The user can click on an erroneous sentence to demand GED results. *LinggleWrite* marks suspicious words with orange, red or green, suggesting to insert a word, delete the word, or replace the word respectively, as shown in Section C of Figure 1 (center right). Subsequently, the user can click on an error to display plausible corrective suggestions returned by a n-gram search engine.

2.4 Corrective Feedback

We present corrective suggestions according to the context and the edit type (i.e., insertion, deletion, replacement), using an existing linguistic search engine, *Linggle* (Boisson et al., 2013). An example of corrective suggestions for the sentence *"I finished school on June"* is shown in Section E in Figure 1 (bottom right). *LinggleWrite* detects "on" probably requiring a replacement edit. We convert the detected error into a Linggle query to search for more appropriate expressions, and provide the user with the search result "school in June' for considerations.

3 Method

To develop *LinggleWrite*, we extract the most common grammar patterns from a corpus in order to provide writing suggestions. Additionally, we develop models for AES and GED based on annotated learner corpora. We retrieve corrective feedback by querying a linguistic search engine according to the predicted edit type of an error. We describe the process in detail in the following subsections.

3.1 Extracting Grammar Patterns

We extract grammatical patterns, collocations and bilingual examples for keywords from a given corpus to provide writing suggestions in the interactive writing session. Our extraction process includes four steps.

In Step (1), we build a dictionary of grammar patterns of verbs, nouns and adjectives based on Francis et al. (1996). For example, the grammar patterns of the word *play* are **V n**, **V n in n**, etc.

In Step (2), we parse sentences from Corpus of Contemporary American English (COCA) and Cambridge online dictionary (CAM) using a dependency parser to extract grammar patterns and collocations based on the templates in Step (1). For example, the extracted grammar pattern and collocation from the sentence "Schools **play** an important role **in** society" are "**V n in n**" and "**society**".

In Step (3), for each keyword, we count and filter out patterns and collocations based on mean and standard deviation. Finally, we use GDEX method (Kilgarriff et al., 2008) to select the best monolingual and bilingual examples from COCA and CAM for each pattern.

3.2 Scoring an Essay

We formulate AES as a regression problem and train a neural model for this task. We investigate two neural network architectures with different input formats: word-based models and sentence-based models, which learn essay representation based on word sequences and sentence sequences respectively. We build our word-based models upon CNN, LSTM and Bi-LSTM (Taghipour and Ng, 2016), while sentence-level models upon the LSTM-LSTM and LSTM-CNN framework (Dong et al., 2017). Moreover, we further extend both sentence-based models and word-based models by adding the attention mechanism after the neural layer, attempting to select the sentences or words to focus on for effective scoring. Our models are similar to other sentence-based and word-based neural AES model (e.g., Taghipour and Ng (2016); Dong et al. (2017)), but we use a different training set, EFCAMDAT (Geertzen et al., 2013) and output format, CEFR levels, to train our model.

3.3 Detecting Grammatical Errors

We formulate GED as a sequence labeling problem and develop a neural sequence labeling model to deal with the problem.

An existing GED method proposed by Rei and Yannakoudakis (2016) takes tokens as input and predicts whether each token is correct in the sentence as output. We extend their model by changing the binary error tag schema (*Incorrect and Correct*) into a more informative DIRC tag schema (*Delete, Insert, Replace, and Correct*), with the goal of providing learners more specific suggestions (i.e., the edit type of an error) to revise their essay. We train a GED model based on Bi-LSTM with a Conditional Random Field layer (CRF). To improve the GED model, we add Bidirectional Encoder Representations from Transformers (BERT), which significantly outperforms other embedding schemes in many tasks (Devlin et al., 2018). In addition, we also add a character-based word embedding, Flair, which captures more contextual information (Akbik et al., 2018). Our training process is divided into two steps.

In Step (1), we convert sentences with error annotations into unedited sentences and DIRC tags (i.e., $<$[-,-]$>$ for *Delete*, tokens preceded by $<${+,+}$>$ for *Insert*, $<$[-,-]{+,+}$>$ for *Replace* and tokens with no edit tag for *Correct*). For example, the sentence "I believe there are {+a+} lot of [-why-]{+ways+} enjoy [-the-] shopping." is converted to "I believe there are lot of why enjoy the shopping ." and "$<$C C C C I C R C D C C$>$". These two sequences are treated as the input and output of a neural GED model respectively. Note that the token to be inserted ({+a+}) is not in the unedited sentence, and the right token *lot* is labeled *I* instead.

In Step (2), we train a neural GED model for a grammatical error detector using a BiLSTM-CRF architecture. We first combine BERT embeddings (Devlin et al., 2018) with Flair embeddings (Akbik et al., 2018) to form word embeddings and then encode each token in a given sentence into a fixed-length vector. Finally, these embeddings are fed

Operators	Corresponding edit types	Description	Example
*	Insertion Edit	match zero or any words	good * this
_	Replacement Edit	match one word	not _ me to
?	Deletion Edit	search for TERM optionally	discuss ?about this issue

Table 1: Query operator instruction

into BiLSTM-CRF network to compute and output a DIRC label sequence.

3.4 Retrieving Suggestions for Detected Errors

To retrieve writing suggestions for detected errors, we design queries for each edit type to search for more plausible corrections using *Linggle*, a linguistic search engine on a web-based dataset of one trillion words (Boisson et al., 2013).

Linggle has different query functions and operators to search word usage in context as shown in Figure 1. These query functions enable the system to query zero, one or multiple words. For example, "play * role" is intended to search for a maximum span of three intervening words. We use three operators ("?", "*", "_") to retrieve corrective suggestions for the three edit types, as described below.

Deletion edit: We use the "?" operator before a word tagged with "D" to search for n-grams with or without the word in question. For example, receiving the sentence *"We discuss about this issue."* as input, our GED model outputs the sequence "C C D C C". Then, we generate the query "discuss ?about this issue" to search *Linggle* for corrective suggestions.

Insertion edit: We use the "*" operator before a word tagged with "I" to search for ngrams with additional words around this word. For example, an insertion edit on "this" is detected in the sentence *"I am good this sport."* (the GED model output "C C C I C"), and thus a *Linggle* query are formulated as "good * this".

Replacement edit: A word tagged with "R" indicates replacement required. We first check if the word is misspelled using *enchant*[2] library. If misspelled, we replace the word with candidates by *enchant* (e.g., 'moey' → 'money/mopey/mosey'). If not, we use the "_" operator to search for alternative n-grams. For example, the GED output of the sentence *"The driver did not accept me to get on*

the bus." would be "C C C C **R** C C C C C C C C". Thus, we use the query "not _ me to" to search for replacement.

4 Experiments

4.1 Datasets

We used the EF-Cambridge Open Language Database (EFCAMDAT) (Geertzen et al., 2013) to train our AES model. This dataset contains about 1.2 million essays with over 83 million words written by approximately 174,000 learners with a wide range of CEFR levels (A1-C2) (language proficiency level). We used the student essays as input and the CEFR level assigned by a grader as output to train the AES model. Due to the imbalanced distribution of levels as shown in Table 2, we randomly selected 1,903 essays from each level and then used 5-fold cross validation for training and evaluation.

CEFR Level	#Essays	#Training
A1	460,614	1,903
A2	300,188	1,903
B1	166,453	1,903
B2	60,844	1,903
C1	14,551	1,903
C2	1,903	1,903

Table 2: Description of the EFCAMDAT dataset

To train the GED model, we use the First Certificate in English dataset (FCE). This dataset contains 1,224 essays written by English learners who took the First Certificate in English (FCE) exam. These essays have been manually tagged based on 77 error types (Yannakoudakis et al., 2011). We used 30,953 sentences from FCE for training, 2,720 for testing, and 2,222 for development. We followed the approach of Rei and Yannakoudakis (2016) in our experiment, but converted the dataset into DIRC format as described in Section 3.3.

---

[2]https://github.com/AbiWord/enchant

Model	Binary Task			DIRC Task								
	Incorrect tag			Insertion tag			Replacement tag			Deletion tag		
	Prec.	Rec.	$F_{0.5}$	Prec.	Rec.	$F_{0.5}$	Prec.	Rec.	$F_{0.5}$	Prec.	Rec.	$F_{0.5}$
Rei and Søgaard (2018)	65.5	28.6	52									
BiLSTM-CRF + word2vec	**89**	13.8	42.6	**57.2**	12.1	32.9	**82.9**	22.4	53.9	**67.6**	3.1	13.2
BiLSTM-CRF + Flair	68.9	24.6	50.7	53.8	20.2	40.4	72.8	28.3	55.4	59.6	10.1	30.17
BiLSTM-CRF + BERT	71.1	35.7	59.4	53.2	23.8	42.7	73.1	36.1	60.7	53.9	24.1	43.2
BiLSTM-CRF + BERT +Flair	72.3	**36.7**	**60.6**	54.6	**25.3**	**44.3**	73.5	**40.6**	**63.3**	59	**24.9**	**46.3**

Table 3: Evaluation on FCE-public test set in DIRC task and binary task

4.2 Hyperparameters

For the AES model, we optimized the trained model using RMSProp (Dauphin et al., 2015) optimizer with learning rate 0.001 and the maximum gradient norm was set to 0.9. We used pre-trained 100-dimensional GloVe vectors (Pennington et al., 2014) as input. The hidden layer size of LSTM and Bi-LSTM was set to 100. For CNN models, we used a window size of 5 and hidden layer size of 100. We applied dropout on the neural network layer to avoid overfitting, with dropout probabilities set to 0.2. The batch size was 32 and each model was trained for 50 epochs.

For the GED model, we set parameters different from previous work (Rei and Yannakoudakis, 2016). We use the publicly available pre-trained word embeddings GoogleNews word vectors (word2vec) (Mikolov et al., 2013), Flair (Akbik et al., 2018), and BERT[3] (Devlin et al., 2018) to represent words. Flair embeddings were trained on the 1-billion word corpus used in Chelba et al. (2013) and the embedding size (both forward and backward) was 2048. As for BERT, we utilized *bert-base-uncased* model which is trained on the English Wikipedia (2.5G words) and *BooksCorpus* (0.8G words). We employed 2-layer Bi-LSTM with CRF to develop for GED model and set the hidden layer size of Bi-LSTM to 256. We used SGD optimizer with learning rate 0.01, with maximum gradient norm set to 1. We applied dropout on both embedding and Bi-LSTM layers with dropout probabilities 0.5. We trained the network for 150 epochs and selected the best model with the highest F1 score on the development set.

5 Evaluation

For the AES task, we adopted quadratic weighted Kappa (QWK) as our evaluation metric, which was used in Automated Student Assessment Prize (ASAP) competition and several AES researches (Taghipour and Ng, 2016; Vaswani et al., 2017; Dong et al., 2017). For the GED task, we follow the previous research by Rei and Yannakoudakis (2016) and use precision, recall and $F_{0.5}$ to evaluate our GED model.

Table 3 presents the results of different GED models on the FCE testset with binary and DIRC format to compare our results with the state-of-the-art method proposed by Rei and Søgaard (2018) using the binary schema. Table 3 shows that **BiLSTM-CRF+BERT+Flair** performs substantially better than the other GED models and achieve state-of-the-art performance on the FCE test set. Interestingly, we note that the model with word2vec pre-trained word embeddings achieves the highest precision but the lowest recall. As for the DIRC schema, **BiLSTM-CRF+BERT+Flair** performs the best among all models. Importantly, the DIRC model performs comparably to the binary model while providing more informative feedback (i.e., the edit type) for learners to self-edit their essays. It is also worth noting that for GED and GEC tasks multiple answers are acceptable and there is low inter-annotator agreement (Rozovskaya and Roth, 2010). Bryant and Ng (2015) pointed out even human annotators can only achieve 72.8 $F_{0.5}$ score at the best against the gold standard annotations of multiple annotators in GEC tasks. Thus, it is fair to say that the performance of our model against one gold standard annotation are underestimated and not far from human annotators, thus acceptable for an application.

Table 4 shows results of different network architectures on the AES task. As we can see in Table 4, **LSTN-LSTM-ATT** achieves the best performance among all models. In addition, we find that sentence-level models perform better than word-level ones in general. Furthermore, we also observe that the model with attention mechanism per-

---

[3]https://github.com/google-research/bert#pre-trained-models

Model	Model Type	Avg. QWK score
CNN	Word-level	0.902
LSTM	Word-level	0.927
Bi-LSTM	Word-level	0.921
LSTM + attention	Word-level	0.931
CNN-CNN	Sentence-level	0.934
LSTM-LSTM	Sentence-level	0.937
CNN-LSTM-ATT	Sentence-level	0.952
LSTM-LSTM-ATT	Sentence-level	**0.957**

Table 4: Average QWK scores on EFCAMDAT

forms slightly better than the other without attention mechanism. Besides, the result (i.e., QWK score 0.957) shows our neural models are efficient to predict scores in EFCAMDAT, comparing with other datasets as Automated Student Assessment Prize[4] (ASAP). Trained on ASAP, the character-based model with CNN-LSTM proposed by Taghipour and Ng (2016) scores QWK 0.761, and the sentence-based model with LSTM-CNN-att proposed by Taghipour and Ng (2016) achieves QWK score 0.764.

6 Conclusion and Future Work

In summary, we have presented an writing environment that supports interactive writing suggestions, scoring, error detection and corrective feedback. For the interactive writing task, we provide grammatical suggestions, collocations, and bilingual examples, to guide the user towards writing fluently. For the GED task, we proposed a new label schema, DIRC. Experiments show that the proposed label schema achieves comparable performance (on binary task) while providing more informative feedback. In addition, we leverage an existing linguistic search engine to provide corrective suggestions for each error type.

Many avenues exist for future research and improvement of our system. For example, the method for introducing additional training data or generating artificial training data could be implemented to improve the performance. An interesting direction to explore is re-ranking corrective suggestions, so that the suggestion more relevant to the original sentence goes to the top. Yet another direction of research would be to detect fine-grained error types. Finally, our system currently providing additional Chinese translations for English examples. Obviously we could easily provide languages trans-

lations by changing a bilingual dictionary.

Acknowledgment

This work is supported by Ministry of Science and Technology, Taiwan under Grant No. 109-2639-M-007-001-, No. 109-2634-F-001-010-, and National Tsing Hua University under Grant No. 109Q2729E1.

References

Alan Akbik, Duncan Blythe, and Roland Vollgraf. 2018. Contextual string embeddings for sequence labeling. In *Proceedings of the 27th International Conference on Computational Linguistics*, pages 1638–1649. Association for Computational Linguistics.

Joanne Boisson, Ting-Hui Kao, Jian-Cheng Wu, Tzu-Hsi Yen, and Jason S Chang. 2013. Linggle: a web-scale linguistic search engine for words in context. In *Proceedings of the 51st Annual Meeting of the Association for Computational Linguistics: System Demonstrations*, pages 139–144.

Christopher Bryant and Hwee Tou Ng. 2015. How far are we from fully automatic high quality grammatical error correction? In *Proceedings of the 53rd Annual Meeting of the Association for Computational Linguistics and the 7th International Joint Conference on Natural Language Processing (Volume 1: Long Papers)*, volume 1, pages 697–707.

Ciprian Chelba, Tomas Mikolov, Mike Schuster, Qi Ge, Thorsten Brants, Phillipp Koehn, and Tony Robinson. 2013. One billion word benchmark for measuring progress in statistical language modeling. Technical report, Google.

Mia Xu Chen, Benjamin N Lee, Gagan Bansal, Yuan Cao, Shuyuan Zhang, Justin Lu, Jackie Tsay, Yinan Wang, Andrew M Dai, Zhifeng Chen, et al. 2019. Gmail smart compose: Real-time assisted writing. In *Proceedings of the 25th ACM SIGKDD International Conference on Knowledge Discovery & Data Mining*, pages 2287–2295.

Yann N. Dauphin, Harm de Vries, and Yoshua Bengio. 2015. Equilibrated adaptive learning rates for non-convex optimization. In *Proceedings of the 28th International Conference on Neural Information Processing Systems - Volume 1*, NIPS'15, pages 1504–1512, Cambridge, MA, USA. MIT Press.

Jacob Devlin, Ming-Wei Chang, Kenton Lee, and Kristina Toutanova. 2018. Bert: Pre-training of deep bidirectional transformers for language understanding. *arXiv preprint arXiv:1810.04805*.

Fei Dong, Yue Zhang, and Jie Yang. 2017. Attention-based recurrent convolutional neural network for automatic essay scoring. In *Proceedings of the 21st*

---

[4]https://www.kaggle.com/c/asap-aes

Conference on Computational Natural Language Learning (CoNLL 2017), pages 153–162. Association for Computational Linguistics.

Gill Francis, Susan Hunston, and Elizabeth Manning. 1996. Grammar patterns 1: verbs. *NY: Harper-Collins Publication*.

Jeroen Geertzen, Theodora Alexopoulou, and Anna Korhonen. 2013. Automatic linguistic annotation of large scale l2 databases: The ef-cambridge open language database. In *Proceedings of SLRF 2012*.

Marti A Hearst. 2015. Can natural language processing become natural language coaching? In *Proceedings of the 53rd Annual Meeting of the Association for Computational Linguistics and the 7th International Joint Conference on Natural Language Processing (Volume 1: Long Papers)*, volume 1, pages 1245–1252.

Adam Kilgarriff, Milos Husák, Katy McAdam, Michael Rundell, and Pavel Rychlý. 2008. Gdex: Automatically finding good dictionary examples in a corpus. In *Proc. Euralex*.

Tomas Mikolov, Ilya Sutskever, Kai Chen, Greg Corrado, and Jeffrey Dean. 2013. Distributed representations of words and phrases and their compositionality. In *Proceedings of the 26th International Conference on Neural Information Processing Systems - Volume 2*, NIPS'13, pages 3111–3119, USA. Curran Associates Inc.

Jeffrey Pennington, Richard Socher, and Christopher D. Manning. 2014. Glove: Global vectors for word representation. In *In EMNLP*.

Marek Rei and Anders Søgaard. 2018. Jointly learning to label sentences and tokens. *CoRR*, abs/1811.05949.

Marek Rei and Helen Yannakoudakis. 2016. Compositional sequence labeling models for error detection in learner writing. In *Proceedings of the 54th Annual Meeting of the Association for Computational Linguistics (Volume 1: Long Papers)*, pages 1181–1191. Association for Computational Linguistics.

Alla Rozovskaya and Dan Roth. 2010. Annotating esl errors: Challenges and rewards. In *Proceedings of the NAACL HLT 2010 fifth workshop on innovative use of NLP for building educational applications*, pages 28–36. Association for Computational Linguistics.

Kaveh Taghipour and Hwee Tou Ng. 2016. A neural approach to automated essay scoring. In *Proceedings of the 2016 Conference on Empirical Methods in Natural Language Processing*, pages 1882–1891. Association for Computational Linguistics.

Ashish Vaswani, Noam Shazeer, Niki Parmar, Jakob Uszkoreit, Llion Jones, Aidan N Gomez, Łukasz Kaiser, and Illia Polosukhin. 2017. Attention is all you need. In *Advances in neural information processing systems*, pages 5998–6008.

Helen Yannakoudakis, Ted Briscoe, and Ben Medlock. 2011. A new dataset and method for automatically grading esol texts. In *Proceedings of the 49th Annual Meeting of the Association for Computational Linguistics: Human Language Technologies-Volume 1*, pages 180–189. Association for Computational Linguistics.

CLIReval: Evaluating Machine Translation as a
Cross-Lingual Information Retrieval Task

Shuo Sun
Johns Hopkins University
`ssun32@jhu.edu`

Suzanna Sia
Johns Hopkins University
`ssia1@jhu.edu`

Kevin Duh
Johns Hopkins University
`kevinduh@cs.jhu.edu`

Abstract

We present **CLIReval**, an easy-to-use toolkit
for evaluating machine translation (MT) with
the proxy task of cross-lingual information retrieval (CLIR). Contrary to what the project
name might suggest, CLIReval does not actually require any annotated CLIR dataset. Instead, it automatically transforms translations
and references used in MT evaluations into
a synthetic CLIR dataset; it then sets up
a standard search engine (Elasticsearch) and
computes various information retrieval metrics (e.g., mean average precision) by treat-
ing the translations as documents to be retrieved. The idea is to gauge the quality of
MT by its impact on the document translation approach to CLIR. As a case study, we
run CLIReval on the "metrics shared task" of
WMT2019; while this extrinsic metric is not
intended to replace popular intrinsic metrics
such as BLEU, results suggest CLIReval is
competitive in many language pairs in terms
of correlation to human judgments of quality. CLIReval is publicly available at `https:`
`//github.com/ssun32/CLIReval`.

1 Introduction

Machine translation (MT) is the task of automatically translating sentences from a source language
to a target language. A natural question that arises
is how do we determine whether an MT system is
translating sentences well? One answer is that we
can engage human translators to evaluate the translated sentences manually. Unfortunately, evaluating translations can be relatively time-consuming
and worse, the fact that the quality of translation is
inherently subjective can lead to variations among
different human translators. The desire for fast and
consistent evaluation has led to the emergence of
a plethora of automatic evaluation metrics such as
BLEU (Papineni et al., 2002), TER (Snover et al.,
2006), METOR (Banerjee and Lavie, 2005) and

BEER (Stanojević and Sima'an, 2014). Out of the
aforementioned metrics, BLEU has become the de
facto evaluation metric for machine translation. It
calculates the weighted average of n-gram precision between a translated sentence and a reference
sentence. Nevertheless, BLEU, too, has its problems. For example, Callison-Burch et al. (2006)
showed that an improved BLEU score does not represent an actual improvement in translation quality.

There are also some proposals to evaluate the
quality of translations with the help of extrinsic
proxy tasks. Berka et al. (2011) collected short
English documents from various domains and created yes and no questions in Czech. They then
translated the English documents into Czech and
evaluated the quality of the MT systems based on
human performances on the documents and questions in Czech. Scarton and Specia (2016) translated a dataset of German reading comprehension
tests into English with various MT systems such as
Google Translate and Bing Translate and judged
the quality of translations based on human performances on the translated reading comprehension
datasets. Unfortunately, these external tasks suffer
from the same scalability and consistency issues as
manual evaluation.

One downstream task that relies heavily on MT
but has not been used as a method to evaluate MT
systems is the task of *Cross-Lingual Information
Retrieval (CLIR)*. CLIR is a task in which search
queries are issued in one language, and the retrieved relevant documents are written in a different
language. Two commonly used methods in CLIR
are *query translation*, where queries are translated
into the same language as the documents and *document translation* where documents are translated
into the same language as the queries (Zhou et al.,
2012; Oard, 1998; McCarley, 1999). A monolingual IR system is then used to obtain search results.

CLIR is an active field of research, and previ-

Proceedings of the 58th Annual Meeting of the Association for Computational Linguistics, pages 134–141
July 5 - July 10, 2020. ©2020 Association for Computational Linguistics

ous works suggest that the performance of CLIR correlates highly with the quality of the MT (Zhu and Wang, 2006; Nie, 2010; Yarmohammadi et al., 2019). Therefore, we expect IR metrics to be good indicators of the quality of translations. Unfortunately, there is currently no publicly available tool to facilitate research in this area, and this motivates us to design and implement CLIReval.

CLIReval is a lightweight python-based MT evaluation toolkit that consumes the same inputs as other automatic MT evaluation tools such as multi-bleu.perl and SacreBLEU (Post, 2018) and *does not require any additional annotated CLIR data.* Instead, it automatically transforms inputs into a synthetic CLIR dataset on the fly with the help of an Information Retrieval (IR) system. It implements the document translation approach to CLIR, where MT translations are viewed as documents and indexed using a commonly-used search engine (Elasticsearch).

As a case study, we test CLIReval on the metrics shared task of WMT2019 (Ma et al., 2019), which measures the Pearson correlations (r) between automatically generated MT metrics and human judgments. Results show that CLIReval consistently performs at the level of $r \geq 0.9$ and is on par or even outperforms popular metrics such as BLEU on multiple language directions. Further, this is achieved without using external data or doing domain-based parameter tuning. These promising results highlight the potential of CLIR as a proxy task for MT evaluation, and we hope CLIReval can facilitate future research in this area.

Our key contributions in this work can be summarized as follows:

1. We release **CLIReval**,[1] an open-source toolkit that evaluates the quality of MT outputs in the context of a CLIR system, *without the need for any actual CLIR dataset.* The only inputs required to the tool are the translations and the references. It is easy to use in that with a single script, the tool will create a synthetic CLIR dataset, index the translations as documents, and report metrics such as mean average precision.

2. We demonstrate that CLIReval can perform as well as popular intrinsic MT metrics on recent WMT metrics shared task, without supervision from external datasets and domain-based

[1]https://github.com/ssun32/CLIReval

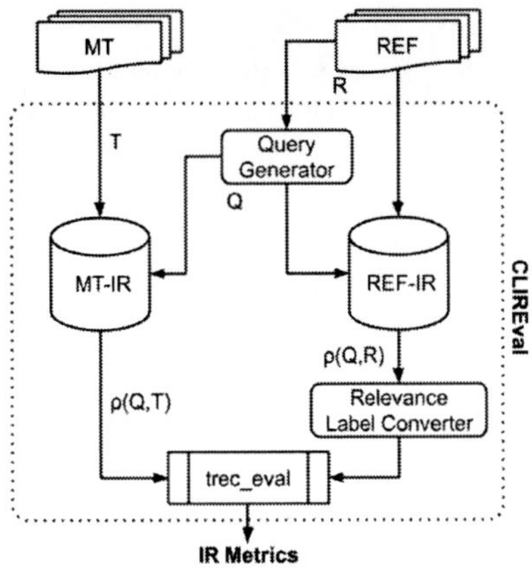

Figure 1: The system architecture of CLIReval. Documents from input files are separately indexed into two instances of IR systems. Generated search queries are used to query both IR instances. Search scores from REF-IR are converted to discrete relevance judgment labels as required by trec_eval. Finally, CLIReval uses trec_eval to calculate IR metrics.

parameter tuning. Results suggest that CLIR is a feasible proxy task for MT evaluation and is worth further exploration in future research.

2   Approach

Given a set of source documents S, an MT system ϕ converts S into a set of translated documents, $T = \phi(S)$. Intrinsic MT metrics directly calculate an aggregated score between the sentences in T and sentences in R, where R is a set of reference documents.[2]

We propose an alternative way to evaluate ϕ by first converting it into a proxy CLIR task and then evaluate the MT system with extrinsic IR metrics. First, CLIReval extracts a set of synthetic search queries Q from R. Second, given a monolingual information retrieval (IR) engine ρ, we can run these queries Q over the document collection R to obtain a set of "relevant" documents for Q. We use the notation $\rho(Q, R)$ to refer to this set of desired returned search results.

Now, our goal is to evaluate the quality of the translation $T = \phi(S)$ under the same IR engine ρ. We index the documents T into the IR engine and submit the same queries to obtain the search

[2]When document boundaries are not defined, CLIReval automatically creates artificial document boundaries. The default option is to treat each sentence as a document for retrieval purposes.

results $\rho(Q, T)$. Finally, we can measure the performance of the CLIR system by comparing $\rho(Q, T)$ to $\rho(Q, R)$, and calculating IR metrics such as mean average precision.

This approach makes several assumptions. First, CLIReval implements the *document translation approach* to CLIR and evaluates MT quality in that context; additionally, we assume that ρ is a robust and reasonable IR engine that can be used across a wide range of situations. Second, we assume R contains the "correct" translations of S, and that $\rho(Q, R)$ is a good approximation of the optimal search results. Third, we assume that automatically-generated Q can mimic that actual information needs of manually-crafted queries. If these caveats are acknowledged, then CLIReval is a reasonable tool for MT evaluation.

3   Design and Implementation Details

Figure 1 presents the system architecture of CLIReval. The only necessary inputs are 1) a system output translation (MT) file and 2) a reference (REF) file. CLIReval executes the following steps:

1. Separately index documents in MT and REF files into two instances of the Information Retrieval (IR) system, we refer to them as MT-IR and REF-IR.

2. Convert text in the REF file into search queries with the *Query Generator* module.

3. Query both instances of IR system with the same set of generated search queries.

4. Convert search scores from REF-IR to discrete relevance labels with the *Relevance Label Converter*.

5. Finally, CLIReval evaluates the search results from MT-IR and relevance judgment labels from REF-IR with trec_eval,[3] a standard evaluation toolkit used by the information retrieval community.

We emphasize that the above steps are achieved with a single easy-to-use script: CLIReval is as simple as executing the following command:

```
python evaluate.py [ref file] [mt
file]
```

where the inputs are standard text files that

one might pass to `multi-bleu.perl`, or standard SGML files that one might pass to `mteval-v13a.pl`, both of which are common BLEU scripts for MT.[4]

3.1   Input files

CLIReval ingests a system output translation (MT) file which contains documents translated by an MT system and a reference (REF) file, which contains reference translations of the same source documents. Our system supports two input file formats:

1. The *SGML format* commonly used by the news translation shared task from the annual conference on machine translation (Barrault et al., 2019). This is also the input format required by the NIST BLEU scoring tool.[5] In a SGML file, every translated sentence segment is placed in a <seg> tag, and sentence segments belonging to the same document are placed in the same <doc> tag. Every <doc> tag must also contain a unique document id attribute used to identify the document.

2. A *text file* where each line contains a sentence. A user can supply an optional mapping file that maps a line number to a (document id and, segment id) tuple. If a mapping file is not specified, CLIReval will create an artificial document boundary every N sentences.[6]

For either format, the number of documents in the MT file must be equivalent to the number of documents in the REF file. Further, the number of sentence segments in a machine translated document must also match the number of sentence segments in the corresponding reference document.

3.2   Query Generator

The query generator module ingests data in the REF file and automatically generates search queries. CLIReval has two modes for query generation, which can be specified with the query_mode argument:

1. In **sentences** mode, the query generator extracts all reference sentences from the input

<hr>

[3]https://github.com/usnistgov/trec_eval

[4]https://github.com/moses-smt/mosesdecoder/blob/master/scripts/generic/

[5]ftp://jaguar.ncsl.nist.gov/mt/resources/mteval-v13.pl

[6]N can be specified with the doc_length argument. The default value is 1, which means every sentence is treated as a document.

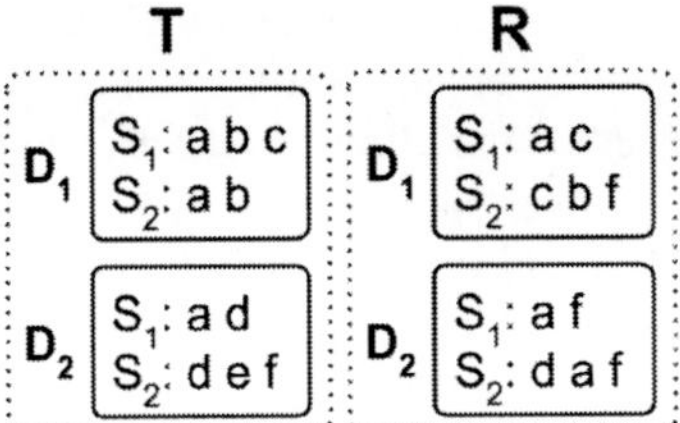

Figure 2: R is a set of sample reference documents and each document contains two sentences, while T is a set of sample translated documents.

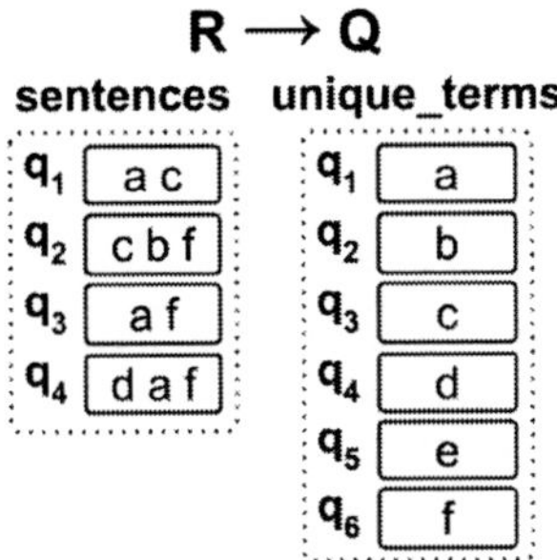

Figure 3: Sample outputs from the *query generator*. In *sentences* mode, all sentences from R (Figure 2) are used as search queries while in the *unique_terms* mode, the unique terms in R are the search queries.

REF file and treats every sentence as a search query string. This is inspired by Sasaki et al. (2018), who use the first sentences of documents as queries.

2. In **unique_terms** mode, the query generator treats all unique terms as queries. For Elasticsearch, these terms can be obtained from the term vectors of all indexed documents.

We recognize that using sentences or unique terms as queries might be less ideal than using real search queries, but getting relevant human-generated queries can be time-consuming and expensive. Our query generation methods are cheap and fast, which enables quick experimentation. Examples of R and T are shown in Figure 2, and the resulting queries generated from R are shown in Figure 3. In the example, we have two documents D_1 and D_2 each with two sentences S_1 and S_2. In the **sentence** mode for query generation, each of the four sentences in R are used as queries; in the **unique_terms** mode, the 6 vocabulary words are extracted as query.

3.3 Information Retrieval (IR) System

To ensure consistent and reproducible results, we choose Elasticsearch[7] as the default backend IR system for CLIReval and adopt well-tested search configurations.[8] Elasticsearch is an open-source, lightweight, and fast search engine written in Java. We pick Elasticsearch for three reasons:

First, Elasticsearch has built-in analyzers for a wide variety of languages, which allows CLIReval to support many translation tasks beyond English as the target language. Analyzers are Elasticsearch modules that preprocess and tokenize queries and documents according to language-specific rules. It also implements stopwords removal and stemming. These are important operations that affect the quality of search results.

Second, Elasticsearch implements many competitive retrieval models used by IR researchers and practitioners. By default, CLIReval uses the Okapi BM25 (Robertson et al., 2009) score to measure the degree of similarity of documents to a given search query. Note that BM25 shows strong performances on many datasets (Chapelle and Chang, 2011; McDonald et al., 2018) and frequently outperforms newer "state of the art" methods (Guo et al., 2016). It is also fast to compute, allowing CLIReval to run in a highly efficient manner.

Third, Elasticsearch is a widely used search engine solution that is supported on various platforms. This increases the ease of installation for users of CLIReval.

CLIReval separately indexes the documents from MT and REF files into two instances of Elasticsearch. It then queries the Elasticsearch instances with the generated query strings. For every query, Elasticsearch returns the top 100 documents ranked by BM25 scores. Since trec_eval only accepts discrete relevance judgment labels, the relevance label converter module is used to convert search scores from REF-IR into discrete labels.

3.4 Relevance Label Converter

We implement three ways of converting raw BM25 scores of REF-IR into discrete *relevance judgment labels*:

The **query_in_document** method (Schamoni et al., 2014; Sasaki et al., 2018) assigns 1 to a document if and only if the given search query

---

[7]https://www.elastic.co/
[8]CLIReval is flexible and users can easily replace Elasticsearch with their own IR system.

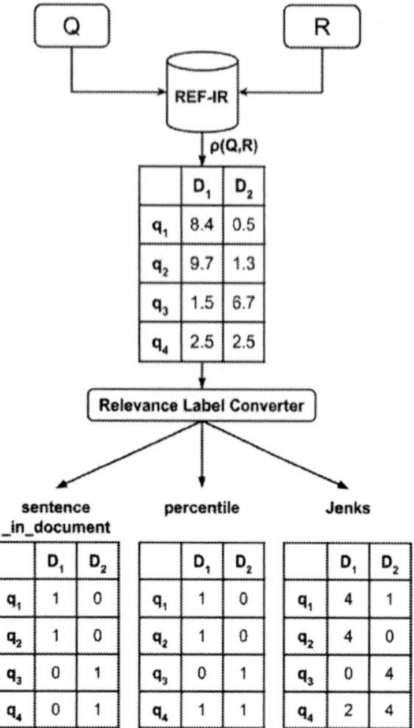

Figure 4: Given queries from the query generator and documents from R, we can obtain relevance scores from an IR system. The *relevance label converter* then converts those relevance scores into discrete relevance labels via different conversion modes.

is extracted from that document. Consequently, there will only be one relevant document per search query.

The **percentile** method assigns 1 to documents with BM25 scores in the top 25 percentile of all document scores returned by the IR system and 0 otherwise. The cutoff percentile value can be adjusted with the *n_percentile* argument.

Th **Jenks** methods uses Jenks natural breaks optimization[9] to automatically break a list of BM25 scores into different classes. This is achieved by minimizing the variance of BM25 scores within a class and at the same time maximize the variance of average BM25 scores between classes (McMaster and McMaster, 2002). Following the conventions of publicly available IR datasets (Chapelle and Chang, 2011; Qin and Liu, 2013), we break the BM25 scores into 5 relevance judgment classes, where 4 indicates that a document is highly relevant to a given query and 0 indicates that a document is not relevant to a given query. For each query, CLIReval normalizes the BM25 scores of

retrieved documents to the range [0, 1] and use Jenks natural breaks optimization to convert the BM25 scores into discrete relevance judgment labels. Users can specify the number of classes with the *jenks_nb_class* argument.

Figure 4 illustrates an example of how relevance labels are generated for each query-document pair using the generated query Q (see Section 3.2 and the reference documents R provided by the user. First, raw BM25 scores are obtained by indexing R in an IR system and searching with Q. These scores are then converted to discrete labels in one of three ways.

3.5 IR Metrics

To summarize: after the queries and relevance labels are prepared (as in Section 3.2 and 3.4), the MT output T (e.g. Figure 2, left) is indexed into another IR system. Finally, we run the queries Q through this MT-IR system to obtain document scores $\rho(Q, T)$ (e.g. Figure 1, left branch), which can be evaluated with respect to the relevance labels. We do this final evaluation with the standard trec_eval toolkit.

The trec_eval toolkit returns a large number of IR metrics but CLIReval is configured to return only two of the most popular IR metrics by default:

- **Mean average precision (MAP)** is the mean of the average precision scores for each query (Buckley and Voorhees, 2005).

- **Normalized discounted cumulative gain (NDCG)** is a metric that measures the usefulness of documents based on their ranks in the search results (Järvelin and Kekäläinen, 2002) and is normalized to [0, 1].

We choose MAP because it is a widely understood metric, and NDCG because it allows for multiple levels of relevance labels. We follow standard practice in IR benchmark datasets such as Chapelle and Chang (2011) and calculate both metrics at the cutoff threshold of 10 documents. We name these metrics as MAP@10 and NDCG@10.

3.6 Installation

CLIReval is written in Python 3 and works on Python 3.5 and later. Elasticsearch requires at least Java 8. We provide a shell script that automatically downloads and installs Elasticsearch 6.5.3 and the latest version of trec_eval. It also installs additional

---

[9]https://en.wikipedia.org/wiki/Jenks_natural_breaks_optimization

Elasticsearch plugins that support additional languages. In total, CLIReval has built-in support for 36 languages and for unsupported languages, it will fall back to the default standard analyzer, which is based on the Unicode text segmentation algorithm.[10] We tested CLIReval extensively in the Unix/Linux environment, but it should work in other environments with minimal modification.

4 Case Study

4.1 WMT metrics shared task

To demonstrate the utility of CLIReval, we test it on the metrics shared task of WMT2019.[11] The metrics task (Ma et al., 2019) is designed to evaluate outputs from automatic MT metrics against actual human ratings on machine translation systems. The goal is to find evaluation methods that have high Pearson correlations with human judgments. For every system in every language direction, we compute multiple system-level scores (different IR metrics) with CLIReval.

In total, there are 18 language directions, and for every language direction, a reference file and 11 to 22 system generated translation files are provided. In every reference file, there are around 1000 to 2000 sentences in 70 to 140 documents. The only exceptions are French-German and German-French, where all sentences are placed in the same document. Since document boundaries are not clearly defined in these language directions, we are excluding them from this case study.

4.2 Run Time

We used an Intel Xeon E5 Linux server with 64GB RAM. For every language direction, CLIReval runs consistently at the rate of around 0.2 to 0.3 seconds per document and it takes less than a minute to get results.

4.3 Results

We use the official evaluation scripts[12] to compute linear correlations between IR metrics and human judgments.

Table 1 presents the results for 16 language directions and IR metrics perform well. On Jenks mode, NDCG@10 outperforms BLEU and NIST on 10 out of the 16 language directions. Further,

the 4 IR metrics collectively hold the top scores for 6 language directions. BEER seems to be a little bit better than the IR metrics, claiming the top spot for 7 language directions. Note that the participating BEER system is trained on provided in-domain data, while we are getting comparable results without any tuning. It is also worth pointing out that the intrinsic MT metrics work at sentence level while in comparison, CLIReval works at the document-level. Nonetheless, the results are encouraging and show the potential of CLIR as a proxy task for MT evaluation.

4.4 Analysis: BLEU vs. NDCG

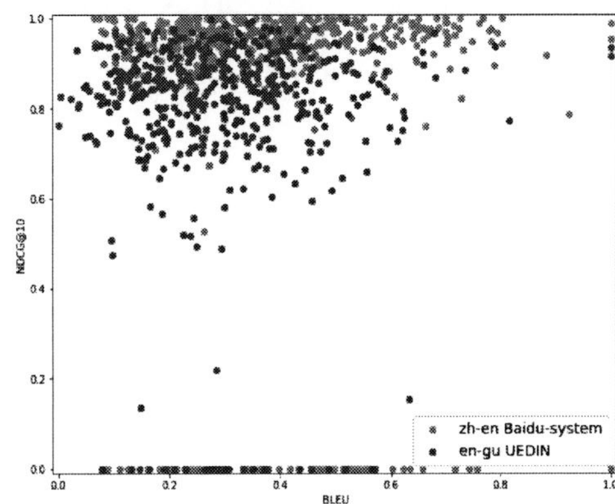

Figure 5: Scatterplot of sentence-level NDCG@10 vs sentence-level BLEU on zh-en and en-gu. For better visualization, only 300 random samples from each language direction are shown.

To get a deeper comparison between CLIReval and the most popular MT metric, BLEU, we randomly select two systems (Baidu-system for zh-en and UEDIN for en-gu) and calculate sentence-level BLEU and sentence-level NDCG@10 scores[13] on both systems. As we can see in Figure 5, there is no clear correlation between sentence-level NDCG@10 and sentence-level BLEU scores. To be more exact, the Pearson correlations between the two metrics is almost non-existent, at -0.021 and -0.032 for zh-en and en-gu respectively. This shows that the two metrics are qualitatively different and contribute different perspectives to MT evaluation.

5 Conclusions

We present CLIReval, an open-source python-based evaluation toolkit for machine translation.

---

[10]https://unicode.org/reports/tr29/
[11]http://www.statmt.org/wmt19/
[12]http://ufallab.ms.mff.cuni.cz/~bojar/wmt18-metrics-task-package.tgz

[13]calculated with CLIReval using default arguments.

LD	BLEU	NIST	TER	BEER	query_in_document		Jenks	
					MAP@10	NDCG@10	MAP@10	NDCG@10
de→cs	0.941	0.954	0.890	0.978	0.971	0.968	0.965	**0.991**
de→en	0.849	0.813	0.874	**0.906**	0.865	0.869	0.654	0.858
en→cs	0.897	0.896	0.980	**0.990**	0.882	0.889	0.909	0.983
en→de	0.921	0.321	0.969	**0.983**	0.953	0.953	0.977	0.982
en→fi	0.969	0.971	0.981	**0.989**	0.915	0.906	0.927	0.944
en→gu	0.737	0.786	0.865	0.829	**0.912**	0.909	0.833	0.847
en→kk	0.852	0.930	0.940	0.971	**0.982**	**0.982**	0.963	0.968
en→lt	0.989	0.993	**0.994**	0.982	0.776	0.791	0.903	0.916
en→ru	0.986	0.988	**0.995**	0.977	0.865	0.862	0.980	0.953
en→zh	0.901	0.884	0.856	0.803	0.928	**0.930**	0.772	0.902
fi→en	0.982	0.986	0.984	**0.993**	0.956	0.955	0.944	0.960
gu→en	0.834	0.930	0.890	**0.952**	0.814	0.809	0.782	0.824
kk→en	0.946	0.942	0.799	**0.986**	0.970	0.968	**0.986**	0.983
lt→en	**0.961**	0.944	0.960	0.947	0.636	0.612	0.929	0.865
ru→en	0.879	0.925	0.917	0.915	0.922	0.920	0.866	**0.961**
zh→en	0.899	0.921	0.840	0.942	0.930	0.922	0.622	**0.957**

Table 1: Pearson correlations (r) of various metrics against human judgments. Best scores for every language direction are highlighted in bold. Note that BEER is trained on in-domain resources from the WMT2019 metrics task. We show MAP@10 and NDCG@10 scores for CLIReval with two relevance label conversion settings.

Rather than directly evaluating translated sentences against reference sentences, CLIReval transforms the inputs into the closely related task of CLIR, without the need for annotated CLIR dataset.

The aim of this project is not to replace current automatic evaluation metrics or fix the limitations in those metrics, but to bridge the gap between machine translation and cross-lingual information retrieval and to show that CLIR is a feasible proxy task for MT evaluation.

Our case study on the WMT2019 metrics shared task further highlights the potential of CLIR as a proxy task for MT evaluation, and we hope that CLIReval can facilitate future research in this area.

Acknowledgement

We want to thank Sorami Hisamoto and Muhammad Mahbubur Rahman for their initial code and guidance on best practices for Elasticsearch.

References

Satanjeev Banerjee and Alon Lavie. 2005. Meteor: An automatic metric for mt evaluation with improved correlation with human judgments. In *Proceedings of the acl workshop on intrinsic and extrinsic evaluation measures for machine translation and/or summarization*, pages 65–72.

Loïc Barrault, Ondřej Bojar, Marta R Costa-jussà, Christian Federmann, Mark Fishel, Yvette Graham, Barry Haddow, Matthias Huck, Philipp Koehn, Shervin Malmasi, et al. 2019. Findings of the 2019 conference on machine translation (wmt19). In *Proceedings of the Fourth Conference on Machine Translation (Volume 2: Shared Task Papers, Day 1)*, pages 1–61.

Jan Berka, Martin Černý, and Ondřej Bojar. 2011. Quiz-based evaluation of machine translation. *The Prague Bulletin of Mathematical Linguistics*, 95:77–86.

Chris Buckley and Ellen Voorhees. 2005. Retrieval system evaluation. *TREC: Experiment and Evaluation in Information Retrieval*, pages 53–75.

Chris Callison-Burch, Miles Osborne, and Philipp Koehn. 2006. Re-evaluation the role of bleu in machine translation research. In *11th Conference of the European Chapter of the Association for Computational Linguistics*.

Olivier Chapelle and Yi Chang. 2011. Yahoo! learning to rank challenge overview. In *Proceedings of the Learning to Rank Challenge*, pages 1–24.

Jiafeng Guo, Yixing Fan, Qingyao Ai, and W Bruce Croft. 2016. A deep relevance matching model for ad-hoc retrieval. In *Proceedings of the 25th ACM International on Conference on Information and Knowledge Management*, pages 55–64.

Kalervo Järvelin and Jaana Kekäläinen. 2002. Cumulated gain-based evaluation of ir techniques. *ACM Transactions on Information Systems (TOIS)*, 20(4):422–446.

Qingsong Ma, Johnny Wei, Ondřej Bojar, and Yvette Graham. 2019. Results of the wmt19 metrics shared task: Segment-level and strong mt systems pose big challenges. In *Proceedings of the Fourth Conference on Machine Translation (Volume 2: Shared Task Papers, Day 1)*, pages 62–90.

J Scott McCarley. 1999. Should we translate the documents or the queries in cross-language information retrieval? In *Proceedings of the 37th annual meeting of the Association for Computational Linguistics on Computational Linguistics*, pages 208–214. Association for Computational Linguistics.

Ryan McDonald, George Brokos, and Ion Androutsopoulos. 2018. Deep relevance ranking using enhanced document-query interactions. In *Proceedings of the 2018 Conference on Empirical Methods in Natural Language Processing*, pages 1849–1860.

Robert McMaster and Susanna McMaster. 2002. A history of twentieth-century american academic cartography. *Cartography and Geographic Information Science*, 29(3):305–321.

Jian-Yun Nie. 2010. Cross-language information retrieval. *Synthesis Lectures on Human Language Technologies*, 3(1):1–125.

Douglas W Oard. 1998. A comparative study of query and document translation for cross-language information retrieval. In *Conference of the Association for Machine Translation in the Americas*, pages 472–483. Springer.

Kishore Papineni, Salim Roukos, Todd Ward, and Wei-Jing Zhu. 2002. Bleu: a method for automatic evaluation of machine translation. In *Proceedings of the 40th annual meeting on association for computational linguistics*, pages 311–318. Association for Computational Linguistics.

Matt Post. 2018. A call for clarity in reporting bleu scores. In *Proceedings of the Third Conference on Machine Translation: Research Papers*, pages 186–191.

Tao Qin and Tie-Yan Liu. 2013. Introducing LETOR 4.0 datasets. *CoRR*, abs/1306.2597.

Stephen Robertson, Hugo Zaragoza, et al. 2009. The probabilistic relevance framework: Bm25 and beyond. *Foundations and Trends® in Information Retrieval*, 3(4):333–389.

Shota Sasaki, Shuo Sun, Shigehiko Schamoni, Kevin Duh, and Kentaro Inui. 2018. Cross-lingual learning-to-rank with shared representations. In *Proceedings of the 2018 Conference of the North American Chapter of the Association for Computational Linguistics: Human Language Technologies, Volume 2 (Short Papers)*, pages 458–463.

Carolina Scarton and Lucia Specia. 2016. A reading comprehension corpus for machine translation evaluation. In *Proceedings of the Tenth International Conference on Language Resources and Evaluation (LREC'16)*, pages 3652–3658.

Shigehiko Schamoni, Felix Hieber, Artem Sokolov, and Stefan Riezler. 2014. Learning translational and knowledge-based similarities from relevance rankings for cross-language retrieval. In *Proceedings of the 52nd Annual Meeting of the Association for Computational Linguistics (Volume 2: Short Papers)*, pages 488–494.

Matthew Snover, Bonnie Dorr, Richard Schwartz, Linnea Micciulla, and John Makhoul. 2006. A study of translation edit rate with targeted human annotation.

Miloš Stanojević and Khalil Sima'an. 2014. Beer: Better evaluation as ranking. In *Proceedings of the Ninth Workshop on Statistical Machine Translation*, pages 414–419.

Mahsa Yarmohammadi, Xutai Ma, Sorami Hisamoto, Muhammad Rahman, Yiming Wang, Hainan Xu, Daniel Povey, Philipp Koehn, and Kevin Duh. 2019. Robust document representations for cross-lingual information retrieval in low-resource settings. In *Proceedings of Machine Translation Summit XVII Volume 1: Research Track*, pages 12–20, Dublin, Ireland. European Association for Machine Translation.

Dong Zhou, Mark Truran, Tim Brailsford, Vincent Wade, and Helen Ashman. 2012. Translation techniques in cross-language information retrieval. *ACM Computing Surveys (CSUR)*, 45(1):1–44.

Jiang Zhu and Haifeng Wang. 2006. The effect of translation quality in mt-based cross-language information retrieval. In *Proceedings of the 21st International Conference on Computational Linguistics and the 44th annual meeting of the Association for Computational Linguistics*, pages 593–600. Association for Computational Linguistics.

ConvLab-2: An Open-Source Toolkit for Building, Evaluating, and Diagnosing Dialogue Systems

Qi Zhu[†] **Zheng Zhang**[†] **Yan Fang**[†] **Xiang Li**[†] **Ryuichi Takanobu**[†]
Jinchao Li[‡] **Baolin Peng**[‡] **Jianfeng Gao**[‡] **Xiaoyan Zhu**[†] **Minlie Huang**[†*]

[†]Dept. of Computer Science and Technology, [†]Institute for Artificial Intelligence,
[†]State Key Lab of Intelligent Technology and Systems,
[†]Beijing National Research Center for Information Science and Technology,
Tsinghua University, Beijing, China
[‡]Microsoft Research, Redmond, USA

[†]{zhu-q18,z-zhang15,fangy17,gxly19}@mails.tsinghua.edu.cn
[‡]{jincli,bapeng,jfgao}@microsoft.com [†]{zxy-dcs,aihuang}@tsinghua.edu.cn

Abstract

We present *ConvLab-2*, an open-source toolkit that enables researchers to build task-oriented dialogue systems with state-of-the-art models, perform an end-to-end evaluation, and diagnose the weakness of systems. As the successor of ConvLab (Lee et al., 2019b), ConvLab-2 inherits ConvLab's framework but integrates more powerful dialogue models and supports more datasets. Besides, we have developed an analysis tool and an interactive tool to assist researchers in diagnosing dialogue systems. The analysis tool presents rich statistics and summarizes common mistakes from simulated dialogues, which facilitates error analysis and system improvement. The interactive tool provides a user interface that allows developers to diagnose an assembled dialogue system by interacting with the system and modifying the output of each system component.

1 Introduction

Task-oriented dialogue systems are gaining increasing attention in recent years, resulting in a number of datasets (Henderson et al., 2014; Wen et al., 2017; Budzianowski et al., 2018b; Rastogi et al., 2019) and a wide variety of models (Wen et al., 2015; Peng et al., 2017; Lei et al., 2018; Wu et al., 2019; Gao et al., 2019). However, very few open-source toolkits provide full support to assembling an end-to-end dialogue system with state-of-the-art models, evaluating the performance in an end-to-end fashion, and analyzing the bottleneck both qualitatively and quantitatively. To fill the gap, we have developed **ConvLab-2** based on our previous dialogue system platform ConvLab (Lee et al., 2019b). ConvLab-2 inherits its predecessor's framework and extend it by integrating many recently proposed state-of-the-art dialogue models. In addition,

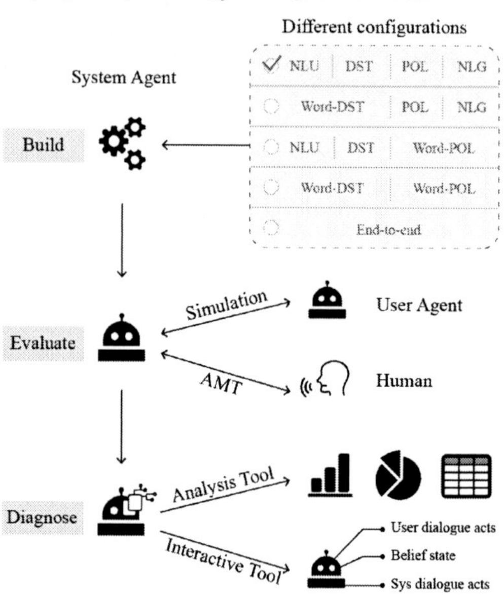

Figure 1: Framework of ConvLab-2. The top block shows different approaches to build a dialogue system.

two powerful tools, namely the analysis tool and the interactive tool, are provided for in-depth error analysis. ConvLab-2 will be the development platform for Multi-domain Task-oriented Dialog Challenge II track in the 9th Dialog System Technology Challenge (DSTC9)[1].

As shown in Figure 1, there are many approaches to building a task-oriented dialogue system, ranging from pipeline methods with multiple components to fully end-to-end models. Previous toolkits focus on either end-to-end models (Miller et al., 2017) or one specific component such as dialogue policy (POL) (Ultes et al., 2017), while the others toolkits that are designed for developers (Bocklisch et al., 2017; Papangelis et al., 2020) do not

---

[*]Corresponding author.

[1]https://sites.google.com/dstc.community/dstc9/home

Proceedings of the 58th Annual Meeting of the Association for Computational Linguistics, pages 142–149
July 5 - July 10, 2020. ©2020 Association for Computational Linguistics

have state-of-the-art models integrated. ConvLab (Lee et al., 2019b) is the first toolkit that provides various powerful models for all dialogue components and allows researchers to quickly assemble a complete dialogue system (using a set of recipes). ConvLab-2 inherits the flexible framework of ConvLab and imports recently proposed models that achieve state-of-the-art performance. In addition, ConvLab-2 supports several large-scale dialogue datasets including CamRest676 (Wen et al., 2017), MultiWOZ (Budzianowski et al., 2018b), DealOrNoDeal (Lewis et al., 2017), and CrossWOZ (Zhu et al., 2020).

To support end-to-end evaluation, ConvLab-2 provides user simulators for automatic evaluation and integrates Amazon Mechanical Turk for human evaluation, similar to ConvLab. Moreover, it provides an analysis tool and a human-machine interactive tool for diagnosing a dialogue system. Researchers can perform quantitative analysis using the analysis tool. It presents useful statistics extracted from the conversations between the user simulator and the dialogue system. This information helps reveal the weakness of the system and signifies the direction for further improvement. With the interactive tool, researchers can perform qualitative analysis by deploying their dialogue systems and conversing with the systems via the webpage. During the conversation, the intermediate output of each component in a pipeline system, such as the user dialogue acts and belief state, are presented on the webpage. In this way, the performance of the system can be examined, and the prediction errors of those components can be corrected manually, which helps the developers identify the bottleneck component. The interactive tool can also be used to collect real-time human-machine dialogues and user feedback for further system improvement.

2 ConvLab-2

2.1 Dialogue Agent

Each speaker in a conversation is regarded as an agent. ConvLab-2 inherits and simplifies ConvLab's framework to accommodate more complicated dialogue agents (e.g., using multiple models for one component) and more general scenarios (e.g., multi-party conversations). Thanks to the flexibility of the agent definition, researchers can build an agent with different types of configurations, such as a traditional pipeline method (as

shown in the first layer of the top block in Figure 1), a fully end-to-end method (the last layer), and between (other layers) once instantiating corresponding models. Researchers can also freely customize an agent, such as incorporating two dialogue systems into one agent to cope with multiple tasks. Based on the unified agent definition that both dialogue systems and user simulators are treated as agents, ConvLab-2 supports conversation between two agents and can be extended to more general scenarios involving three or more parties.

2.2 Models

ConvLab-2 provides the following models for every possible component in a dialogue agent. Note that compared to ConvLab, newly integrated models in ConvLab-2 are marked in bold. Researchers can easily add their models by implementing the interface of the corresponding component. We will keep adding state-of-the-art models to reflect the latest progress in task-oriented dialogue.

2.2.1 Natural Language Understanding

The natural language understanding (NLU) component, which is used to parse the other agent's intent, takes an utterance as input and outputs the corresponding dialogue acts. ConvLab-2 provides three models: Semantic Tuple Classifier (STC) (Mairesse et al., 2009), MILU (Lee et al., 2019b), and **BERTNLU**. BERT (Devlin et al., 2019) has shown strong performance in many NLP tasks. Thus, ConvLab-2 proposes a new BERTNLU model. BERTNLU adds two MLPs on top of BERT for intent classification and slot tagging, respectively, and fine-tunes all parameters on the specified tasks. BERTNLU achieves the best performance on MultiWOZ in comparison with other models.

2.2.2 Dialogue State Tracking

The dialogue state tracking (DST) component updates the belief state, which contains the constraints and requirements of the other agent (such as a user). ConvLab-2 provides a rule-based tracker that takes dialogue acts parsed by the NLU as input.

2.2.3 Word-level Dialogue State Tracking

Word-level DST obtains the belief state directly from the dialogue history. ConvLab-2 integrates four models: MDBT (Ramadan et al., 2018), **SUMBT** (Lee et al., 2019a), and **TRADE** (Wu et al., 2019). TRADE generates the belief state from utterances using a copy mechanism and achieves state-of-the-art performance on Multi-WOZ.

2.2.4 Dialogue Policy

Dialogue policy receives the belief state and outputs system dialogue acts. ConvLab-2 provides a rule-based policy, a simple neural policy that learns directly from the corpus using imitation learning, and reinforcement learning policies including REINFORCE (Williams, 1992), PPO (Schulman et al., 2017), and **GDPL** (Takanobu et al., 2019). GDPL achieves state-of-the-art performance on Multi-WOZ.

2.2.5 Natural Language Generation

The natural language generation (NLG) component transforms dialogue acts into a natural language sentence. ConvLab-2 provides a template-based method and SC-LSTM (Wen et al., 2015).

2.2.6 Word-level Policy

Word-level policy directly generates a natural language response (rather than dialogue acts) according to the dialogue history and the belief state. ConvLab-2 integrates three models: MDRG (Budzianowski et al., 2018a), **HDSA** (Chen et al., 2019), and **LaRL** (Zhao et al., 2019). MDRG is the baseline model proposed by Budzianowski et al. (2018b) on MultiWOZ, while HDSA and LaRL achieve much stronger performance on this dataset.

2.2.7 User Policy

User policy is the core of a user simulator. It takes a pre-set user goal and system dialogue acts as input and outputs user dialogue acts. ConvLab-2 provides an agenda-based (Schatzmann et al., 2007) model and neural network-based models including HUS and its variational variants (Gür et al., 2018). To perform end-to-end simulation, researchers can equip the user policy with NLU and NLG components to assemble a complete user simulator.

2.2.8 End-to-end Model

A fully end-to-end dialogue model receives the dialogue history and generates a response in natural language directly. ConvLab-2 extends Sequicity (Lei et al., 2018) to multi-domain scenarios: when the model senses that the current domain has switched, it resets the belief span, which records information of the current domain. ConvLab-2 also integrates **DAMD** (Zhang et al., 2019) which obtains state-of-the-art results on MultiWOZ. As for the DealOrNoDeal dataset, we provide the **ROLLOUTS RL** policy proposed by Lewis et al. (2017).

2.3 Datasets

Compared with ConvLab, ConvLab-2 can integrate a new dataset more conveniently. For each dataset, ConvLab-2 provides a unified data loader that can be used by all the models, thus separating data processing from the model definition. Currently, ConvLab-2 supports four task-oriented dialogue datasets, including CamRest676 (Wen et al., 2017), MultiWOZ (Eric et al., 2019), DealOrNoDeal (Lewis et al., 2017), and CrossWOZ (Zhu et al., 2020).

2.3.1 CamRest676

CamRest676 (Wen et al., 2017) is a Wizard-of-Oz dataset, consisting of 676 dialogues in a restaurant domain. ConvLab-2 offers an agenda-based user simulator and a complete set of models for building a traditional pipeline dialogue system on the CamRest676 dataset.

2.3.2 MultiWOZ

MultiWOZ (Budzianowski et al., 2018b) is a large-scale multi-domain Wizard-of-Oz dataset. It consists of 10,438 dialogues with system dialogue acts and belief states. However, user dialogue acts are missing, and belief state annotations and dialogue utterances are noisy. To address these issues, Convlab (Lee et al., 2019b) annotated user dialogue acts automatically using heuristics. Eric et al. (2019) further re-annotated the belief states and utterances, resulting in the MultiWOZ 2.1 dataset.

2.3.3 DealOrNoDeal

DealOrNoDeal (Lewis et al., 2017) is a dataset of human-human negotiations on a multi-issue bargaining task. It contains 5,805 dialogues based on 2,236 unique scenarios. On this dataset, ConvLab-2 implements ROLLOUTS RL (Lewis et al., 2017) and LaRL (Zhao et al., 2019) models.

2.3.4 CrossWOZ

CrossWOZ (Zhu et al., 2020) is the first large-scale Chinese multi-domain Wizard-of-Oz dataset proposed recently. It contains 6,012 dialogues spanning over five domains. Besides dialogue acts and belief states, the annotations of user states, which indicate the completion of a user goal, are also provided. ConvLab-2 offers a rule-based user simulator and a complete set of models for building a pipeline system on the CrossWOZ dataset.

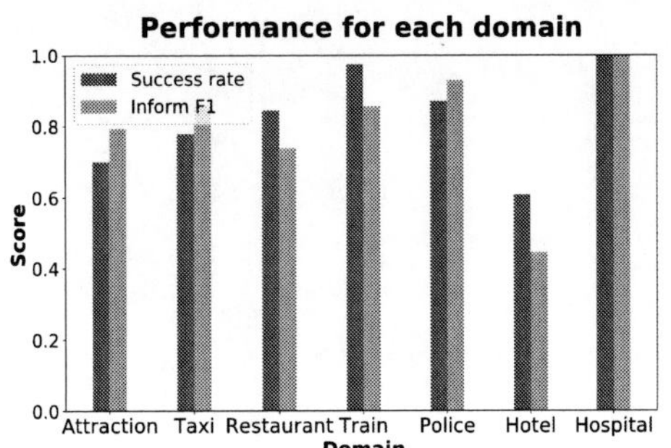

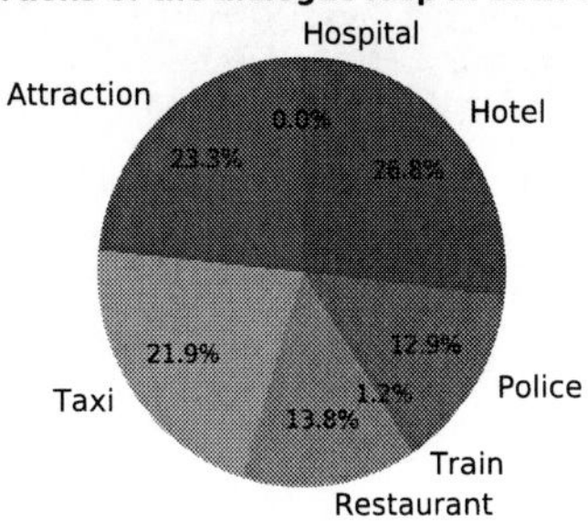

Figure 2: Performance of the demo system in Section 3. **Left:** Success rate and inform F1 for each domain. **Right:** Proportions of the dialogue loop in each domain.

Overall results:

Success Rate: 60.8%; inform F1: 44.5%

Most confusing user dialogue acts:

Request-Hotel-Post-?
- 34%: Request-Hospital-Post-?
- 32%: Request-Attraction-Post-?

Request-Hotel-Addr-?
- 29%: Request-Attraction-Addr-?
- 28%: Request-Restaurant-Addr-?

Request-Hotel-Phone-?
- 26%: Request-Restaurant-Phone-?
- 26%: Request-Attraction-Phone-?

Invalid system dialogue acts:
- 31%: Inform-Hotel-Parking
- 28%: Inform-Hotel-Internet

Redundant system dialogue acts:
- 34%: Inform-Hotel-Stars

Missing system dialogue acts:
- 25%: Inform-Hotel-Phone

Most confusing system dialogue acts:

Recommend-Hotel-Parking-yes
- 21%: Recommend-Hotel-Parking-none
- 18%: Inform-Hotel-Parking-none

Inform-Hotel-Parking-yes
- 17%: Inform-Hotel-Parking-none

Inform-Hotel-Stars-4
- 16%: Inform-Hotel-Internet-none

User dialogue acts that cause loop:
- 53% Request-Hotel-Phone-?
- 21% Request-Hotel-Post-?
- 14% Request-Hotel-Addr-?

Table 1: Comprehensive results (partial) of the demo system in Section 3 for the Hotel domain. To save space, only the most frequent errors are presented.

2.4 Analysis Tool

To evaluate a dialogue system quantitatively, ConvLab-2 offers an analysis tool to perform an end-to-end evaluation with a specified user simulator and generate an HTML report which contains rich statistics of simulated dialogues. Charts and tables are used in the test report for better demonstration. Partial results of a demo system in Section 3 are shown in Figure 2 and Table 1. Currently, the report contains the following pieces of information for each task domain:

- Metrics for overall performance such as success rate, inform F1, average turn number, etc.

- Common errors of the NLU component, such as the confusion matrix of user dialogue acts. For the example in Table 1, 34% of the requests for the Postcode in the Hotel domain are misinterpreted as the requests in the Hospital domain.

- Frequent invalid, redundant, and missing system dialogue acts predicted by the dialogue policy.

- The system dialogue acts from which the NLG component generates responses that confuse the user simulator. For the example in Table 1, it is hard to inform the user that the hotel has free parking.

- The causes of dialogue loops. Dialogue loop is the situation that the user keeps repeating the same request until the max turn number is reached. This result shows the requests that are hard for the system to handle.

145

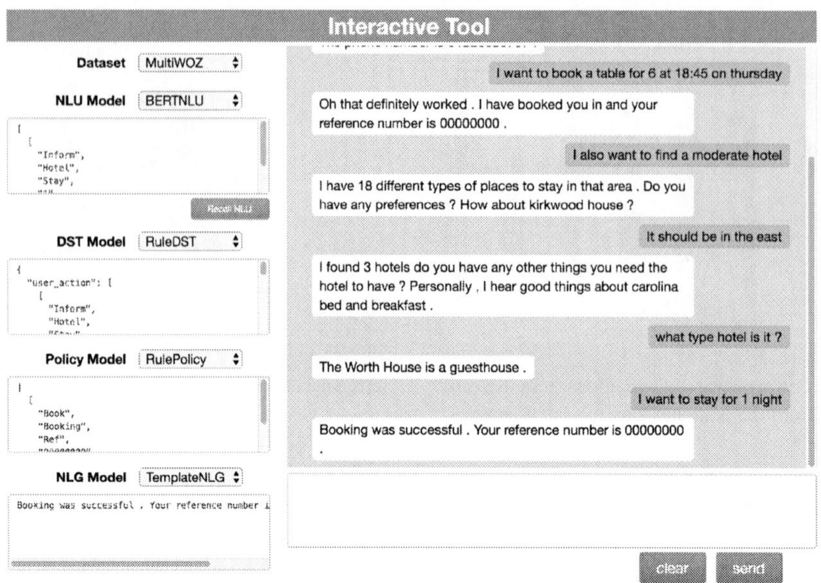

Figure 3: The interface of the Interactive Tool.

The analysis tool also supports the comparison between different dialogue systems that interact with the same user simulator. The above statistics and comparison results can significantly facilitate error analysis and system improvement.

2.5 Interactive Tool

ConvLab-2 provides an interactive tool that enables researchers to converse with a dialogue system through a graphical user interface and modify intermediate results to correct system errors.

As shown in Figure 3, researchers can customize their dialogue system by selecting the dataset and the model of each component. Then, they can interact with the system via the user interface. During a conversation, the output of each component is displayed on the left side as a JSON formatted string, including the user dialogue acts parsed by the NLU, the belief state tracked by the DST, the system dialogue acts selected by the policy and the final system response generated by the NLG. By showing both the dialogue history and the component outputs, the researchers can get a good understanding of how their system works.

In addition to the fine-grained system output, the interactive tool also supports intermediate output modification. When a component makes a mistake and the dialogue fails to continue, the researchers can correct the JSON output of that component to redirect the conversation by replacing the original output with the correct one. This function is helpful when the researchers are debugging a specific component.

In consideration of the compatibility across platforms, the interactive tool is deployed as a web service that can be accessed via a web browser. To use self-defined models, the researchers have to edit a configuration file, which defines all available models for each component. The researchers can also add their own models into the configuration file easily.

3 Demo

This section demonstrates how to use ConvLab-2 to build, evaluate, and diagnose a traditional pipeline dialogue system developed on the MultiWOZ dataset.

```
import ... # import necessary modules
# Create models for each component
# Parameters are omitted for simplicity
sys_nlu = BERTNLU(...)
sys_dst = RuleDST(...)
sys_policy = RulePolicy(...)
sys_nlg = TemplateNLG(...)
# Assemble a pipeline system named "sys"
sys_agent = PipelineAgent(sys_nlu, sys_dst,
    sys_policy, sys_nlg, name="sys")
# Build a user simulator similarly but without DST
user_nlu = BERTNLU(...)
user_policy = RulePolicy(...)
user_nlg = TemplateNLG(...)
user_agent = PipelineAgent(user_nlu, None,
    user_policy, user_nlg, name="user")
# Create an evaluator and a conversation environment
evaluator = MultiWozEvaluator()
sess = BiSession(sys_agent, user_agent, evaluator)
# Start simulation
sess.init_session()
```

```
sys_utt = ""
while True:
    sys_utt, user_utt, sess_over, reward = sess.
    next_turn(sys_utt)
    if sess_over:
        break
print(sess.evaluator.task_success())
print(sess.evaluator.inform_F1())
# Use the analysis tool to generate a test report
analyzer = Analyzer(user_agent, dataset="MultiWOZ")
analyzer.comprehensive_analyze(sys_agent,
    total_dialog=1000)
# Compare multiple systems
sys_agent2 = PipelineAgent(MILU(...), sys_dst,
    sys_policy, sys_nlg, name="sys")
analyzer.compare_models(agent_list=[sys_agent,
    sys_agent2], model_name=["bertnlu", "milu"],
    total_dialog=1000)
```

Listing 1: Example code for the demo.

To build such a dialogue system, we need to instantiate a model for each component and assemble them into a complete agent. As shown in the above code, the system consists of a BERTNLU, a rule-based DST, a rule-based system policy, and a template-based NLG. Likewise, we can build a user simulator that consists of a BERTNLU, an agenda-based user policy, and a template-based NLG. Thanks to the flexibility of the framework, the DST of the simulator can be `None`, which means passing the parsed dialogue acts directly to the policy without the belief state.

For end-to-end evaluation, ConvLab-2 provides a `BiSession` class, which takes a system, a simulator, and an evaluator as inputs. Then this class can be used to simulate dialogues and calculate end-to-end evaluation metrics. For example, the task success rate of the system is 64.2%, and the inform F1 is 67.0% for 1000 simulated dialogues. In addition to automatic evaluation, ConvLab-2 can perform human evaluation via Amazon Mechanical Turk using the same system agent.

Then the analysis tool can be used to perform a comprehensive evaluation. Equipped with a user simulator, the tool can analyze and compare multiple systems. Some results are shown in Figure 2 and Table 1. We collected statistics from 1000 simulated dialogues and found that

- The demo system performs the poorest in the Hotel domain but always completes the goal in the Hospital domain.

- The sub-task in the Hotel domain is more likely to cause dialogue loops than in other domains. More than half of the loops in the Hotel domain are caused by the user request for the phone number.

- One of the most common errors of the NLU component is misinterpreting the domain of user dialogue acts. For example, the user request for the Postcode, address, and phone number in the Hotel domain is often parsed as in other domains.

- In the Hotel domain, the dialogue acts whose slots are `Parking` are much harder to be perceived than other dialogue acts.

The researchers can further diagnose their system by observing fine-grained output and rescuing a failed dialogue using our provided interactive tool. An example is shown in Figure 3, in which at first the BERTNLU falsely identified the domain as *Restaurant*. After correcting the domain to *Hotel* manually, a *Recall NLU* button appears. By clicking the button, the dialogue system reruns this turn by skipping the NLU module and directly use the corrected NLU output. Combined with the observations from the analysis tool, alleviating the domain confusion problem of the NLU component may significantly improve system performance.

4 Code and Resources

ConvLab-2 is publicly available on `https://github.com/thu-coai/ConvLab-2`. Resources such as datasets, trained models, tutorials, and demo video are also released. We will keep track of new datasets and state-of-the-art models. Contributions from the community are always welcome.

5 Conclusion

We present ConvLab-2, an open-source toolkit for building, evaluating, and diagnosing a task-oriented dialogue system. Based on ConvLab (Lee et al., 2019b), ConvLab-2 integrates more powerful models, supports more datasets, and develops an analysis tool and an interactive tool for comprehensive end-to-end evaluation. For demonstration, we give an example of using ConvLab-2 to build, evaluate, and diagnose a system on the MultiWOZ dataset. We hope that ConvLab-2 is instrumental in promoting the research on task-oriented dialogue.

Acknowledgments

This work was jointly supported by the NSFC projects (Key project with No. 61936010 and regular project with No. 61876096), and the National Key R&D Program of China (Grant No. 2018YFC0830200). We thank THUNUS NExT Joint-Lab for the support.

References

Tom Bocklisch, Joey Faulkner, Nick Pawlowski, and Alan Nichol. 2017. Rasa: Open source language understanding and dialogue management.

Pawel Budzianowski, Iñigo Casanueva, Bo-Hsiang Tseng, and Milica Gasic. 2018a. Towards end-to-end multi-domain dialogue modelling.

Paweł Budzianowski, Tsung-Hsien Wen, Bo-Hsiang Tseng, Iñigo Casanueva, Stefan Ultes, Osman Ramadan, and Milica Gašić. 2018b. MultiWOZ - a large-scale multi-domain wizard-of-Oz dataset for task-oriented dialogue modelling. In *Proceedings of the 2018 Conference on Empirical Methods in Natural Language Processing*, pages 5016–5026, Brussels, Belgium. Association for Computational Linguistics.

Wenhu Chen, Jianshu Chen, Pengda Qin, Xifeng Yan, and William Yang Wang. 2019. Semantically conditioned dialog response generation via hierarchical disentangled self-attention. In *Proceedings of the 57th Annual Meeting of the Association for Computational Linguistics*, pages 3696–3709, Florence, Italy. Association for Computational Linguistics.

Jacob Devlin, Ming-Wei Chang, Kenton Lee, and Kristina Toutanova. 2019. BERT: Pre-training of deep bidirectional transformers for language understanding. In *Proceedings of the 2019 Conference of the North American Chapter of the Association for Computational Linguistics: Human Language Technologies, Volume 1 (Long and Short Papers)*, pages 4171–4186, Minneapolis, Minnesota. Association for Computational Linguistics.

Mihail Eric, Rahul Goel, Shachi Paul, Abhishek Sethi, Sanchit Agarwal, Shuyag Gao, and Dilek Hakkani-Tur. 2019. Multiwoz 2.1: Multi-domain dialogue state corrections and state tracking baselines. *arXiv preprint arXiv:1907.01669*.

Jianfeng Gao, Michel Galley, and Lihong Li. 2019. Neural approaches to conversational ai. *Foundations and Trends® in Information Retrieval*, 13(2-3):127–298.

Izzeddin Gür, Dilek Hakkani-Tür, Gokhan Tür, and Pararth Shah. 2018. User modeling for task oriented dialogues. In *2018 IEEE Spoken Language Technology Workshop (SLT)*, pages 900–906. IEEE.

Matthew Henderson, Blaise Thomson, and Jason D. Williams. 2014. The second dialog state tracking challenge. In *Proceedings of the 15th Annual Meeting of the Special Interest Group on Discourse and Dialogue (SIGDIAL)*, pages 263–272, Philadelphia, PA, U.S.A. Association for Computational Linguistics.

Hwaran Lee, Jinsik Lee, and Tae-Yoon Kim. 2019a. SUMBT: Slot-utterance matching for universal and scalable belief tracking. In *Proceedings of the 57th Annual Meeting of the Association for Computational Linguistics*, pages 5478–5483, Florence, Italy. Association for Computational Linguistics.

Sungjin Lee, Qi Zhu, Ryuichi Takanobu, Zheng Zhang, Yaoqin Zhang, Xiang Li, Jinchao Li, Baolin Peng, Xiujun Li, Minlie Huang, and Jianfeng Gao. 2019b. ConvLab: Multi-domain end-to-end dialog system platform. In *Proceedings of the 57th Annual Meeting of the Association for Computational Linguistics: System Demonstrations*, pages 64–69, Florence, Italy. Association for Computational Linguistics.

Wenqiang Lei, Xisen Jin, Min-Yen Kan, Zhaochun Ren, Xiangnan He, and Dawei Yin. 2018. Sequicity: Simplifying task-oriented dialogue systems with single sequence-to-sequence architectures. In *Proceedings of the 56th Annual Meeting of the Association for Computational Linguistics (Volume 1: Long Papers)*, pages 1437–1447, Melbourne, Australia. Association for Computational Linguistics.

Mike Lewis, Denis Yarats, Yann Dauphin, Devi Parikh, and Dhruv Batra. 2017. Deal or no deal? end-to-end learning of negotiation dialogues. In *Proceedings of the 2017 Conference on Empirical Methods in Natural Language Processing*, pages 2443–2453, Copenhagen, Denmark. Association for Computational Linguistics.

F. Mairesse, M. Gasic, F. Jurcicek, S. Keizer, B. Thomson, K. Yu, and S. Young. 2009. Spoken language understanding from unaligned data using discriminative classification models. In *2009 IEEE International Conference on Acoustics, Speech and Signal Processing*, pages 4749–4752.

Alexander Miller, Will Feng, Dhruv Batra, Antoine Bordes, Adam Fisch, Jiasen Lu, Devi Parikh, and Jason Weston. 2017. ParlAI: A dialog research software platform. In *Proceedings of the 2017 Conference on Empirical Methods in Natural Language Processing: System Demonstrations*, pages 79–84, Copenhagen, Denmark. Association for Computational Linguistics.

Alexandros Papangelis, Mahdi Namazifar, Chandra Khatri, Yi-Chia Wang, Piero Molino, and Gokhan Tur. 2020. Plato dialogue system: A flexible conversational ai research platform.

Baolin Peng, Xiujun Li, Lihong Li, Jianfeng Gao, Asli Celikyilmaz, Sungjin Lee, and Kam-Fai Wong. 2017. Composite task-completion dialogue policy learning via hierarchical deep reinforcement learning. In *Proceedings of the 2017 Conference on Empirical Methods in Natural Language Processing*, pages 2231–2240, Copenhagen, Denmark. Association for Computational Linguistics.

Osman Ramadan, Paweł Budzianowski, and Milica Gašić. 2018. Large-scale multi-domain belief tracking with knowledge sharing. In *Proceedings of the 56th Annual Meeting of the Association for Computational Linguistics (Volume 2: Short Papers)*, pages 432–437, Melbourne, Australia. Association for Computational Linguistics.

Abhinav Rastogi, Xiaoxue Zang, Srinivas Sunkara, Raghav Gupta, and Pranav Khaitan. 2019. Towards scalable multi-domain conversational agents: The schema-guided dialogue dataset. *arXiv preprint arXiv:1909.05855*.

Jost Schatzmann, Blaise Thomson, Karl Weilhammer, Hui Ye, and Steve Young. 2007. Agenda-based user simulation for bootstrapping a POMDP dialogue system. In *Human Language Technologies 2007: The Conference of the North American Chapter of the Association for Computational Linguistics; Companion Volume, Short Papers*, pages 149–152, Rochester, New York. Association for Computational Linguistics.

John Schulman, Filip Wolski, Prafulla Dhariwal, Alec Radford, and Oleg Klimov. 2017. Proximal policy optimization algorithms. *arXiv preprint arXiv:1707.06347*.

Ryuichi Takanobu, Hanlin Zhu, and Minlie Huang. 2019. Guided dialog policy learning: Reward estimation for multi-domain task-oriented dialog. In *Proceedings of the 2019 Conference on Empirical Methods in Natural Language Processing and the 9th International Joint Conference on Natural Language Processing (EMNLP-IJCNLP)*, pages 100–110, Hong Kong, China. Association for Computational Linguistics.

Stefan Ultes, Lina M. Rojas-Barahona, Pei-Hao Su, David Vandyke, Dongho Kim, Iñigo Casanueva, Paweł Budzianowski, Nikola Mrkšić, Tsung-Hsien Wen, Milica Gašić, and Steve Young. 2017. PyDial: A multi-domain statistical dialogue system toolkit. In *Proceedings of ACL 2017, System Demonstrations*, pages 73–78, Vancouver, Canada. Association for Computational Linguistics.

Tsung-Hsien Wen, Milica Gašić, Nikola Mrkšić, Pei-Hao Su, David Vandyke, and Steve Young. 2015. Semantically conditioned LSTM-based natural language generation for spoken dialogue systems. In *Proceedings of the 2015 Conference on Empirical Methods in Natural Language Processing*, pages 1711–1721, Lisbon, Portugal. Association for Computational Linguistics.

Tsung-Hsien Wen, David Vandyke, Nikola Mrkšić, Milica Gašić, Lina M. Rojas-Barahona, Pei-Hao Su, Stefan Ultes, and Steve Young. 2017. A network-based end-to-end trainable task-oriented dialogue system. In *Proceedings of the 15th Conference of the European Chapter of the Association for Computational Linguistics: Volume 1, Long Papers*, pages 438–449, Valencia, Spain. Association for Computational Linguistics.

Ronald J. Williams. 1992. Simple statistical gradient-following algorithms for connectionist reinforcement learning. *Machine Learning*, 8(3):229–256.

Chien-Sheng Wu, Andrea Madotto, Ehsan Hosseini-Asl, Caiming Xiong, Richard Socher, and Pascale Fung. 2019. Transferable multi-domain state generator for task-oriented dialogue systems. In *Proceedings of the 57th Annual Meeting of the Association for Computational Linguistics*, pages 808–819, Florence, Italy. Association for Computational Linguistics.

Yichi Zhang, Zhijian Ou, and Zhou Yu. 2019. Task-Oriented Dialog Systems that Consider Multiple Appropriate Responses under the Same Context. In *Proceedings of the AAAI Conference on Artificial Intelligence*.

Tiancheng Zhao, Kaige Xie, and Maxine Eskenazi. 2019. Rethinking action spaces for reinforcement learning in end-to-end dialog agents with latent variable models. In *Proceedings of the 2019 Conference of the North American Chapter of the Association for Computational Linguistics: Human Language Technologies, Volume 1 (Long and Short Papers)*, pages 1208–1218, Minneapolis, Minnesota. Association for Computational Linguistics.

Qi Zhu, Kaili Huang, Zheng Zhang, Xiaoyan Zhu, and Minlie Huang. 2020. CrossWOZ: A large-scale chinese cross-domain task-oriented dialogue dataset. *Transactions of the Association for Computational Linguistics*.

OpusFilter: A Configurable Parallel Corpus Filtering Toolbox

Mikko Aulamo and **Sami Virpioja** and **Jörg Tiedemann**
Department of Digital Humanities
University of Helsinki, Helsinki / Finland
{mikko.aulamo, sami.virpioja, jorg.tiedemann}@helsinki.fi

Abstract

This paper introduces OpusFilter, a flexible and modular toolbox for filtering parallel corpora. It implements a number of components based on heuristic filters, language identification libraries, character-based language models, and word alignment tools, and it can easily be extended with custom filters. Bitext segments can be ranked according to their quality or domain match using single features or a logistic regression model that can be trained without manually labeled training data. We demonstrate the effectiveness of OpusFilter on the example of a Finnish-English news translation task based on noisy web-crawled training data. Applying our tool leads to improved translation quality while significantly reducing the size of the training data, also clearly outperforming an alternative ranking given in the crawled data set. Furthermore, we show the ability of OpusFilter to perform data selection for domain adaptation.

1 Introduction

Data filtering tools are important to reduce the noise fed into machine learning algorithms such as the ones used in neural machine translation. This is especially true for data sets with suspicious sources like unrestricted web crawls or data sets that are automatically extracted from complex data formats such as PDF or HTML with all their different flavors and implementations. Cleaning parallel corpora is a special case in which not only the raw data but also the quality of alignment between source and target language needs to checked. The aligned translations drive the mapping from input to the output language as a strong supervision during the training steps, and the amount of noise will have a decisive impact on the adequacy of the translations. The effect is especially severe for low resource settings, in which little data is available, and each mistake might directly influence the end result.

The interest in automatic bitext (i.e. bilingual parallel corpora) filtering is constantly growing pushed by the advances in neural machine translation. Khayrallah and Koehn (2018) show that noisy training data is often more harmful for neural translation models than statistical translation models. As a consequence, international evaluation campaigns like the ones organised by WMT now feature shared tasks on data cleaning and ranking (Koehn et al., 2018, 2019). Various approaches have been proposed based on such challenges and directly benefit the development of MT engines in low-resource settings.

This paper presents a framework for bitext cleaning, OpusFilter, focusing on processing data collected in OPUS (Tiedemann, 2012), the world's largest resource of openly available parallel corpora. In contrast to tools such as bicleaner (Sánchez-Cartagena et al., 2018) and Zipporah (Xu and Koehn, 2017), that implement a single method for parallel corpus filtering, OpusFilter is designed as a toolbox that is useful for testing and using many different approaches. Below we describe the design of OpusFilter and present its application in the test case of filtering Finnish-English parallel data included in ParaCrawl.

2 OpusFilter Toolbox

The OpusFilter toolbox is implemented in Python 3 and is available at `https://github.com/Helsinki-NLP/OpusFilter` under the permissive MIT open-source license. The main script provided by the package is `opusfilter`, which takes a configuration file as an input. The configuration files are written in YAML syntax.[1] A configuration contains common global options (currently only the output directory) and a list of steps that are run one by one. There are different step types

---

[1] See https://yaml.org/

Proceedings of the 58th Annual Meeting of the Association for Computational Linguistics, pages 150–156
July 5 - July 10, 2020. ©2020 Association for Computational Linguistics

(functions) for downloading parallel corpora from the OPUS database, combining and taking subsets of the corpora, filtering and scoring segment pairs with a combination of different filters, and training and using a classifier based on the scores. The configuration files for all our experiments are included in the GitHub repository.

The input and output files for the functions are defined in the configuration, and it is simple to also use external data files. In contrast to common text file processing tools, the OpusFilter functions support the processing of parallel files that have corresponding data on the same lines. Special attention has been paid to make the processing of large files memory-efficient: Full corpora are never loaded into memory, but the segment pairs and scores are processed one at a time if possible, and in fixed-size chunks otherwise.

In this section, we describe the current functionality of the OpusFilter toolbox. In the future, we plan to include more functions for common monolingual and parallel data processing operations. The ultimate goal is that all pre-processing steps could be defined in a single configuration file making it easy to share them for reproducing MT experiments.

2.1 Downloading and selecting data

The first steps typically refer to data selection and their preparation. Relevant data sets can be downloaded, concatenated, and divided into subsets.

opus_read uses the OpusTools[2] library to download a specified parallel corpus from the OPUS corpus collection, and stores it into two files (source and target segments, one segment per line). There are options for selecting a specified version of the corpus and whether to download pre-tokenized or untokenized segments.

Multiple files can be concatenated by the **concatenate** function. The **head**, **tail**, and **slice** functions can be used to the lines from the top, bottom or middle of the parallel input files. Furthermore, **subset** takes a random subset of the selected size from a corpus. It has an option to shuffle the target language segments to produce examples of poor translation pairs that can be used as negative examples in training a segment pair classifier. Finally, **split** divides parallel files into two parts when given the approximate proportions as fractions. The split is based on a hash function, making it deterministic

on the content of the input lines.

2.2 Filtering and Scoring

All filter classes implemented in OpusFilter are applicable both for direct filtering of the data and for producing a quality score for each segment pair. If a filtering method does not produce any sensible score, it should output 1 for acceptable pairs and 0 for unacceptable pairs. Any method that produces one or more scores provides options for selecting filtering thresholds for the scores.

The current filters implemented in OpusFilter include (a) simple length-based filters (maximum and minimum length and segment length ratio in words or characters), (b) script and language identification filters, (c) filters that consider special characters such as numbers and punctuation marks, (d) filters that use probabilities from n-gram language models, and (e) filters that use word alignment probabilities. For a complete list, see the documentation of the software.

The filters can be used by two functions:

filter applies a specified list of filters to a parallel corpus and outputs those segments that pass all the filters (or optionally those that do not).

score produces scores for the segment pairs in a parallel corpus from the specified list of filters. The scores are written in JSON Lines format, which is easy to process, and for example simple to load as a `pandas`[3] `DataFrame` object.

There are also methods for using and processing the score files: **join** is a function to combine separate score files to a single file, and **sort** sorts the given input files based on the scores. Reordering the data makes it convenient to remove noisy pairs from the end of the sentence files.

In addition, OpusFilter implements **remove_duplicates** for filtering out duplicate lines from parallel corpora. The matching can be based on any combination of the lines in the input files, so that it is possible, for example, to make sure that each target sentence occurs only once in a bitext.

2.3 Classification

The scores calculated by different filters can be used as features for a classifier that predicts whether a given segment pair is clean enough to be used, for example, for training machine translation models. Moreover, the classification probability

---

[2]https://github.com/Helsinki-NLP/OpusTools

[3]https://pandas.pydata.org/

can be applied for sorting the data according to their expected cleanliness.

The classification approach currently supported by OpusFilter is inspired by Vázquez et al. (2019). First, we take a set of sentence pairs and score them using features produced by filters. This set is then split into clean and noisy examples in order to be used as the training data for a logistic regression classifier. To choose the positive and negative example pairs, we set a percentage threshold value for all filter scores. Each sentence pair has to obtain scores that are above the threshold percentile for all filters in order to be considered clean; otherwise, they are labeled noisy.

Unlike Vázquez et al. (2019), who manually placed the threshold between the two peaks of a score distribution in cases where the distribution is bimodal, we implemented an automatic selection of the optimal threshold to ensure a more convenient usage of the OpusFilter toolbox. Multiple models with different training data splits using different thresholds can be trained in order to find the best performing model. The minimum, maximum, and initial percentage thresholds can be specified for each score in the configuration file, and optimized with a search algorithm. The optimization criterion can be cross-entropy of the classifier[4] or the area under the receiver operating characteristics curve (ROC AUC) based on a development set of scores labeled as noisy or clean by the user.

Finally, once the logistic regression model is trained and selected, it can be applied to each segment pair in a larger set of data to produce a single cleanness score, which is the probability prediction from the model. For classification, the following functions have been implemented:

train_classifier optimizes a classifier to predict the cleanliness of the segment pairs using the procedure described above. The inputs are training scores, the criterion to be used in the model optimization, search algorithm details for the optimization, and a development set if the ROC AUC criterion is used. The optimized classifier is written to the specified output file.

classify assigns either a cleanness score or label to each sentence in a data set. The inputs are the classifier file and the sentence pairs to be classified, and the resulting scores or labels are written line by line into a specified output file.

2.4 Custom Filters

The toolbox is extendable with custom filter classes defined in Python. The filter classes should be based on the abstract base class `FilterABC` and implement two methods: `score` and `accept`. The `score` method takes an iterator over segment pairs, and yields a score object for each pair. The score may either be a single number, or if multiple score values need to be yielded, a dictionary that has the numbers as values. The `accept` method takes a single output yielded by the `score` method, and returns whether the segment pair should be accepted based on the score.

2.5 Studying Filter Scores

In addition to the main `opusfilter` script, there is a separate tool `opusfilter-scores` for calculating and plotting statistics from scored segment pairs. The commands include `describe` for printing the basic statistics of the scores, `hist` for plotting score histograms (see the example in Figure 1a), `corr` for plotting a correlation matrix of the scores (Figure 1b), and `scatter-matrix` for drawing a matrix of scatter plots between the values of different scores.

3 Experiments

To demonstrate the usefulness of the OpusFilter toolbox, we show results from two main experiments on the Finnish-English news translation task (in both directions): (i) Filtering noisy data, and (ii) applying domain adaptation.

For training, we use data from version 4 of the ParaCrawl corpus (Esplà-Gomis et al., 2019). The data is taken from a general internet crawl and contains segments that are noisy and potentially harmful for machine translation models. We use the subset of the corpus that is already filtered by the bicleaner tool[5] (Sánchez-Cartagena et al., 2018). This data set contains 2,156,069 segment pairs and is ordered by the score from bicleaner, which enables us to directly compare it to our tool. We create five versions of the training data by removing 10%, 20%, 30%, 40% and 50% of the pairs from the noisy end of the collection and train translation models with the full data and with the five reduced

---

[4]Also, Akaike Information Criterion (AIC) or Bayes Information Criterion (BIC) can be applied, similarly to how Vázquez et al. (2019) operate in cases where the score distribution is not bimodal. However, they differ from the cross-entropy only in the case that a feature can be completely removed.

[5]https://github.com/bitextor/bicleaner

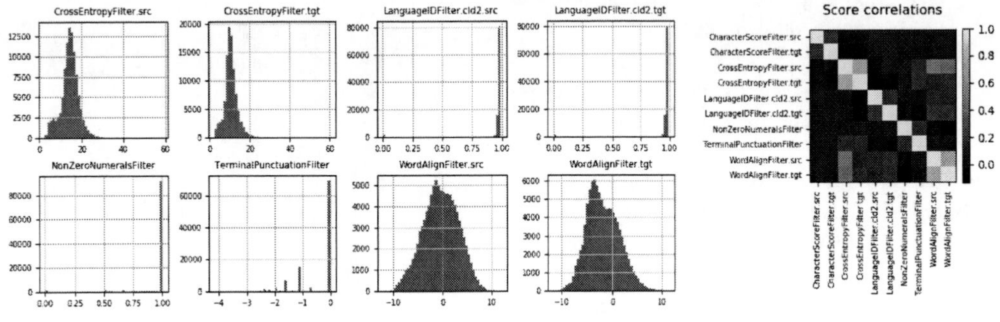

(a) Histograms of the scores. (b) Correlations between the scores.

Figure 1: Histograms and correlations of the score values used for training classifiers in the Finnish-English noise filtering. CharacterScoreFilters have been excluded from histograms as their values are almost always one.

training sets. Next, we reorder the data with our toolkit and again create new data sets by removing data with the same proportions as previously.

We then apply data provided for the WMT news translation task[6] for validation and testing. In particular, we use newstest2018 as the development set and newstest2019 as our test set for both language directions. The translation models are trained with the OpenNMT toolkit (Klein et al., 2017) using RNN encoders and decoders with LSTM gates. All training sets are tokenized with the tokenizer from the mosesdecoder toolkit (Koehn et al., 2007) and segmented with BPE (Sennrich et al., 2016) using subword-nmt[7] before feeding them to OpenNMT.

3.1 Ranking

Following Vázquez et al. (2019), we first produce an initial filtering of the ParaCrawl corpus. For this, we use the following heuristic filters from the OpusFilter toolbox:

- LengthFilter: The length of the segments have to be between 1 and 100 words.
- LengthRatioFilter: The maximum ratio between the source and target segments has to be below 3.
- LongWordFilter: Exclude segment pair if any word is longer than 40 characters.
- HtmlTagFilter: Exclude segment pairs with any HTML tags.
- CharacterScoreFilter: All alphabetic characters have to be in Latin script.

The initial filtering removed only 8,055 (0.4%) of the Finnish to English segment pairs, proba-

bly because similar filters are already applied in bicleaner when preparing the original data set. Nevertheless, these steps are useful for creating data to train models used in the later filtering methods. First, we train word alignment priors for the model 3 of the eflomal tool[8] (Östling and Tiedemann, 2016) and variable-length character n-gram models for the source and target languages using the VariKN toolkit[9] (Siivola et al., 2007). In addition, we train a background language model that combines the source and target languages of the unfiltered corpus. We interpolate it with the language-specific models with coefficient 0.01 to ensure that we cover all characters that appear in the data.

Next, we take a random subset of 100,000 segment pairs from the corpus for training a logistic regression classifier. To extract features for the logistic regression to be trained on, we use another set of filters from the OpusFilter toolbox:

- CharacterScoreFilter: The proportion of Latin characters among all alphabetic characters
- LanguageIDFilter: Confidence score from the CLD2 language identification library[10] if the correct language is identified, or 0 otherwise
- TerminalPunctuationFilter: The "term-punct" score from Vázquez et al. (2019)
- NonZeroNumeralsFilter: The "non-zero" score from Vázquez et al. (2019)
- CrossEntropyFilter: Word-based cross-entropies of the source and target sentences from the respective character n-gram models
- WordAlignFilter: Unnormalized source-to-

[6]http://www.statmt.org/wmt19/translation-task.html
[7]https://github.com/rsennrich/subword-nmt
[8]https://github.com/robertostling/eflomal
[9]https://github.com/vsiivola/variKN
[10]https://github.com/CLD2Owners/cld2

target and target-to-source alignment probabilities obtained by eflomal

Figure 1a shows histograms of the scores over
the 100,000 training segments pairs in the data, produced by the `opusfilter-scores` tool. The
distribution of the cross-entropy values is quite
unimodal, indicating that such a score alone does
not make a clear division of the segment pairs as
clean or noisy. Language identification scores are
mostly close to one, but zero for a small fraction of
the segments, indicating that they contain incorrect
languages. Also, non-zero numerals and terminal
punctuation scores show that a small number of
samples look problematic. Word alignment scores
have an interesting close-to-bimodal distribution.
Smaller values indicate better alignment, so the
lower peak is for more problematic segment pairs.

The correlations of the scores over the training
data are illustrated in Figure 1b. As excepted, the
same scores for source and target segments correlate slightly for all scores and highly for the
cross-entropy and alignment scores. Also, non-
zero numerals and terminal punctuation filters correlate slightly, indicating segment pairs that have
both different punctuation marks and numbers, thus
likely to be poor translations. Finally, cross-entropy
scores for the source language (Finnish) have a
moderate correlation with the alignment scores. As
it is likely that the English side has mostly been the
original text, problems in the fluency of the translation seem to also indicate issues in its adequacy.

3.2 Results

In this section, we compare the results of models
trained with data in the original (bicleaner) order
and in the order of our classifier using the different data splits described above. We also test the
ROC AUC model for which we created a small
development set of 200 randomly selected segment
pairs that have manually been annotated as noisy
or clean (100 examples each). A pair was annotated noisy only in the case of serious problems;
sentences with single translation errors or relatively
poor fluency were still considered clean.

Figure 2 provides an overview of the results for
Finnish to English. We can see that our filtering
method is very effective. Removing noisy data
according to the ranking produced by our tool improves the BLEU score compared to the model that
applies the whole ParaCrawl data. In contrast, removing data based on the original ParaCrawl order

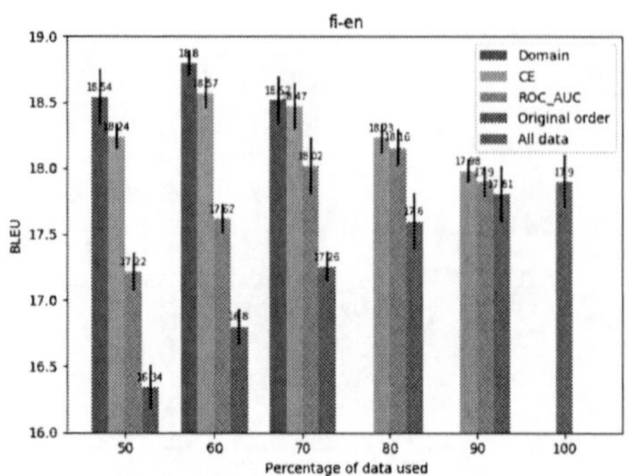

Figure 2: BLEU scores for Finnish-English translation
models trained with data that is pruned based on different ranking orders. The reported BLEU values show
the mean of six translation models. The 100-mark bar
shows the score when using the whole ParaCrawl corpus for training.

degrades the BLEU score at all cutoff points. When
using cross-entropy based sorting of the data, cutting off 40% of the lowest scoring training pairs
increased BLEU by 0.67 points when compared to
using the full training set. If more than 40% of the
data is removed, the BLEU score starts to decrease.
Surprisingly, ROC AUC based sorting, which requires a manually annotated development set, produces worse results than cross-entropy. ROC AUC
reaches a maximum gain of 0.26 BLEU points over
using the whole data set when 20% of the data is
truncated from the noisy end.

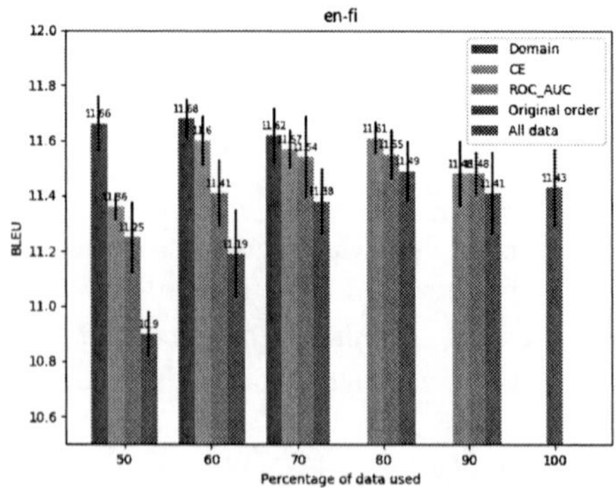

Figure 3: BLEU scores for English-Finnish translation
models.

English to Finnish translations show similar results, as illustrated in figure 3, although the BLEU
scores are overall lower as it is common in systems
translating into morphologically rich languages.
Again, cross-entropy based models perform better
than ROC AUC based ones: at 80% cutoff cross-

entropy model has 0.18 point and ROC AUC model has 0.12 point improvement over using the whole data. The increases in scores are more modest in English to Finnish translations than in Finnish to English translations.

As seen in Table 1, the cross-entropy based logistic regression model sets the weights of the cross-entropy language model filters and the word alignment filters very close to zero, while setting stronger weights for all other filters compared to the ROC AUC model. Detecting the correct language and having similar numerals in both sides of the sentence pairs seem to be the most important factors for the cleaning task, as their corresponding filters have by far the highest weights.

	CE	ROC AUC
Intercept	-4.63	-4.73
CharacterScoreFilter.src	1.75	0.77
CharacterScoreFilter.tgt	1.22	0.65
CrossEntropyFilter.src	-0.12	0.40
CrossEntropyFilter.tgt	-0.01	0.83
LanguageIDFilter.cld2.src	31.33	11.30
LanguageIDFilter.cld2.tgt	8.39	6.57
NonZeroNumeralsFilter	14.36	13.03
TerminalPunctuationFilter	2.57	0.82
WordAlignFilter.src	-0.15	0.53
WordAlignFilter.tgt	-0.04	0.87

Table 1: Logistic regression weights for models chosen with cross-entropy and ROC AUC for each filter score in the Finnish-English experiment. Positive weight is for the pairs that are predicted as clean.

3.3 OpusFilter for Domain Adaptation

Besides of generally cleaning noisy training data, OpusFilter can also be used to select training data that is similar and appropriate for translation tasks in specific domains. To demonstrate this, we conduct the following domain adaptation experiment.

We use, again, newstest2019 for testing and newstest2018 as development data. To adapt to the news domain, we now take in-domain data from previous years of the news translation task concatenating test sets from 2015, 2016 and 2017 for both Finnish and English. In total, this gives us 7372 sentence pairs that we apply to train n-gram language models for the news domain for both languages using the OpusFilter's **train_ngram** feature.

In Finnish to English translations, the best BLEU score is achieved using 60% of the full training data. To see whether we can reach a higher score by removing training examples that do not fit the news domain, we first select 70% of the cleanest

ParaCrawl data based on the order from our cross-entropy optimized classifier. Next, we use our previously trained news domain language models to assign a new score with CrossEntropyFilters for each sentence in both languages in our 70% data. We sort the data based on the language model scores and remove data from the noisy end to create 60% and 50% data sets that reflect the additional domain adaptation. Note that these percentage cutoff points refer to proportions from the full ParaCrawl data set, so the absolute number of sentence pairs is the same as in the other data sets used in the previous experiments. Finally, we apply those news-domain-adapted data sets to train translation models in the same way as before.[11]

The results are included in Figures 2 and 3. In all cases, the domain filtering leads to an improvement compared to the corresponding noise-filtered model. At the 70% mark, the results are very similar as the training sets are essentially the same. The Finnish to English model improves the score by 0.23 BLEU points over the noise-filtered model at the 60% mark. The English to Finnish model produces similar results but with lower scores. Those results demonstrate the effectiveness of OpusFilter to also perform data selection for domain adaptation without further annotation and additional components.

4   Conclusions and Future Work

This paper introduces OpusFilter, a modular tool for parallel data selection and ranking. OpusFilter can easily be configured to work with OPUS data and various filters to train effective classifiers in order to rank bitext segments. We demonstrate its use in a Finnish-English translation task based on the noisy ParaCrawl data used for training. The classifiers can be trained without human annotation, and the automatic model selection methods implemented in the toolbox lead to a similar performance compared to classifiers based on small manually labeled validation data. OpusFilter is open source and distributed with a permissive license to make it widely applicable. In future work, we would like to extend the toolbox with additional filters and classification options. One option could be the inclusion of sentence embedding based filtering (Guo et al., 2018). Additionally, we would like to explore OpusFilter's use in different scenarios and for other language pairs. Especially interesting

---

[11]The WMT testsets are not included in training the models.

would be the application in low-resource settings and various levels of noise in the original data. Furthermore, the use for domain adaptation and data selection should be further explored.

Acknowledgments

This work is part of the FoTran project, funded by the European Research Council (ERC) under the European Union's Horizon 2020 research and innovation programme (grant agreement № 771113), as well as the MeMAD project, funded by the European Union's Horizon 2020 Research and Innovation Programme (grant agreement № 780069).

References

Miquel Esplà-Gomis, Mikel L Forcada, Gema Ramírez-Sánchez, and Hieu Hoang. 2019. Paracrawl: Web-scale parallel corpora for the languages of the eu. In *Proceedings of Machine Translation Summit XVII Volume 2: Translator, Project and User Tracks*, pages 118–119.

Mandy Guo, Qinlan Shen, Yinfei Yang, Heming Ge, Daniel Cer, Gustavo Hernández Ábrego, Keith Stevens, Noah Constant, Yun-Hsuan Sung, Brian Strope, and Ray Kurzweil. 2018. Effective parallel corpus mining using bilingual sentence embeddings. *CoRR*, abs/1807.11906.

Huda Khayrallah and Philipp Koehn. 2018. On the impact of various types of noise on neural machine translation. In *Proceedings of the 2nd Workshop on Neural Machine Translation and Generation*, pages 74–83, Melbourne, Australia. Association for Computational Linguistics.

Guillaume Klein, Yoon Kim, Yuntian Deng, Jean Senellart, and Alexander M. Rush. 2017. Opennmt: Open-source toolkit for neural machine translation. In *Proc. ACL*.

Philipp Koehn, Francisco Guzmán, Vishrav Chaudhary, and Juan Pino. 2019. Findings of the wmt 2019 shared task on parallel corpus filtering for low-resource conditions. In *Proceedings of the Fourth Conference on Machine Translation (Volume 3: Shared Task Papers, Day 2)*, pages 56–74, Florence, Italy. Association for Computational Linguistics.

Philipp Koehn, Hieu Hoang, Alexandra Birch, Chris Callison-Burch, Marcello Federico, Nicola Bertoldi, Brooke Cowan, Wade Shen, Christine Moran, Richard Zens, Chris Dyer, Ondřej Bojar, Alexandra Constantin, and Evan Herbst. 2007. Moses: Open source toolkit for statistical machine translation. In *Proceedings of the 45th Annual Meeting of the Association for Computational Linguistics Companion Volume Proceedings of the Demo and Poster Sessions*, pages 177–180, Prague, Czech Republic. Association for Computational Linguistics.

Philipp Koehn, Huda Khayrallah, Kenneth Heafield, and Mikel L. Forcada. 2018. Findings of the wmt 2018 shared task on parallel corpus filtering. In *Proceedings of the Third Conference on Machine Translation, Volume 2: Shared Task Papers*, pages 739–752, Belgium, Brussels. Association for Computational Linguistics.

Robert Östling and Jörg Tiedemann. 2016. Efficient word alignment with Markov Chain Monte Carlo. *Prague Bulletin of Mathematical Linguistics*, 106:125–146.

Víctor M. Sánchez-Cartagena, Marta Bañón, Sergio Ortiz-Rojas, and Gema Ramírez-Sánchez. 2018. Prompsit's submission to wmt 2018 parallel corpus filtering shared task. In *Proceedings of the Third Conference on Machine Translation, Volume 2: Shared Task Papers*, Brussels, Belgium. Association for Computational Linguistics.

Rico Sennrich, Barry Haddow, and Alexandra Birch. 2016. Neural machine translation of rare words with subword units. *Proceedings of the 54th Annual Meeting of the Association for Computational Linguistics (Volume 1: Long Papers)*.

Vesa Siivola, Teemu Hirsimäki, and Sami Virpioja. 2007. On growing and pruning Kneser-Ney smoothed n-gram models. *IEEE Transactions on Audio, Speech and Language Processing*, 15(5):1617–1624.

Jörg Tiedemann. 2012. Parallel data, tools and interfaces in OPUS. In *Proceedings of the 8th International Conference on Language Resources and Evaluation (LREC'12)*, Istanbul, Turkey. European Language Resources Association (ELRA).

Raúl Vázquez, Umut Sulubacak, and Jörg Tiedemann. 2019. The university of Helsinki submission to the WMT19 parallel corpus filtering task. In *Proceedings of the Fourth Conference on Machine Translation (Volume 3: Shared Task Papers, Day 2)*, pages 294–300, Florence, Italy. Association for Computational Linguistics.

Hainan Xu and Philipp Koehn. 2017. Zipporah: a fast and scalable data cleaning system for noisy webcrawled parallel corpora. In *Proceedings of the 2017 Conference on Empirical Methods in Natural Language Processing*, pages 2945–2950, Copenhagen, Denmark. Association for Computational Linguistics.

Label Noise in Context

Michael Desmond[*]
mdesmond@us.ibm.com

Catherine Finegan-Dollak[*]
cfd@ibm.com

Jeff Boston
daddyb@us.ibm.com

Matthew Arnold
marnold@us.ibm.com

IBM Research AI
1101 Kitchawan Rd, Yorktown Heights, NY 10598, USA

Abstract

Label noise—incorrectly or ambiguously labeled training examples—can negatively impact model performance. Although noise detection techniques have been around for decades, practitioners rarely apply them, as manual noise remediation is a tedious process. Examples incorrectly flagged as noise waste reviewers' time, and correcting label noise without guidance can be difficult.

We propose LNIC, a noise-detection method that uses an example's neighborhood within the training set to (a) reduce false positives and (b) provide an explanation as to why the example was flagged as noise. We demonstrate on several short-text classification datasets that LNIC outperforms the state of the art on measures of precision and $F_{0.5}$-score. We also show how LNIC's training set context helps a reviewer to understand and correct label noise in a dataset. The LNIC tool lowers the barriers to label noise remediation, increasing its utility for NLP practitioners.

1 Introduction

Label noise—examples with incorrect or ambiguous labels in a training set—degrades the performance of the learned model, resulting in inaccurate predictions (Frénay and Verleysen, 2014). Automated data collection risks generating noisy datasets, and human annotators may introduce noise through a lack of attention or expertise.

Automatic noise-detection algorithms analyze a training set and flag "suspicious" examples that are likely mislabeled (Brodley and Friedl, 1999; Frénay and Verleysen, 2014). Suspicious examples can be deleted, automatically corrected by an algorithm, or reviewed by a human. Human review is the most effective of these mitigation options but is comparatively expensive.

	sports	fitness
⇒	Unexpected increase in running ability	• Why doesn't my stamina seem to improve?
	• Is it possible for the libero to score points in volleyball?	• Is there a rule of thumb for setting running goals?
	• How counter-productive would having two coaches be?	

Table 1: Training set context can help an annotator decide if the highlighted suspicious training example is correctly labeled *sports* or should be labeled *fitness*.

Two problems contribute to making human review time consuming: false positives and a lack of explanation. False positives are examples that are incorrectly flagged as noise; reviewing such examples wastes the annotator's time. Showing a reviewer a suspicious example without an explanation is effective in the simplest cases, but is likely to cause difficulty and frustration in the more common case of non-obvious noise that requires a deeper comprehension of the data.

To date, few noise-detection algorithms have been designed with human review in mind. Sluban et al. (2010) is the only work we are aware of that recognized that a noise-detection algorithm for use in a human review process should emphasize precision (*i.e.*, reduce the proportion of false positives). However, we are unaware of any existing work that addresses the explainability of detected label noise.

We propose the Label Noise in Context system, or LNIC, which uses the neighborhood surrounding a suspicious example in the training set to improve both precision and explainability. By calculating a similarity matrix for the dataset, we are able to identify a suspicious example's neighborhood and use a method similar to a nearest-neighbors classifier to filter out false positives. Applying a set of simple heuristics to the same similarity matrix allows us to construct a *training set context*, like that in Table 1. Seen in isolation, an example about

---

[*]The first two authors contributed equally.

Proceedings of the 58th Annual Meeting of the Association for Computational Linguistics, pages 157–186
July 5 - July 10, 2020. ©2020 Association for Computational Linguistics

running ability labeled as belonging to the *sports* class is not obviously wrong; however, once the annotator understands that she is seeing it because there are more similar examples in the *fitness* class, it becomes apparent that there is a better label.

The main contributions of this work are

- We describe LNiC's nearest-neighbors-based algorithm to improve precision and explainability of automatically detected label noise (Sec. 3).
- We show that neighborhood-based filtering after noise-detection improves precision and $F_{0.5}$ over the state of the art for five short-text classification datasets (Sec. 4 and 5).
- We present the LNiC tool for reviewing noise in context, demonstrating the value of explanations for understanding and fixing label noise (Sec. 6).

A demo video is available at `https://www.youtube.com/watch?v=20cigQaCc_k`, and a live web demo is at `http://lnic.mybluemix.net/`

2   Related Work

Noise Detection.   Frénay and Verleysen (2014) conducted a comprehensive survey of the various approaches to detecting and remediating label noise. Many works advocate removing label noise to improve model performance (Brodley and Friedl, 1999; Sánchez et al., 2003; Smith and Martinez, 2011). Teng (2000) advocates automatic relabeling, while others present the case for human-in-the-loop (Ekambaram et al., 2016; Fefilatyev et al., 2012; Matic et al., 1992; Sluban et al., 2010) and hybrid techniques (Miranda et al., 2009). In work contemporaneous with ours, Northcutt et al. (2019) remove examples where a classifier's confidence is low.

The most directly related work is Brodley and Friedl (1999), describing a noise detection method using predictions from an ensemble of classifiers, and Sluban et al. (2010), proposing the High Agreement Random Forest (HARF) system; both systems are described in detail in Section 3.1.

Brodley and Friedl (1999) dropped suspicious examples but propose correction instead as future work. Sluban et al. (2010) note that precision of noise-detection is important when a human will review all suspicious examples. Garcia et al. (2016)'s experiments show that HARF also achieved state-of-the-art F_1 scores on a variety of datasets.

Active Learning   Similar to label noise remediation, active learning (Settles, 2014) seeks to minimize the effort a human needs to expend on data labeling activities in order to improve model performance. However, active learning aims to select the most informative *unlabeled* data to label next, while label noise detection identifies *already-labeled* data that may require additional labeling effort. We consider active learning and label noise detection as complimentary technologies, that might be woven together within a robust model improvement flow.

At a technical level, some active learning and label noise detection techniques are based on similar foundations. Query By Committee (QBC) (Seung et al., 1992) active learning uses an ensemble of classifiers, selecting examples on which the ensemble *disagrees* for labeling. Similarly ensemble-based noise detection algorithms select examples where the ensemble *agrees* (but disagrees with the given label). Model uncertainty, which underpins many effective active learning strategies such as *least confident*, *margin*, and *entropy*, is also the basis of label noise detection methods such as cleanlab (Northcutt et al., 2019).

Explainability.   With the rise of increasingly complex classification models, explaining classifier predictions has received a great deal of attention. Perhaps the most well-known system is LIME (Ribeiro et al., 2016). The LIME authors noted that explaining classifier predictions increases human trust and provides insights that can be used to improve the model. To explain a classifier's prediction on a particular example, the algorithm collects nearby examples and the model's predictions for them. It trains a linear model on a simpler representation of this data, allowing it to indicate which words or super-pixels are important in the classifier's decision.

Numerous recent works in NLP and machine learning emphasize explainability. Dhurandhar et al. (2018) explained classifier predictions with positive features that push an example towards its assigned class and negative features whose absence prevent an example from being placed in a different class. Lei et al. (2016) jointly trained a generator and an encoder in order to generate rationales for sentiment prediction and a similar-question-retrieval task. Mullenbach et al. (2018) used a convolutional neural network to predict codes describing the diagnosis and treatment of patients given the clinical notes on the patent encounter. Their attention mechanism not only improved the system's precision and F_1, but also highlighted the text that was most relevant to each code. Chiyah Garcia et al. (2018)'s system used an expert-generated decision tree and a set of templates to generate natural language explanations of what an autonomous underwater vehicle was doing and why.

Despite the interest in explainable models, no work that we are aware of has attempted to make detected label noise explainable.

3 Algorithms

LNiC uses a three-step process. First, a noise-detection algorithm flags suspicious examples. Second, a neighborhood-based filter decides which of these examples to ignore and which to flag for human review. Finally, we generate a context, using rules to select neighbors to present to the user.

3.1 Noise-Detection Algorithms

LNiC's noise-detection phase can use any noise-detection algorithm. Here, we report on three ensemble algorithms derived from the literature: consensus (Brodley and Friedl, 1999), agreed correction, and HARF (Sluban et al., 2010).[1]

Ensemble noise detection algorithms train several classifiers on cross-validation splits of the train set. Each classifier predicts labels for the left-out examples. The predicted label is the classifier's "vote" for that example. If it matches the current label, the classifier voted that the example is *not* suspicious; otherwise, the classifier voted that it is. In Brodley and Friedl (1999)'s consensus algorithm, if all votes agree that an example is suspicious, the algorithm flags that example as suspicious. Our agreed correction variant requires all votes from the ensemble to agree not only that an example is mislabeled, but also on what the correct label would be. HARF (Sluban et al., 2010) relies on the fact that a random forest is an ensemble of decision trees; it flags an example as suspicious if a super-majority of trees vote that it is.

3.2 Neighborhood Filtering

Neighborhood filtering reduces the number of examples that are incorrectly flagged as noise. If a majority of neighbors of an example have the same label as that example, it suggests that the example is correctly labeled, so LNiC filters it out of the list of suspicious examples.

The neighborhood filter calculates the pairwise cosine similarity of all examples in the training

data, then finds the k neighbors closest to each suspicious example s, where k is a tunable hyperparameter. If s's current label y_c is also the most common among those neighbors, s is filtered from the pool of suspicious examples as a false positive, otherwise s is flagged for human review.[2]

LNiC supports filtering on the *feature neighborhood* or the *activation neighborhood*. The feature neighborhood represents each example using its original feature vector (here, USE embeddings (Cer et al., 2018)). The activation neighborhood represents each example in the training set using final layer activations from a neural classifier trained on the entire data set, the idea being to project training examples into a classification space.

3.3 Context Generation

The final step of the LNiC algorithm is to apply heuristics to the neighborhood to generate a training set context. This context acts as an explanation, showing (a) which classes the noise-detection ensemble proposed as a better label for the suspicious example, and (b) the most similar examples from the current class and those proposed classes.

The ensembles in the noise-detection algorithms generate a list of predicted labels for each suspicious example. These labels plus the example's current label comprise the *permitted labels* for that example. The heuristic selects the example from each permitted label that is closest to the suspicious example. If there are fewer than k permitted labels (where k is the desired context size), the balance of the context is filled out by selecting the remaining $k - n$ nearest neighbors from the permitted labels.

We build the explanation based on both the activation neighborhood and the feature neighborhood; an example that already appears in the activation context is omitted from the feature context and replaced by the next-nearest neighbor. Figures 4 and 5 show a examples of this contextual explanation.

4 Experiments

We hypothesize that adding a neighborhood-based filter after noise detection reduces the rates of false positives while retaining true noisy examples. We test this by injecting noise into datasets, running algorithms over them, and measuring the correctly and incorrectly flagged suspicious examples.

---

[1] Models and hyperparameters are listed in Appendix A

[2] When using raw features, this filter acts like a k-nearest neighbors classifier with veto power over the ensemble. Experiments with a vote by weighted cosine similarity correlated closely with this simpler technique, and we did not pursue it.

4.1 Datasets

We evaluate on the short-text classification datasets listed in Table 2.[3] Phase one of the evaluation introduces label noise—effectively "corrupting" the datasets. The amount of introduced label noise was controlled by an error-rate parameter, interpreted as the fraction of the training set to mislabel.

We used two strategies to introduce label noise: *random* and *next-best*. Both selected a random sample of the training data to mislabel. The random strategy assigned a random incorrect label to each selected example. The next-best strategy assigned the "next-best" incorrect label, as predicted by a classifier trained on the entire train set; this simulates a best effort but incorrect labeling, as might be performed by a confused human labeler.

4.2 Metrics

Because the goal of the algorithm is to avoid wasting human time, our evaluation should heavily punish false positives. We therefore measure the precision of each algorithm. We also follow Sluban et al. (2010) in reporting $F_{0.5}$, an F-score that values precision twice as much as recall.

$$F_{0.5} = (1 + 0.5^2) \frac{precision \cdot recall}{(0.5^2 \cdot precision) + recall} \quad (1)$$

Not every situation calls for precision to be valued twice as much as recall. Therefore, we also report F_β (Rijsbergen, 1979) for $\beta \in \{1.0, 0.2, 0.1\}$ to reflect the preferences of users who value precision and recall equally, precision five times more than recall, and precision ten times more.

5 Results

Figure 1 shows average precision and $F_{0.5}$ scores across the five datasets, and Table 3 further summarizes by averaging across error rates. Appendix B shows results split by dataset and error rate.

Table 3 shows that, averaged across datasets and error rates, adding neighborhood filtering of any kind improves precision of all of the underlying algorithms. For randomly generated noise, this is true for $F_{0.5}$ as well. Figure 1a also shows that the neighborhood activation filter gives a large boost to precision over all three noise-detection algorithms, and the feature neighborhood filter gives a smaller

but still observable benefit. For next-best noise, adding the feature neighborhood filtering improves $F_{0.5}$, but activation neighborhood filtering slightly worsens $F_{0.5}$. From the graph in Figure 1d, it is apparent that activation neighborhood filtering has a benefit to $F_{0.5}$ at low error rates but declines relative to the other systems as the error rate increases, crossing at error rates near 15%. Addition of too much next-best noise negatively impacts the neural network trained on the uncorrected data, distorting the activation space. While this distortion does not harm precision, it is detrimental to recall.

For both random and next-best noise, agreed correction with activation neighborhood filtering achieves the best average precision. For random noise, HARF with activation-neighborhood filtering gives the best $F_{0.5}$ across noise rates. However, for next-best noise, HARF suffered a dramatic loss in recall when error rates exceeded about 12% (Figure 1d), leading it to have low overall $F_{0.5}$. This may be due to the random forest's use of bagging: if a subset of trees trains on samples with a great deal of non-random noise, those trees could learn to misclassify systematically. Agreed correction with feature neighborhood filtering gave the highest average $F_{0.5}$ for next-best noise.

The upward trend in precision as error rates increase suggests that the same core of false positives are consistently detected. As the number of true positives increases with higher error rates, the core of false positives makes up a smaller fraction of the total number of examples flagged as suspicious.

Table 4 lists F_β scores. As expected, using a neighborhood filter, which reduces the number of suspicious examples shown to a user, is particularly advantageous when precision is valued more than recall ($F_{0.2}$ and $F_{0.1}$), but often extracts a cost when recall and precision are equally important ($F_{1.0}$). Thus, agreed correction with no neighborhood filter is the best system to optimize $F_{1.0}$ when using next-best noise. Nevertheless, the strongest system for $F_{1.0}$ on random noise is still HARF with activation neighborhood filtering, followed closely by consensus with activation neighborhood filtering.

6 The LNiC Tool

The LNiC tool implements the algorithms described above and provides a web interface to review label noise in context. The interface visually summarizes the overall label noise within a dataset and links to groups of suspicious examples in con-

---

	Source	Description	Train	Classes
Stack Exchange	Collected by the authors from `https://archive.org/details/stackexchange`	Question titles from general-interest forums classified by topic	5000	15
Stack Overflow	Subset of (Xu et al., 2015)	Question titles from programming forum classified by topic	10000	20
Jeopardy	Subset of `www.j-archive.com`	Gameshow question-answer pairs classified by category	5080	21
ATIS	(Price, 1990; Hakkani-Tur et al., 2016)	Questions from air travel domain classified by intent	4952	17
Snips-2017	`https://github.com/snipsco/nlu-benchmark/`	Requests to a digital assistant classified by intent	13784	7

Table 2: Dataset details.

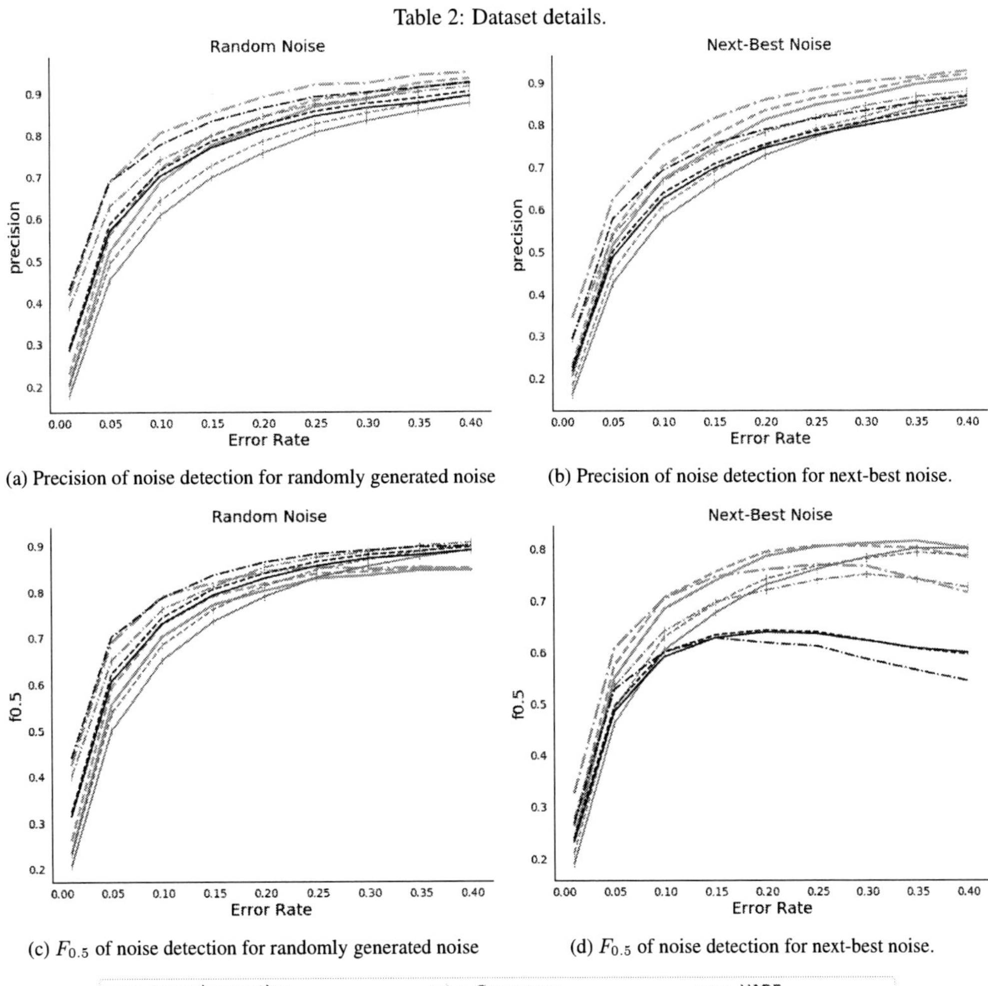

(a) Precision of noise detection for randomly generated noise

(b) Precision of noise detection for next-best noise.

(c) $F_{0.5}$ of noise detection for randomly generated noise

(d) $F_{0.5}$ of noise detection for next-best noise.

Figure 1: Precision and $F_{0.5}$ at various noise levels, averaged across the five datasets.

text. LNIC's representation of the noise summary (Figure 2) is similar to a confusion matrix. In the *label noise matrix* each cell indicates the number of noisy examples discovered where the context includes the classes specified by the row and the column.[4] Clicking on a cell brings the user to a list of examples flagged as noise. Each of these examples can be expanded to show the context, as

---

[4]The agreed-correction algorithm guarantees that each context contains exactly two classes. When using larger contexts, the summary can be a list of class tuples.

	buddhism	cooking	diy	fitness	gardening	health	history	interpersonal	mythology	outdoors	parenting	pets	productivity	sports	travel
buddhism		0	0	2	2	4	10	6	10	4	5	4	12	4	1
cooking	0		7	2	5	10	1	1	0	12	4	2	1	2	4
diy	0	7		1	10	3	1	0	0	11	4	1	0	1	1
fitness	2	2	1		0	52	0	0	0	17	4	0	15	29	0
gardening	2	5	10	0		3	0	1	1	14	0	2	1	1	0
health	4	10	3	52	3		2	2	0	12	7	7	20	7	1
history	10	1	1	0	0	2		0	25	1	2	0	1	4	5
interpersonal	6	1	0	0	1	2	0		0	1	14	4	20	5	1
mythology	10	0	0	0	1	0	25	0		0	0	0	0	1	1
outdoors	4	12	11	17	14	12	1	1	0		2	10	3	18	18
parenting	5	4	4	4	0	7	2	14	0	2		4	13	1	3
pets	4	2	1	0	2	7	0	4	0	10	4		0	0	1
productivity	12	1	0	15	1	20	1	20	0	3	13	0		0	1
sports	4	2	1	29	1	7	4	5	1	18	1	0	0		1
travel	1	4	1	0	0	1	5	1	1	18	3	1	1	1	

Figure 2: The label noise matrix summarizing noise discovered in approximately 30k examples from the Stack Exchange dataset.

	Random Noise		Next-Best Noise	
	P	$F_{0.5}$	P	$F_{0.5}$
Agreed correction	0.732	0.713	0.717	0.691
+ *Neighborhood filtering using*				
feature	0.753	0.729	0.738	**0.698**
activation	**0.819**	0.773	**0.779**	0.681
Consensus	0.672	0.702	0.647	0.645
+ *Neighborhood filtering using*				
feature	0.698	0.725	0.668	0.654
activation	0.774	0.781	0.713	0.646
HARF	0.734	0.751	0.667	0.559
+ *Neighborhood filtering using*				
feature	0.746	0.761	0.677	0.563
activation	0.801	**0.798**	0.718	0.549

Table 3: Mean precision and $F_{0.5}$ for the five datasets, averaged across all error rates. The top row in each section is a baseline system with no filtering.

	Random Noise			Next-Best Noise		
	$F_{1.0}$	$F_{0.2}$	$F_{0.1}$	$F_{1.0}$	$F_{0.2}$	$F_{0.1}$
Agreed correction	0.695	0.728	0.731	**0.666**	0.712	0.716
+ *Neighborhood filtering using*						
feature	0.706	0.748	0.752	0.658	0.729	0.736
activation	0.721	**0.809**	**0.817**	0.585	**0.757**	**0.773**
Consensus	0.760	0.678	0.674	0.652	0.646	0.647
+ *Neighborhood filtering using*						
feature	0.776	0.703	0.699	0.647	0.665	0.667
activation	0.800	0.775	0.774	0.581	0.698	0.709
HARF	0.787	0.737	0.734	0.477	0.639	0.659
+ *Neighborhood filtering using*						
feature	0.794	0.748	0.746	0.477	0.647	0.669
activation	**0.803**	0.800	0.800	0.430	0.672	0.705

Table 4: Average F-scores across the datasets valuing precision to different degrees.

illustrated in Figures 3 and 4.

Data from Stack Exchange illustrates how context helps a reviewer understand problems in a dataset. Sometimes, context shows that an example is mislabeled. Without context, it is easy for an annotator to be uncertain of whether a question about the existence of a myth belongs in the *history* class; it is a question about a historical civilization, after all. However, from the context in Figure 4, it is clear that even questions about the history of myths are categorized as *mythology*, and so the example's label should be changed to maintain consistency.

Other times, context can reveal more complex issues with the class structure of the data. Figure 5 shows a suspicious example from the *health* class that the noise detection algorithm suggests may belong in the *fitness* class. The context shows that in fact, both classes include questions about the timing of meals with regard to exercise. A human reviewer should make a decision about where the boundary between these two classes should lie and assign these utterances consistently to one class.

7 Conclusion

Although NLP practitioners know that label noise harms performance, and noise detection algorithms have long been available, this technology is not

history / mythology

Suspicious examples between history and mythology.

Mayan calendar coinciding with winter solstice
The concept that scripture is made to adapt to changes of society, technology, and language
What gift did Saladin send to Richard when he was ill?
Are there any texts/translations of the 4 main Egyptian creation myths?
How were the Welsh Triads used by the Welsh?
Is there a Greek myth of Poseidon "dating" his daughter in the form of a dolphin?
What is this symbol in red box?
What is known about the Antiu?
Is Krampus real?

Figure 3: Suspicious examples at the intersection of *history* and *mythology* classes without context.

history	mythology
• Is there a Greek myth of Poseidon "dating" his daughter in the form of a dolphin? (1.000)	• Who is the oldest being in Greek mythology? (0.958)
	• Are there any female heroines in Shinto mythology? (0.953)
	• Who worshipped the Titans? (0.953)
	• Are there any saints or heroes in mythology who ally with death? (0.953)
	• Did any ancient cultures or scholars recognize the Hero's Journey monomyth? (0.951)
• How did Greeks make greek fire? (0.463)	• Does Poseidon rule over all the sea gods? (0.602)
	• Is Greek mythology derivative of/influence by Ugaritic/Canaanite mythology? (0.591)
	• Where does Poseidon get called the God of Kin? (0.570)
	• Why is Roman Mythology so similar to Greek Mythology or vice versa? (0.565)
	• Is there a world tree in Greek mythology? (0.563)

Figure 4: An example from Figure 3, with context. In red is the suspicious example. Examples in the white box are its context from activation space, and those in the blue box are context from raw embedding space. Numbers in parentheses indicate cosine similarity.

being applied in practice, perhaps because human

How long should one wait to eat after exercise

fitness	health
• Should I eat before or after my exercise? (0.989)	• How long should one wait to eat after exercise (1.000)
• How long should I wait to exercise after eating? (0.955)	• What are the health benefits of consuming smaller meals more often throughout the day? (0.957)
• What are the benefits to eating immediately after exercising? (0.954)	• What happens when you eat carbs everyday? (0.955)
• How long should I wait after dinner before I start exercising? (0.833)	• Why am I advised not to eat immediately before exercise? (0.626)
• Is it okay to eat after exercising? (0.768)	
• How long do I wait after a failed lift? (0.646)	
• How early should I eat before Hockey training (0.629)	
• What is the best thing to eat before a long bike ride? (0.617)	

Figure 5: Context shows overlapping class definitions.

review of detected errors is difficult and time consuming. LNιC makes human review of possible label noise easier and more efficient. It reduces the number of false positive examples that the reviewer must look at, providing state-of-the-art precision and $F_{0.5}$ across several short text datasets. And by providing an explanation of why the model flagged an example as suspicious, it makes the output of label noise detectors understandable and actionable.

Acknowledgments

We thank Evelyn Duesterwald as well as the anonymous reviewers for helpful feedback.

References

Carla E. Brodley and Mark A. Friedl. 1999. Identifying mislabeled training data. *Journal of Artificial Intelligence Research*, 11:131–167.

Daniel Cer, Yinfei Yang, Sheng-yi Kong, Nan Hua, Nicole Limtiaco, Rhomni St. John, Noah Constant, Mario Guajardo-Cespedes, Steve Yuan, Chris Tar, Yun-Hsuan Sung, Brian Strope, and Ray Kurzweil. 2018. Universal sentence encoder. *arXiv preprint*, abs/1803.11175.

Francisco Javier Chiyah Garcia, David A. Robb, Xingkun Liu, Atanas Laskov, Pedro Patron, and Helen Hastie. 2018. Explainable Autonomy: A Study of Explanation Styles for Building Clear Mental Models. In *Proceedings of the 11th International Conference on Natural Language Generation*, pages 99–108, Tilburg University, The Netherlands. Association for Computational Linguistics.

Amit Dhurandhar, Pin-Yu Chen, Ronny Luss, Chun-Chen Tu, Paishun Ting, Karthikeyan Shanmugam, and Payel Das. 2018. Explanations based on the missing: Towards contrastive explanations with pertinent negatives. In *Advances in Neural Information Processing Systems 31*, pages 592–603. Curran Associates, Inc.

Rajmadhan Ekambaram, Sergiy Fefilatyev, Matthew Shreve, Kurt Kramer, Lawrence O. Hall, Dmitry B. Goldgof, and Rangachar Kasturi. 2016. Active cleaning of label noise. *Pattern Recognition*, 51:463–480.

Sergiy Fefilatyev, Matthew Shreve, Kurt Kramer, Lawrence Hall, Dmitry Goldgof, Rangachar Kasturi, Kendra Daly, Andrew Remsen, and Horst Bunke. 2012. Label-noise reduction with support vector machines. In *Proceedings of the 21st International Conference on Pattern Recognition (ICPR2012)*, pages 3504–3508. IEEE.

Benoît Frénay and Michel Verleysen. 2014. Classification in the presence of label noise: A survey. *IEEE transactions on neural networks and learning systems*, 25(5):845–869.

Luís P.F. Garcia, André C.P.L.F. de Carvalho, and Ana C. Lorena. 2016. Noise detection in the meta-learning level. *Neurocomputing*, 176:14–25.

Dilek Hakkani-Tur, Gokhan Tur, Asli Celikyilmaz, Yun-Nung Chen, Jianfeng Gao, and Ye-Yi Wang. 2016. Multi-domain joint semantic frame parsing using bi-directional RNN-LSTM. In *Proceedings of Interspeech*.

Tao Lei, Regina Barzilay, and Tommi Jaakkola. 2016. Rationalizing Neural Predictions. In *Proceedings of the 2016 Conference on Empirical Methods in Natural Language Processing*, pages 107–117, Austin, Texas. Association for Computational Linguistics.

N. Matic, I. Guyon, L. Bottou, J. Denker, and V. Vapnik. 1992. Computer aided cleaning of large databases for character recognition. In *Proceedings., 11th IAPR International Conference on Pattern Recognition. Vol. II. Conference B: Pattern Recognition Methodology and Systems*, pages 330–333. IEEE.

André L.B. Miranda, Luís Paulo F. Garcia, André C.P.L.F. Carvalho, and Ana C. Lorena. 2009. Use of classification algorithms in noise detection and elimination. In *International Conference on Hybrid Artificial Intelligence Systems*, pages 417–424. Springer.

James Mullenbach, Sarah Wiegreffe, Jon Duke, Jimeng Sun, and Jacob Eisenstein. 2018. Explainable Prediction of Medical Codes from Clinical Text. In *Proceedings of the 2018 Conference of the North American Chapter of the Association for Computational Linguistics: Human Language Technologies, Volume 1 (Long Papers)*, pages 1101–1111, New Orleans, Louisiana. Association for Computational Linguistics.

Curtis G Northcutt, Lu Jiang, and Isaac L Chuang. 2019. Confident learning: Estimating uncertainty in dataset labels. *arXiv preprint arXiv:1911.00068*.

F. Pedregosa, G. Varoquaux, A. Gramfort, V. Michel, B. Thirion, O. Grisel, M. Blondel, P. Prettenhofer, R. Weiss, V. Dubourg, J. Vanderplas, A. Passos, D. Cournapeau, M. Brucher, M. Perrot, and E. Duchesnay. 2011. Scikit-learn: Machine learning in Python. *Journal of Machine Learning Research*, 12:2825–2830.

P. J. Price. 1990. Evaluation of spoken language systems: The ATIS domain. In *Proceedings of the Workshop on Speech and Natural Language*, HLT '90, pages 91–95, Stroudsburg, PA, USA. Association for Computational Linguistics.

Marco Tulio Ribeiro, Sameer Singh, and Carlos Guestrin. 2016. "Why Should I Trust You?" Explaining the Predictions of Any Classifier Marco. In *Proceedings of the 22nd ACM SIGKDD International Conference on Knowledge Discovery and Data Mining*, pages 1135–1144, San Francisco, California, USA. ACM.

C. J. Van Rijsbergen. 1979. *Information Retrieval*, 2nd edition. Butterworth-Heinemann, Newton, MA, USA.

José Salvador Sánchez, Ricardo Barandela, Ana I. Marqués, Roberto Alejo, and Jorge Badenas. 2003. Analysis of new techniques to obtain quality training sets. *Pattern Recognition Letters*, 24(7):1015–1022.

Burr Settles. 2014. Active learning literature survey. 2010. *Computer Sciences Technical Report*, 1648.

H Sebastian Seung, Manfred Opper, and Haim Sompolinsky. 1992. Query by committee. In *Proceedings of the fifth annual workshop on Computational learning theory*, pages 287–294.

Borut Sluban, Dragan Gamberger, and Nada Lavra. 2010. Advances in class noise detection. In *Proceedings of the 19th European Conference on Artificial Intelligence*, pages 1105–1106. IOS Press.

Michael R. Smith and Tony Martinez. 2011. Improving classification accuracy by identifying and removing instances that should be misclassified. In *The 2011 International Joint Conference on Neural Networks*, pages 2690–2697. IEEE.

Choh Man Teng. 2000. Evaluating noise correction. In *Pacific Rim International Conference on Artificial Intelligence*, pages 188–198. Springer.

Jiaming Xu, Peng Wang, Guanhua Tian, Bo Xu, Jun Zhao, Fangyuan Wang, and Hongwei Hao. 2015. Short text clustering via convolutional neural networks. In *Proceedings of the 1st Workshop on Vector Space Modeling for Natural Language Processing*, pages 62–69, Denver, Colorado. Association for Computational Linguistics.

A Appendix: Model Details

For ease of replication, this appendix specifies the details of the models used in our experiments.

For consensus and agreed-only noise detection, our ensemble consisted of three classifiers from Scikit Learn (Pedregosa et al., 2011): LogisticRegression, RandomForestClassifier, and MLPClassifier. We used default parameters, except that we set MLPClassifier's `max_iter` parameter to 1000 to speed up experiments.

For HARF, we used a RandomForestClassifier model with 500 trees and required 90% agreement. Sluban et al. (2010) reported on models requiring lower levels of agreement, but preliminary testing demonstrated that 90% improved results on our datasets.

For the neighborhood filter, we set $k = 5$.

Our raw vector representation of all utterances was USE (Cer et al., 2018). The activations for activation-based filtering and context generation were generated using an MLPClassifier with `hidden_layer_sizes = [100, 512]`.

B Appendix: Detailed Results

Results were summarized in the body of the paper for conciseness. In this appendix, we present precision and $F_{0.5}$ for each of the five datasets and for each of the error rates.

Underlying Algorithm	Context Filter	error rate	precision	$F_{0.5}$
Agreed correction	(baseline)	0.01	0.203559	0.235175
		0.05	0.516995	0.551899
		0.10	0.678281	0.692148
		0.15	0.758825	0.754214
		0.20	0.815761	0.792989
		0.25	0.855683	0.815505
		0.30	0.874819	0.821995
		0.35	0.902361	0.829439
		0.40	0.914755	0.823054
	activation	0.01	0.379626	0.374314
		0.05	0.653646	0.647463
		0.10	0.777705	0.745331
		0.15	0.831916	0.782190
		0.20	0.873480	0.801011
		0.25	0.899718	0.810401
		0.30	0.910957	0.806536
		0.35	0.925808	0.796353
		0.40	0.936250	0.779562
	feature	0.01	0.228381	0.261363
		0.05	0.551033	0.582140
		0.10	0.709730	0.716853
		0.15	0.785696	0.772165
		0.20	0.836971	0.804862
		0.25	0.871780	0.821373
		0.30	0.887976	0.823381
		0.35	0.912542	0.825164
		0.40	0.925177	0.816177
	nonsuspicious	0.01	0.219619	0.252413
		0.05	0.541191	0.573870
		0.10	0.700703	0.710048
		0.15	0.777494	0.767097
		0.20	0.832716	0.802072
		0.25	0.870279	0.820193
		0.30	0.885262	0.822268
		0.35	0.909316	0.823756
		0.40	0.922156	0.814744
Consensus	(baseline)	0.01	0.169058	0.197610
		0.05	0.438177	0.479689
		0.10	0.591796	0.626953
		0.15	0.678183	0.704604
		0.20	0.741275	0.758822
		0.25	0.787061	0.794762
		0.30	0.818512	0.818545
		0.35	0.847556	0.837087
		0.40	0.865010	0.843633
	activation	0.01	0.340710	0.337163
		0.05	0.581698	0.591143
		0.10	0.702483	0.699962
		0.15	0.765191	0.752932
		0.20	0.811529	0.785388
		0.25	0.843820	0.806149
		0.30	0.864403	0.817224
		0.35	0.882211	0.818990
		0.40	0.895110	0.814209
	feature	0.01	0.191324	0.221609
		0.05	0.472302	0.511817
		0.10	0.624910	0.655624
		0.15	0.707260	0.727099
		0.20	0.766436	0.776426
		0.25	0.806752	0.805997
		0.30	0.834342	0.824318
		0.35	0.862185	0.838768
		0.40	0.879229	0.843028
	nonsuspicious	0.01	0.185901	0.215997
		0.05	0.463941	0.504450
		0.10	0.614485	0.646574
		0.15	0.701349	0.722953
		0.20	0.762975	0.773727
		0.25	0.804869	0.804780
		0.30	0.833155	0.824230
		0.35	0.859147	0.835885
		0.40	0.875436	0.839302

Underlying Algorithm	Context Filter	error rate	precision	$F_{0.5}$
HARF590	(baseline)	0.01	0.250247	0.272751
		0.05	0.527276	0.544201
		0.10	0.662522	0.659799
		0.15	0.732189	0.709038
		0.20	0.777402	0.732818
		0.25	0.808914	0.744331
		0.30	0.830042	0.745807
		0.35	0.846649	0.742334
		0.40	0.867032	0.742929
	activation	0.01	0.360629	0.352368
		0.05	0.631307	0.613590
		0.10	0.733487	0.692197
		0.15	0.792436	0.730627
		0.20	0.825070	0.739711
		0.25	0.851299	0.745366
		0.30	0.865749	0.736683
		0.35	0.879965	0.729277
		0.40	0.893418	0.720200
	feature	0.01	0.256974	0.279874
		0.05	0.542058	0.557569
		0.10	0.676098	0.671038
		0.15	0.744827	0.718450
		0.20	0.788157	0.739972
		0.25	0.819442	0.750494
		0.30	0.839792	0.750249
		0.35	0.857306	0.745631
		0.40	0.876019	0.744641
	nonsuspicious	0.01	0.263552	0.286632
		0.05	0.542341	0.557493
		0.10	0.676441	0.670760
		0.15	0.744850	0.717847
		0.20	0.788948	0.739795
		0.25	0.818234	0.748751
		0.30	0.839663	0.749268
		0.35	0.856773	0.743603
		0.40	0.875930	0.743391

Table 5: ATIS, Next-Best Noise

Underlying Algorithm	Context Filter	error rate	precision	$F_{0.5}$
Agreed correction	(baseline)	0.01	0.203559	0.235175
		0.05	0.516995	0.551899
		0.10	0.678281	0.692148
		0.15	0.758825	0.754214
		0.20	0.815761	0.792989
		0.25	0.855683	0.815505
		0.30	0.874819	0.821995
		0.35	0.902361	0.829439
		0.40	0.914755	0.823054
	activation	0.01	0.379626	0.374314
		0.05	0.653646	0.647463
		0.10	0.777705	0.745331
		0.15	0.831916	0.782190
		0.20	0.873480	0.801011
		0.25	0.899718	0.810401
		0.30	0.910957	0.806536
		0.35	0.925808	0.796353
		0.40	0.936250	0.779562
	feature	0.01	0.228381	0.261363
		0.05	0.551033	0.582140
		0.10	0.709730	0.716853
		0.15	0.785696	0.772165
		0.20	0.836971	0.804862
		0.25	0.871780	0.821373
		0.30	0.887976	0.823381
		0.35	0.912542	0.825164
		0.40	0.925177	0.816177
	nonsuspicious	0.01	0.219619	0.252413
		0.05	0.541191	0.573870
		0.10	0.700703	0.710048
		0.15	0.777494	0.767097
		0.20	0.832716	0.802072
		0.25	0.870279	0.820193
		0.30	0.885262	0.822268
		0.35	0.909316	0.823756
		0.40	0.922156	0.814744

Consensus	(baseline)	0.01	0.169058	0.197610
		0.05	0.438177	0.479689
		0.10	0.591796	0.626953
		0.15	0.678183	0.704604
		0.20	0.741275	0.758822
		0.25	0.787061	0.794762
		0.30	0.818512	0.818545
		0.35	0.847556	0.837087
		0.40	0.865010	0.843633
	activation	0.01	0.340710	0.337163
		0.05	0.581698	0.591143
		0.10	0.702483	0.699962
		0.15	0.765191	0.752932
		0.20	0.811529	0.785388
		0.25	0.843820	0.806149
		0.30	0.864403	0.817224
		0.35	0.882211	0.818990
		0.40	0.895110	0.814209
	feature	0.01	0.191324	0.221609
		0.05	0.472302	0.511817
		0.10	0.624910	0.655624
		0.15	0.707260	0.727099
		0.20	0.766436	0.776426
		0.25	0.806752	0.805997
		0.30	0.834342	0.824318
		0.35	0.862185	0.838768
		0.40	0.879229	0.843028
	nonsuspicious	0.01	0.185901	0.215997
		0.05	0.463941	0.504450
		0.10	0.614485	0.646574
		0.15	0.701349	0.722953
		0.20	0.762975	0.773727
		0.25	0.804869	0.804780
		0.30	0.833155	0.824230
		0.35	0.859147	0.835885
		0.40	0.875436	0.839302
HARF590	(baseline)	0.01	0.250247	0.272751
		0.05	0.527276	0.544201
		0.10	0.662522	0.659799
		0.15	0.732189	0.709038
		0.20	0.777402	0.732818
		0.25	0.808914	0.744331
		0.30	0.830042	0.745807
		0.35	0.846649	0.742334
		0.40	0.867032	0.742929
	activation	0.01	0.360629	0.352368
		0.05	0.631307	0.613590
		0.10	0.733487	0.692197
		0.15	0.792436	0.730627
		0.20	0.825070	0.739711
		0.25	0.851299	0.745366
		0.30	0.865749	0.736683
		0.35	0.879965	0.729277
		0.40	0.893418	0.720200
	feature	0.01	0.256974	0.279874
		0.05	0.542058	0.557569
		0.10	0.676098	0.671038
		0.15	0.744827	0.718450
		0.20	0.788157	0.739972
		0.25	0.819442	0.750494
		0.30	0.839792	0.750249
		0.35	0.857306	0.745631
		0.40	0.876019	0.744641
	nonsuspicious	0.01	0.263552	0.286632
		0.05	0.542341	0.557493
		0.10	0.676441	0.670760
		0.15	0.744850	0.717847
		0.20	0.788948	0.739795
		0.25	0.818234	0.748751
		0.30	0.839663	0.749268
		0.35	0.856773	0.743603
		0.40	0.875930	0.743391

Table 6: ATIS, Random Noise

Underlying Algorithm	Context Filter	error rate	precision	$F_{0.5}$
Agreed correction	(baseline)	0.01	0.203559	0.235175
		0.05	0.516995	0.551899
		0.10	0.678281	0.692148
		0.15	0.758825	0.754214
		0.20	0.815761	0.792989
		0.25	0.855683	0.815505
		0.30	0.874819	0.821995
		0.35	0.902361	0.829439
		0.40	0.914755	0.823054
	activation	0.01	0.379626	0.374314
		0.05	0.653646	0.647463
		0.10	0.777705	0.745331
		0.15	0.831916	0.782190
		0.20	0.873480	0.801011
		0.25	0.899718	0.810401
		0.30	0.910957	0.806536
		0.35	0.925808	0.796353
		0.40	0.936250	0.779562
	feature	0.01	0.228381	0.261363
		0.05	0.551033	0.582140
		0.10	0.709730	0.716853
		0.15	0.785696	0.772165
		0.20	0.836971	0.804862
		0.25	0.871780	0.821373
		0.30	0.887976	0.823381
		0.35	0.912542	0.825164
		0.40	0.925177	0.816177
	nonsuspicious	0.01	0.219619	0.252413
		0.05	0.541191	0.573870
		0.10	0.700703	0.710048
		0.15	0.777494	0.767097
		0.20	0.832716	0.802072
		0.25	0.870279	0.820193
		0.30	0.885262	0.822268
		0.35	0.909316	0.823756
		0.40	0.922156	0.814744
Consensus	(baseline)	0.01	0.169058	0.197610
		0.05	0.438177	0.479689
		0.10	0.591796	0.626953
		0.15	0.678183	0.704604
		0.20	0.741275	0.758822
		0.25	0.787061	0.794762
		0.30	0.818512	0.818545
		0.35	0.847556	0.837087
		0.40	0.865010	0.843633
	activation	0.01	0.340710	0.337163
		0.05	0.581698	0.591143
		0.10	0.702483	0.699962
		0.15	0.765191	0.752932
		0.20	0.811529	0.785388
		0.25	0.843820	0.806149
		0.30	0.864403	0.817224
		0.35	0.882211	0.818990
		0.40	0.895110	0.814209
	feature	0.01	0.191324	0.221609
		0.05	0.472302	0.511817
		0.10	0.624910	0.655624
		0.15	0.707260	0.727099
		0.20	0.766436	0.776426
		0.25	0.806752	0.805997
		0.30	0.834342	0.824318
		0.35	0.862185	0.838768
		0.40	0.879229	0.843028
	nonsuspicious	0.01	0.185901	0.215997
		0.05	0.463941	0.504450
		0.10	0.614485	0.646574
		0.15	0.701349	0.722953
		0.20	0.762975	0.773727
		0.25	0.804869	0.804780
		0.30	0.833155	0.824230
		0.35	0.859147	0.835885
		0.40	0.875436	0.839302

Underlying Algorithm	Context Filter	error rate	precision	$F_{0.5}$
HARF590	(baseline)	0.01	0.250247	0.272751
		0.05	0.527276	0.544201
		0.10	0.662522	0.659799
		0.15	0.732189	0.709038
		0.20	0.777402	0.732818
		0.25	0.808914	0.744331
		0.30	0.830042	0.745807
		0.35	0.846649	0.742334
		0.40	0.867032	0.742929
	activation	0.01	0.360629	0.352368
		0.05	0.631307	0.613590
		0.10	0.733487	0.692197
		0.15	0.792436	0.730627
		0.20	0.825070	0.739711
		0.25	0.851299	0.745366
		0.30	0.865749	0.736683
		0.35	0.879965	0.729277
		0.40	0.893418	0.720200
	feature	0.01	0.256974	0.279874
		0.05	0.542058	0.557569
		0.10	0.676098	0.671038
		0.15	0.744827	0.718450
		0.20	0.788157	0.739972
		0.25	0.819442	0.750494
		0.30	0.839792	0.750249
		0.35	0.857306	0.745631
		0.40	0.876019	0.744641
	nonsuspicious	0.01	0.263552	0.286632
		0.05	0.542341	0.557493
		0.10	0.676441	0.670760
		0.15	0.744850	0.717847
		0.20	0.788948	0.739795
		0.25	0.818234	0.748751
		0.30	0.839663	0.749268
		0.35	0.856773	0.743603
		0.40	0.875930	0.743391

Table 7: Jeopardy, Next-Best Noise

Underlying Algorithm	Context Filter	error rate	precision	$F_{0.5}$
Agreed correction	(baseline)	0.01	0.203559	0.235175
		0.05	0.516995	0.551899
		0.10	0.678281	0.692148
		0.15	0.758825	0.754214
		0.20	0.815761	0.792989
		0.25	0.855683	0.815505
		0.30	0.874819	0.821995
		0.35	0.902361	0.829439
		0.40	0.914755	0.823054
	activation	0.01	0.379626	0.374314
		0.05	0.653646	0.647463
		0.10	0.777705	0.745331
		0.15	0.831916	0.782190
		0.20	0.873480	0.801011
		0.25	0.899718	0.810401
		0.30	0.910957	0.806536
		0.35	0.925808	0.796353
		0.40	0.936250	0.779562
	feature	0.01	0.228381	0.261363
		0.05	0.551033	0.582140
		0.10	0.709730	0.716853
		0.15	0.785696	0.772165
		0.20	0.836971	0.804862
		0.25	0.871780	0.821373
		0.30	0.887976	0.823381
		0.35	0.912542	0.825164
		0.40	0.925177	0.816177
	nonsuspicious	0.01	0.219619	0.252413
		0.05	0.541191	0.573870
		0.10	0.700703	0.710048
		0.15	0.777494	0.767097
		0.20	0.832716	0.802072
		0.25	0.870279	0.820193
		0.30	0.885262	0.822268
		0.35	0.909316	0.823756
		0.40	0.922156	0.814744

Consensus	(baseline)	0.01	0.169058	0.197610
		0.05	0.438177	0.479689
		0.10	0.591796	0.626953
		0.15	0.678183	0.704604
		0.20	0.741275	0.758822
		0.25	0.787061	0.794762
		0.30	0.818512	0.818545
		0.35	0.847556	0.837087
		0.40	0.865010	0.843633
	activation	0.01	0.340710	0.337163
		0.05	0.581698	0.591143
		0.10	0.702483	0.699962
		0.15	0.765191	0.752932
		0.20	0.811529	0.785388
		0.25	0.843820	0.806149
		0.30	0.864403	0.817224
		0.35	0.882211	0.818990
		0.40	0.895110	0.814209
	feature	0.01	0.191324	0.221609
		0.05	0.472302	0.511817
		0.10	0.624910	0.655624
		0.15	0.707260	0.727099
		0.20	0.766436	0.776426
		0.25	0.806752	0.805997
		0.30	0.834342	0.824318
		0.35	0.862185	0.838768
		0.40	0.879229	0.843028
	nonsuspicious	0.01	0.185901	0.215997
		0.05	0.463941	0.504450
		0.10	0.614485	0.646574
		0.15	0.701349	0.722953
		0.20	0.762975	0.773727
		0.25	0.804869	0.804780
		0.30	0.833155	0.824230
		0.35	0.859147	0.835885
		0.40	0.875436	0.839302
HARF590	(baseline)	0.01	0.250247	0.272751
		0.05	0.527276	0.544201
		0.10	0.662522	0.659799
		0.15	0.732189	0.709038
		0.20	0.777402	0.732818
		0.25	0.808914	0.744331
		0.30	0.830042	0.745807
		0.35	0.846649	0.742334
		0.40	0.867032	0.742929
	activation	0.01	0.360629	0.352368
		0.05	0.631307	0.613590
		0.10	0.733487	0.692197
		0.15	0.792436	0.730627
		0.20	0.825070	0.739711
		0.25	0.851299	0.745366
		0.30	0.865749	0.736683
		0.35	0.879965	0.729277
		0.40	0.893418	0.720200
	feature	0.01	0.256974	0.279874
		0.05	0.542058	0.557569
		0.10	0.676098	0.671038
		0.15	0.744827	0.718450
		0.20	0.788157	0.739972
		0.25	0.819442	0.750494
		0.30	0.839792	0.750249
		0.35	0.857306	0.745631
		0.40	0.876019	0.744641
	nonsuspicious	0.01	0.263552	0.286632
		0.05	0.542341	0.557493
		0.10	0.676441	0.670760
		0.15	0.744850	0.717847
		0.20	0.788948	0.739795
		0.25	0.818234	0.748751
		0.30	0.839663	0.749268
		0.35	0.856773	0.743603
		0.40	0.875930	0.743391

Table 8: Jeopardy, Random Noise

Underlying Algorithm	Context Filter	error rate	precision	$F_{0.5}$
Agreed correction	(baseline)	0.01	0.203559	0.235175
		0.05	0.516995	0.551899
		0.10	0.678281	0.692148
		0.15	0.758825	0.754214
		0.20	0.815761	0.792989
		0.25	0.855683	0.815505
		0.30	0.874819	0.821995
		0.35	0.902361	0.829439
		0.40	0.914755	0.823054
	activation	0.01	0.379626	0.374314
		0.05	0.653646	0.647463
		0.10	0.777705	0.745331
		0.15	0.831916	0.782190
		0.20	0.873480	0.801011
		0.25	0.899718	0.810401
		0.30	0.910957	0.806536
		0.35	0.925808	0.796353
		0.40	0.936250	0.779562
	feature	0.01	0.228381	0.261363
		0.05	0.551033	0.582140
		0.10	0.709730	0.716853
		0.15	0.785696	0.772165
		0.20	0.836971	0.804862
		0.25	0.871780	0.821373
		0.30	0.887976	0.823381
		0.35	0.912542	0.825164
		0.40	0.925177	0.816177
	nonsuspicious	0.01	0.219619	0.252413
		0.05	0.541191	0.573870
		0.10	0.700703	0.710048
		0.15	0.777494	0.767097
		0.20	0.832716	0.802072
		0.25	0.870279	0.820193
		0.30	0.885262	0.822268
		0.35	0.909316	0.823756
		0.40	0.922156	0.814744
Consensus	(baseline)	0.01	0.169058	0.197610
		0.05	0.438177	0.479689
		0.10	0.591796	0.626953
		0.15	0.678183	0.704604
		0.20	0.741275	0.758822
		0.25	0.787061	0.794762
		0.30	0.818512	0.818545
		0.35	0.847556	0.837087
		0.40	0.865010	0.843633
	activation	0.01	0.340710	0.337163
		0.05	0.581698	0.591143
		0.10	0.702483	0.699962
		0.15	0.765191	0.752932
		0.20	0.811529	0.785388
		0.25	0.843820	0.806149
		0.30	0.864403	0.817224
		0.35	0.882211	0.818990
		0.40	0.895110	0.814209
	feature	0.01	0.191324	0.221609
		0.05	0.472302	0.511817
		0.10	0.624910	0.655624
		0.15	0.707260	0.727099
		0.20	0.766436	0.776426
		0.25	0.806752	0.805997
		0.30	0.834342	0.824318
		0.35	0.862185	0.838768
		0.40	0.879229	0.843028
	nonsuspicious	0.01	0.185901	0.215997
		0.05	0.463941	0.504450
		0.10	0.614485	0.646574
		0.15	0.701349	0.722953
		0.20	0.762975	0.773727
		0.25	0.804869	0.804780
		0.30	0.833155	0.824230
		0.35	0.859147	0.835885
		0.40	0.875436	0.839302

Underlying Algorithm	Context Filter	error rate	precision	$F_{0.5}$
HARF590	(baseline)	0.01	0.250247	0.272751
		0.05	0.527276	0.544201
		0.10	0.662522	0.659799
		0.15	0.732189	0.709038
		0.20	0.777402	0.732818
		0.25	0.808914	0.744331
		0.30	0.830042	0.745807
		0.35	0.846649	0.742334
		0.40	0.867032	0.742929
	activation	0.01	0.360629	0.352368
		0.05	0.631307	0.613590
		0.10	0.733487	0.692197
		0.15	0.792436	0.730627
		0.20	0.825070	0.739711
		0.25	0.851299	0.745366
		0.30	0.865749	0.736683
		0.35	0.879965	0.729277
		0.40	0.893418	0.720200
	feature	0.01	0.256974	0.279874
		0.05	0.542058	0.557569
		0.10	0.676098	0.671038
		0.15	0.744827	0.718450
		0.20	0.788157	0.739972
		0.25	0.819442	0.750494
		0.30	0.839792	0.750249
		0.35	0.857306	0.745631
		0.40	0.876019	0.744641
	nonsuspicious	0.01	0.263552	0.286632
		0.05	0.542341	0.557493
		0.10	0.676441	0.670760
		0.15	0.744850	0.717847
		0.20	0.788948	0.739795
		0.25	0.818234	0.748751
		0.30	0.839663	0.749268
		0.35	0.856773	0.743603
		0.40	0.875930	0.743391

Table 9: SNIPS, Next-Best Noise

Underlying Algorithm	Context Filter	error rate	precision	$F_{0.5}$
Agreed correction	(baseline)	0.01	0.203559	0.235175
		0.05	0.516995	0.551899
		0.10	0.678281	0.692148
		0.15	0.758825	0.754214
		0.20	0.815761	0.792989
		0.25	0.855683	0.815505
		0.30	0.874819	0.821995
		0.35	0.902361	0.829439
		0.40	0.914755	0.823054
	activation	0.01	0.379626	0.374314
		0.05	0.653646	0.647463
		0.10	0.777705	0.745331
		0.15	0.831916	0.782190
		0.20	0.873480	0.801011
		0.25	0.899718	0.810401
		0.30	0.910957	0.806536
		0.35	0.925808	0.796353
		0.40	0.936250	0.779562
	feature	0.01	0.228381	0.261363
		0.05	0.551033	0.582140
		0.10	0.709730	0.716853
		0.15	0.785696	0.772165
		0.20	0.836971	0.804862
		0.25	0.871780	0.821373
		0.30	0.887976	0.823381
		0.35	0.912542	0.825164
		0.40	0.925177	0.816177
	nonsuspicious	0.01	0.219619	0.252413
		0.05	0.541191	0.573870
		0.10	0.700703	0.710048
		0.15	0.777494	0.767097
		0.20	0.832716	0.802072
		0.25	0.870279	0.820193
		0.30	0.885262	0.822268
		0.35	0.909316	0.823756
		0.40	0.922156	0.814744

173

Consensus	(baseline)	0.01	0.169058	0.197610
		0.05	0.438177	0.479689
		0.10	0.591796	0.626953
		0.15	0.678183	0.704604
		0.20	0.741275	0.758822
		0.25	0.787061	0.794762
		0.30	0.818512	0.818545
		0.35	0.847556	0.837087
		0.40	0.865010	0.843633
	activation	0.01	0.340710	0.337163
		0.05	0.581698	0.591143
		0.10	0.702483	0.699962
		0.15	0.765191	0.752932
		0.20	0.811529	0.785388
		0.25	0.843820	0.806149
		0.30	0.864403	0.817224
		0.35	0.882211	0.818990
		0.40	0.895110	0.814209
	feature	0.01	0.191324	0.221609
		0.05	0.472302	0.511817
		0.10	0.624910	0.655624
		0.15	0.707260	0.727099
		0.20	0.766436	0.776426
		0.25	0.806752	0.805997
		0.30	0.834342	0.824318
		0.35	0.862185	0.838768
		0.40	0.879229	0.843028
	nonsuspicious	0.01	0.185901	0.215997
		0.05	0.463941	0.504450
		0.10	0.614485	0.646574
		0.15	0.701349	0.722953
		0.20	0.762975	0.773727
		0.25	0.804869	0.804780
		0.30	0.833155	0.824230
		0.35	0.859147	0.835885
		0.40	0.875436	0.839302
HARF590	(baseline)	0.01	0.250247	0.272751
		0.05	0.527276	0.544201
		0.10	0.662522	0.659799
		0.15	0.732189	0.709038
		0.20	0.777402	0.732818
		0.25	0.808914	0.744331
		0.30	0.830042	0.745807
		0.35	0.846649	0.742334
		0.40	0.867032	0.742929
	activation	0.01	0.360629	0.352368
		0.05	0.631307	0.613590
		0.10	0.733487	0.692197
		0.15	0.792436	0.730627
		0.20	0.825070	0.739711
		0.25	0.851299	0.745366
		0.30	0.865749	0.736683
		0.35	0.879965	0.729277
		0.40	0.893418	0.720200
	feature	0.01	0.256974	0.279874
		0.05	0.542058	0.557569
		0.10	0.676098	0.671038
		0.15	0.744827	0.718450
		0.20	0.788157	0.739972
		0.25	0.819442	0.750494
		0.30	0.839792	0.750249
		0.35	0.857306	0.745631
		0.40	0.876019	0.744641
	nonsuspicious	0.01	0.263552	0.286632
		0.05	0.542341	0.557493
		0.10	0.676441	0.670760
		0.15	0.744850	0.717847
		0.20	0.788948	0.739795
		0.25	0.818234	0.748751
		0.30	0.839663	0.749268
		0.35	0.856773	0.743603
		0.40	0.875930	0.743391

Table 10: SNIPS, Random Noise

Underlying Algorithm	Context Filter	error rate	precision	$F_{0.5}$
Agreed correction	(baseline)	0.01	0.203559	0.235175
		0.05	0.516995	0.551899
		0.10	0.678281	0.692148
		0.15	0.758825	0.754214
		0.20	0.815761	0.792989
		0.25	0.855683	0.815505
		0.30	0.874819	0.821995
		0.35	0.902361	0.829439
		0.40	0.914755	0.823054
	activation	0.01	0.379626	0.374314
		0.05	0.653646	0.647463
		0.10	0.777705	0.745331
		0.15	0.831916	0.782190
		0.20	0.873480	0.801011
		0.25	0.899718	0.810401
		0.30	0.910957	0.806536
		0.35	0.925808	0.796353
		0.40	0.936250	0.779562
	feature	0.01	0.228381	0.261363
		0.05	0.551033	0.582140
		0.10	0.709730	0.716853
		0.15	0.785696	0.772165
		0.20	0.836971	0.804862
		0.25	0.871780	0.821373
		0.30	0.887976	0.823381
		0.35	0.912542	0.825164
		0.40	0.925177	0.816177
	nonsuspicious	0.01	0.219619	0.252413
		0.05	0.541191	0.573870
		0.10	0.700703	0.710048
		0.15	0.777494	0.767097
		0.20	0.832716	0.802072
		0.25	0.870279	0.820193
		0.30	0.885262	0.822268
		0.35	0.909316	0.823756
		0.40	0.922156	0.814744
Consensus	(baseline)	0.01	0.169058	0.197610
		0.05	0.438177	0.479689
		0.10	0.591796	0.626953
		0.15	0.678183	0.704604
		0.20	0.741275	0.758822
		0.25	0.787061	0.794762
		0.30	0.818512	0.818545
		0.35	0.847556	0.837087
		0.40	0.865010	0.843633
	activation	0.01	0.340710	0.337163
		0.05	0.581698	0.591143
		0.10	0.702483	0.699962
		0.15	0.765191	0.752932
		0.20	0.811529	0.785388
		0.25	0.843820	0.806149
		0.30	0.864403	0.817224
		0.35	0.882211	0.818990
		0.40	0.895110	0.814209
	feature	0.01	0.191324	0.221609
		0.05	0.472302	0.511817
		0.10	0.624910	0.655624
		0.15	0.707260	0.727099
		0.20	0.766436	0.776426
		0.25	0.806752	0.805997
		0.30	0.834342	0.824318
		0.35	0.862185	0.838768
		0.40	0.879229	0.843028
	nonsuspicious	0.01	0.185901	0.215997
		0.05	0.463941	0.504450
		0.10	0.614485	0.646574
		0.15	0.701349	0.722953
		0.20	0.762975	0.773727
		0.25	0.804869	0.804780
		0.30	0.833155	0.824230
		0.35	0.859147	0.835885
		0.40	0.875436	0.839302

Underlying Algorithm	Context Filter	error rate	precision	$F_{0.5}$
HARF590	(baseline)	0.01	0.250247	0.272751
		0.05	0.527276	0.544201
		0.10	0.662522	0.659799
		0.15	0.732189	0.709038
		0.20	0.777402	0.732818
		0.25	0.808914	0.744331
		0.30	0.830042	0.745807
		0.35	0.846649	0.742334
		0.40	0.867032	0.742929
	activation	0.01	0.360629	0.352368
		0.05	0.631307	0.613590
		0.10	0.733487	0.692197
		0.15	0.792436	0.730627
		0.20	0.825070	0.739711
		0.25	0.851299	0.745366
		0.30	0.865749	0.736683
		0.35	0.879965	0.729277
		0.40	0.893418	0.720200
	feature	0.01	0.256974	0.279874
		0.05	0.542058	0.557569
		0.10	0.676098	0.671038
		0.15	0.744827	0.718450
		0.20	0.788157	0.739972
		0.25	0.819442	0.750494
		0.30	0.839792	0.750249
		0.35	0.857306	0.745631
		0.40	0.876019	0.744641
	nonsuspicious	0.01	0.263552	0.286632
		0.05	0.542341	0.557493
		0.10	0.676441	0.670760
		0.15	0.744850	0.717847
		0.20	0.788948	0.739795
		0.25	0.818234	0.748751
		0.30	0.839663	0.749268
		0.35	0.856773	0.743603
		0.40	0.875930	0.743391

Table 11: Stack Exchange, Next-Best Noise

Underlying Algorithm	Context Filter	error rate	precision	$F_{0.5}$
Agreed correction	(baseline)	0.01	0.203559	0.235175
		0.05	0.516995	0.551899
		0.10	0.678281	0.692148
		0.15	0.758825	0.754214
		0.20	0.815761	0.792989
		0.25	0.855683	0.815505
		0.30	0.874819	0.821995
		0.35	0.902361	0.829439
		0.40	0.914755	0.823054
	activation	0.01	0.379626	0.374314
		0.05	0.653646	0.647463
		0.10	0.777705	0.745331
		0.15	0.831916	0.782190
		0.20	0.873480	0.801011
		0.25	0.899718	0.810401
		0.30	0.910957	0.806536
		0.35	0.925808	0.796353
		0.40	0.936250	0.779562
	feature	0.01	0.228381	0.261363
		0.05	0.551033	0.582140
		0.10	0.709730	0.716853
		0.15	0.785696	0.772165
		0.20	0.836971	0.804862
		0.25	0.871780	0.821373
		0.30	0.887976	0.823381
		0.35	0.912542	0.825164
		0.40	0.925177	0.816177
	nonsuspicious	0.01	0.219619	0.252413
		0.05	0.541191	0.573870
		0.10	0.700703	0.710048
		0.15	0.777494	0.767097
		0.20	0.832716	0.802072
		0.25	0.870279	0.820193
		0.30	0.885262	0.822268
		0.35	0.909316	0.823756
		0.40	0.922156	0.814744

Consensus	(baseline)	0.01	0.169058	0.197610
		0.05	0.438177	0.479689
		0.10	0.591796	0.626953
		0.15	0.678183	0.704604
		0.20	0.741275	0.758822
		0.25	0.787061	0.794762
		0.30	0.818512	0.818545
		0.35	0.847556	0.837087
		0.40	0.865010	0.843633
	activation	0.01	0.340710	0.337163
		0.05	0.581698	0.591143
		0.10	0.702483	0.699962
		0.15	0.765191	0.752932
		0.20	0.811529	0.785388
		0.25	0.843820	0.806149
		0.30	0.864403	0.817224
		0.35	0.882211	0.818990
		0.40	0.895110	0.814209
	feature	0.01	0.191324	0.221609
		0.05	0.472302	0.511817
		0.10	0.624910	0.655624
		0.15	0.707260	0.727099
		0.20	0.766436	0.776426
		0.25	0.806752	0.805997
		0.30	0.834342	0.824318
		0.35	0.862185	0.838768
		0.40	0.879229	0.843028
	nonsuspicious	0.01	0.185901	0.215997
		0.05	0.463941	0.504450
		0.10	0.614485	0.646574
		0.15	0.701349	0.722953
		0.20	0.762975	0.773727
		0.25	0.804869	0.804780
		0.30	0.833155	0.824230
		0.35	0.859147	0.835885
		0.40	0.875436	0.839302
HARF590	(baseline)	0.01	0.250247	0.272751
		0.05	0.527276	0.544201
		0.10	0.662522	0.659799
		0.15	0.732189	0.709038
		0.20	0.777402	0.732818
		0.25	0.808914	0.744331
		0.30	0.830042	0.745807
		0.35	0.846649	0.742334
		0.40	0.867032	0.742929
	activation	0.01	0.360629	0.352368
		0.05	0.631307	0.613590
		0.10	0.733487	0.692197
		0.15	0.792436	0.730627
		0.20	0.825070	0.739711
		0.25	0.851299	0.745366
		0.30	0.865749	0.736683
		0.35	0.879965	0.729277
		0.40	0.893418	0.720200
	feature	0.01	0.256974	0.279874
		0.05	0.542058	0.557569
		0.10	0.676098	0.671038
		0.15	0.744827	0.718450
		0.20	0.788157	0.739972
		0.25	0.819442	0.750494
		0.30	0.839792	0.750249
		0.35	0.857306	0.745631
		0.40	0.876019	0.744641
	nonsuspicious	0.01	0.263552	0.286632
		0.05	0.542341	0.557493
		0.10	0.676441	0.670760
		0.15	0.744850	0.717847
		0.20	0.788948	0.739795
		0.25	0.818234	0.748751
		0.30	0.839663	0.749268
		0.35	0.856773	0.743603
		0.40	0.875930	0.743391

Table 12: Stack Exchange, Random Noise

Underlying Algorithm	Context Filter	error rate	precision	$F_{0.5}$
Agreed correction	(baseline)	0.01	0.203559	0.235175
		0.05	0.516995	0.551899
		0.10	0.678281	0.692148
		0.15	0.758825	0.754214
		0.20	0.815761	0.792989
		0.25	0.855683	0.815505
		0.30	0.874819	0.821995
		0.35	0.902361	0.829439
		0.40	0.914755	0.823054
	activation	0.01	0.379626	0.374314
		0.05	0.653646	0.647463
		0.10	0.777705	0.745331
		0.15	0.831916	0.782190
		0.20	0.873480	0.801011
		0.25	0.899718	0.810401
		0.30	0.910957	0.806536
		0.35	0.925808	0.796353
		0.40	0.936250	0.779562
	feature	0.01	0.228381	0.261363
		0.05	0.551033	0.582140
		0.10	0.709730	0.716853
		0.15	0.785696	0.772165
		0.20	0.836971	0.804862
		0.25	0.871780	0.821373
		0.30	0.887976	0.823381
		0.35	0.912542	0.825164
		0.40	0.925177	0.816177
	nonsuspicious	0.01	0.219619	0.252413
		0.05	0.541191	0.573870
		0.10	0.700703	0.710048
		0.15	0.777494	0.767097
		0.20	0.832716	0.802072
		0.25	0.870279	0.820193
		0.30	0.885262	0.822268
		0.35	0.909316	0.823756
		0.40	0.922156	0.814744
Consensus	(baseline)	0.01	0.169058	0.197610
		0.05	0.438177	0.479689
		0.10	0.591796	0.626953
		0.15	0.678183	0.704604
		0.20	0.741275	0.758822
		0.25	0.787061	0.794762
		0.30	0.818512	0.818545
		0.35	0.847556	0.837087
		0.40	0.865010	0.843633
	activation	0.01	0.340710	0.337163
		0.05	0.581698	0.591143
		0.10	0.702483	0.699962
		0.15	0.765191	0.752932
		0.20	0.811529	0.785388
		0.25	0.843820	0.806149
		0.30	0.864403	0.817224
		0.35	0.882211	0.818990
		0.40	0.895110	0.814209
	feature	0.01	0.191324	0.221609
		0.05	0.472302	0.511817
		0.10	0.624910	0.655624
		0.15	0.707260	0.727099
		0.20	0.766436	0.776426
		0.25	0.806752	0.805997
		0.30	0.834342	0.824318
		0.35	0.862185	0.838768
		0.40	0.879229	0.843028
	nonsuspicious	0.01	0.185901	0.215997
		0.05	0.463941	0.504450
		0.10	0.614485	0.646574
		0.15	0.701349	0.722953
		0.20	0.762975	0.773727
		0.25	0.804869	0.804780
		0.30	0.833155	0.824230
		0.35	0.859147	0.835885
		0.40	0.875436	0.839302

Underlying Algorithm	Context Filter	error rate	precision	$F_{0.5}$
HARF590	(baseline)	0.01	0.250247	0.272751
		0.05	0.527276	0.544201
		0.10	0.662522	0.659799
		0.15	0.732189	0.709038
		0.20	0.777402	0.732818
		0.25	0.808914	0.744331
		0.30	0.830042	0.745807
		0.35	0.846649	0.742334
		0.40	0.867032	0.742929
	activation	0.01	0.360629	0.352368
		0.05	0.631307	0.613590
		0.10	0.733487	0.692197
		0.15	0.792436	0.730627
		0.20	0.825070	0.739711
		0.25	0.851299	0.745366
		0.30	0.865749	0.736683
		0.35	0.879965	0.729277
		0.40	0.893418	0.720200
	feature	0.01	0.256974	0.279874
		0.05	0.542058	0.557569
		0.10	0.676098	0.671038
		0.15	0.744827	0.718450
		0.20	0.788157	0.739972
		0.25	0.819442	0.750494
		0.30	0.839792	0.750249
		0.35	0.857306	0.745631
		0.40	0.876019	0.744641
	nonsuspicious	0.01	0.263552	0.286632
		0.05	0.542341	0.557493
		0.10	0.676441	0.670760
		0.15	0.744850	0.717847
		0.20	0.788948	0.739795
		0.25	0.818234	0.748751
		0.30	0.839663	0.749268
		0.35	0.856773	0.743603
		0.40	0.875930	0.743391

Table 13: Stack Overflow, Next-Best Noise

Underlying Algorithm	Context Filter	error rate	precision	$F_{0.5}$
Agreed correction	(baseline)	0.01	0.203559	0.235175
		0.05	0.516995	0.551899
		0.10	0.678281	0.692148
		0.15	0.758825	0.754214
		0.20	0.815761	0.792989
		0.25	0.855683	0.815505
		0.30	0.874819	0.821995
		0.35	0.902361	0.829439
		0.40	0.914755	0.823054
	activation	0.01	0.379626	0.374314
		0.05	0.653646	0.647463
		0.10	0.777705	0.745331
		0.15	0.831916	0.782190
		0.20	0.873480	0.801011
		0.25	0.899718	0.810401
		0.30	0.910957	0.806536
		0.35	0.925808	0.796353
		0.40	0.936250	0.779562
	feature	0.01	0.228381	0.261363
		0.05	0.551033	0.582140
		0.10	0.709730	0.716853
		0.15	0.785696	0.772165
		0.20	0.836971	0.804862
		0.25	0.871780	0.821373
		0.30	0.887976	0.823381
		0.35	0.912542	0.825164
		0.40	0.925177	0.816177
	nonsuspicious	0.01	0.219619	0.252413
		0.05	0.541191	0.573870
		0.10	0.700703	0.710048
		0.15	0.777494	0.767097
		0.20	0.832716	0.802072
		0.25	0.870279	0.820193
		0.30	0.885262	0.822268
		0.35	0.909316	0.823756
		0.40	0.922156	0.814744

Consensus	(baseline)	0.01	0.169058	0.197610
		0.05	0.438177	0.479689
		0.10	0.591796	0.626953
		0.15	0.678183	0.704604
		0.20	0.741275	0.758822
		0.25	0.787061	0.794762
		0.30	0.818512	0.818545
		0.35	0.847556	0.837087
		0.40	0.865010	0.843633
	activation	0.01	0.340710	0.337163
		0.05	0.581698	0.591143
		0.10	0.702483	0.699962
		0.15	0.765191	0.752932
		0.20	0.811529	0.785388
		0.25	0.843820	0.806149
		0.30	0.864403	0.817224
		0.35	0.882211	0.818990
		0.40	0.895110	0.814209
	feature	0.01	0.191324	0.221609
		0.05	0.472302	0.511817
		0.10	0.624910	0.655624
		0.15	0.707260	0.727099
		0.20	0.766436	0.776426
		0.25	0.806752	0.805997
		0.30	0.834342	0.824318
		0.35	0.862185	0.838768
		0.40	0.879229	0.843028
	nonsuspicious	0.01	0.185901	0.215997
		0.05	0.463941	0.504450
		0.10	0.614485	0.646574
		0.15	0.701349	0.722953
		0.20	0.762975	0.773727
		0.25	0.804869	0.804780
		0.30	0.833155	0.824230
		0.35	0.859147	0.835885
		0.40	0.875436	0.839302
HARF590	(baseline)	0.01	0.250247	0.272751
		0.05	0.527276	0.544201
		0.10	0.662522	0.659799
		0.15	0.732189	0.709038
		0.20	0.777402	0.732818
		0.25	0.808914	0.744331
		0.30	0.830042	0.745807
		0.35	0.846649	0.742334
		0.40	0.867032	0.742929
	activation	0.01	0.360629	0.352368
		0.05	0.631307	0.613590
		0.10	0.733487	0.692197
		0.15	0.792436	0.730627
		0.20	0.825070	0.739711
		0.25	0.851299	0.745366
		0.30	0.865749	0.736683
		0.35	0.879965	0.729277
		0.40	0.893418	0.720200
	feature	0.01	0.256974	0.279874
		0.05	0.542058	0.557569
		0.10	0.676098	0.671038
		0.15	0.744827	0.718450
		0.20	0.788157	0.739972
		0.25	0.819442	0.750494
		0.30	0.839792	0.750249
		0.35	0.857306	0.745631
		0.40	0.876019	0.744641
	nonsuspicious	0.01	0.263552	0.286632
		0.05	0.542341	0.557493
		0.10	0.676441	0.670760
		0.15	0.744850	0.717847
		0.20	0.788948	0.739795
		0.25	0.818234	0.748751
		0.30	0.839663	0.749268
		0.35	0.856773	0.743603
		0.40	0.875930	0.743391

Table 14: Stack Overflow, Random Noise

C   Appendix: Enlarged Figures

This appendix contains the same images as the body of the paper, enlarged to improve accessibility.

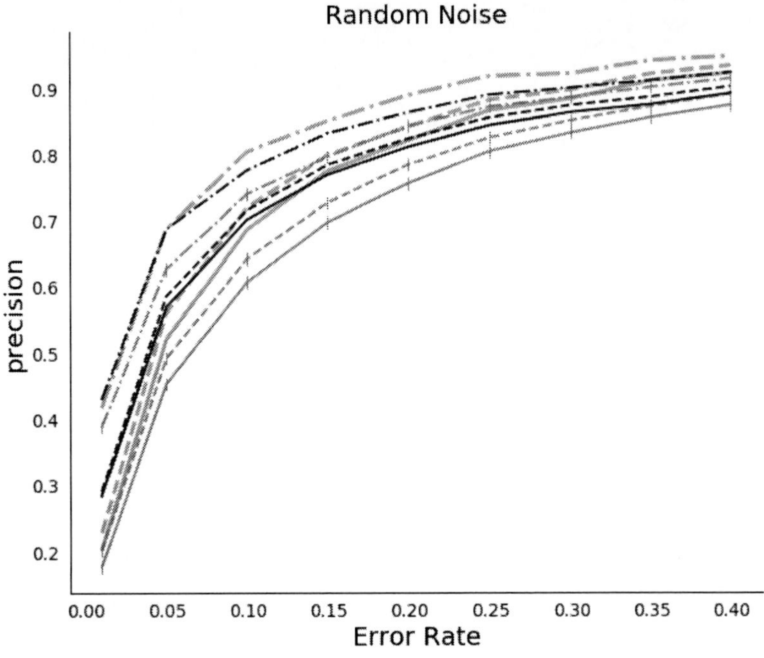

(a) Precision of noise detection for randomly generated noise

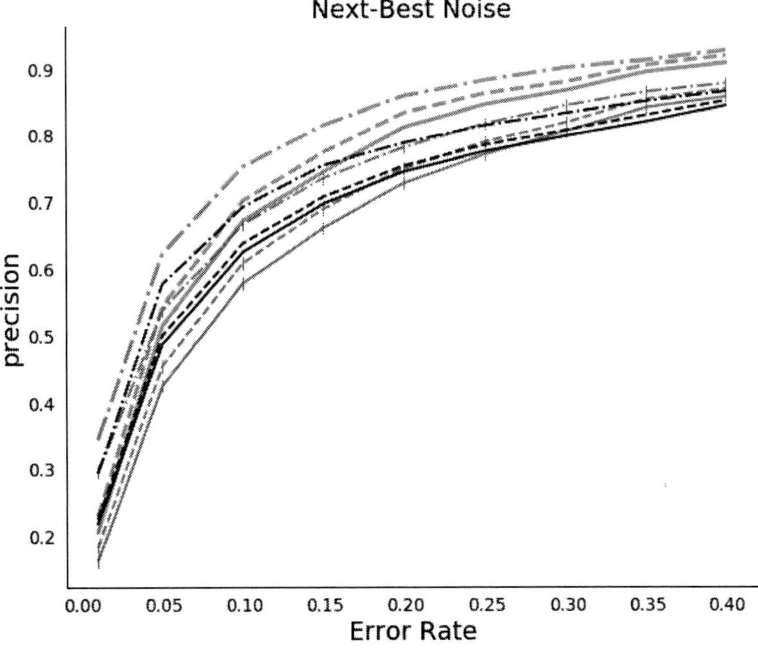

(b) Precision of noise detection for next-best noise.

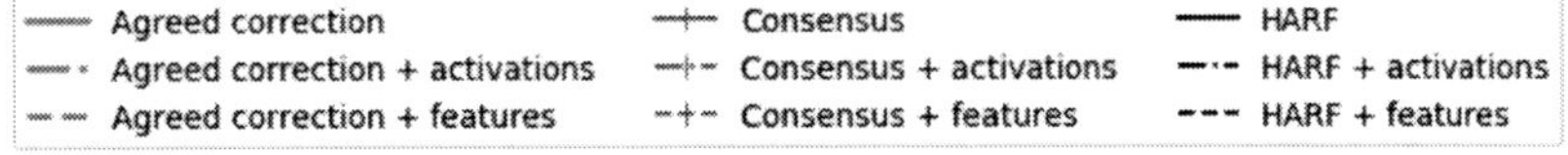

Figure 6: Precision at various noise levels, averaged across the five datasets.

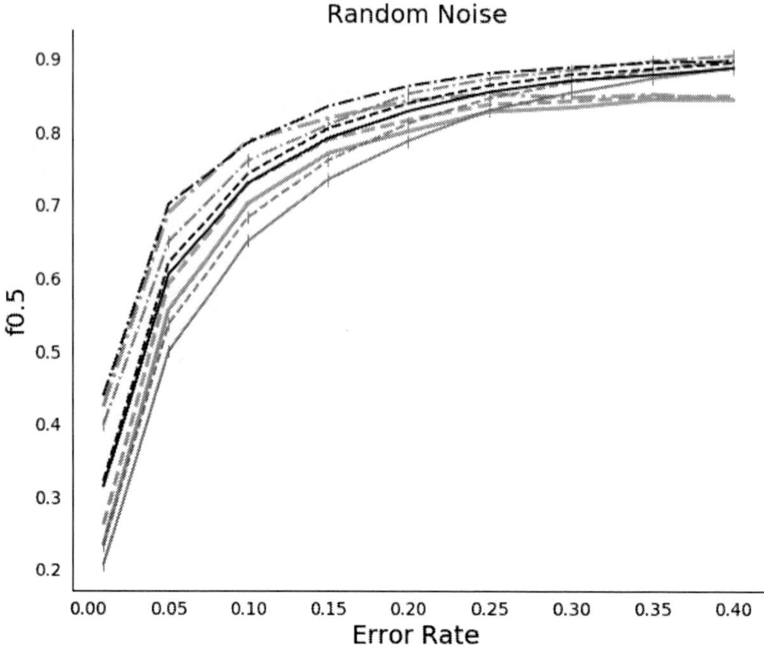

(c) $F_{0.5}$ of noise detection for randomly generated noise

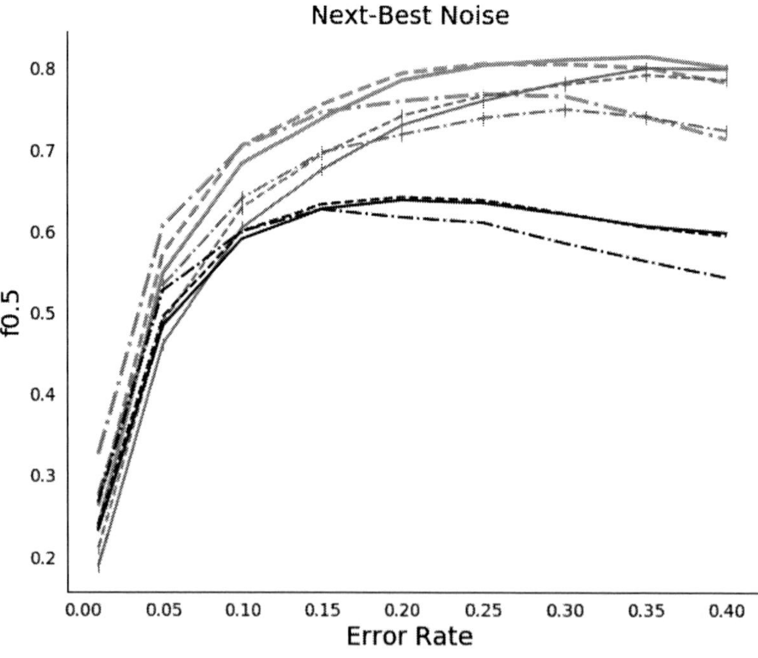

(d) $F_{0.5}$ of noise detection for next-best noise.

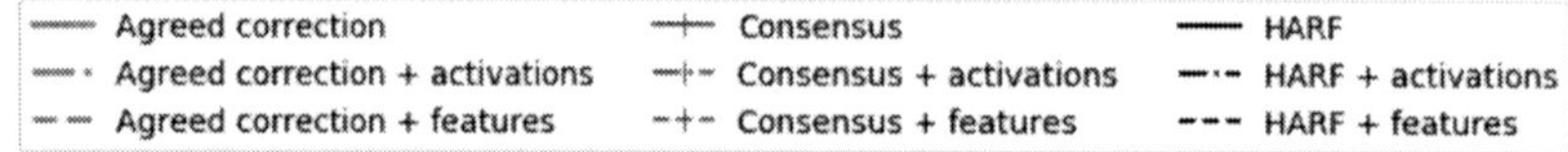

Figure 6: $F_{0.5}$ at various noise levels, averaged across the five datasets.

	buddhism	cooking	diy	fitness	gardening	health	history	interpersonal	mythology	outdoors	parenting	pets	productivity	sports	travel
buddhism		0	0	2	2	4	10	6	10	4	5	4	12	4	1
cooking	0		7	2	5	10	1	1	0	12	4	2	1	2	4
diy	0	7		1	10	3	1	0	0	11	4	1	0	1	1
fitness	2	2	1		0	52	0	0	0	17	4	0	15	29	0
gardening	2	5	10	0		3	0	1	1	14	0	2	1	1	0
health	4	10	3	52	3		2	2	0	12	7	7	20	7	1
history	10	1	1	0	0	2		0	25	1	2	0	1	4	5
interpersonal	6	1	0	0	1	2	0		0	1	14	4	20	5	1
mythology	10	0	0	0	1	0	25	0		0	0	0	0	1	1
outdoors	4	12	11	17	14	12	1	1	0		2	10	3	18	18
parenting	5	4	4	4	0	7	2	14	0	2		4	13	1	3
pets	4	2	1	0	2	7	0	4	0	10	4		0	0	1
productivity	12	1	0	15	1	20	1	20	0	3	13	0		0	1
sports	4	2	1	29	1	7	4	5	1	18	1	0	0		1
travel	1	4	1	0	0	1	5	1	1	18	3	1	1	1	

Figure 7: A summary of noise discovered in approximately 30k examples from Stack Exchange.

history / mythology

Suspicious examples between history and mythology.

Mayan calendar coinciding with winter solstice

The concept that scripture is made to adapt to changes of society, technology, and language

What gift did Saladin send to Richard when he was ill?

Are there any texts/translations of the 4 main Egyptian creation myths?

How were the Welsh Triads used by the Welsh?

Is there a Greek myth of Poseidon "dating" his daughter in the form of a dolphin?

What is this symbol in red box?

What is known about the Antiu?

Is Krampus real?

Figure 8: Suspicious examples at the intersection of *history* and *mythology* classes without context.

history	mythology
• Is there a Greek myth of Poseidon "dating" his daughter in the form of a dolphin? (1.000)	• Who is the oldest being in Greek mythology? (0.956)
	• Are there any female heroines in Shinto mythology? (0.953)
	• Who worshipped the Titans? (0.953)
	• Are there any saints or heroes in mythology who ally with death? (0.953)
	• Did any ancient cultures or scholars recognize the Hero's Journey monomyth? (0.951)
• How did Greeks make greek fire? (0.463)	• Does Poseidon rule over all the sea gods? (0.602)
	• Is Greek mythology derivative of/influence by Ugartic/Canaanite mythology? (0.591)
	• Where does Poseidon get called the God of Kin? (0.570)
	• Why is Roman Mythology so similar to Greek Mythology or vice versa? (0.565)
	• Is there a world tree in Greek mythology? (0.563)

Figure 9: An example from Figure 3, with context. In red is the suspicious example. Examples in the white box are its context from activation space, and those in the blue box are context from raw embedding space. Numbers in parentheses indicate cosine similarity.

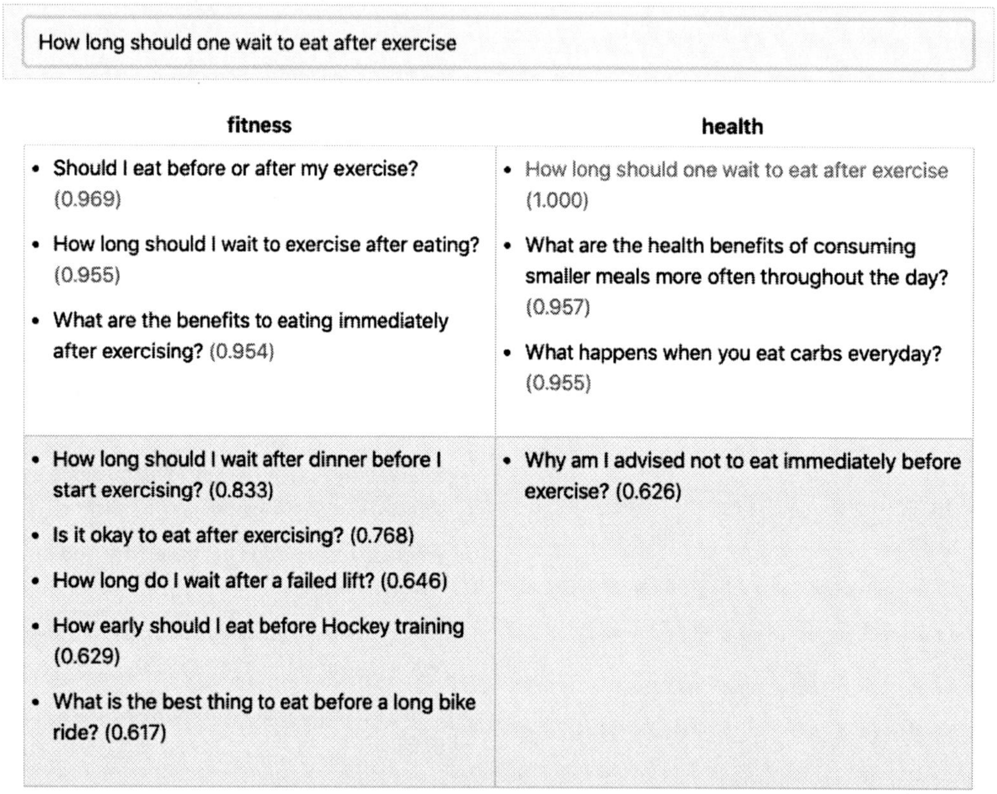

How long should one wait to eat after exercise
fitness
health
Should I eat before or after my exercise? (0.969)
How long should I wait to exercise after eating? (0.955)
What are the benefits to eating immediately after exercising? (0.954)
How long should one wait to eat after exercise (1.000)
What are the health benefits of consuming smaller meals more often throughout the day? (0.957)
What happens when you eat carbs everyday? (0.955)
How long should I wait after dinner before I start exercising? (0.833)
Is it okay to eat after exercising? (0.768)
How long do I wait after a failed lift? (0.646)
How early should I eat before Hockey training (0.629)
What is the best thing to eat before a long bike ride? (0.617)
Why am I advised not to eat immediately before exercise? (0.626)

Figure 10: Context shows overlapping class definitions.

EXBERT: A Visual Analysis Tool to Explore Learned Representations in Transformer Models

Ben Hoover
IBM Research
MIT-IBM Watson AI Lab

Hendrik Strobelt
IBM Research
MIT-IBM Watson AI Lab

Sebastian Gehrmann
Harvard SEAS

`{benjamin.hoover,hendrik.strobelt}@ibm.com`
`gehrmann@seas.harvard.edu`

Abstract

Large Transformer-based language models can route and reshape complex information via their multi-headed attention mechanism. Although the attention never receives explicit supervision, it can exhibit recognizable patterns following linguistic or positional information. Analyzing the learned representations and attentions is paramount to furthering our understanding of the inner workings of these models. However, analyses have to catch up with the rapid release of new models and the growing diversity of investigation techniques. To support analysis for a wide variety of models, we introduce EXBERT, a tool to help humans conduct flexible, interactive investigations and formulate hypotheses for the model-internal reasoning process. EXBERT provides insights into the meaning of the contextual representations and attention by matching a human-specified input to similar contexts in large annotated datasets. By aggregating the annotations of the matched contexts, EXBERT can quickly replicate findings from literature and extend them to previously not analyzed models.

1 Introduction

Learned contextualized representations of a neural network can contain meaningful information. Uncovering this information plays a vital role in understanding and interpreting the learned structure of neural networks (Belinkov and Glass, 2019). One way to identify information is to probe the representations by using them as features in classifiers for linguistic tasks, or by identifying contexts that lead to similar patterns (Tenney et al., 2019b; Conneau et al., 2018; Strobelt et al., 2017).

With Transformers (Vaswani et al., 2017) overtaking recurrent models as the primary architectures for many NLP tasks, analyzing attention has become another common strategy for interpretability (Raganato and Tiedemann, 2018a; Clark et al., 2019). These efforts focus on selecting a model, such as BERT (Devlin et al., 2019), and exploring the Transformer's contextual embeddings and attentions across layers to determine whether and where it learns to represent linguistic features. Previous studies have uncovered specific attention heads that learn particular dependencies (Vig and Belinkov, 2019; Clark et al., 2019).

However, once the standard linguistic probing tasks are exhausted, it is challenging to develop new hypotheses to test. Toward that end, interactive visualizations provide a successful strategy to develop new insights and strategies. Visualization tools can offer concise summaries of useful information and allow interaction with large models. Attention visualizations have thus taken significant steps toward these goals of making explorations fast and interactive for the user (Vig, 2019). However, interpreting attention patterns without understanding the attended-to embeddings, or relying on attention alone as a faithful explanation, can lead to faulty interpretations (Brunner et al., 2019; Jain and Wallace, 2019; Wiegreffe and Pinter, 2019; Li et al., 2019).

To address this challenge, we developed **EXBERT**, a tool that combines the advantages of static analyses with a dynamic and intuitive view into both the attentions and internal representations of the underlying model. EXBERT provides these insights for any user-specified model and corpus by probing whether the representations capture meaningful information. We demonstrate that EXBERT can replicate insights from the analysis by Clark et al. (2019) and easily extend it to other models. It is open-source, extensible, and compatible with many current Transformer architectures, both autoregressive and masked language models. **EXBERT** is available at `exbert.net`.

Proceedings of the 58th Annual Meeting of the Association for Computational Linguistics, pages 187–196
July 5 - July 10, 2020. ©2020 Association for Computational Linguistics

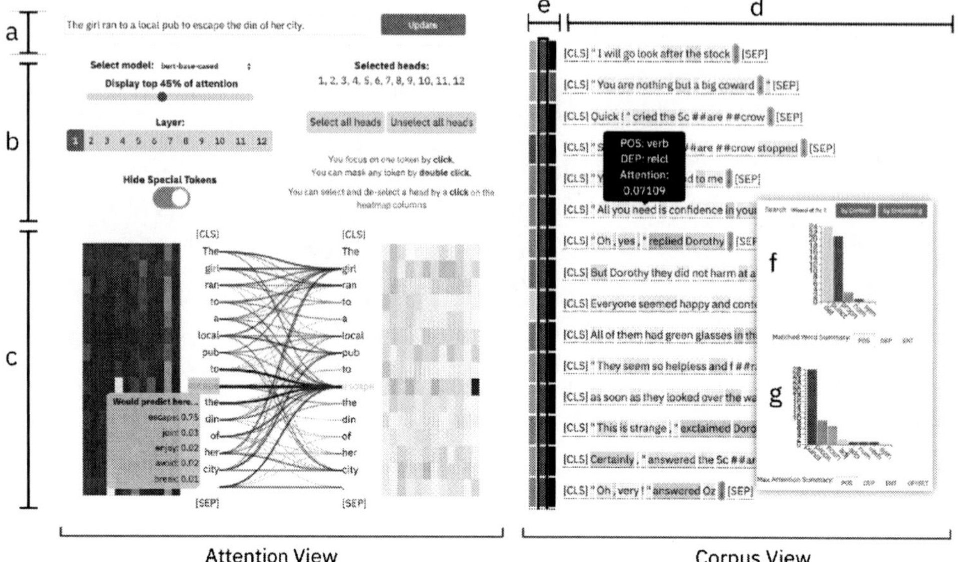

Attention View   Corpus View

Figure 1: An overview of the different components of the tool. Users can enter a sentence in (a) and modify the attention view through selections in (b). Self attention is displayed in (c), with attentions directed as coming *from* the left column and pointing *to* the right. The blue matrix on the left shows a head's attention (column) out of a token (row), whereas the right-hand matrix shows attention into each token by each head. The top-k predictions for each token are shown on hover in the gray box. The most similar tokens to the MASKed "escape" token in (c) are shown and summarized in (d-g), taken from an annotated corpus (shown: Wizard of Oz). Every token in (d) displays its linguistic metadata on hover. The metadata of the results in (d) are summarized in the histograms (f) and (g) for the matched token (green highlight) and the token of max attention. The colored bars on the histogram correspond to colors in the columns of (e), where the center column summarizes the metadata of the matched token, and the adjacent columns represent the metadata of the words to the left and right of the matched token.

2 Background

2.1 Transformer Models

The Transformer architecture, as defined by Vaswani et al. (2017), relies on multiple sequential applications of *self attention* layers. Self-attention is the process by which each token within an input sequence Y of length N computes attention weights over all tokens in the input. As part of this process, the inputs are projected into a key, query, and value representation with W_k, W_q, and W_v. The Transformer applies I of these *attention heads* in parallel, using separate weights. We denote each head with the superscript (i).

$$\mathbf{A}^{(i)} = \text{softmax}\left((YW_q^{(i)})(YW_k^{(i)})^\top\right).$$

This computation yields a matrix in $\mathbb{R}^{N \times N}$ where the entry $\mathbf{A}_{ij}$ represents the attention out of token y_i into token y_j.[1] The representation for each attention head $h^{(i)}$ is then multiplied by the value,

$$h^{(i)} = \mathbf{A}^{(i)}(YW_v^{(i)}).$$

The representations $h^{(1)}, \ldots, h^{(I)}$ are concatenated and followed by a linear projection layer. The output of this projection we call the *token embedding* $E^{(l)}$, which is used as input to layer $l + 1$.

2.2 Transformer Analysis

The analysis of learned contextual representation in neural networks has been a widely investigated topic in NLP (Belinkov and Glass, 2019). Before the advent of large pretrained models, analyses focused on models trained for specific tasks like machine translation. Some showed that Transformer models, similar to recurrent models, can

---

[1]For autoregressive models like GPT-2 (Radford et al., 2019), this matrix is triangular since attention cannot point toward unseen tokens.

effectively encode syntactic properties in their representations (Raganato and Tiedemann, 2018b; Mareček and Rosa, 2018). Researchers have developed suites of probing techniques, agnostic to the underlying model, that can capture these properties across many different linguistic tasks (Tenney et al., 2019b; Conneau et al., 2018). Over the past year, similar tests have primarily been applied to BERT (Devlin et al., 2019) and its derivatives (e.g., Sanh et al., 2019; Liu et al., 2019). Similar to task-specific models, Goldberg (2019) found that BERT clearly encodes syntax within some of its attentions. Moreover, Tenney et al. (2019a) demonstrated that linguistic information is very localized within the representations in different layers.

In parallel, individual attention heads of Transformer models have also received much focus. Clark et al. (2019) showed that individual heads recognize standard Part of Speech (POS) and Dependency (DEP) relationships (e.g., Objects of the Preposition (POBJ) and Determinants (DET)) with high fidelity. Vig and Belinkov (2019) also explored the dependency relations across heads and discovered that initial layers typically encode positional relations, middle layers capture the most dependency relations, and later layers look for unique patterns and structures. These insights are exposed interactively through EXBERT.

3 Overview

EXBERT focuses on displaying a succinct view of both the attention and the internal representations of each token. Figure 1 shows an overview of the tool's two main components. The **Attention View** provides an interactive view of the self-attention of the model, where users can change layers, select heads, and view the aggregated attention. The **Corpus View** presents a user with aggregate statistics that aim to describe and summarize the hidden representations of a currently selected token or set of attention heads. For simplicity, the tool defaults to focus on single-sentence examples.

3.1 Attention View

The attention $\mathbf{A}$ can be understood as an adjacency matrix, which is conducive to a representation of curves pointing from each token to every other token. However, since $\mathbf{A}$ is not symmetric, a visualization has to separate the *outgoing* and *incoming* attention of a token. We achieve this by duplicating the tokens of input Y and presenting it in two vertical sections, connected through the attention.

Hovering over a token will reduce the displayed attention graph to the incoming/outgoing attention of that token. We display the top predictions of the model at that position. Clicking on a token freezes the filtered attention view.

Many models introduce special tokens (e.g., "[CLS]", "<|endoftext|>") for downstream classification or generation tasks. These tokens often receive very high attention and act as a null operation (Clark et al., 2019). We provide a switch to hide the special tokens of the model and renormalize based on the other attentions to provide easier visualization of subtle attention patterns.

3.2 Corpus View

Representations, on the other hand, cannot be easily visualized footnoteSee Strobelt et al. (2017) for a discussion why heat-maps are not an appropriate visualization of hidden states. but they can be understood by searching for similar representations in an annotated corpus. The results of this search are presented in the **Corpus View** with the highest-similarity matches shown first. The histograms display the accumulated features of the matched representations and the token that receives the most attention.

Searching Inspired by Strobelt et al. (2017, 2018), EXBERT performs a nearest neighbor search of embeddings on a reference corpus as follows. A corpus is first split by sentence and its tokens labeled for desired metadata (e.g., POS, DEP, NER). The model then processes this corpus, and its embeddings $E^{(l)}$ are stored at every layer l and indexed for a Cosine Similarity (CS) search using faiss (Johnson et al., 2019). The top 50 most similar tokens matching a query embedding are displayed and summarized for the user in the context of their use in the annotated corpus.

To supplement the layer embeddings $E^{(l)}$ and enable exploration of the attention heads, we derive a *Context Embedding* $C^{(l)}$, which we define as the concatenation of heads before the linear projection at the layer's output. Formally, this is defined as:

$$C^{(l)} = \text{Concat}(\widetilde{\mathrm{h}}^{(l,1)}, \ldots, \widetilde{\mathrm{h}}^{(l,n)}),$$

where $\widetilde{\mathrm{h}}^{(l,i)}$ is defined as the $L2$ normalized representation of head i at layer l to enable CS searching by head. To search the corpus for any subset of heads $H_s \subseteq \{1, \ldots, n\}$, we set all values of $\widetilde{h}^{(l,i)}$ to 0 in C^l, where $i \notin H_s$.

Bidirectional vs. Autoregressive Behavior EXBERT is flexible to accommodate both bidirectional and autoregressive Transformer architectures, but the tool behaves slightly differently for each. Bidirectional models have histogram summaries for the nearest neighbor matches across the corpus and allow interactive MASKing of tokens. When hovering over any token, the interface will show what the language model would predict at that token.

Autoregressive models will also search for the nearest neighbors to a selected token's embedding, but the interface will instead summarize the metadata of the following token (indicated in red font). Hovering over any token in the **Attention View** will display what the model would predict *next*.

3.3 Extending EXBERT

EXBERT runs Huggingface's unified API for Transformer models (Wolf et al., 2019) which allows any Transformer model from that API to take full advantage of the **Attention View**.

Similarity searching requires the user to first annotate a corpus with the desired model. Scripts to aid annotation of a corpus from a custom model is provided in the code repository.[2]

To display metadata from a corpus in a custom domain, users will need to align the transformer model's tokenization scheme to extracted metadata (e.g., DNA Sequences and their properties). EXBERT accomplishes this by first tokenizing, normalizing, and labeling the sentence with spaCy (Honnibal and Montani, 2017). If these tokens are split further by the Transformer's tokenization scheme, each word-piece receives the metadata of its parent token. Note that special tokens like "[CLS]" and "<|endoftext|>" have no linguistic features assigned to them.

4 Case Study: BERT

Clark et al. (2019) performed an extensive analysis to determine which heads in a base sized BERT Transformer model learned which dependencies. We show here how some of their insights are easily accessible through the EXBERT interface (Devlin et al., 2019) for the case-sensitive BERT-base model, which has 12 layers and 12 heads per layer.

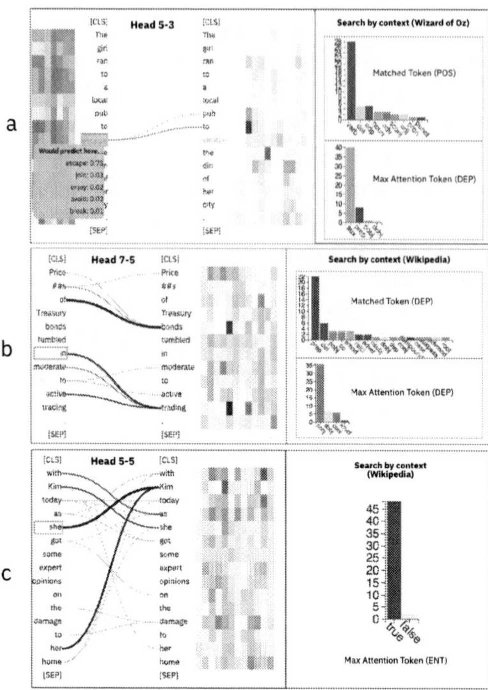

Figure 2: Exploration of different attention heads for pretrained model BERT$_{\text{base}}$ and different corpora. (a) shows head 5-3 expecting looks at the presents of an auxiliary verb (AUX) to predict that the MASK should be a verb. Head 7-5 in (b) shows a head that has learned to attend to Objects of the Preposition (POBJ). Finally, (c) shows Head 5-5 learning correct co-reference.

We use the notation <layer>-<head> to refer to a single head at a single layer, and <layer>-[<heads>] to describe the cumulative attention of heads at a layer (e.g., 4-[1,3,9] to describe the aggregated attention of heads 1, 3, and 9 at layer 4).

4.1 Behind the Heads

Figure 2 shows examples where distinct heads learn evident linguistic features. Figure 2a shows that the MASKed verb "escape" points to the auxiliary verb (AUX) "to". If we search over the annotated Wizard of Oz[3], we see that the tokens matching the MASK's most similar contexts at Head 5-3 are verbs and that the attention out of these matched words goes primarily to an AUX dependency.

Figure 2b shows that Head 7-5 finds relationships between prepositions (PREP) and their objects (POBJ) in the input sentence. By searching for the token "in" across a subset of the "Wikipedia" corpus (Merity et al., 2016), we confirm that many

---

[2]https://github.com/bhoov/exbert.

[3]http://www.gutenberg.org/ebooks/55

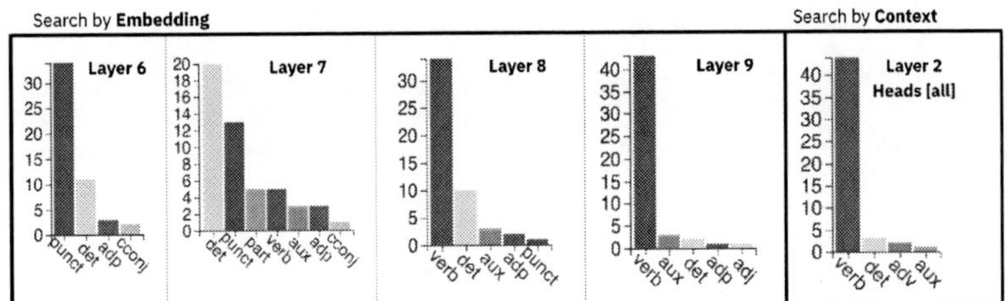

Figure 3: A progression of the information encoded by a nearest neighbor embedding (left) and context (right) searches for the MASKed token "escape" in Figure 2a and the sentence, "The girl ran to a local pub to escape the din of her city." Note that heads encode verb information (dark green) significantly earlier than the embeddings.

other annotated sentences exhibit this pattern.

Figure 2c seemingly finds a head that determines co-reference to entity relationships, as both "she" and "her" are pointing strongly at "Kim" and little to everything else. Because the parse tree is absent in the annotated corpus, we are unable to search for co-reference patterns. However, the corpus search does reveal that this head learns to match pronouns to Entities rather than common gendered words such as "woman" or "mother".

4.2 Behind the Mask

Earlier layers of a BERT model can capture particular linguistic information (Clark et al., 2019; Vig and Belinkov, 2019). We now explore this behavior for a MASKed token across layers. We look at the following sentence, also shown in Figure 2a:

The girl ran to a local pub to escape the din of her city.

We begin by masking the "escape" token in the example sentence at layer 1 and search what information is behind the "[MASK]" token's embedding (Figure 1). Note that at this early layer, there is no meaningful linguistic information encoded in a MASK token's embedding, and the matching embeddings are most similar to punctuation (PUNCT) and determinants (DET), which are the most common tokens in English (Figure 1f). Additionally, the maximum attention out of the MASKed token points to itself (Figure 1c).

As layers progress, more VERB information is encoded in the token's embedding, as shown in Figure 3. At layer 6, the model does not relate the MASKed word to verbs, but by layer 9 it is convinced that the MASK should be a verb. Note that accumulated head information confidently captured a "verb" pattern in a significantly earlier layer.

5 Case Study: GPT-2

5.1 Gender Bias

We now use EXBERT to explore the problem of gender bias and co-reference in autoregressive Transformers (Zhao et al., 2018), a problem inherent in the training data that infects the model's understanding of language (Font and Costa-jussà, 2019). Take the following sentence:

The man visited the nurse and told him to attend to his patients.

We aim to detect whether the model thinks "nurse" is male or female before it sees the masculine pronoun "him" referring to "nurse". Because GPT-2 is trained to predict the next word, we can do this by selecting the token "told" and hovering over it to see the prediction of that pronoun. These results are shown in Figure 4a, and from the probabilities, we can see that GPT-2 predicts "her" with 90% probability. The next closest token "him" is only 6%. Figure 4b shows that replacing "nurse" with "doctor" alters the prediction to be strongly in favor of predicting "him" at 68% probability, while "her" falls to 18%. The attention patterns in the final three layers remain ostensibly the same for both sentences.

5.2 Heads up

In contrast to BERT, GPT-2 is an autoregressive language model. This makes it more difficult to detect some dependencies by looking at attention patterns (e.g., PREP looking for its POBJ in the future). However, EXBERT can offer similar insights as above using slightly altered methods. The following experiments use the smaller configuration of GPT-2 with 12 layers and 12 heads (Radford et al., 2019).

Exploring the heads in GPT-2 reveals that GPT-

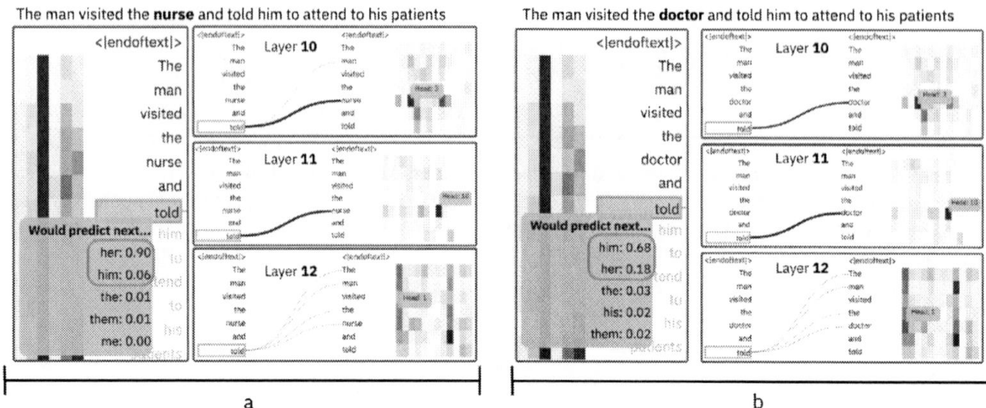

Figure 4: Highlights the bias of the GPT-2 model for generation. (a) "nurse" prompts the model to predict "her". (b) shows "doctor" causing the model to predict "him"

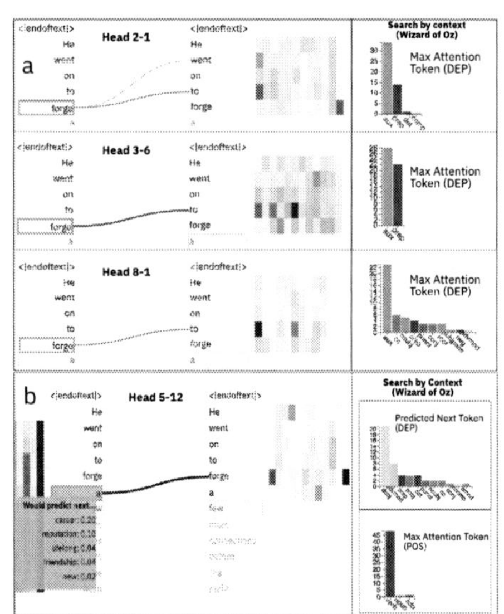

Figure 5: Discovering simple head patterns in GPT-2 using the sentence. (a) shows strong detection of the AUX dependency. (b) shows a head detecting the DOBJ dependency

2's heads also learn distinct syntactic structure. Figure 5a shows a few heads at different layers that seemingly learn the AUX dependency. Heads at earlier layers show an affinity for the AUX pattern, but also confuse "to" with a preposition even though a verb directly follows. This behavior hints that these heads look primarily to match the word "to" rather than its contextual meaning.

Similarly, Figure 5b shows a head that attends predominantly to a preceding verb and matches contexts in which the following word is a DOBJ. Interestingly, the more complex DOBJ dependency is picked up by a head as early as layer 5-12, whereas a simpler dependency like the AUX pattern is only clearly detected later in Layer 8.

6 Discussion

In this paper, we introduced an interactive visualization tool, EXBERT, that can reveal an intelligible structure in the learned representations of Transformer models. We demonstrated, through an attention visualization and nearest neighbor searching techniques, that EXBERT can replicate research that explores what attentions and representations learn and detect biases in text inputs.

We acknowledge that EXBERT is limited compared to more global analyses since it only presents statistics across a small number of neighbors for a single token at a time. These neighbors do not necessarily reveal a head's or an embedding's global behavior. However, EXBERT can effectively narrow the scope and refine hypotheses through quick testing iterations. These hypotheses about the model behavior can, in a later step, be evaluated by robust statistical tests on a global level.

To assist researchers with their model investigations, we host a demo of the tool with multiple models at `exbert.net`.

References

Yonatan Belinkov and James Glass. 2019. Analysis methods in neural language processing: A survey. *Transactions of the Association for Computational Linguistics*, 7:49–72.

Gino Brunner, Yang Liu, DamiÃąn Pascual, Oliver Richter, and Roger Wattenhofer. 2019. On the validity of self-attention as explanation in transformer models.

Kevin Clark, Urvashi Khandelwal, Omer Levy, and Christopher D. Manning. 2019. What does BERT look at? an analysis of bert's attention. *CoRR*, abs/1906.04341.

Alexis Conneau, Germán Kruszewski, Guillaume Lample, Loïc Barrault, and Marco Baroni. 2018. What you can cram into a single vector: Probing sentence embeddings for linguistic properties. In *Proceedings of the 56th Annual Meeting of the Association for Computational Linguistics (Volume 1: Long Papers)*, pages 2126–2136.

Jacob Devlin, Ming-Wei Chang, Kenton Lee, and Kristina Toutanova. 2019. Bert: Pre-training of deep bidirectional transformers for language understanding. In *Proceedings of the 2019 Conference of the North American Chapter of the Association for Computational Linguistics: Human Language Technologies, Volume 1 (Long and Short Papers)*, pages 4171–4186.

Joel Escudé Font and Marta R. Costa-jussà. 2019. Equalizing gender biases in neural machine translation with word embeddings techniques. *CoRR*, abs/1901.03116.

Yoav Goldberg. 2019. Assessing bert's syntactic abilities. *arXiv preprint arXiv:1901.05287*.

Matthew Honnibal and Ines Montani. 2017. spaCy 2: Natural language understanding with Bloom embeddings, convolutional neural networks and incremental parsing. To appear.

Sarthak Jain and Byron C Wallace. 2019. Attention is not explanation. In *Proceedings of the 2019 Conference of the North American Chapter of the Association for Computational Linguistics: Human Language Technologies, Volume 1 (Long and Short Papers)*, pages 3543–3556.

Jeff Johnson, Matthijs Douze, and Hervé Jégou. 2019. Billion-scale similarity search with gpus. *IEEE Transactions on Big Data*.

Xintong Li, Guanlin Li, Lemao Liu, Max Meng, and Shuming Shi. 2019. On the word alignment from neural machine translation. In *Proceedings of the 57th Annual Meeting of the Association for Computational Linguistics*, pages 1293–1303, Florence, Italy. Association for Computational Linguistics.

Yinhan Liu, Myle Ott, Naman Goyal, Jingfei Du, Mandar Joshi, Danqi Chen, Omer Levy, Mike Lewis, Luke Zettlemoyer, and Veselin Stoyanov. 2019. Roberta: A robustly optimized bert pretraining approach. *arXiv preprint arXiv:1907.11692*.

David Mareček and Rudolf Rosa. 2018. Extracting syntactic trees from transformer encoder self-attentions. In *Proceedings of the 2018 EMNLP Workshop BlackboxNLP: Analyzing and Interpreting Neural Networks for NLP*, pages 347–349.

Stephen Merity, Caiming Xiong, James Bradbury, and Richard Socher. 2016. Pointer sentinel mixture models. *CoRR*, abs/1609.07843.

Alec Radford, Jeffrey Wu, Rewon Child, David Luan, Dario Amodei, and Ilya Sutskever. 2019. Language models are unsupervised multitask learners. *OpenAI Blog*, 1(8).

Alessandro Raganato and Jorg Tiedemann. 2018a. An analysis of encoder representations in transformer-based machine translation. In EMNLP Workshop: BlackboxNLP.

Alessandro Raganato and Jörg Tiedemann. 2018b. An analysis of encoder representations in transformer-based machine translation. In *Proceedings of the 2018 EMNLP Workshop BlackboxNLP: Analyzing and Interpreting Neural Networks for NLP*, pages 287–297.

Victor Sanh, Lysandre Debut, Julien Chaumond, and Thomas Wolf. 2019. Distilbert, a distilled version of bert: smaller, faster, cheaper and lighter. *arXiv preprint arXiv:1910.01108*.

Hendrik Strobelt, Sebastian Gehrmann, Michael Behrisch, Adam Perer, Hanspeter Pfister, and Alexander M. Rush. 2018. Seq2seq-vis: A visual debugging tool for sequence-to-sequence models. *CoRR*, abs/1804.09299.

Hendrik Strobelt, Sebastian Gehrmann, Hanspeter Pfister, and Alexander M Rush. 2017. LSTMVis: A tool for visual analysis of hidden state dynamics in recurrent neural networks. *IEEE transactions on visualization and computer graphics*, 24(1):667–676.

Ian Tenney, Dipanjan Das, and Ellie Pavlick. 2019a. Bert rediscovers the classical nlp pipeline. In *Proceedings of the 57th Annual Meeting of the Association for Computational Linguistics*, pages 4593–4601.

Ian Tenney, Patrick Xia, Berlin Chen, Alex Wang, Adam Poliak, R Thomas McCoy, Najoung Kim, Benjamin Van Durme, Sam Bowman, Dipanjan Das, and Ellie Pavlick. 2019b. What do you learn from context? probing for sentence structure in contextualized word representations. In *International Conference on Learning Representations*.

Ashish Vaswani, Noam Shazeer, Niki Parmar, Jakob Uszkoreit, Llion Jones, Aidan N Gomez, Łukasz Kaiser, and Illia Polosukhin. 2017. Attention is all you need. In *Advances in neural information processing systems*, pages 5998–6008.

Jesse Vig. 2019. A multiscale visualization of attention in the transformer model. *CoRR*, abs/1906.05714.

Jesse Vig and Yonatan Belinkov. 2019. Analyzing the structure of attention in a transformer language model. *CoRR*, abs/1906.04284.

Sarah Wiegreffe and Yuval Pinter. 2019. Attention is not not explanation.

Thomas Wolf, Lysandre Debut, Victor Sanh, Julien Chaumond, Clement Delangue, Anthony Moi, Pierric Cistac, Tim Rault, RÃl'mi Louf, Morgan Funtowicz, and Jamie Brew. 2019. Transformers: State-of-the-art natural language processing.

Jieyu Zhao, Tianlu Wang, Mark Yatskar, Vicente Ordonez, and Kai-Wei Chang. 2018. Gender bias in coreference resolution: Evaluation and debiasing methods. In *Proceedings of the 2018 Conference of the North American Chapter of the Association for Computational Linguistics: Human Language Technologies, Volume 2 (Short Papers)*, pages 15–20, New Orleans, Louisiana. Association for Computational Linguistics.

A Recreating the experiments

We allow direct linking to an experimental setup in the interface. A list of the links to reproduce our results is given below (all links in the supplementary material are correct at the time of publishing, but may be changed in the distant future):

- Overview (Figure 1):
  `https://bit.ly/2OfD6Vt`

- Behind the Heads (Figure 2)
    - (a): `https://bit.ly/2GJUihs`
    - (b): `https://bit.ly/38Ycss8`
    - (c): `https://bit.ly/2S8qGzO`

- Behind the Mask (Figure 3):
  `https://bit.ly/2RJ952n`

- GPT-2 Bias (Figure 4):
  `https://bit.ly/36ELwMo`

- Heads Up (Figure 5):
    - (a): `https://bit.ly/2vAcgRe`
    - (b): `https://bit.ly/2S9qHDs`

B Additional Material

In addition to the content presented in the main paper, we have recorded a short **video demo** showing how to use the tool to probe for particular patterns at `https://youtu.be/e31oyfo_thY`.

A **Lite version** of the tool, without the corpus searching, demoing many common Transformer models is hosted by Huggingface at `huggingface.co/exbert`.

Figure 6: The most similar embeddings, in context, to the MASKed token "escape" in the sentence: "The girl ran to a local pub to escape the din of her city" at the output of layer 12 of $BERT_{base}$ (shown in Figure 2a). Corpus results are annotated excerpts from the Wizard of Oz. Notice how at the output layer all attentions are primarily to the word itself or the final punctuation mark of the sentence, indicating that the most important information is likely already encoded in the selected token's embedding.

Nakdan: Professional Hebrew Diacritizer

Avi Shmidman[1]   **Shaltiel Shmidman**[1]   **Moshe Koppel**[1]   **Yoav Goldberg**[1,2]

[1]Bar Ilan University / Ramat Gan, Israel
DICTA / Jerusalem, Israel
[2]Allen Institute for Artificial Intelligence
`avi.shmidman@biu.ac.il`, `{shmidms1,koppel,yogo}@cs.biu.ac.il`

Abstract

We present a system for automatic diacritization of Hebrew text. The system combines modern neural models with carefully curated declarative linguistic knowledge and comprehensive manually constructed tables and dictionaries. Besides providing state of the art diacritization accuracy, the system also supports an interface for manual editing and correction of the automatic output, and has several features which make it particularly useful for preparation of scientific editions of Hebrew texts. The system supports Modern Hebrew, Rabbinic Hebrew and Poetic Hebrew. The system is freely accessible for all use at `http://nakdanpro.dicta.org.il`.

1 Introduction

We present a web-based system for diacritization of Hebrew text, which caters to both casual and expert users. The diacritization engine driving the system combines manually curated linguistic resources with modern machine learning models.

Diacritization   In Hebrew writing, the letters are almost entirely consonantal; the vowels are indicated by diacritic marks, generally positioned underneath the letters. However, in most cases, printed Hebrew omits the diacritic marks and includes only the letters, resulting in a highly ambiguous text, in which any given non-diacritized word can represent a host of different Hebrew words, each with a different meaning and pronunciation. For example, the form בצל can be diacritized as בָּצָל (noun, "onion"), בְּצֵל (prefix+noun, "in a shadow"), בַּצֵל (prefix+definitive+noun, "in the shadow") and others. The task of diacritization is thus a task of disambiguation: choosing from among the valid word possibilities for each non-diacritized word, and then adding in the diacritic marks accordingly. The multiple possibilities for

diacritizing any given word often represent different morphological possibilities. Thus, to an extent, choosing the correct diacritization entails morphological disambiguation; conversely, prior morphological disambiguation greatly reduces the total possible diacritization possibilities. We provide further details in §2.

Hybrid Neural and Rule-based Approach   Our approach, described in §3, uses several bi-LSTM-based deep-learning modules for disambiguating the correct diacritization in context. However, it is also supplemented by comprehensive inflection tables and lexicons, when appropriate.

Web Interface   We provide a web interface for the user to input a text for diacritization and refine the resulting diacritized text (Figure 1). Our system parses the text and automatically adds diacritics throughout. Afterward, the user can proofread the text in the interface. For each word, all alternate diacritization possibilities are provided for immediate selection, ordered according to their predicted probability. Keyboard shortcuts allow efficient navigation of the text and fast selection of alternate options. Users can choose to see morphological analyses for each of the diacritization options, to assist in distinguishing between options.

Diacritics in Scientific Editions   We aim to provide a tool that is useful to casual users and language enthusiasts, but also to experts and professionals who may use it to set scientific editions of historical Hebrew texts. This latter requirement poses several challenges: handling of editorial sigla interspersed within the words; flexible handling of matres lectionis (letters which function as semi-vowels); and dealing with the orthography of medieval Hebrew, which often diverges widely from that of Modern Hebrew. Our tool meets scholarly requirements on all these fronts, as detailed in §8.

Proceedings of the 58th Annual Meeting of the Association for Computational Linguistics, pages 197–203
July 5 - July 10, 2020. ©2020 Association for Computational Linguistics

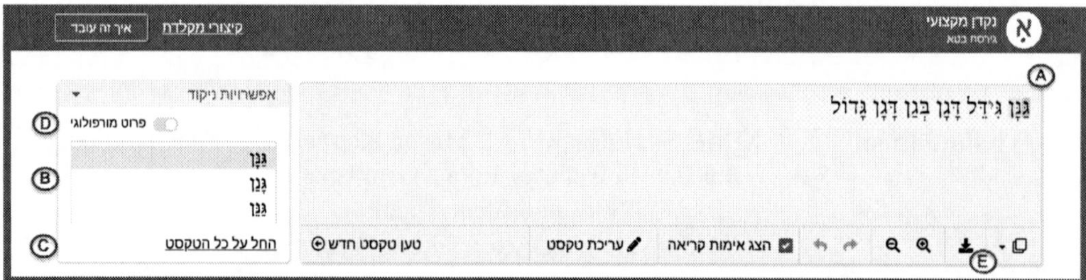

Figure 1: The main web interface of our diacritization tool, showing the automatic diacritized text (A) and allowing the user to proofread and potentially correct the text. The user can navigate the words using the mouse or the left/right keys, and can select an alternate diacritization option from the listbox on the left (B) using either the mouse or the up/down keys. Changes for a given word can be marked for application over the entire text (C), and are marked in color (not shown in this example). The user can also choose to see the morphological analysis of each form (D). The resulting diacritized text can be exported to various formats (E).

2 The Hebrew Diacritics System

The diacritics system of modern Hebrew marks vowels and gemination, and includes 12 primary diacritic symbols:

Symbol	Name	Symbol	Name
◌	Patach	◌	Shuruq
◌	Qamatz	◌	Holam
◌	Segol	◌	Hataf-Patach
◌	Tzereh	◌	Hataf-Qamatz
◌	Qibbutz	◌	Hataf-Segol
◌	Hiriq	◌	Shva

Additionally, a dot in the middle of a letter indicates gemination. For the case of the 'shin' letter, an upper dot distinguishes between pronunciation as 's' or as 'sh'. Diacritized Hebrew aims to position a diacritic on every single letter of the word, with the exception of final letters and matres lectionis.

Ambiguity In our tests, knowing the correct diacritics reduces the full-morphological-analysis ambiguity from 9.1 to 2.4 average analyses per word form, while knowing the full-morphological-analysis reduces the diacritization ambiguity from 6.2 to 1.4 average options per word form. Note that these numbers reflect fine-grained morphological tagging. If we utilize coarse-grained tagging, sufficing with the part of speech for each word, then knowing the correct diacritization reduces the average morphological ambiguity from 3.2 options to 1.97, while knowing the correct POS tag reduces the average diacritization ambiguity from 6.2 options to 2.75. Thus, the need for an automated diacritization utility is particularly crucial in order to properly disambiguate a Hebrew text.

3 Approach

Recent trends in NLP suggest moving towards machine-learned models that automatically learn to extract the regularities in the data. Such approaches have also been applied to diacritization of Arabic (Belinkov and Glass, 2015; Rashwan et al., 2015; Abandah et al., 2015; Mubarak et al., 2019). However, while these generally provide very strong results, they also often make mistakes that contradict our prior knowledge of the linguistic system. While the machine-learned models generalize very well and can learn to perform tasks in which humans cannot articulate the underlying regularities, there are also many cases that language-experts *can* articulate precisely, and these tend to correlate with the cases that the learned models fail on.

We therefore take a hybrid approach. Similar to traditional diacritization systems (Choueka and Neeman, 1995), we use our explicit knowledge about the language and the diacritization system whenever we can. However, we also supplement our knowledge with learned model predictions for the challenging cases for which we cannot articulate the rules and regularities: selecting the appropriate diacritization in context, and providing diacritization for out-of-vocabulary words. This methodology departs from recent diacritization works that rely on HMM and neural-network methods (Gal, 2002; Belinkov and Glass, 2015), while ignoring forms of explicit linguistic knowledge.

We use such a combination of machine-learned and human-specified knowledge in all the components of the system, either by supplementing the predictor with manually constructed options, or by filtering its output space.

Of course, a prerequisite for an effective machine-learned system is high-quality training data. Our system is trained on a collection of 1,5M diacritized tokens which we annotated in-house.

4 High-quality Data Sources

We make use of the following language resources and corpora, which we collected.

Language Resources Our main resource is a high-coverage and accurate lexicon of Hebrew word forms, their diacritization and their corresponding morphological analyses. Employing a staff of language experts, we began by assembling a list of all nouns, adjectives and verbal roots in the Hebrew language. This list includes 50K lexemes altogether (10K roots, 30,5K nouns, and 9,5K adjectives). We then built comprehensive inflection tables to generate all possible inflected forms from each of these lexemes, including all valid combinations of possessive and accusative suffixes, with full diacritization. Altogether, this process generated some 5,5 million inflected forms (3,8M verbal forms; 1,3M nominal forms; and 460K adjectival forms). We also added 1,7K adverbs, and another 4,5K function words (conjunctions, prepositions, existentials, quantifiers, etc., including all possible suffix combinations). Finally, we collected a set of 17,5K frequent proper nouns (countries and major cities; heads of state and other notable people; and frequently-mentioned companies and organizations), and our language experts diacritized these as well. These tables suffice for modern Hebrew; however, in historical Hebrew texts, we often find Aramaic terms interspersed within the Hebrew. Therefore, we also built a similarly comprehensive and diacritized wordlist for Babylonian Aramaic. Our Aramaic wordlist contains 750K verbal inflected forms; 200K nominals; 1,5K adjectives; and another 2K adverbs and function words. We additionally assembled an exhaustive list of non-diacritized Hebrew names of persons and locations (including collections of both street names and city names).

Annotated Corpora For morphological tagging, we make use of a corpus of 200K tokens of modern Hebrew, composed of Hebrew fiction, news, wikipedia, and blogs. These tokens were manually annotated with fine-grained morphological information according to the scheme of (Elhadad et al., 2005). Additionally, as noted, we annotated a 1,5M word diacritized modern Hebrew corpus, consisting of Hebrew prose (both fiction and non-fiction), newspapers (both news and op-ed), wikipedia, blogs (including many female-dominant blogs, to ensure coverage of feminine word forms), law protocols, Parliament proceedings, TV transcripts, academic texts, and biographical sketches. We have similarly collected and annotated corpora of historical Hebrew, consisting of Jewish legal writings and commentaries from the 3rd-12th centuries: 110K words with fine-grained morphological tagging, and 2M words with diacritization. Finally, regarding poetic Hebrew, we collected and annotated a corpus of 1,3M words, containing Hebrew poetry from both medieval and modern periods.

The undiacritized base texts were collected largely through partnerships with cooperating organizations in Israel; the morphological tagging and diacritization was done primarily in-house by our Hebrew language experts.

5 System Architecture

On a high level, our system works in the following stages, which we will elaborate on below. Each stage combines engineered linguistic information and a trained neural model.

1. POS-tagging and morphological disambiguation.

2. Filtering the possible diacritization analyses based on high coverage accurate tables and the output of stage (1).

3. Ranking the possible diacritizations for each word, in context.

Part-of-speech tagging and morphological disambiguation As diacritic marks closely interact with the morphological analysis and part-of-speech (POS) of the token, we first perform POS-tagging and morphological disambiguation, using a two-stage process. In the first stage, each word is assigned its core part-of-speech, and in the second stage it is enriched with additional morphological properties, where the set of considered morphological properties is determined based on the coarse-grained POS (e.g., nouns take gender, number and definiteness, while verbs do not take definiteness but do take tense and person).[1]

---

[1] We consider the following POS-tags: *Adj, Adv, Conj, At_Prep, Neg, Noun, Num, Prep, Pron, ProperNoun, Verb,*

Training is performed on our annotated corpus of 200K tokens. The resulting tagger has an accuracy of 92% for the coarse-grained part-of-speech, and 79% for full morphological disambiguation.[2]

Both taggers are 2-layer bi-LSTM transducers (Goldberg, 2017), where the first stage coarse-grained tagger maps each token w_i to a coarse POS-tag t_i, while the second stage morphological tagger adds additional morphological properties $m_i^1, ..., m_i^k$. Each bi-LSTM takes as inputs vectors $x_1, ..., x_n$ corresponding to tokens $w_1, ..., w_n$ and produces vectors $h(x_1), ..., h(x_n)$. These vectors are then fed into multi-layer perceptrons (MLP) for predicting the POS-tags and morphological properties, where each property is predicted by a different MLP:

$$t_i = \arg\max_j \text{softmax}(MLP_{\text{pos}}(h(x_i))_{[j]}$$

$$m_i^k = \arg\max_j \text{softmax}(MLP_{m_k}(h(x_i))_{[j]}$$

The set of MLPs m_i^k for a word is determined based on its predicted coarse-grained POS-tag.

In the coarse-grained tagger, each token w_i is mapped to an input vector x_i which encodes character level information, distributional word-level information, possible morphological analyses of w_i,[3] and lexicon-based features of w_i. Specifically, x_i is a concatenation of: (a) for a word w_i made of characters $c_1^{w_i}, ..., c_m^{w_i}$ the sum of bi-LSTM states $\sum_j h(c_j^{w_i})$ from a char-level bi-LSTM that runs over the entire sentence; (b) bi-LSTM state at w_i, for a word-level bi-LSTM that runs on pre-trained word2vec vectors for all of the words in the sentence; (c) a vector representing the possible fine-grained morphological analyses for the word,[4] according to our wide-coverage lexicon; (d) bits

indicating whether w_i is in our comprehensive list of proper-nouns (names of streets, cities and people), and whether it is in our wide-coverage lexicon at all (the latter is used to mark rare and unknown words). In the fine-grained tagger, x_i is a concatenation of vector (b) above and: for a word w_i where the predicted POS tag is t_i, and the possible fine-grained morphological analyses for w_i limited by t_i is represented by m_i, the bi-LSTM state for a bi-LSTM that runs on the concatenation of $(t_i; m_i)$. Significantly, note that in the fine-grained tagger, x_i does not include the information of the word form on the character-level. We find this to be more accurate, because it removes bias in cases where a specific character form happens to appear in the training corpus in only one configuration. This is particularly relevant regarding verbs which can be resolved as either a masculine or a feminine verb, each with a distinct diacritization. In many cases, the training corpus contains the verb only in one stereotypical gender configuration. By hiding the character-level information, we force the system to make a more logical morphological determination, because it is not able to mechanically set the feature equal to what was seen in the training corpus.

Constraints The tagger predictions are constrained by a wide-coverage lexicon that maps word forms to their possible morphological analyses. When a word is not in the lexicon, we allow all POS-tags for the word. We also apply additional filters to rule out POS-tags for words that participate in a hand-crafted list of about 10K word collocations, and in all of their possible inflected forms (e.g., in the context of the tokens (בית מרקחת) *byt mrkĥt*, the word בית *byt* should not be tagged as the absolute form בַּיִת *bayit*, but rather as the construct form בֵּית *beyt*. And thus too for the plural inflection of the same collocation - בתי מרקחת *bty mrkĥt*, the word בתי *bty* should not be tagged as בָּתֵּי *byty* (feminine noun with possessive suffix), but rather as the plural-construct form בָּתֵּי *batey*).

Filtering For each word w_i in the text, we retrieve from our wordlists (see §4) a set of possible diacritizations $D_i = d_1^i, ..., d_\ell^i$ and their corresponding morphological analyses. This set is then further refined by intersecting it with the predicted morphological analysis for the word. Words that are not in our list get an empty set, indicating that their diacritization is not constrained. This stage leaves us with an average of 1.2 diacritic sequences

---

Interrogative, Interj, Quantifier, Existential, Modal, Prefix, Participle, Copula, Titular, Shel_Prep, and the following morphological properties: *Gender, Number, Person, Construct/Absolute, Suffix (possessive / accusative / pronominal)*.

[2]While these numbers may seem low, we note that they are (a) on-par with other Hebrew systems (Adler and Elhadad, 2006; More and Tsarfaty, 2016) and (b) are only intended to support the diacritization process, where we find they do well.

[3]We find that providing the coarse-grained tagger with information about possible fine-grained analyses of neighbouring words helps to disambiguate cases where a given word can be resolved as more than one POS. For instance, a given word may be resolvable as a noun or adjective; however, if the adjective possibility involves a feminine conjugation, and the preceding noun is a masculine noun, then the probability of the adjectival POS is severely reduced.

[4]We assign trainable embeddings of 3-5 dimensions to each morphological category (gender, number, person, etc.), and we concatenate these together to form the input vector.

200

for each known word. If we were to perform random selection from this list, we would achieve 87.1% exact-match word-level diacritization accuracy on our Modern Hebrew test corpus.

Diacritization Ranking Finally, we run an LSTM-based diacritization module to rank the possible diacritization sequences from the previous stage, and to assign diacritics to unknown words.

The LSTM-based module assigns a diacritic mark for each character in the sequence.[5] The diacritics for each word w_i are predicted separately, using beam-search over the predictions of the diacritic for each letter with the word, to ensure word-level consistency. For known words, the beam-search is constrained to valid diacritic predictions from the set D_i, while for unknown words it is unconstrained. Note that when predicting the diacritics for a letter $c_j^{w_i}$ in token w_i the model is aware of the other diacritic assignments in that word, but not of diacritic assignments for the other words of the sentence. However, the model *is* context-aware, as it considers the character-level and word-level information from the entire sentence via a sentence-level bi-LSTM layer.

To be more precise, each letter $c_j^{w_i}$ is mapped to a vector $h'(c_j^{w_i})$ which is a concatenation of the followings two items: (a) bi-LSTM state at $c_j^{w_i}$ for a char-level bi-LSTM that runs over the entire sentence; (b) bi-LSTM state at w_i for a word-level bi-LSTM that runs on the pre-trained word2vec vectors for all words in the sentence. Then, for a given word w_i we have a list of vectors representing each letter $h'(c_1^{w_i})...h'(c_m^{w_i})$. We then predict the diacritization sequence as follows. If this is a known word, then we have a list of k possible diacritization sequences, and we choose the one with the highest score:

$$s = \arg\max_k score(c_{1:m}^{w_i}, t_{1:m}^k)$$

where $t_{1:m}^k$ is the kth diacritic sequence, and $score(c_{1:m}^{w_i}, t_{1:m}^k)$ is calculated as:

$$\sum_{j=1}^{m} MLP(h'(c_j^{w_i}); LSTM(t_{0:j-1}^k))_{[t_j]}$$

For unknown words, we run beam-search with $k = 8$ to predict the k most likely diacritization sequences, and we choose the top beam-ray.

---

[5]Combinations of gemination with an additional diacritic mark are considered distinct diacritic symbols for prediction. An independent MLP predicts the position of the upper dot for the 'shin' character.

	Letter Accuracy	Word Accuracy
Dicta	**95.12%**	**88.23%**
Morfix	90.32%	80.9%
Snopi	78.96%	66.41%

Table 1: Accuracy on Modern Hebrew Test Corpus

6 Evaluation

We evaluate the system quantitatively against two commercial Hebrew diacritization systems, Morfix[6] and Snopi[7], considered state-of-the-art.

We also provide qualitative evaluation, demonstrating the ability to diacritize unknown words, and to produce context-sensitive diacritization.

Quantitative Evaluation We use two quantitative measures to evaluate our model. (1) Word-level accuracy: for a given word[8], we consider the prediction correct if and only if all the diacritic marks on the word are correct, including gemination and the 'shin' dot, with all matres lectionis removed. (2) Character-level accuracy: For each Hebrew letter in the input text we check if the model predicted the correct set of diacritic marks for the letter (and, for matres lectionis, we check that the model predicted their removal).

We evaluated the system on a 6,000-word unseen gold-test corpus, manually diacritized by a professional linguist (Table 1). The corpus consists of a random selection of Hebrew wiki articles. We have made the test corpus publicly available.[9]

Qualitative Evaluation For the qualitative evaluation, we demonstrate that the system knows how to handle diacritization for unknown words, and this, in a context-sensitive manner. For this example we choose an invalid word which conforms to Hebrew letter patterns but which does not actually exist in modern Hebrew: סרדינות. No such word exists in Hebrew dictionaries, nor in our wordlist. We put the word into a sentence in two contexts - in the first, it fills the role of an adverb, and in the second, it fills the role of a noun. Hebrew diacritization norms would dictate two different diacritizations for these two usages: for the adverb, the final vowel should be 'u', while for the noun, it should be 'o'. Our system handles both correctly (Figure 2).

---

[6]https://nakdan.morfix.co.il/
[7]http://www.nakdan.com/
[8]For this calculation, punctuation and non-Hebrew words or symbols are ignored.
[9]The test corpus can be downloaded at this link: http://tiny.cc/hebrew-test-git

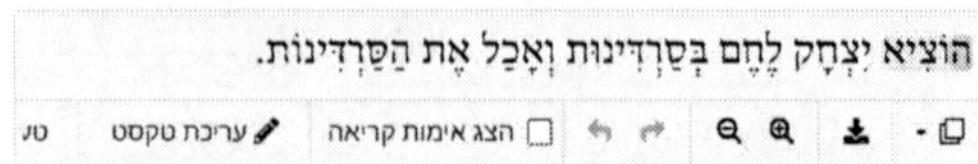

Figure 2: Diacritization of the fictional word סרדינות in two different contexts, with two different prefixes; the word is diacritized as expected in both contexts.

	Letter Accuracy	Word Accuracy
Dicta	94.94%	87.94%
Morfix	80.25%	68.1%
Snopi	72.53%	58.39%

Table 2: Accuracy on Rabbinic Hebrew Test Corpus

7 Additional Text Genres

In addition to modern Hebrew, we also support Rabbinic Hebrew and poetic Hebrew. These genres require specialized handling. Firstly, we cannot use our modern Hebrew morphology model, because the morphological and syntactic norms of these genres differ from those of modern Hebrew. Secondly, we cannot use our modern Hebrew wordlist filters. There is no standardized orthography for Rabbinic Hebrew, nor for medieval poetic Hebrew. Additionally, poets often specifically choose less common words in order to meet prosodic constraints; thus, our rare-word filters are not relevant. Finally, many words which would be considered invalid in modern Hebrew are found within these other genres. Rabbinic Hebrew includes many Aramaic words, as well as Hebrew words with Aramaic prefixes. Poetic Hebrew includes oddities such as past-tense verbs with temporal prefixes.

For Rabbinic Hebrew, we train a specialized morphology model based on our tagged historical Hebrew corpus. For poetry, where morphological sequences are less constrained and less predictable, we skip the morphology layer and diacritize the text directly based on the diacritization LSTM.

In order to test our performance, we created test corpora for each of the genres. The poetry test corpus includes a set of liturgical poems of the 'yotzer' genre, transcribed from Cairo Genizah manuscripts.[10] The Rabbinic Hebrew test corpus is taken from the 'Bet Yosef', a 16th century commentary on Jewish law.[11] In Tables 2 and 3 we display our quantitative results on these two corpora.

---

[10] Full data on these texts is available here: `http://weekdayyotzrot.com`

[11] Both test corpora are available for download here: `http://tiny.cc/hebrew-test-git`

	Letter Accuracy	Word Accuracy
Dicta	85.76%	70.23%
Morfix	80.9%	65.3%
Snopi	69.24%	52%

Table 3: Accuracy on Poetic Hebrew Test Corpus

8 Advanced Features

1. Scientific Editions: In scientific editions, editorial sigla are interspersed throughout the text. For instance, letters which are rubbed out in the textual witnesses will be supplied within brackets (מד[ר]ש). Existing diacritization tools fail here because they parse such sigla as word separators. Secondly, normative Hebrew diacritization entails the omission of matres lectionis, and indeed existing tools omit these letters when returning the diacritized text. However, in scientific editions, matres lectionis must be maintained in order to represent the manuscript evidence. Finally, the orthography of medieval Hebrew manuscripts can diverge wildly from modern norms; for example, we often find a yod inserted after the initial letter of a hitpael construction (e.g. היתלבש), a phenomenon which would never occur in a modern Hebrew text. Our tool meets all of these needs, and allows the user to either remove or maintain matres lectionis.
2. The web interface automatically highlights Biblical quotes within the Hebrew text. Biblical phrases are often incorporated into Hebrew texts, whether as explicit prooftexts or as rhetorical flourishes. We automatically identify such quotes, diacritize them according to the canonized diacritization of the Hebrew Bible, and display them in the distinctive Koren font (a font well-known for its use in modern Hebrew Bibles). See figure 3 for an example.

Figure 3: Integrated Biblical quote marked with font.

9 Conclusion

We are pleased to release our Hebrew diacritization system for free unrestricted use. It is powered by a combination of advanced machine learning and manually curated linguistic resources, and thus succeeds in setting a new state of the art for Hebrew diacritization. We have released also our diacritized test corpora for benchmarking.

References

Gheith Abandah, Alex Graves, Balkees Al-Shagoor, Alaa Arabiyat, Fuad Jamour, and Majid Al-Taee. 2015. Automatic diacritization of arabic text using recurrent neural networks. *International Journal on Document Analysis and Recognition (IJDAR)*, 18:183–197.

Meni Adler and Michael Elhadad. 2006. An unsupervised morpheme-based HMM for hebrew morphological disambiguation. In *ACL 2006, 21st International Conference on Computational Linguistics and 44th Annual Meeting of the Association for Computational Linguistics, Proceedings of the Conference, Sydney, Australia, 17-21 July 2006*.

Yonatan Belinkov and James R. Glass. 2015. Arabic diacritization with recurrent neural networks. In *EMNLP*.

Yaacov Choueka and Yoni Neeman. 1995. Nakdantext,(an in-context text-vocalizer for modern hebrew). In *BISFAI-95, The Fifth Bar Ilan Symposium for Artificial Intelligence*.

Michael Elhadad, Yael Netzer, David Gabay, and Meni Adler. 2005. Hebrew morphological tagging guidelines. Technical report, Technical report, Ben-Gurion University, Dept. of Computer Science.

Ya'akov Gal. 2002. An hmm approach to vowel restoration in arabic and hebrew. In *Proceedings of the ACL-02 workshop on Computational approaches to semitic languages*, pages 1–7. Association for Computational Linguistics.

Yoav Goldberg. 2017. Neural network methods for natural language processing. *Synthesis Lectures on Human Language Technologies*, 10(1):1–309.

Amir More and Reut Tsarfaty. 2016. Data-driven morphological analysis and disambiguation for morphologically rich languages and universal dependencies. In *Proceedings of COLING 2016*.

Hamdy Mubarak, Ahmed Abdelali, Hassan Sajjad, Younes Samih, and Kareem Darwish. 2019. Highly effective Arabic diacritization using sequence to sequence modeling. In *Proceedings of the 2019 Conference of the North American Chapter of the Association for Computational Linguistics: Human Language Technologies, Volume 1 (Long and Short Papers)*, pages 2390–2395, Minneapolis, Minnesota. Association for Computational Linguistics.

Mohsen Rashwan, Ahmad Sallab, Hazem Raafat, and Ahmed Rafea. 2015. Deep learning framework with confused sub-set resolution architecture for automatic arabic diacritization. *IEEE Transactions on Audio Speech and Language Processing*, 23.

PHOTON: A Robust Cross-Domain Text-to-SQL System

Jichuan Zeng[1*†]   Xi Victoria Lin[2*]   Caiming Xiong[2]   Richard Socher[2]
Michael R. Lyu[1]   Irwin King[1]   Steven C.H. Hoi[2]
[1] The Chinese University of Hong Kong
[2] Salesforce Research
[1] {jczeng,lyu,king}@cse.cuhk.edu.hk
[2] {xilin,cxiong,rsocher,shoi}@salesforce.com

Abstract

Natural language interfaces to databases (NLIDB) democratize end user access to relational data. Due to fundamental differences between natural language communication and programming, it is common for end users to issue questions that are ambiguous to the system or fall outside the semantic scope of its underlying query language. We present PHOTON, a robust, modular, cross-domain NLIDB that can flag natural language input to which a SQL mapping cannot be immediately determined. PHOTON consists of a strong neural semantic parser (63.2% structure accuracy on the Spider dev benchmark), a human-in-the-loop question corrector, a SQL executor and a response generator. The question corrector is a discriminative neural sequence editor which detects confusion span(s) in the input question and suggests rephrasing until a translatable input is given by the user or a maximum number of iterations are conducted. Experiments on simulated data show that the proposed method effectively improves the robustness of text-to-SQL system against untranslatable user input. The live demo of our system is available at http://www.naturalsql.com.

1   Introduction

Natural language interfaces to databases (Popescu et al., 2003; Li and Jagadish, 2014) democratize end user access to relational data and have attracted significant research attention for decades (Hemphill et al., 1990; Dahl et al., 1994; Zelle and Mooney, 1996; Popescu et al., 2003; Bertomeu et al., 2006; Zhong et al., 2017; Yu et al., 2018, 2019a). Most existing NLIDBs adopt a modular architecture consisting of rule-based natural language parsing, ambiguity detection and pragmatics modeling (Li and

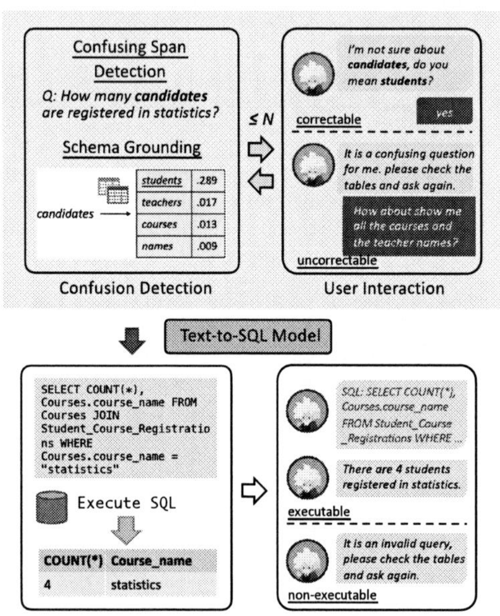

Figure 1: PHOTON workflow. The question corrector (upper block) detects the untranslatable questions from user input, scans the confusion span(s) that need clarification or correction. The accepted question is mapped into a SQL query through a text-to-SQL model, and finally the SQL execution results are returned to the user.

Jagadish, 2014; Setlur et al., 2016, 2019). While they have been shown effective in pilot study and production, rule-based approaches are limited in terms of coverage, scalability and naturalness — they are not robust against the diversity of human language expressions and are difficult to scale across domains.

Recent advances in neural natural language processing (Sutskever et al., 2014; Dong and Lapata, 2016; See et al., 2017a; Liang et al., 2017; Lin et al., 2019; Bogin et al., 2019a), pre-training (Devlin et al., 2019; Hwang et al., 2019), and the availability of large-scale supervised datasets (Zhong

---

* Equal contribution. Jichuan implemented the demo interaction flow and the neural question corrector. Victoria designed and implemented the neural semantic parser.

† Work done during internship at Salesforce Research.

Proceedings of the 58th Annual Meeting of the Association for Computational Linguistics, pages 204–214
July 5 - July 10, 2020. ©2020 Association for Computational Linguistics

et al., 2017; Finegan-Dollak et al., 2018; Yu et al., 2018, 2019b,a) enabled deep learning based approaches to significantly improve the state-of-the-art in nearly all subtasks of building an NLIDB. These include semantic parsing (Dong and Lapata, 2018; Zhang et al., 2019), ambiguity detection and confidence estimation (Dong et al., 2018; Yao et al., 2019), natural language response generation (Liu et al., 2019) and so on. Moreover, by jointly modeling the natural language question and database schema in the neural space, latest text-to-SQL semantic parsers can work cross domains (Yu et al., 2018; Zhang et al., 2019).

In this work, we present PHOTON, a modular, cross-domain NLIDB that adopts deep learning in its core components. PHOTON consists of (1) a neural semantic parser, (2) a human-in-the-loop question corrector, (3) a SQL query executor and (4) a natural language response generator. The *neural semantic parser* assumes limited DB content access due to data privacy concerns (§ 3.1). It employs a BERT-based (Devlin et al., 2019) DB schema-aware question encoder and a pointer-generator decoder (See et al., 2017a) with static SQL correctness check. It achieves competitive performance on the popular cross-domain text-to-SQL benchmark, Spider (Yu et al., 2018) (63.2% structure accuracy on the dev set based on the official evaluation).[1] The *question corrector* is a neural sequence editor which detects potential confusion span(s) in the input question and suggests possible corrections for the user to give feedback. When an input question is successfully translated into an executable SQL query, the *response generator* generates a natural language response conditioned on the output of the SQL *query executor*.

A pilot study with non-expert SQL users shows that the system effectively increases the flexibility of user's natural language expression and is easy to be adapted to unseen databases. Being able to detect and correct untranslatable questions reduces unexpected error cases during user interaction.

2 System Design

In this section, we will elaborate on the system design of PHOTON.

---

[1] We are continuously improving the performance of the neural semantic parser. Currently the semantic parser only accepts standalone question as input. We plan to also model the interaction context in future work.

2.1 Overview

Figure 1 shows the overall workflow of our system. PHOTON is an end-to-end system that takes a user question and database schema as input, and output the query result after executing the generated SQL on the database. PHOTON is a modular framework designed towards practical industrial applications. The core modules in PHOTON are the SQL parser and confusion detection mechanism. The SQL parser parses the input question and database schema, maps them into executable SQL query via an encoder-decoder framework. The confusion detection module identifies the untranslatable questions and captures the confusing span of the untranslatable question. The confusing tokens together with the context are fed into the auto-correction module to make a prediction of user attempted question.

To make it more applicable and accessible for user to query the database in a natural way, PHOTON also provides user interaction module enabling user to refine their queries in the interaction with the system. Response generation handles the output of the system by transducing the database-style query result into natural language or post warning when the query is non-executable on the database, making the system more user-friendly. Notice that the response generation module in the current version is implemented using a template-based approach and can be improved by using more advanced response generation models.

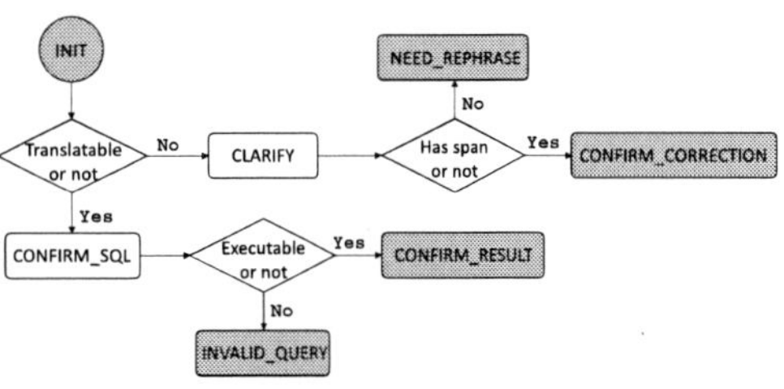

Response Template

CONFIRM_RESULT	"SQL: {PRED_SQL}. {NL_RESPONSE}"
CONFIRM_CORRECTION	"Sorry, {CONF_TOKENS} is confusing in our scenario, do you mean {CORR_TOKENS}?"
NEED_REPHRASE	"Sorry, it is a confusing question for me, please rephrase your question and ask again."
INVALID_QUERY	"Sorry, it is an invalidate query, please check the table names and associated fields of interest."

Figure 2: State transition map of interaction in PHOTON. States with darker background are the end states that can receive user reply, and switch to INIT state automatically. The bottom part is the system response templates in each end state.

2.2 User Interaction

Figure 2 illustrates the interaction process, which involves four types of response states: `CONFIRM_RESULT`, `CONFIRM_CORRECTION`, `NEED_REPHRASE`, and `INVALID_QUERY`. The set of response templates can be found at the bottom of Figure 2. When a user initiates the conversation by entering one query, PHOTON will first predict whether the query is translatable or not. If translatable, PHOTON generates the corresponding SQL command and checks the command's executability; otherwise, PHOTON will provide a correction strategy (i.e., `CONFIRM_CORRECTION`) based on the detected confusing span or ask the users to further rephrase the inquiry (i.e., `NEED_REPHRASE`) if no span is captured.

2.3 UI Design

Our system UI consists of three panels: chat window, schema viewer and results viewer.

- *Chat window*: This is a standard chat window that facilitates communication between the user and PHOTON. The user types the natural language input and the natural language responses of the system are displayed.

- *Schema viewer*: This view provides a graph visualization of the underlying relational DB schema. The panel is hideable and will not be shown in case the DB schema is confidential.

- *Result viewer*: This view displays the returned results of an executable SQL query mapped from a confirmed input question. The SQL query is formatted and displayed in the top for user verification. Multi-record results are presented as sub-tables. Result consists of a single table cell is presented as a 1-cell sub-table. If the result comes from an aggregation operation such as a counting, the data records supporting the calculation are also shown for explanability. Confidential DB records are hidden from the display and the user is informed of the number of hidden records.

2.4 Cross Domain

A relational DB for user queries should be set before usage. PHOTON consists of a collection of default databases and allows users to upload their own DBs for testing. Users can select which database they want to query by clicking the "Selected Database" drop down button.

3 Model

3.1 Neural Semantic Parser

The neural semantic parser is an end-to-end model whose input consists of a user question and the DB schema, and outputs a SQL query. Due to data privacy concerns, we assume that the neural semantic parser does not have full access to the DB content. Instead, we assume for each DB field, the parser have access to the set of possible values of the field, for example, "Country.Region": {"Carribean", "Porto Rico", ...}[2]. We call such value sets "picklists" by industry convention.

3.1.1 Schema-Question Encoder

Following previous work (Hwang et al., 2019; Zhang et al., 2019), we serialize the relational DB schema and concatenate it to the user question. As shown in Figure 3 , we represent each table with the table name followed by a sequence of field names. Each table name is preceded by the special token `[T]` and each field name is preceded by the special token `[C]`. The representations of multiple tables are concatenated together to form the serialization of the schema, which is surrounded by `[SEP]` tokens and concatenated to the question. Finally, the question is preceded by the `[CLS]` token following convention of BERT encoder (Devlin et al., 2019).

This sequence is fed into the pretrained BERT, followed by a bi-directional LSTM to form a joint encoding of the question and schema $\mathbf{h}_{\text{input}}$. The text portion of $\mathbf{h}_{\text{input}}$ is passed through another bi-LSTM to obtain the question encoding $\mathbf{h}_{\text{Q}}$. We represent each schema component (tables and fields) using the slices of $\mathbf{h}_{\text{input}}$ corresponding to the special token `[T]` and `[C]`.

Meta-data Features We further trained dense look-up features to represent if a field is a primary key ($\mathbf{f}_{\text{pri}}$), if a field appears in a foreign key pair ($\mathbf{f}_{\text{for}}$) and the data type of the field ($\mathbf{f}_{\text{type}}$). These meta-data features are fused with the representations in $\mathbf{h}_{\text{input}}$ via a projection layer g to obtain the final representation of each schema component:

$$\mathbf{h}^{C_p} = g([\mathbf{h}^m_{\text{input}}; \mathbf{f}^i_{\text{pri}}; \mathbf{f}^j_{\text{for}}; \mathbf{f}^k_{\text{type}}]) \tag{1}$$

$$= \text{ReLU}(\mathbf{W}_g[\mathbf{h}^m_{\text{input}}; \mathbf{f}^i_{\text{pri}}; \mathbf{f}^j_{\text{for}}; \mathbf{f}^k_{\text{type}}] + \mathbf{b}_g)$$

$$\mathbf{h}^{T_q} = g([\mathbf{h}^n_{\text{input}}; \mathbf{0}; \mathbf{0}; \mathbf{0}]), \tag{2}$$

---

[2] In practice, we can limit the access to only certain fields.

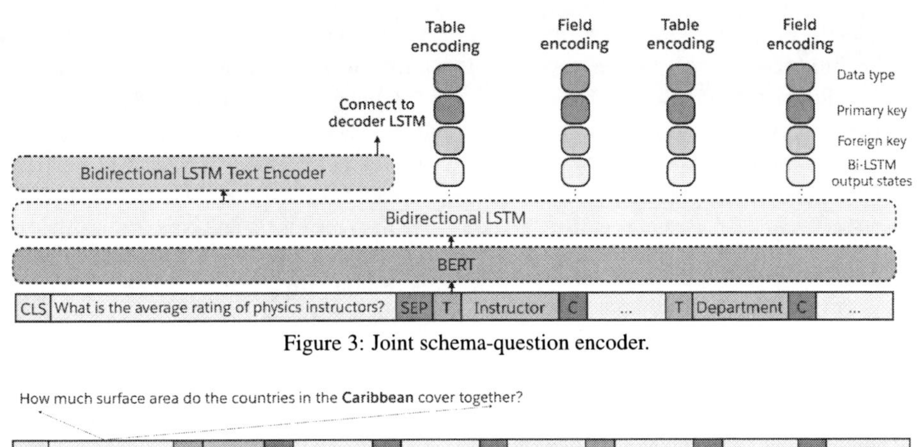

Figure 3: Joint schema-question encoder.

Figure 4: Joint schema-question encoder augmented with picklist values.

where m is the index of the special token corresponding to the p-th column in the input and n is the index of the special token corresponding to the q-th table in the input. i, j and k are the feature indices indicating the corresponding properties of C_p. $[\mathbf{h}_{input}^m; \mathbf{f}_{pri}^i; \mathbf{f}_{for}^j; \mathbf{f}_{type}^k]$ is the concatenation of the four vectors. The meta-data features we include are specific to fields and the table representations are fused with zero place-holder vectors.

3.1.2 Decoder

We use an LSTM-based sequential pointer-generator (See et al., 2017b) as the decoder. The generation vocabulary of our decoder consists of 70 SQL keywords and reserved tokens, plus the 10 digits[3]. At each step, the decoder computes a probability distribution over actions that consists of generating a token from the reserved vocabulary, copying a token from the input text or copying a schema component.

3.1.3 Static SQL Correctness Check

The sequential pointer-generator we adopted does not guarantee the output SQL is syntactically correct. In practice, we perform beam-search decoding and run a static SQL correctness check[4] to eliminate erroneous predictions from the beam. Specifi-

cally, we employ a tool implemented on top of the Mozilla SQL Parser[5] to analyze the output SQL queries and ensure they satisfy the following criteria:

1. The SQL query is syntactically correct.
2. The SQL query satisfies schema consistency[6].

We found this approach is very effective and results in an absolute improvement of 4∼5% in the evaluation score on Spider dev set (Yu et al., 2018).

3.1.4 Picklist Incorporation

We use picklists to inform the semantic parser regarding potential matches in the DB. For an input question Q and a field C_p, we compute the longest character sequence match between Q and each value in the picklist of C_p. We select the value with top-1 matching score above a certain threshold θ as a match. For each field with a matched picklist value, we append the surface form of the value to it in the input sequence representation, separated by the special token [V]. The augmented sequence is used as the input to the schema-question encoder. In practice, we found picklist augmentation results in an absolute performance improvement of 1% on the Spider dev set.

Figure 4 illustrates the input sequence with aug-

---

[3]Such that the parser is able to generate numbers corresponding to utterances such as "first", "second" etc.

[4]Some prior work such as (Wang et al., 2018) performs a similar check by executing the decoded SQL queries on the target DB. We implement the static checking as it can reduce the traffic between the interface and the DB.

[5]https://github.com/mozilla/moz-sql-parser

[6]The fields appeared in a SELECT SQL query must come from the tables in the corresponding FROM clause. The fields in a JOIN condition clause must come from tables mentioned in front of them in the JOIN clause.

mented picklist values. In this example, the matching algorithm identifies "Carribean" associated with the column "Country.Region" as a match. Hence it inserts "Carribean" after [... [C], "Region"] with [V] as a separation token[7]. The representations of fields with no picklist value match are unchanged.

3.2 Confusion Detection: Handling Untranslatable and Ambiguous Input

In order to handle ambiguous and untranslatable input questions, PHOTON adopts a discriminatively trained classifier to detect user input to which a SQL mapping cannot be immediately determined. This covers questions that are incomplete (e.g. *What is the total?*), ambiguous or vague (e.g. *Show me homes with good schools*), beyond the representation scope of SQL (e.g. *How many tourists visited all of the 10 attractions?*), or simply noisy (e.g. *Cyrus teaches physics in department*).

3.2.1 Untranslatable Question Detection

Inspired by (Rajpurkar et al., 2018), we create a synthetic dataset which consists of untranslatable questions generated by applying rule-based transformations and adversarial filtering (Zellers et al., 2018) to examples in existing text-to-SQL datasets. We then train a stagewise model that first classifies if the input is translatable or not, and then predicts confusing spans in an untranslatable input.

Dataset Construction. In order to construct the untranslatable questions, we firstly exam the types of untranslatable questions seen on the manually constructed CoSQL (Yu et al., 2019a) and Multi-WOZ (Budzianowski et al., 2018) datasets (Table 4 of A.1). We then design our modification strategies to generate the untranslatable questions from the original text-to-SQL dataset automatically. Specifically, for a text-to-SQL example that contains a natural language question, a DB schema and a SQL query, we first identify all non-overlapping question spans that possibly refer to a table field occurred in the SELECT and WHERE clauses of the SQL query using string-matching heuristics. Then we apply *Swap* and *Drop* operations on the question and DB schema respectively to generate different types of untranslatable questions. The modification tokens are marked as the confusion spans of the

synthetic untranslatable questions, except for the question *Drop* strategy.

Table 5 in A.1 provides a detailed summary of all transformations applied[8]. For example, given the original question "How many countries exist?", "countries" is detected to be referring to a table field. We drop the token, and pass the modified question "How many exist?" to back-translation for grammar smoothing. After that, we obtain the untranslatable question "How many are there?". Once we have the synthetic untranslatable questions, adversarial filtering is employed to iteratively refine the set of untranslatable examples to be more indiscernible by trivial stylistic classifiers (Zellers et al., 2018).

Predicting Untranslatable Questions and Confusing Spans. We utilize the BERT contextualized representations of [CLS] token, followed by a single-layer classifier to tell whether a given user question and table schema can be translated into SQL or not. To identify the questionable token spans of untranslatable question, following Zhang et al. (2019), we employ a hierarchical bi-LSTM structure to encode each column header and use the hidden states as the column header embedding. We then use a bi-LSTM to encode the question's BERT embedding, and the hidden states are fed into a dot-product co-attention (Luong et al., 2015) layer over the column header embedding. The output of co-attention augmented question embedding is fed into a linear layer follow by softmax operator to predict the start and end tokens indices of the confusing spans in the question.

3.2.2 Database-aware Token Correction

Figure 5 illustrates the proposed tokens correction module in PHOTON. We use the masked language model (MLM) of BERT (Devlin et al., 2019) to auto-correct the confusing tokens. Specifically, we replace the confusing tokens with the [MASK] special token. The output distribution of MLM head on the mask token is employed to score the candidate spans. We construct the candidate span list by extracting all the table names and columns names from the database schema. After user confirmation, the confusing tokens in the input are replaced by the predicted tokens of MLM.

---

[7]In practice, we found a question typically has 0 to 4 picklist value matches. As a result, the picklist augmented schema-question representation still stays under the maximum input length of BERT.

[8]To introduce semantic variation and ensure grammar fluency, we apply back-translation on the generated question using Google Cloud Translation API https://cloud. google.com/translate/. We use Chinese as the intermediate language.

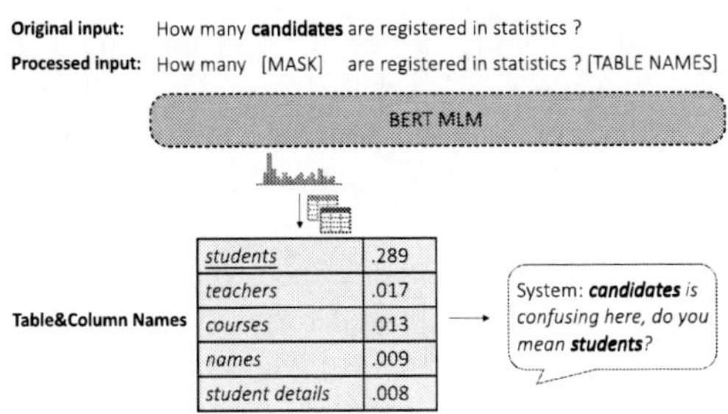

Figure 5: Token Correction in PHOTON.

4   Evaluation

In this section, we empirically evaluate the robustness and effectiveness of PHOTON.

In particular, we examine two key modules of PHOTON: the confusion detection module and the neural semantic parser. The former aims to detect the untranslatable questions and predicts the confusing spans; if the question is translatable, it then applies the proposed neural semantic parser to perform the text-to-SQL parsing. Since PHOTON is designed as a stagewise system, we can evaluate the performance of each module separately.

4.1   Experimental Setup

Dataset.   We conduct experiments on Spider (Yu et al., 2018) and $\text{Spider}_{\text{UTran}}$ dataset. Spider is a large-scale, human annotated, cross-domain text-to-SQL benchmark. $\text{Spider}_{\text{UTran}}$ is our modified dataset to evaluate robustness, created by injecting the untranslatable questions into Spider. We obtained 5,330 additional untranslatable questions (4,733 for training and 597 for development) from the original Spider dataset. To ensure the quality of our synthetic dataset, we hired SQL experts from Upwork[9] to annotate the auto-generated untranslatable examples in the dev set. We conduct our evaluation by following the database split setting, as illustrated in Table 1. The split follows the original dataset hence there is no test set of $\text{Spider}_{\text{UTran}}$ (the test set of Spider is not publicly accessible).

Training and Inference Details.   Our neural semantic parser is trained on Spider. We permute table order (up to 16 different ones) during training. We use the uncased BERT-base model from Huggingface's transformer library (Wolf et al., 2019). We set all LSTMs to 1-layer and set the dimension of $\mathbf{h}_{\text{input}}$, $\mathbf{f}_{\text{pri}}$, $\mathbf{f}_{\text{for}}$, $\mathbf{f}_{\text{type}}$ and the decoder to 512. We employ Adam-SGD (Kingma and Ba, 2015) with a

	Spider		$\text{Spider}_{\text{UTran}}$	
	Train	Dev	Train	Dev
# Q	8,659	1,034	13,392	1,631
# UTran Q	0	0	4,733	597
# Schema	146	20	918	112

Table 1: Data split of Spider and $\text{Spider}_{\text{UTran}}$. Q represents the all the questions, UTran Q represents the untranslatable questions.

mini-batch size of 32 and default Adam parameters. We train a maximum of 50,000 steps and set the learning rate to $5e - 4$ in the first 5,000 iterations and linearly decays it to 0 afterwards. We fine-tune BERT with a fine-tuning rate linearly increasing from $3e - 5$ to $8e - 5$ in the first 5,000 iterations and linearly decaying to 0 afterwards. We use a beam size of 128 in the beam search decoding.

4.2   Experimental Results

Confusion Detection.   We examine the robustness of PHOTON by evaluating the performance of the Confusion Detection module in handling ambiguous and untranslatable input. In particular, we aim to examine if PHOTON is effective in handling untranslatable questions by measuring the translatability detection accuracy and the confusing span prediction accuracy & F1 score[10]. We compare to a baseline that uses a single-layer attentive bidirectional LSTM ("Att-biLSTM"). Table 2 shows the evaluation results on the $\text{Spider}_{\text{UTran}}$ dataseet.

	Tran Acc	Span Acc	Span F1
Att-biLSTM	66.6	58.7	59.2
PHOTON	**79.7**	**69.1**	**72.9**

Table 2: Translatability prediction accuracy ("Tran Acc") and the confusing spans prediction accuracy and F1 on our $\text{Spider}_{\text{UTran}}$ dataset (%).

As observed from Table 2, PHOTON achieves encouraging performance in determining the translatability of a question and predicting the confusing spans of untranslatable ones. In comparison to the Att-biLSTM baseline, PHOTON obtains significant improvements in both translatability accuracy and the confusing spans prediction accuracy. These improvements are partly attribute to the proposed effective schema encoding strategy.

---

[10]We use the same way as SQuAD 2.0 (Rajpurkar et al., 2018) to compute the span accuracy and F1.

Neural Semantic Parser. We then evaluate the performance of the proposed neural semantic parser of PHOTON on the original Spider dataset. In particular, we compare PHOTON and other existing text-to-SQL approaches by measuring the exact set match (EM) accuracy (Yu et al., 2018). We compare with several existing approaches, including Global GNN (Bogin et al., 2019b), EditSQL (Zhang et al., 2019), IRNet (Guo et al., 2019), and RYANSQL (Choi et al., 2020). Table 3 shows the evaluation results on Spider Dev set.

Model	EM Acc.
GNN (Bogin et al., 2019a)	40.7
Global-GNN (Bogin et al., 2019b)	52.7
EditSQL + BERT (Zhang et al., 2019)	57.6
GNN+Bertrand-DR[†] (Kelkar et al., 2020)	57.9
EditSQL+Bertrand-DR[†] (Kelkar et al., 2020)	58.5
IRNet + BERT (Guo et al., 2019)	61.9
RYANSQL + BERT [†] (Choi et al., 2020)	66.6
PHOTON	63.2

[†] denotes unpublished work on arXiv.

Table 3: Experimental results on the Spider Dev set (%). EM Acc. denotes the exact set match accuracy.

As observed from Table 3, PHOTON achieves a very competitive text-to-SQL performance on the Spider benchmark with 63.2% exact set match accuracy on the Spider dev set, which validates the effectiveness of our neural semantic parser for translating an input question into a valid SQL query.

5 Related Work

Natural Language Interfaces to Databases. NLIDBs has been studied extensively in the past decades. Thanks to the availability of large-scale datasets (Zhong et al., 2017; Finegan-Dollak et al., 2018; Yu et al., 2018), data-driven approaches have dominated the field, in which deep learning based models achieve the best performance in both strongly (Hwang et al., 2019; Zhang et al., 2019; Guo et al., 2019) and weakly (Liang et al., 2017; Min et al., 2019) supervised settings. However, most of existing text-to-SQL datasets include only questions that can be translated into a valid SQL query. Spider (Finegan-Dollak et al., 2018) specifically controlled question clarify during data collection to exclude poorly phrased and ambiguous questions. WikiSQL (Zhong et al., 2017) was constructed on top of manually written synchronous grammars, and the mapping between its questions and SQL queries can be effectively resolved via lexical matching in vector space (Hwang et al., 2019). CoSQL (Yu et al., 2019a) is by far the only existing corpus to our knowledge which entables data-driven modeling and evaluation of untranslatable question detection. Yet the dataset is of context-dependent nature and contains untranslatable questions of limited variety. We fill in this gap by proposing PHOTON to cover a diverse set of untranslatable user input in text-to-SQL.

Noisy User Input in Semantic Parsing. Despite being absent from most large-scale text-to-SQL benchmarks, noisy user input has been frequently encountered and battled with by the semantic parsing community. Underspecification (Archangeli, 1988) and vagueness (Varzi, 2001) have solid linguistic theory foundation. Lexicon-based semantic parsers (Zettlemoyer and Collins, 2005; Roberts and Patra, 2017) may reject the input if the lexicon match is unsuccessful. Other approaches for handling untranslatable user input include inference and generating defaults (Setlur et al., 2019), paraphrasing (Arthur et al., 2015, 2016), verification (Arthur et al., 2015) and confidence estimation (Dong et al., 2018). We adopt a data-augmentation and discriminative learning based approach, which has demonstrated superior performance in related domains (Rajpurkar et al., 2018)

6 Conclusion and Future Work

We present PHOTON, a robust modular cross-domain text-to-SQL system, consisting of semantic parser, untranslatable question detector, human-in-the-loop question corrector, and natural language response generator. PHOTON has the potential to scale up to hundreds of different domains. It is the first cross-domain text-to-SQL system designed towards industrial applications with rich features, and bridges the demand of sophisticated database analysis and people without any SQL background knowledge.

The current PHOTON system is still a prototype, with very limited user interactions and functions. We will continue to add more features to PHOTON, such as voice input, spelling checking, and visualizing the output when appropriate to inspect the translation process. We also plan to improve the performance of core models in PHOTON, such as semantic parsing (text-to-SQL), response generation (table-to-text) and context-aware user interaction (text-to-text). A comprehensive evaluation will also be conducted among the users of our system.

References

Diana Archangeli. 1988. Aspects of underspecification theory. *Phonology*, 5(2):183–207.

Philip Arthur, Graham Neubig, Sakriani Sakti, and Satoshi Nakamura. 2016. Semantic parsing of ambiguous input using multi synchronous grammars.

Philip Arthur, Graham Neubig, Sakriani Sakti, Tomoki Toda, and Satoshi Nakamura. 2015. Semantic parsing of ambiguous input through paraphrasing and verification. *TACL*, 3:571–584.

Núria Bertomeu, Hans Uszkoreit, Anette Frank, Hans-Ulrich Krieger, and Brigitte Jörg. 2006. Contextual phenomena and thematic relations in database QA dialogues: results from a wizard-of-Oz experiment. In *Proceedings of the Interactive Question Answering Workshop at HLT-NAACL 2006*, pages 1–8, New York, NY, USA. Association for Computational Linguistics.

Ben Bogin, Jonathan Berant, and Matt Gardner. 2019a. Representing schema structure with graph neural networks for text-to-sql parsing. In *Proceedings of the 57th Conference of the Association for Computational Linguistics, ACL 2019, Florence, Italy, July 28- August 2, 2019, Vol. 1*, pages 4560–4565.

Ben Bogin, Matt Gardner, and Jonathan Berant. 2019b. Global reasoning over database structures for text-to-sql parsing. *CoRR*, abs/1908.11214.

Pawel Budzianowski, Tsung-Hsien Wen, Bo-Hsiang Tseng, Iñigo Casanueva, Stefan Ultes, Osman Ramadan, and Milica Gasic. 2018. Multiwoz - A large-scale multi-domain wizard-of-oz dataset for task-oriented dialogue modelling. In *Proceedings of the 2018 Conference on Empirical Methods in Natural Language Processing, Brussels, Belgium, October 31 - November 4, 2018*, pages 5016–5026.

DongHyun Choi, Myeong Cheol Shin, EungGyun Kim, and Dong Ryeol Shin. 2020. RYANSQL: recursively applying sketch-based slot fillings for complex text-to-sql in cross-domain databases. *CoRR*, abs/2004.03125.

Deborah A. Dahl, Madeleine Bates, Michael Brown, William M. Fisher, Kate Hunicke-Smith, David S. Pallett, Christine Pao, Alexander I. Rudnicky, and Elizabeth Shriberg. 1994. Expanding the scope of the ATIS task: The ATIS-3 corpus. In *Human Language Technology, Proceedings of a Workshop held at Plainsboro, New Jerey, USA, March 8-11, 1994*.

Jacob Devlin, Ming-Wei Chang, Kenton Lee, and Kristina Toutanova. 2019. BERT: pre-training of deep bidirectional transformers for language understanding. In *Proceedings of the 2019 Conference of the North American Chapter of the Association for Computational Linguistics: Human Language Technologies, NAACL-HLT 2019, Minneapolis, MN, USA, June 2-7, 2019, Volume 1*, pages 4171–4186.

Li Dong and Mirella Lapata. 2016. Language to logical form with neural attention. In *Proceedings of the 54th Annual Meeting of the Association for Computational Linguistics, ACL 2016, August 7-12, 2016, Berlin, Germany, Volume 1: Long Papers*. The Association for Computer Linguistics.

Li Dong and Mirella Lapata. 2018. Coarse-to-fine decoding for neural semantic parsing. In *Proceedings of the 56th Annual Meeting of the Association for Computational Linguistics, ACL 2018, Melbourne, Australia, July 15-20, 2018, Volume 1: Long Papers*, pages 731–742.

Li Dong, Chris Quirk, and Mirella Lapata. 2018. Confidence modeling for neural semantic parsing. In (Gurevych and Miyao, 2018), pages 743–753.

Catherine Finegan-Dollak, Jonathan K. Kummerfeld, Li Zhang, Karthik Ramanathan, Sesh Sadasivam, Rui Zhang, and Dragomir R. Radev. 2018. Improving text-to-sql evaluation methodology. In (Gurevych and Miyao, 2018), pages 351–360.

Jiaqi Guo, Zecheng Zhan, Yan Gao, Yan Xiao, Jian-Guang Lou, Ting Liu, and Dongmei Zhang. 2019. Towards complex text-to-sql in cross-domain database with intermediate representation. In *Proceedings of the 57th Conference of the Association for Computational Linguistics, ACL 2019, Florence, Italy, July 28- August 2, 2019, Volume 1: Long Papers*, pages 4524–4535.

Iryna Gurevych and Yusuke Miyao, editors. 2018. *Proceedings of the 56th Annual Meeting of the Association for Computational Linguistics, ACL 2018, Melbourne, Australia, July 15-20, 2018, Volume 1: Long Papers*. Association for Computational Linguistics.

Charles T. Hemphill, John J. Godfrey, and George R. Doddington. 1990. The ATIS spoken language systems pilot corpus. In *Speech and Natural Language: Proceedings of a Workshop Held at Hidden Valley, Pennsylvania, USA, June 24-27, 1990*.

Wonseok Hwang, Jinyeung Yim, Seunghyun Park, and Minjoon Seo. 2019. A comprehensive exploration on wikisql with table-aware word contextualization. *CoRR*, abs/1902.01069.

Amol Kelkar, Rohan Relan, Vaishali Bhardwaj, Saurabh Vaichal, and Peter Relan. 2020. Bertrand-dr: Improving text-to-sql using a discriminative re-ranker. *arXiv preprint arXiv:2002.00557*.

Diederik P. Kingma and Jimmy Ba. 2015. Adam: A method for stochastic optimization. In *3rd International Conference on Learning Representations, ICLR 2015, San Diego, CA, USA, May 7-9, 2015, Conference Track Proceedings*.

Anna Korhonen, David R. Traum, and Lluís Màrquez, editors. 2019. *Proceedings of the 57th Conference of the Association for Computational Linguistics, ACL 2019, Florence, Italy, July 28- August 2, 2019, Volume 1: Long Papers*. Association for Computational Linguistics.

Fei Li and Hosagrahar Visvesvaraya Jagadish. 2014. Nalir: an interactive natural language interface for querying relational databases. In *International Conference on Management of Data, SIGMOD 2014, Snowbird, UT, USA, June 22-27, 2014*, pages 709–712. ACM.

Chen Liang, Jonathan Berant, Quoc V. Le, Kenneth D. Forbus, and Ni Lao. 2017. Neural symbolic machines: Learning semantic parsers on freebase with weak supervision. In *Proceedings of the 55th Annual Meeting of the Association for Computational Linguistics, ACL 2017, Vancouver, Canada, July 30 - August 4, Volume 1: Long Papers*, pages 23–33. Association for Computational Linguistics.

Kevin Lin, Ben Bogin, Mark Neumann, Jonathan Berant, and Matt Gardner. 2019. Grammar-based neural text-to-sql generation. *CoRR*, abs/1905.13326.

Tianyu Liu, Fuli Luo, Pengcheng Yang, Wei Wu, Baobao Chang, and Zhifang Sui. 2019. Towards comprehensive description generation from factual attribute-value tables. In (Korhonen et al., 2019), pages 5985–5996.

Thang Luong, Hieu Pham, and Christopher D. Manning. 2015. Effective approaches to attention-based neural machine translation. In *Proceedings of the 2015 Conference on Empirical Methods in Natural Language Processing, EMNLP 2015, Lisbon, Portugal, September 17-21, 2015*, pages 1412–1421.

Sewon Min, Danqi Chen, Hannaneh Hajishirzi, and Luke Zettlemoyer. 2019. A discrete hard EM approach for weakly supervised question answering. *CoRR*, abs/1909.04849.

Ana-Maria Popescu, Oren Etzioni, and Henry A. Kautz. 2003. Towards a theory of natural language interfaces to databases. In *Proceedings of the 8th International Conference on Intelligent User Interfaces, IUI 2003, Miami, FL, USA, January 12-15, 2003*, pages 149–157. ACM.

Pranav Rajpurkar, Robin Jia, and Percy Liang. 2018. Know what you don't know: Unanswerable questions for squad. In *Proceedings of the 56th Annual Meeting of the Association for Computational Linguistics, ACL 2018, Melbourne, Australia, July 15-20, 2018, Volume 2: Short Papers*, pages 784–789.

Kirk Roberts and Braja Gopal Patra. 2017. A semantic parsing method for mapping clinical questions to logical forms. In *AMIA 2017, American Medical Informatics Association Annual Symposium, Washington, DC, USA, November 4-8, 2017*. AMIA.

Abigail See, Peter J. Liu, and Christopher D. Manning. 2017a. Get to the point: Summarization with pointer-generator networks. In *Proceedings of the 55th Annual Meeting of the Association for Computational Linguistics, ACL 2017, Vancouver, Canada, July 30 - August 4, Volume 1: Long Papers*, pages 1073–1083.

Abigail See, Peter J. Liu, and Christopher D. Manning. 2017b. Get to the point: Summarization with pointer-generator networks. In *Proceedings of the 55th Annual Meeting of the Association for Computational Linguistics (Volume 1: Long Papers)*, pages 1073–1083, Vancouver, Canada. Association for Computational Linguistics.

Vidya Setlur, Sarah E. Battersby, Melanie Tory, Rich Gossweiler, and Angel X. Chang. 2016. Eviza: A natural language interface for visual analysis. In *Proceedings of the 29th Annual Symposium on User Interface Software and Technology, UIST 2016, Tokyo, Japan, October 16-19, 2016*, pages 365–377. ACM.

Vidya Setlur, Melanie Tory, and Alex Djalali. 2019. Inferencing underspecified natural language utterances in visual analysis. In *Proceedings of the 24th International Conference on Intelligent User Interfaces, IUI 2019, Marina del Ray, CA, USA, March 17-20, 2019*, pages 40–51. ACM.

Ilya Sutskever, Oriol Vinyals, and Quoc V. Le. 2014. Sequence to sequence learning with neural networks. In *Advances in Neural Information Processing Systems 27: Annual Conference on Neural Information Processing Systems 2014, December 8-13 2014, Montreal, Quebec, Canada*, pages 3104–3112.

Achille C Varzi. 2001. Vagueness, logic, and ontology.

Chenglong Wang, Po-Sen Huang, Alex Polozov, Marc Brockschmidt, and Rishabh Singh. 2018. Execution-guided neural program decoding. *CoRR*, abs/1807.03100.

Thomas Wolf, Lysandre Debut, Victor Sanh, Julien Chaumond, Clement Delangue, Anthony Moi, Pierric Cistac, Tim Rault, R'emi Louf, Morgan Funtowicz, and Jamie Brew. 2019. Huggingface's transformers: State-of-the-art natural language processing. *ArXiv*, abs/1910.03771.

Ziyu Yao, Yu Su, Huan Sun, and Wen-tau Yih. 2019. Model-based interactive semantic parsing: A unified framework and A text-to-sql case study. In *Proceedings of the 2019 Conference on Empirical Methods in Natural Language Processing and the 9th International Joint Conference on Natural Language Processing, EMNLP-IJCNLP 2019, Hong Kong, China, November 3-7, 2019*, pages 5446–5457. Association for Computational Linguistics.

Tao Yu, Rui Zhang, Heyang Er, Suyi Li, Eric Xue, Bo Pang, Xi Victoria Lin, Yi Chern Tan, Tianze Shi, Zihan Li, Youxuan Jiang, Michihiro Yasunaga, Sungrok Shim, Tao Chen, Alexander Richard Fabbri, Zifan Li, Luyao Chen, Yuwen Zhang, Shreya Dixit, Vincent Zhang, Caiming Xiong, Richard Socher, Walter S. Lasecki, and Dragomir R. Radev. 2019a. Cosql: A conversational text-to-sql challenge towards cross-domain natural language interfaces to databases. *CoRR*, abs/1909.05378.

Tao Yu, Rui Zhang, Kai Yang, Michihiro Yasunaga, Dongxu Wang, Zifan Li, James Ma, Irene Li, Qingning Yao, Shanelle Roman, Zilin Zhang, and Dragomir R. Radev. 2018. Spider: A large-scale human-labeled dataset for complex and cross-domain semantic parsing and text-to-sql task. In *Proceedings of the 2018 Conference on Empirical Methods in Natural Language Processing, Brussels, Belgium, Oct 31 - Nov 4, 2018*, pages 3911–3921.

Tao Yu, Rui Zhang, Michihiro Yasunaga, Yi Chern Tan, Xi Victoria Lin, Suyi Li, Heyang Er, Irene Li, Bo Pang, Tao Chen, Emily Ji, Shreya Dixit, David Proctor, Sungrok Shim, Jonathan Kraft, Vincent Zhang, Caiming Xiong, Richard Socher, and Dragomir R. Radev. 2019b. Sparc: Cross-domain semantic parsing in context. In (Korhonen et al., 2019), pages 4511–4523.

John M. Zelle and Raymond J. Mooney. 1996. Learning to parse database queries using inductive logic programming. In *Proceedings of the Thirteenth National Conference on Artificial Intelligence and Eighth Innovative Applications of Artificial Intelligence Conference, AAAI 96, IAAI 96, Portland, Oregon, USA, August 4-8, 1996, Volume 2.*, pages 1050–1055.

Rowan Zellers, Yonatan Bisk, Roy Schwartz, and Yejin Choi. 2018. SWAG: A large-scale adversarial dataset for grounded commonsense inference. In *Proceedings of the 2018 Conference on Empirical Methods in Natural Language Processing, Brussels, Belgium, October 31 - November 4, 2018*, pages 93–104. Association for Computational Linguistics.

Luke S. Zettlemoyer and Michael Collins. 2005. Learning to map sentences to logical form: Structured classification with probabilistic categorial grammars. In *UAI '05, Proceedings of the 21st Conference in Uncertainty in Artificial Intelligence, Edinburgh, Scotland, July 26-29, 2005*, pages 658–666. AUAI Press.

Rui Zhang, Tao Yu, Heyang Er, Sungrok Shim, Eric Xue, Xi Victoria Lin, Tianze Shi, Caiming Xiong, Richard Socher, and Dragomir R. Radev. 2019. Editing-based SQL query generation for cross-domain context-dependent questions. *CoRR*, abs/1909.00786.

Victor Zhong, Caiming Xiong, and Richard Socher. 2017. Seq2sql: Generating structured queries from natural language using reinforcement learning. *CoRR*, abs/1709.00103.

A Appendices

A.1 Construct Untranslatable Questions

Table 4 shows a summary of different types of untranslatable questions based on analysis of CoSQL (Yu et al., 2019a) and Multi-WOZ (Budzianowski et al., 2018).

Table 5 shows examples of applying question-side and schema-side transformations to convert a translatable question from existing text-to-SQL datasets to an untranslatable question.

Reason	Description	Example
Underspecification	Input does not specify which data entries/attributes to query.	Q: What is the total? Schema: ||Course_ID||Staring_Data||Course||…
Overspecification	Input asks for information that cannot be found in the DB.	Q: What is the name of the singer with the largest **net worth**? Schema: ||Singer_ID||Name||Birth_Year||Citizenship||
Ambiguity & Vagueness	Input contains ambiguous or vague expressions.	Q: Show me homes with **good** schools Schema: ||Address||Community||School Name||School Rating||
Beyond representation scope of SQL	Input asks for information that cannot be obtained by SQL logic.	Q: What is the **trend** of housing price this year? Schema: ||House ID||Location||Price||Number of amenties||
Not a query	Input is not a linguistically valid question.	Q: Cyrus teaches physics in department.
Others	Other cases that the question cannot be translated.	Q: How many **Russias** have Summer's transfer window? Schema: ||Name||Country||Type||Transfer Window||Transfer Fee||

Table 4: Types of untranslatable questions in text-to-SQL identified from manual analysis of CoSQL (Yu et al., 2019a) and Multi-WOZ (Budzianowski et al., 2018). A question span that is problematic for the translation is highlighted when applicable.

Transformation		Original data	Transformed data	Confusing text span
Question	Swap	Q1: How many *conductors* are there? S1: || Conductor_ID || Name || Age || Nationlity|| Year_of_Work ||	Q1: How many soloists are there ?	soloists
		Q2: What are the maximum and minimum values of *area codes* ? S2: || Vote_ID || Phone_Number || Area_Code || State || Created ||	Q2: What are the maximum and minimum values of types?	types
	Drop	Q1: How many *countries* exist? S1: || CoutryId || CountryName || Continent ||	Q1: How many are there?	WHOLE SENTENCE
		Q2: What is the *official language* spoken in the country whose head of state is Beatrix? S2: || CountryCode || HeadOfState || Captital || Language || IsOfficial || Percentage ||	Q2: What are the people in the country where Beatrix is located?	WHOLE SENTENCE
Schema Drop		Q1: How much *surface area* do the countires in the Carribean cover together? S1: || Name ||Continent || Region || *SurfaceArea* || Population || LifeExpectancy ||	S1: || Name ||Continent || Region || Population || LifeExpectancy ||	surface area
		Q2: Find the name and *age* of the visitor who bought the most tickets at once. S2: ||Customer_ID||Name||Level_of_membership|| *Age* ||	S2: ||Customer_ID||Name||Level_of_membership||	age

Table 5: Examples of question-side and schema-side transformations for generating training data for untranslatable question detection. Let Q denote the question and S denote the schema. For each transformation, we provide two examples, i.e., (Q1, S1) and (Q2, S2). The italic and bold fonts highlight phrases before and after transformations.

Interactive Task Learning from GUI-Grounded Natural Language Instructions and Demonstrations

Toby Jia-Jun Li, Tom M. Mitchell, Brad A. Myers
School of Computer Science
Carnegie Mellon University
{tobyli, tom.mitchell, bam}@cs.cmu.edu

Abstract

We show SUGILITE, an intelligent task automation agent that can learn new tasks and relevant associated concepts interactively from the user's natural language instructions and demonstrations, using the graphical user interfaces (GUIs) of third-party mobile apps. This system provides several interesting features: (1) it allows users to teach new task procedures and concepts through verbal instructions together with demonstration of the steps of a script using GUIs; (2) it supports users in clarifying their intents for demonstrated actions using GUI-grounded verbal instructions; (3) it infers parameters of tasks and their possible values in utterances using the hierarchical structures of the underlying app GUIs; and (4) it generalizes taught concepts to different contexts and task domains. We describe the architecture of the SUGILITE system, explain the design and implementation of its key features, and show a prototype in the form of a conversational assistant on Android.

1 Introduction

Interactive task learning (ITL) is an emerging research topic that focuses on enabling task automation agents to learn new tasks and their corresponding relevant concepts through natural interaction with human users (Laird et al., 2017). This topic is also known as *end user development* (EUD) for task automation (Ko et al., 2011; Myers et al., 2017). Work in this domain includes both physical agents (e.g., robots) that learn tasks that might involve sensing and manipulating objects in the real world (Chai et al., 2018; Argall et al., 2009), as well as software agents that learn how to perform tasks through software interfaces (Azaria et al., 2016; Allen et al., 2007; Labutov et al., 2018; Leshed et al., 2008). This paper focuses on the latter category.

A particularly useful application of ITL is for conversational virtual assistants (e.g., Apple Siri, Google Assistant, Amazon Alexa). These systems have been widely adopted by end users to perform tasks in a variety of domains through natural language conversation. However, a key limitation of these systems is that their task fulfillment and language understanding capabilities are limited to a small set of pre-programmed tasks (Li et al., 2018b; Labutov et al., 2018). This limited support is not adequate for the diverse "long-tail" of user needs and preferences (Li et al., 2017a). Although some software agents provide APIs to enable third-party developers to develop new "skills" for them, this requires significant programming expertise and relevant APIs, and therefore is not usable by the vast majority of end users.

Natural language instructions play a key role in some ITL systems for virtual assistants, because this modality represents an natural way for humans to teach new tasks (often to other humans), and has a low learning barrier compared to existing textual or visual programming languages for task automation. Some prior systems (Azaria et al., 2016; Labutov et al., 2018; Le et al., 2013; Srivastava et al., 2017, 2018) relied solely natural language instruction, while others (Allen et al., 2007; Kirk and Laird, 2019; Sereshkeh et al., 2020) also used demonstrations of direct manipulations to supplement the natural language instructions. We surveyed the prior work, and identified the following five key design challenges:

1. **Usability**: The system should be usable for users without significant programming expertise. It should be easy and intuitive to use with a low learning barrier. This requires careful design of the dialog flow to best match the user's natural model of task instruction.

2. **Applicability**: The system should handle a

Proceedings of the 58th Annual Meeting of the Association for Computational Linguistics, pages 215–223
July 5 - July 10, 2020. ©2020 Association for Computational Linguistics

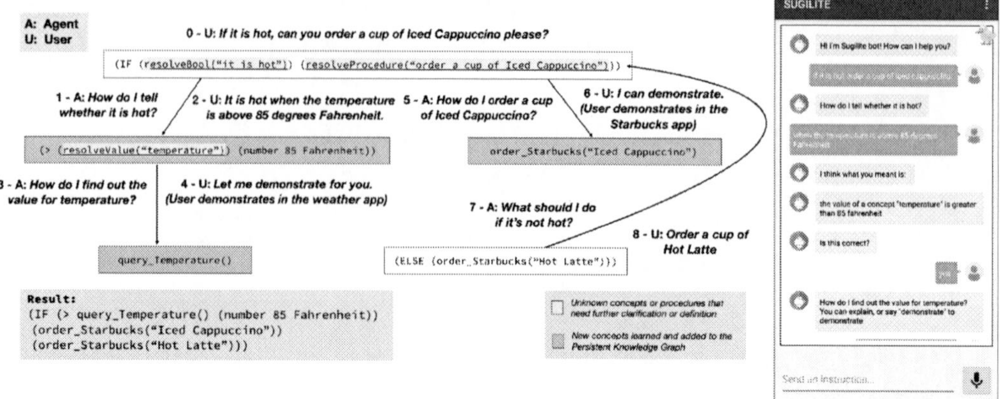

Figure 1: An example dialog structure while SUGILITE learns a new task that contains a conditional and new concepts. The numbers indicate the sequence of the utterances. The screenshot on the right shows the conversational interface during these steps.

wide range of common and long-tail tasks across different domains. Many existing systems can only work with pre-specified task domains (Labutov et al., 2018; Azaria et al., 2016; Gulwani and Marron, 2014), or services that provide open API access to their functionalities (Campagna et al., 2017; Le et al., 2013). This limits the applicability of those systems to a smaller subset of tasks.

The same problem also applies to the language understanding capability of the system. It should be able to understand, ground, and act upon instructions in different task domains (e.g., different phone apps) without requiring pre-built parsers for each domain.

3. **Generalizability**: The system should learn generalized procedures and concepts to handle new task contexts that go beyond the example context used for instruction. This includes inferring parameters of tasks, allowing the use of different parameter values, and adapting learned concepts to new task domains.

4. **Flexibility**: The system should be sufficiently expressive to allow users to specify flexible rules, conditions, and other control structures that reflect their intentions.

5. **Robustness**: The system should be resilient to minor changes in target applications, and be able to recover from errors caused by previously unseen or unexpected situations, possibly with some help from the user.

To address these challenges, we present the prototype of a new task automation agent named SUGILITE[1][2]. This prototype integrates and implements the results from several of our prior research works (Li et al., 2017a, 2018a, 2017b; Li and Riva, 2018; Li et al., 2019), and we are current preparing for a field deployment study with this prototype. The implementation of our system is also open-sourced on GitHub[3]. The high-level approach used in SUGILITE is to combine conversational natural language instructions with demonstrations on mobile app GUIs, and to use each of the two modalities to disambiguate, ground, and supplement the user's inputs from the other modality through mixed-initiative interactions.

2   System Overview

This section explains how SUGILITE learns new tasks and concepts from the multi-modal interactive instructions from the users.

The user starts with speaking a command. The command can describe either an action (e.g., "check the weather") or an automation rule with a condition (e.g., "If it is hot, order a cup of Iced Cappuccino"). Suppose that the agent has no prior knowledge in any of the involved task

---

[1]Sugilite is a gemstone, and here stands for **S**martphone **U**sers **G**enerating **I**ntelligent **L**ikeable **I**nterfaces **T**hrough **E**xamples.

[2]A demo video is available at https://www.youtube.com/watch?v=tdHEk-GeaqE

[3]https://github.com/tobyli/Sugilite_development

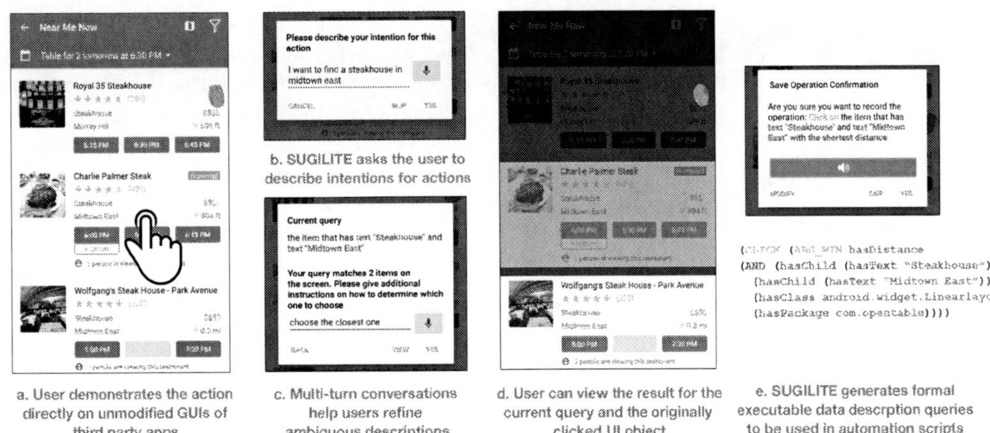


```
(CLICK (ARG_MIN hasDistance
(AND (hasChild (hasText "Steakhouse"))
   (hasChild (hasText "Midtown East"))
   (hasClass android.widget.Linearlayout)
   (hasPackage com.opentable)))))
```

a. User demonstrates the action directly on unmodified GUIs of third party apps

b. SUGILITE asks the user to describe intentions for actions

c. Multi-turn conversations help users refine ambiguous descriptions

d. User can view the result for the current query and the originally clicked UI object

e. SUGILITE generates formal executable data descrption queries to be used in automation scripts

Figure 2: The screenshots of SUGILITE's demonstration mechanism and its multi-modal mixed-initiative intent clarification process for the demonstrated actions.

domains, then it will recursively resolve the unknown concepts and procedures used in the command. Although it does not know these concepts, it can recognize the structure of the command (e.g., conditional), and parse each part of the command into the corresponding typed `resolve` functions, as shown in Figure 1. SUGILITE uses a grammar-based executable semantic parsing architecture (Liang, 2016); therefore its conversation flow operates on the recursive execution of the `resolve` functions. Since the `resolve` functions are typed, the agent can generate prompts based on their types (e.g., "How do I tell whether..." for `resolveBool` and "How do I find out the value for..." for `resolveValue`).

When the SUGILITE agent reaches the `resolve` function for a value query or a procedure, it asks the users if they can demonstrate them. The users can then demonstrate how they would normally look up the value, or perform the procedure manually with existing mobile apps on the phone by direct manipulation (Figure 2a). For any ambiguous demonstrated action, the user verbally explains the intent behind the action through multi-turn conversations with the help from an interaction proxy overlay that guides the user to focus on providing more effective input (see Figure 2bcde, more details in Section 3.2). When the user demonstrates a value query (e.g., finding out the value of the temperature), SUGILITE highlights the GUI elements showing values with the compatible types (see Figure 3) to assist the user in finding the appropriate GUI element during the demonstration.

All user-instructed value concepts, Boolean concepts, and procedures automatically get generalized by SUGILITE. The procedures are parameterized so that they can be reused with different parameter values in the future. For example, for Utterance 8 in Figure 1, the user does not need to demonstrate again since the system can invoke the newly-learned `order_Starbucks` function with a different parameter value (details in Section 3.3). The learned concepts and value queries are also generalized so that the system recognizes the different definitions of concepts like "hot" and value queries like "temperature" in different contexts (details in Section 3.4).

3 Key Features

3.1 Using Demonstrations in Natural Language Instructions

SUGILITE allows users to use demonstrations to teach the agent any unknown procedures and concepts in their natural language instructions. As discussed earlier, a major challenge in ITL is that understanding natural language instructions and carrying out the tasks accordingly require having knowledge in the specific task domains. Our use of programming by demonstration (PBD) is an effective way to address this "out-of-domain" problem in both the task-fulfillment and the natural language understanding processes (Li et al., 2018b). In SUGILITE, procedural actions are represented as sequences of GUI operations, and declarative con-

Figure 3: The user teaches the value concept "commute time" by demonstrating querying the value in Google Maps. SUGILITE highlights all the duration values on the Google Maps GUI.

cepts can be represented as references to GUI contents. This approach supports ITL for a wide range of tasks – virtually anything that can be performed with one or more existing third-party mobile apps.

Our prior study (Li et al., 2019) also found that the availability of app GUI references can result in end users providing clearer natural language commands. In one study where we asked participants to instruct an intelligent agent to complete everyday computing tasks in natural language, the participants who saw screenshots of relevant apps used *fewer* unclear, vague, or ambiguous concepts in their verbal instructions than those who did not see the screenshots. Details of the study design and the results can be found in Li et al. (2019).

3.2 Spoken Intent Clarification for Demonstrated Actions

A major limitation of demonstrations is that they are too literal, and are therefore brittle to any changes in the task context. They encapsulate *what* the user did, but not *why* the user did it. When the context changes, the agent often may not know what to do, due to this lack of understanding of the user intents behind their demonstrated actions. This is known as the *data description problem* in the PBD community, and it is regarded as a key problem in PBD research (Cypher and Halbert, 1993; Lieberman, 2001). For example, just looking at the action shown in Figure 2a, one cannot tell if the user meant "the restaurant with the most

reviews", "the promoted restaurant", "the restaurant with 1,000 bonus points", "the cheapest Steakhouse", or any other criteria, so the system cannot generate a description for this action that accurately reflects the user's intent. A prior approach is to ask for multiple examples from the users (McDaniel and Myers, 1999), but this is often not feasible due to the user's inability to come up with useful and complete examples, and the amount of examples required for complex tasks (Myers and McDaniel, 2001; Lee et al., 2017).

SUGILITE's approach is to ask users to verbally explain their intent for the demonstrated actions using speech. Our formative study (Li et al., 2018a) found that end users were able to provide useful and generalizable explanations for the intents of their demonstrated actions. They also commonly used in their utterances semantic references to GUI contents (e.g., "the close by restaurant" for an entry showing the text "596 ft") and implicit spatial references (e.g., "the score for Lakers" for a text object that contains a numeric value and is right-aligned to another text object "Lakers").

Based on these findings, we designed and implemented a multi-modal mixed-initiative intent clarification mechanism for demonstrated actions. As shown in Figure 2, the user describes their intention in natural language, and iteratively refines the descriptions to remove ambiguity with the help of an interactive overlay (Figure 2d). The overlay highlights the result from executing the current data description query, and helps the user focus on explaining the key differences between the target object (highlighted in red) and the false positives (highlighted in yellow) of the query.

To ground the user's natural language explanations about GUI elements, SUGILITE represents each GUI screen as a *UI snapshot graph*. This graph captures the GUI elements' text labels, meta-information (including screen position, type, and package name), and the spatial (e.g., `nextTo`), hierarchical (e.g., `hasChild`), and semantic relations (e.g., `containsPrice`) among them (Figure 4). A semantic parser translates the user's explanation into a graph query on the UI snapshot graph, executes it on the graph, and verifies if the result matches the correct entity that the user originally demonstrated. The goal of this process is to generate a query that uniquely matches the target UI element and also reflects the user's underlying intent.

Our semantic parser uses a Floating Parser ar-

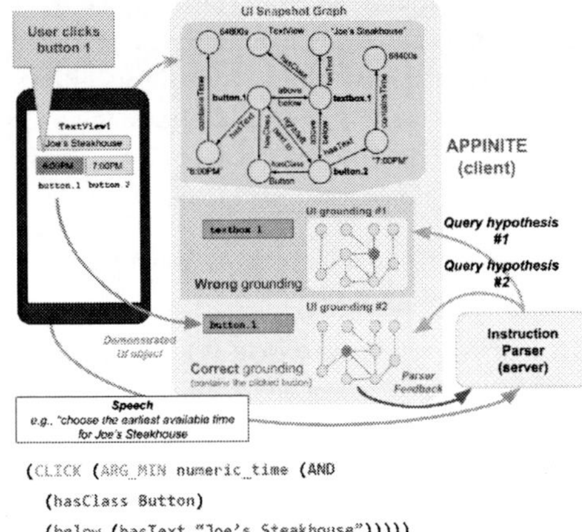


```
(CLICK (ARG_MIN numeric_time (AND
  (hasClass Button)
  (below (hasText "Joe's Steakhouse")))))
```

Figure 4: SUGILITE's instruction parsing and grounding process for intent clarifications illustrated on an example UI snapshot graph constructed from a simplified GUI snippet.

chitecture (Pasupat and Liang, 2015) and is implemented with the SEMPRE framework (Berant et al., 2013). We represent UI snapshot graph queries in a simple but flexible LISP-like query language (S-expressions) that can represent joins, conjunctions, superlatives and their compositions, constructed by the following 7 grammar rules:

$$E \to e; E \to S; S \to (\text{join } r\ E); S \to (\text{and } S\ S)$$

$$T \to (\text{ARG\_MAX } r\ S); T \to (\text{ARG\_MIN } r\ S); Q \to S \mid T$$

where Q is the root non-terminal of the query expression, e is a terminal that represents a UI object entity, r is a terminal that represents a relation, and the rest of the non-terminals are used for intermediate derivations. SUGILITE's language forms a subset of a more general formalism known as Lambda Dependency-based Compositional Semantics (Liang et al., 2013), which is a notationally simpler alternative to lambda calculus which is particularly well-suited for expressing queries over knowledge graphs. More technical details and the user evaluation are discussed in Li et al. (2018a).

3.3 Task Parameterization through GUI Grounding

Another way SUGILITE leverages GUI groundings in the natural language instructions is to infer task parameters and their possible values. This allows the agent to learn generalized procedures (e.g., to order *any kind of beverage* from Starbucks) from a demonstration of a specific instance of the task (e.g., ordering an iced cappuccino).

SUGILITE achieves this by comparing the user utterance (e.g., "order a cup of iced cappuccino") against the *data descriptions* of the target UI elements (e.g., click on the menu item that has the text "Iced Cappuccino") and the arguments (e.g., put "Iced Cappuccino" into a search box) of the demonstrated actions for matches. This process grounds different parts in the utterances to specific actions in the demonstrated procedure. It then analyzes the hierarchical structure of GUI at the time of demonstration, and looks for alternative GUI elements that are in parallel to the original target GUI element structurally. In this way, it extracts the other possible values for the identified parameter, such as the names of all the other drinks displayed in the same menu as "Iced Cappuccino"

The extracted sets of possible parameter values are also used for disambiguating the procedures to invoke, such as invoking the `order_Starbucks` procedure for the command "order a cup of *latte*", but invoking the `order_PapaJohns` procedure for the command "order a *cheese pizza*."

3.4 Generalizing the Learned Concepts

In addition to the procedures, SUGILITE also automatically generalizes the learned *concepts* in order to reuse parts of existing concepts as much as possible to avoid requiring users to perform redundant demonstrations (Li et al., 2019).

For Boolean concepts, SUGILITE assumes that the Boolean operation and the types of the arguments stay the same, but the arguments themselves may differ. For example, the concept "hot" used in Figure 1 can be generalize to "`arg0` is greater than `arg1`" where `arg0` and `arg1` can be value queries or constant values of the *temperature type*. This allows the various constant thresholds of temperature, or dynamic queries for temperatures depending on the specific task context. This mechanism allows concepts to be used across different contexts (e.g., determining whether to order iced coffee vs. whether to open the window) task domains (e.g., "the weather is hot" vs. "the oven is hot").

Similarly, named value queries (resolved from `resolveValue` such as "temperature" in Figure 1) can be generalized to have different implementations depending on the task domain. In "the temperature outside", `query_Temperature()`

can invoke the weather app, whereas in "the temperature of the oven" it can invoke the smart oven app to look up the current temperature of the oven (Li et al., 2017b).

4 Evaluation

We conducted several lab user studies to evaluate the usability, efficiency and effectiveness of SUG-ILITE. The results of these study showed that end users without significant programming expertise were able to successfully teach the agent the procedures of performing common tasks (e.g., ordering pizza, requesting Uber, checking sports score, ordering coffee) (Li et al., 2017a), conditional rules for triggering the tasks (Li et al., 2019), and concepts relevant to the tasks (e.g., the weather is *hot*, the traffic is *heavy*) (Li et al., 2019) using SUG-ILITE. The users were also able to clarify their intents when ambiguities arise (Li et al., 2018a). Most of our participants found SUGILITE easy and natural to use (Li et al., 2017a, 2018a, 2019). Efficiency wise, teaching a task usually took the user 3–6 times longer than how long it took to perform the task manually in our studies (Li et al., 2017a), which indicates that teaching a task using SUG-ILITE can save time for many repetitive tasks.

5 Discussion and Future Work

5.1 Using GUIs for Language Grounding

SUGILITE illustrates the great promise of using GUIs as a resource for grounding and understanding natural language instructions in ITL. The GUIs encapsulate rich knowledge about the flows of the underlying tasks and the properties and relations of relevant entities, so they can be used to bootstrap the domain-specific knowledge needed by ITL systems that rely on natural language instructions for learning. Users are also familiar with GUIs, which makes GUIs the ideal medium to which users can refer during task instructions. A major challenge in natural language instruction is that the users do not know what concepts or knowledge the agent already knows so that they can use it in their instructions (Li et al., 2019). Therefore, they often introduce additional unknown concepts that are either unnecessary or entirely beyond the capability of the agent (e.g., explaining "hot" as "when I'm sweating" when teaching the agent to "open the window when it is hot"). By using the app GUIs as the medium, the system can effectively constrain the users to refer to things

that can be found out from some app GUIs (e.g., "hot" can mean "the temperature is high"), which mostly overlaps with the "capability ceiling" of smartphone-based agents, and allows the users to define new concepts for the agent by referring to app GUIs (Li et al., 2017a, 2019).

5.2 More Robust Natural Language Understanding

The current version of SUGILITE uses a grammar-based executable semantic parser to understand the users' natural language explanations of their intents for the demonstrated actions. While this approach comes with many benefits, such as only requiring a small amount of training data and not relying on any domain knowledge, it has rigid patterns and therefore sometimes encounters problems with the flexible structures and varied expressions in the user utterances.

We are looking at alternative approaches for parsing natural language instructions into our domain-specific language (DSL) for representing data description queries and task execution procedures. A promising strategy is to take advantage of the abstract syntax tree (AST) structure in our DSL for constructing a neural parser (Xu et al., 2020; Yin and Neubig, 2017), which reduces the amount of training data needed and enforces the well-formedness of the output code.

The current model also only uses the semantic information from the local user instructions and their corresponding app GUIs. Another promising approach to enable more robust natural language understanding is to leverage the pre-trained general-purpose language models (e.g., BERT (Devlin et al., 2018)) to encode the user instructions and the information extracted from app GUIs.

5.3 Extracting Task Semantics from GUIs

An interesting future direction is to better extract semantics from app GUIs so that the user can focus on high-level task specifications and personal preferences without dealing with low-level mundane details (e.g., "buy 2 burgers" means setting the value of the textbox below the text "quantity" and next to the text "Burger" to be "2"). Some works have made early progress in this domain (Liu et al., 2018b; Deka et al., 2016; Chen et al., 2020) thanks to the availability of large datasets of GUIs like RICO (Deka et al., 2017). Recent reinforcement learning-based approaches and semantic parsing techniques have also shown promising results in learning models for navigating through GUIs for user-specified task objectives (Liu et al., 2018a; Pasupat et al., 2018). For ITL, an interesting future challenge is to combine these user-independent domain-agnostic machine-learned models with the user's personalized instructions for a specific task. This will likely require a new kind of mixed-initiative instruction (Horvitz, 1999) where the agent is more proactive in guiding the user and takes more initiative in the dialog. This could be supported by improved background knowledge and task models, and more flexible dialog frameworks that can handle the continuous refinement and uncertainty inherent in natural language interaction, and the variations in user goals. Collecting and aggregating personal task instructions across many users also introduce important concerns on user privacy, as discussed in (Li et al., 2020).

5.4 Multi-Modal Interactions in Conversational Learning

SUGILITE combines speech and direct manipulation to enable a "speak and point" interaction style, which has been studied since early interactive systems like Put-That-There (Bolt, 1980). As described in Section 3.2, a key pattern used in SUGILITE's multi-modal interface is *mutual disambiguation* (Oviatt, 1999) where it utilizes inputs in complementary modalities to infer robust and generalizable scripts that can accurately represent user intentions.

We are currently exploring other ways of using multi-modal interactions to supplement natural language instructions in ITL. A promising direction is to use GUI references to help with repairing conversational breakdowns (Beneteau et al., 2019; Ashktorab et al., 2019; Myers et al., 2018) caused by incorrect semantic parsing, intent classification, or entity recognition. Since GUIs encapsulate rich semantic information about the users' intents, the task flows, and the task constraints, we can potentially ask the users to point to the relevant GUI screens as a part of the error handling process, explaining the errors with references to the GUIs, and helping the system recover from the breakdowns.

6   Conclusion

We described SUGILITE, a task automation agent that can learn new tasks and relevant concepts interactively from users through their GUI-grounded natural language instructions and demonstrations.

This system provides capabilities such as intent clarification, task parameterization, and concept generalization. SUGILITE shows the promise of using app GUIs for grounding natural language instructions, and the effectiveness of resolving unknown concepts, ambiguities, and vagueness in natural language instructions using a mixed-initiative multi-modal approach.

Acknowledgments

This research was supported in part by Verizon and Oath through the InMind project, a J.P. Morgan Faculty Research Award, NSF grant IIS-1814472, and AFOSR grant FA95501710218. Any opinions, findings or recommendations expressed here are those of the authors and do not necessarily reflect views of the sponsors. We thank Amos Azaria, Igor Labutov, Xiaohan Nancy Li, Xiaoyi Zhang, Jingya Chen, and Marissa Radensky for their contributions to the development of this system.

References

James Allen, Nathanael Chambers, George Ferguson, Lucian Galescu, Hyuckchul Jung, Mary Swift, and William Taysom. 2007. PLOW: A Collaborative Task Learning Agent. In *Proceedings of the 22nd National Conference on Artificial Intelligence - Volume 2*, AAAI'07, pages 1514–1519, Vancouver, British Columbia, Canada. AAAI Press.

Brenna D. Argall, Sonia Chernova, Manuela Veloso, and Brett Browning. 2009. A Survey of Robot Learning from Demonstration. *Robot. Auton. Syst.*, 57(5):469–483.

Zahra Ashktorab, Mohit Jain, Q Vera Liao, and Justin D Weisz. 2019. Resilient chatbots: Repair strategy preferences for conversational breakdowns. In *Proceedings of the 2019 CHI Conference on Human Factors in Computing Systems*, page 254. ACM.

Amos Azaria, Jayant Krishnamurthy, and Tom M. Mitchell. 2016. Instructable Intelligent Personal Agent. In *Proc. The 30th AAAI Conference on Artificial Intelligence (AAAI)*, volume 4.

Erin Beneteau, Olivia K Richards, Mingrui Zhang, Julie A Kientz, Jason Yip, and Alexis Hiniker. 2019. Communication breakdowns between families and alexa. In *Proceedings of the 2019 CHI Conference on Human Factors in Computing Systems*, pages 1–13.

Jonathan Berant, Andrew Chou, Roy Frostig, and Percy Liang. 2013. Semantic parsing on freebase from question-answer pairs. In *Proceedings of the 2013 Conference on Empirical Methods in Natural Language Processing*, pages 1533–1544.

Richard A. Bolt. 1980. "Put-that-there": Voice and Gesture at the Graphics Interface. In *Proceedings of the 7th Annual Conference on Computer Graphics and Interactive Techniques*, SIGGRAPH '80, pages 262–270, New York, NY, USA. ACM.

Giovanni Campagna, Rakesh Ramesh, Silei Xu, Michael Fischer, and Monica S. Lam. 2017. Almond: The architecture of an open, crowdsourced, privacy-preserving, programmable virtual assistant. In *Proceedings of the 26th International Conference on World Wide Web*, pages 341–350.

Joyce Y Chai, Qiaozi Gao, Lanbo She, Shaohua Yang, Sari Saba-Sadiya, and Guangyue Xu. 2018. Language to action: Towards interactive task learning with physical agents. In *IJCAI*, pages 2–9.

Jieshan Chen, Chunyang Chen, Zhenchang Xing, Xiwei Xu, Liming Zhu, Guoqiang Li, and Jinshui Wang. 2020. Unblind your apps: Predicting natural-language labels for mobile gui components by deep learning. In *Proceedings of the 42nd International Conference on Software Engineering*, ICSE '20.

Allen Cypher and Daniel Conrad Halbert. 1993. *Watch what I do: programming by demonstration*. MIT press.

Biplab Deka, Zifeng Huang, Chad Franzen, Joshua Hibschman, Daniel Afergan, Yang Li, Jeffrey Nichols, and Ranjitha Kumar. 2017. Rico: A Mobile App Dataset for Building Data-Driven Design Applications. In *Proceedings of the 30th Annual ACM Symposium on User Interface Software and Technology*, UIST '17, pages 845–854, New York, NY, USA. ACM.

Biplab Deka, Zifeng Huang, and Ranjitha Kumar. 2016. ERICA: Interaction Mining Mobile Apps. In *Proceedings of the 29th Annual Symposium on User Interface Software and Technology*, UIST '16, pages 767–776, New York, NY, USA. ACM.

Jacob Devlin, Ming-Wei Chang, Kenton Lee, and Kristina Toutanova. 2018. Bert: Pre-training of deep bidirectional transformers for language understanding. *arXiv preprint arXiv:1810.04805*.

Sumit Gulwani and Mark Marron. 2014. Nlyze: Interactive programming by natural language for spreadsheet data analysis and manipulation. In *Proceedings of the 2014 ACM SIGMOD international conference on Management of data*, pages 803–814.

Eric Horvitz. 1999. Principles of mixed-initiative user interfaces. In *Proceedings of the SIGCHI conference on Human Factors in Computing Systems*, pages 159–166. ACM.

James R. Kirk and John E. Laird. 2019. Learning hierarchical symbolic representations to support interactive task learning and knowledge transfer. In *Proceedings of the Twenty-Eighth International Joint Conference on Artificial Intelligence, IJCAI-19*, pages 6095–6102. International Joint Conferences on Artificial Intelligence Organization.

Amy J. Ko, Robin Abraham, Laura Beckwith, Alan Blackwell, Margaret Burnett, Martin Erwig, Chris Scaffidi, Joseph Lawrance, Henry Lieberman, Brad Myers, Mary Beth Rosson, Gregg Rothermel, Mary Shaw, and Susan Wiedenbeck. 2011. The State of the Art in End-user Software Engineering. *ACM Comput. Surv.*, 43(3):21:1–21:44.

Igor Labutov, Shashank Srivastava, and Tom Mitchell. 2018. Lia: A natural language programmable personal assistant. In *Proceedings of the 2018 Conference on Empirical Methods in Natural Language Processing: System Demonstrations*, pages 145–150. Association for Computational Linguistics.

John E Laird, Kevin Gluck, John Anderson, Kenneth D Forbus, Odest Chadwicke Jenkins, Christian Lebiere, Dario Salvucci, Matthias Scheutz, Andrea Thomaz, Greg Trafton, et al. 2017. Interactive task learning. *IEEE Intelligent Systems*, 32(4):6–21.

Vu Le, Sumit Gulwani, and Zhendong Su. 2013. SmartSynth: Synthesizing Smartphone Automation Scripts from Natural Language. In *Proceeding of the 11th Annual International Conference on Mobile Systems, Applications, and Services*, MobiSys '13, pages 193–206, New York, NY, USA. ACM.

Tak Yeon Lee, Casey Dugan, and Benjamin B. Bederson. 2017. Towards Understanding Human Mistakes of Programming by Example: An Online User Study. In *Proceedings of the 22nd International Conference on Intelligent User Interfaces*, IUI '17, pages 257–261, New York, NY, USA. ACM.

Gilly Leshed, Eben M. Haber, Tara Matthews, and Tessa Lau. 2008. CoScripter: Automating & Sharing How-to Knowledge in the Enterprise. In *Proceedings of the SIGCHI Conference on Human Factors in Computing Systems*, CHI '08, pages 1719–1728, New York, NY, USA. ACM.

Toby Jia-Jun Li, Amos Azaria, and Brad A. Myers. 2017a. SUGILITE: Creating Multimodal Smartphone Automation by Demonstration. In *Proceedings of the 2017 CHI Conference on Human Factors in Computing Systems*, CHI '17, pages 6038–6049, New York, NY, USA. ACM.

Toby Jia-Jun Li, Jingya Chen, Brandon Canfield, and Brad A. Myers. 2020. Privacy-preserving script sharing in gui-based programming-by-demonstration systems. *Proc. ACM Hum.-Comput. Interact.*, 4(CSCW).

Toby Jia-Jun Li, Igor Labutov, Xiaohan Nancy Li, Xiaoyi Zhang, Wenze Shi, Tom M. Mitchell, and Brad A. Myers. 2018a. APPINITE: A Multi-Modal Interface for Specifying Data Descriptions in Programming by Demonstration Using Verbal Instructions. In *Proceedings of the 2018 IEEE Symposium on Visual Languages and Human-Centric Computing (VL/HCC 2018)*.

Toby Jia-Jun Li, Igor Labutov, Brad A. Myers, Amos Azaria, Alexander I. Rudnicky, and Tom M. Mitchell. 2018b. Teaching Agents When They Fail: End User Development in Goal-oriented Conversational Agents. In *Studies in Conversational UX Design*. Springer.

Toby Jia-Jun Li, Yuanchun Li, Fanglin Chen, and Brad A. Myers. 2017b. Programming IoT Devices by Demonstration Using Mobile Apps. In *End-User Development*, pages 3–17, Cham. Springer International Publishing.

Toby Jia-Jun Li, Marissa Radensky, Justin Jia, Kirielle Singarajah, Tom M. Mitchell, and Brad A. Myers. 2019. PUMICE: A Multi-Modal Agent that Learns Concepts and Conditionals from Natural Language and Demonstrations. In *Proceedings of the 32nd Annual ACM Symposium on User Interface Software and Technology (UIST 2019)*, UIST 2019. ACM.

Toby Jia-Jun Li and Oriana Riva. 2018. KITE: Building conversational bots from mobile apps. In *Proceedings of the 16th ACM International Conference on Mobile Systems, Applications, and Services (MobiSys 2018)*. ACM.

Percy Liang. 2016. Learning executable semantic parsers for natural language understanding. *Communications of the ACM*, 59(9):68–76.

Percy Liang, Michael I. Jordan, and Dan Klein. 2013. Learning dependency-based compositional semantics. *Computational Linguistics*, 39(2):389–446.

Henry Lieberman. 2001. *Your wish is my command: Programming by example*. Morgan Kaufmann.

Evan Zheran Liu, Kelvin Guu, Panupong Pasupat, and Percy Liang. 2018a. Reinforcement learning on web interfaces using workflow-guided exploration. In *International Conference on Learning Representations*.

Thomas F Liu, Mark Craft, Jason Situ, Ersin Yumer, Radomir Mech, and Ranjitha Kumar. 2018b. Learning design semantics for mobile apps. In *The 31st Annual ACM Symposium on User Interface Software and Technology*, pages 569–579. ACM.

Richard G. McDaniel and Brad A. Myers. 1999. Getting More out of Programming-by-demonstration. In *Proceedings of the SIGCHI Conference on Human Factors in Computing Systems*, CHI '99, pages 442–449, New York, NY, USA. ACM.

Brad A. Myers, Amy J. Ko, Chris Scaffidi, Stephen Oney, YoungSeok Yoon, Kerry Chang, Mary Beth Kery, and Toby Jia-Jun Li. 2017. Making End User Development More Natural. In *New Perspectives in End-User Development*, pages 1–22. Springer, Cham.

Brad A. Myers and Richard McDaniel. 2001. Sometimes you need a little intelligence, sometimes you need a lot. *Your Wish is My Command: Programming by Example. San Francisco, CA: Morgan Kaufmann Publishers*, pages 45–60.

Chelsea Myers, Anushay Furqan, Jessica Nebolsky, Karina Caro, and Jichen Zhu. 2018. Patterns for how users overcome obstacles in voice user interfaces. In *Proceedings of the 2018 CHI Conference on Human Factors in Computing Systems*, pages 1–7.

Sharon Oviatt. 1999. Mutual disambiguation of recognition errors in a multimodel architecture. In *Proceedings of the SIGCHI conference on Human Factors in Computing Systems*, pages 576–583. ACM.

Panupong Pasupat, Tian-Shun Jiang, Evan Liu, Kelvin Guu, and Percy Liang. 2018. Mapping natural language commands to web elements. In *Proceedings of the 2018 Conference on Empirical Methods in Natural Language Processing*, pages 4970–4976, Brussels, Belgium. Association for Computational Linguistics.

Panupong Pasupat and Percy Liang. 2015. Compositional Semantic Parsing on Semi-Structured Tables. In *Proceedings of the 53rd Annual Meeting of the Association for Computational Linguistics and the 7th International Joint Conference on Natural Language Processing*. ArXiv: 1508.00305.

Alborz Rezazadeh Sereshkeh, Gary Leung, Krish Perumal, Caleb Phillips, Minfan Zhang, Afsaneh Fazly, and Iqbal Mohomed. 2020. Vasta: a vision and language-assisted smartphone task automation system. In *Proceedings of the 25th International Conference on Intelligent User Interfaces*, pages 22–32.

Shashank Srivastava, Igor Labutov, and Tom Mitchell. 2017. Joint concept learning and semantic parsing from natural language explanations. In *Proceedings of the 2017 Conference on Empirical Methods in Natural Language Processing*, pages 1527–1536.

Shashank Srivastava, Igor Labutov, and Tom Mitchell. 2018. Zero-shot learning of classifiers from natural language quantification. In *Proceedings of the 56th Annual Meeting of the Association for Computational Linguistics (Volume 1: Long Papers)*, pages 306–316, Melbourne, Australia. Association for Computational Linguistics.

Frank F Xu, Zhengbao Jiang, Pengcheng Yin, Bogdan Vasilescu, and Graham Neubig. 2020. Incorporating external knowledge through pre-training for natural language to code generation. *arXiv preprint arXiv:2004.09015*.

Pengcheng Yin and Graham Neubig. 2017. A syntactic neural model for general-purpose code generation. In *Proceedings of the 55th Annual Meeting of the Association for Computational Linguistics (Volume 1: Long Papers)*, pages 440–450, Vancouver, Canada. Association for Computational Linguistics.

MIXINGBOARD:
a Knowledgeable Stylized Integrated Text Generation Platform

Xiang Gao   Michel Galley   Bill Dolan
Microsoft Research, Redmond, WA, USA
{xiag,mgalley,billdol}@microsoft.com

Abstract

We present MIXINGBOARD, a platform for quickly building demos with a focus on knowledge grounded stylized text generation. We unify existing text generation algorithms in a shared codebase and further adapt earlier algorithms for constrained generation. To borrow advantages from different models, we implement strategies for cross-model integration, from the token probability level to the latent space level. An interface to external knowledge is provided via a module that retrieves on-the-fly relevant knowledge from passages on the web or any document collection. A user interface for local development, remote webpage access, and a RESTful API are provided to make it simple for users to build their own demos [1].

1 Introduction

Neural text generation algorithms have seen great improvements over the past several years (Radford et al., 2019; Gao et al., 2019a). However each algorithm and neural model usually focuses on a specific task and may differ significantly from each other in terms of architecture, implementation, interface, and training domains. It is challenging to unify these algorithms theoretically, but a framework to organically integrate multiple algorithms and components can benefit the community in several ways, as it provides (1) a shared codebase to reproduce and compare the state-of-the-art algorithms from different groups without time consuming trial and errors, (2) a platform to experiment the cross-model integration of these algorithms, and (3) a framework to build demo quickly upon these components. This framework can be built upon existing deep learning libraries (Paszke et al., 2019;

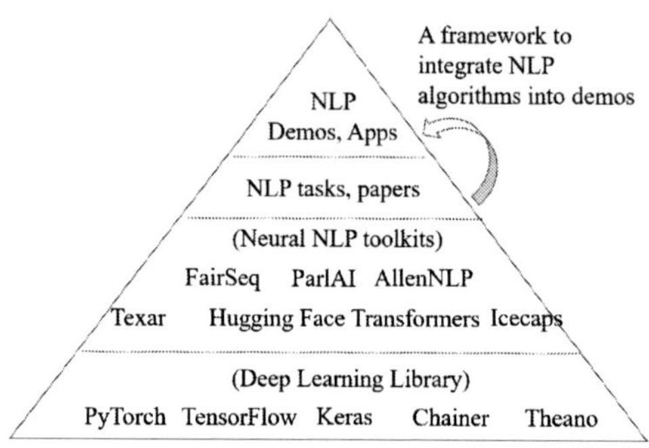

Figure 1: MIXINGBOARD is designed as a platform to organically and quickly integrate separate NLP algorithms into compelling demos

Abadi et al., 2015) and neural NLP toolkits (HuggingFace, 2019; Gardner et al., 2018; Hu et al., 2018; Ott et al., 2019; Shiv et al., 2019; Miller et al., 2017)[2], as illustrated in Fig. 1.

There are several challenges to do such integration. Firstly, engineering efforts are needed to unify the interface of different implementation. Secondly, a top-level manager needs to be designed to utilize different models together. Finally, different models are trained using different data with different performance. Cross-model integration, instead of calling each isolated model individually, can potentially improve the overall performance. In this work, we unified the models of different implementation in a single codebase, implemented demos as top-level managers to access different models, and provide strategies to allow more organic integration across the models, including token probability interpolation, cross-mode scoring, latent interpolation, and unified hypothesis ranking.

This work is also aimed to promote the development of grounded text generation. The exist-

---

[1] Source code available at github.com/microsoft/MixingBoard

[2] Although multiple libraries and toolkits are mentioned in Fig. 1, the current implementation is primarily based on PyTorch models

224

Proceedings of the 58th Annual Meeting of the Association for Computational Linguistics, pages 224–231
July 5 - July 10, 2020. ©2020 Association for Computational Linguistics

ing works focusing on the knowledge grounded text generation (Prabhumoye et al., 2019; Qin et al., 2019; Galley et al., 2019) usually assume the knowledge passage is given. However in practice this is not true. We provide the component to retrieve knowledge passage on-the-fly from web or customized document, to allow engineers or researchers test existing or new generation models. Keyphrase constrained generation (Hokamp and Liu, 2017) is another type of grounded generation, broadly speaking. Similarly the keyphrase needs to be provided to apply such constraints. We provide tools to extract constraints from knowledge passage or stylized corpus.

Finally, friendly user interface is a component usually lacking in the implementation of neural models but it is necessary for a demo-centric framework. We provide scripts to build local terminal demo, webpage demo, and RESTful API demo.

2 Design

Our goal is to build a framework that will allow users to quickly build text generation demos using existing modeling techniques. This design allows the framework to be almost agnostic to the ongoing development of text generation techniques (Gao et al., 2019a). Instead, we focus on the organic integration of models and the interfaces for the final demo/app.

From a top-down view, our design are bounded to two markets: text processing assistant, and conversational AI, as illustrated in Fig. 2. Two demos are present as examples in these domains: document auto-completion and Sherlock Holmes. We further breakdown these demos into several tasks, designed to be shared across different demos. We also designed several strategies to integrate multiple models to generate text. These strategies allow each model to plug-in without heavy constraints on the architecture of the models, as detailed in Section 4.

As the goal is not another deep learning NLP toolkit, we rely on existing ones (HuggingFace, 2019; Paszke et al., 2019; Gardner et al., 2018) and online API services Bing Web Search provided in Azure Cognitive Service[3] and TagME.[4] Similarly, most tasks are using existing algorithms: language modeling (Zhang et al., 2019; Radford et al.,

2019), knowledge grounded generation (Qin et al., 2019; Prabhumoye et al., 2019) or span retrieval (Seo et al., 2016; Devlin et al., 2018), style transfer (Gao et al., 2019c,b) and constrained generation (Hokamp and Liu, 2017).

3 Modules

3.1 Knowledge passage retrieval

We use the following free-text, unstructured text sources to retrieve relevant knowledge passage.

- Search engine. Free-text form "knowledge" is retrieved from the following sources 1) text snippets from the (customized) webpage search; 2) text snippets (customized) news search; 3) user-provided documents.
- Specialized websites. For certain preferred domains, e.g., wikipedia.org, we will further download the whole webpage (rather than just the text snippet returned from search engine) to obtain more text snippets.
- Users can also provide their customized knowledge base, like a README file, which can be updated on-the-fly, to allow the agent using latest knowledge.

User may select one or multiple sources listed above to obtain knowledge passage candidates. Then the text snippets are then ranked by relevancy as well as diversity.

3.2 Stylized synonym

We provide a component to retrieve synonym of given target style for a query word. This component is useful for the style transfer module (Section 3.4) as well as the constrained generation module (Section 3.7).

The similarity based on word2vec, $\text{sim}_{\text{word2vec}}$, is defined as the cosine similarity between the vectors of two words. The similarity based on human-edited dictionary, sim_{dict}, is defined as 1 if the candidate word in the synonym list of the query word, otherwise 0. The final similarity between the two words is defined as the weighted average of these two similarities:

$$\text{sim} = (1 - w_{\text{dict}})\,\text{sim}_{\text{word2vec}} + w_{\text{dict}}\,\text{sim}_{\text{dict}}$$

We only choose the candidate word with a similarity higher than certain threshold as the synonym of the query word. Then we calculate the style score of these synonym using a style classifier. We

---

[3] https://azure.microsoft.com/en-us/services/cognitive-services/
[4] https://tagme.d4science.org/tagme/

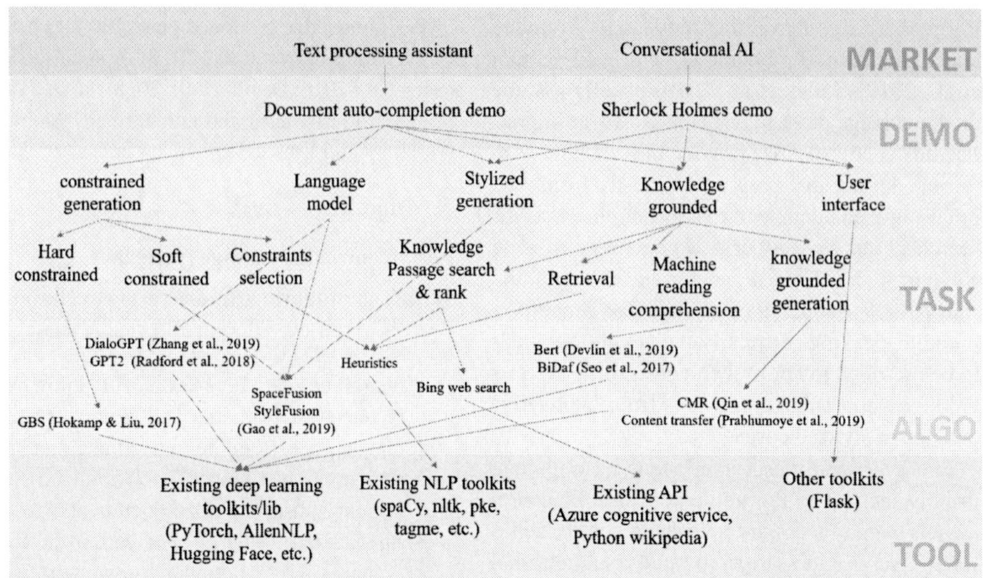

Figure 2: The architecture of MIXINGBOARD, consisting of layers from basic tools, algorithms, tasks to integrated demos with market into consideration.

provided a logistic regression model taking 1gram multi-hot vector as features, trained on non-stylized corpus vs. stylized corpus.

3.3 Latent interpolation

For a given two latent vectors, z_a and z_b, we expect the decoded results from the interpolated vector $z_i = uz_a + (1 - u)z_b$ can retain the desired features from both z_a and z_b. However this requires a interpolatable, smooth latent space. For this purpose, we apply the SpaceFusion (Gao et al., 2019b) and StyleFusion (Gao et al., 2019c) to learn such latent space. The latent interpolation is then used to transfer style, apply soft constraints, and interpolating hypothesis obtained using different models.

3.4 Stylized generation

Gao et al. (2019c) proposed StyleFusion to generate stylized response for a given conversation context by structuring a shared latent space for non-stylized conversation data and stylized samples. We extend it to a style transfer method, i.e., modify the style of a input sentence while maintaining its content, via latent interpolation (see Section 3.3).

- **Soft-edit** refers to a two-step algorithm, 1) edit the input sentence by replace each word by a synonym of the target style (e.g. "cookie" replaced by "biscuit" if the target style is

British), if there exists any; 2) the edited sentence from step 1 may not be fluent, so we then apply latent interpolation between the input sentence and edited sentence to seek a sentence that is both stylized and fluent.

- **Soft-retrieval** refers to a similar two-step algorithm, but step 1) is to retrieve a "similar" sentence from a stylized corpus, and then apply step 2) to do the interpolation. One example is given in Fig. 5. The hypothesis "he was once a schoolmaster in the north of england" is retrieved given the DialoGPT hypothesis "he's a professor at the university of london".

3.5 Conditioned text generation

Generate a set of candidate responses conditioned on the conversation history, or a follow-up sentence conditioned on the existing text.

- GPT-2 (Radford et al., 2019) is a transformer (Vaswani et al., 2017) based text generation model.
- DialoGPT (Zhang et al., 2019) is a large-scale pre-trained conversation model obtained by training GPT-2 (Radford et al., 2019) on Reddit comments data.
- SpaceFusion (Gao et al., 2019b) is a regularized multi-task learning framework proposed to learn a smooth and interpolatable latent space.

226

3.6 Knowledge grounded generation

We consider the following methods to consume the retrieved knowledge passage and relevant long-form text on the fly as a source of external knowledge.

- Machine reading comprehension. In the codebase, we fine-tuned BERT on SQuAD.
- Content transfer is a task proposed in (Prabhumoye et al., 2019) designed to, given a context, generate a sentence using knowledge from an external article. We implemented this algorithm in the codebase.
- Knowledge grounded response generation is a task firstly proposed in (Ghazvininejad et al., 2018) and later extended in Dialog System Technology Challenge 7 (DSTC7)(Galley et al., 2019). We implemented the CMR algorithm (Conversation with on-demand Machine Reading) proposed in (Qin et al., 2019).

3.7 Constrained generation

Besides the grounded generation, it is also useful to apply constraints at the decoding stage that encourage the generated hypotheses contain the desired phrases. We provide the following two ways to obtain constraints.

- Key phrases extracted from the Knowledge passage. We use the PKE package (Boudin, 2016) to identify the keywords.
- In some cases, users may want to use a stylized version of the topic phrases or phrase of a desired style as the constraints. We use the stylized synonym algorithm as introduced in Section 3.4 to provide such stylized constraints.

With the constraints obtained above, we provide the following two ways to apply such constraints during decoding.

- **Hard constraint** is applied via Grid Beam Search (GBS) (Hokamp and Liu, 2017), which is a lexically constrained decoding algorithm that can be applied to almost any models at the decoding stage and generate hypotheses that contain desired paraphrases (i.e. the constraints). We implemented GBS to provide a hard constrained decoding.
- **Soft constraint** refers the case that generation is likely, but not always, to satisfy constraints (e.g. include given keywords in the

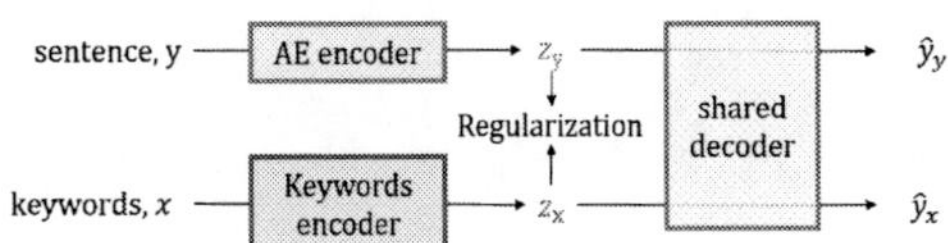

Figure 3: A soft keywords constrained generation model based on SpaceFusion (Gao et al., 2019b).

hypothesis). We provide an adapted version of SpaceFusion (Gao et al., 2019b) for this purpose. Gao et al. (2019b) proposed to align the latent space of a Sequence-to-Sequence (S2S) model and that of an Autoencoder (AE) model to improve dialogue generation performance. Inspired by this work, we proposed to replace the S2S model by a keywords-to-sequence model, which takes multi-hot input of the keywords x identified from sentence y, as illustrated in Fig. 3. During training, we simply choose the top-k rare words (rareness measured by inverse document frequency) as the keywords, and k is randomly choose from a Uniform distribution $k \sim U(1, K)$.

4 Cross-model integration

Multiple models may be called for the same query and returns different responses. We propose the following ways to organically integrate multiple models, as illustrated in Fig. 4. User can apply these strategies with customized models.

- **Token probability interpolation** refers prediction of the next token using a (weighted) average of the token probability distributions from two or more models given the same time step and given the same context and incomplete hypothesis. Previously, it has been proposed to bridge a conversation model and stylized language model (Niu and Bansal, 2018). This technique does not require the models to share the latent space but the vocabulary should be shared across different models.
- **Latent interpolation** refers the technique introduced in Section 3.3. It provides a way to interpolate texts in the latent space. Unlike the token-level strategy introduced above, this technique focuses on the latent level and ingests information from the whole sentence. However if the two candidates are too dissimilar, the interpolation may result in undesired outputs. The soft constraint algorithm intro-

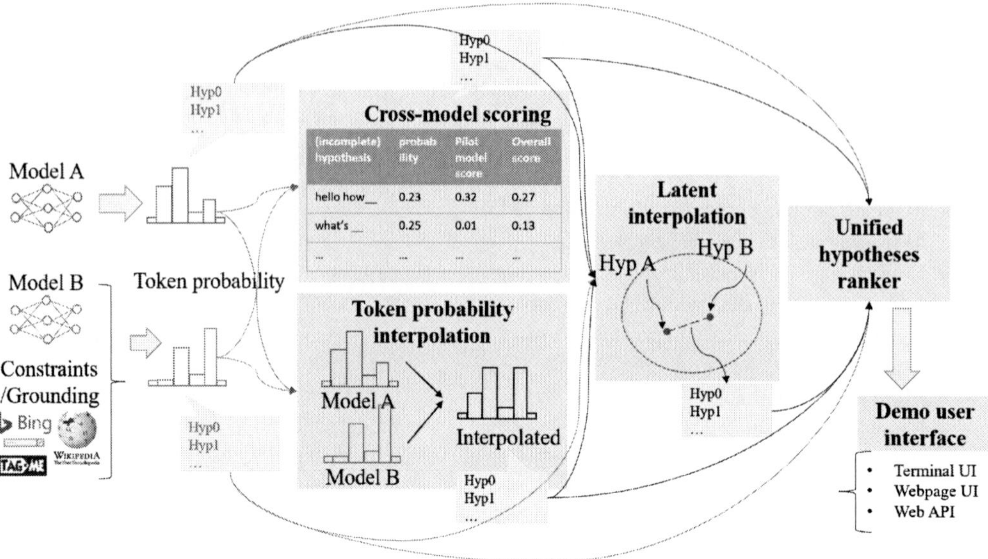

Figure 4: An example flow chart showing the integration of two models at different stages (blue boxes).

duced in Section 3.7 is one option to apply such interpolation.

- **Cross model pruning** refers pruning the hypothesis candidates (can be incomplete hypothesis, e.g. during beam search) not just based on the joint token probability, but also the evaluated probability from a secondary model. This strategy does not require a shared vocabulary or a shared latent space. Interpolating two models trained on dissimilar domains may be risky but the cross model pruning strategy is safer as the secondary model is only used roughly as a discriminator rather than a generator.
- **Unified hypothesis ranking** is the final step which sum up the hypotheses generated from each single model and these from the integration of multiple models using the above strategies. We consider the following criteria for the hypothesis ranking: 1) likelihood, measured by the conditional token probability given the context; 2) informativeness, measured by average inverse document frequency (IDF) of the tokens in the hypothesis; 3) repetition penalty, measured by the ratio of the number of unique ngrams and the number of total ngrams. and 4) style intensity, measured by a style classifiers, if style is considered.

5 Demos

5.1 Virtual Sherlock Holmes

This demo is a step towards a virtual version of Sherlock Holmes, able to chat in Sherlock Holmes style, with Sherlock Holmes background knowledge in mind. As an extended version of the one introduced by Gao et al. (2019c), the current demo is grounded on knowledge and coupled with more advanced language modeling (Zhang et al., 2019). It is designed to integrate the following components: open-domain conversation, stylized response generation, knowledge-grounded conversation, and question answering. Specifically, for a given query, the following steps are executed:

- Call DialoGPT (Zhang et al., 2019) and StyleFusion (Gao et al., 2019c) to get a set of hypotheses.
- Call the knowledge passage selection module to get a set of candidate passages. Then feed these passages to the span selection algorithm (Bert-based MRC (Devlin et al., 2018)) and CMR (Qin et al., 2019) to get a set of knowledge grounded response.
- Optionally, use the cross-model integration strategies, such as interpolating the token probability of DialoGPT and CMR.
- Based on TF-IDF similarity, best answer is retrieved from a user provided corpus of question-answer pairs. If the similarity is

lower than certain threshold, the retrieved result will not be returned.

- Apply the style transfer module to obtain stylized version of the the hypotheses obtained from steps above.

- feed all hypotheses to the unified ranker and return the top ones.

5.2 Document auto-completion assistant

This demo is designed as a writing assistant, which provides suggestion of the next sentence given the context. The assistant is expected to be knowledgeable (able to retrieve relevant knowledge passage from web or a given unstructured text source) and stylized (if a given target style is specified). For a given query, the following steps are executed:

- Call language model GPT2 (Radford et al., 2019) to get a set of hypotheses

- Call the knowledge passage selection module to get a set of candidate passages. Then feed these passages to content transfer algorithm (Prabhumoye et al., 2019) to get a set of knowledge grounded response.

- Optionally, use the cross-model integration strategies, such as latent interpolation to interpolate hypotheses from above models.

- Apply the style transfer module to obtain stylized version of the the hypotheses obtained from steps above.

- Feed all hypotheses to the unified ranker and return the top ones.

6   User interface

We provided the following three ways to access the demos introduced above for local developer, remote human user, and interface for other programs.

- **Command line interface** is provided for local interaction. This is designed for developer to test the codebase.

- **Webpage interface** is implemented using the Flask toolkit.[5] A graphic interface is provided with html webpage for remote access for human user. As illustrated in Fig. 5, the Sherlock Holmes webpage consists of a input panel where the user can provide context and control style, a hypothesis list which specify the model and scores of the ranked hypotheses, and a knowledge passage list showing

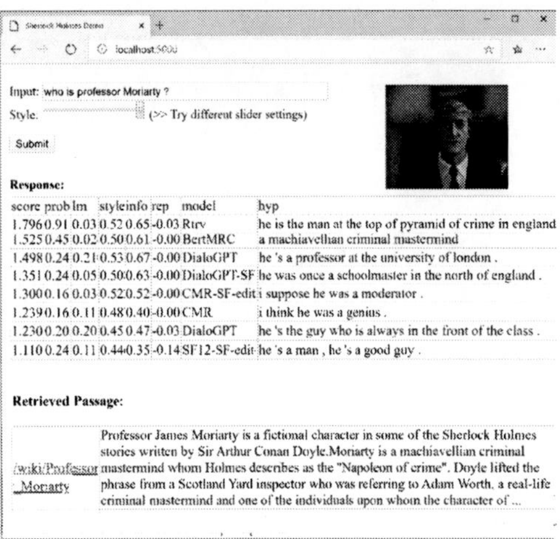

Figure 5: Sherlock Holmes webpage demo with wikipedia knowledge example.

the retrieved knowledge passages. Another example is given in Fig. 6 for document auto-completion demo, where multiple options of knowledge passage is given.

- **RESTful API** is implemented using the Flask-RESTful toolkit.[6] JSON object will be returned for remote request. This interface is designed to allow remote access for other programs. One example is to host this RESTful API on a dedicated GPU machine, so the webpage interface can be hosted on another less powerful machine to send request through RESTful API.

7   Conclusion

MIXINGBOARD is a new open-source platform to organically integrate multiple state-of-the-art NLP algorithms to build demo quickly with user friendly interface. We unified these NLP algorithms in a single codebase, implemented demos as top-level managers to access different models, and provide strategies to allow more organic integration across the models. We provide the component to retrieve knowledge passage on-the-fly from web or customized document for grounded text generation. For future work, we plan to keep adding the state-of-the-art algorithms, reduce latency and fine-tune the implemented models on larger and/or more comprehensive corpus to improve performance.

---

[5]https://flask.palletsprojects.com/en/1.1.x/

[6]https://flask-restful.readthedocs.io/en/latest/

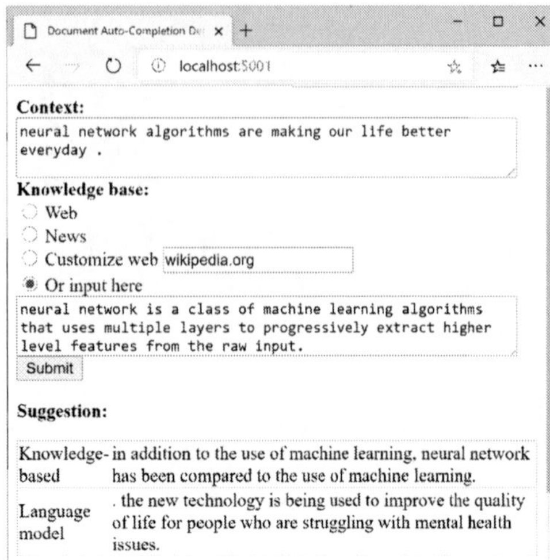

Figure 6: Document Auto-completion webpage demo with user input knowledge passage.

References

Martín Abadi, Ashish Agarwal, Paul Barham, Eugene Brevdo, Zhifeng Chen, Craig Citro, Greg S. Corrado, Andy Davis, Jeffrey Dean, Matthieu Devin, Sanjay Ghemawat, Ian Goodfellow, Andrew Harp, Geoffrey Irving, Michael Isard, Yangqing Jia, Rafal Jozefowicz, Lukasz Kaiser, Manjunath Kudlur, Josh Levenberg, Dan Mané, Rajat Monga, Sherry Moore, Derek Murray, Chris Olah, Mike Schuster, Jonathon Shlens, Benoit Steiner, Ilya Sutskever, Kunal Talwar, Paul Tucker, Vincent Vanhoucke, Vijay Vasudevan, Fernanda Viégas, Oriol Vinyals, Pete Warden, Martin Wattenberg, Martin Wicke, Yuan Yu, and Xiaoqiang Zheng. 2015. TensorFlow: Large-scale machine learning on heterogeneous systems. Software available from tensorflow.org.

Florian Boudin. 2016. pke: an open source python-based keyphrase extraction toolkit. In *Proceedings of COLING 2016, the 26th International Conference on Computational Linguistics: System Demonstrations*, pages 69–73, Osaka, Japan.

Jacob Devlin, Ming-Wei Chang, Kenton Lee, and Kristina Toutanova. 2018. BERT: Pre-training of deep bidirectional transformers for language understanding. *arXiv preprint arXiv:1810.04805*.

Michel Galley, Chris Brockett, Xiang Gao, Jianfeng Gao, and Bill Dolan. 2019. Grounded response generation task at DSTC7. In *AAAI Dialog System Technology Challenges (DSTC7) Workshop*.

Jianfeng Gao, Michel Galley, and Lihong Li. 2019a. Neural approaches to conversational AI. *Foundations and Trends in Information Retrieval*, 13(2-3):127–298.

Xiang Gao, Sungjin Lee, Yizhe Zhang, Chris Brockett, Michel Galley, Jianfeng Gao, and Bill Dolan. 2019b. Jointly optimizing diversity and relevance in neural response generation. *NAACL-HLT 2019*.

Xiang Gao, Yizhe Zhang, Sungjin Lee, Michel Galley, Chris Brockett, Jianfeng Gao, and Bill Dolan. 2019c. Structuring latent spaces for stylized response generation. *arXiv preprint arXiv:1909.05361*.

Matt Gardner, Joel Grus, Mark Neumann, Oyvind Tafjord, Pradeep Dasigi, Nelson Liu, Matthew Peters, Michael Schmitz, and Luke Zettlemoyer. 2018. Allennlp: A deep semantic natural language processing platform. *arXiv preprint arXiv:1803.07640*.

Marjan Ghazvininejad, Chris Brockett, Ming-Wei Chang, Bill Dolan, Jianfeng Gao, Wen-tau Yih, and Michel Galley. 2018. A knowledge-grounded neural conversation model. In *Thirty-Second AAAI Conference on Artificial Intelligence*.

Chris Hokamp and Qun Liu. 2017. Lexically constrained decoding for sequence generation using grid beam search. *arXiv preprint arXiv:1704.07138*.

Zhiting Hu, Haoran Shi, Zichao Yang, Bowen Tan, Tiancheng Zhao, Junxian He, Wentao Wang, Lianhui Qin, Di Wang, et al. 2018. Texar: A modularized, versatile, and extensible toolkit for text generation. *arXiv preprint arXiv:1809.00794*.

HuggingFace. 2019. PyTorch transformer repository. https://github.com/huggingface/pytorch-transformers.

Alexander H Miller, Will Feng, Adam Fisch, Jiasen Lu, Dhruv Batra, Antoine Bordes, Devi Parikh, and Jason Weston. 2017. Parlai: A dialog research software platform. *arXiv preprint arXiv:1705.06476*.

Tong Niu and Mohit Bansal. 2018. Polite dialogue generation without parallel data. *Transactions of the Association of Computational Linguistics*, 6:373–389.

Myle Ott, Sergey Edunov, Alexei Baevski, Angela Fan, Sam Gross, Nathan Ng, David Grangier, and Michael Auli. 2019. fairseq: A fast, extensible toolkit for sequence modeling. In *Proceedings of NAACL-HLT 2019: Demonstrations*.

Adam Paszke, Sam Gross, Francisco Massa, Adam Lerer, James Bradbury, Gregory Chanan, Trevor Killeen, Zeming Lin, Natalia Gimelshein, Luca Antiga, et al. 2019. Pytorch: An imperative style, high-performance deep learning library. In *Advances in Neural Information Processing Systems*, pages 8024–8035.

Shrimai Prabhumoye, Chris Quirk, and Michel Galley. 2019. Towards content transfer through grounded text generation. In *Proc. of NAACL*.

Lianhui Qin, Michel Galley, Chris Brockett, Xiaodong Liu, Xiang Gao, Bill Dolan, Yejin Choi, and Jianfeng Gao. 2019. Conversing by reading: Contentful neural conversation with on-demand machine reading. In *Proc. of ACL*.

Alec Radford, Jeffrey Wu, Rewon Child, David Luan, Dario Amodei, and Ilya Sutskever. 2019. Language models are unsupervised multitask learners. *OpenAI Blog*, 1(8).

Minjoon Seo, Aniruddha Kembhavi, Ali Farhadi, and Hannaneh Hajishirzi. 2016. Bidirectional attention flow for machine comprehension. *arXiv preprint arXiv:1611.01603*.

Vighnesh Leonardo Shiv, Chris Quirk, Anshuman Suri, Xiang Gao, Khuram Shahid, Nithya Govindarajan, Yizhe Zhang, Jianfeng Gao, Michel Galley, Chris Brockett, et al. 2019. Microsoft icecaps: An open-source toolkit for conversation modeling. In *Proceedings of the 57th Conference of the Association for Computational Linguistics: System Demonstrations*, pages 123–128.

Ashish Vaswani, Noam Shazeer, Niki Parmar, Jakob Uszkoreit, Llion Jones, Aidan N Gomez, Łukasz Kaiser, and Illia Polosukhin. 2017. Attention is all you need. In *Advances in neural information processing systems*, pages 5998–6008.

Yizhe Zhang, Siqi Sun, Michel Galley, Yen-Chun Chen, Chris Brockett, Xiang Gao, Jianfeng Gao, Jingjing Liu, and Bill Dolan. 2019. DialoGPT: Large-scale generative pre-training for conversational response generation. *arXiv preprint arXiv:1911.00536*.

NLP Scholar: An Interactive Visual Explorer for
Natural Language Processing Literature

Saif M. Mohammad
National Research Council Canada
`saif.mohammad@nrc-cnrc.gc.ca`

Abstract

As part of the NLP Scholar project, we created a single unified dataset of NLP papers and their meta-information (including citation numbers), by extracting and aligning information from the ACL Anthology and Google Scholar. In this paper, we describe several interconnected interactive visualizations (dashboards) that present various aspects of the data. Clicking on an item within a visualization or entering query terms in the search boxes filters the data in all visualizations in the dashboard. This allows users to search for papers in the area of their interest, published within specific time periods, published by specified authors, etc. The interactive visualizations presented here, and the associated dataset of papers mapped to citations, have additional uses as well including understanding how the field is growing (both overall and across sub-areas), as well as quantifying the impact of different types of papers on subsequent publications.

1 Introduction

NLP is a broad interdisciplinary field that draws knowledge from Computer Science, Linguistics, Information Science, Psychology, Social Sciences, and more.[1] Over the years, scientific publications in NLP have grown in number and diversity; we now see papers published on a vast array of research questions and applications in a growing list of venues—in journals such as CL and TACL, in large conferences such as ACL and EMNLP, as well as a number of small area-focused workshops.

The ACL Anthology (AA) is a digital repository of public domain, free to access, articles on NLP.[2] It includes papers published in the family of ACL conferences as well as in other NLP conferences such as LREC and RANLP. As of June 2019, it provided access to the full text and metadata for close to 50K articles published since 1965.[3] It is the largest single source of scientific literature on NLP. However, the meta-data does not include citation statistics.

Citation statistics are the most commonly used metrics of research impact. They include: number of citations, average citations, h-index, relative citation ratio, and impact factor. Note, however, that the number of citations is not always a reflection of the quality or importance of a piece of work. Furthermore, the citation process can be abused, for example, by egregious self-citations (Ioannidis et al., 2019). Nonetheless, given the immense volume of scientific literature, the relative ease with which one can track citations using services such as Google Scholar (GS), and given the lack of other easily applicable and effective metrics, citation analysis is an imperfect but useful window into research impact.

Google Scholar is a free web search engine for academic literature.[4] Through it, users can access the metadata associated with an article such as the number of citations it has received. Google Scholar does not provide information on how many articles are included in its database. However, scientometric researchers estimated that it included about 389 million documents in January 2018 (Gusenbauer, 2019)—making it the world's largest source of academic information. Thus, it is not surprising that there is growing interest in the use of Google Scholar information to draw inferences about scholarly research in general (Martín-Martín et al., 2018; Mingers and Leydesdorff, 2015; Orduña-Malea et al., 2014; Khabsa and Giles, 2014; Howland, 2010) and on scholarly impact in particular (Bos

---

[1] One can make a distinction between NLP and Computational Linguistics; however, for this work we will consider them to be synonymous.

[2] https://www.aclweb.org/anthology/

[3] ACL licenses its papers with a Creative Commons Attribution 4.0 International License.

[4] https://scholar.google.com

Proceedings of the 58th Annual Meeting of the Association for Computational Linguistics, pages 232–255
July 5 - July 10, 2020. ©2020 Association for Computational Linguistics

and Nitza, 2019; Ioannidis et al., 2019; Ravenscroft et al., 2017; Bulaitis, 2017; Yogatama et al., 2011; Priem and Hemminger, 2010).

Services such as Google Scholar and Semantic Scholar cover a wide variety of academic disciplines. Wile there are benefits to this, the lack of focus on NLP literature has some drawbacks as well: e.g, the potential for too many search results that include many irrelevant papers. For example, if one is interested in NLP papers on *emotion* and *privacy*, searching for them on Google Scholar is less efficient than searching for them on a platform dedicated to NLP papers. Further, services such as Google Scholar provide minimal interactive visualizations. NLP Scholar with its focus on AA data, is not meant to replace these tools, but act as a complementary tool for dedicated visual search of NLP literature.

ACL 2020 has a special theme asking researchers to reflect on the state of NLP. In the spirit of that theme, and as part of a broader project on analyzing NLP Literature, we extracted and aligned information from the ACL Anthology (AA) and Google Scholar to create a dataset of tens of thousands of NLP papers and their citations (Mohammad, 2020c, 2019). In separate work, we have used the data to explores questions such as: how well cited are papers of different types (journal articles, conference papers, demo papers, etc.)? how well cited are papers published in different time spans? how well cited are papers from different areas of research within NLP? etc. (Mohammad, 2020a). We also explored gender gaps in Natural Language Processing research, in terms of authorship and citations (Mohammad, 2020b). In this paper we describe how we built an interactive visual explorer for this unified data, which we refer to as *NLP Scholar*. Some notable uses of NLP Scholar are listed below:

- Search for relevant related work in various areas within NLP.

- Identify the highly cited articles on an interactive timeline.

- Identify past papers published in a venue of interest (such as ACL or LREC).

- Identify papers from the past (say ten years back) published in a venue of interest (say ACL or LREC) that have made substantial impact through citations.

- Examine changes in number of articles and number of citations in a chosen area of interest over time.

- Identify citation impact of different types of papers—e.g., short papers, shared task papers, demo papers, etc.

Even beyond the dedicated interactive visualizer described here, the underlying data with its alignment between AA and GS has potential uses in:

- Creating a web browser extension that allows users of GS to look up the aligned AA information (the full ACL BibTeX, poster, slides, access to proceedings from the same venue, etc.).

- Similarly, in the reverse direction, allowing access from AA to the GS information on the aligned paper. This could include number of citations, lists of papers citing the paper, etc.

Perhaps most importantly, though, NLP Scholar serves as a visual record of the state of NLP literature in terms of citations. We note again though, that even though this work seeks to make citation metrics more accessible for ACL Anthology papers, citation metrics are not always accurate reflections of the quality, importance, or impact of individual papers.

All of the data and interactive visualizations associated with this work are freely available through the project homepage.[5]

2 Background and Related Work

Much of the work in visualizing scientific literature has focused on showing topics of research (Wu et al., 2019; Heimerl et al., 2012; Lee et al., 2005). There is also notable work on visualizing communities through citation networks (Heimerl et al., 2015; Radev et al., 2016).

Various subsets of AA have been used in the past for a number of tasks, including: to study citation patterns and intent (Radev et al., 2016; Zhu et al., 2015; Nanba et al., 2011; Mohammad et al., 2009; Teufel et al., 2006; Aya et al., 2005; Pham and Hoffmann, 2003), to generate summaries of scientific articles (Qazvinian et al., 2013), to study gender disparities in NLP (Schluter, 2018), to study subtopics within NLP (Anderson et al.,

---

[5]http://saifmohammad.com/WebPages/nlpscholar.html

2012), and to create corpora of scientific articles (Mariani et al., 2018; Bird et al., 2008).

However, none of these works provide an interactive visualization for users to explore NLP literature and their citations.

3 Data

We now briefly describe how we extracted information from the ACL Anthology and Google Scholar. (Further details about the dataset, as well as an analysis of the volume of research in NLP over the years, are available in Mohammad (2020c).)

3.1 ACL Anthology Data

The ACL Anthology provides access to its data through its website and a github repository (Gildea et al., 2018).[6] We extracted paper title, names of authors, year of publication, and venue of publication from the repository.[7]

As of June 2019, AA had ~50K entries; however, this includes forewords, schedules, etc. that are not truly research publications. After discarding them we are left with a set of 44,895 papers.

3.2 Google Scholar Data

Google Scholar does not provide an API to extract information about the papers. This is likely because of its agreement with publishing companies that have scientific literature behind paywalls (Martín-Martín et al., 2018). We extracted citation information from Google Scholar profiles of authors who published at least three papers in the ACL Anthology. (This is explicitly allowed by GS's robots exclusion standard. This is also how past work has studied Google Scholar (Khabsa and Giles, 2014; Orduña-Malea et al., 2014; Martín-Martín et al., 2018).) This yielded citation information for 1.1 million papers in total. We will refer to this dataset as *GS-NLP*. Note that GS-NLP includes citation counts not just for NLP papers, but also for non-NLP papers published by the authors.

GS-NLP includes 32,985 of the 44,895 papers in AA (about 74%). We will refer to this subset of the

ACL Anthology papers as AA'. The citation analyses presented in this paper are on AA'. (Future work will explore visualizations on GS-NLP.)

Entries across AA and GS are aligned by matching the paper title, year of publication, and first author last name.[8]

4 Building an Interactive Visualization to Explore Scientific Literature

We now describe how we created an interactive visualization—NLP Scholar—that allows one to visually explore the data from the ACL Anthology along with citation information from Google Scholar. We first created a relational database (involving multiple tables) that stores the AA and GS data (§4.1). We then loaded the database in Tableau—an interactive data visualization software—to build the visualizations (§4.2).[9]

4.1 NLP Scholar Relational Database

Data from AA and GS is stored in four tables (tsv files): papers, authors, title-unigrams, and title-bigrams. They contain the following information:

papers: Each row corresponds to a unique paper. The columns include: paper title, year of publication, list of authors, venue of publication, number of citations at the time of data collection (June 2019), NLP Scholar paper id, ACL paper id, and some other meta-data associated with the paper.

The *NLP Scholar paper id* is a concatenation of the paper title, year of publication, and first author last name. (This id was also used to align entries across AA and GS).

authors: Each row corresponds to a paper–author combination. The columns include: NLP Scholar paper id, author first name, and author last name. A paper with three authors contributes three rows to the table (all three have the same paper id, but different author names).

title-unigrams: Each row corresponds to a paper title and unigram combination. The columns include: NLP Scholar paper id and paper title unigram (a word that occurs in the title of the paper). A paper with five unique words in the title

---

[6]https://www.aclweb.org/anthology/
https://github.com/acl-org/acl-anthology

[7]Multiple authors can have the same name and the same authors may use multiple variants of their names in papers. The AA volunteer team handles such ambiguities using both semi-automatic and manual approaches (fixing some instances on a case-by-case basis). Additionally, the AA repository includes a file that has canonical forms of author names. Authors can provide AA with their aliases, change-of-name information, and preferred canonical name, which is then eventually recorded in the canonical-name file.

[8]There were marked variations in how the same venue was described in the meta-information across AA and GS; thus, venue information was not used for alignment.

[9]Tableau: https://www.tableau.com
Even though there are paid versions of Tableau, the visualizations built with Tableau can be freely shared with others on the world wide web. Users do not require any special software to interact with these visualization on the web.

contributes five rows to the table (all five have the same paper id, but different words).

title-bigrams: Each row corresponds to a paper title and bigram combination. The columns include: NLP Scholar paper id and paper title bigram (a two-word sequence that occurs in the title of the paper). A paper with four unique bigrams in the title contributes four rows to the table (all four have the same paper id, but different bigrams).

Once the tables are loaded in Tableau, the following pairs of tables are each joined (inner join) using the NLP Scholar paper id:[10] papers–authors, papers–title-unigrams, and papers–title-bigrams.

4.2 NLP Scholar Interactive Visualization

We developed multiple visualizations to explore various aspects of the data. We group and connect several individual visualizations in dashboards that allow one to explore several aspects of the data together. Clicking on data attributes such as year of publication or venue of publication in one visualization, filters the data in all visualizations within a dashboard to show only the relevant data.

Figure 1 shows a screenshot of the main dashboard. At the top are the number of papers—total (A1) and by year of publication (A2). This allows one to see the growth/decline of the papers over the years.

Below it, we see the number of citations—total (B1) and by year of publication (B2). For a given year, the bar is partitioned into segments corresponding to individual papers. Each segment (paper) has a height that is proportional to the number of citations it has received and assigned a colour at random. This allows one to quickly identify high-citation papers.[11]

Hovering over individual papers in B2 pops open an information box showing the paper title, authors, year of publication, publication venue, and #citations. Figure 6 in the Appendix shows a blow up of B2 along with examples of the hover information box. Similarly, hovering over other parts of the dashboard shows corresponding information. (This is especially helpful, when parts of the text

are truncated or otherwise not visible due to space constraints.)

Further below, we see lists of papers (C) and authors (D)—both are ordered by number of citations. Search boxes in the bottom right (E) allow searching for papers that have particular terms in the title or searching for papers by author name. One can also restrict the search to a span of years using the slider.

Four other dashboards are also created that have the same five elements as the main dashboard (A through E), and additionally include a six element F to provide a focused search facility. This sixth element is a treemap that shows the most common: venues and paper types (F1), title unigrams (F2), title bigrams (F3), or language mentions in the title (F4). (We only show one of the four treemaps at a time to prevent overwhelming the user.) The treemaps are shown in Figures 2 to 5, respectively.

5 Data Explorations with NLP Scholar

Figure 1 A1 shows that the dataset includes 44,895 papers. A2 shows that the volume of papers published was considerably lower in the early years (1965 to 1989); there was a spurt in the 1990s; and substantial numbers since the year 2000. Also, note that the number of publications is considerably higher in alternate years. This is due to certain biennial conferences. Since 1998 the largest of such conferences has been LREC (In 2018 alone LREC had over 700 main conferences papers and additional papers from its 29 workshops). COLING, another biennial conference (also occurring in the even years) has about 45% of the number of main conference papers as LREC.

B1 shows that AA′ papers have received ∼1.2 million citations (as of June 2019). The timeline graph in B2 shows that, with time, not only have the number of papers grown, but also the number of high-citation papers. We see a marked jump in the 1990s over the previous decades, but the 2000s are the most notable in terms of the high number of citations. The 2010s papers will likely surpass the 2000s papers in the years to come.

The most cited papers list (C) shows influential papers from machine translation, sentiment analysis, word embeddings, syntax, and semantics.

Among the authors (D), observe that Christopher Manning has not only received the most number of citations, he has also received almost three times as many citations as the next person in the list.

---

[10]An inner join selects all rows from both participating tables whose join column values match across the two tables.

[11]Note that since the number of colours is smaller than the number of papers, multiple papers may have the same color; however, the probability of adjacent papers receiving the same colour is small—even then, the system will provide visual clues distinguishing each segment when hovering over the area.

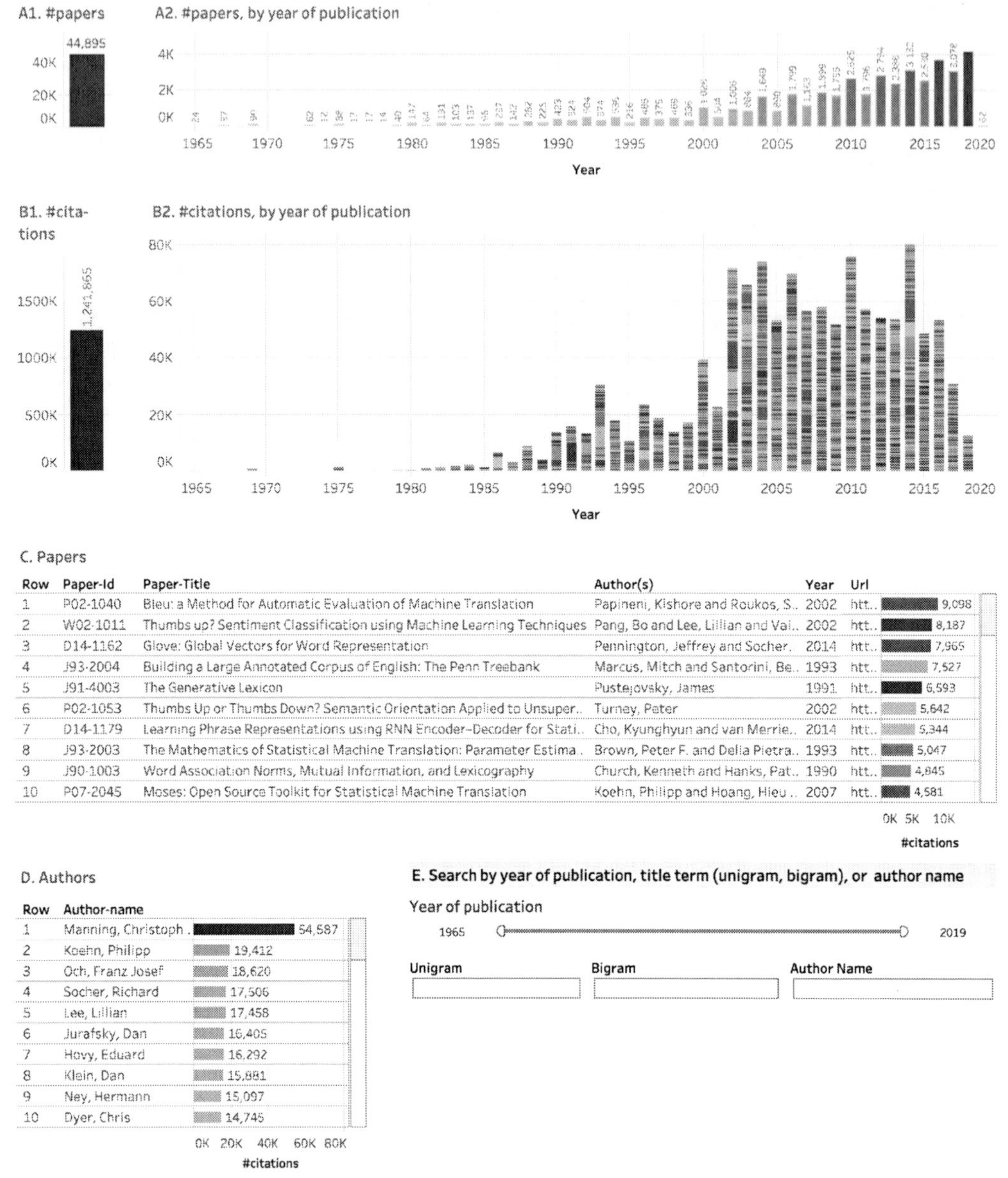

Figure 1: A screenshot of NLP Scholar's principle dashboard.

Search: NLP Scholar allows for search in a number of ways. Suppose we are interested in the topic of sentiment analysis. Then we can enter the relevant keywords in the search box: *sentiment, valence, emotion, emotions, affect,* etc. Then the visualizations are filtered to present details of only those papers that have at least one of these keywords in the title. (Future work will allow for search in the abstract and the whole text.)

Figure 7 in the Appendix shows the filtered result. The system identified 1,481 papers that each have at least one of the query terms in the title. They have received more than 85K citations. The citations timeline (B2 in Figure 7) shows that there were just a few scattered papers in early years (1987–2000) that received a small number of citations. However, two papers in 2002 received a massive number of citations, and likely led to

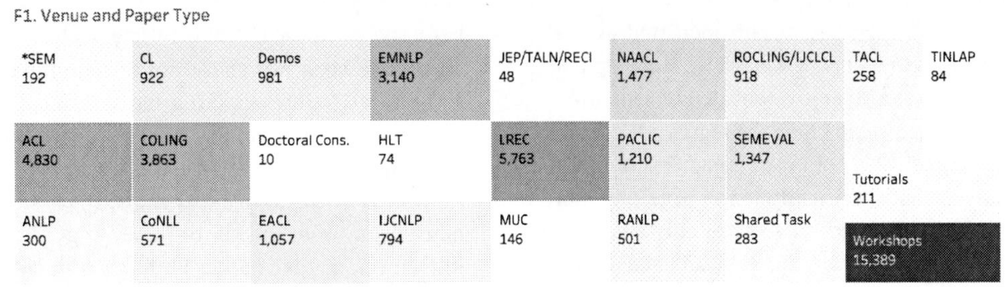

F1. Venue and Paper Type

*SEM	CL	Demos	EMNLP	JEP/TALN/RECI	NAACL	ROCLING/IJCLCL	TACL	TINLAP
192	922	981	3,140	48	1,477	918	258	84
ACL	COLING	Doctoral Cons.	HLT	LREC	PACLIC	SEMEVAL	Tutorials	
4,830	3,863	10	74	5,763	1,210	1,347	211	
ANLP	CoNLL	EACL	IJCNLP	MUC	RANLP	Shared Task	Workshops	
300	571	1,057	794	146	501	283	15,389	

Figure 2: A treemap of popular NLP venues and paper types. Darker shades of green: higher volumes of papers.

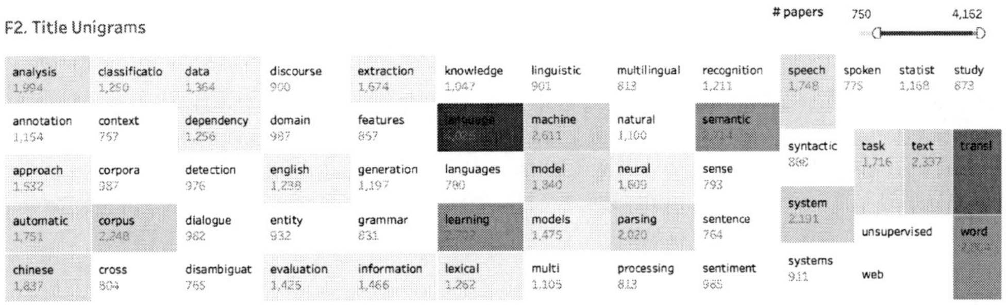

F2. Title Unigrams — # papers 750 … 4,162

analysis	classificatio	data	discourse	extraction	knowledge	linguistic	multilingual	recognition	speech	spoken	statist	study
1,994	1,250	1,364	900	1,674	1,047	901	813	1,211	1,748	775	1,168	873
annotation	context	dependency	domain	features	language	machine	natural	semantic	syntactic	task	text	transl
1,164	757	1,256	987	857		2,611	1,100		868	1,716	2,337	
approach	corpora	detection	english	generation	languages	model	neural	sense	system			
1,532	887	976	1,238	1,197	780	1,340	1,609	793	2,191			
automatic	corpus	dialogue	entity	grammar	learning	models	parsing	sentence	systems	unsupervised	word	
1,751	2,248	962	932	831		1,475	2,020	764	911			
chinese	cross	disambiguat	evaluation	information	lexical	multi	processing	sentiment	web			
1,837	804	765	1,425	1,466	1,262	1,105	813	965				

Figure 3: A treemap of the most common unigrams in paper titles. Darker shades of green: higher frequencies.

F3. Title Bigrams — #papers 175 … 200,150

2016 task	coreference resolution	finite state	language models	named entity	question answering	semeval 2017	shared task	social media	speech recogn.	spoken dialog.
2017 task	cross lingual	information extraction	language processing	natural language	relation extraction	semeval 2018				
2018 task	dependency parsing	information retrieval	large scale	neural machine	role labeling	semi supervised	spoken language	word alignmt.	word embeds.	
case study	dialogue systems	language generation	machine learning	neural network	semantic role	sense disambiguation	statistical machine	word segmentn.		
chinese word	entity recognition	language model	machine translation	neural networks	semeval 2016	sentiment analysis	translation system	word sense		

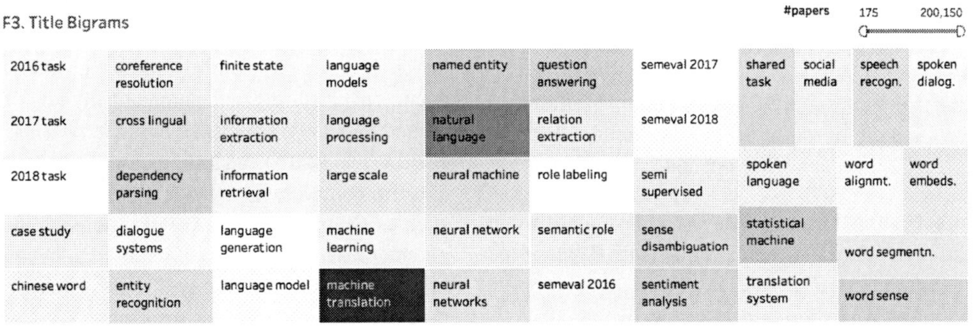

Figure 4: A treemap of the most common bigrams in paper titles. Darker shades of green: higher frequencies.

F4. Languages — #papers 5 … 1,837

afrikaans	bulgarian	czech	filipino	hebrew	interlingua	korean	mandarin	portuguese	slovak	sloven	spanis	swahili
10	48	111	15	47	20	231	212	162	7	21	230	5
amharic	cantonese	danish	finnish	hindi	inuktitut	kurdish	mongolian	romanian	swedish	thai	turki	urdu
16	19	68	44	177	6	7	9	63	146	68	87	64
arabic	catalan	dutch	french	hungarian	irish	latin	norwegian	russian	tagalog			
550	20	135	362	56	17	32	54	120	9			
assamese	chinese	english	galician	icelandic	italian	malay	persian	sanskrit	tamil	uyghur	wels	
8	1,837	1,238	7	17	141	8	60	25	24	9	6	
basque	croatian	estonian	german	indonesian	japanese	malayalam	polish	serbian	telugu	vietnamese		
64	57	35	405	35	711	15	98	20	20	51		

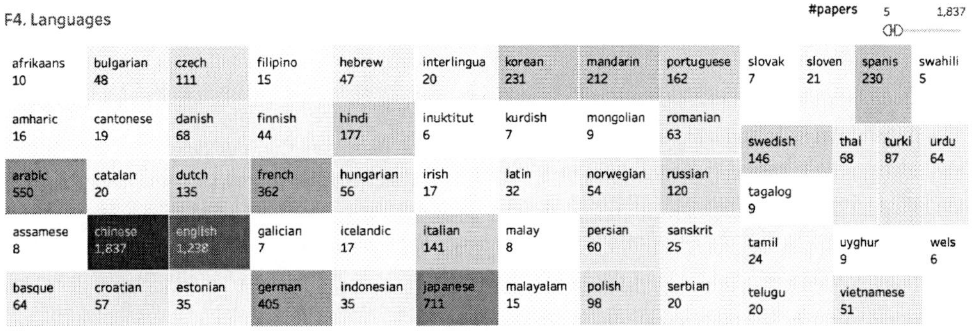

Figure 5: A treemap of the most common language terms in titles. Darker shades of green: higher frequencies.

the substantially increased interest in the field. The number of papers has steadily increased since 2002, with close to 250 papers in 2018, showing that the area continues to enjoy considerable attention.

One can also fine tune the search as desired. Say we are interested not in the broad area of sentiment analysis, but specifically in the work on emotions and affect. Then they can enter only emotion- and affect-related keywords. A disadvantage of using terms for search is that some terms are ambiguous and they can pull in irrelevant articles; also if a paper is about the topic of interest but its title does not have one of the standard keywords associated with the topic, then it might be left out. That said, if one does come across a paper that has the query term but is not in the topic of interest, they can right click and exclude that paper from the visualization; and as mentioned before, future work will allow for searches in the abstract and full text as well. We are also currently working on clustering papers using the words in the articles as features.[12]

Below are some more examples of interactions with NLP Scholar (Figures are in the Appendix after references):

- Figure 8 shows the state of the visualization when one clicks the year 2016 in A1.

- Figures 9 and 10 show examples of author search by clicking on the authors list (D) (*Christopher Manning* and *Lillian Lee*).

- Figures 11 and 12 show the dashboard when one clicks on the Venue and Paper Type treemap (F1): *ACL main conference papers* and *Workshop papers*, respectively.

- Figures 13, 14 and 15 in the Appendix also show examples of search for the terms *parsing, statistical* and *neural*, respectively (accessed by clicking on the title unigrams treemap (F2)).

- Figures 16, 17, and 18 show the dashboard when one clicks on the Title Bigrams treemap (F3): *machine translation, question answering,* and *word embeddings*, respectively.

- Figures 19 and 20 show the dashboard when one clicks on the Languages treemap (F4): *Chinese* and *Swahili*, respectively.

Once the system goes live, we hope to collect further usage scenarios from the users at large.

For this work, we chose not to stem the terms in the titles before applying the search. This is because in some search scenarios, it is beneficial to distinguish the different morphological forms of a word. For example, papers with *emotions* in the titles are more likely to be dealing with multiple emotions than papers with the term *emotion*. When such distinctions do not need to be made, it is easy for users to include morphological variants as additional query terms.

6 Conclusions and Future Work

We presented NLP Scholar—an interactive visual explorer for the ACL Anthology. Notably, the tool also has access to citation information from Google Scholar. It includes several interconnected interactive visualizations (dashboards) that allow users to quickly and efficiently search for relevant related work by clicking on items within a visualization or through search boxes. All of the data and interactive visualizations associated with this work are freely available through the project homepage.[13]

Future work will provide additional functionalities such as search within abstracts and whole texts, document clustering, and automatically identifying related papers. We see NLP Scholar, with its dedicated visual search capabilities for NLP papers, as a useful complementary tool to existing resources such as Google Scholar. We also note that the approach presented here is not required to be applied only to the ACL Anthology or NLP papers; it can be used to display papers from other sources too such as pre-print archives and anthologies of papers from other fields of study.

Acknowledgments

This work was possible due to the helpful discussion and encouragement from a number of awesome people including: Dan Jurafsky, Tara Small, Michael Strube, Cyril Goutte, Eric Joanis, Matt Post, Torsten Zesch, Ellen Riloff, Iryna Gurevych, Rebecca Knowles, Isar Nejadgholi, and Peter Turney. Also, a big thanks to the ACL Anthology and Google Scholar Teams for creating and maintaining wonderful resources.

---

[12]Note that clustering approaches also have limitations, such as differing results depending on the parameters used.

[13]http://saifmohammad.com/WebPages/nlpscholar.html

References

Ashton Anderson, Dan McFarland, and Dan Jurafsky. 2012. Towards a computational history of the acl: 1980-2008. In *Proceedings of the ACL-2012 Special Workshop on Rediscovering 50 Years of Discoveries*, pages 13–21. Association for Computational Linguistics.

Selcuk Aya, Carl Lagoze, and Thorsten Joachims. 2005. Citation classification and its applications. In *Knowledge Management: Nurturing Culture, Innovation, and Technology*, pages 287–298. World Scientific.

Steven Bird, Robert Dale, Bonnie J Dorr, Bryan Gibson, Mark Thomas Joseph, Min-Yen Kan, Dongwon Lee, Brett Powley, Dragomir R Radev, and Yee Fan Tan. 2008. The acl anthology reference corpus: A reference dataset for bibliographic research in computational linguistics.

Arthur R Bos and Sandrine Nitza. 2019. Interdisciplinary comparison of scientific impact of publications using the citation-ratio. *Data Science Journal*, 18(1).

Zoe Bulaitis. 2017. Measuring impact in the humanities: Learning from accountability and economics in a contemporary history of cultural value. *Palgrave Communications*, 3(1):7.

Daniel Gildea, Min-Yen Kan, Nitin Madnani, Christoph Teichmann, and Martín Villalba. 2018. The ACL anthology: Current state and future directions. In *Proceedings of Workshop for NLP Open Source Software (NLP-OSS)*, pages 23–28, Melbourne, Australia. Association for Computational Linguistics.

Michael Gusenbauer. 2019. Google scholar to overshadow them all? comparing the sizes of 12 academic search engines and bibliographic databases. *Scientometrics*, 118(1):177–214.

Florian Heimerl, Qi Han, Steffen Koch, and Thomas Ertl. 2015. Citerivers: Visual analytics of citation patterns. *IEEE transactions on visualization and computer graphics*, 22(1):190–199.

Florian Heimerl, Steffen Koch, Harald Bosch, and Thomas Ertl. 2012. Visual classifier training for text document retrieval. *IEEE Transactions on Visualization and Computer Graphics*, 18(12):2839–2848.

Jared L Howland. 2010. How scholarly is google scholar? a comparison to library databases.

John PA Ioannidis, Jeroen Baas, Richard Klavans, and Kevin W Boyack. 2019. A standardized citation metrics author database annotated for scientific field. *PLoS biology*, 17(8):e3000384.

Madian Khabsa and C Lee Giles. 2014. The number of scholarly documents on the public web. *PloS one*, 9(5):e93949.

Bongshin Lee, Mary Czerwinski, George Robertson, and Benjamin B Bederson. 2005. Understanding research trends in conferences using paperlens. In *CHI'05 extended abstracts on Human factors in computing systems*, pages 1969–1972.

Joseph Mariani, Gil Francopoulo, and Patrick Paroubek. 2018. The nlp4nlp corpus (i): 50 years of publication, collaboration and citation in speech and language processing. *Frontiers in Research Metrics and Analytics*, 3:36.

Alberto Martín-Martín, Enrique Orduna-Malea, Mike Thelwall, and Emilio Delgado López-Cózar. 2018. Google scholar, web of science, and scopus: A systematic comparison of citations in 252 subject categories. *Journal of Informetrics*, 12(4):1160–1177.

John Mingers and Loet Leydesdorff. 2015. A review of theory and practice in scientometrics. *European journal of operational research*, 246(1):1–19.

Saif Mohammad, Bonnie Dorr, Melissa Egan, Ahmed Hassan, Pradeep Muthukrishan, Vahed Qazvinian, Dragomir Radev, and David Zajic. 2009. Using citations to generate surveys of scientific paradigms. In *Proceedings of human language technologies: The 2009 annual conference of the North American chapter of the association for computational linguistics*, pages 584–592.

Saif M. Mohammad. 2019. The state of nlp literature: A diachronic analysis of the acl anthology. *arXiv preprint arXiv:1911.03562*.

Saif M. Mohammad. 2020a. Examining citations of natural language processing literature. In *Proceedings of the 2020 Annual Conference of the Association for Computational Linguistics*, Seattle, USA.

Saif M. Mohammad. 2020b. Gender gap in natural language processing research: Disparities in authorship and citations. In *Proceedings of the 2020 Annual Conference of the Association for Computational Linguistics*, Seattle, USA.

Saif M. Mohammad. 2020c. Nlp scholar: A dataset for examining the state of nlp research. In *Proceedings of the 12th Language Resources and Evaluation Conference (LREC-2020)*, Marseille, France.

Hidetsugu Nanba, Noriko Kando, and Manabu Okumura. 2011. Classification of research papers using citation links and citation types: Towards automatic review article generation. *Advances in Classification Research Online*, 11(1):117–134.

Enrique Orduña-Malea, Juan Manuel Ayllón, Alberto Martín-Martín, and Emilio Delgado López-Cózar. 2014. About the size of google scholar: playing the numbers. *arXiv preprint arXiv:1407.6239*.

Son Bao Pham and Achim Hoffmann. 2003. A new approach for scientific citation classification using cue phrases. In *Australasian Joint Conference on Artificial Intelligence*, pages 759–771. Springer.

Jason Priem and Bradely H Hemminger. 2010. Scientometrics 2.0: New metrics of scholarly impact on the social web. *First monday*, 15(7).

Vahed Qazvinian, Dragomir R Radev, Saif M Mohammad, Bonnie Dorr, David Zajic, Michael Whidby, and Taesun Moon. 2013. Generating extractive summaries of scientific paradigms. *Journal of Artificial Intelligence Research*, 46:165–201.

Dragomir R Radev, Mark Thomas Joseph, Bryan Gibson, and Pradeep Muthukrishnan. 2016. A bibliometric and network analysis of the field of computational linguistics. *Journal of the Association for Information Science and Technology*, 67(3):683–706.

James Ravenscroft, Maria Liakata, Amanda Clare, and Daniel Duma. 2017. Measuring scientific impact beyond academia: An assessment of existing impact metrics and proposed improvements. *PloS one*, 12(3):e0173152.

Natalie Schluter. 2018. The glass ceiling in NLP. In *Proceedings of the 2018 Conference on Empirical Methods in Natural Language Processing*, pages 2793–2798.

Simone Teufel, Advaith Siddharthan, and Dan Tidhar. 2006. Automatic classification of citation function. In *Proceedings of the 2006 Conference on Empirical Methods in Natural Language Processing*, pages 103–110.

Shaopeng Wu, Youbing Zhao, Farzad Parvinzamir, Nikolaos Th Ersotelos, Hui Wei, and Feng Dong. 2019. Literature explorer: effective retrieval of scientific documents through nonparametric thematic topic detection. *The Visual Computer*, pages 1–18.

Dani Yogatama, Michael Heilman, Brendan O'Connor, Chris Dyer, Bryan R Routledge, and Noah A Smith. 2011. Predicting a scientific community's response to an article. In *Proceedings of the 2011 Conference on Empirical Methods in Natural Language Processing*, pages 594–604.

Xiaodan Zhu, Peter Turney, Daniel Lemire, and André Vellino. 2015. Measuring academic influence: Not all citations are equal. *Journal of the Association for Information Science and Technology*, 66(2):408–427.

A Appendix

Figures 6 through 20 (in the pages ahead) show example interactions with NLP Scholar that were discussed in Section 5.

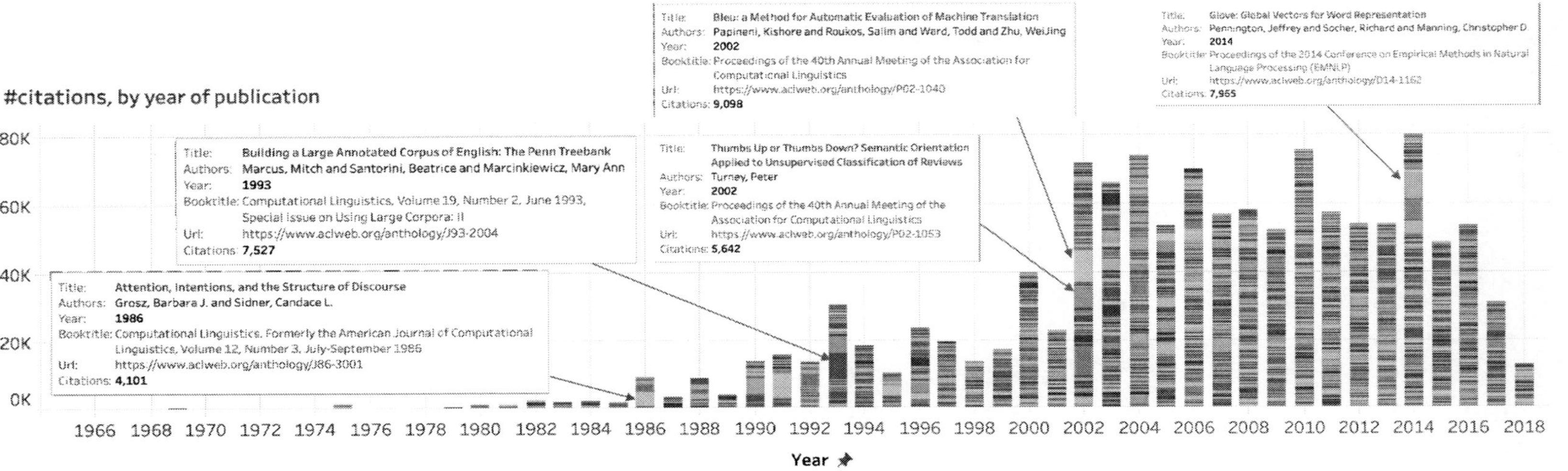

Figure 6: NLP Scholar: Hovering over individual papers in B2 pops open an information box showing the paper title, authors, year of publication, publication venue, and #citations.

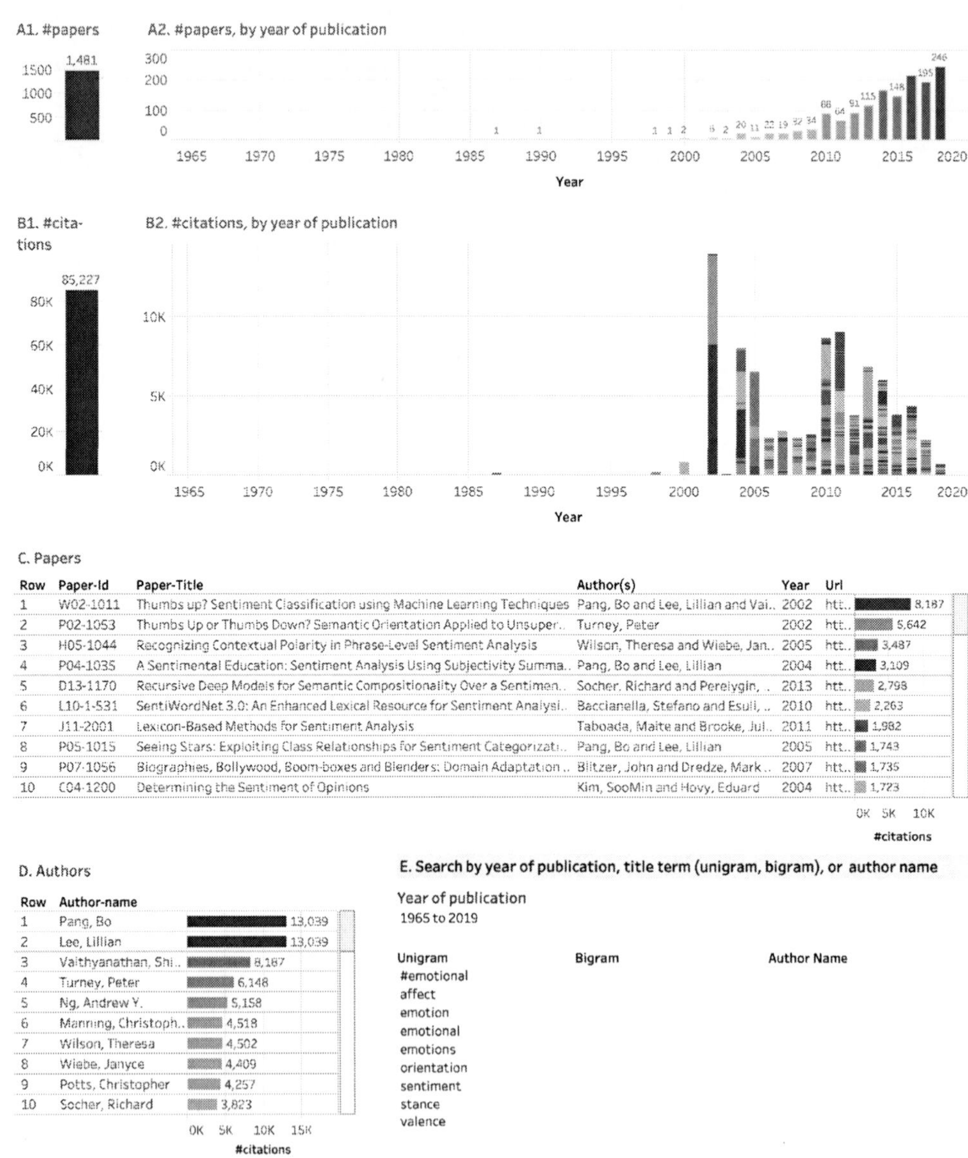

C. Papers

Row	Paper-Id	Paper-Title	Author(s)	Year	Url	#citations
1	W02-1011	Thumbs up? Sentiment Classification using Machine Learning Techniques	Pang, Bo and Lee, Lillian and Vai..	2002	htt..	8,187
2	P02-1053	Thumbs Up or Thumbs Down? Semantic Orientation Applied to Unsuper..	Turney, Peter	2002	htt..	5,642
3	H05-1044	Recognizing Contextual Polarity in Phrase-Level Sentiment Analysis	Wilson, Theresa and Wiebe, Jan..	2005	htt..	3,487
4	P04-1035	A Sentimental Education: Sentiment Analysis Using Subjectivity Summa..	Pang, Bo and Lee, Lillian	2004	htt..	3,109
5	D13-1170	Recursive Deep Models for Semantic Compositionality Over a Sentimen..	Socher, Richard and Pereiygin, .	2013	htt..	2,798
6	L10-1-531	SentiWordNet 3.0: An Enhanced Lexical Resource for Sentiment Analysi..	Baccianella, Stefano and Esuli, ..	2010	htt..	2,263
7	J11-2001	Lexicon-Based Methods for Sentiment Analysis	Taboada, Maite and Brooke, Jul..	2011	htt..	1,982
8	P05-1015	Seeing Stars: Exploiting Class Relationships for Sentiment Categorizati..	Pang, Bo and Lee, Lillian	2005	htt..	1,743
9	P07-1056	Biographies, Bollywood, Boom-boxes and Blenders: Domain Adaptation ..	Blitzer, John and Dredze, Mark..	2007	htt..	1,735
10	C04-1200	Determining the Sentiment of Opinions	Kim, SooMin and Hovy, Eduard	2004	htt..	1,723

D. Authors

Row	Author-name	#citations
1	Pang, Bo	13,039
2	Lee, Lillian	13,039
3	Vaithyanathan, Shi..	8,187
4	Turney, Peter	6,148
5	Ng, Andrew Y.	5,158
6	Manning, Christoph..	4,518
7	Wilson, Theresa	4,502
8	Wiebe, Janyce	4,409
9	Potts, Christopher	4,257
10	Socher, Richard	3,823

Figure 7: NLP Scholar: After entering terms associated with sentiment analysis in the search box.

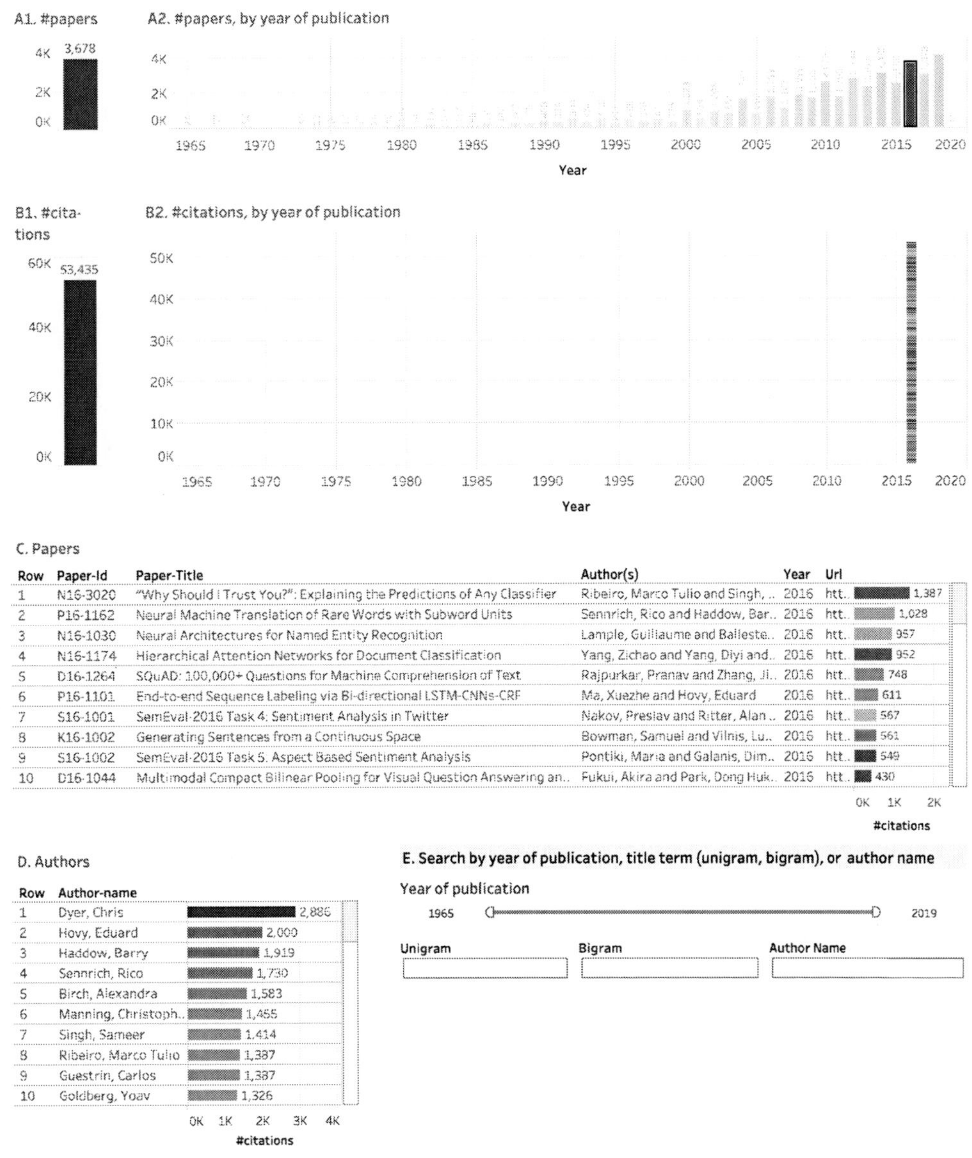

Figure 8: NLP Scholar: After clicking on the 2016 bar in the #papers by year viz (A2).

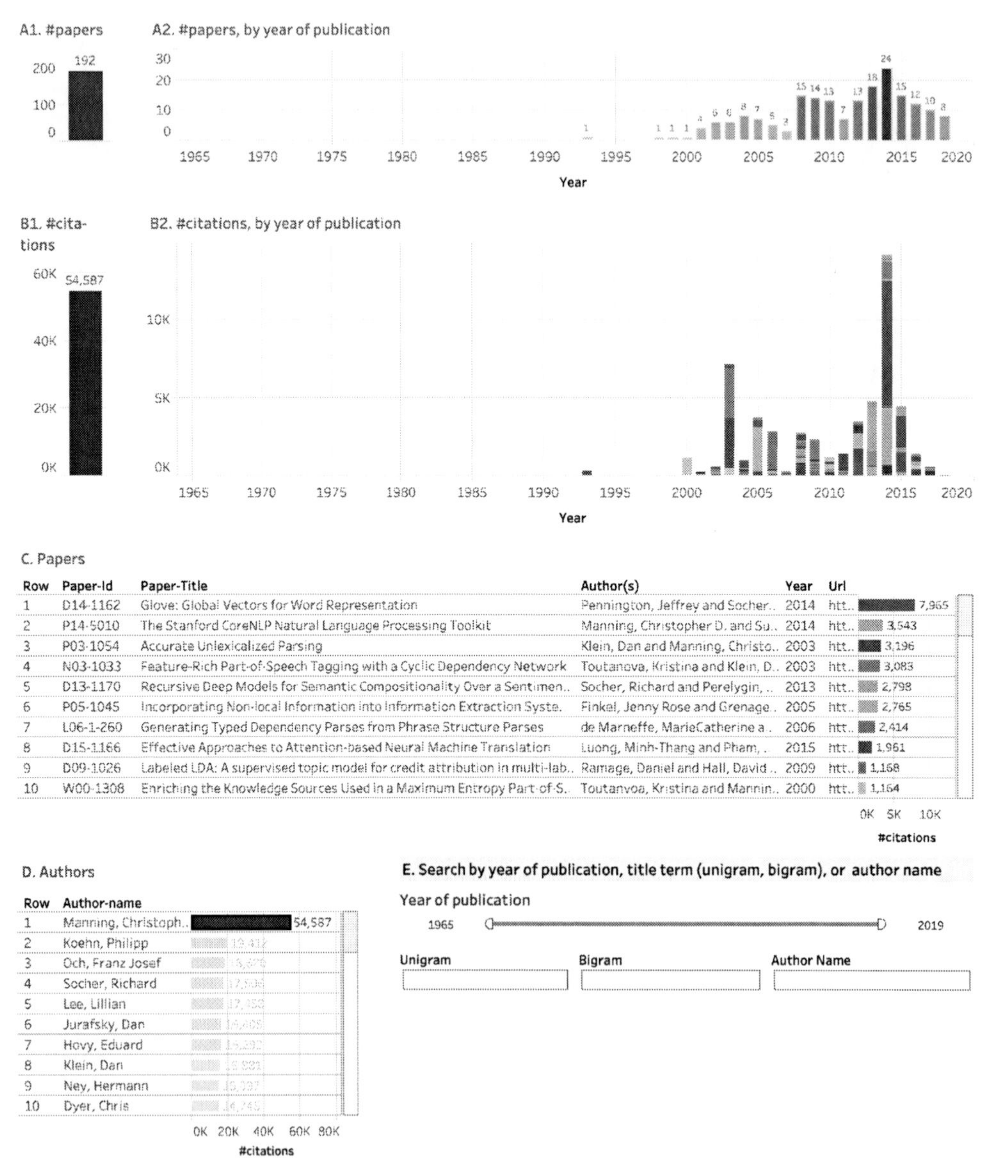

Figure 9: NLP Scholar: After clicking on 'Manning, Christopher' in the Authors list (D).

Figure 10: NLP Scholar: After clicking on 'Lee, Lillian' in the Authors list (D).

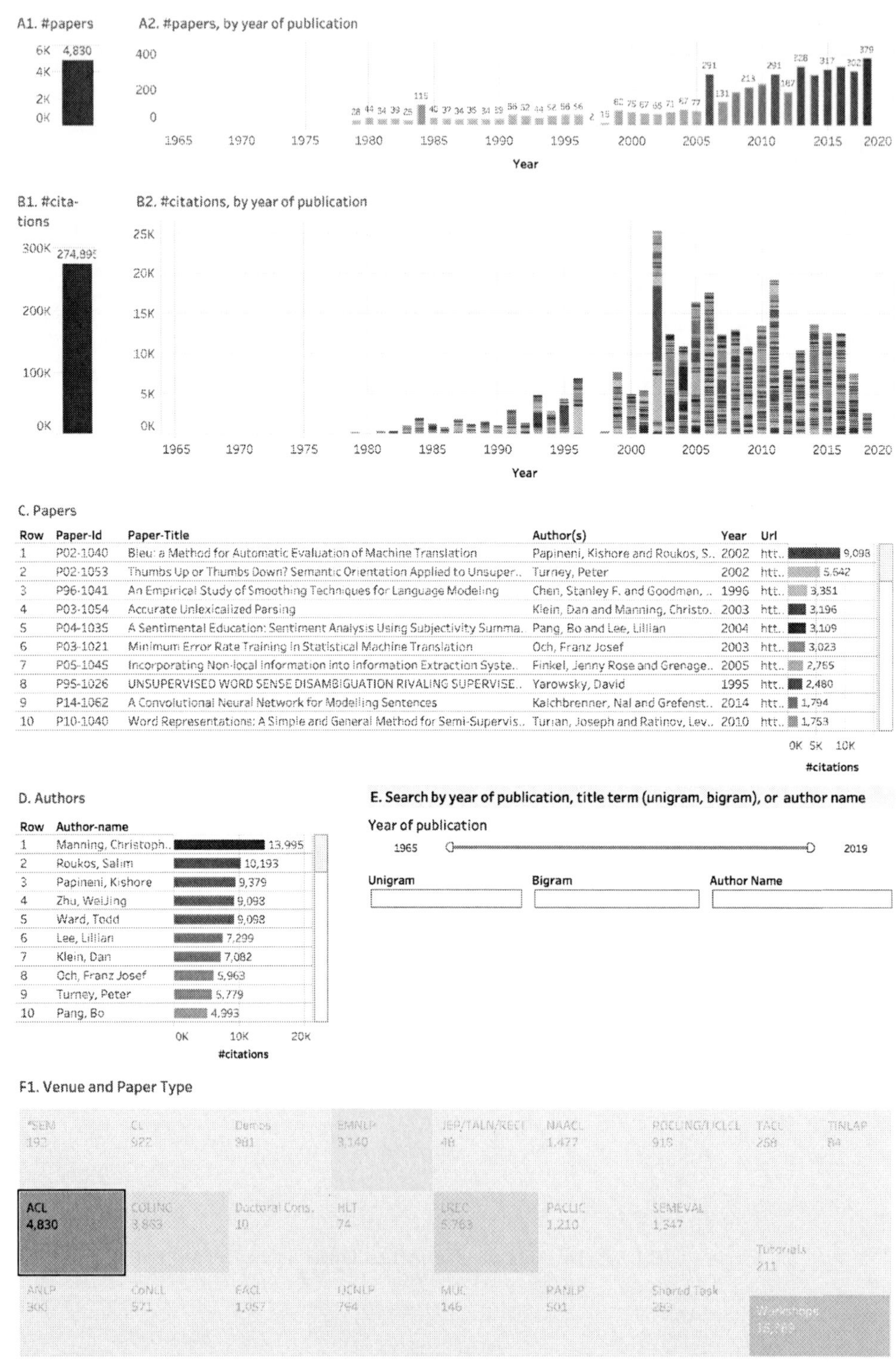

Figure 11: NLP Scholar: After clicking on 'ACL' in the venue and paper type treemap (F1).

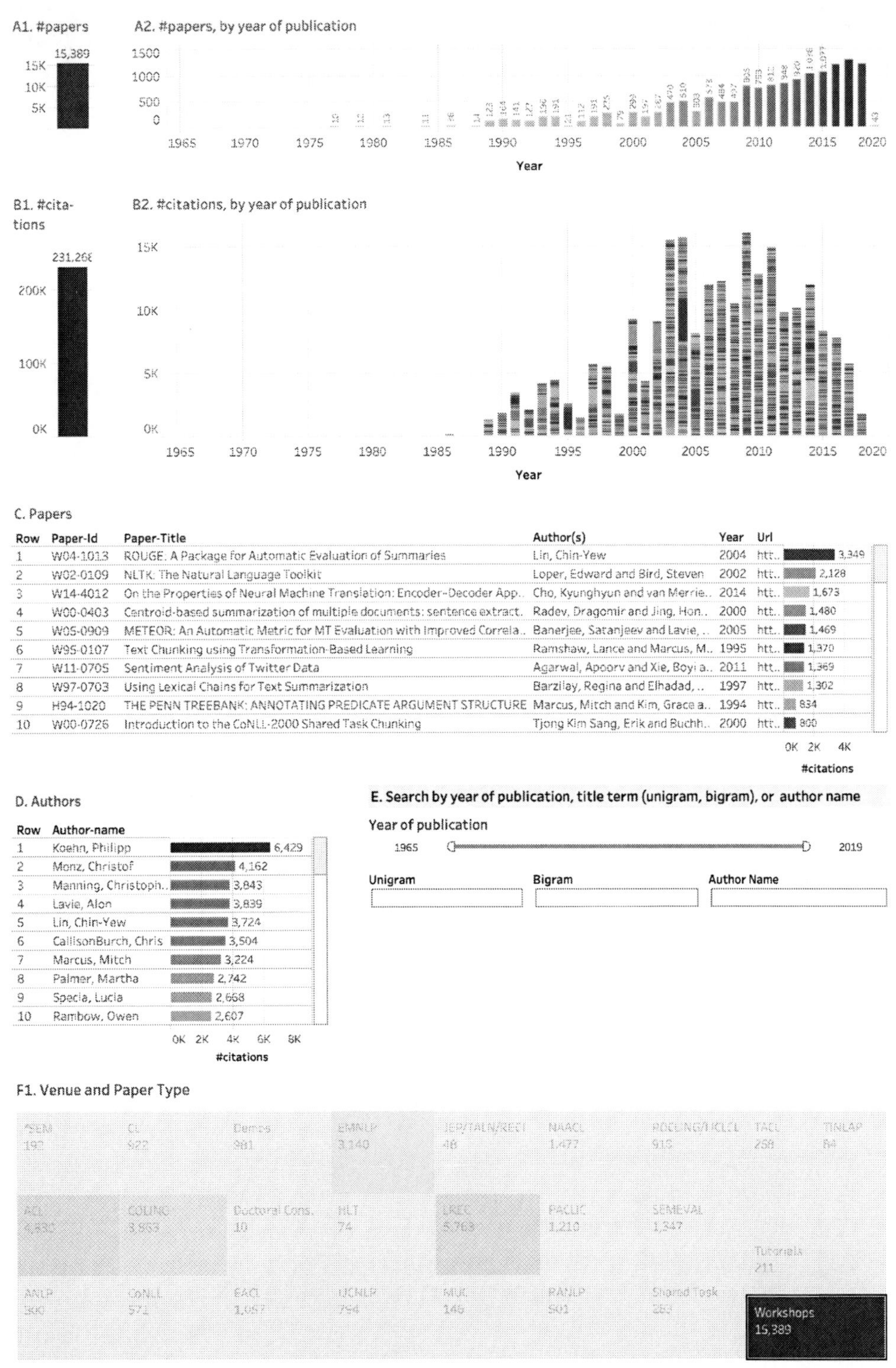

Figure 12: NLP Scholar: After clicking on 'Workshops' in the venue and paper type treemap (F1).

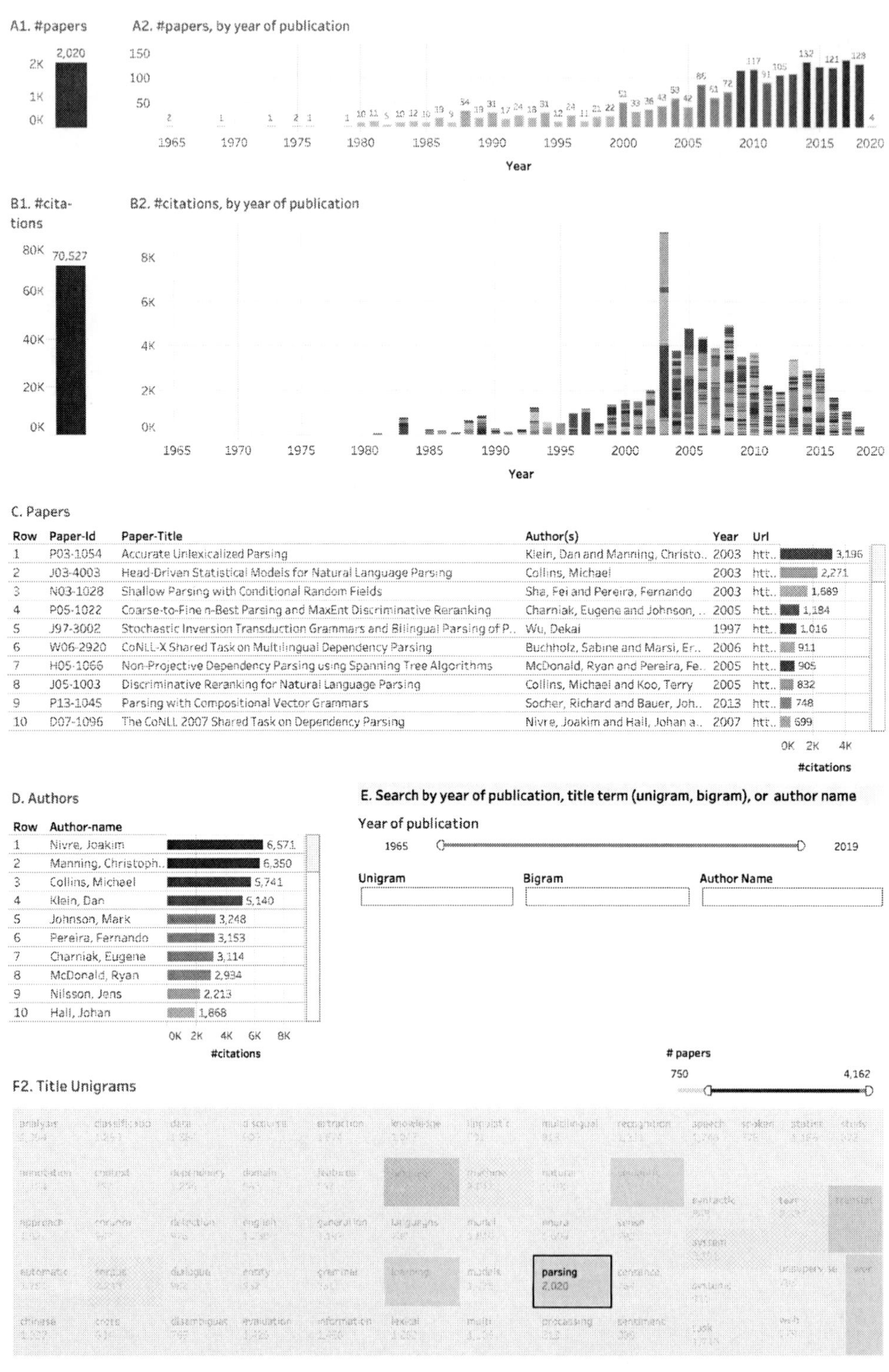

Figure 13: NLP Scholar: After clicking on 'parsing' in the unigrams treemap (F2).

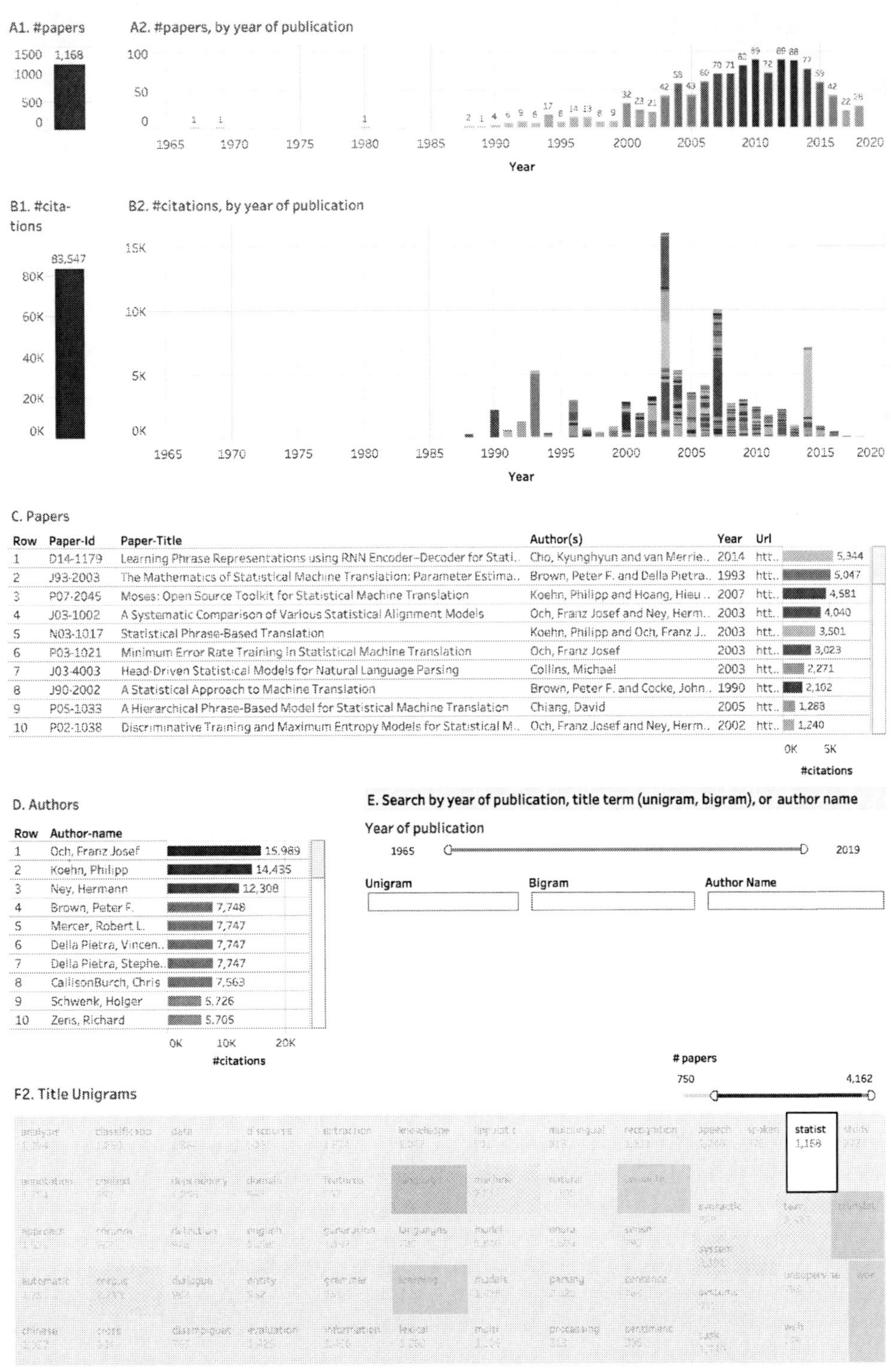

Figure 14: NLP Scholar: After clicking on 'statistical' in the unigrams treemap (F2).

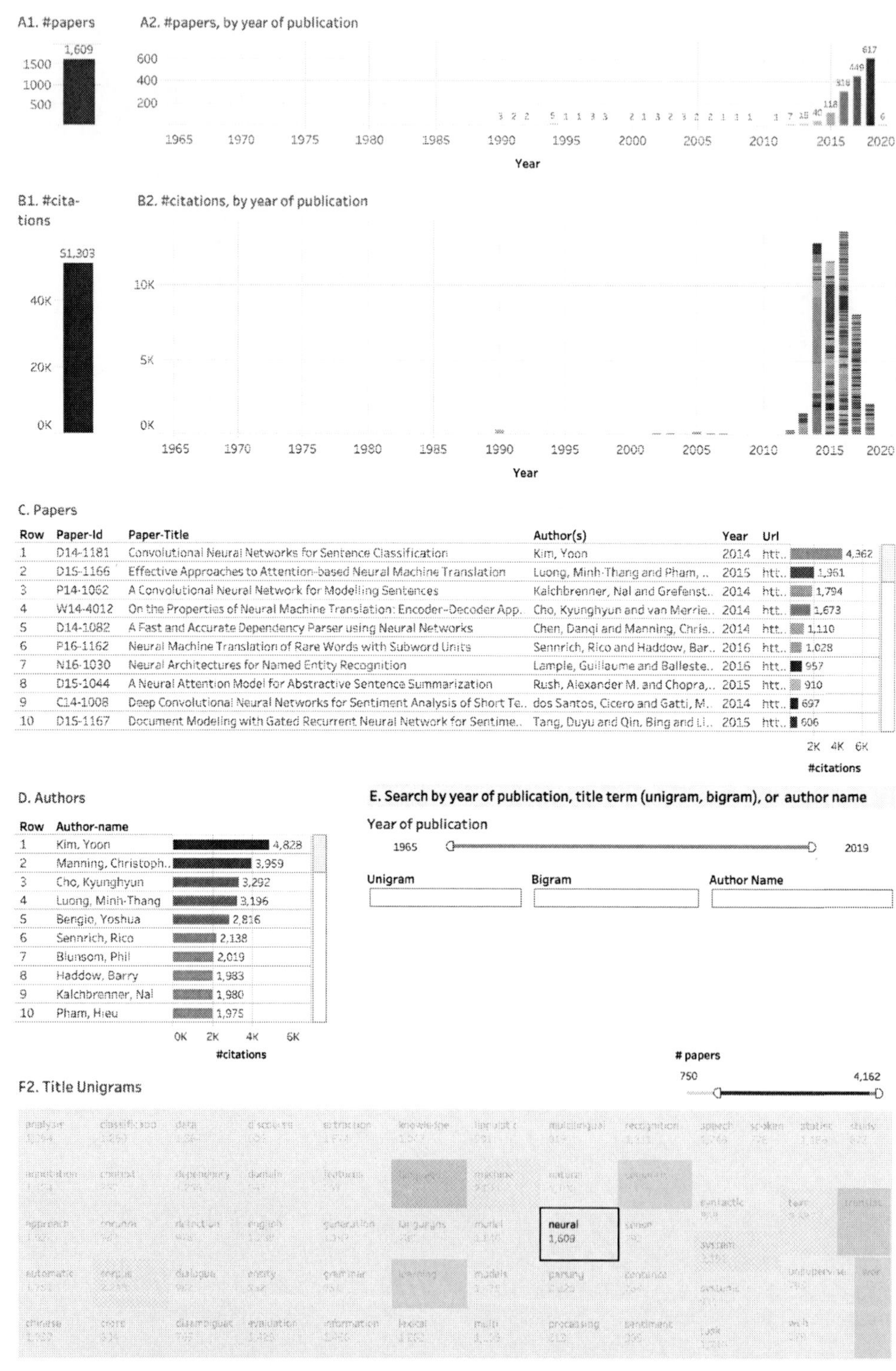

Figure 15: NLP Scholar: After clicking on 'neural' in the unigrams treemap (F2).

Figure 16: NLP Scholar: After clicking on 'machine translation' in the bigrams treemap (F3).

Figure 17: NLP Scholar: After clicking on 'question answering' in the bigrams treemap (F3).

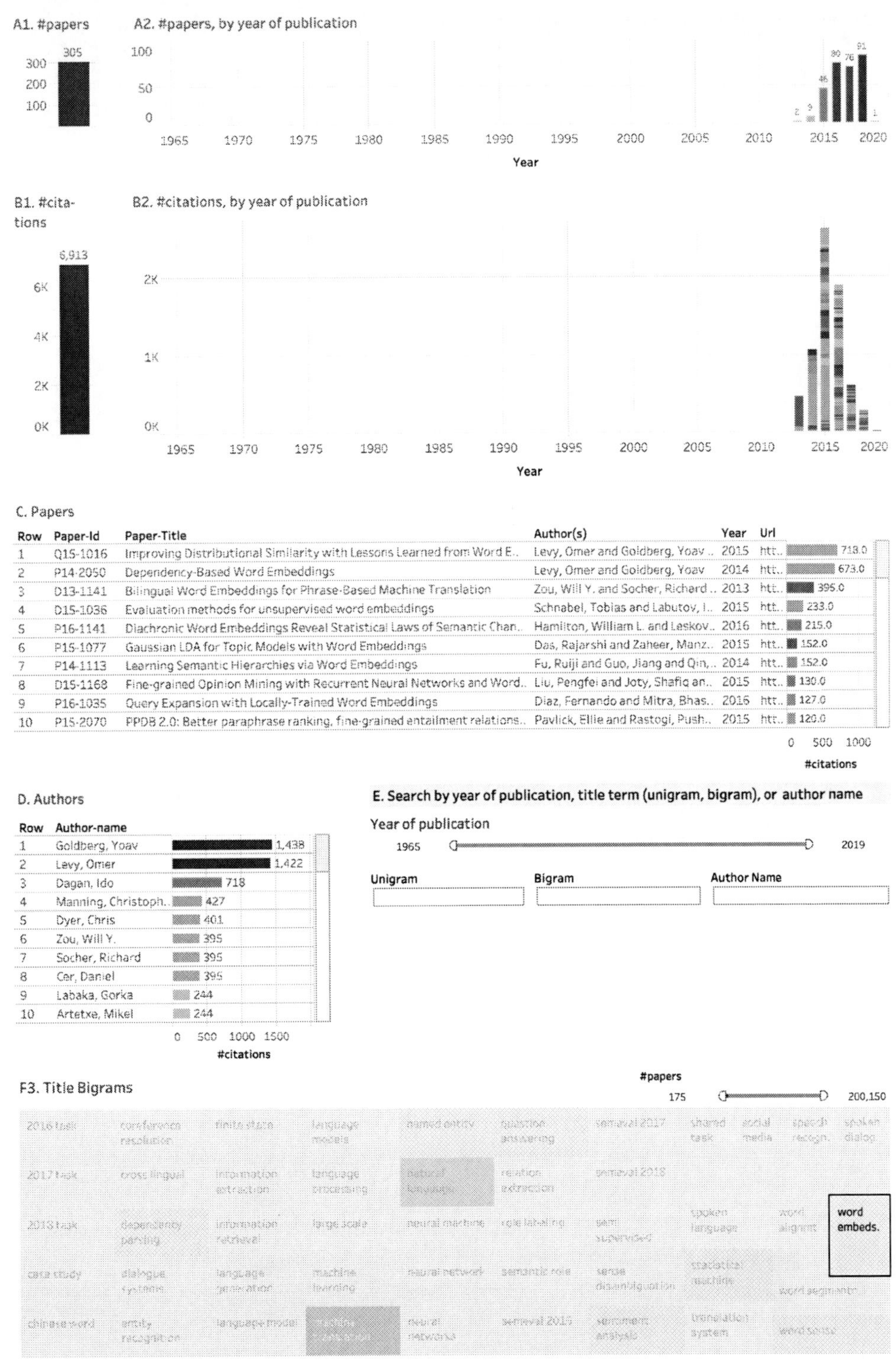

Figure 18: NLP Scholar: After clicking on 'word embeddings' in the bigrams treemap (F3).

253

Figure 19: NLP Scholar: After clicking on 'Chinese' in the languages treemap (F4).

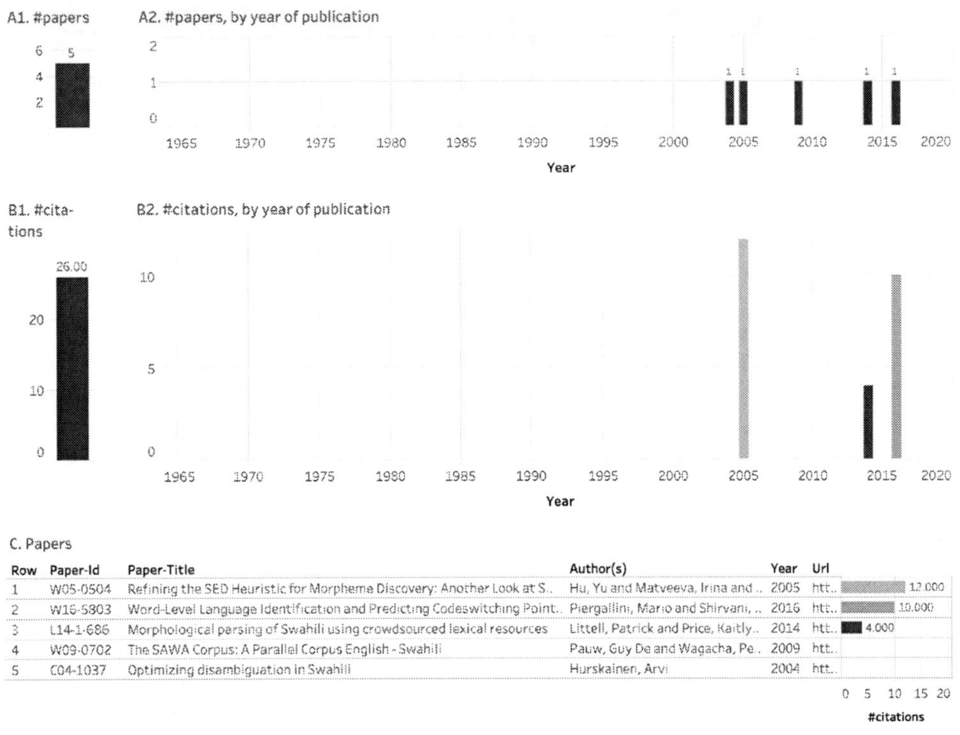

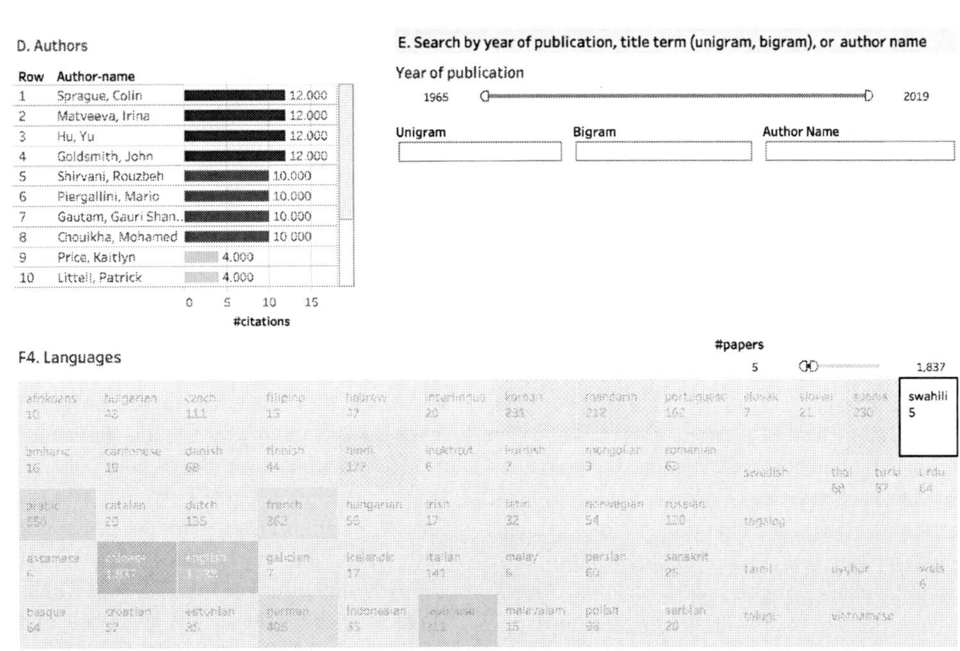

Figure 20: NLP Scholar: After clicking on 'Swahili' in the languages treemap (F4).

Stimulating Creativity with FunLines:
A Case Study of Humor Generation in Headlines

Nabil Hossain[*], **John Krumm**[†], **Tanvir Sajed**[‡] and **Henry Kautz**[*]

[*]Department of Computer Science, University of Rochester
[†]Microsoft Research AI, Microsoft Corporation, Redmond, WA
[‡]Department of Computing Science, University of Alberta

{nhossain,kautz}@cs.rochester.edu, jckrumm@microsoft.com, tsajed@ualberta.ca

Abstract

Building datasets of creative text, such as humor, is quite challenging. We introduce **FunLines**, a competitive game where players edit news headlines to make them funny, and where they rate the funniness of headlines edited by others. FunLines makes the humor generation process fun, interactive, collaborative, rewarding and educational, keeping players engaged and providing humor data at a very low cost compared to traditional crowdsourcing approaches. FunLines offers useful performance feedback, assisting players in getting better over time at generating and assessing humor, as our analysis shows. This helps to further increase the quality of the generated dataset. We show the effectiveness of this data by training humor classification models that outperform a previous benchmark, and we release this dataset to the public.

1 Introduction

While some data for machine learning tasks, like image object detection, is relatively easy to annotate, generating data that depends on human creativity is quite difficult. Unlike many objective tasks, creativity is much less constrained, people do not always agree on the quality of creative output, and measuring creativity often requires more effort. One such creative endeavor is humor, which is subjective and hard to define, making consensus difficult. Factors such as human preferences, mood, world knowledge, and complex interrelationships play important roles in determining what is funny, making it challenging to generate humor datasets.

One approach to crowdsourcing creative data is to hire workers, as we did for humorous headlines in Hossain et al. (2019). An alternative is to make a game for gathering the data. Games are especially suitable for gathering creative output because it is enjoyable to both generate and rate creative artifacts, particularly humor. The effectiveness of games for labeling data has been shown in previous work (Von Ahn and Dabbish, 2004, 2008).

In this paper, we introduce Funlines[1], an online game for generating funny news headlines for humor research. We explore and evaluate this fun, competitive way of motivating people to contribute creative text, addressing some of the special challenges of generating humor data mentioned above.

Generating a dataset of creative artifacts for machine learning requires ratings of the artifacts. This has been done for sites like Reddit (reddit.com) for jokes and Photofeeler (photofeeler.com) for photos, both of which allow casual users to upvote/downvote creative content from others. The Hafez research project lets users rate machine generated poetry (Ghazvininejad et al., 2017). In Fun-Lines, one of the two main tasks for players is to rate the funniness of headlines that have been edited by other players. Humor is inherently social, and the headlines' collective exposure to, and rating from, humans preserves this important feature.

The other main task in FunLines is to edit regular headlines to make them funny. To simplify machine learning and humor analysis, we want funny headlines that are highly constrained. In FunLines, players start with a regular headline from a news source and they change a single word or entity to make it funny, giving data that is particularly suitable for understanding the tipping point between serious and humorous. This contrasts with Unfun.me, which is also a game for generating pairs of funny and unfunny headlines (West and Horvitz, 2019). With Unfun.me, players start with a funny headline and make it serious, where their edits are unconstrained but encouraged to be minimal. Because it starts with regular headlines, FunLines has

---

[1] https://funlines.co
FunLines demo video: https://youtu.be/5OXJMxDBaLY

Proceedings of the 58th Annual Meeting of the Association for Computational Linguistics, pages 256–262
July 5 - July 10, 2020. ©2020 Association for Computational Linguistics

(a) The Headline Editing Task.

(b) The Headline Rating Task.

Figure 1: Screenshots of the FunLines humor tasks.

an enormous amount of raw source material. Also related to FunLines' editing tasks are projects that help users create humor, like HumorTools (Chilton et al., 2016) and Libitum (Hossain et al., 2017).

By deploying FunLines, we learned how players behaved, and we responded with modifications to encourage players to provide creative, high quality data. We show that over time, players made significant improvements in both the quality of their humor and consistency of their ratings. We also show that the resulting data is effective for training humor detection systems. In fact, FunLines uses one of our humor detectors to give instant feedback when players edit a headline. We compare the FunLines data to **Humicroedit**, which is a humorous headlines dataset we collected previously from crowd workers (Hossain et al., 2019). FunLines data is less expensive, higher quality, and leads to improved automated humor detection. Overall, we show that a competitive game is effective for gathering data for a human creativity task based on an experiment with a large number of users.

2   The FunLines Humor Game

FunLines is designed to collect a large volume of rated, humorous headlines. It makes the humor generation process fun, interactive, competitive, rewarding and educational, keeping players engaged.

In FunLines, players can attempt two tasks: (i) edit regular news headlines to make them funny, and (ii) rate the funniness of headlines edited by other players. They receive feedback for these actions, which helps them get better at the game. Players are ranked in our performance-based leader-boards, which offer prize money. We now describe the various aspects of the game that make it work.

2.1   Editing Headlines

Similar to our previous work (Hossain et al., 2019), we restrict the headline editing task to the substitution of a noun, verb or entity in the headline with a single word. This constraint enables focused analysis on humor triggered by atomic changes in text.

Shown in Figure 1(a), the headline editing interface highlights the headline's replaceable words in blue. It allows a single word substitute to be submitted by the player. To help put the headline in context, we provide information such as the news source, category and date of publication, including a link to the article (H16 in Fig. 1(a)). Upon submitting the edited headline, the player receives an estimated funniness score from a humor classifier built into FunLines (see Section 5.1).

2.2   Rating Headlines

As in Hossain et al. (2019), players rate a headline's funniness on a 4 point scale, as shown in Fig. 1(b):

0 - Not funny at all   **2** - Funny
1 - Only slightly funny   **3** - Very funny

We provide instant rating feedback to players when they rate a headline that already has a consensus rating from other players. This feedback includes whether the player's rating is reasonably close, higher, or lower compared to ratings from others.

Each edited headline is made available in the game until it has **five** funniness ratings, which constitutes a **fully rated** edited headline.

2.3 Competition Setting

We designed FunLines as a humor competition to motivate players to perform well. Players are scored based on their editing and rating, and they are ranked on the game's leaderboard page.

2.3.1 Leaderboard

We maintain two performance-based leaderboards:

1. **Top points scorers:** This ranks players by points scored based on volume and quality of editing and rating as well as keeping a good balance between the volume of editing and rating.

2. **Highest average ratings:** This ranks players who received the highest mean funniness ratings for their edited headlines.

Players who rank in the top 10 positions in any of the two leaderboards at the end of the 5-week long contest receive prize money between US$ 5-100.

The leaderboard page also lists the recent top 10 funny headlines to show players examples of successful edits so that they can adjust their editing style, and to encourage them to make it to this list.

2.3.2 Qualification Requirements

Our competition requires participants to edit between 50-150 headlines and to rate between 200-500 headlines to be considered for prize money. The upper limits prevent players from running up their scores simply based on volume rather than quality. The lower limits help us collect more data, and since players get better at the game over time (details in Section 4.1), the quality of data improves with a larger volume of work from each player.

2.3.3 Scoring

Players receive humor points when they edit or rate headlines. We do not reveal the precise scoring formulae to the players to discourage them from "gaming" the game. The three scoring factors are:
Editing Points: This score component exponentially increases with a headline's funniness ratings, encouraging players to make each edited headline as funny as possible.
Rating Points: This is a function of the difference between the player's ratings and ratings from other players for the headline. The lower the difference, the higher the points earned, and a large difference gives the player negative points. This incentivizes players to be objective, rating headlines based on how others (*e.g.*, a crowd) would rate them instead of letting their own biases influence their decisions.

Task Balancing Points: Players are rewarded for maintaining a good balance between the numbers of edits and ratings. These points are maximized if the ratio of total ratings to total edits is between 3-10. This discourages players from ignoring one of the tasks, helping to keep our dataset balanced.

2.4 Protecting Against Abusive Behavior

During pilot tests, we noticed certain abusive player behavior, which we minimized, as described below:
Abusive Edits: We prevent players from submitting slang words, crude sexual references, bathroom jokes and other cheap forms of humor using blacklists. Also, players are encouraged to flag an edited headline if it demonstrates abusive behavior, and such headlines are removed from the rating pool, depriving their editors of potential points.
Abusive Ratings: We forced a time delay to prevent players from rapidly rating headlines without reading them. Attempts at lowering others' points by consistently assigning low ratings cause players to accumulate large negative points as these ratings mostly disagree with ratings from other players.

Players who repeatedly show abusive behavior are warned, and, in some cases, suspended in order to maintain a healthy competition environment.

2.5 Performance Feedback

FunLines gives players feedback on their performance so that they can improve their play:
Editing: Players see their top 5 most funny edited headlines and their 10 most recent edited headlines and the corresponding ratings for all. This helps them monitor how their edited headlines appeal to other players, and to adjust their editing style. They also see which of their edits are marked as abusive.
Rating: Players see the histogram of their rating selections and the percentage of their ratings that are significantly above or below the ratings of others who rated the same headlines. This helps them spot and rectify errors such as frequently overestimating or underestimating ratings, a common user behavior we saw initially in the competition. Players also see the 10 most recent headlines they rated and the ratings they assigned.

Players are advised on how many more edits or ratings to do to optimize their task balancing score.

2.6 Ordering Headlines for Rating

The ordering of headlines displayed for rating greatly influences which headlines receive more ratings. Using their sampling weights, we re-compute the display order of headlines for rating every few minutes. Headlines are assigned higher sampling weights if they: (i) are from players with high volumes of edited headlines, (ii) are from players who received very few ratings, (iii) are recently submitted, or (iv) have received more ratings.

Ratings are diversified by limiting each player from rating more than 10 headlines of another player. These design decisions make the game fair, engaging, and rewarding to all players.

2.7 Popular Headlines and Player Flexibility

FunLines provides headlines from 5 diverse topics: politics, world news, entertainment, technology and sports. It daily adds about 300 trending English headlines from major news outlets posted to Reddit.

FunLines gives players the flexibility to choose which headlines to edit or rate, a freedom that the crowd workers in Hossain et al. (2019) did not have. Not all headlines are easy to edit or judge for humor, and by providing a large pool of headlines, FunLines allows players be strategic and selective. For example, they can focus only on headlines they appreciate and understand, and they can use the SKIP button to permanently ignore headlines that are confusing or simply too difficult to edit or rate.

Our editable headlines are sorted by most recently published first, making it easier for players to generate humor with stories that are fresh in their minds. FunLines also offers players the option of choosing to work on headlines by their preferred news categories. Overall, these features help tackle human preferences and knowledge related challenges associated with humor understanding.

3 Gathering Data

In this section, we describe our player recruiting strategies, our gathered dataset, and its comparison against Humicroedit (Hossain et al., 2019).

3.1 Attracting Players

To jump start data collection, we hired players from Amazon Mechanical Turk (AMT). Our competition budget was US\$ 1,000, and since the total prize money was US\$ 560, we spent the remaining US\$ 440 to hire 100 US turkers. These turkers were intended to seed the game, and many of them continued playing after their paid work was finished.

We sought additional players by advertising FunLines in our networks, making a TV news appearance, and posting on relevant social media pages.

Original Headline (replaced word in bold)	Edit	RT
Sanders says he has more donors than Trump	hair	3.0
'What is the green new deal?'	ham	2.4
Japan begins controversial Taiji dolphin hunt	ninja	2.0
Bolton confirms he's willing to testify	lie	1.6
A\$AP Rocky found guilty of assault in Sweden	singing	1.0
Netherlands to drop 'Holland' as nickname	Gangster	0.4
The useful idiot from Louisiana	Louis	0.0
K-pop star Sulli found dead aged 25	*skipped*	–

Table 1: Headlines in FunLines with ratings.

Metric	Humicroedit	FunLines
Size	15,095	8,248
Mean funniness	0.94	1.26
Cost per datum	29.8c	12.1c
Agreement α	0.20	0.25
Unique words used	41.2%	53.4%
No. of editors	73	214
No. of raters	131	246

Table 2: Humicroedit and FunLines data comparison.

Overall, we had 290 players, out of whom 204 completed at least 20 edits and ratings, 89 met the competition qualification requirements, and 33 completed the maximum 150 edits and 500 ratings.

3.2 Dataset Quality

Here we examine the FunLines dataset[2] and we compare it to Humicroedit (Hossain et al., 2019), the same type of headline data we previously obtained using only AMT workers and without a game. Table 1 shows sample headlines in FunLines and Table 2 shows several quality measures.

In total, we received 13,063 edited headlines and 46,359 headline ratings, leading to 8,248 fully rated headlines and only 55 abusive headlines. On average, players took about 25 seconds per edit and 5 seconds per rating, implying that they collectively spent about 168 hours playing the game. Given that our budget was US\$ 1,000, this makes the hourly participation rate only US\$ 5.95. The cost of each fully rated headline in FunLines is 12.1 cents vs 29.8 cents in Humicroedit, a nearly 60% cost reduction. The mean funniness rating for Humicroedit is 0.94 vs. 1.27 in FunLines, meaning that our competition based approach enabled us to achieve a 35% boost in funniness on average. Funnier headlines are hard to obtain, which makes our FunLines dataset more valuable for machine learning.

The annotator agreement score in FunLines, measured by Krippendorf's α (Krippendorff, 1970), is 0.25 vs. 0.20 in Humicroedit, implying higher

---

[2]Dataset: cs.rochester.edu/u/nhossain/funlines.html

agreement without spending funds for qualifying players, which we did for Humicroedit. Instead, the game's real-time feedback helps people learn how to be better editors and raters. 53.4% of the words used in FunLines are unique vs. 41.2% in Humicroedit, indicating more diversity of edits.

All these factors show that our competition based approach to humor data collection is a better option than simply hiring crowd workers who are not incentivized and rewarded based on performance.

Finally, our data size could be increased by raising the editing and rating caps, running the competition longer, reaching out to more people, or being more efficient at rating partially rated headlines.

4 Analysis of Player Behavior

We examine how players adapted to the FunLines competition and the headlines they attempted.

4.1 Player Improvement over Time

Figure 2(a) shows that over time, the mean funniness of fully rated headlines steadily increases, indicating that players are getting better at making funnier edited headlines as the competition proceeds. In addition, Figure 2(b) shows that as players edit more headlines, they generally get better at making funnier edits. Finally, Figure 2(c) shows that as players rate more headlines, the difference of their ratings from the mean ratings of others for the same headline decreases, indicating that players become more consistent at rating over time.

Overall, Figure 2 demonstrates the educational aspect of FunLines, suggesting that by playing the game, people can learn to be better at generating humor and agreeing on its ratings. These results emphasize the advantages of this competitive and collaborative approach in helping us collect quality humor data, mirroring the social nature of humor.

4.2 Choosing Headline Categories

We analyze whether players were strategic about choosing headlines to edit. Table 3 shows the proportions of the five headline categories in the headlines supplied by FunLines (H), the proportions of headlines from each category that were edited (E), the proportions of each category in the fully rated FunLines dataset (FR), and the mean funniness ratings of headlines from each category.

The two classes with the highest mean funniness ratings are politics and world news. The E (edited) column shows that players are ignoring about 30%

Category	% H	% E	% FR	Mean RT
Politics	70.0	71.5	56.4	1.32
World news	22.3	71.0	22.4	1.29
Technology	4.6	92.9	11.0	1.22
Sports	1.1	96.7	3.4	1.14
Entertainment	2.0	95.2	6.8	0.96

Table 3: FunLines headline categories with ratings.

of headlines from these categories, while they are almost exhausting the headlines from the other three categories. Not all headlines can be easily made funny, and attempting almost all the headlines from these three categories is likely hurting players' funniness scores. Besides, politics and world news are very popular topics, whereas the others are somewhat niche categories with smaller audiences, and thus the raters are perhaps not familiar with the entities and events mentioned in their articles, and thus might not be "getting" the jokes.

5 Detecting Humorous Headlines

We investigate if the FunLines dataset of 8,248 fully rated headlines is suitable for humor detection.

5.1 Instant Editing Feedback

Whenever a player submits an edited headline, FunLines uses a humor detection system to provide instant funniness feedback. This is a fine-tuned BERT next sentence prediction model (Devlin et al., 2019) in the regression setting that uses the input:

<original headline> [SEP] <edited headline>

We re-train this model as blocks of new data becomes available. We start by training on the first 1,000 fully rated headlines, and we test our model against the next 1,000. Then we train on the first 2,000 and test on the next 1,000, and so on. The results, shown in Figure 3, suggest that the model gets increasingly accurate in its funniness estimations over time as more data becomes available, and thus its feedback to the user improves over time. We attribute this to both the increased volume of data and the increased quality and consistency of edited and rated headlines, as illustrated in Figure 2.

5.2 Improving Classification for Humicroedit

We explore whether using the FunLines data can improve binary humor classification in Humicroedit (Hossain et al., 2019). We augment the training data of Humicroedit with the FunLines data, and we evaluate classification performance with and without this dataset augmentation.

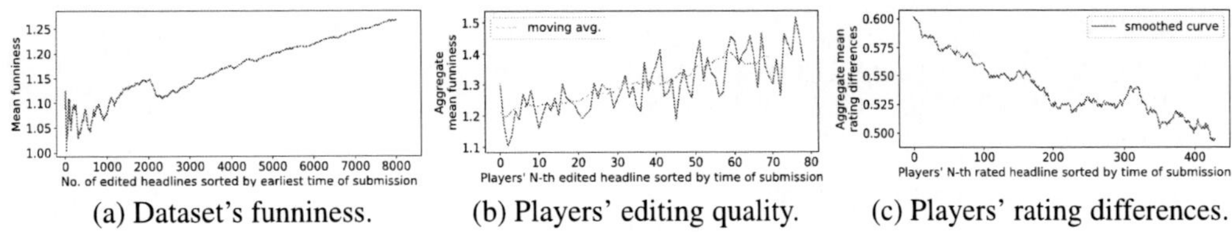

(a) Dataset's funniness. (b) Players' editing quality. (c) Players' rating differences.

Figure 2: Players get better at editing and rating headlines over time, helping to increase funniness in the dataset.

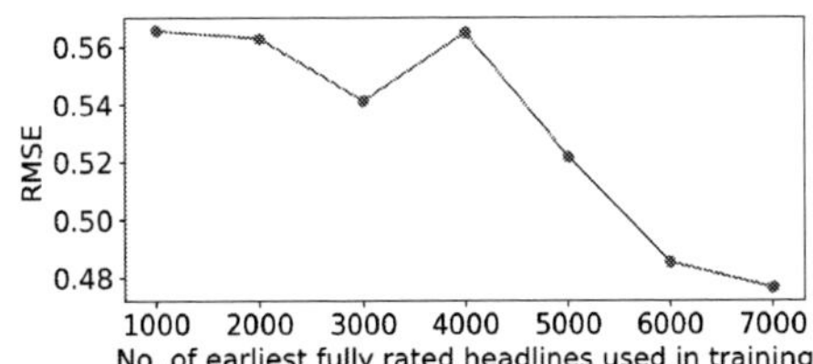

Figure 3: Results of re-training BERT funniness regression as more data becomes available in FunLines.

X	MaxUF	MinF	LSTM	BERT	BERT Aug.
10	0.2	1.8	68.54	76.48	77.32
20	0.4	1.4	67.21	73.76	75.66
30	0.6	1.2	66.11	69.37	70.75
40	0.8	1.0	64.07	66.38	68.00
50	0.8	0.8	60.6	63.93	64.40

Table 4: Humicroedit classification accuracy with and without using augmented training data from FunLines.

Humicroedit was trained on the top and bottom $X\%$ funny and unfunny headlines in its dataset. Each $X\%$ gives an upper and lower funniness threshold, and we use these same thresholds (MaxUF and MinF in Table 4) to select the augmentation data from FunLines. We trimmed the FunLines data so there was balanced augmentation for funny and unfunny.

For a fair comparison with Hossain et al. (2019), we ignore the original headlines and use only the edited versions of headlines as classifier input. We fine-tune the BERT sentence classification model on both the original and augmented Humicroedit dataset. In Table 4, we show the funniness thresholds for each subset X, the benchmark results in Hossain et al. (2019) obtained using LSTM with GloVe word vectors, and we report our new results.

These results suggest that while BERT trained on Humicroedit alone outperforms LSTM, the FunLines data helps further BERT's classification accuracy (BERT Aug.) by up to 2% for each of the sub-datasets. This is good improvement given that we are only augmenting Humicroedit with part of the FunLines dataset and the 0-3 funniness scale between the two datasets are not calibrated. Further, in Humicroedit, each original headline was edited three times, so there is overlap in its training and test sets, which makes the task a bit easier. In FunLines, headlines were mostly edited only once.

Our experiments used the BERT base model with a learning rate of $1e^{-4}$, max seq length of 64, batch size of 8, and we trained models for up to 3 epochs.

6 Conclusion and Future Work

FunLines is an online game for generating funny headlines. While creative data can be difficult to obtain, FunLines makes it easier by taking advantage of the inherent fun of creativity and competition. We described the game, including a rich set of feedback for players to assess their own performance along with controls and incentives for them to create funny headlines. Our deployment attracted 290 players for a total cost of US$ 1,000. Compared to our earlier work for gathering the same type of data from only turkers, FunLines produced funnier headlines with better rating agreement and at nearly 60% lower cost per headline. We showed how players' performance improves over time, both in terms of their headline quality and rating consistency. We showed how the FunLines data is effective for training machine learning models to detect and to rate humorous headlines. Furthermore, this data has already found use in a recent SemEval shared task on humor recognition (Hossain et al., 2020)[3].

Having built models for detecting humor, we see this data as the foundation of the automatic *creation* of humorous headlines in a generate-and-test approach. More generally, FunLines is a prototype for gathering datasets of creative artifacts from people that is engaging, interactive, competitive, rewarding, educational and inexpensive. In future, we would like to extend the FunLines data collection setup to a more general crowdsourcing framework, for example, to collect style transfer data.

---

[3]https://competitions.codalab.org/competitions/20970

References

Lydia B Chilton, James A Landay, and Daniel S Weld. 2016. Humortools: A microtask workflow for writing news satire.

Jacob Devlin, Ming-Wei Chang, Kenton Lee, and Kristina Toutanova. 2019. BERT: Pre-training of deep bidirectional transformers for language understanding. In *Proceedings of the 2019 Conference of the North American Chapter of the Association for Computational Linguistics: Human Language Technologies, Volume 1 (Long and Short Papers)*, pages 4171–4186, Minneapolis, Minnesota. Association for Computational Linguistics.

Marjan Ghazvininejad, Xing Shi, Jay Priyadarshi, and Kevin Knight. 2017. Hafez: an interactive poetry generation system. In *Proceedings of ACL 2017, System Demonstrations*, pages 43–48, Vancouver, Canada. Association for Computational Linguistics.

Nabil Hossain, John Krumm, and Michael Gamon. 2019. "President vows to cut <taxes> hair": Dataset and analysis of creative text editing for humorous headlines. In *Proceedings of the 2019 Conference of the North American Chapter of the Association for Computational Linguistics: Human Language Technologies, Volume 1 (Long and Short Papers)*, pages 133–142, Minneapolis, Minnesota. Association for Computational Linguistics.

Nabil Hossain, John Krumm, Michael Gamon, and Henry Kautz. 2020. Semeval-2020 task 7: Assessing humor in edited news headlines (to appear). In *Proceedings of the 14th International Workshop on Semantic Evaluation*.

Nabil Hossain, John Krumm, Lucy Vanderwende, Eric Horvitz, and Henry Kautz. 2017. Filling the blanks (hint: plural noun) for Mad Libs humor. In *Proceedings of the 2017 Conference on Empirical Methods in Natural Language Processing*, pages 638–647, Copenhagen, Denmark. Association for Computational Linguistics.

Klaus Krippendorff. 1970. Estimating the reliability, systematic error and random error of interval data. *Educational and Psychological Measurement*, 30(1):61–70.

Luis Von Ahn and Laura Dabbish. 2004. Labeling images with a computer game. In *Proceedings of the SIGCHI conference on Human factors in computing systems*, pages 319–326.

Luis Von Ahn and Laura Dabbish. 2008. Designing games with a purpose. *Communications of the ACM*, 51(8):58–67.

Robert West and Eric Horvitz. 2019. Reverse-engineering satire, or "paper on computational humor accepted despite making serious advances". In *Proceedings of the AAAI Conference on Artificial Intelligence*, volume 33, pages 7265–7272.

Usnea: An Authorship Tool for Interactive Fiction using Retrieval Based Semantic Parsing

Ben Swanson[*]
Google
pwnr@google.com[*]

Boris Smus[*]
Google
smus@google.com

Abstract

The reader of a choose your own adventure novel and the user of a modern virtual assistant have a subtle similarity; both may, through the right lens, be viewed as engaging with a work of Interactive Fiction. This literary form emerged in the 1970s and has grown like a vine along the branch of modern technology, one guided by the advances of the other. In this work we weave together threads from the Interactive Fiction community and neural semantic parsing for dialog systems, defining the data model and necessary algorithms for a novel type of Interactive Fiction and open sourcing its accompanying authoring tool. Specifically, our work integrates retrieval based semantic parsing predicates into the branching story structures well known to the Interactive Fiction community, relaxing the relatively strict lexical options of preexisting systems.

1 Introduction

Interactive Fiction (IF) is a diverse genre of art and entertainment that is most well known in the context of video games, from text adventures (e.g. *Zork*), to classic point and click adventures such as *Monkey Island* to award winning modern games like *80 Days* (Time Magazine Game of the Year 2014). Less familiar to the general public is the literary tradition that recognizes IF as high art on par with the novel and poem, and produces compelling work collected in ever-growing online repositories[1]. The signature techniques of IF include branching story structure, multiple endings, and the use of lamps to solve complex problems.

IF was born, they say, in 1979 as ADVENT, a text based cave exploration game written by a father to amuse and delight his daughters (Niesz and Holland, 1984). Over the last 40 years, the interactive affordances of technology have grown from text in a terminal to include modern marvels such as graphics, audio, touchscreens, virtual reality, and speech recognition, and with their added complexity has come the creation of authorship software that allows nontechnical authors to harness these media. This is exemplified in Inform[2], a compiled programming language whose lines of code are themselves grammatical English sentences.

Authorship tools for IF define some structure of a story and provide suggested algorithms or software itself to realize this structure in a form that a reader can digest, which taken together we will call a *model specification*. Our particular model specification is inspired by recent work in neural dialog systems for virtual assistants. While ADVENT and Alexa may seem to have little in common, they are both clearly a turn taking interaction between a *system* and a *reader*[3]. Their internal workings are also similar, as it is no coincidence that the sub-genre of parser games like *Zork* shares a token in its name with the semantic parsers used in a dialog agents; they share the common ancestor of tree-structure parsers from the early days of computational linguistics (Woods, 1973).

We make use of retrieval based semantic parsing (Yao et al., 2019), a variant of nearest neighbor classification using inverse semantic similarity as its distance metric. One particular strength of this method is that the semantic similarity metric, or semantic kernel (Altınel et al., 2015), can be pretrained on general domain text pairs. Instantiating a domain specific semantic parser is tantamount to the definition of *exemplars*, strings paired with class labels that indicate their known semantics. Crucially, this is a task that can be done with no machine learning or programming background. It

---

* equal contribution
[1] https://www.ifarchive.org

[2] http://inform7.com

[3] We avoid the term "user" in this work in order to differentiate between users of the authoring tool (*authors*) and users of the resulting literary work (*readers*).

Proceedings of the 58th Annual Meeting of the Association for Computational Linguistics, pages 263–269
July 5 - July 10, 2020. ©2020 Association for Computational Linguistics

also avoids explicit formal semantic representations such as FrameNet (Baker et al., 1998), eliminating the learning curve required to bootstrap supervised discriminative semantic parsing systems such as Wang et al. (2015).

Our model grants the reader a more freeform mode of interaction compared to many other examples of IF; as long as the author can guide and anticipate the readers' inputs into close neighborhoods of their exemplars, the reader can both decide what to say and how to say it. For the author, we optimize for efficiency with features that collapse common patterns observed in user testing and components designed for the iterative tuning of the semantic parser exemplars. We also consider a third user type, the programmer who wishes to extend our open source library, by implementing our tool in Angular with extensive modularity via dependency injection. The general tool architecture is as an AppEngine hosted website, with Firebase for persistence.

2 Interactive Fiction

2.1 Overview

In its broadest sense, IF is an entertainment experience in which the reader is not a passive observer, or equivalently a sequence of *reader turns* and *system turns*. The reader turns need not be self-composed, as in the Choose Your Own Adventure novel where the system turns are the book chapters and the reader turns are selected from pre-written choices. While the system turns need not be simple text and often include audiovisual components, for clarity we restrict the scope of our discussion of IF in this work to the class in which our model lies where both user and system turns are purely textual.

Of the many members of this class, the two that we keep top of mind in our model design are parser games and dialogues. In parser games (Zorklikes), the reader commonly plays as the protagonist and system turns describe the reader's current observations of the world around them. The reader has a semantically rich but linguistically constrained set of options supplied by a semantic parser that recognizes combinatoric verb / object pairings. Our second focus is on dialogues, where the system and reader turns are both conversational utterances. This is motivated by the emergence of virtual assistants as a potential delivery mechanism for IF and the existing use of branching dialogues in story

rich video games.

2.2 History, Abridged

While IF has rarely gained recognition in the mainstream media outside video games, it has been an area of literary and academic interest for several decades. Ziegfeld (1989) is especially prescient; in their discussion of the then nascent intersection of computer technology and storytelling, they explore possibilities for the use of branching that both include and expand on some of our own ideas, as well as raise thoughtful questions that remain unanswered today as to the eventual place of IF in art history.

The first documented piece of IF was ADVENT, written in the late seventies. Ziegfeld (1989) describes some other early IF work done in collaboration with well-known authors such as Michael Crichton, Ray Bradbury, and Arthur C Clarke. This early notoriety has faded, but the community of writers has remained continuously productive; Montfort (2005) provides a tour of the first two and a half decades of IF, and the conference Narrascope[4] is a hub for modern authors.

Many authorship tools have been created for IF, often with general purpose features that have enabled unanticipated expressions of their models' underlying mechanisms. Of particular importance is the authorship tool Twine[5], whose easy to use interface has inspired a surge of IF work.

Outside of pure entertainment, IF has proven potential in education(Squire, 2003), specifically as a language learning tool(Baltra, 1990). One recent example that uses a state based model specification similar to our own is Ramanarayanan and LaMar (2018), in which IF is used an assessment tool and a correlation is demonstrated between proficiency level and a learned student specific MDP parameter.

3 Related Work

In NLP literature, perhaps the closest touchpoint to this work is Jonell et al. (2018), where a open domain chatbot is constructed by crowdsourcing appropriate responses for known chat histories. They describe a nightly iteration process in which the day's user utterances are clustered using a similarity function into paraphrase clusters and then passed to crowdworkers to provide appropriate followup system turns. They incrementally grow a

---

[4]https://narrascope.org/
[5]http://twinery.org

directed graph based chatbot model of a similar structure to our own, but approach the authorship process in a drastically different manner and target only the desiderata of chitchat dialog as opposed to the general class of IF.

(Koller et al., 2018) also creates a directed graph editing tool for dialogs, with API hooks allowing the control of Lego Mindstorms robots. While this application would at first glance seem quite different, the data model is similar. The visual similarity of our tools alone demonstrates their near isomorphism; in both cases the authorship process is tantamount to the definition of a graph topology and the filling of schema for graph components. The major difference arises instead from our use of retrieval based semantic matching and focus on IF.

Our use of retrieval based (or paraphrase based) methods draws from recent work in semantic parsing (Berant and Liang, 2014) (Fader et al., 2013) and one-shot classification (Koch et al., 2015) powered by the growing availability of general domain semantic similarity training data (Yang et al., 2018) (Cer et al., 2018). One notable addition in our work is the introduction of anti-examples for tuning parser quality.

4   Model Specification

Our model can be considered a marriage between the intuitive design principles of Twine and modern methods in dialog systems. A typical dialog system design consists of components responsible for Language Understanding, Dialog Management, and Language Generation (Bohus and Rudnicky, 2009) (Shum et al., 2018).

4.1   Language Understanding

We employ retrieval based semantic matching for Language Understanding (LU), a close variant of nearest neighbor classification. We assume a finite set of unique semantic intents that our LU system can recognize. Formally, this method requires

$$\mathcal{U}: \text{a set of exemplar strings}$$
$$\mathcal{A}: \text{a set of anti-exemplar strings}$$
$$\mathcal{E}: \text{a set of semantic intents}$$
$$\mathcal{M}: \cup\{\mathcal{U}, \mathcal{A}\} \to \mathcal{E}: \text{a mapping to semantic intents}$$
$$\mathcal{D}(x, y) \to \mathbb{R}: \text{a string similarity function}$$

and semantic parsing is done with Nearest Neighbor (NN) classification using $\frac{1}{\mathcal{D}}$ as the distance metric. The classifier has an additional rejection option, triggered when no member of $\mathcal{U}$ produces a similarity with the user utterance that exceeds some author determined τ.

We augment the traditional NN classification algorithm with anti-examples, letting $\mathcal{A}$ be a set of anti-example strings. Their specific functionality is outlined below in Algorithm 1, which shows the full semantic parsing algorithm for an input x.

Algorithm 1: Semantic Parsing of input x

Result: Semantic intent e $\in \mathcal{E}$ or REJECT
$\mathcal{S} \leftarrow \cup\{\mathcal{U}, \mathcal{A}\}$;
while $\mathcal{S} \neq \varnothing$ **do**
    $z^* \leftarrow \arg\max_{z \in \mathcal{S}} \mathcal{D}(x, z)$;
    if $\mathcal{D}(x, z^*) \geq \tau$ **then**
        if $z^* \in A$ **then**
            forall $w \in \mathcal{S} \mid \mathcal{M}(w) = \mathcal{M}(z^*)$
            do
                $\mathcal{S} \leftarrow \mathcal{S} - w$
            end
        else
            return $\mathcal{M}(z)$
        end
    else
        return REJECT
    end
end
return REJECT

4.2   Dialogue Management

Our Dialogue Management (DM) system is based on a directed graph, representing the definition and evolution of dialog state by enumerating the finite set of all possible states (the graph nodes), and the allowed transitions between them (the graph edges). We assume a unique global start node and allow multiple end nodes. A node's outgoing edges are either directly associated with a semantic enum index as described above or marked as a RepeatedFail edge. The DM traverses the former when its outbound edge is returned by the semantic parser and the latter when the semantic parser has returned REJECT n times in a row, for some author controlled n.

The fundamental task of the DM is to determine $\mathcal{U}$ and $\mathcal{A}$ to be used in Algorithm 1, and a Markov-like memoryless model that returns all outgoing edges of the current node is sufficient for simple dialogues. However, to enable more complex storytelling opportunities we add a global state which we call the *World*.

The World is implemented as a string to string map, and each edge may assigned a *Condition* and *Mutation*. A Condition is any boolean predicate on the World, which allows its edge as a candidate only if it is satisfied. A full Condition is the conjunction of boolean subconditions, where each subcondition is the presence or absence of a specific key or key/value pair in the World. A Mutation is a list of operations to be performed on the World, and is executed upon its edge's traversal. We permit the use of mutations that set key value pairs or delete keys from the World.

We add one further augmentation: a boolean AutoAdvance property on a node that, if enabled, immediately randomly traverses an outgoing edge instead of waiting for the reader turn. This simple feature provides flexibility in graph design, allowing patterns we observed a desire for in user testing.

4.3 Language Generation

Language Generation is simplified nearly to its limit in our specification; each node is directly associated with a system turn, its Prompt, produced when the node is visited. To allow for more forgiving reader experiences we add two additional optional sources of system text. The first is a Reprompt, shown in response to a REJECT from the semantic parser, allowing the author to guide the reader towards a sucessfully parseable utterance. The second source of system text is an optional message attached to RepeatedFail edges, to allow acknowledgement of the perhaps unexpected transition.

5 Authoring Tool

Authoring under our model specification requires both defining the topology of a directed graph and filling the schema of node and edge properties (Figure 1). Some schema fields have complex types, which have multiple isomorphic data models of negligible difference provided they fulfill their functional purpose. MUTATIONS specifies a set of string to string map mutations and CONDITIONS a set of simple boolean key/value lookups, while MATCHCANDIDATES are tuples of exemplar strings and booleans indicating if they are anti-examples.

5.1 Main Authoring Tool

The home screen of the tool (Figure 2) consists of two panels. On the left is the graph editor, which vi-

- **Node**
    - PROMPT : STRING
    - REPROMPT : STRING
    - AUTOADVANCE? : BOOLEAN
- **Edge**
    - MUTATIONS : ♦
    - CONDITIONS : ♦
    - EITHER
        * MATCHCANDIDATES : ♦
    - OR
        * REPEATEDFAILMESSAGE : STRING
        * REPEATEDFAILN : NUMBER

Figure 1: Schema for graph specification, omitting standard graph topology information for a single source directed graph. Fields with complex types ♦ are discussed in Section 5.

sualizes and provides editing options for the graph topology. On the right is the the graph inspector, which allows the editing of the schema data outlined in Figure 1.

The graph inspector has a focus that determines the schema editing options that it displays. Clicking on a node or edge in the graph editor will focus it on that node or edge, while clicking on the background will focus the inspector on an editor for global hyperparameters such as the project name and persistence filename. Both node and edge editors contain buttons that delete them from the graph, a sole exception to topology being the domain of the graph editor alone.

The graph editor has its own toolbar containing the following actions: Save, CopyToClipboard, AutoZoom, AutoLayout. We consider all of these to be self-documenting with the exception of AutoLayout, whose intention is to produce a well packed organization of the graph through the following process.

Our AutoLayout algorithm first topologically sorts the graph and checks it for cycles. If no cycles exist then for each node n we calculate $l(n)$, the length of the longest path from the start node. The nodes are then arranged in rows of regular spacing such that each n appears in row $l(n)$. A best effort is made to choose a relative ordering of nodes in each row that minimizes visually tangled webs of edges, and we allow and rely on manual adjustment to achieve the author's ideal visual organization.

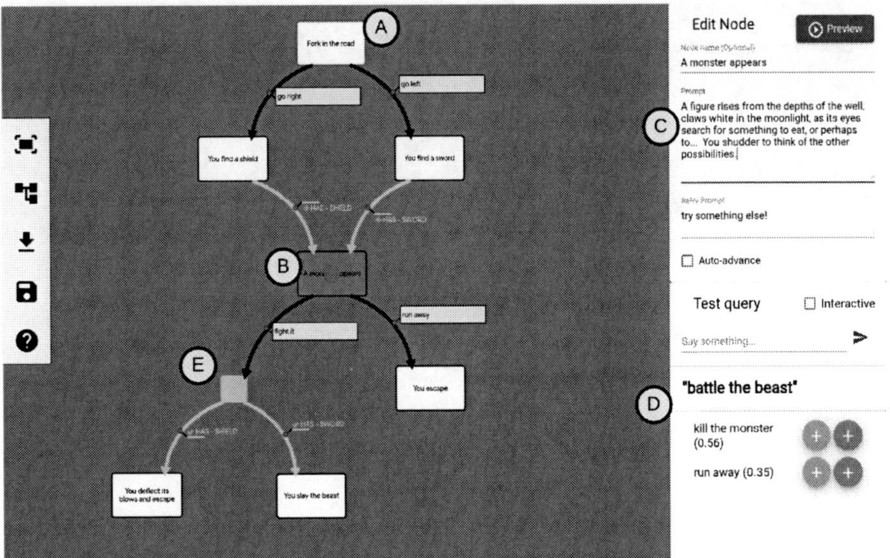

Figure 2: The main editor window, showing a story with start node A. The node B is selected, and so its details appear in the inspector on the right. Note that its display name is distinct from the richer game text (C). The results of using the Node Tester on the potential input "battle the beast" are shown in (D). They demonstrate that this utterance would cause a transition to node E, an AutoAdvance node that would immediately transition to one of two end states depending on the player's previous choices.

5.2 Node Tester

The authorship process is by nature iterative, and we recognize the importance of facilitating the editing of existing content. In particular, we anticipate a feedback loop in which the author observes or imagines reader turns and wishes to test them and tune the semantic matching model based on the results. For example, an author might want to verify that some reader turn matches, or does not match, a particular edge and add it to that edge as either a positive or anti-example if the desired behavior is not observed.

In aid of this use case, we provide an interactive node tester, found in the graph inspector when focused on a node (lower right in Figure 2). This tool allows the author to probe with a potential utterance and view the most similar exemplar from each possible edge and their similarity scores. With one click, the author can then add their probe utterance to an existing edge as a positive or anti-example, or create a new edge and target node with the probe utterance as a positive exemplar on the new edge.

5.3 Preview Mode

We follow the footsteps of Twine in the integration of a modest implementation of a reading program in the authoring tool, and allow the author to trigger this "Preview Mode" starting from any node in the graph. While we intend the debugging of semantic matches to be more easily performed using the Node Tester, Preview Mode is useful for authors to get early feedback on their work without investing in bespoke reader software.

As an alternative, we also add a toggle for Interactive Mode to the Node Tester described above; in this mode if the probe user utterance would match an edge, the editor selection and inspector focus automatically move to that edge's target node. This is functionally equivalent to (although certainly less immersive than) the full Preview Mode and allows the authors to maintain their cognitive connection with the graph editor and inspector while testing the boundaries of the semantic parser.

5.4 Implementation Considerations

We implement our tool in Angular, a web application platform that supports dependency injection. This not only facilitates the introduction of custom node metadata and UI, but also enables modularity in the services that drive the editor. Two key services, the persistence (save/load) mechanism, and the semantic similarity function $\mathcal{D}$, are injected and as such easy to override with custom code. We hope that allowing flexibility in the storage medium

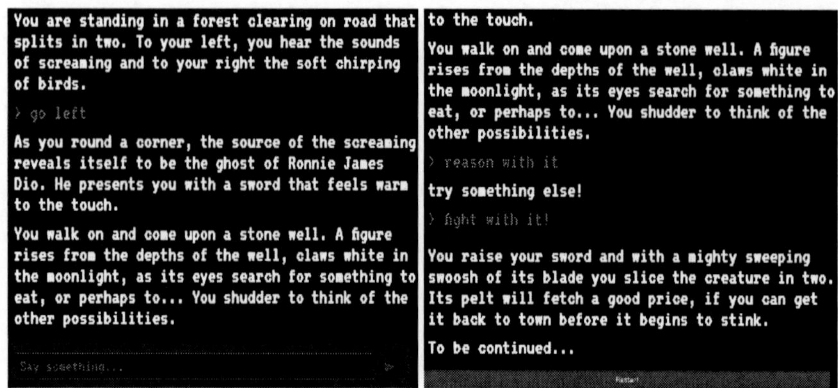

Figure 3: Preview Mode, displaying two successive screenshots of a reading of the story shown in Figure 2. Note that in the second panel the reader response "reason with it" is rejected, leading to the use of the retry prompt.

will allow for easier integration with custom reader software and injection of $\mathcal{D}$ is in anticipation of future superior models, some options for which are discussed below.

We provide one instantiation of each service. Our persistence service implementation uses Firebase, a popular cloud database, with instructions on how to configure Firebase credentials when launching a server in the repository's README. For $\mathcal{D}$, our implementation uses the open source Universal Sentence Encoder of Cer et al. (2018).

We note that significantly better similarity models are easily attainable as Cer et al. (2018) predates recent breakthrough techniques in pretraining (Devlin et al., 2018) (Yang et al., 2019). Furthermore, the dataset of paraphrase pairs used to train the encoder of Cer et al. (2018) is drawn from the SNLI corpus (Bowman et al., 2015) with additional unsupervised multi-task training data taken from sources such as Wikipedia and web news; this broad coverage will likely give reasonable results for any domain, but the specific flavor of IF or its subtypes (e.g. dialouge) would likely benefit from domain specific fine-tuning.

6 Discussion

We present a flexible model specification for a new flavor of Interactive Fiction inspired by recent trends in retrieval based dialog systems, and provide an accompanying authorship tool. Our tool is deployed as an AppEngine app, is written in Angular, and is open source [6].

Our model specification makes use of semantic matching based predicates to traverse a directed graph, tracing out a "reading" of the piece. The use of semantic matching allows active reader ideation of their role while remaining within guard rails that maintain narrative cohesion. Furthermore, its use of text based exemplars in a non-parametric model with a pretrained semantic kernel permits the iterative tuning of the semantic parsing system by an author with no programming or machine learning background.

Interactive Fiction is an art form with an uncertain future that is connected in no small way to its proximity to games and the social norms separating games and fine art. Ziegfeld (1989) muses that IF may either be like American poetry waiting for its Walt Whitman, or like the cutup poetry fad of the beat poets, bound for obscurity. They perhaps did not expect that the question would remain unanswered for thirty years. We hope foremost that authors will enjoy using our tool to create something they care about, and that readers will enjoy their creations.

References

Berna Altınel, Murat Can Ganiz, and Banu Diri. 2015. A corpus-based semantic kernel for text classification by using meaning values of terms. *Engineering Applications of Artificial Intelligence*, 43:54–66.

Collin F Baker, Charles J Fillmore, and John B Lowe. 1998. The berkeley framenet project. In *Proceedings of the 17th international conference on Computational linguistics-Volume 1*, pages 86–90. Association for Computational Linguistics.

Armando Baltra. 1990. Language learning through computer adventure games. *Simulation & Gaming*, 21(4):445–452.

---

[6]http://borismus.github.io/usnea

Jonathan Berant and Percy Liang. 2014. Semantic parsing via paraphrasing. In *Proceedings of the 52nd Annual Meeting of the Association for Computational Linguistics (Volume 1: Long Papers)*, pages 1415–1425.

Dan Bohus and Alexander I Rudnicky. 2009. The ravenclaw dialog management framework: Architecture and systems. *Computer Speech & Language*, 23(3):332–361.

Samuel R Bowman, Gabor Angeli, Christopher Potts, and Christopher D Manning. 2015. A large annotated corpus for learning natural language inference. *arXiv preprint arXiv:1508.05326*.

Daniel Cer, Yinfei Yang, Sheng-yi Kong, Nan Hua, Nicole Limtiaco, Rhomni St John, Noah Constant, Mario Guajardo-Cespedes, Steve Yuan, Chris Tar, et al. 2018. Universal sentence encoder. *arXiv preprint arXiv:1803.11175*.

Jacob Devlin, Ming-Wei Chang, Kenton Lee, and Kristina Toutanova. 2018. Bert: Pre-training of deep bidirectional transformers for language understanding. *arXiv preprint arXiv:1810.04805*.

Anthony Fader, Luke Zettlemoyer, and Oren Etzioni. 2013. Paraphrase-driven learning for open question answering. In *Proceedings of the 51st Annual Meeting of the Association for Computational Linguistics (Volume 1: Long Papers)*, pages 1608–1618.

Patrik Jonell, Mattias Bystedt, Fethiye Irmak Dogan, Per Fallgren, Jonas Ivarsson, Marketa Slukova, Ulme Wennberg, José Lopes, Johan Boye, and Gabriel Skantze. 2018. Fantom: A crowdsourced social chatbot using an evolving dialog graph. *Proc. Alexa Prize*.

Gregory Koch, Richard Zemel, and Ruslan Salakhutdinov. 2015. Siamese neural networks for one-shot image recognition. In *ICML deep learning workshop*, volume 2. Lille.

Alexander Koller, Timo Baumann, and Arne Köhn. 2018. Dialogos: Simple and extensible dialog modeling.

Nick Montfort. 2005. *Twisty Little Passages: an approach to interactive fiction*. Mit Press.

Anthony J Niesz and Norman N Holland. 1984. Interactive fiction. *Critical Inquiry*, 11(1):110–129.

Vikram Ramanarayanan and Michelle LaMar. 2018. Toward automatically measuring learner ability from human-machine dialog interactions using novel psychometric models. In *Proceedings of the Thirteenth Workshop on Innovative Use of NLP for Building Educational Applications*, pages 117–126.

Heung-Yeung Shum, Xiao-dong He, and Di Li. 2018. From eliza to xiaoice: challenges and opportunities with social chatbots. *Frontiers of Information Technology & Electronic Engineering*, 19(1):10–26.

Kurt Squire. 2003. Video games in education. *Int. J. Intell. Games & Simulation*, 2(1):49–62.

Yushi Wang, Jonathan Berant, and Percy Liang. 2015. Building a semantic parser overnight. In *Proceedings of the 53rd Annual Meeting of the Association for Computational Linguistics and the 7th International Joint Conference on Natural Language Processing (Volume 1: Long Papers)*, pages 1332–1342.

William A Woods. 1973. Progress in natural language understanding: an application to lunar geology. In *Proceedings of the June 4-8, 1973, national computer conference and exposition*, pages 441–450. ACM.

Yinfei Yang, Steve Yuan, Daniel Cer, Sheng-Yi Kong, Noah Constant, Petr Pilar, Heming Ge, Yun-Hsuan Sung, Brian Strope, and Ray Kurzweil. 2018. Learning semantic textual similarity from conversations. *arXiv preprint arXiv:1804.07754*.

Zhilin Yang, Zihang Dai, Yiming Yang, Jaime Carbonell, Russ R Salakhutdinov, and Quoc V Le. 2019. Xlnet: Generalized autoregressive pretraining for language understanding. In *Advances in neural information processing systems*, pages 5754–5764.

Jiaqi Yao, Keren Wang, Zhengguo Xu, and Jikun Yan. 2019. Classvector: A parameterized prototype-based model for text classification. In *Proceedings of the 2019 11th International Conference on Machine Learning and Computing*, pages 322–326. ACM.

Richard Ziegfeld. 1989. Interactive fiction: A new literary genre? *New Literary History*, 20(2):341–372.

DIALOGPT : Large-Scale Generative Pre-training for Conversational Response Generation

Yizhe Zhang   Siqi Sun   Michel Galley   Yen-Chun Chen
Chris Brockett   Xiang Gao   Jianfeng Gao   Jingjing Liu   Bill Dolan
Microsoft Corporation, Redmond, WA, USA *
{yizzhang,siqi.sun,mgalley,yenchen,chrisbkt,xiag,jfgao,jingjl,billdol}@microsoft.com

Abstract

We present a large, tunable neural conversational response generation model, DIALOGPT (dialogue generative pre-trained transformer). Trained on 147M conversation-like exchanges extracted from Reddit comment chains over a period spanning from 2005 through 2017, DialoGPT extends the Hugging Face PyTorch transformer to attain a performance close to human both in terms of automatic and human evaluation in single-turn dialogue settings. We show that conversational systems that leverage DialoGPT generate more relevant, contentful and context-consistent responses than strong baseline systems. The pre-trained model and training pipeline are publicly released to facilitate research into neural response generation and the development of more intelligent open-domain dialogue systems.

1 Introduction

We introduce DIALOGPT, a tunable gigaword-scale neural network model for generation of conversational reponses, trained on Reddit data.

Recent advances in large-scale pre-training using transformer-based architectures (Radford et al., 2018; Devlin et al., 2019; Raffel et al., 2019) have achieved great empirical success. OpenAI's GPT-2 (Radford et al., 2018), for example, has demonstrated that transformer models trained on very large datasets can capture long-term dependencies in textual data and generate text that is fluent, lexically diverse, and rich in content. Such models have the capacity to capture textual data with fine granularity and produce output with a high-resolution that closely emulates real-world text written by humans.

DIALOGPT extends GPT-2 to address the challenges of conversational neural response genera-

tion. Neural response generation is a subcategory of text-generation that shares the objective of generating natural-looking text (distinct from any training instance) that is *relevant* to the prompt. Modelling conversations, however, presents distinct challenges in that human dialogue, which encapsulates the possibly competing goals of two participants, is intrinsically more diverse in the range of potential responses (Li et al., 2016a; Zhang et al., 2018; Gao et al., 2019a,b). It thus poses a greater *one-to-many* problem than is typical in other text generation tasks such as neural machine translation, text summarization and paraphrasing. Human conversations are also generally more informal, noisy, and, when in the form of textual chat, often contain informal abbreviations or syntactic/lexical errors.

Most open-domain neural response generation systems suffer from content or style inconsistency (Li et al., 2016b; Zhang et al., 2019; Gao et al., 2019c), lack of long-term contextual information (Serban et al., 2017), and blandness (Li et al., 2016a; Zhang et al., 2018; Qin et al., 2019). While these issues can be alleviated by modelling strategies specifically designed to boost information content, a transformer-based architecture like GPT-2 (Radford et al., 2018), which uses a multi-layer self-attentive mechanism to allow fully-connected cross-attention to the full context in a computationally efficient manner, seems like a natural choice for exploring a more general solution. Transformer models, for example, allow long-term dependency information to be better be preserved across time (Radford et al., 2018), thereby improving content consistency. They also have higher model capacity due to their deep structure (up to 48 layers in GPT-2) and are more effective in leveraging large-scale datasets (more than 100 million training instances) than RNN-based approaches (Vaswani et al., 2017).

---

* A collaboration between Microsoft Research and Microsoft Dynamics 365 AI Research.

Proceedings of the 58th Annual Meeting of the Association for Computational Linguistics, pages 270–278
July 5 - July 10, 2020. ©2020 Association for Computational Linguistics

Like GPT-2, DIALOGPT is formulated as an autoregressive (AR) language model, and uses the multi-layer transformer as model architecture. Unlike GPT-2, however, DIALOGPT is trained on large-scale dialogue pairs/sessions extracted from Reddit discussion chains. Our assumption is that this should enable DIALOGPT to capture the joint distribution of $P(\text{Target}, \text{Source})$ in conversational flow with finer granularity. In practice, this is what we observe: sentences generated by DIALOGPT are diverse and contain information specific to the source prompt, analogous what GPT-2 generates for continuous text. We have evaluated the pre-trained model on a public benchmark dataset (DSTC-7), and a new 6k multi-reference test dataset extracted from Reddit postings. DIALOGPT achieves state-of-the-art results in both automatic and human evaluation, lifting performance to near-human response quality.

We have released the source code and a pre-trained model to facilitate future research.[1]. Our model can be easily leveraged and adapted to new dialogue datasets, especially datasets with few training examples. The DIALOGPT package also contains an open-source training pipeline (data extraction/preparation and model training/evaluation) built upon the Huggingface PyTorch transformer (HuggingFace, 2019). [2]

2 Dataset

The dataset is extracted from comment chains scraped from Reddit spanning from 2005 till 2017. Reddit discussions can be naturally expanded as tree-structured reply chains, since a thread replying to one thread forms the root node of subsequent threads. We extract each path from the root node to the leaf node as a training instance containing multiple turns of dialogue.

We filter the data by removing the instances where (1) there is a URL in source or target, (2) where the target contains word repetitions of at least three words, (3) where the response does not contain at least one of the top-50 most frequent English words (e.g., "the", "of", "a"), since this probably indicates it might not be an English sentence, (4) where the response contains special markers such as "[" or "]", as this could be markup

language, (5) where source and target sequences together are longer than 200 words, (6) where the target contains offensive language, identified by phrase matching against a large blocklist. We also excluded a large number of subreddits that had been identified as likely to contain offensive content. In addition, we aggressively filtered out blandness, e.g., removing instances where the responses contained 90% of tri-grams that have been seen more than 1000 times. Often uninformative, such responses account for about 1% of the data. After filtering, the dataset comprises 147,116,725 dialogue instances, in total 1.8 billion words.

3 Method

3.1 Model Architecture

We trained our DIALOGPT model on the basis of the GPT-2 (Radford et al., 2018) architecture.The GPT-2 transformer model adopts the generic transformer language model (Vaswani et al., 2017) and leverages a stack of masked multi-head self-attention layers to train on massive web-text data. The text generated either from scratch or based on a user-specific prompt is realistic-looking. The success of GPT-2 demonstrates that a transformer language model is able to characterize human language data distributions at a fine-grained level, presumably due to large large model capacity and superior efficiency.

Our model inherits from GPT-2 (Radford et al., 2018), a 12-to-48 layer transformer with layer normalization, a initialization scheme that accounts for model depth that we modified, and byte pair encodings (Sennrich et al., 2016) for the tokenizer. We follow the OpenAI GPT-2 to model a multi-turn dialogue session as a long text and frame the generation task as language modeling. We first concatenate all dialog turns within a dialogue session into a long text $x_1, \cdots, x_N$ (N is the sequence length), ended by the end-of-text token. We denote the source sentence (dialogue history) as $S = x_1, \cdots, x_m$ and target sentence (ground truth response) as $T = x_{m+1}, \cdots, x_N$, the conditional probability of $P(T|S)$ can be written as the product of a series of conditional probabilities:

$$p(T|S) = \prod_{n=m+1}^{N} p(x_n|x_1, \cdots, x_{n-1}) \quad (1)$$

For a multi-turn dialogue session $T_1, \cdots, T_K$, (1) can be written as $p(T_K, \cdots, T_2|T_1)$, which is

---

[1]GitHub: `https://github.com/microsoft/DialoGPT`; **Blog:** `https://aka.ms/dialogpt`

[2]Our model is also available over Hugging face Transformers. `https://huggingface.co/microsoft/DialoGPT-medium`

essentially the product of conditional probabilities of $p(T_i|T_1, \cdots, T_{i-1})$. Consequently, optimizing a single objective $p(T_K, \cdots, T_2|T_1)$ can be perceived as optimizing all $p(T_i|T_1, \cdots, T_{i-1})$ source-target pairs.

Our implementation is based on the open-source PyTorch-transformer repository.[3]

3.2 Mutual Information Maximization

Open-domain text generation models are notorious for generating bland, uninformative samples. To address this problem, we implement a maximum mutual information (MMI) scoring function (Li et al., 2016a; Zhang et al., 2018). MMI employs a pre-trained *backward* model to predict source sentences from given responses, i.e., $P(\text{Source}|\text{target})$. We first generate a set of hypotheses using top-K sampling. Then we use the probability of $P(\text{Source}|\text{Hypothesis})$ to rerank all hypotheses. Intuitively, maximizing backward model likelihood penalizes the bland hypotheses, as frequent and repetitive hypotheses can be associated with many possible queries, thus yielding a lower probability for any specific query.

We also attempted to optimize the reward $R \triangleq P(\text{Source}|\text{Hypothesis})$ using a policy gradient (Williams, 1992) with a sample-averaged baseline, following Zhang et al. (2018). The validation reward can be stably improved, but unlike the training under RNN architecture, we observed that reinforcement learning (RL) training easily converges to a degenerate locally-optimal solution, where the hypothesis simply repeats the source sentence (i.e., a parroting model) and mutual information is maximized. We hypothesize that transformers can become trapped in local optima due to their strong model representation power. We leave the investigation of regularized RL training to future work.

4 Result

4.1 Experimental Details

We trained 3 different sizes of the model with total parameters of 117M, 345M and 762M respectively. The model specification follows Radford et al. (2018) (Table 1).

Our model uses a vocabulary of 50,257 entries, and was trained on 16 Nvidia V100 machines with

Model	Layers	D_{emb}	B
117M	12	768	128
345M	24	1024	64
762M	36	1280	32

Table 1: Model configurations. "B" denotes batch size per GPU.

NVLink. We used the Noam learning rate scheduler with 16000 warm-up steps. The learning rate is selected based on validation loss. Each model is trained until there is no progress in validation loss. For small and medium models, we trained the models for up to 5 epochs. For the large model we trained for at most 3 epochs.

Speeding up training　To accelerate the training process and accommodate GPU memory limitations, we first compress all training data into a lazy-loading database file, so that data is loaded only when needed (pre-fetching large chunks to reduce access frequency). We also leverage separate asynchronous data processes to scale the training. As a result, training time declines approximately linearly w.r.t. the number of GPUs. We further employed a dynamic batching strategy to group conversations of similar lengths into the same batch, thus increasing training throughput.

4.2 DSTC-7 Dialogue Generation Challenge

The DSTC (Dialog System Technology Challenges) 7 track (Galley et al., 2019) is an end-to-end conversational modeling task,[4] in which the goal is to generate conversation responses that go beyond chitchat by injecting information that is grounded in external knowledge. This task is distinct from what is commonly thought of as goal-oriented, task-oriented, or task-completion dialogs in that there is no specific or predefined goal (e.g., booking a flight, or reserving a table at a restaurant). Instead, it targets human-like interactions where the underlying goal is often ill-defined or unknown in advance, of the kind seen in work and other productive environments (e.g., brainstorming meetings) where people share information.

The DSTC-7 test data contains conversation threads from Reddit data. In order to create a multi-reference test set, we utilized conversation sessions that contain 6 or more responses. Given

---

[3] https://github.com/huggingface/pytorch-transformers

[4] https://github.com/mgalley/DSTC7-End-to-End-Conversation-Modeling/tree/master/evaluation

other filtering criteria such as turn length, this yields a 5-reference test set of size 2208. (For each instance, one of the 6 human responses is set aside to assess human performance on this task.) Note that our training data is collected from a different time span from the test set.

We performed automatic evaluation using standard machine translation metrics, including BLEU (Papineni et al., 2002), METEOR (Lavie and Agarwal, 2007), and NIST (Doddington, 2002). NIST is a variant of BLEU that weights n-gram matches by their information gain, i.e., it indirectly penalizes uninformative n-grams. We also use Entropy (Zhang et al., 2018) and Dist-n (Li et al., 2016a) to evaluate lexical diversity. More details are provided in Galley et al. (2019).

We compared DIALOGPT with our in-house competitive sequence-to-sequence model PERSONALITYCHAT based on (Li et al., 2016a) and trained on Twitter data, which has been used in production as a Cognitive Service for Microsoft Azure.[5] Table 2 summarizes the automatic evaluation results. DIALOGPT with 345M parameters and beam search achieved the highest automatic score across most metrics. Scores for DIALOGPT with 345M parameters are better across the board than with 117M parameters. Beam search (with beam width 10) dramatically improves BLEU and DIST scores, and marginally improves NIST and METEOR. Note that our model is fine-tuned on source-target pairs, and does not leverage grounding information from the DSTC training set. Presumably, the model learns background information during pre-training and is unhindered by the lack of a grounding document.

The automatic scores of DIALOGPT are higher than those for humans. This does not mean that the generation is more "realistic" than human, but is probably attributable to the one-to-many nature of conversation. As illustrated in Figure 1, multiple human responses (R1-R4) can correspond well to a source utterance. Without loss of generality, suppose R1-R3 are the "ground truth" references that will be tested on, while R4 is the "held-out" human response that serves to compute a "human" score. In semantic space, a generated response R_g from a well-trained model will presumably tend to lie in the vicinity the geometric center

[5]Project   PERSONALITYCHAT: https://docs.microsoft.com/en-us/azure/cognitive-services/project-personality-chat/overview

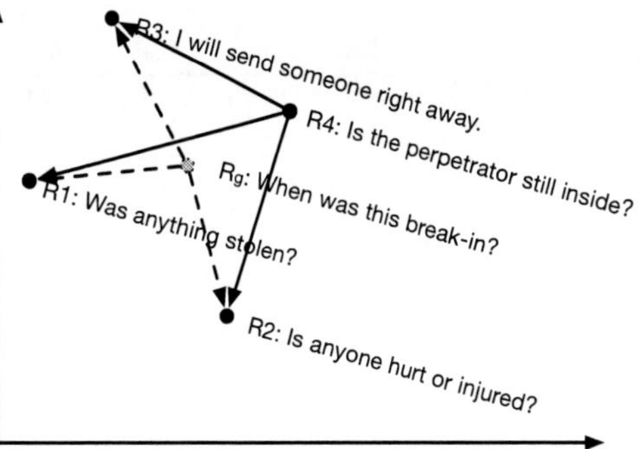

Figure 1: A generated response can surpass a human response in automatic metrics. Example responses are from Gupta et al. (2019)

of all possible responses, because the training objective seeks to generate the most likely response. This may be close to the geometric mean of all training instances, thus "averaging out" these instances. Consequently, a generated response R_g might have a lower "semantic distance" (manifested in higher automatic scores like BLEU) from R1-R3 than the targeted human response R4.

4.3 A New Reddit Multi-reference Dataset

We further evaluate DIALOGPT on a multi-reference test set with 6K examples. The results are shown in Table 3. We test our method on two settings: training from scratch and fine-tuning using GPT-2 as the pre-trained model. In both settings, a larger model consistently outperforms a smaller one. Comparing training from scratch to fine-tuning from the pre-trained GPT-2 model, when applying to smaller model, using GPT-2 model gives larger performance gains. Again, the best system DIALOGPT (345M, w/ beam search) scores higher on BLEU than humans. Larger models trained from scratch (345M and 762M) perform comparably to one finetuned on GPT-2.

4.4 Re-ranking The Response Using MMI

We perform mutual information maximization as described in Section 3.2. Specifically, we generate 16 samples for each input source sentence by using top-K sampling ($K = 10$) using the 345M model fine-tuned from the GPT-2 medium model. This is followed by a re-ranking step using a backward model, which is also a 345M model finetuned from the GPT-2 medium model. The response that yields lowest backward model loss is

Method	NIST		BLEU		METEOR	Entropy	Dist		Avg Len
	N-2	N-4	B-2	B-4		E-4	D-1	D-2	
PERSONALITYCHAT	0.19	0.20	10.44%	1.47%	5.42%	6.89	5.9%	16.4%	8.2
Team B	2.51	2.52	14.35%	1.83%	8.07%	9.03	10.9%	32.5%	15.1
DIALOGPT (117M)	1.58	1.60	10.36%	2.02%	7.17%	6.94	6.2%	18.94%	13.0
GPT(345M)	1.78	1.79	9.13%	1.06%	6.38%	9.72	11.9%	44.2%	14.7
DIALOGPT (345M)	2.80	2.82	14.16%	2.31%	8.51%	**10.08**	9.1%	39.7%	16.9
DIALOGPT (345M,Beam)	**2.92**	**2.97**	**19.18%**	**6.05%**	**9.29%**	9.57	**15.7%**	**51.0%**	14.2
Human	2.62	2.65	12.35%	3.13%	8.31%	10.45	16.7%	67.0%	18.8

Table 2: DSTC evaluation. "Team B" is the winner system of the DSTC-7 challenge. "Beam" denotes beam search. "Human" represents the held-out ground truth reference.

Method	NIST		BLEU		METEOR	Entropy	Dist		Avg Len
	N-2	N-4	B-2	B-4		E-4	D-1	D-2	
PERSONALITYCHAT	0.78	0.79	11.22%	1.95%	6.93%	8.37	5.8%	18.8%	8.12
Training from scratch:									
DIALOGPT (117M)	1.23	1.37	9.74%	1.77%	6.17%	7.11	5.3%	15.9%	9.41
DIALOGPT (345M)	2.51	3.08	16.92%	4.59%	9.34%	9.03	6.7%	25.6%	11.16
DIALOGPT (762M)	2.52	3.10	17.87%	5.19%	9.53%	9.32	7.5%	29.3%	10.72
Training from OpenAI GPT-2:									
DIALOGPT (117M)	2.39	2.41	10.54%	1.55%	7.53%	10.77	8.6%	39.9%	12.82
DIALOGPT (345M)	3.00	3.06	16.96%	4.56%	9.81%	9.12	6.8%	26.3%	12.19
DIALOGPT (345M, Beam)	**3.4**	**3.5**	**21.76%**	**7.92%**	10.74%	10.48	**12.38%**	**48.74%**	11.34
DIALOGPT (762M)	2.84	2.90	18.66%	5.25%	9.66%	9.72	7.76%	29.93%	11.19
DIALOGPT (762M, Beam)	2.90	2.98	21.08%	7.57%	10.11%	10.06	11.62%	44.07%	10.68
DIALOGPT (345M, MMI)	3.28	3.33	15.68%	3.94%	**11.23%**	**11.25**	9.39%	45.55%	17.21
Human	3.41	4.25	17.90%	7.48%	10.64%	10.99	14.5%	63.0%	13.10

Table 3: 6K Reddit multi-reference evaluation. "Beam" denotes beam search. "Human" represents the held-out ground truth reference.

selected for evaluation. The results are summarized in the second to last row in Table 3. It can be seen that compared with Greedy generation, MMI re-ranking produces more diverse responses with higher NIST, METEOR and Entropy and Dist scores, but with a slight drop in BLEU.

4.5 Generation Examples

We provide sample generated dialogues in Table 4 (interactive chat) and Table 5 (a self-playing bot with user prompt). The output is based on top-K sampling.[6] Interestingly, our model exhibits the ability to address commonsense questions to some extent, presumably owing to the rich amount of information that can be learned from Reddit data. In some cases, instead of giving the "desired" answer, the system generates an alternative, reasonable answer. Our observations suggest that the system is able to deal with multi-turn generation better than an RNN counterpart and tends to be

more consistent with respect to context (Table 5).[7]

source	Response
who is the first president of the United States?	George Washington
what is the boiling point of water?	I think it's about 212 F.
which one is bigger, sun or moon?	The sun .
which animal has black and white stripes?	A black and white striped cat .

Table 4: Addressing commonsense questions

4.6 Human Evaluation

Human evaluations We evaluated 2000 randomly sampled test sources from the Reddit 6K test dataset using crowd-sourcing. Systems were paired and each pair of system outputs was randomly presented to 3 judges, who ranked them

---

[6]Owing to occasional toxic outputs, we are unable to release the generation code at this time.

[7]We provide a live invitation-only demonstration site for a conversational agents with toxicity controls and mutual information maximization features discussed in this paper. Check our GitHub repository for more information.

Role	response
User	Does money buy happiness?
Bot	Depends how much money you spend on it .
User	What is the best way to buy happiness ?
Bot	You just have to be a millionaire by your early 20s, then you can be happy .
User	This is so difficult !
Bot	You have no idea how hard it is to be a millionaire and happy . There is a reason the rich have a lot of money

Table 5: An interactive example of multi-turn dialogue

Role	Response
User	what is the meaning of life ?
Bot	The meaning is to be with your family and friends .
Bot	I'm going to guess : It means that your parents and friends have loved you . That's the meaning , I believe .
Bot	I think the meaning is to make sure you're alive when you die . So you'll be with your family , friends , and yourself .
Bot	It's not , but thanks for trying to help .

Table 6: An example of multi-turn self-playing dialogue with user prompt

for relevance, informativeness and how human-like the generating is using a 3-point Likert-like scale. Judges were required to pass a qualification test, and a regime of spam detection was imposed.[8] Overall judge preferences for relevance, informativeness and human-likeness, presented as raw numbers and a percentage of the total, are shown in Table 7. A strong preference can be observed for DialoGPT over PersonalityChat. Table 7 also suggests that the "vanilla" DialoGPT medium model may already be close to human response quality. Unexpectedly, we found that judges may prefer the MMI variant over human responses, probably because of many of the true human responses are erratic or idiosyncratic, or are tied to internet memes that happened to be unfamiliar to the judges.[9] (See Section 4.2 for the conditions underlying this effect.) Further details, including a test of significance and the human evaluation template used, are provided in the Appendix.

---

[8] We used held-out hand-vetted data from the human and PersonalityChat datasets to provide clear-cut cases for spam prevention and judge training examples. We suspect that this may have helped bias the results towards the extremes.

[9] For example, one judge protested that the internet meme "I was today years old when I realized this." did not seem human-like.

5 Related work

There are several open-sourced toolkits for large-scale pre-trained transformer models. Hugging-face Conv-AI transfer learning repository (Wolf et al., 2019) contains the code for training conversational AI systems with transfer learning based on the GPT-2 transformer language model, which achieves the state-of-the-art performance on ConvAI-2 dialogue competition. DLGnet (Olabiyi and Mueller, 2019) is a large transformer model trained on dialogue dataset and achieves good performance in multi-turn dialogue generation. AllenNLP (Gardner et al., 2018) is developed as a toolkit for many natural language processing tasks, including the large-scale pre-trained bi-LSTM sentence representation learning framework ELMo (Peters et al., 2018). Texar (Hu et al., 2018) focuses on text generation including style transferring and controllable generation. It includes reinforcement learning capabilities along with its sequence modelling tools. DeepPavlov (Burtsev et al., 2018) is a popular framework focusing on task-oriented dialogue. This public repository contains several demos and pre-trained models for question answering and sentiment classification. Icecaps (Shiv et al., 2019) is a response generation toolkit with techniques such as grounding on personalities or external knowledge and multi-task training. The ConvAI2 challenge (Dinan et al., 2019) has a focus on personalized conversations. ParlAI (Miller et al., 2017) is another library for developing task-oriented dialogue systems. It contains pre-trained models for knowledge-grounded chatbot trained with crowd-sourced data. The Text-to-Text Transformer (Raffel et al., 2019) unifies multiple text modeling tasks, and achieves the state-of-the-art results in various natural language generation and understanding benchmarks.

6 Limitations and risks

DIALOGPT is released as a model only; the onus of decoder implementation resides with the user. Despite our efforts to minimize the amount of overtly offensive data prior to training, DI-ALOGPT retains the potential to generate output that may trigger offense. Output may reflect gender and other historical biases implicit in the data. Responses generated using this model may exhibit a propensity to express agreement with propositions that are unethical, biased or offensive (or the

Relevance: *A and B, which is more relevant and appropriate to the immediately preceding turn?*				
System A		Neutral		System B
DialoGPT (345M)	3281 (**72%**)	394 (9%)	882 (19%)	PersonalityChat ****
DialoGPT (345M)	2379 (40%)	527 (9%)	3094 (**52%**)	DialoGPT (345M, w/ MMI) ****
DialoGPT (345M)	3019 (**50%**)	581 (10%)	2400 (40%)	DialoGPT (345M, Beam) ****
DialoGPT (345M)	2726 (**45%**)	576 (10%)	2698 (45%)	DialoGPT (762M)
DialoGPT (345M)	2671 (45%)	513 (9%)	2816 (**47%**)	Human response
DialoGPT (345M, w/ MMI)	2871 (**48%**)	522 (9%)	2607 (43%)	Human response ***

Informative: *A and B, which is more contentful, interesting and informative?*				
System A		Neutral		System B
DialoGPT (345M)	3490 (**77%**)	206 (5%)	861 (19%)	PersonalityChat ****
DialoGPT (345M)	2474 (41%)	257 (4%)	3269(**54%**)	DialoGPT (345M, w/ MMI) ****
DialoGPT (345M)	3230 (**54%**)	362 (6%)	2408(40%)	DialoGPT (345M, Beam) *****
DialoGPT (345M)	2856 (**48%**)	303 (5%)	2841(47%)	DialoGPT (762M)
DialoGPT (345M)	2722 (45%)	234 (4%)	3044(**51%**)	Human response ****
DialoGPT (345M, w/ MMI)	3011 (**50%**)	234 (4%)	2755(46%)	Human response **

Human-like: *A and B, which is more likely to be generated by human rather than a chatbot?*				
System A		Neutral		System B
DialoGPT (345M)	3462 (**76%**)%	196 (4%)	899 (20%)	PersonalityChat ****
DialoGPT (345M)	2478 (41%)%	289 (5%)	3233 (**54%**)	DialoGPT (345M, w/ MMI) ****
DialoGPT (345M)	3233 (**54%**)%	340 (6%)	2427 (40%)	DialoGPT (345M, Beam) ****
DialoGPT (345M)	2847 (**47%**)%	321 (5%)	2832 (47%)	DialoGPT (762M)
DialoGPT (345M)	2716 (45%)%	263 (4%)	3021 (**50%**)	Human response ***
DialoGPT (345M, w/ MMI)	2978 (**50%**)%	241 (4%)	2781 (46%)	Human response *

Table 7: Results of **Human Evaluation** for relevance, informativeness and human-response possibility, showing preferences (%) for our model (DialoGPT) vis-a-vis its variants and real human responses. Distributions skew towards DialoGPT with MMI, even when compared with human outputs. Numbers in bold indicate the preferred systems. Statistically significant results are indicated: * $p \leq 0.01$, ** $p \leq 0.001$, *** $p \leq 0.0001$, **** $p \leq 0.00001$.

reverse, disagreeing with otherwise ethical statements). These are known issues in current state-of-the-art end-to-end conversation models trained on large naturally-occurring datasets. A major motive for releasing DIALOGPT is to enable researchers to investigate these issues and develop mitigation strategies. In no case should inappropriate content generated as a result of using DIALOGPT be construed to reflect the views or values of either the authors or Microsoft Corporation.

7 Conclusion

We have released an open-domain pre-trained model, DIALOGPT, trained on massive real-world Reddit dataset. The package consists of a distributed training pipeline and several pre-trained models that can be fine-tuned to obtain a conversation model on a moderately-sized customized dataset in few hours. DIALOGPT is fully open-sourced and easy to deploy, allowing users to ex-tend the pre-trained conversational system to boot-strap training using various datasets. It serves as a building block to novel applications and methodologies. Detection and control of toxic output will be a major focus of future investigation. We will investigate leveraging reinforcement learning to further improve the relevance of the generated responses and prevent the model from generating egregious responses.

Acknowledgements

We would like to thank Yu Wang, Vighnesh Leonardo Shiv, Chris Quirk, and the anonymous reviewers for their helpful discussions and comments.

References

M. Burtsev, A. Seliverstov, R. Airapetyan, M. Arkhipov, D. Baymurzina, N. Bushkov, O. Gureenkova, T. Khakhulin, Y. Kuratov,

D. Kuznetsov, A. Litinsky, V. Logacheva, A. Lymar, V. Malykh, M. Petrov, V. Polulyakh, L. Pugachev, A. Sorokin, M. Vikhreva, and M. Zaynutdinov. 2018. DeepPavlov: Open-source library for dialogue systems. In *Proceedings of the 56th Annual Meeting of the Association for Computational Linguistics-System Demonstrations.*

Jacob Devlin, Ming-Wei Chang, Kenton Lee, and Kristina Toutanova. 2019. BERT: Pre-training of deep bidirectional transformers for language understanding. *NAACL 2019.*

E. Dinan, V. Logacheva, V. Malykh, A. Miller, K. Shuster, J. Urbanek, D. Kiela, A. Szlam, I. Serban, R. Lowe, S. Prabhumoye, A. W. Black, A. Rudnicky, J. Williams, J. Pineau, M. Burtsev, and J. Weston. 2019. The second conversational intelligence challenge (ConvAI2).

George Doddington. 2002. Automatic evaluation of machine translation quality using n-gram co-occurrence statistics. In *Proceedings of the second international conference on Human Language Technology Research.* Morgan Kaufmann Publishers Inc.

Michel Galley, Chris Brockett, Xiang Gao, Jianfeng Gao, and Bill Dolan. 2019. Grounded response generation task at DSTC7. In *AAAI Dialog System Technology Challenges Workshop.*

J. Gao, M. Galley, and L. Li. 2019a. Neural approaches to conversational AI. *Foundations and Trends in Information Retrieval.*

Xiang Gao, Sungjin Lee, Yizhe Zhang, Chris Brockett, Michel Galley, Jianfeng Gao, and Bill Dolan. 2019b. Jointly optimizing diversity and relevance in neural response generation. *NAACL-HLT 2019.*

Xiang Gao, Yizhe Zhang, Sungjin Lee, Michel Galley, Chris Brockett, Jianfeng Gao, and Bill Dolan. 2019c. Structuring latent spaces for stylized response generation. *EMNLP-IJCNLP.*

M. Gardner, J. Grus, M. Neumann, O. Tafjord, P. Dasigi, N. F. Liu, M. Peters, M. Schmitz, and L. S. Zettlemoyer. 2018. AllenNLP: A deep semantic natural language processing platform. In *Proceedings of Workshop for NLP Open Source Software.*

Prakhar Gupta, Shikib Mehri, Tiancheng Zhao, Amy Pavel, Maxine Eskenazi, and Jeffrey P Bigham. 2019. Investigating evaluation of open-domain dialogue systems with human generated multiple references. *arXiv preprint arXiv:1907.10568.*

Z. Hu, H. Shi, Z. Yang, B. Tan, T. Zhao, J. He, W. Wang, L. Qin, D. Wang, et al. 2018. Texar: A modularized, versatile, and extensible toolkit for text generation. *ACL.*

HuggingFace. 2019. PyTorch transformer repository. https://github.com/huggingface/pytorch-transformers.

Alon Lavie and Abhaya Agarwal. 2007. Meteor: An automatic metric for mt evaluation with high levels of correlation with human judgments. In *Proceedings of the Second Workshop on Statistical Machine Translation*, pages 228–231. Association for Computational Linguistics.

Jiwei Li, Michel Galley, Chris Brockett, Jianfeng Gao, and Bill Dolan. 2016a. A diversity-promoting objective function for neural conversation models. *NAACL.*

Jiwei Li, Michel Galley, Chris Brockett, Georgios P Spithourakis, Jianfeng Gao, and Bill Dolan. 2016b. A persona-based neural conversation model. *ACL.*

A. H. Miller, W. Feng, A. Fisch, J. Lu, D. Batra, A. Bordes, D. Parikh, and J. Weston. 2017. ParlAI: A dialog research software platform. In *Proceedings of the 2017 EMNLP System Demonstration.*

Oluwatobi Olabiyi and Erik T Mueller. 2019. Multi-turn dialogue response generation with autoregressive transformer models. *arXiv preprint:1908.01841.*

Kishore Papineni, Salim Roukos, Todd Ward, and Wei-Jing Zhu. 2002. Bleu: a method for automatic evaluation of machine translation. *ACL.*

M. E. Peters, M. Neumann, M. Iyyer, M. Gardner, C. Clark, K. Lee, and L. Zettlemoyer. 2018. Deep contextualized word representations. *NAACL.*

Lianhui Qin, Michel Galley, Chris Brockett, Xiaodong Liu, Xiang Gao, Bill Dolan, Yejin Choi, and Jianfeng Gao. 2019. Conversing by reading: Contentful neural conversation with on-demand machine reading. *ACL.*

A. Radford, J. Wu, R. Child, D. Luan, D. Amodei, and I. Sutskever. 2018. Language models are unsupervised multitask learners. Technical report, OpenAI.

Colin Raffel, Noam Shazeer, Adam Roberts, Katherine Lee, Sharan Narang, Michael Matena, Yanqi Zhou, Wei Li, and Peter J. Liu. 2019. Exploring the limits of transfer learning with a unified text-to-text transformer. *arXiv preprint:1910.10683.*

R. Sennrich, B. Haddow, and A. Birch. 2016. Neural machine translation of rare words with subword units. *ACL.*

Iulian Vlad Serban, Alessandro Sordoni, Ryan Lowe, Laurent Charlin, Joelle Pineau, Aaron Courville, and Yoshua Bengio. 2017. A hierarchical latent variable encoder-decoder model for generating dialogues. *AAAI.*

Vighnesh Leonardo Shiv, Chris Quirk, Anshuman Suri, Xiang Gao, Khuram Shahid, Nithya Govindarajan, Yizhe Zhang, Jianfeng Gao, Michel Galley, Chris Brockett, et al. 2019. Microsoft icecaps: An open-source toolkit for conversation modeling. *ACL.*

Ashish Vaswani, Noam Shazeer, Niki Parmar, Jakob Uszkoreit, Llion Jones, Aidan N Gomez, Łukasz Kaiser, and Illia Polosukhin. 2017. Attention is all you need. *NeurIPS*.

Ronald J Williams. 1992. Simple statistical gradient-following algorithms for connectionist reinforcement learning. *Machine learning*.

Thomas Wolf, Victor Sanh, Julien Chaumond, and Clement Delangue. 2019. TransferTransfo: A transfer learning approach for neural network based conversational agents. *CoRR*, abs/1901.08149.

Yizhe Zhang, Michel Galley, Jianfeng Gao, Zhe Gan, Xiujun Li, Chris Brockett, and Bill Dolan. 2018. Generating informative and diverse conversational responses via adversarial information maximization. *NeurIPS*.

Yizhe Zhang, Xiang Gao, Sungjin Lee, Chris Brockett, Michel Galley, Jianfeng Gao, and Bill Dolan. 2019. Consistent dialogue generation with self-supervised feature learning. *arXiv preprint:1903.05759*.

ADVISER: A Toolkit for Developing *Multi-modal, Multi-domain* and *Socially-engaged* Conversational Agents

Chia-Yu Li, Daniel Ortega, Dirk Väth, Florian Lux,
Lindsey Vanderlyn, Maximilian Schmidt, Michael Neumann, Moritz Völkel,
Pavel Denisov, Sabrina Jenne, Zorica Kacarevic and Ngoc Thang Vu*
Institute for Natural Language Processing (IMS), University of Stuttgart
`thangvu@ims.uni-stuttgart.de`

Abstract

We present ADVISER[1] - an open-source, multi-domain dialog system toolkit that enables the development of multi-modal (incorporating speech, text and vision), socially-engaged (e.g. emotion recognition, engagement level prediction and backchanneling) conversational agents. The final Python-based implementation of our toolkit is flexible, easy to use, and easy to extend not only for technically experienced users, such as machine learning researchers, but also for less technically experienced users, such as linguists or cognitive scientists, thereby providing a flexible platform for collaborative research.

1 Introduction

Dialog systems or chatbots, both text-based and multi-modal, have received much attention in recent years, with an increasing number of dialog systems in both industrial contexts such as Amazon *Alexa*, Apple *Siri*, Microsoft *Cortana*, Google *Duplex*, *XiaoIce* (Zhou et al., 2018) and Furhat[2], as well as academia such as *MuMMER* (Foster et al., 2016) and *Alana* (Curry et al., 2018). However, open-source toolkits and frameworks for developing such systems are rare, especially for developing multi-modal systems comprised of speech, text, and vision. Most of the existing toolkits are designed for developing dialog systems focused only on core dialog components, with or without the option to access external speech processing services (Bohus and Rudnicky, 2009; Baumann and Schlangen, 2012; Lison and Kennington, 2016; Ultes et al., 2017; Ortega et al., 2019; Lee et al., 2019).

To the best of our knowledge, there are only two

toolkits, proposed in (Foster et al., 2016) and (Bohus et al., 2017), that support developing dialog agents using multi-modal processing and social signals (Wagner et al., 2013). Both provide a decent platform for building systems, however, to the best of our knowledge, the former is not open-source, and the latter is based on the .NET platform, which could be less convenient for non-technical users such as linguists and cognitive scientists, who play an important role in dialog research.

In this paper, we introduce a new version of ADVISER - previously a text-based, multi-domain dialog system toolkit (Ortega et al., 2019) - that supports multi-modal dialogs, including speech, text and vision information processing. This provides a new option for building dialog systems that is open-source and Python-based for easy use and fast prototyping. The toolkit is designed in such a way that it is modular, flexible, transparent, and user-friendly for both technically experienced and less technically experienced users.

Furthermore, we add novel features to ADVISER, allowing it to process social signals and to incorporate them into the dialog flow. We believe that these features will be key to developing human-like dialog systems because it is well-known that social signals, such as emotional states and engagement levels, play an important role in human computer interaction (McTear et al., 2016). However in contrast to open-ended dialog systems (Weizenbaum, 1966), our toolkit focuses on task-oriented applications (Bobrow et al., 1977), such as searching for a lecturer at the university (Ortega et al., 2019). The purpose we envision for dialog systems developed using our toolkit is not the same as the objective of a social chatbot such as *XiaoIce* (Zhou et al., 2018). Rather than promoting "an AI companion with an emotional connection to satisfy the human need for communication, affection, and social belonging" (Zhou et al., 2018), ADVISER

---

* All authors contributed equally.

[1]Link to open-source code: `https://github.com/DigitalPhonetics/adviser`

[2]https://docs.furhat.io

Proceedings of the 58th Annual Meeting of the Association for Computational Linguistics, pages 279–286
July 5 - July 10, 2020. ©2020 Association for Computational Linguistics

helps develop dialog systems that support users in efficiently fulfilling concrete goals, while at the same time considering social signals such as emotional states and engagement levels so as to remain friendly and likeable.

2 Objectives

The main objective of this work is to develop a multi-domain dialog system toolkit that allows for multi-modal information processing and that provides different modules for extracting social signals such as emotional states and for integrating them into the decision making process. The toolkit should be easy to use and extend for users of all levels of technical experience, providing a flexible collaborative research platform.

2.1 Toolkit Design

We extend and substantially modify our previous, text-based dialog system toolkit (Ortega et al., 2019) while following the same design choices. This means that our toolkit is meant to optimize the following four criteria: *Modularity, Flexibility, Transparency* and *User-friendliness at different levels*. This is accomplished by decomposing the dialog system into independent modules (services), which in turn are either rule-based, machine learning-based or both. These services can easily be combined in different orders/architectures, providing users with flexible options to design new dialog architectures.

2.2 Challenges & Proposed Solutions

Multi-modality The main challenges in handling multi-modality are a) the design of a synchronization infrastructure and b) the large range of different latencies from different modalities. To alleviate the former, we use the publisher/subscriber software pattern presented in section 4 to synchronize signals coming from different sources. This software pattern also allows for services to run in a distributed manner. By assigning computationally heavy tasks such as speech recognition and speech synthesis to a more powerful computing node, it is possible to reduce differences in latency when processing different modalities, therefore achieving more natural interactions.

Socially-Engaged Systems Determining the ideal scope of a socially-engaged dialog system is a complex issue, that is which information should be extracted from users and how the system can best

Figure 1: Tracking emotion states and engagement levels using multi-modal information.

react to these signals. Here we focus on two major social signals: emotional states and engagement levels (see section 3.1), and maintain an internal user state to track them over the course of a dialog. Note that the toolkit is designed in such a way that any social signal could be extracted and leveraged in the dialog manager. In order to react to social signals extracted from the user, we provide an initial affective policy module (see section 3.5) and an initial affective NLG module (see section 3.7), which could be easily extended to more sophisticated behavior. Furthermore, we provide a backchanneling module that enables the dialog system to give feedback to users during conversations. Utilizing these features could lead to increased trust and enhance the impression of an empathetic system.

3 Functionalities

3.1 Social Signal Processing

We present the three modules of ADVISER for processing social signals: (a) emotion recognition, (b) engagement level prediction, and (c) backchanneling. Figure 1 illustrates an example of our system tracking emotion states and engagement levels.

Multi-modal Emotion Recognition For recognizing a user's emotional state, all three available modalities – text, audio, and vision – can potentially be exploited, as they can deliver complementary information (Zeng et al., 2009). Therefore, the emotion recognition module can subscribe to the particular input streams of interest (see section 4 for details) and apply emotion prediction either in a time-continuous fashion or discretely per turn.

In our example implementation in the toolkit, we integrate speech emotion recognition, i.e. using the acoustic signal as features. Based on the work presented in (Neumann and Vu, 2017) we use log Mel filterbank coefficients as input to convolutional neural networks (CNNs). For the sake of modularity, three separate models are employed for predicting different types of labels: (a) basic emotions {angry, happy, neutral, sad}, (b) arousal levels {low, medium, high}, and (c) valence levels {negative, neutral, positive}. The models are trained on the IEMOCAP dataset (Busso et al., 2008). The output of the emotion recognition module consists of three predictions per user turn, which can then be used by the user state tracker (see section 3.4). For future releases, we plan to incorporate multiple training datasets as well as visual features.

Engagement Level Prediction   User engagement is closely related to states such as boredom and level of interest, with implications for user satisfaction and task success (Forbes-Riley et al., 2012; Schuller et al., 2009). In ADVISER, we assume that eye activity serves as an indicator of various mental states (Schuller et al., 2009; Niu et al., 2018) and implement a gaze tracker that monitors the user's direction of focus via webcam.

Using OpenFace 2.2.0, a toolkit for facial behavior analysis (Baltrusaitis et al., 2018), we extract the features *gaze_angle_x* and *gaze_angle_y*, which capture left-right and up-down eye movement, for each frame and compute the deviation from the central point of the screen. If the deviation exceeds a certain threshold for a certain number of seconds, the user is assumed to look away from the screen, thereby disengaging. Thus, the output of our engagement level prediction module is the binary decision {looking, not looking}. Both the spatial and temporal sensitivity can be adjusted, such that developers have the option to decide *how far* and *how long* the user's gaze can stray from the central point until they are considered to be disengaged. In an adaptive system, this information could be used to select re-engagement strategies, e.g. using an affective template (see section 3.7).

Backchanneling   In a conversation, a backchannel (BC) is a soft interjection from the listener to the speaker, with the purpose of signaling acknowledgment or reacting to what was just uttered. Backchannels contribute to a successful conversation flow (Clark and Krych, 2004). Therefore, we add an acoustic backchannel module to create a more human-like dialog experience. For backchannel prediction, we extract 13 Mel-frequency-cepstral coefficients from the user's speech signal, which form the input to

the convolutional neural network based on Ortega et al. (2020). The model assigns one of three categories from the proactive backchanneling theory (Goodwin, 1986) to each user utterance {no-backchannel, backchannel-continuer and backchannel-assessment}. The predicted category is used to add the backchannel realization, such as *Right* or *Uh-huh*, to the next system response.

3.2   Speech Processing

Automatic Speech Recognition (ASR)   The speech recognition module receives a speech signal as input, which can come from an internal or external microphone, and outputs decoded text. The specific realization of ASR can be interchanged or adapted, for example for new languages or different ASR methods. We provide an end-to-end ASR model for English based on the Transformer neural network architecture. We use the end-to-end speech processing toolkit ESPnet (Watanabe et al., 2018) and the IMS-speech English multi-dataset recipe (Denisov and Vu, 2019), updated to match the LibriSpeech Transformer-based system in ESPnet (Karita et al., 2019) and to include more training data. Training data comprises the LibriSpeech, Switchboard, TED-LIUM 3, AMI, WSJ, Common Voice 3, SWC, VoxForge and M-AILABS datasets with a total amount of 3249 hours. As input features, 80-dimensional log Mel filterbank coefficients are used. Output of the ASR model is a sequence of subword units, which include single characters as well as combinations of several characters, making the model lexicon independent.

Speech Synthesis   For ADVISER's voice output, we use the ESPnet-TTS toolkit (Hayashi et al., 2019), which is an extension of the ESPnet toolkit mentioned above. We use FastSpeech as the synthesis model speeding up mel-spectrogram generation by a factor of 270 and voice generation by a factor of 38 compared to autoregressive Transformer TTS (Ren et al., 2019). We use a Parallel Wave-GAN (Yamamoto et al., 2020) to generate waveforms that is computationally efficient and achieves a high mean opinion score of 4.16. The FastSpeech and WaveGAN models were trained with 24 hours of the LJSpeech dataset from a single speaker (Ito, 2017) and are capable of generating voice output in real-time when using a GPU. The synthesis can run on any device in a distributed system. Additionally, we optimize the synthesizer for abbreviations, such as *Prof., Univ., IMS, NLP, ECTS* and *PhD*, as well as for German proper names, such as street names. These optimizations can be easily extended.

Turn Taking To make interacting with the system more natural, we use a naive end-of-utterance detection. Users indicate the start of their turn by pressing a hotkey, so they can choose to pause the interaction. The highest absolute peak of each recording chunk is then compared with a predefined threshold. If a certain number of sequential chunks do not peak above the threshold, the recording stops. We are currenlty in the process of planning more sophisticated turn taking models, such as Skantze et al. (2015).

3.3 Natural Language Understanding

The natural language understanding (NLU) unit parses the textual user input (De Mori et al., 2008) - or the output from the speech recognition system - and extracts the user action type, generally referred to as intent in goal-oriented dialog systems (e.g. *Inform* and *Request*), as well as the corresponding slots and values. The domain-independent, rule-based NLU presented in Ortega et al. (2019) is integrated into ADVISER and adapted to the new domains presented in section 5.

3.4 State Tracking

Belief State Tracking (BST): The BST tracks the history of user informs and the user action types, requests, with one BST entry per turn. This information is stored in a dictionary structure that is built up, as the user provides more details and the system has a better understanding of user intent.

User State Tracking (UST): Similar to the BST, the UST tracks the history of the user's state over the course of a dialog, with one entry per turn. In the current implementation, the user state consists of the user's engagement level, valence, arousal, and emotion category (details in section 3.1).

3.5 Dialog Policies

Policies To determine the correct system action, we provide three types of policy services: a handcrafted and a reinforcement learning policy for finding entities from a database (Ortega et al., 2019), as well as a handcrafted policy for looking up information through an API call. Both handcrafted policies use a series of rules to help the user find a single entity or, once an entity has been found (or directly provided by the user), find information about that entity. The reinforcement learning (RL)

policy's action-value function is approximated by a neural network which outputs a value for each possible system action, given the vectorized representation of a turn's belief state as input. The neural network is constructed as proposed in Väth and Vu (2019) following a duelling architecture (Wang et al., 2016). It consists of two separate calculation streams, each with its own layers, where the final layer yields the action-value function. For off-policy batch-training, we make use of prioritized experience replay (Schaul et al., 2015).

Affective Policy In addition, we have also implemented a rule-based affective policy service that can be used to determine the system's emotional response. As this policy is domain-agnostic, predicting the next system *emotion* output rather than the next system *action*, it can be used alongside any of the previously mentioned policies.

User Simulator To support automatic evaluation and to train the RL policy, we provide a user simulator service outputting at the user acts level. As we are concerned with task-oriented dialogs here, the user simulator has an agenda-based (Schatzmann et al., 2007) architecture and is randomly assigned a goal at the beginning of the dialog. Each turn, it then works to first respond to the system utterance, and then after to fulfill its own goal. When the system utterance also works toward fulfilling the user goal, the RL policy is rewarded by achieving a shorter total dialog turn count (Ortega et al., 2019).

3.6 External Information Resources

ADVISER supports three options to access information from external information sources. In addition to being able to query information from SQL-based databases, we add two new options that includes querying information via APIs and from knowledge bases (e.g. Wikidata (Vrandečić and Krötzsch, 2014)). For example, when a user asks a simple question - *Where was Dirk Nowitzki born?*, our pretrained neural network predicts the topic entity - *Dirk Nowitzki* - and the relation - *place of birth*. Then, the answer is automatically looked up using Wikidata's SPARQL endpoint.

3.7 Natural Language Generation (NLG)

In the NLG service, the semantic representation of the system act is transformed into natural language. ADVISER currently uses a template-based approach to NLG in which each possible system act is mapped to exactly one utterance. A special

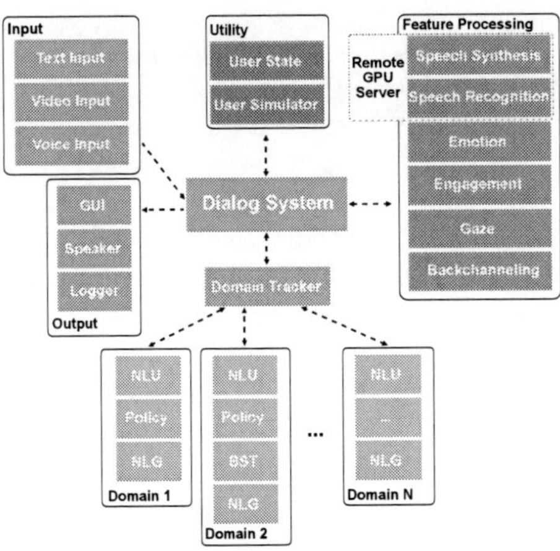

Figure 2: Example ADVISER toolkit configuration: Grey represents backend components, blue represents domain-specific services, and all other colors represent domain-agnostic services. Two components are run remotely.

syntax using placeholders reduces the number of templates needed and accounts for correct morphological inflections (Ortega et al., 2019). Additionally, we developed an affective NLG service, which allows for different templates to be used depending on the user's emotional state. This enables a more sensitive/adaptive system. For example, if the user is sad and the system does not understand the user's input, it might try to establish common ground to prevent their mood from getting worse due to the bad news. An example response would be "As much as I would love to help, I am a bit confused" rather than the more neutral "Sorry I am a bit confused". One set of NLG templates can be specified for each possible emotional state. At runtime, the utterance is then generated from the template associated with the current system emotion and system action.

4   Software Architecture

4.1   Dialog as a Collection of Services

To allow for maximum flexibility in combining and reusing components, we consider a dialog system as a group of services which communicate asynchronously by publishing/subscribing to certain topics. A service is called as soon as at least one message for all its subscribed topics is received and may additionally publish to one or more topics. Services can elect to receive the most recent message for a topic (e.g. up-to-date belief state) or

a list of all messages for that topic since the last service call (e.g. a list of video frames). Constructing a dialog system in this way allows us to break free from a pipeline architecture. Each step in the dialog process is represented by one or more services which can operate in parallel or sequentially. For example, tasks like video and speech capture may be performed and processed in parallel before being synchronized by a user state tracking module subscribing to input from both sources. Figure 2 illustrates the system architecture. For debugging purposes, we provide a utility to draw the dialog graph, showing the information flow between services, including remote services, and any inconsistencies in publish/subscribe connections.

4.2   Support for Distributed Systems

Services are location-transparent and may thus be distributed across multiple machines. A central dialog system discovers local and remote services and provides synchronization guarantees for dialog initialization and termination. Distribution of services enables, for instance, a more powerful computer to handle tasks such as real-time text-to-speech generation (see Figure 2). This is particularly helpful when multiple resource-heavy tasks are combined into a single dialog system.

4.3   Support for Multi-Domain Systems

In addition to providing multi-modal support, the publish/subscribe framework also allows for multi-domain support by providing a structure which enables arbitrary branching and rejoining of graph structures. When a service is created, users simply specify which domain(s) it should publish/subscribe to. This, in combination with a domain tracking service, allows for seamless integration of domain-agnostic services (such as speech input/output) and domain-specific services (such as NLU/NLG for the lecturers domain).

5   Example Use Cases

5.1   Example Domains

We provide several example domains to demonstrate ADVISER's functionalities. Databases for lecturers and courses at the Institute for Natural Language Processing (IMS), which we used in the previous version of ADVISER, were adapted to the new system architecture. As example APIs, we implemented a weather domain that makes calls to the OpenWeatherMap API[3] and a mensa domain for gathering information from the dining hall at the university of Stuttgart. Note that affective templates were only added to the lecturers and mensa domain. All domains can be used within the same dialog, simply by switching the topic.

5.2 An Example Implementation

Our toolkit allows for easy creation of a dialog system within a few lines of code as follows.

```
# domains
weather = WeatherDomain()
mensa = MensaDomain()
# create system from desired services
ds = DialogSystem(services=[
    DomainTracker(domains=[mensa,
    weather]),
    SpeechRecorder(),
    VideoInput(),
    EngagementTracker(),
    EmotionTracker(),
    WeatherNLU(domain=weather),
    MensaNLU(domain=mensa),
    ...,
    SpeechOutputPlayer()])

ds.run_dialog(...)
```

As a first step, a dialog system object is initialized, which is responsible for coordinating the initialization and graceful termination of all dialog services. Talking about multiple domains in one dialog is enabled by creating a simple keyword-based domain tracker which is introduced as the first argument to the dialog system. To make the dialog multi-modal, speech and vision modules are introduced next, along with modules to extract engagement and emotion. So far, all of these modules are domain-agnostic and can be used as shared resources between all domains. Next, domain-dependent services such as NLUs, BSTs and NLGs for weather and mensa, are added. The following shows an example dialog.

SYSTEM: Hello, please let me know how I can help you, I can discuss the following domains: Mensa Food and Weather.
USER: I could have something to eat. What does the mensa offer today?
SYSTEM: What type of dish are you looking for?
USER: I would like a main dish.
SYSTEM: Should the meal be vegan?
USER: Yes.
SYSTEM: The meal mediterranean Ebly wheat is served today, is a main dish and is vegan.
USER: Okay, cool, I will go there now! What is the weather like?

---

[3]https://openweathermap.org/api

SYSTEM: The weather in Stuttgart on January 28 at 3 PM is 3 degrees celsius with light snow.
USER: Thank you, ADVISER, good bye!
SYSTEM: Thank you, good bye.

---

6 Related Work

Other tools for building dialog systems include *ConvLab* (Lee et al., 2019), an open-source, text-based dialog system platform that supports both pipelined architectures and an end-to-end neural architecture. *ConvLab* also provides reusable components and supports multi-domain settings. Other systems are largely text-based, but offer the incorporation of external speech components. *InproTK* (Baumann and Schlangen, 2012), for instance, in which modules communicate by networks via configuration files, uses ASR based on Sphinx-4 and synthesis based on MaryTTS. Similarly, *RavenClaw* (Bohus and Rudnicky, 2009) provides a framework for creating dialog managers; ASR and synthesis components can be supplied, for example, by connecting to Sphinx and Kalliope. *OpenDial* (Lison and Kennington, 2016) relies on probabilistic rules and provides options to connect to speech components such as Sphinx. Multi-domain dialog toolkit - *PyDial* (Ultes et al., 2017) supports connection to DialPort.

As mentioned in the introduction, Microsoft Research's \psi is an open and extensible platform that supports the development of multi-modal AI systems (Bohus et al., 2017). It further offers audio and visual processing, such as speech recognition and face tracking, as well as output, such as synthesis and avatar rendering. And the *MuMMER* (multi-modal Mall Entertainment Robot) project (Foster et al., 2016) is based on the SoftBank Robotics *Pepper* platform, and thereby comprises processing of audio-, visual- and social signals, with the aim to develop a socially engaging robot that can be deployed in public spaces.

7 Conclusions

We introduce ADVISER – an open-source, multi-domain dialog system toolkit that allows users to easily develop multi-modal and socially-engaged conversational agents. We provide a large variety of functionalities, ranging from speech processing to core dialog system capabilities and social signal processing. With this toolkit, we hope to provide a flexible platform for collaborative research in multi-domain, multi-modal, socially-engaged conversational agents.

References

Tadas Baltrusaitis, Amir Zadeh, Yao Chong Lim, and Louis-Philippe Morency. 2018. OpenFace 2.0: Facial Behavior Analysis Toolkit.

Timo Baumann and David Schlangen. 2012. The InproTK 2012 Release. In *NAACL-HLT Workshop on Future Directions and Needs in the Spoken Dialog Community: Tools and Data.*

Daniel G. Bobrow, Ronald M. Kaplan, Martin Kay, Donald A. Norman, Henry Thompson, and Terry Winograd. 1977. Gus, a frame-driven dialog system. *Artificial Intelligence.*

Dan Bohus, Sean Andrist, and Mihai Jalobeanu. 2017. Rapid Development of Multimodal Interactive Systems: A Demonstration of Platform for Situated Intelligence. In *ICMI '17: Proceedings of the 19th ACM International Conference on Multimodal Interaction*, pages 493–494.

Dan Bohus and Alexander I Rudnicky. 2009. The ravenclaw dialog management framework: Architecture and systems. *Computer Speech & Language*, 23(3):332–361.

Carlos Busso, Murtaza Bulut, Chi-Chun Lee, Abe Kazemzadeh, Emily Mower, Samuel Kim, Jeannette N Chang, Sungbok Lee, and Shrikanth S Narayanan. 2008. Iemocap: Interactive emotional dyadic motion capture database. *Language resources and evaluation*, 42(4).

H. H Clark and M. A Krych. 2004. Speaking while monitoring addressees for understanding. *Journal of Memory and Language.*

Amanda Cercas Curry, Ioannis Papaioannou, Alessandro Suglia, Shubham Agarwal, Igor Shalyminov, Xinnuo Xu, Ondřej Dušek, Arash Eshghi, Ioannis Konstas, Verena Rieser, and Oliver Lemon. 2018. Alana v2: Entertaining and Informative Open-domain Social Dialogue using Ontologies and Entity Linking. In *1st Proceedings of Alexa Prize.*

Renato De Mori, Frédéric Bechet, Dilek Hakkani-Tur, Michael McTear, Giuseppe Riccardi, and Gokhan Tur. 2008. Spoken language understanding. *IEEE Signal Processing Magazine.*

Pavel Denisov and Ngoc Thang Vu. 2019. Imsspeech: A speech to text tool. *Studientexte zur Sprachkommunikation: Elektronische Sprachsignalverarbeitung 2019*, pages 170–177.

Kate Forbes-Riley, Diane Litman, Heather Friedberg, and Joanna Drummond. 2012. Intrinsic and Extrinsic Evaluation of an Automatic User Disengagement Detector for an Uncertainty-Adaptive Spoken Dialogue System. In *Conference of the North American Chapter of the Association for Computational Linguistics: Human Language Technologies*, pages 91–102, Montréal.

Mary Ellen Foster, Rachid Alami, Olli Gestranius, Oliver Lemon, Marketta Niemelä, Jean Marc Odobez, and Amit Kumar Pandey. 2016. The MuMMER project: Engaging human-robot interaction in real-world public spaces. In *Processings of the Eighth International Conference on Social Robotics (ICSR 2016)*, pages 753–763. Springer.

Charles Goodwin. 1986. Between and within: Alternative sequential treatments of continuers and assessments. *Journal of Human Studies.*

Tomoki Hayashi, Ryuichi Yamamoto, Katsuki Inoue, Takenori Yoshimura, Shinji Watanabe, Tomoki Toda, Kazuya Takeda, Yu Zhang, and Xu Tan. 2019. Espnet-tts: Unified, reproducible, and integratable open source end-to-end text-to-speech toolkit.

Keith Ito. 2017. The lj speech dataset. `https://keithito.com/LJ-Speech-Dataset/`.

Shigeki Karita, Nanxin Chen, Tomoki Hayashi, Takaaki Hori, Hirofumi Inaguma, Ziyan Jiang, Masao Someki, Nelson Enrique Yalta Soplin, Ryuichi Yamamoto, Xiaofei Wang, et al. 2019. A comparative study on transformer vs rnn in speech applications. In *IEEE Automatic Speech Recognition and Understanding Workshop (ASRU).*

Sungjin Lee, Qi Zhu, Ryuichi Takanobu, Zheng Zhang, Yaoqin Zhang, Xiang Li, Jinchao Li, Baolin Peng, Xiujun Li, Minlie Huang, and Jianfeng Gao. 2019. ConvLab: Multi-Domain End-to-End Dialog System Platform. In *Proceedings of the 57th Annual Meeting of the Association for Computational Linguistics: System Demonstrations*, pages 64–69.

Pierre Lison and Casey Kennington. 2016. Opendial: A toolkit for developing spoken dialogue systems with probabilistic rules. In *Proceedings of ACL-2016 system demonstrations*, pages 67–72.

Michael Frederick McTear, Zoraida Callejas, and David Griol. 2016. *The conversational interface*, volume 6. Springer.

Michael Neumann and Ngoc Thang Vu. 2017. Attentive convolutional neural network based speech emotion recognition: A study on the impact of input features, signal length, and acted speech. In *Proceedings of Interspeech.*

Xuesong Niu, Hu Han, Jiabei Zeng, Xuran Sun, Shiguang Shan, Yan Huang, Songfan Yang, and Xilin Chen. 2018. Automatic Engagement Prediction with GAP Feature. In *ICMI*, pages 599–603, Boulder. Association for Computing Machinery.

Daniel Ortega, Chia-Yu Li, and Thang Vu. 2020. Oh, Jeez! or uh-huh? A listener-aware Backchannel predictor on ASR transcriptions. In *ICASSP 2020 - IEEE International Conference on Acoustics, Speech and Signal Processing*, pages 8064–8068.

Daniel Ortega, Dirk Väth, Gianna Weber, Lindsey Vanderlyn, Maximilian Schmidt, Moritz Völkel, Zorica Karacevic, and Ngoc Thang Vu. 2019. Adviser: A dialog system framework for education & research. In *Proceedings of the 57th Annual Meeting of the Association for Computational Linguistics: System Demonstrations*, pages 93–98.

Yi Ren, Yangjun Ruan, Xu Tan, Tao Qin, Sheng Zhao, Zhou Zhao, and Tie-Yan Liu. 2019. Fastspeech: Fast, robust and controllable text to speech. In *Advances in Neural Information Processing Systems*, pages 3165–3174.

Jost Schatzmann, Blaise Thomson, Karl Weilhammer, Hui Ye, and Steve Young. 2007. Agenda-based user simulation for bootstrapping a pomdp dialogue system. In *Proceedings of NAACL*.

Tom Schaul, John Quan, Ioannis Antonoglou, and David Silver. 2015. Prioritized experience replay. In *Proceedings of ICLR*.

Björn Schuller, Ronald Müller, Florian Eyben, Jürgen Gast, Benedikt Hörnler, Martin Wöllmer, Gerhard Rigoll, Anja Höthker, and Hitoshi Konosu. 2009. Being bored? Recognising natural interest by extensive audiovisual integration for real-life application. *Image and Vision Computing*, 27:1760–1774.

Gabriel Skantze, Martin Johansson, and Jonas Beskow. 2015. Exploring turn-taking cues in multi-party human-robot discussions about objects. In *Proceedings of the 2015 ACM on International Conference on Multimodal Interaction*, pages 67–74.

Stefan Ultes, Lina M. Rojas Barahona, Pei-Hao Su, David Vandyke, Dongho Kim, Iñigo Casanueva, Paweł Budzianowski, Nikola Mrkšić, Tsung-Hsien Wen, Milica Gasic, and Steve Young. 2017. PyDial: A Multi-domain Statistical Dialogue System Toolkit. In *Proceedings of ACL*.

Dirk Väth and Ngoc Thang Vu. 2019. To combine or not to combine? a rainbow deep reinforcement learning agent for dialog policies. In *Proceedings of the 20th Annual SIGdial Meeting on Discourse and Dialogue*, pages 62–67.

Denny Vrandečić and Markus Krötzsch. 2014. Wikidata: a free collaborative knowledgebase. *Communications of the ACM*, 57(10):78–85.

Johannes Wagner, Florian Lingenfelser, Tobias Baur, Ionut Damian, Felix Kistler, and Elisabeth André. 2013. The social signal interpretation (ssi) framework: multimodal signal processing and recognition in real-time. In *Proceedings of the 21st ACM international conference on Multimedia*.

Ziyu Wang, Tom Schaul, Matteo Hessel, Hado Van Hasselt, Marc Lanctot, and Nando De Freitas. 2016. Dueling network architectures for deep reinforcement learning. In *Proceedings of ICML*.

Shinji Watanabe, Takaaki Hori, Shigeki Karita, Tomoki Hayashi, Jiro Nishitoba, Yuya Unno, Nelson Enrique Yalta Soplin, Jahn Heymann, Matthew Wiesner, Nanxin Chen, Adithya Renduchintala, and Tsubasa Ochiai. 2018. Espnet: End-to-end speech processing toolkit. In *Interspeech*, pages 2207–2211.

Joseph Weizenbaum. 1966. ELIZA: A Computer Program for the Study of Natural Language Communication Between Man and Machine. *Communications of the ACM*, 9(1).

Ryuichi Yamamoto, Eunwoo Song, and Jae-Min Kim. 2020. Parallel wavegan: A fast waveform generation model based on generative adversarial networks with multi-resolution spectrogram. In *ICASSP 2020 - IEEE International Conference on Acoustics, Speech and Signal Processing*, pages 6199–6203.

Zhihong Zeng, Maja Pantic, Glenn I Roisman, and Thomas S Huang. 2009. A survey of affect recognition methods: Audio, visual, and spontaneous expressions. *IEEE transactions on pattern analysis and machine intelligence*, 31(1):39–58.

Li Zhou, Jianfeng Gao, Di Li, and Heung-Yeung Shum. 2018. The Design and Implementation of XiaoIce, an Empathetic Social Chatbot. *Computational Linguistics*, pages 1–62.

`Prta`: A System to Support the Analysis of Propaganda Techniques in the News

Giovanni Da San Martino[1]   Shaden Shaar[1]   Yifan Zhang[1]
Seunghak Yu[2]   Alberto Barrón-Cedeño[3]   Preslav Nakov[1]

[1] Qatar Computing Research Institute, HBKU, Qatar
[2] MIT Computer Science and Artificial Intelligence Laboratory, Cambridge, MA, USA
[3] Università di Bologna, Forlì, Italy

{gmartino,sshaar,yzhang,pnakov}@hbku.edu.qa
seunghak@csail.mit.edu
a.barron@unibo.it

Abstract

Recent events, such as the 2016 US Presidential Campaign, Brexit and the COVID-19 "infodemic", have brought into the spotlight the dangers of online disinformation. There has been a lot of research focusing on fact-checking and disinformation detection. However, little attention has been paid to the specific rhetorical and psychological techniques used to convey propaganda messages. Revealing the use of such techniques can help promote media literacy and critical thinking, and eventually contribute to limiting the impact of "fake news" and disinformation campaigns.

`Prta` (Propaganda Persuasion Techniques Analyzer) allows users to explore the articles crawled on a regular basis by highlighting the spans in which propaganda techniques occur and to compare them on the basis of their use of propaganda techniques. The system further reports statistics about the use of such techniques, overall and over time, or according to filtering criteria specified by the user based on time interval, keywords, and/or political orientation of the media. Moreover, it allows users to analyze any text or URL through a dedicated interface or via an API. The system is available online: https://www.tanbih.org/prta.

1 Introduction

Brexit and the 2016 US Presidential campaign (Muller, 2018), as well as major events such the COVID-19 outbreak (World Health Organization, 2020), were marked by disinformation campaigns at an unprecedented scale. This has brought the public attention to the problem, which became known under the name "fake news". Even though declared word of the year 2017 by Collins dictionary,[1] we find that term unhelpful, as it can easily mislead people, and even fact-checking organizations, to only focus on the veracity aspect.

At the EU level, a more precise term is preferred, *disinformation*, which refers to information that is both (*i*) false, and (*ii*) intents to harm. The often-ignored aspect (*ii*) is the main reasons why disinformation has become an important issue, namely because the news was *weaponized*.

Another aspect that has been largely ignored is the mechanism through which disinformation is being conveyed: using propaganda techniques. *Propaganda* can be defined as (*i*) trying to influence somebody's opinion, and (*ii*) doing so on purpose (Da San Martino et al., 2020). Note that this definition is orthogonal to that of disinformation: Propagandist news can be both true and false, and it can be both harmful and harmless (it could even be good). Here our focus is on the propaganda techniques: on their typology and use in the news.

Propaganda messages are conveyed via specific rhetorical and psychological techniques, ranging from leveraging on emotions —such as using *loaded language* (Weston, 2018, p. 6), *flag waving* (Hobbs and Mcgee, 2008), *appeal to authority* (Goodwin, 2011), slogans (Dan, 2015), and clichés (Hunter, 2015)— to using logical fallacies —such as *straw men* (Walton, 1996) (misrepresenting someone's opinion), *red herring* (Weston, 2018, p. 78),(Teninbaum, 2009) (presenting irrelevant data), *black-and-white fallacy* (Torok, 2015) (presenting two alternatives as the only possibilities), and *whataboutism* (Richter, 2017).

Here, we present `Prta` —the PRopaganda persuasion Techniques Analyzer. `Prta` makes online readers aware of propaganda by automatically detecting the text fragments in which propaganda techniques are being used as well as the type of propaganda technique in use. We believe that revealing the use of such techniques can help promote media literacy and critical thinking, and eventually contribute to limiting the impact of "fake news" and disinformation campaigns.

---

[1] https://www.bbc.com/news/uk-41838386

Proceedings of the 58th Annual Meeting of the Association for Computational Linguistics, pages 287–293
July 5 - July 10, 2020. ©2020 Association for Computational Linguistics

loaded language • **Outrage** as Donald Trump suggests injecting disinfectant to kill virus.
name calling, labeling • WHO: Coronavirus emergency is '**Public Enemy Number 1**'
repetition • I still have a **dream**. It is a **dream** deeply rooted in the American **dream**. I have a **dream** that ...
exaggeration, minimization • Coronavirus '**risk to the American people remains very low**', Trump said.
doubt • **Can the same be said for the Obama Administration?**
appeal to fear/prejudice • **A dark, impenetrable and "irreversible" winter of persecution of the faithful by their own shepherds will fall.**
flag-waving • Mueller attempts **to stop the will of We the People!!!** It's time to jail Mueller.
causal oversimplification • **If France had not have declared war on Germany then World War II would have never happened.**
slogans • **"BUILD THE WALL!"** Trump tweeted.
appeal to authority • **Monsignor Jean-François Lantheaume, who served as first Counsellor of the Nunciature in Washington, confirmed that "Viganò said the truth. That's all."**
black-and-white fallacy • Francis said these words: "**Everyone is guilty for the good he could have done and did not do ... If we do not oppose evil, we tacitly feed it.**"
obfuscation, Intentional vagueness, Confusion • **Women and men are physically and emotionally different. The sexes are not "equal," then, and therefore the law should not pretend that we are!**
thought-terminating cliches • **I do not really see any problems there.** Marx is the President.
whataboutism • President Trump —**who himself avoided national military service** in the 1960's— keeps beating the war drums over North Korea.
reductio ad hitlerum • "Vichy journalism," a term which now fits so much of the mainstream media. **It collaborates in the same way that the Vichy government in France collaborated with the Nazis.**
red herring • **"You may claim that the death penalty is an ineffective deterrent against crime – but what about the victims of crime? How do you think surviving family members feel when they see the man who murdered their son kept in prison at their expense? Is it right that they should pay for their son's murderer to be fed and housed?"**
bandwagon • **He tweeted, "EU no longer considers #Hamas a terrorist group. Time for US to do same."**
straw man • "Take it seriously, but with a large grain of salt." **Which is just Allen's more nuanced way of saying: "Don't believe it."**

Table 1: Our 18 propaganda techniques with example snippets. The propagandist span appears highlighted.

With Prta, users can explore the contents of articles about a number of topics, crawled from a variety of sources and updated on a regular basis, and to compare them on the basis of their use of propaganda techniques. The application reports overall statistics about the occurrence of such techniques, as well as their usage over time, or according to user-defined filtering criteria such as time span, keywords, and/or political orientation of the media. Furthermore, the application allows users to input and to analyze any text or URL of interest; this is also possible via an API, which allows other applications to be built on top of the system.

Prta relies on a supervised multi-granularity gated BERT-based model, which we train on a corpus of news articles annotated at the fragment level with 18 propaganda techniques, a total of 350K word tokens (Da San Martino et al., 2019).

Our work is in contrast to previous efforts, where propaganda has been tackled primarily at the article level (Rashkin et al., 2017; Barrón-Cedeño et al., 2019; Barrón-Cedeño et al., 2019). It is also different from work in the related field of computational argumentation, which deals with some specific logical fallacies related to propaganda, such as *ad hominem* fallacy (Habernal et al., 2018b).

Consider the game *Argotario*, which educates people to recognize and create fallacies such as *ad hominem*, *red herring* and *irrelevant authority*, which directly relate to propaganda (Habernal et al., 2017, 2018a). Unlike them, we have a richer inventory of techniques and we show them in the context of actual news.

The remainder of this paper is organized as follows. Section 2 introduces the machine learning model at the core of the Prta system. Section 3 sketches the full architecture of Prta, with focus on the process of collection and processing of the input articles. Section 4 describes the system interface and its functionality, and presents some examples. Section 5 draws conclusions and discusses possible directions for future work.

2 Data and Model

Data We train our model on a corpus of 350K tokens (Da San Martino et al., 2019; Yu et al., 2019), manually annotated by professional annotators with the instances of use of eighteen propaganda techniques. See Table 1 for a complete list and examples for each of these techniques.[2]

---

[2]Detailed list with definitions and examples is available at http://propaganda.qcri.org/annotations/definitions.html

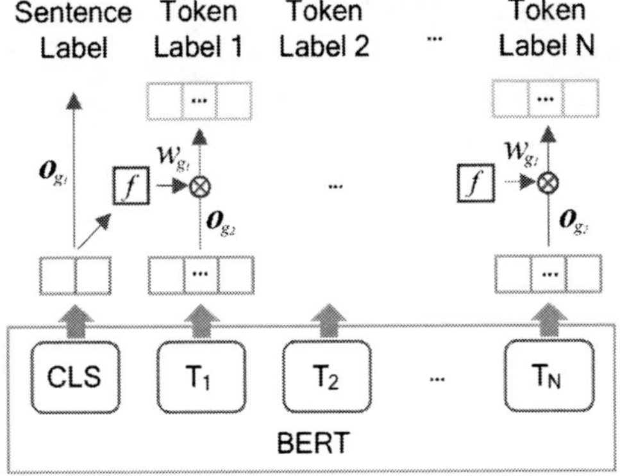

Figure 1: The architecture of our model.

Model Our model is based on multi-task learning with the following two tasks:

FLC *Fragment-level classification.* Given a sentence, identify all spans of use of propaganda techniques in it and the type of technique.

SLC *Sentence-level classification.* Given a sentence, predict whether it contains at least one propaganda technique.

Our model adds on top of BERT (Devlin et al., 2019) a set of layers that combine information from the fragment- and the sentence-level annotations to boost the performance of the FLC task on the basis of the SLC task. The network architecture is shown in Figure 1, and we refer to it as a multi-granularity network. It features 19 output units for each input token in the FLC task, standing for one of the 18 propaganda techniques or "no technique." A complementary output focuses on the SLC task, which is used to generate, through a trainable gate, a weight w that is multiplied by the input of the FLC task. The gate consists of a projection layer to one dimension and an activation function. The effect of this modeling is that if the sentence-level classifier is confident that the sentence does not contain propaganda, i.e., $w \sim 0$, then no propaganda technique would be predicted for any of the word tokens in the sentence.

The model we use in `Prta` outperforms BERT-based baselines on both at the sentence-level (F_1 of 60.71 vs. 57.74) and at the fragment-level (F_1 of 22.58 vs. 21.39). At the fragment-level, the model outperforms the best solution of a hackathon organized on this data.[3]

For the `Prta` system, we applied a softmax operator to turn its output into a bounded value in the range [0,1], which allows us to show a confidence for each prediction. Further details about the techniques, the model, the data, and the experiments can be found in (Da San Martino et al., 2019).[4]

3 System Architecture

`Prta` collects news articles from a number of news outlets, discards near-duplicates and finally identifies both specific propaganda techniques and sentences containing propaganda.

We crawl a growing list (now 250) of RSS feeds, Twitter accounts, and websites, and we extract the plain text from the crawled Web pages using the Newspaper3k library[5]. We then perform deduplication based on a combination of URL partial matching and content analysis using a hash function.

Finally, we use the model from Section 2 to identify sentences with propaganda and instances of use of specific propaganda techniques in the text and their types. We further organize the articles into topics; currently, the topics are defined using keyword matching, e.g., an article mentioning *COVID-19* or *Brexit* is assigned to a corresponding topic. By accumulating the techniques identified in multiple articles, `Prta` can show the volume of propaganda techniques used by each medium —as well as aggregated over all media for a specific topic— thus, allowing the user to do comparisons and analysis, as described in the next section.

4 Interface

`Prta` offers the following functionality.

For each crawled news article:

1. It flags all text spans in which a propaganda technique has been spotted.

2. It flags all sentences containing propaganda.

For a user-provided text or a URL:

3. It flags the same as in 1 and 2 above.

At the medium and at the topic level:

4. It displays aggregated statistics about the propaganda techniques used by all media on a specific topic, and also for individual media, or for media with specific political ideology.

---

[3]https://www.datasciencesociety.net/events/
hack-the-news-datathon-2019

[4]The corpus and the models are available online at
propaganda.qcri.org/fine-grained-propaganda-emnlp.html
[5]http://newspaper.readthedocs.io

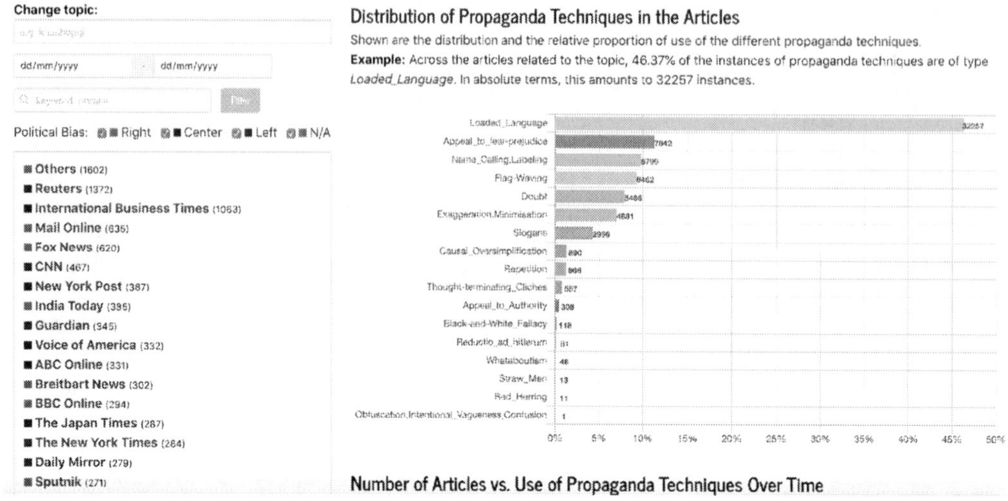

Figure 2: Overall view for a topic.

This functionality is implemented in the three interfaces we expose to the user: the main topic page, the article page, and the custom article page, which we describe in Sections 4.1–4.3. Although points 1 and 2 above are run offline, they can also be invoked for a custom text using our API.[6]

4.1 Main Topic Page

Figure 2 shows a snapshot of the main page for a given topic: here, the *Coronavirus Outbreak in 2019-20*. We can see on the left panel, a list of the media covering the topic, sorted by number of articles. This allows the user to get a general idea about the degree of coverage of the topic by different media.

The right panel in Figure 2 shows statistics about the articles from the left panel. In particular, we can see the global distribution of the propaganda techniques in the articles, both in relative and in absolute terms. The right panel further shows a graph with the number of articles about the topic and the average number of propaganda techniques per article over time. Finally, it shows another graph with the relative proportion of propagandistic content per article; it is possible to click and to navigate from this graph to the target article. The latter two graphs are not shown in Figure 2, as they could not fit in this paper, but the reader is welcome to check them online.

The set of articles on the left panel can be filtered by time interval, by keyword, by political orientation of the media (left/center/right), as well as by any combination thereof.

Clicking on a medium on the left panel expands it, displaying its articles ranked on the basis of Eq. (1). Given the output of the multi-granularity network, we compute a simple score to assess the proportion of propaganda techniques in an article or in an individual media source. Let $F(x)$ be a set of fragment-level annotations in article x, where each annotation is a sequence of tokens. We compute the propaganda score for x as the ratio between the number of tokens covered by some propagandist fragment (regardless of the technique) and the total number of tokens in the article:

$$Q_a(x) = \frac{|\bigcup_{f \in F(x)} f|}{|x|}. \quad (1)$$

Selecting a medium, or any other filtering criterion, further updates the graph on the center-right panel. For example, Figures 3a and 3b show the distribution of the techniques used by the BBC vs. Fox News when covering the topic of *Gun Control and Gun Rights*. We can see that both media use a lot of `loaded language`, which is the most common technique media use in general. However, the BBC also makes heavy use of `labeling` and `doubt`, whereas Fox News has a higher preference for `flag waving` and `slogans`.

---

[6]Link to the API available at https://www.tanbih.org/prta

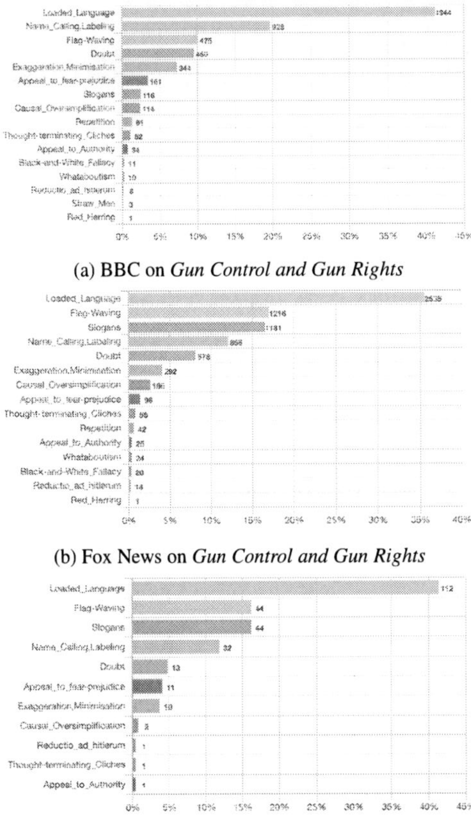

(a) BBC on *Gun Control and Gun Rights*

(b) Fox News on *Gun Control and Gun Rights*

(c) Fox News on *Jamal Khashoggi's Murder*

Figure 3: Example of the distribution of the techniques as used by two media and on two different topics. Note that the scales are different.

Next, Figure 3c shows the propaganda techniques used by Fox News when covering the Khashoggi's Murder, which has a very similar technique distribution to the plot in Figure 3b.

This similarity between the distribution of propaganda techniques in Figures 3b and 3c might be a coincidence, or it could represent a consistent style, regardless of the topic. We leave the exploration of this and other hypotheses to the interested user, which is an easy exercise with the `Prta` system.

4.2 Article Page

When the user selects an article title on the left panel (Figure 2), its full content will appear on a middle panel with the propaganda fragments highlighted, as shown in Figure 4. Meanwhile, a right panel will appear, showing the color codes used for each of the techniques found in the article (the techniques that are not present are shown in gray).

Moreover, using the slider bar on top of the right panel, the user can set a confidence threshold, and then only those propaganda fragments in the article whose confidence is equal or higher than this set threshold would be highlighted. When the user hovers the mouse over a propagandist span, a short description of the technique would pop up. If the user wishes to find more information about the propaganda techniques, she can simply click on the corresponding question mark in the right panel.

4.3 Custom Article Analysis

Our interface allows the user to submit her own text for analysis. This allows her to find the techniques used in articles published by media that we do not currently cover or to analyze other kinds of texts. Texts can be submitted by copy-pasting in the text box on top, or, alternatively, by using a URL. In the latter case, the text box will be automatically filled with the content extracted from the URL using the Newspaper3k library (see Section 3), but the user can still edit the content before submitting the text for analysis. The maximum allowed length is the one enforced by the browser. Yet, we recommend to keep texts shorter than 4k in order to avoid blocking the server with too large requests.

Figure 5 shows the analysis for an excerpt of Winston Churchill's speech on May 10, 1940. All the techniques found in this speech are highlighted in the same way as described in Section 4.2. Notice that, in this case, we have set the confidence threshold to 0.4 and some of the techniques are consequently not highlighted. We can see that the system has identified heavy use of propaganda techniques. In particular, we can observe the use of *Flag Waving* and *Appeal to Fear*, which is understandable as the purpose of this speech was to prepare the British population for war.

5 Conclusion and Future Work

We have presented the `Prta` system for detecting and highlighting the use of propaganda techniques in online news. The system further shows aggregated statistics about the use of such techniques in articles filtered according to several criteria, including date ranges, media sources, bias of the sources, and keyword searches. The system also allows users to analyze their own text or the contents of a URL of interest.

We have made publicly available our data and models, as well as an API to the live system.

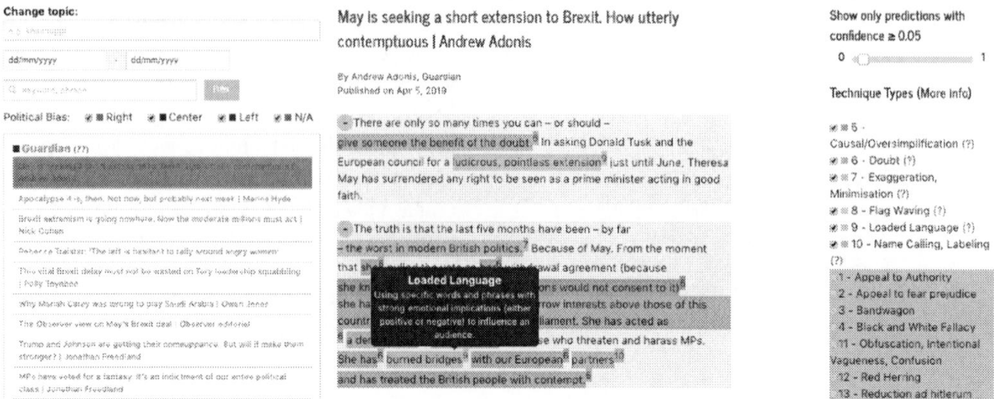

Figure 4: Selecting an article from the left panel, loads it and highlights its propaganda techniques.

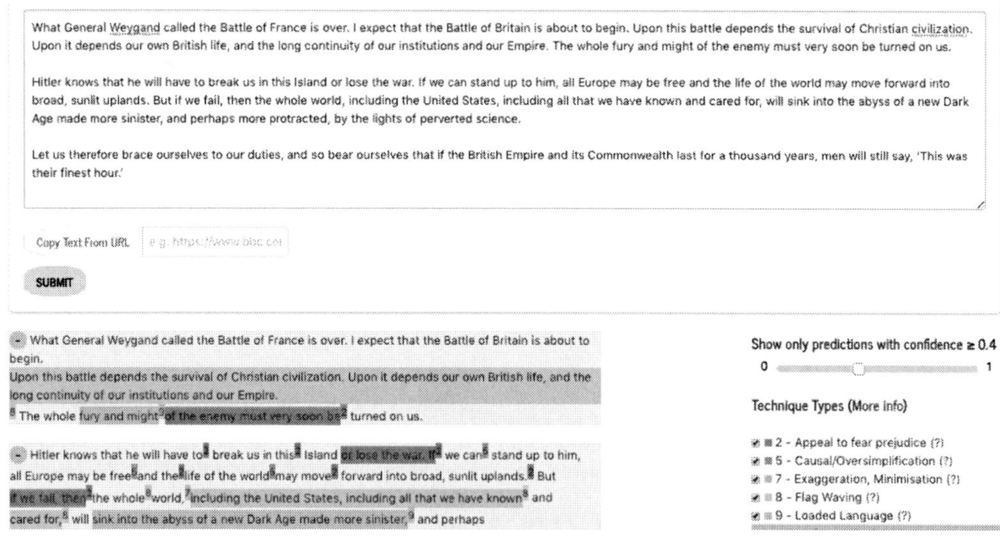

Figure 5: Analysis of a custom text, an excerpt from a speech by W. Churchill at the beginning of World War II. The confidence threshold is set to 0.4, and thus fragments for which the confidence is lower are not highlighted.

We hope that the `Prta` system would help raise awareness about the use of propaganda techniques in the news, thus promoting media literacy and critical thinking, which are arguably the best long-term answer to "fake news" and disinformation.

In future work, we plan to add more media sources, especially from non-English media and regions. We further want to extend the tool to support other propaganda techniques such as *cherry-picking* and *omission*, among others, which would require analysis beyond the text of a single article.

Acknowledgments

The `Prta` system is developed within the Propaganda Analysis Project[7], part of the Tanbih project[8]. Tanbih aims to limit the effect of "fake news", propaganda, and media bias by making users aware of what they are reading, thus promoting media literacy and critical thinking. Different organizations collaborate in Tanbih, including the Qatar Computing Research Institute (HBKU) and MIT-CSAIL.

---

[7]http://propaganda.qcri.org
[8]http://tanbih.qcri.org

References

Alberto Barrón-Cedeño, Israa Jaradat, Giovanni Da San Martino, and Preslav Nakov. 2019. Proppy: Organizing the news based on their propagandistic content. *Information Processing & Management*, 56(5):1849–1864.

Alberto Barrón-Cedeño, Giovanni Da San Martino, Israa Jaradat, and Preslav Nakov. 2019. Proppy: A system to unmask propaganda in online news. In *Proceedings of the 33rd AAAI Conference on Artificial Intelligence*, AAAI '19, pages 9847–9848, Honolulu, HI, USA.

Giovanni Da San Martino, Stefano Cresci, Alberto Barrón-Cedeño, Seunghak Yu, Roberto Di Pietro, and Preslav Nakov. 2020. A survey on computational propaganda detection. In *Proceedings of the 29th International Joint Conference on Artificial Intelligence and the 17th Pacific Rim International Conference on Artificial Intelligence*, IJCAI-PRICAI '20, Yokohama, Japan.

Giovanni Da San Martino, Seunghak Yu, Alberto Barrón-Cedeño, Rostislav Petrov, and Preslav Nakov. 2019. Fine-grained analysis of propaganda in news articles. In *Proceedings of the 2019 Conference on Empirical Methods in Natural Language Processing and 9th International Joint Conference on Natural Language Processing*, EMNLP-IJCNLP '2019, Hong Kong, China.

Lavinia Dan. 2015. Techniques for the Translation of Advertising Slogans. In *Proceedings of the International Conference Literature, Discourse and Multicultural Dialogue*, LDMD '15, pages 13–23, Mures, Romania.

Jacob Devlin, Ming-Wei Chang, Kenton Lee, and Kristina Toutanova. 2019. BERT: Pre-training of deep bidirectional transformers for language understanding. In *Proceedings of the 2019 Conference of the North American Chapter of the Association for Computational Linguistics: Human Language Technologies*, NAACL-HLT '19, pages 4171–4186, Minneapolis, MN, USA.

Jean Goodwin. 2011. Accounting for the force of the appeal to authority. In *Proceedings of the 9th International Conference of the Ontario Society for the Study of Argumentation*, OSSA '11, pages 1–9, Ontario, Canada.

Ivan Habernal, Raffael Hannemann, Christian Pollak, Christopher Klamm, Patrick Pauli, and Iryna Gurevych. 2017. Argotario: Computational argumentation meets serious games. In *Proceedings of the Conference on Empirical Methods in Natural Language Processing*, EMNLP '17, pages 7–12, Copenhagen, Denmark.

Ivan Habernal, Patrick Pauli, and Iryna Gurevych. 2018a. Adapting serious game for fallacious argumentation to German: pitfalls, insights, and best practices. In *Proceedings of the Eleventh International Conference on Language Resources and Evaluation*, LREC '18, Miyazaki, Japan.

Ivan Habernal, Henning Wachsmuth, Iryna Gurevych, and Benno Stein. 2018b. Before name-calling: Dynamics and triggers of ad hominem fallacies in web argumentation. In *Proceedings of the 2018 Conference of the North American Chapter of the Association for Computational Linguistics: Human Language Technologies*, NAACL-HLT '18, pages 386–396, New Orleans, LA, USA.

Renee Hobbs and Sandra Mcgee. 2008. Teaching about propaganda: An examination of the historical roots of media literacy. *Journal of Media Literacy Education*, 6(62):56–67.

John Hunter. 2015. Brainwashing in a large group awareness training? The classical conditioning hypothesis of brainwashing. Master's thesis, University of Kwazulu-Natal, Pietermaritzburg, South Africa.

Robert Muller. 2018. Indictment of Internet Research Agency. https://commons.wikimedia.org/wiki/File:Internet_research_agency_indictment.pdf.

Hannah Rashkin, Eunsol Choi, Jin Yea Jang, Svitlana Volkova, and Yejin Choi. 2017. Truth of varying shades: Analyzing language in fake news and political fact-checking. In *Proceedings of the 2017 Conference on Empirical Methods in Natural Language Processing*, EMNLP '17, pages 2931–2937, Copenhagen, Denmark.

Monika L Richter. 2017. The Kremlin's platform for 'useful idiots' in the West: An overview of RT's editorial strategy and evidence of impact. Technical report, Kremlin Watch.

Gabriel H Teninbaum. 2009. Reductio ad Hitlerum: Trumping the judicial Nazi card. *Michigan State Law Review*, page 541.

Robyn Torok. 2015. Symbiotic radicalisation strategies: Propaganda tools and neuro linguistic programming. In *Proceedings of the Australian Security and Intelligence Conference*, pages 58–65, Perth, Australia.

Douglas Walton. 1996. *The straw man fallacy*. Royal Netherlands Academy of Arts and Sciences.

Anthony Weston. 2018. *A rulebook for arguments*. Hackett Publishing.

World Health Organization. 2020. Novel coronavirus (2019-ncov): situation report, 13. https://apps.who.int/iris/handle/10665/330778. Accessed: 2020-04-01.

Seunghak Yu, Giovanni Da San Martino, and Preslav Nakov. 2019. Experiments in detecting persuasion techniques in the news. In *Proceedings of the NeurIPS 2019 Joint Workshop on AI for Social Good*, Vancouver, Canada.

Clinical-Coder: Assigning Interpretable ICD-10 Codes to Chinese Clinical Notes

Pengfei Cao[*1,2], **Chenwei Yan**[*3],

Xiangling Fu[3], **Yubo Chen**[1,2], **Kang Liu**[1,2], **Jun Zhao**[1,2], **Shengping Liu**[4], **Weifeng Chong**[4],

[1] National Laboratory of Pattern Recognition, Institute of Automation,
Chinese Academy of Sciences, Beijing, China

[2] School of Artificial Intelligence, University of Chinese Academy of Sciences, Beijing, China

[3] Key Laboratory of Trustworthy Distributed Computing and Service(BUPT),
Ministry of Education, Beijing University of Posts and Telecommunications, Beijing, China

[4] Beijing Unisound Information Technology Co., Ltd, Beijing, China

{pengfei.cao, yubo.chen, kliu, jzhao}@nlpr.ia.ac.cn, {2013213347, fuxiangling}@bupt.edu.cn,
{liushengping, chongweifeng}@unisound.com

Abstract

In this paper, we introduce Clinical-Coder, an online system aiming to assign ICD codes to Chinese clinical notes. ICD coding has been a research hotspot of clinical medicine, but the interpretability of prediction hinders its practical application. We exploit a **D**ilated **C**onvolutional **A**ttention network with **N**-gram **M**atching Mechanism (DCANM) to capture semantic features for non-continuous words and continuous n-gram words, concentrating on explaining the reason why each ICD code to be predicted. The experiments demonstrate that our approach is effective and that our system is able to provide supporting information in clinical decision making.

1 Introduction

International Classification of Disease (ICD) is the diagnostic classification standard in the field of clinical medicine, which assigns unique code to each disease. The popularization of ICD codes immensely promotes the information sharing and clinical research of disease worldwide and has a positive influence on health condition research, insurance claims, morbidity and mortality statistics (Shi et al., 2017). Therefore, ICD coding – which assigns proper ICD codes to a clinical note – has drawn much attention.

It is always that ICD coding relies on the manual work of professional staff. The manual coding is very error-prone and time-consuming since the continuous updating version of ICD codes results in a substantial increase in code numbers. The number of ICD-10 codes is up to 72,184, more than five times the previous version (i.e., ICD-9). It allows for more detailed classifications of patients' conditions, injuries, and diseases. However, there

is no doubt that the increased granularity increases the difficulty of manual coding.

Existing studies came up with several approaches of automatic coding prediction to replace the repetitive manual work, from the traditional machine learning methods (Perotte et al., 2013; Koopman et al., 2015), to neural network methods (Shi et al., 2017; Yu et al., 2019). Although these methods achieve great success, they are still confronted with a critical challenge, which is the interpretability of predicted codes. Explainable model and results are essential for clinical medicine decision making (Mullenbach et al., 2018). Thus, the practical approach is supposed to predict correct codes and simultaneously give the reason why each code is predicted.

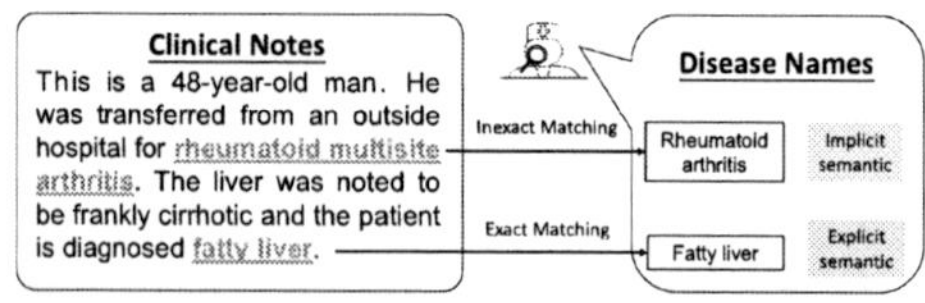

Figure 1: Two kind of semantic phenomenon: explicit semantic features and implicit semantic features.

In this paper, we try to provide the interpretability of predictions from a semantic perspective. It is a phenomenon that the exact disease names or similar expressions of disease names often appear in the discharge summary. For example, as shown in Figure 1, the exact matching with disease name such as "fatty liver" is a direct evidence of inference. We call the continuous consistent words as explicit semantic features. Moreover, the inexact matching such as "rheumatoid multisite arthritis" is also very useful to predict the codes and should be taken into consideration. We refer to the non-continuous

---

*co-first authors, they contributed equally to this work

Proceedings of the 58th Annual Meeting of the Association for Computational Linguistics, pages 294–301
July 5 - July 10, 2020. ©2020 Association for Computational Linguistics

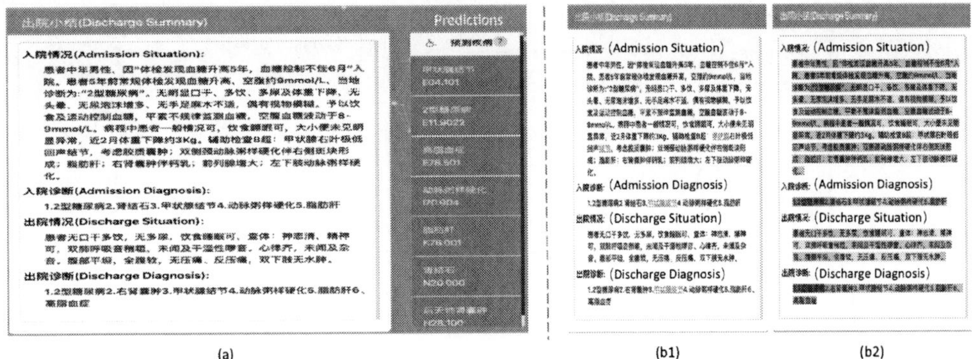

(a) (b1) (b2)

Figure 2: The screenshot of Clinical-Coder system, the English version can be found in the appendix A. (a) gives the predicted diseases after users enter the clinical notes which contains four parts, admission situation, admission diagnosis, discharge situation and discharge diagnosis. (b1) and (b2) are the visualization of supporting information for predictions.

words as implicit semantic features. The two kinds of semantic features are both clues to explain the reason why to assign each code, which is also the basis of experts in manual coding process. To capture the two semantic phenomena, we exploit dilated convolution and n-gram matching mechanism to extract implicit semantic features and explicit semantic features, respectively. Furthermore, we develop a system to assist the professional coders in assigning the correct codes. In summary, the main contributions are as follows:

- We collect a large-scale Chinese Clinical notes dataset, making up for the lack of Chinese ICD coding corpus.

- We propose a novel method to simultaneously capture implicit and explicit semantic features, which enables to give interpretability for each predicted code.

- We develop an open-access online system, called clinical-coder, that automatically assigns codes to the free-text clinical notes with an indication of the supporting information for each code to be predicted. It uses vivid visualization to provide interpretability of prediction for each ICD code. The site can be accessed by `http://159.226.21.226/disease-prediction`, and instructions video is provided at `https://youtu.be/U4TImTwEysE`.

Figure 2 illustrates an example of the automatic coding for a Chinese Clinical note in our system

(For the convenience of readers, the English version is included in the appendix A). The left of Figure 2 (a) is the free-text notes user entered, and the right of Figure 2 (a) is predicted codes and corresponding disease names. Figure 2 (b1) and Figure 2 (b2) are the visualization of supporting information for predictions. The detailed description is presented in the section 3.2.

2 Related Work

2.1 Automatic ICD coding

Automatic ICD coding has recently been a research hotspot in the field of clinical medicine, where neural network architecture methods show promising results than traditional machine learning methods.

Most studies treat automatic ICD coding as a multi-label classification problem and use only the free-text in summaries to predict codes (Subotin and Davis, 2015; Kavuluru et al., 2015; Yu et al., 2019), while many methods benefit from extra information. Shi et al. (2017) encode label description with character-level and word-level long short-term memory network. Rios and Kavuluru (2018) encode label description with averaging words embedding. Furthermore, adversarial learning is employed to unify writing styles of diagnosis descriptions and ICD code descriptions (Xie et al., 2018). Besides code descriptions, Wikipedia comes to be regarded as an external knowledge source (Prakash et al., 2017; Bai and Vucetic, 2019).

Additionally, inferring interpretability is a crucial challenge and obstacle for practical automatic coding, since professionals are willing to be con-

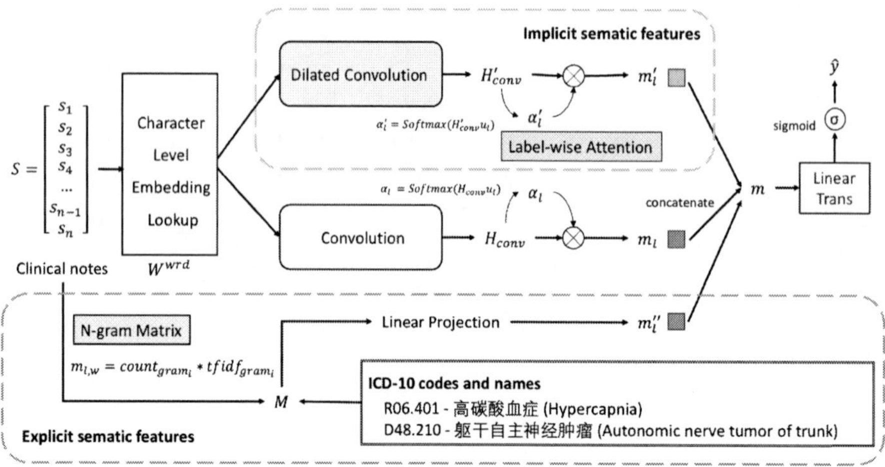

Figure 3: The whole architecture of the model. The input is the clinical text, and output is the ICD codes. The yellow dotted box indicates how to use attention-based dilated convolution to capture the implicit semantic of non-continuous words. The green dotted box indicates how to use n-gram matching mechanism to capture the explicit semantic of continuous n-gram words.

vinced by the model insights of vital supporting information or decision-making process (Vani et al., 2017; Mullenbach et al., 2018). Baumel et al. (2018) employ bidirectional Gated Recurrent Unit with sentence-level attention to obtain relevant sentences for each code. Mullenbach et al. (2018) use attention at the word level, which is more fine-grained. Our work is inspired by (Mullenbach et al., 2018), assigning the importance value for each label to the discharge summaries to assists in explaining the model prediction process.

2.2 Dilated Convolution

Dilated convolution is designed for image classification to aggregate multi-scale contextual information without losing resolution in computer vision (Yu and Koltun, 2016). It inserts "holes" in the standard convolution map to increase the reception field. The hole-structure brings a breakthrough improvement to the semantic segmentation task.

Similarly, several hole-structured convolution neural networks (CNNs) (Lei et al., 2015; Guo et al., 2017) are designed to handle natural language processing tasks. In the text, there exists non-continuous semantic where useless information may be interspersed among the sentences. Holes in the dilated convolution can ignore the extra word between the non-continuous words and well adapt to match non-continuous semantic. Since the semantic infomation is crutial when understanding

natural language(Zuo et al., 2019), we apply the dilated convolution to encode the text, capturing the non-continuous semantic information.

3 Clinical Coder System

3.1 Method

We propose a **Dilated Convolutional Attention** network with **N-gram Matching Mechanism** (DCANM) for ICD coding task. Figure 3 describes the architecture of the model. The input of model is all sentences in clinical notes, which are spliced together. The input sentences interact with ICD code names to capture explicit semantic features and generate an n-gram matrix. At the same time, the input sentences are transformed into vector and processed by dilated CNN to capture implicit semantic features. Attention mechanism is used to improve the performance. Then all features are concatenated to form the final features. Finally, we use a sigmoid classifier to predict the probability of each code. Next, we give the detailed descriptions.

Word Embedding. Word embedding is a low-dimensional vector representation of a word. We use the pre-trained embedded matrix $W^{wrd} \in \mathbb{R}^{d^w \times |V|}$, where d^w is the dimension of word embedding and $|V|$ is the size of vocabulary. Given a sentence, $S = [w_1, w_2, ..., w_N]$, where N is the number of words in the sentence, we can get the word embedding by:

$$w_e = W^{wrd}v_i, \qquad (1)$$

where v_i is the one-hot representation of the current word in the corresponding column of W^{wrd}.

Explicit Semantic Features. N-gram matching mechanism is applied to capture explicit semantic features. We use disease names (D) to sampling on the text (T). First, move the sliding window on the disease name $d_l \in D$ to get a n-gram substring. Then, calculate the frequency of each n-gram substring in the free-text. The sum of frequencies of gram with same length n (denoted as $gram_n$) has reflected the emergence of disease names in the text, nevertheless some grams have their unique particularity. For example, given a 2-gram string, "糖尿" (Diabetes) is more representative than "慢性"(Chronic) though they have the same length. To represent the degree of importance of different n-gram, each n-gram is given a term frequency-inverse document frequency (tf-idf) weight. Finally, for each free-text clinical note, we calculate an explicit semantic n-gram matrix (M) with size of $L \times W$, where L is numbers of labels and W is the numbers of sliding windows. For example, we have four sliding windows which lengths are 2, 3, 4, 5, so W is 4. For the l-th row the w-th column item in the feature map, we have:

$$m_{l,w} = \sum_{i=1}^{L_{gram_{ln}}} count_{gram_{lni}} * tf\_idf_{gram_{lni}} \qquad (2)$$

$$tf\_idf_{gram_i} = \frac{n}{L_{n_l}} * \frac{L}{freq_{gram_{lni}}}, \qquad (3)$$

where w is the index of n-length sliding window, $gram_{ln}$ is all n-length substrings of the l-th disease name, $gram_{lni}$ is the i-th $gram_{ln}$, $L_{gram_{ln}}$ is the number of $gram_{ln}$, $count_{gram_{lni}}$ is the frequencies of $gram_{lni}$ in the text, L_{n_l} is the length of the l-th disease name, $freq_{gram_{lni}}$ is the frequencies of $gram_{lni}$ in all disease names.

In this calculation, we can distinguish the importance degree of n-gram substring. It also works on English clinical notes, for instance, in a specific case from MIMIC-III (Johnson et al., 2016), the tf-idf value of "history of" is 1.79 while "atrial fibrillation" is 9.32 because "history of" appears 249 times in all ICD disease names and "atrial fibrillation" only appears two times. The higher the value is, the more representative the word is. Therefore "atrial fibrillation" is more likely to indicate a disease than "history of".

Implicit Semantic Features. Dilated convolution is applied to capture implicit semantic features. For a long clinical text, dilated convolution extends the reception field in the situation of not using pooling operation so that every kernel has a wider range of information. More importantly, it has "holes" in convolution map, which means it can be adapted to match the non-continuous semantic information. For example, "类风湿性多部位关节炎"(Rheumatoid multisite arthritis) in the clinical notes refers to "类风湿性关节炎"(Rheumatoid arthritis) in ICD, the convolution map with holes can tolerate the redundant parts, as shown in Figure 4. It is a distinct advantage of dilated convolution for processing texts.

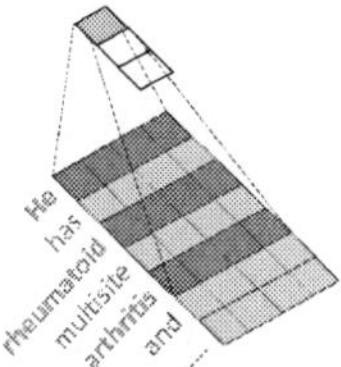

Figure 4: An example of the dilated convolution in processing text.

Formally, the actual filter width of dilated convolutional neural network is computed as,

$$k_d = r(k-1) + 1, \qquad (4)$$

where $r \in [1, 2, 3, ...]$ is the dilated rate, k is the origin filter width.

For each step n, the typical convolution is computed as formula 5 and dilated convolution is computed as formula 6. The dilated CNN is same as typical CNN when the dilated rate is 1, since k_d equals to k when $r = 1$:

$$h_n = tanh(W_c * x_{n:n+k-1} + b_c) \qquad (5)$$

$$h'_n = tanh(W_c * x_{n:n+k_d-1} + b_c), \qquad (6)$$

where $W_c \in \mathbb{R}^{k_d \times d_e \times d_c}$ is the convolutional filter map, k_d is the actual filter width, d_e is the size of the word embedding, an d_c the size of the filter output and $b_c \in \mathbb{R}^{d_c}$ is the bias.

Attention. After convolution, the sentence is represented as $H \in \mathbb{R}^{d_c \times N}$. We employ the per-label attention mechanism (Mullenbach et al., 2018) to find the most contributed characters for each label.

For each label l, the distributed attention weight is computed as:

$$\alpha_l = SoftMax(H^T u_l), \qquad (7)$$

where $u_l \in \mathbb{R}^{d_c}$ is the vector representation of label l. Finally, the sentence is represented as:

$$m_l = H\alpha_l \qquad (8)$$

We employ attention both for typical CNN and dilated CNN, for convenience of distinction, we denote them as m_l and m_l', respectively.

Classification. m_l and m_l' is concatenated with the linear transformed n-gram matrix horizontally. The aim of this step is to combining all the features together. Then we exploit sigmoid classifier and the prediction of label i is computed as,

$$\hat{y}_i = \sigma(W^T[m_l; m_l'; m_l''] + b), \qquad (9)$$

where $i \in [1, 2, ..., L]$, $W \in \mathbb{R}^{3d_c}$, b is the bias, m_l'' is the linear projection of n-gram matrix(M).

The loss function is the multi-label binary cross-entropy (Nam et al., 2013).

$$\mathcal{L} = \sum_{i=1}^{L}[-y_i log(\hat{y}_i) - (1 - y_i)log(1 - \hat{y}_i)], \qquad (10)$$

where $y_i \in \{0, 1\}$ is the ground truth for the i-th label and $\hat{y}_i$ is the sigmoid score for the i-th label.

3.2 User Interface

Figure 2 illustrates the user interface of our system.

User Input. The left of Figure 2(a) displays the user input. The user enters the whole free clinical note, which includes at least one from admission situation, admission diagnosis, discharge situation, and discharge diagnosis into the input box.

Predicted Labels. The predicted labels are presented in the list of Figure 2(a), including disease name and homologous ICD codes. The number of predicted codes are not always the same as the diseases in discharge diagnosis, because clinicians may leave out certain diseases and several diagnoses should be combined into one ICD code(Shi et al., 2017). Our model can list all these diseases, and give the reason why they should be predicted.

Interpretability. Interpretability is a critical aspect of the decision-making system, especially in the clinical medicine domain. In our system, we give two ways, n-gram matching mechanism and attention, to assist users in understanding why each code is predicted. A user can know why the model predicted the labels, and what the key information in its decision was:

(1) **N-gram Matching Mechanism.** When a patient suffering from a disease, the corresponding text span related to disease names often appear in the discharge summary. As shown in Figure 2 (b1), the gram in disease name is highlighted to give a hint to users if it appears in the clinical text. Highlighting not only tells users why we predict each code but also prompts the place of the important information.

(2) **Attention.** As shown in Figure 2 (b2), the red background is attention distribution, and the darker the color is, the more useful the word is to predict the current label. The darker color is also helpful and attractive for human-being to double-check the correction of labels.

4 Experiments

4.1 Dataset

We evaluate our model on both Chinese and English datasets. The Chinese dataset, collected by us, contains 50,678 Chinese clinical notes and 6,200 unique ICD-10 codes. For each clinical note, it contains five parts: admission situation, admission diagnosis, discharge situation, discharge diagnosis and annotated ICD-10 codes. Admission situation involves chief complaints, past medical history, etc. Discharge situation involves the results of general examination. Admission diagnosis and discharge diagnosis involve disease names, which may not be totally consistent with standard names in ICD-10. The manually annotated codes are based on ICD-10, which are tagged by professional coders after reading through the whole clinical note.

	CN-Full	CN-50	MIMIC-III-50
# Samples	50,678	36,758	9,795
# Labels	6200	50	50
Vocabulary size	3,957	3,957	51,917
# Average tokens per sample	621	655	1,530
# Average labels per sample	4.3	2.6	5.7

Table 1: Detailed information for three datasets.

The dataset (CN-Full) is formed with full labels mentioned above, and it is divided into train set and test set with the radio of 9:1. In addition, due to the phenomenon that massive codes are infrequent, and a small amount of codes are high-frequent, we reconstructed a sub-dataset (CN-50) with the most frequent 50 codes from the original dataset. The specific process is that filtering the origin train set and test set, and maintain the data which has at least one of the top 50 most frequent codes.

Dataset	CN-Full						CN-50					
Model	F1		AUC		R@k		F1		AUC		R@k	
	Macro	Micro	Macro	Micro	k=5	k=10	Macro	Micro	Macro	Micro	k=5	k=8
CAML(Mullenbach et al., 2018)	0.0600	0.6755	0.8832	0.9808	0.6099	0.7651	0.8305	0.8458	0.9846	0.9902	0.8796	0.9579
Dilated CNN	0.1017	0.6997	0.8637	0.9772	0.6268	0.7864	0.8399	0.8523	0.9849	0.9904	0.8807	0.9550
N-gram Matching	**0.1200**	0.7050	**0.9574**	**0.9915**	0.6393	0.8036	0.8385	0.8543	0.9867	0.9922	0.8900	0.9640
DACNM	0.1116	**0.7127**	0.9520	0.9909	**0.6430**	**0.8043**	**0.8452**	**0.8602**	**0.9878**	**0.9932**	**0.8895**	**0.9657**

Table 2: Evaluation on Chinese dataset CN-Full and CN-50.

To better compare with the previous works, we also evaluate our method on the MIMIC-III dataset (Johnson et al., 2016), which is the most authoritative English dataset for evaluating the performance of automatic ICD coding approaches. The detailed description for these datasets is listed in Table 1.

4.2 Data Preprocess and Parameters

We splice the admission situation, admission diagnosis, discharge situation and discharge diagnosis together, which is the input of the model. The max length of the input is 1000. The word embedding is pre-trained using Word2Vec (Mikolov et al., 2013) with the dimensions of 100. The text is from all clinical notes. The batch size is 16. The dropout rate is 0.5. The optimizer is Adam (Kingma and Ba, 2015) with a learning rate of 0.0001.

We use Micro-F1, Macro-F1, area under the ROC (Receiver Operating Characteristic) curve (AUC) and P@k as the metrics. P@k (Precision at k) is the fraction of the k highest-scored labels that are present in the ground truth.

4.3 Results

First, for the Chinese dataset (CN-Full and CN-50), CAML (Mullenbach et al., 2018) is set as our baseline, which use traditional convolutional attention network. Moreover, we test the dilated CNN and n-gram matching mechanism separately. The results in Table 2 indicate that dilated CNN and n-gram matching mechanism both have a positive effect on improving performance from baseline, and the best results are obtained when they combined.

We also evaluate our method on English dataset (MIMIC-III-50). The results are shown in Table 3. The CNN and Bi-GRU are the classic methods and the results are the same as (Mullenbach et al., 2018). Our proposed model achieves the Micro-F1 score of 0.641, which outperforms all previous works, more importantly providing interpretability.

Besides, we notice that macro-F1 measure is always lower than micro-F1, especially in the full labels datasets. It means the smaller classes have

Model	F1		AUC		P@k
	Macro	Micro	Macro	Micro	k=5
CNN	0.576	0.625	0.876	0.907	**0.620**
Bi-GRU	0.484	0.549	0.828	0.868	0.591
C-MemNN(Prakash et al., 2017)	-	-	0.833	-	0.42
(Shi et al., 2017)	-	0.532	-	0.900	-
HA-GRU(Baumel et al., 2018)	-	0.366	-	-	-
CAML(Mullenbach et al., 2018)	0.532	0.614	0.875	0.909	0.609
DR-CAML(Mullenbach et al., 2018)	0.576	0.633	0.884	0.916	0.618
DACNM (Proposed model)	**0.579**	**0.641**	**0.890**	**0.916**	0.616

Table 3: Evaluation on MIMIC-III-50 dataset

poorer performance than larger classes, which is consistent with the facts. Either MIMIC-III or the Chinese dataset, the sample distributions are extremely imbalanced. Minority of codes are highly frequent, while most codes are infrequent. N-gram matching mechanism helps improve macro-F1 on CN-Full dataset obviously, reaching two times than baseline. It can be inferred that utilizing grams in disease names is useful for the smaller class.

5 Conclusion

In this paper, we propose a **D**ilated **C**onvolutional **A**ttention network with **N**-gram **M**atching Mechanism (DCANM) for automatic ICD coding. The dilated CNN, which is first applied to the ICD coding task, aims to capture semantic information for non-continuous words, and the n-gram matching mechanism aims to capture the continuous semantic. They both provide a pretty good interpretability for prediction. Moreover, we develop an open-access system to help users assign ICD codes. We will try to utilize external resources to solve the few-shot and zero-shot problem in the future.

Acknowledgments

This work is supported by the National Natural Science Foundation of China (No.61922085, No.61533018, No.61976211) and the Key Research Program of the Chinese Academy of Sciences (Grant NO.ZDBS-SSW-JSC006). This work is also supported by Beijing Academy of Artificial Intelligence (BAAI2019QN0301) and a grant from Ant Financial Services Group.

References

Tian Bai and Slobodan Vucetic. 2019. Improving medical code prediction from clinical text via incorporating online knowledge sources. In *The World Wide Web Conference*, WWW'19, pages 72–82.

Tal Baumel, Jumana Nassour-Kassis, Raphael Cohen, Michael Elhadad, and Noémie Elhadad. 2018. Multi-label classification of patient notes: Case study on ICD code assignment. In *Proceedings of the Workshops of the Thirty-Second AAAI Conference on Artificial Intelligence*, pages 409–416.

Jiahui Guo, Bin Yue, Guandong Xu, Zhenglu Yang, and Jin-Mao Wei. 2017. An enhanced convolutional neural network model for answer selection. In *Proceedings of the 26th International Conference on World Wide Web Companion*, WWW'17, pages 789–790.

Alistair Johnson, Tom Pollard, Lu Shen, Li-wei Lehman, Mengling Feng, Mohammad Ghassemi, Benjamin Moody, Peter Szolovits, Leo Celi, and Roger Mark. 2016. MIMIC-III, a freely accessible critical care database. *Scientific Data*, 3:16–35.

Ramakanth Kavuluru, Anthony Rios, and Yuan Lu. 2015. An empirical evaluation of supervised learning approaches in assigning diagnosis codes to electronic medical records. *Artificial Intelligence in Medicine*, 65(2):155–166.

Diederik P. Kingma and Jimmy Ba. 2015. Adam: A method for stochastic optimization. *arXiv preprint arXiv:1511.07122*.

Bevan Koopman, Guido Zuccon, Anthony Nguyen, Anton Bergheim, and Narelle Grayson. 2015. Automatic icd-10 classification of cancers from free-text death certificates. *International Journal of Medical Informatics*, 84(11):956–965.

Tao Lei, Regina Barzilay, and Tommi Jaakkola. 2015. Molding CNNs for text: Non-linear, nonconsecutive convolutions. In *Proceedings of the 2015 Conference on Empirical Methods in Natural Language Processing*, pages 1565–1575.

Tomas Mikolov, G.s Corrado, Kai Chen, and Jeffrey Dean. 2013. Efficient estimation of word representations in vector space. In *Proceedings of Workshop at International Conference on Learning Representations*, pages 1–12.

James Mullenbach, Sarah Wiegreffe, Jon Duke, Jimeng Sun, and Jacob Eisenstein. 2018. Explainable prediction of medical codes from clinical text. In *Proceedings of the 2018 Conference of the North American Chapter of the Association for Computational Linguistics: Human Language Technologies, Volume 1 (Long Papers)*, pages 1101–1111.

Jinseok Nam, Jungi Kim, Iryna Gurevych, and Johannes Fürnkranz. 2013. Large-scale multi-label text classification - revisiting neural networks. In *Proceedings of the 2014 European Conference on Machine Learning and Knowledge Discovery in Databases - Volume Part II*, pages 437–452.

Adler Perotte, Rimma Pivovarov, Karthik Natarajan, Nicole Weiskopf, Frank Wood, and No é mie Elhadad. 2013. Diagnosis code assignment: models and evaluation metrics. *Journal of the American Medical Informatics Association*, 21(2):231–237.

Aaditya Prakash, Siyuan Zhao, Sadid Hasan, Vivek Datla, Kathy Lee, Ashequl Qadir, Joey Liu, and Oladimeji Farri. 2017. Condensed memory networks for clinical diagnostic inferencing. In *Proceedings of the Thirty-First AAAI Conference on Artificial Intelligence*, pages 3274–3280.

Anthony Rios and Ramakanth Kavuluru. 2018. Fewshot and zero-shot multi-label learning for structured label spaces. In *Proceedings of the Conference on Empirical Methods in Natural Language Processing*, volume 2018, pages 3132–3142.

Haoran Shi, Pengtao Xie, Zhiting Hu, Ming Zhang, and Eric Xing. 2017. Towards automated ICD coding using deep learning. *arXiv preprint arXiv:1711.04075*.

Michael Subotin and Anthony Davis. 2015. A method for modeling co-occurrence propensity of clinical codes with application to icd-10-pcs auto-coding. *Journal of the American Medical Informatics Association*, 23(5):866–871.

Ankit Vani, Yacine Jernite, and David Sontag. 2017. Grounded recurrent neural networks. *arXiv preprint arXiv:1705.08557*.

Pengtao Xie, Haoran Shi, Ming Zhang, and Eric P. Xing. 2018. A neural architecture for automated ICD coding. In *Proceedings of the 56th Annual Meeting of the Association for Computational Linguistics(Volume 1:Long Papers)*, pages 1066–1076.

Fisher Yu and Vladlen Koltun. 2016. Multi-scale context aggregation by dilated convolutions. *arXiv preprint arXiv:1511.07122*.

Ying Yu, Min Li, Liangliang Liu, Zhihui Fei, Fang-Xiang Wu, and Jianxin Wang. 2019. Automatic ICD code assignment of chinese clinical notes based on multilayer attention birnn. *Journal of Biomedical Informatics*, 91:103–114.

Xinyu Zuo, Yubo Chen, Kang Liu, and Jun Zhao. 2019. Event co-reference resolution via a multi-loss neural network without using argument information. *Science China Information Sciences*, 62.

A Appendix: English Version of Figure 2(a)

Since the online system is for Chinese clinical notes, we provide corresponding English version for reading convenience.

Admissions situation:

The middle-aged man was admitted to the hospital because of a "blood glucose increase of 5 years and poor glycemic control in June". The patient's routine physical examination five years ago revealed an increase in blood glucose, about 9 mmol / L on an empty stomach, and the local diagnosis was: "type 2 diabetes". No obvious dry mouth, frequent drinking, polyuria and weight loss, no dizziness, no increased urine foam, no numbness in hands, feet, and occasionally blurred vision. Diet and exercise were used to control blood glucose. Normally, blood glucose was monitored irregularly, and fasting blood glucose fluctuated between 8-9mmol / L. During the course of the disease, the general condition of the patient is OK, the diet and sleep are OK, and there is no obvious abnormality in the stool. The weight loss in the last 2 months is about 3Kg. Auxiliary examination B: Ultralow hypoechoic nodules in the right lobe of the thyroid gland, considering glial cysts; bilateral carotid atherosclerosis with right plaque formation; fatty liver; right renal cyst with calcium milk; enlarged prostate; Atherosclerosis.

Admission diagnosis:

1. Type 2 diabetes **2.** Kidney stones **3.** Thyroid nodules **4.** Atherosclerosis **5.** Fatty liver

Discharge situation:

The patient had no dry mouth and frequent drinking, no polyuria, diet and sleep were OK, physical examination: clear mind, good spirits, slightly thicker breathing sounds in both lungs, and no wet and dry rales. Heart rhythm is uniform, and no noise is heard. The abdomen is flat, the whole abdomen is soft, no tenderness, no tenderness, no edema in both lower limbs.

Discharge diagnosis:

1.Type 2 diabetes **2.** Right renal cyst **3.** Thyroid nodule **4.** Atherosclerosis **5.** Fatty liver **6.** Hyperlipidemia

Predicted diseases and codes:

1. Thyroid nodule E04.101
2. Type 2 diabetes E11.9022
3. Hyperlipidemia E78.501
4. Atherosclerosis I70.904
5. Fatty liver K76.001
6. Kidney stones N20.000
7. Acquired renal cysts N28.100

ESPnet-ST: All-in-One Speech Translation Toolkit

Hirofumi Inaguma[1] **Shun Kiyono**[2] **Kevin Duh**[3] **Shigeki Karita**[4]
Nelson Yalta[5] **Tomoki Hayashi**[6,7] **Shinji Watanabe**[3]
[1] Kyoto University   [2] RIKEN AIP   [3] Johns Hopkins University
[4] NTT Communication Science Laboratories   [5] Waseda University
[6] Nagoya University   [7] Human Dataware Lab. Co., Ltd.
`inaguma@sap.ist.i.kyoto-u.ac.jp`

Abstract

We present *ESPnet-ST*, which is designed for the quick development of speech-to-speech translation systems in a single framework. *ESPnet-ST* is a new project inside end-to-end speech processing toolkit, ESPnet, which integrates or newly implements automatic speech recognition, machine translation, and text-to-speech functions for speech translation. We provide all-in-one recipes including data pre-processing, feature extraction, training, and decoding pipelines for a wide range of benchmark datasets. Our reproducible results can match or even outperform the current state-of-the-art performances; these pre-trained models are downloadable. The toolkit is publicly available at `https://github.com/espnet/espnet`.

1 Introduction

Speech translation (ST), where converting speech signals in a language to text in another language, is a key technique to break the language barrier for human communication. Traditional ST systems involve cascading automatic speech recognition (ASR), text normalization (e.g., punctuation insertion, case restoration), and machine translation (MT) modules; we call this Cascade-ST (Ney, 1999; Casacuberta et al., 2008; Kumar et al., 2014). Recently, sequence-to-sequence (S2S) models have become the method of choice in implementing both the ASR and MT modules (c.f. (Chan et al., 2016; Bahdanau et al., 2015)). This convergence of models has opened up the possibility of designing end-to-end speech translation (E2E-ST) systems, where a single S2S directly maps speech in a source language to its translation in the target language (Bérard et al., 2016; Weiss et al., 2017).

E2E-ST has several advantages over the cascaded approach: (1) a single E2E-ST model can reduce latency at inference time, which is useful for time-critical use cases like simultaneous interpretation. (2) A single model enables back-propagation training in an end-to-end fashion, which mitigates the risk of error propagation by cascaded modules. (3) In certain use cases such as endangered language documentation (Bird et al., 2014), source speech and target text translation (without the intermediate source text transcript) might be easier to obtain, necessitating the adoption of E2E-ST models (Anastasopoulos and Chiang, 2018). Nevertheless, the verdict is still out on the comparison of translation quality between E2E-ST and Cascade-ST. Some empirical results favor E2E (Weiss et al., 2017) while others favor Cascade (Niehues et al., 2019); the conclusion also depends on the nuances of the training data condition (Sperber et al., 2019).

We believe the time is ripe to develop a unified toolkit that facilitates research in both E2E and cascaded approaches. We present *ESPnet-ST*, a toolkit that implements many of the recent models for E2E-ST, as well as the ASR and MT modules for Cascade-ST. Our goal is to provide a toolkit where researchers can easily incorporate and test new ideas under different approaches. Recent research suggests that pre-training, multi-task learning, and transfer learning are important techniques for achieving improved results for E2E-ST (Bérard et al., 2018; Anastasopoulos and Chiang, 2018; Bansal et al., 2019; Inaguma et al., 2019). Thus, a unified toolkit that enables researchers to seamlessly mix-and-match different ASR and MT models in training both E2E-ST and Cascade-ST systems would facilitate research in the field.[1]

ESPnet-ST is especially designed to target the ST task. ESPnet was originally developed for the

---

[1] There exist many excellent toolkits that support both ASR and MT tasks (see Table 1). However, it is not always straightforward to use them for E2E-ST and Cascade-ST, due to incompatible training/inference pipelines in different modules or lack of detailed preprocessing/training scripts.

Proceedings of the 58th Annual Meeting of the Association for Computational Linguistics, pages 302–311
July 5 - July 10, 2020. ©2020 Association for Computational Linguistics

Toolkit	Supported task						Example (w/ corpus pre-processing)						Pre-trained model
	ASR	LM	E2E-ST	Cascade-ST	MT	TTS	ASR	LM	E2E-ST	Cascade-ST	MT	TTS	
ESPnet-ST (ours)	✓	✓	✓	✓	✓	✓	✓	✓	✓	✓	✓	✓	✓
Lingvo[1]	✓	✓	✓♣	✓♣	✓	✓♣	✓	✓	–	–	✓	–	–
OpenSeq2seq[2]	✓	✓	–	–	✓	✓	✓	✓	–	–	✓	–	✓
NeMo[3]	✓	✓	–	–	✓	✓	✓	✓	–	–	✓	–	✓
RETURNN[4]	✓	✓	✓	–	✓	–	–	–	–	–	–	–	✓
SLT.KIT[5]	✓	–	✓	✓	✓	–	✓	–	✓	✓	✓	–	✓
Fairseq[6]	✓	✓	–	–	✓	–	✓	✓	–	–	✓	–	✓
Tensor2Tensor[7]	✓	✓	–	–	✓	–	–	–	–	–	✓	–	✓◇
OpenNMT-{py, tf}[8]	✓	✓	–	–	✓	–	–	–	–	–	–	–	✓
Kaldi[9]	✓	✓	–	–	–	–	✓	✓	–	–	–	–	✓
Wav2letter++[10]	✓	✓	–	–	–	–	✓	✓	–	–	–	–	✓

Table 1: Framework comparison on supported tasks in January, 2020. ♣Not publicly available. ◇Available only in Google Cloud storage. [1](Shen et al., 2019) [2](Kuchaiev et al., 2018) [3](Kuchaiev et al., 2019) [4](Zeyer et al., 2018) [5](Zenkel et al., 2018) [6](Ott et al., 2019) [7](Vaswani et al., 2018) [8](Klein et al., 2017) [9](Povey et al., 2011) [10](Pratap et al., 2019)

ASR task (Watanabe et al., 2018), and recently extended to the text-to-speech (TTS) task (Hayashi et al., 2020). Here, we extend ESPnet to ST tasks, providing code for building translation systems and recipes (i.e., scripts that encapsulate the entire training/inference procedure for reproducibility purposes) for a wide range of ST benchmarks. This is a non-trivial extension: with a unified codebase for ASR/MT/ST and a wide range of recipes, we believe ESPnet-ST is an *all-in-one toolkit* that should make it easier for both ASR and MT researchers to get started in ST research.

The contributions of *ESPnet-ST* are as follows:

- To the best of our knowledge, this is the first toolkit to include ASR, MT, TTS, and ST recipes and models in the same codebase. Since our codebase is based on the unified framework with a common stage-by-stage processing (Povey et al., 2011), it is very easy to customize training data and models.

- We provide recipes for ST corpora such as Fisher-CallHome (Post et al., 2013), Libri-trans (Kocabiyikoglu et al., 2018), How2 (Sanabria et al., 2018), and Must-C (Di Gangi et al., 2019a)[2]. Each recipe contains a single script (`run.sh`), which covers all experimental processes, such as corpus preparation, data augmentations, and transfer learning.

- We provide the open-sourced toolkit and the pre-trained models whose hyper-parameters

are intensively tuned. Moreover, we provide interactive demo of speech-to-speech translation hosted by Google Colab.[3]

2 Design

2.1 Installation

All required tools are automatically downloaded and built under `tools` (see Figure 1) by a make command. The tools include (1) neural network libraries such as PyTorch (Paszke et al., 2019), (2) ASR-related toolkits such as Kaldi (Povey et al., 2011), and (3) MT-related toolkits such as Moses (Koehn et al., 2007) and sentence-piece (Kudo, 2018). *ESPnet-ST* is implemented with Pytorch backend.

2.2 Recipes for reproducible experiments

We provide various recipes for all tasks in order to quickly and easily reproduce the strong baseline systems with a single script. The directory structure is depicted as in Figure 1. `egs` contains corpus directories, in which the corresponding task directories (e.g., `st1`) are included. To run experiments, we simply execute `run.sh` under the desired task directory. Configuration yaml files for feature extraction, data augmentation, model training, and decoding etc. are included in `conf`. Model directories including checkpoints are saved under `exp`. More details are described in Section 2.4.

---

[2]We also support ST-TED (Jan et al., 2018) and low-resourced Mboshi-French (Godard et al., 2018) recipes.

[3]`https://colab.research.google.com/ github/espnet/notebook/blob/master/st_ demo.ipynb`

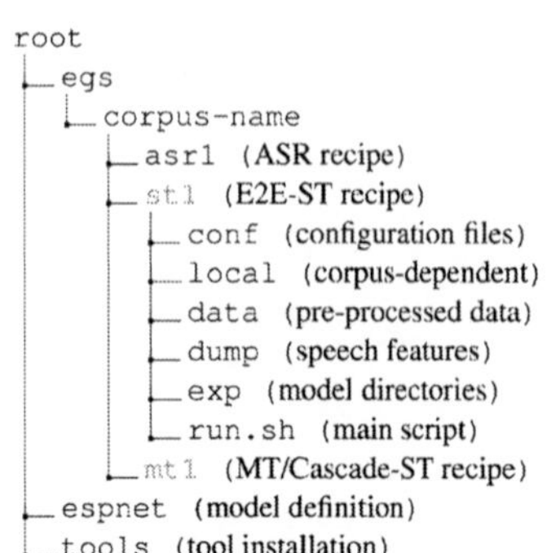

Figure 1: Directory structure of ESPnet-ST

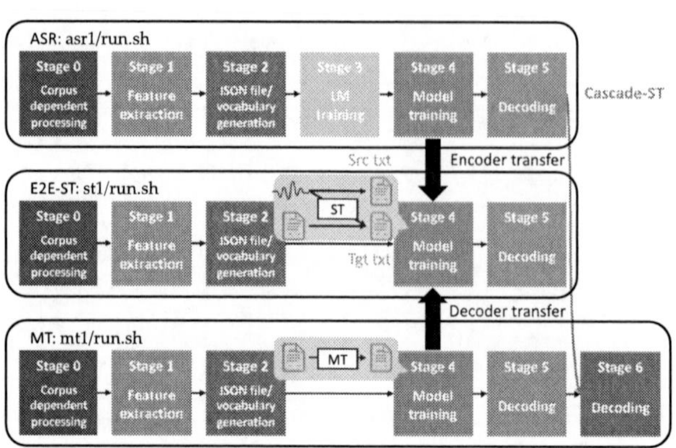

Figure 2: All-in-one process pipelines in ESPnet-ST

2.3 Tasks

We support language modeling (LM), neural text-to-speech (TTS) in addition to ASR, ST, and MT tasks. To the best of our knowledge, none of frameworks support all these tasks in a single toolkit. A comparison with other frameworks are summarized in Table 1. Conceptually, it is possible to combine ASR and MT modules for Cascade-ST, but few frameworks provide such examples. Moreover, though some toolkits indeed support speech-to-text tasks, it is not trivial to switch ASR and E2E-ST tasks since E2E-ST requires the auxiliary tasks (ASR/MT objectives) to achieve reasonable performance.

2.4 Stage-by-stage processing

ESPnet-ST is based on a stage-by-stage processing including corpus-dependent pre-processing, feature extraction, training, and decoding stages. We follow Kaldi-style data preparation, which makes it easy to augment speech data by leveraging other data resources prepared in `egs`.

Once `run.sh` is executed, the following processes are started.

Stage 0: Corpus-dependent pre-processing is conducted using scripts under `local` and the resulting text data is automatically saved under `data`. Both transcriptions and the corresponding translations with three different treatments of casing and punctuation marks (hereafter, punct.) are generated after text normalization and tokenization with `tokenizer.perl` in Moses; (a) **tc**: truecased text with punct., (b) **lc**: lowercased text with punct., and (3) **lc.rm**: lowercased text without punct. except for apostrophe. `lc.rm` is designed for the ASR task since the conventional ASR system does not generate punctuation marks. However, it is possible to train ASR models so as to generate truecased text using `tc`.[4]

Stage 1: Speech feature extraction based on Kaldi and our own implementations is performed.

Stage 2: Dataset JSON files in a format ingestable by ESPnet's Pytorch back-end (containing token/utterance/speaker/language IDs, input and output sequence lengths, transcriptions, and translations) are dumped under `dump`.

Stage 3: (ASR recipe only) LM is trained.

Stage 4: Model training (RNN/Transformer) is performed.

Stage 5: Model averaging, beam search decoding, and score calculation are conducted.

Stage 6: (Cascade-ST recipe only) The system is evaluated by feeding ASR outputs to the MT model.

2.5 Multi-task learning and transfer learning

In ST literature, it is acknowledged that the optimization of E2E-ST is more difficult than individually training ASR and MT models. Multitask training (MTL) and transfer learning from ASR and MT tasks are promising approaches for this problem (Weiss et al., 2017; Bérard et al., 2018; Sperber et al., 2019; Bansal et al., 2019). Thus, in **Stage 4** of the E2E-ST recipe, we allow options to add auxiliary ASR and MT objectives. We also support options to initialize the parameters of the ST encoder with a pre-trained ASR encoder in `asr1`, and to initialize the parameters of the ST decoder with a pre-trained MT decoder in `mt1`.

---

[4]We found that this degrades the ASR performance.

2.6 Speech data augmentation

We implement techniques that have shown to give improved robustness in the ASR component.

Speed perturbation We augmented speech data by changing the speed with factors of 0.9, 1.0, and 1.1, which results in 3-fold data augmentation. We found this is important to stabilize E2E-ST training.

SpecAugment Time and frequency masking blocks are randomly applied to log mel-filterbank features. This has been originally proposed to improve the ASR performance and shown to be effective for E2E-ST as well (Bahar et al., 2019b).

2.7 Multilingual training

Multilingual training, where datasets from different language pairs are combined to train a single model, is a potential way to improve performance of E2E-ST models (Inaguma et al., 2019; Di Gangi et al., 2019c). Multilingual E2E-ST/MT models are supported in several recipes.

2.8 Additional features

Experiment manager We customize the data loader, trainer, and evaluator by overriding Chainer (Tokui et al., 2019) modules. The common processes are shared among all tasks.

Large-scale training/decoding We support job schedulers (e.g., SLURM, Grid Engine), multiple GPUs and half/mixed-precision training/decoding with `apex` (Micikevicius et al., 2018).[5] Our beam search implementation vectorizes hypotheses for faster decoding (Seki et al., 2019).

Performance monitoring Attention weights and all kinds of training/validation scores and losses for ASR, MT, and ST tasks can be collectively monitored through TensorBoard.

Ensemble decoding Averaging posterior probabilities from multiple models during beam search decoding is supported.

3 Example Models

To give a flavor of the models that are supported with ESPnet-ST, we describe in detail the construction of an example E2E-ST model, which is used later in the Experiments section. Note that there are many customizable options not mentioned here.

---

[5] `https://github.com/NVIDIA/apex`

Automatic speech recognition (ASR) We build ASR components with the Transformer-based hybrid CTC/attention framework (Watanabe et al., 2017), which has been shown to be more effective than RNN-based models on various speech corpora (Karita et al., 2019). Decoding with the external LSTM-based LM trained in the **Stage 3** is also conducted (Kannan et al., 2017). The transformer uses 12 self-attention blocks stacked on the two VGG blocks in the speech encoder and 6 self-attention blocks in the transcription decoder; see (Karita et al., 2019) for implementation details.

Machine translation (MT) The MT model consists of the source text encoder and translation decoder, implemented as a transformer with 6 self-attention blocks. For simplicity, we train the MT model by feeding lowercased source sentences without punctuation marks (`lc.rm`) (Peitz et al., 2011). There are options to explore characters and different subword units in the MT component.

End-to-end speech translation (E2E-ST) Our E2E-ST model is composed of the speech encoder and translation decoder. Since the definition of parameter names is exactly same as in the ASR and MT components, it is quite easy to copy parameters from the pre-trained models for transfer learning. After ASR and MT models are trained as described above, their parameters are extracted and used to initialize the E2E-ST model. The model is then trained on ST data, with the option of incorporating multi-task objectives as well.

Text-to-speech (TTS) We also support end-to-end text-to-speech (E2E-TTS), which can be applied after ST outputs a translation. The E2E-TTS model consists of the feature generation network converting an input text to acoustic features (e.g., log-mel filterbank coefficients) and the vocoder network converting the features to a waveform. Tacotron 2 (Shen et al., 2018), Transformer-TTS (Li et al., 2019), FastSpeech (Ren et al., 2019), and their variants such as a multi-speaker model are supported as the feature generation network. WaveNet (van den Oord et al., 2016) and Parallel WaveGAN (Yamamoto et al., 2020) are available as the vocoder network. See Hayashi et al. (2020) for more details.

4 Experiments

In this section, we demonstrate how models from our ESPnet recipes perform on benchmark speech

	Model	Es → En				
		Fisher			CallHome	
		dev	dev2	test	devtest	evltest
E2E	Char RNN + ASR-MTL (Weiss et al., 2017)	48.30	49.10	48.70	16.80	17.40
	ESPnet-ST (Transformer)					
	ASR-MTL (multi-task w/ ASR)	46.64	47.64	46.45	16.80	16.80
	+ MT-MTL (multi-task w/ MT)	47.17	48.20	46.99	17.51	17.64
	ASR encoder init. (①)	46.25	47.11	46.21	17.35	16.94
	+ MT decoder init. (②)	46.25	47.60	46.72	17.62	17.50
	+ SpecAugment (③)	48.94	49.32	48.39	18.83	18.67
	+ Ensemble 3 models (① + ② + ③)	**50.76**	**52.02**	**50.85**	**19.91**	**19.36**
Cascade	Char RNN ASR → Char RNN MT (Weiss et al., 2017)	**45.10**	**46.10**	**45.50**	16.20	16.60
	Char RNN ASR → Char RNN MT (Inaguma et al., 2019)♣	37.3	39.6	38.6	16.8	16.5
	ESPnet-ST					
	Transformer ASR◇ → Transformer MT	41.96	43.46	42.16	19.56	19.82

Table 2: BLEU of ST systems on Fisher-CallHome Spanish corpus. ♣Implemented w/ ESPnet. ◇w/ SpecAugment.

	Model	En → Fr
E2E	Transformer + ASR/MT-trans + KD[1]	17.02
	+ Ensemble 3 models	**17.8**
	Transformer + PT△ + adaptor[2]	16.80
	Transformer + PT△ + SpecAugment[3]	17.0
	RNN + TCEN[4,♣]	17.05
	ESPnet-ST (Transformer)	
	ASR-MTL	15.30
	+ MT-MLT	15.47
	ASR encoder init. (①)	15.53
	+ MT decoder init. (②)	16.22
	+ SpecAugment (③)	16.70
	+ Ensemble 3 models (① + ② + ③)	17.40
Cascade	Transformer ASR → Transformer MT[1]	**17.85**
	ESPnet-ST	
	Transformer ASR◇ → Transformer MT	16.96

Table 3: BLEU of ST systems on Libri-trans corpus. ♣Implemented w/ ESPnet. △Pre-training. ◇w/ SpecAugment. [1](Liu et al., 2019) [2](Bahar et al., 2019a) [3](Bahar et al., 2019b) [4](Wang et al., 2020)

	Model	En → Pt
E2E	RNN (Sanabria et al., 2018)	36.0
	ESPnet-ST	
	Transformer	40.59
	+ ASR-MTL	44.90
	+ MT-MLT	45.10
	Transformer + ASR encoder init. (①)	45.03
	+ MT decoder init. (②)	45.63
	+ SpecAugment (③)	45.68
	+ Ensemble 3 models (① + ② + ③)	**48.04**
Cascade	**ESPnet-ST**	
	Transformer ASR → Transformer MT	44.90

Table 4: BLEU of ST systems on How2 corpus

translation corpora: Fisher-CallHome Spanish En→Es, Libri-trans En→Fr, How2 En→Pt, and Must-C En→8 languages. Moreover, we also performed experiments on IWSLT16 En-De to validate the performance of our MT modules.

All sentences were tokenized with the `tokenizer.perl` script in the Moses toolkit (Koehn et al., 2007). We used the joint source and target vocabularies based on byte pair encoding (BPE) (Sennrich et al., 2016) units. ASR vocabularies were created with English sentences only with `lc.rm`. We report 4-gram BLEU (Papineni et al., 2002) scores with the `multi-bleu.perl` script in Moses. For speech features, we extracted 80-channel log-mel filterbank coefficients with 3-dimensional pitch features using Kaldi, resulting 83-dimensional features per frame. Detailed training and decoding configurations are available in `conf/train.yaml` and `conf/decode.yaml`, respectively.

4.1 Fisher-CallHome Spanish (Es→En)

Fisher-CallHome Spanish corpus contains 170-hours of Spanish conversational telephone speech, the corresponding transcription, as well as the English translations (Post et al., 2013). All punctuation marks except for apostrophe were removed (Post et al., 2013; Kumar et al., 2014; Weiss et al., 2017). We report case-insensitive BLEU on Fisher-{*dev*, *dev2*, *test*} (with four references), and CallHome-{*devtest*, *evltest*} (with a single reference). We used 1k vocabulary for all tasks.

Results are shown in Table 2. It is worth noting that we did not use any additional data resource. Both MTL and transfer learning improved the performance of vanilla Transformer. Our best system with SpecAugment matches the current state-of-the-art performance (Weiss et al., 2017). Moreover, the total training/inference time is much shorter since our E2E-ST models are based on the BPE1k unit rather than characters.[6]

---

[6]Weiss et al. (2017) trained their model for more than 2.5

	Model	De	Pt	Fr	Es	Ro	Ru	Nl	It
E2E	Transformer + ASR encoder init.[1,♣]	17.30	20.10	26.90	20.80	16.50	10.50	18.80	16.80
	ESPnet-ST (Transformer) ASR encoder/MT decoder init.	22.33	27.26	31.54	27.84	20.91	15.32	26.86	22.81
	+ SpecAugment	**22.91**	**28.01**	**32.69**	**27.96**	**21.90**	**15.75**	**27.43**	**23.75**
Cascade	Transformer → Transformer ASR[1]	18.5	21.5	27.9	22.5	16.8	11.1	22.2	18.9
	ESPnet-ST Transformer ASR → Transformer MT	**23.65**	**29.04**	**33.84**	**28.68**	**22.68**	**16.39**	**27.91**	**24.04**

Table 5: BLEU of ST systems on Must-C corpus. ♣Implemented w/ Fairseq. [1](Di Gangi et al., 2019b)

Framework	En→De			De→En		
	test2012	test2013	test2014	test2012	test2013	test2014
Fairseq	27.73	29.45	25.14	32.25	34.23	29.49
ESPnet-ST	26.92	28.88	24.70	32.19	33.46	29.22

Table 6: BLEU of MT systems on IWSLT 2016 corpus

4.2 Libri-trans (En→ Fr)

Libri-trans corpus contains 236-hours of English read speech, the corresponding transcription, and the French translations (Kocabiyikoglu et al., 2018). We used the clean 100-hours of speech data and augmented translation references with Google Translate for the training set (Bérard et al., 2018; Liu et al., 2019; Bahar et al., 2019a,b). We report case-insensitive BLEU on the *test* set. We used 1k vocabulary for all tasks.

Results are shown in Table 3. Note that all models used the same data resource and are competitive to previous work.

4.3 How2 (En→ Pt)

How2 corpus contains English speech extracted from YouTube videos, the corresponding transcription, as well as the Portuguese translation (Sanabria et al., 2018). We used the official 300-hour subset for training. Since speech features in the How2 corpus is pre-processed as 40-channel log-mel filterbank coefficients with 3-dimensional pitch features with Kaldi in advance, we used them without speed perturbation. We used 5k and 8k vocabularies for ASR and E2E-ST/MT models, respectively. We report case-sensitive BLEU on the *dev5* set.

Results are shown in Table 4. Our systems significantly outperform the previous RNN-based model (Sanabria et al., 2018). We believe that our systems can be regarded as the reliable baselines for future research.

4.4 Must-C (En→ 8 langs)

Must-C corpus contains English speech extracted from TED talks, the corresponding transcription, and the target translations in 8 language directions (De, Pt, Fr, Es, Ro, Ru, Nl, and It) (Di Gangi et al., 2019a). We conducted experiments in all 8 directions. We used 5k and 8k vocabularies for ASR and E2E-ST/MT models, respectively. We report case-sensitive BLEU on the *tst-COMMON* set.

Results are shown in Table 5. Our systems outperformed the previous work (Di Gangi et al., 2019b) implemented with the custermized Fairseq[7] with a large margin.

4.5 MT experiment: IWSLT16 En ↔ De

IWSLT evaluation campaign dataset (Cettolo et al., 2012) is the origin of the dataset for our MT experiments. We used En-De language pair. Specifically, IWSLT 2016 training set for training data, test2012 as the development data, and test2013 and test2014 sets as our test data respectively.

We compare the performance of Transformer model in *ESPnet-ST* with that of Fairseq in Table 6. *ESPnet-ST* achieves the performance almost comparable to the Fairseq. We assume that the performance gap is due to the minor difference in the implementation of two frameworks. Also, we carefully tuned the hyper-parameters for the MT task in the small ST corpora, which is confirmed from the reasonable performances of our Cascaded-ST systems. It is acknowledged that Transformer model is extremely sensitive to the hyper-parameters such as the learning rate and the number of warmup

---

weeks with 16 GPUs, while *ESPnet-ST* requires just 1-2 days with a single GPU. The fast inference of ESPnet-ST can be confirmed in our interactive demo page (RTF 0.7755).

[7]https://github.com/mattiadg/ FBK-Fairseq-ST

steps (Popel and Bojar, 2018). Thus, it is possible that the suitable sets of hyper-parameters are different across frameworks.

5 Conclusion

We presented *ESPnet-ST* for the fast development of end-to-end and cascaded ST systems. We provide various all-in-one example scripts containing corpus-dependent pre-processing, feature extraction, training, and inference. In the future, we will support more corpora and implement novel techniques to bridge the gap between end-to-end and cascaded approaches.

Acknowledgment

We thank Jun Suzuki for providing helpful feedback for the paper.

References

Antonios Anastasopoulos and David Chiang. 2018. Tied multitask learning for neural speech translation. In *Proceedings of the 2018 Conference of the North American Chapter of the Association for Computational Linguistics: Human Language Technologies (NAACL-HLT 2018)*, pages 82–91.

Parnia Bahar, Tobias Bieschke, and Hermann Ney. 2019a. A comparative study on end-to-end speech to text translation. In *Proceedings of 2019 IEEE Automatic Speech Recognition and Understanding Workshop (ASRU 2019)*, pages 792–799.

Parnia Bahar, Albert Zeyer, Ralf Schlüter, and Hermann Ney. 2019b. On using SpecAugment for end-to-end speech translation. In *Proceedings of 16th International Workshop on Spoken Language Translation 2019 (IWSLT 2019)*.

Dzmitry Bahdanau, Kyunghyun Cho, and Yoshua Bengio. 2015. Neural machine translation by jointly learning to align and translate. In *Proceedings of the 3rd International Conference on Learning Representations (ICLR 2015)*.

Sameer Bansal, Herman Kamper, Karen Livescu, Adam Lopez, and Sharon Goldwater. 2019. Pretraining on high-resource speech recognition improves low-resource speech-to-text translation. In *Proceedings of the 2019 Conference of the North American Chapter of the Association for Computational Linguistics: Human Language Technologies (NAACL-HLT 2019)*, pages 58–68.

Alexandre Bérard, Laurent Besacier, Ali Can Kocabiyikoglu, and Olivier Pietquin. 2018. End-to-end automatic speech translation of audiobooks. In *Proceedings of 2018 IEEE International Conference on Acoustics, Speech and Signal Processing (ICASSP 2018)*, pages 6224–6228.

Alexandre Bérard, Olivier Pietquin, Christophe Servan, and Laurent Besacier. 2016. Listen and translate: A proof of concept for end-to-end speech-to-text translation. In *Proceedings of NIPS 2016 End-to-end Learning for Speech and Audio Processing Workshop*.

Steven Bird, Lauren Gawne, Katie Gelbart, and Isaac McAlister. 2014. Collecting bilingual audio in remote indigenous communities. In *Proceedings of COLING 2014, the 25th International Conference on Computational Linguistics (COLING 2014)*, pages 1015–1024.

F. Casacuberta, M. Federico, H. Ney, and E. Vidal. 2008. Recent efforts in spoken language translation. *IEEE Signal Processing Magazine*, 25(3):80–88.

Mauro Cettolo, Christian Girardi, and Marcello Federico. 2012. Wit3: Web inventory of transcribed and translated talks. In *Conference of european association for machine translation*, pages 261–268.

William Chan, Navdeep Jaitly, Quoc Le, and Oriol Vinyals. 2016. Listen, attend and spell: A neural network for large vocabulary conversational speech recognition. In *Proceedings of 2016 IEEE International Conference on Acoustics, Speech and Signal Processing (ICASSP 2016)*, pages 4960–4964.

Mattia A. Di Gangi, Roldano Cattoni, Luisa Bentivogli, Matteo Negri, and Marco Turchi. 2019a. MuST-C: a Multilingual Speech Translation Corpus. In *Proceedings of the 2019 Conference of the North American Chapter of the Association for Computational Linguistics: Human Language Technologies (NAACL-HLT 2019)*, pages 2012–2017.

Mattia A Di Gangi, Matteo Negri, and Marco Turchi. 2019b. Adapting transformer to end-to-end spoken language translation. In *Proceedings of 20th Annual Conference of the International Speech Communication Association (INTERSPEECH 2019)*, pages 1133–1137.

Mattia Antonino Di Gangi, Matteo Negri, and Marco Turchi. 2019c. One-to-many multilingual end-to-end speech translation. In *Proceedings of 2019 IEEE Automatic Speech Recognition and Understanding Workshop (ASRU 2019)*, pages 585–592.

Pierre Godard, Gilles Adda, Martine Adda-Decker, Juan Benjumea, Laurent Besacier, Jamison Cooper-Leavitt, Guy-Noel Kouarata, Lori Lamel, Hélène Maynard, Markus Mueller, Annie Rialland, Sebastian Stueker, François Yvon, and Marcely Zanon-Boito. 2018. A very low resource language speech corpus for computational language documentation experiments. In *Proceedings of the Eleventh International Conference on Language Resources and Evaluation (LREC 2018)*, Miyazaki, Japan. European Language Resources Association (ELRA).

Tomoki Hayashi, Ryuichi Yamamoto, Katsuki Inoue, Takenori Yoshimura, Shinji Watanabe, Tomoki Toda,

Kazuya Takeda, Yu Zhang, and Xu Tan. 2020. ESPnet-TTS: Unified, reproducible, and integratable open source end-to-end text-to-speech toolkit. In *Proceedings of 2020 IEEE International Conference on Acoustics, Speech and Signal Processing (ICASSP 2020)*.

Hirofumi Inaguma, Kevin Duh, Tatsuya Kawahara, and Shinji Watanabe. 2019. Multilingual end-to-end speech translation. In *Proceedings of 2019 IEEE Automatic Speech Recognition and Understanding Workshop (ASRU 2019)*, pages 570–577.

Niehues Jan, Roldano Cattoni, Stüker Sebastian, Mauro Cettolo, Marco Turchi, and Marcello Federico. 2018. The IWSLT 2018 evaluation campaign. In *Proceedings of 15th International Workshop on Spoken Language Translation 2018 (IWSLT 2018)*, pages 2–6.

Anjuli Kannan, Yonghui Wu, Patrick Nguyen, Tara N Sainath, Zhifeng Chen, and Rohit Prabhavalkar. 2017. An analysis of incorporating an external language model into a sequence-to-sequence model. In *Proceedings of 2017 IEEE International Conference on Acoustics, Speech and Signal Processing (ICASSP 2017)*, pages 5824–5828.

Shigeki Karita, Nanxin Chen, Tomoki Hayashi, Takaaki Hori, Hirofumi Inaguma, Ziyan Jiang, Masao Someki, Nelson Enrique Yalta Soplin, Ryuichi Yamamoto, Xiaofei Wang, et al. 2019. A comparative study on Transformer vs RNN in speech applications. In *Proceedings of 2019 IEEE Automatic Speech Recognition and Understanding Workshop (ASRU 2019)*, pages 499–456.

Guillaume Klein, Yoon Kim, Yuntian Deng, Jean Senellart, and Alexander Rush. 2017. OpenNMT: Open-source toolkit for neural machine translation. In *Proceedings of ACL 2017, System Demonstrations*, pages 67–72.

Ali Can Kocabiyikoglu, Laurent Besacier, and Olivier Kraif. 2018. Augmenting Librispeech with French translations: A multimodal corpus for direct speech translation evaluation. In *Proceedings of the Eleventh International Conference on Language Resources and Evaluation (LREC 2018)*.

Philipp Koehn, Hieu Hoang, Alexandra Birch, Chris Callison-Burch, Marcello Federico, Nicola Bertoldi, Brooke Cowan, Wade Shen, Christine Moran, Richard Zens, Chris Dyer, Ondřej Bojar, Alexandra Constantin, and Evan Herbst. 2007. Moses: Open source toolkit for statistical machine translation. In *Proceedings of the 45th Annual Meeting of the Association for Computational Linguistics Companion Volume Proceedings of the Demo and Poster Sessions*, pages 177–180.

Oleksii Kuchaiev, Boris Ginsburg, Igor Gitman, Vitaly Lavrukhin, Carl Case, and Paulius Micikevicius. 2018. OpenSeq2Seq: Extensible toolkit for distributed and mixed precision training of sequence-to-sequence models. In *Proceedings of Workshop for NLP Open Source Software (NLP-OSS)*, pages 41–46.

Oleksii Kuchaiev, Jason Li, Huyen Nguyen, Oleksii Hrinchuk, Ryan Leary, Boris Ginsburg, Samuel Kriman, Stanislav Beliaev, Vitaly Lavrukhin, Jack Cook, et al. 2019. NeMo: a toolkit for building AI applications using Neural Modules. *arXiv preprint arXiv:1909.09577*.

Taku Kudo. 2018. Subword regularization: Improving neural network translation models with multiple subword candidates. In *Proceedings of the 56th Annual Meeting of the Association for Computational Linguistics (ACL 2018)*, pages 66–75.

Gaurav Kumar, Matt Post, Daniel Povey, and Sanjeev Khudanpur. 2014. Some insights from translating conversational telephone speech. In *Proceedings of 2014 IEEE International Conference on Acoustics, Speech and Signal Processing (ICASSP 2014)*, pages 3231–3235.

Naihan Li, Shujie Liu, Yanqing Liu, Sheng Zhao, and Ming Liu. 2019. Neural speech synthesis with transformer network. In *Proceedings of the AAAI Conference on Artificial Intelligence*, volume 33, pages 6706–6713.

Yuchen Liu, Hao Xiong, Zhongjun He, Jiajun Zhang, Hua Wu, Haifeng Wang, and Chengqing Zong. 2019. End-to-end speech translation with knowledge distillation. In *Proceedings of 20th Annual Conference of the International Speech Communication Association (INTERSPEECH 2019)*, pages 1128–1132.

Paulius Micikevicius, Sharan Narang, Jonah Alben, Gregory Diamos, Erich Elsen, David Garcia, Boris Ginsburg, Michael Houston, Oleksii Kuchaiev, Ganesh Venkatesh, and Hao Wu. 2018. Mixed precision training. In *Proceedings of the 6th International Conference on Learning Representations (ICLR 2018)*.

Hermann Ney. 1999. Speech translation: Coupling of recognition and translation. In *Proceedings of 1999 IEEE International Conference on Acoustics, Speech and Signal Processing (ICASSP 1999)*, pages 517–520.

J. Niehues, R. Cattoni, S. Stüker, M. Negri, M. Turchi, E. Salesky, R. Sanabria, L. Barrault, L. Specia, and M Federico. 2019. The IWSLT 2019 evaluation campaign. In *Proceedings of 16th International Workshop on Spoken Language Translation 2019 (IWSLT 2019)*.

Aaron van den Oord, Sander Dieleman, Heiga Zen, Karen Simonyan, Oriol Vinyals, Alex Graves, Nal Kalchbrenner, Andrew W. Senior, and Koray Kavukcuoglu. 2016. Wavenet: A generative model for raw audio. *arXiv preprint arXiv:1609.03499*.

Myle Ott, Sergey Edunov, Alexei Baevski, Angela Fan, Sam Gross, Nathan Ng, David Grangier, and Michael Auli. 2019. Fairseq: A fast, extensible toolkit for sequence modeling. In *Proceedings of the 2019 Conference of the North American Chapter of the Association for Computational Linguistics (Demonstrations)*, pages 48–53.

Kishore Papineni, Salim Roukos, Todd Ward, and Wei-Jing Zhu. 2002. Bleu: a method for automatic evaluation of machine translation. In *Proceedings of the 40th Annual Meeting of the Association for Computational Linguistics (ACL 2002)*, pages 311–318.

Adam Paszke, Sam Gross, Francisco Massa, Adam Lerer, James Bradbury, Gregory Chanan, Trevor Killeen, Zeming Lin, Natalia Gimelshein, Luca Antiga, et al. 2019. PyTorch: An imperative style, high-performance deep learning library. In *Proceedings of Advances in Neural Information Processing Systems 32 (NeurIPS 2019)*, pages 8024–8035.

Stephan Peitz, Markus Freitag, Arne Mauser, and Hermann Ney. 2011. Modeling punctuation prediction as machine translation. In *Proceedings of 8th International Workshop on Spoken Language Translation 2011 (IWSLT 2011)*, pages 238–245.

Martin Popel and Ondřej Bojar. 2018. Training Tips for the Transformer Model. *The Prague Bulletin of Mathematical Linguistics*, 110(1):43–70.

Matt Post, Gaurav Kumar, Adam Lopez, Damianos Karakos, Chris Callison-Burch, and Sanjeev Khudanpur. 2013. Improved speech-to-text translation with the Fisher and Callhome Spanish–English speech translation corpus. In *Proceedings of 10th International Workshop on Spoken Language Translation 2013 (IWSLT 2013)*.

Daniel Povey, Arnab Ghoshal, Gilles Boulianne, Lukas Burget, Ondrej Glembek, Nagendra Goel, Mirko Hannemann, Petr Motlicek, Yanmin Qian, Petr Schwarz, et al. 2011. The kaldi speech recognition toolkit. In *Proceedings of 2011 IEEE Automatic Speech Recognition and Understanding Workshop (ASRU 2011)*.

Vineel Pratap, Awni Hannun, Qiantong Xu, Jeff Cai, Jacob Kahn, Gabriel Synnaeve, Vitaliy Liptchinsky, and Ronan Collobert. 2019. Wav2Letter++: A fast open-source speech recognition system. In *Proceedings of 2019 IEEE International Conference on Acoustics, Speech and Signal Processing (ICASSP 2019)*, pages 6460–6464.

Yi Ren, Yangjun Ruan, Xu Tan, Tao Qin, Sheng Zhao, Zhou Zhao, and Tie-Yan Liu. 2019. Fastspeech: Fast, robust and controllable text to speech. In *Advances in Neural Information Processing Systems 32 (NeurIPS 2019)*, pages 3165–3174.

Ramon Sanabria, Ozan Caglayan, Shruti Palaskar, Desmond Elliott, Loïc Barrault, Lucia Specia, and Florian Metze. 2018. How2: A large-scale dataset for multimodal language understanding. In *Proceedings of the Workshop on Visually Grounded Interaction and Language (ViGIL)*.

Hiroshi Seki, Takaaki Hori, Shinji Watanabe, Niko Moritz, and Jonathan Le Roux. 2019. Vectorized Beam Search for CTC-Attention-Based Speech Recognition. In *Proceedings of 20th Annual Conference of the International Speech Communication Association (INTERSPEECH 2019)*, pages 3825–3829.

Rico Sennrich, Barry Haddow, and Alexandra Birch. 2016. Neural machine translation of rare words with subword units. In *Proceedings of the 54th Annual Meeting of the Association for Computational Linguistics (ACL 2016)*, pages 1715–1725.

Jonathan Shen, Patrick Nguyen, Yonghui Wu, Zhifeng Chen, Mia X Chen, Ye Jia, Anjuli Kannan, Tara Sainath, Yuan Cao, Chung-Cheng Chiu, et al. 2019. Lingvo: a modular and scalable framework for sequence-to-sequence modeling. *arXiv preprint arXiv:1902.08295*.

Jonathan Shen, Ruoming Pang, Ron J. Weiss, Mike Schuster, Navdeep Jaitly, Zongheng Yang, Zhifeng Chen, Yu Zhang, Yuxuan Wang, R. J. Skerry-Ryan, Rif A. Saurous, Yannis Agiomyrgiannakis, and Yonghui Wu. 2018. Natural TTS synthesis by conditioning WaveNet on Mel spectrogram predictions. In *Proceedings of 2017 IEEE International Conference on Acoustics, Speech and Signal Processing (ICASSP 2017)*, pages 4779–4783.

Matthias Sperber, Graham Neubig, Jan Niehues, and Alex Waibel. 2019. Attention-passing models for robust and data-efficient end-to-end speech translation. *Transactions of the Association for Computational Linguistics*, 7:313–325.

Seiya Tokui, Ryosuke Okuta, Takuya Akiba, Yusuke Niitani, Toru Ogawa, Shunta Saito, Shuji Suzuki, Kota Uenishi, Brian Vogel, and Hiroyuki Yamazaki Vincent. 2019. Chainer: A deep learning framework for accelerating the research cycle. In *Proceedings of the 25th ACM SIGKDD International Conference on Knowledge Discovery & Data Mining (KDD 2019)*, pages 2002–2011.

Ashish Vaswani, Samy Bengio, Eugene Brevdo, Francois Chollet, Aidan Gomez, Stephan Gouws, Llion Jones, Łukasz Kaiser, Nal Kalchbrenner, Niki Parmar, Ryan Sepassi, Noam Shazeer, and Jakob Uszkoreit. 2018. Tensor2Tensor for neural machine translation. In *Proceedings of the 13th Conference of the Association for Machine Translation in the Americas (Volume 1: Research Papers)*, pages 193–199, Boston, MA. Association for Machine Translation in the Americas.

Chengyi Wang, Yu Wu, Shujie Liu, Zhenglu Yang, and Ming Zhou. 2020. Bridging the gap between pretraining and fine-tuning for end-to-end speech translation. In *Proceedings of the AAAI conference on artificial intelligence 2020 (AAAI 2020)*.

Shinji Watanabe, Takaaki Hori, Shigeki Karita, Tomoki Hayashi, Jiro Nishitoba, Yuya Unno, Nelson Enrique Yalta Soplin, Jahn Heymann, Matthew Wiesner, Nanxin Chen, et al. 2018. ESPnet: End-to-end speech processing toolkit. In *Proceedings of 19th Annual Conference of the International Speech Communication Association (INTERSPEECH 2018)*, pages 2207–2211.

Shinji Watanabe, Takaaki Hori, Suyoun Kim, John R Hershey, and Tomoki Hayashi. 2017. Hybrid CTC/attention architecture for end-to-end speech recognition. *IEEE Journal of Selected Topics in Signal Processing*, 11(8):1240–1253.

Ron J Weiss, Jan Chorowski, Navdeep Jaitly, Yonghui Wu, and Zhifeng Chen. 2017. Sequence-to-sequence models can directly translate foreign speech. In *Proceedings of 18th Annual Conference of the International Speech Communication Association (INTERSPEECH 2017)*, pages 2625–2629.

Ryuichi Yamamoto, Eunwoo Song, and Jae-Min Kim. 2020. Parallel WaveGAN: A fast waveform generation model based on generative adversarial networks with multi-resolution spectrogram. In *Proceedings of 2020 IEEE International Conference on Acoustics, Speech and Signal Processing (ICASSP 2020)*.

Thomas Zenkel, Matthias Sperber, Jan Niehues, Markus Müller, Ngoc-Quan Pham, Sebastian Stüker, and Alex Waibel. 2018. Open source toolkit for speech to text translation. *Prague Bull. Math. Linguistics*, 111:125–135.

Albert Zeyer, Tamer Alkhouli, and Hermann Ney. 2018. RETURNN as a generic flexible neural toolkit with application to translation and speech recognition. In *Proceedings of ACL 2018, System Demonstrations*, pages 128–133.

Penman: An Open-Source Library and Tool for AMR Graphs

Michael Wayne Goodman
Nanyang Technological University
Singapore
`goodmami@uw.edu`

Abstract

Abstract Meaning Representation (AMR) (Banarescu et al., 2013) is a framework for semantic dependencies that encodes its rooted and directed acyclic graphs in a format called PENMAN notation. The format is simple enough that users of AMR data often write small scripts or libraries for parsing it into an internal graph representation, but there is enough complexity that these users could benefit from a more sophisticated and well-tested solution. The open-source Python library *Penman* provides a robust parser, functions for graph inspection and manipulation, and functions for formatting graphs into PENMAN notation. Many functions are also available in a command-line tool, thus extending its utility to non-Python setups.

1 Introduction

Abstract Meaning Representation (AMR; Banarescu et al., 2013) is a framework for encoding English language[1] meaning as structural-semantic graphs using a fork of Propbank (Kingsbury and Palmer, 2002; O'Gorman et al., 2018) for its semantic frames with additional AMR-specific roles. The graphs are connected, directed, with node and edge labels, and may have multiple roots but always have exactly one distinguished top node. AMR corpora, such as the recent AMR Annotation Release 3.0 (LDC2020T02),[2] encode the graphs in a format called PENMAN notation (Matthiessen and Bateman, 1991). PENMAN notation is a text stream and is thus linear, but it first uses bracketing to capture a spanning tree over the graph, then inverted edge labels and references to node IDs to capture re-entrancies. Proper interpretation

of the "pure" graph therefore requires the deinversion of inverted edges and the resolution of node IDs. Some tools that work with AMR use the interpreted pure graph (Cai and Knight, 2013; Song and Gildea, 2019; Chiang et al., 2013), but many others work at the tree level for surface alignment (Flanigan et al., 2014), for transformations from syntax trees (Wang et al., 2015), or to make use of tree-based algorithms (Pust et al., 2015; Takase et al., 2016). Others, particularly sequential neural systems (Konstas et al., 2017; van Noord and Bos, 2017), use the linear form directly.

Furthermore, while AMRs ostensibly describe semantic graphs abstracted away from any particular sentence's surface form, human annotators tend to "leak information" (Konstas et al., 2017) about the source sentence. This means that an annotator might be expected to produce the AMR in Fig. 1 for sentence (1), but then swap the relative order of the adjunct relations `:location` and `:time` for (2).[3] Van Noord and Bos (2017) embraced these biases and intentionally reordered relations, even frame arguments such as `:ARG0` and `:ARG1`, by their surface alignments, leading to a boost in their evaluation scores.

(1) I swam in the pool today.

(2) Today I swam in the pool.

```
(s / swim-01
   :ARG0 (i / i)
   :location (p / pool)
   :time (t / today))
```

Figure 1: An AMR for (1) or (2)

As illustrated above, work involving AMR may use the PENMAN string, the tree structure, or the

---

[1]Variations exist for other languages (e.g., Li et al., 2016; Cabezudo and Pardo, 2019), but AMR is primarily English and is not an interlingua (Xue et al., 2014).

[2]`https://catalog.ldc.upenn.edu/LDC2020T02`

[3]Graphically there is no difference, and a metric like smatch (Cai and Knight, 2013) would return a perfect score when comparing the two.

Proceedings of the 58th Annual Meeting of the Association for Computational Linguistics, pages 312–319
July 5 - July 10, 2020. ©2020 Association for Computational Linguistics

pure graph, or possibly multiple representations. This paper therefore describes and demonstrates *Penman*, a Python library and command-line utility for working with AMR data at both the tree and graph levels and for encoding and decoding these structures using PENMAN notation. Converting a tree into a graph loses information that the tree implicitly encodes, so Penman introduces the *epigraph*:[4] optional information that exists on top of the graph and controls how the pure graph is expressed as a tree. Penman is freely available under a permissive open-source license at `https://github.com/goodmami/penman/`.

2   Decoding and Encoding Graphs

Penman uses three-stage processes to decode PENMAN notation to a graph and to encode a graph to PENMAN, as illustrated in Fig. 2. **Parsing** is the process of getting a tree from a PENMAN string, and **interpretation** is getting a graph from a tree, while **decoding** is the whole string-to-graph process. Going the other way, **configuration** is the process of getting a tree from a graph and **formatting** is getting a string from a tree, while **encoding** is the whole graph-to-string process. Splitting the decoding and encoding processes into two steps each allows one to work with AMR data at any stage. The variant of PENMAN notation used by Penman is described in §2.1. The tree, graph, and epigraph data structures are described in §2.2. Getting a tree from a string (and vice-versa) depends only on understanding PENMAN notation, but getting a graph from a tree (and vice-versa) requires an understanding of the semantic model. Semantic models are described in §2.4.

2.1   PENMAN Notation

The Penman project uses a less-strict variant of PENMAN notation than is used by AMR in order to robustly handle some kinds of erroneous output by AMR parsers. The syntactic and lexical rules for PENMAN notation in PEG syntax[5] are shown in Fig. 3. Optional whitespace (not shown) is allowed around expressions in the syntactic rules.

In AMR, the `Concept` expression on `Node`, the `Atom` expression on `Concept`, and the `(Node / Atom)` expression on `Reln` are obligatory, but they are optional for Penman and will get a

null value when missing. Also in AMR, the initial `Symbol` on `Node` may be further constrained with a specific `Variable` pattern for node identifiers and the `Symbol` in `Atom` would become a choice: `Variable` / `Symbol`. How Penman handles variables is discussed in §2.2.

AMR corpora conventionally use blank lines to delineate multiple graphs, but Penman relies on bracketing instead and whitespace is not significant. Penman also parses comments (not described in Fig. 3), which are lines prefixed with # characters, and extracts metadata where keys are tokens prefixed with two colons (e.g., `::id`) and values are anything after the key until the next key or a newline.

2.2   Decoding: Trees, Graphs, and Epigraphs

In Penman, a **tree** data structure is a $\langle n, B \rangle$ tuple where n is the node's identifier (variable) and B is a list of branches. Each branch is a $\langle l, b \rangle$ tuple where l is a branch label (a possibly inverted role) and b is a (sub)tree or an atom. The first branch on B is the node's concept, thus a tree is a near-direct conversion of the `Node` rule in Fig. 3 where B is the concatenation of `Concept` and `Reln`. The tree corresponding to the AMR in Fig. 2 is shown in Fig. 4.

A **graph** is a tuple $\langle v, T \rangle$ where v is the top variable and T is a flat list of triples. For each triple $\langle s, r, t \rangle$, the source s is always the head variable of a dependency, r is the normalized role, and t is the dependent. When interpreting a triple from a tree branch, n becomes s and t comes from b unless the branch label l is deinverted according to the semantic model (described in §2.4) to produce r, in which case s and t are swapped. In the graph, t is designated a variable if it appears as the source of any other triple; otherwise it is an atom. Triples where t is a variable are called **edge relations**. If t is an atom and r is the special role `:instance`, then t is the node's concept and the triple is an **instance relation**. All other triples are **attribute relations**. Fig. 5 shows the graph corresponding to the AMR in Fig. 2.

Conversion from a PENMAN string to a tree is straightforward: the only information lost in parsing is formatting details like the amount of whitespace. The interpretation of a graph from a tree, however, loses information about the specific tree configuration for the graph, as there are often many possible configurations for the same graph.

---

[4]A different sense than for an inscription on a building or a short passage at the start of a book.

[5]See `https://bford.info/packrat/`

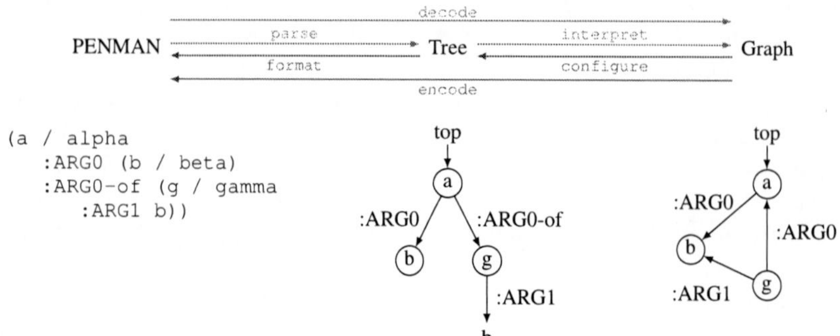

Figure 2: The three-stage decoding/encoding processes

```
# Syntactic rules
Start     <- Node
Node      <- '(' Symbol Concept? Reln* ')'
Concept   <- '/' Atom?
Reln      <- Role Algn? (Node / Atom)?
Atom      <- (String / Symbol) Algn?

# Lexical rules
Symbol    <- NameChr+
Role      <- ':' NameChr*
Algn      <- '~' Prefix? Indices
Prefix    <- [a-zA-Z] '.'?
Indices   <- Digit+ (',' Digit+)*
String    <- '"' (!'"' ('\\' . / .))* '"'
NameChr   <- ![ \n\t\r\f\v()/:~] .
Digit     <- [0-9]
```

Figure 3: Syntactic and lexical rules of PENMAN

```
('a', [
  ('/', 'alpha'),
  (':ARG0', ('b', [
    ('/', 'beta')])),
  (':ARG0-of', ('g', [
    ('/', 'gamma'),
    (':ARG1', 'b')]))])
```

Figure 4: Tree structure for the AMR in Fig. 2

```
('a',
 [('a', ':instance', 'alpha'),
  ('a', ':ARG0', 'b'),
  ('b', ':instance', 'beta'),
  ('g', ':ARG0', 'a'),
  ('g', ':instance', 'gamma'),
  ('g', ':ARG1', 'b')])
```

Figure 5: Graph structure for the AMR in Fig. 2

Therefore, upon interpretation, Penman stores in two places the information that would be lost: in the order of triples (meaning the graph's triples are a sequence, not an unordered bag or set), and in the **epigraph**, which is a mapping of triples to lists of **epigraphical markers**. The choice of the term *epigraph* is by analogy to the *epigenome*: just as epigenetic markers control how genes are expressed in an organism, epigraphical markers control how triples are expressed in a tree. In interpreting a graph from a tree, when a branch's target is another subtree (e.g., when (is encountered in the string), a **Push** marker is assigned to the triple resulting from the branch, indicating that that triple pushed a new node context onto a stack representing the tree structure. The final triple resulting from branches in the subtree, even considering further nested subtrees (e.g., at the point where) is encountered in the string), gets a **Pop** marker indicating the end of the node context. In addition to tree-layout markers, the epigraph is also where surface alignment information is stored, as these alignments are not part of the pure graph. Fig. 6 shows the epigraph for the AMR in Fig. 2.

```
{
('a', ':instance', 'alpha'):[],
('a', ':ARG0', 'b'):       [Push('b')],
('b', ':instance', 'beta'): [Pop],
('g', ':ARG0', 'a'):       [Push('g')],
('g', ':instance', 'gamma'):[],
('g', ':ARG1', 'b'):       [Pop]
}
```

Figure 6: Epigraph structure for the AMR in Fig. 2

2.3 Encoding: No Surprises

When configuring a tree from a graph, the epigraph is used to control where triples occur in the tree. If at each step the layout markers in the epigraph allow the configuration process to navigate a tree with no surprises (that is, when the source or target of each triple is the current node on a node-context stack), then it will produce the same tree that was decoded to get the graph.[6] Otherwise, such as when a graph is modified or constructed without an epigraph, the algorithm will switch to another procedure that repeatedly passes over the list of remaining triples and configures those whose source or target are already in the tree under construction. If no triples are inserted in a pass, the remaining triples are discarded and a warning is logged that the graph is disconnected. The semantic model is used to properly configure inverted branches as necessary.

Once a tree is configured, formatting it to a string is simple, and users may customize the formatter to adjust the amount of whitespace used. The default indentation width is an adaptive mode that indents based on the initial column of the current node context; otherwise an explicit width is multiplied by the nesting level, or a user may select to print the whole AMR on one line. Another customization option is a "compact" mode which joins any attribute relations, but not edges, that immediately follow the concept onto the same line as the concept.

2.4 Semantic Models

In order to interpret a tree into a graph, a semantic model is used to get normalized, or deinverted, triples. Penman provides a default model which only checks if the role ends in `-of` (the conventional indicator of role inversion in PENMAN notation). Ideally this would be all that is needed, but AMR defines several primary (non-inverted) roles ending in `-of`, such as `:consist-of` and `:prep-on-behalf-of`, where the inverted forms are `:consist-of-of` and `:prep-on-behalf-of-of`, respectively. The model therefore first checks if a role is listed as a primary role; if not and if it ends in `-of`, it is inverted, otherwise it is not. When the role of a triple

is deinverted, Penman also swaps its source and target so the dependency relation remains intact.

The model has other uses, such as inverting triples (useful when encoding), defining transformations as described in §3, and checking graphs for compliance with the model. In addition to the default model, Penman includes an AMR model with the roles and transformations defined in the AMR documentation.[7]

3 Graph and Tree Transformations

Goodman (2019a) described four transformations of AMR graphs and trees—namely, **role canonicalization**, **edge reification** (including dereification), **attribute reification**, and **tree structure indication**[8]—and how they could be used to improve the comparability of parser-produced AMR corpora by normalizing differences that are meaning-equivalent in AMR and by allowing for partial credit when, for example, a relation has a correct role but an incorrect target value. Penman incorporates all of those transformations but it (a) depends on the semantic model to define canonical roles and reifications, whereas Goodman 2019a used hard-coded transformations; and (b) inserts layout markers for a "no-surprises" configuration that results in the expected tree. A separately-defined model allows Penman to use the same transformation methods with different versions of AMR, for different tasks, or even with non-AMR representations, by creating different models. For the implementation details of these transformations, refer to Goodman 2019a.

In addition to those four transformations, Penman adds a few more methods. The **rearrange** method operates on a tree and sorts the order of branches by their branch labels. Besides changing the order of branches, their structure is unchanged by this method. Van Noord and Bos (2017) similarly rearranged tree branches based on surface alignments. The **reconfigure** method configures a tree from a graph after discarding the layout markers in the epigraph and sorting the triples based on their roles. Unlike the **rearrange** method, **reconfigure** affects the entire structure of the graph except for which node is the graph's top. For both of these, the sorting methods are defined by the

---

[6]There is currently one known situation where this is not the case: when a graph has duplicate triples with the same source, role, and target, as the epigraph cannot uniquely map the triple to its epigraphical markers. These, however, are likely bad graphs in AMR.

[7]`https://isi.edu/~ulf/amr/lib/roles.html`

[8]With the introduction of the epigraph, tree structure indication is somewhat redundant, however it differs in that the transformation puts this information in the graph triples.

model, and Penman includes three such methods: original order, random order, and canonical order. For **rearrange** there are additional sorting methods applicable to trees: alphanumeric order, attributes-first order, and inverted-last order. Since node variables in AMR are conventionally assigned in order of their appearance and the above methods can change this order, the **reset-variables** method reassigns the variables based on the new tree.

4 Use Cases

Here I describe a handful of use cases that motivate the use of Penman.

4.1 Graph Construction

Users of the Penman library can programmatically construct graphs and then encode them to PENMAN notation. Penman allows users to directly append to the list of triples and assign epigraphical markers, or to assemble small graphs and use set-union operations to combine them together. Another option is to assemble the tree directly, which may make more sense for some systems. Once the tree is configured or constructed, users can use transformations such as **rearrange** and **reset-variables** to make the PENMAN string more canonical in form. Fig. 7 illustrates using the Python API to construct and encode a graph.

```
>>> import penman
>>> g = penman.Graph(
...       [('s', ':instance', 'swim-01'),
...        ('s', ':ARG0', 'i'),
...        ('i', ':instance', 'i'),
...        ('s', ':location', 'p'),
...        ('p', ':instance', 'pool')])
>>> print(penman.encode(g))
(s / swim-01
   :ARG0 (i / i)
   :location (p / pool))
```

Figure 7: Example of using Penman's Python API for graph construction

Another possibility is for graph augmentation, where users rely on Penman to parse a string to a graph which they then modify, e.g., to add surface alignments or wiki links, then serialize to a string again. This allows them to focus on their primary task without worrying about the details of parsing and formatting.

4.2 Graph Validation

Whether one is generating AMR graphs with hand annotation or by automatic means, the end result is not guaranteed to be valid with respect to the model, so Penman offers a function to check for compliance. Currently, this check evaluates three criteria:

1. Is each role defined by the model?

2. Is the top set to a node in the graph?

3. Is the graph fully connected?

To facilitate both library and tool usage, the library function returns a dictionary mapping triples (for context) to error messages, as shown in Fig. 8, while the tool encodes the errors as metadata comments and has a nonzero exit-code on errors.

```
>>> from penman.models.amr import model
>>> g = penman.decode(
...      '(s / swim-01'
...      '   :ARG0 (i / i)'
...      '   :stroke (b / butterfly))')
>>> model.errors(g)
{('s', ':stroke', 'b'): ['invalid role']}
```

Figure 8: Example of using Penman's Python API for checking model compliance

4.3 Formatting for a Consistent Style

The official AMR corpora, such as the AMR Annotation Release 3.0, are distributed with the graphs serialized in a human-readable style that uses increasing levels of indentation to show the nesting of subgraphs. Furthermore, relations on a node appear in a canonical order depending on their roles (e.g., ARG1 appears before ARG2) or their surface alignments, where the appearance of a node roughly follows the order of corresponding words in a sentence. The **rearrange** and **reconfigure** transformations can change the order of relations in the graph to be more canonical, the **reset-variables** method can ensure variable forms are as expected, and the whitespace options of tree formatting can emulate the same indentation style as the official corpora. These features may be useful for users distributing new AMR corpora.

4.4 Normalization for Fairer Evaluation

The normalization options in §3 can be useful when evaluating the results of AMR parsing, as described in Goodman 2019a. Penman is thus well-situated as a preprocessor to an evaluation step using, e.g., smatch (Cai and Knight, 2013), SemBLEU (Song and Gildea, 2019), or SEMA (Anchiêta et al., 2019).

Fig. 9 shows the command-line tool performing role canonicalization.

```
$ echo '(c / chapter :domain-of 7)' \
> | penman --amr --canonicalize-roles
(c / chapter
   :mod 7)
```

Figure 9: Example of using Penman's command-line tool for normalization

4.5 Preprocessing for Machine Learning

Sequential neural models which use linearized AMR graphs have been popular for both parsing and generation (Barzdins and Gosko, 2016; Peng et al., 2017; Konstas et al., 2017; van Noord and Bos, 2017; Song et al., 2018; Damonte and Cohen, 2019; Zhang et al., 2019), but data sparsity is a significant issue (Peng et al., 2017). One way to address data sparsity is to remove senses on concepts (Lyu and Titov, 2018). Fig. 10 shows how the Python API can remove these senses in the tree.

```
>>> import re
>>> sense = re.compile(r'-\d+($|~)')
>>> def desense(branch):
...     role, tgt = branch
...     if role == '/':
...         tgt = sense.sub(r'\1', tgt)
...     return role, target
...
>>> t = penman.parse(
...     '(s / swim-01~e.1'
...     '   :ARG0 (i / i))')
>>> for _, branches in t.nodes():
...     branches[:] = map(desense,
...                       branches)
...
>>> print(penman.format(t))
(s / swim~e.1
   :ARG0 (i / i))
```

Figure 10: Example of using Penman's Python API to remove concept senses

Other techniques include, but are not limited to, normalizing linear forms, as discussed in §4.4; rearranging graphs with alignments to match the input string (van Noord and Bos, 2017); or randomizing branch orders to avoid overfitting to annotator biases, as suggested by (Konstas et al., 2017). Penman supports all these use cases via commands, as in Fig. 9, without any coding required.

5 Applicability beyond AMR

This paper has described PENMAN as a notation for encoding AMR graphs, but it is also applicable to other dependency graphs that share the same constraints (e.g., connected, directed). PENMAN notation can encode Dependency Minimal Recursion Semantics (DMRS; Copestake, 2009; Copestake et al., 2016), such as for learning graph-to-graph machine translation rules (Goodman, 2018) and neural generation (Hajdik et al., 2019), and it can encode Elementary Dependency Structures (EDS; Oepen et al., 2004; Oepen and Lønning, 2006), as shown in Fig. 11 using PyDelphin (Goodman, 2019b) for conversion. It is also useful for extensions of AMR, such as Uniform Meaning Representation (UMR; Pustejovsky et al., 2019).

```
$ echo '{e: x:pron[]
>         _1:pronoun_q[BV x]
>         e:_swim_v_1[ARG1 x]}' \
> | delphin convert --from eds \
>                   --to eds-penman \
>                   --indent 3
(e / _swim_v_1
   :ARG1 (x / pron
      :BV-of (_1 / pronoun_q)))
```

Figure 11: Example of EDS in Penman notation

6 Conclusion

In this paper I have presented Penman, a Python library and command-line tool for working with AMR and other graphs serialized in the PENMAN format. Existing work on AMR has targeted the PENMAN string, the parsed tree, or the interpreted graph, and Penman accommodates all of these use cases by allowing users to work with the tree or graph data structures or to encode them back to strings. Transformations defined at both the graph and tree level make it applicable for pre- and post-processing steps for corpus creation, evaluation, machine learning projects, and more. Penman is available under the MIT open-source license at https://github.com/goodmami/penman. Interactive notebook demonstrations and informational videos are available at https://github.com/goodmami/penman#demo.

Acknowledgments

Thanks to the three anonymous reviewers for their helpful comments, and to the contributors and users of the Penman project for their support.

References

Rafael Torres Anchiêta, Marco Antonio Sobrevilla Cabezudo, and Thiago Alexandre Salgueiro Pardo. 2019. SEMA: an extended semantic evaluation for AMR. In *Proceedings of the 20th Computational Linguistics and Intelligent Text Processing*. Springer International Publishing.

Laura Banarescu, Claire Bonial, Shu Cai, Madalina Georgescu, Kira Griffitt, Ulf Hermjakob, Kevin Knight, Philipp Koehn, Martha Palmer, and Nathan Schneider. 2013. Abstract meaning representation for sembanking. In *Proceedings of the 7th Linguistic Annotation Workshop and Interoperability with Discourse*, pages 178–186, Sofia, Bulgaria. Association for Computational Linguistics.

Guntis Barzdins and Didzis Gosko. 2016. RIGA at SemEval-2016 task 8: Impact of Smatch extensions and character-level neural translation on AMR parsing accuracy. In *Proceedings of the 10th International Workshop on Semantic Evaluation (SemEval-2016)*, pages 1143–1147, San Diego, California. Association for Computational Linguistics.

Marco Antonio Sobrevilla Cabezudo and Thiago Pardo. 2019. Towards a general Abstract Meaning Representation corpus for Brazilian Portuguese. In *Proceedings of the 13th Linguistic Annotation Workshop*, pages 236–244.

Shu Cai and Kevin Knight. 2013. Smatch: an evaluation metric for semantic feature structures. In *Proceedings of the 51st Annual Meeting of the Association for Computational Linguistics (Volume 2: Short Papers)*, volume 2, pages 748–752.

David Chiang, Jacob Andreas, Daniel Bauer, Karl Moritz Hermann, Bevan Jones, and Kevin Knight. 2013. Parsing graphs with hyperedge replacement grammars. In *Proceedings of the 51st Annual Meeting of the Association for Computational Linguistics (Volume 1: Long Papers)*, pages 924–932.

Ann Copestake. 2009. **Invited Talk:** slacker semantics: Why superficiality, dependency and avoidance of commitment can be the right way to go. In *Proceedings of the 12th Conference of the European Chapter of the ACL (EACL 2009)*, pages 1–9, Athens, Greece. Association for Computational Linguistics.

Ann Copestake, Guy Emerson, Michael Wayne Goodman, Matic Horvat, Alexander Kuhnle, and Ewa MuszyAĎska. 2016. Resources for building applications with Dependency Minimal Recursion Semantics. In *Proceedings of the Tenth International Conference on Language Resources and Evaluation (LREC 2016)*, Paris, France. European Language Resources Association (ELRA).

Marco Damonte and Shay B. Cohen. 2019. Structural neural encoders for AMR-to-text generation. In *Proceedings of the 2019 Conference of the North American Chapter of the Association for Computational Linguistics: Human Language Technologies, Volume 1 (Long and Short Papers)*, pages 3649–3658, Minneapolis, Minnesota. Association for Computational Linguistics.

Jeffrey Flanigan, Sam Thomson, Jaime G Carbonell, Chris Dyer, and Noah A Smith. 2014. A discriminative graph-based parser for the abstract meaning representation. In *Proceedings of the 52nd Annual Meeting of the Association for Computational Linguistics (Volume 1: Long Papers)*, pages 1426–1436.

Michael Wayne Goodman. 2018. *Semantic Operations for Transfer-based Machine Translation*. Ph.D. thesis, University of Washington, Seattle.

Michael Wayne Goodman. 2019a. AMR normalization for fairer evaluation. In *Proceedings of the 33rd Pacific Asia Conference on Language, Information, and Computation*, Hakodate.

Michael Wayne Goodman. 2019b. A Python library for deep linguistic resources. In *2019 Pacific Neighborhood Consortium Annual Conference and Joint Meetings (PNC)*, Singapore.

Valerie Hajdik, Jan Buys, Michael Wayne Goodman, and Emily M. Bender. 2019. Neural text generation from rich semantic representations. In *Proceedings of the 2019 Conference on the North American Chapter of the Association for Computational Linguistics: Human Language Technologies (NAACL-HLT))*, Minneapolis, Minnesota.

Paul Kingsbury and Martha Palmer. 2002. From Treebank to Propbank. In *LREC*, pages 1989–1993. Citeseer.

Ioannis Konstas, Srinivasan Iyer, Mark Yatskar, Yejin Choi, and Luke Zettlemoyer. 2017. Neural AMR: Sequence-to-sequence models for parsing and generation. In *Proceedings of the 55th Annual Meeting of the Association for Computational Linguistics (Volume 1: Long Papers)*, pages 146–157, Vancouver, Canada. Association for Computational Linguistics.

Bin Li, Yuan Wen, Weiguang Qu, Lijun Bu, and Nianwen Xue. 2016. Annotating the Little Prince with Chinese AMRs. In *Proceedings of the 10th Linguistic Annotation Workshop held in conjunction with ACL 2016 (LAW-X 2016)*, pages 7–15.

Chunchuan Lyu and Ivan Titov. 2018. AMR parsing as graph prediction with latent alignment. In *Proceedings of the 56th Annual Meeting of the Association for Computational Linguistics (Volume 1: Long Papers)*, pages 397–407.

Christian Matthiessen and John A Bateman. 1991. *Text generation and systemic-functional linguistics: experiences from English and Japanese*. Pinter Publishers.

Rik van Noord and Johan Bos. 2017. Neural semantic parsing by character-based translation: Experiments with abstract meaning representations. *Computational Linguistics in the Netherlands Journal*, 7:93–108.

Stephan Oepen, Dan Flickinger, Kristina Toutanova, and Christopher D Manning. 2004. LinGO Redwoods. *Research on Language and Computation*, 2(4):575–596.

Stephan Oepen and Jan Tore Lønning. 2006. Discriminant-based MRS banking. In *Proceedings of the 5th International Conference on Language Resources and Evaluation*, pages 1250–1255.

Tim O'Gorman, Sameer Pradhan, Martha Palmer, Julia Bonn, Katie Conger, and James Gung. 2018. The new Propbank: Aligning Propbank with AMR through POS unification. In *Proceedings of the Eleventh International Conference on Language Resources and Evaluation (LREC 2018)*.

Xiaochang Peng, Chuan Wang, Daniel Gildea, and Nianwen Xue. 2017. Addressing the data sparsity issue in neural AMR parsing. In *Proceedings of the 15th Conference of the European Chapter of the Association for Computational Linguistics: Volume 1, Long Papers*, pages 366–375, Valencia, Spain. Association for Computational Linguistics.

Michael Pust, Ulf Hermjakob, Kevin Knight, Daniel Marcu, and Jonathan May. 2015. Parsing English into abstract meaning representation using syntax-based machine translation. In *Proceedings of the 2015 Conference on Empirical Methods in Natural Language Processing*, pages 1143–1154.

James Pustejovsky, Ken Lai, and Nianwen Xue. 2019. Modeling quantification and scope in abstract meaning representations. In *Proceedings of the First International Workshop on Designing Meaning Representations*, pages 28–33, Florence, Italy. Association for Computational Linguistics.

Linfeng Song and Daniel Gildea. 2019. SemBleu: A robust metric for AMR parsing evaluation. In *Proceedings of the 57th Annual Meeting of the Association for Computational Linguistics*, pages 4547–4552.

Linfeng Song, Yue Zhang, Zhiguo Wang, and Daniel Gildea. 2018. A graph-to-sequence model for AMR-to-text generation. In *Proceedings of the 56th Annual Meeting of the Association for Computational Linguistics (Volume 1: Long Papers)*, pages 1616–1626, Melbourne, Australia. Association for Computational Linguistics.

Sho Takase, Jun Suzuki, Naoaki Okazaki, Tsutomu Hirao, and Masaaki Nagata. 2016. Neural headline generation on abstract meaning representation. In *Proceedings of the 2016 conference on empirical methods in natural language processing*, pages 1054–1059.

Chuan Wang, Nianwen Xue, and Sameer Pradhan. 2015. A transition-based algorithm for AMR parsing. In *Proceedings of the 2015 Conference of the North American Chapter of the Association for Computational Linguistics: Human Language Technologies*, pages 366–375, Denver, Colorado. Association for Computational Linguistics.

Nianwen Xue, Ondrej Bojar, Jan Hajic, Martha Palmer, Zdenka Uresova, and Xiuhong Zhang. 2014. Not an interlingua, but close: Comparison of English AMRs to Chinese and Czech. In *LREC*, volume 14, pages 1765–1772. Reykjavik, Iceland.

Sheng Zhang, Xutai Ma, Kevin Duh, and Benjamin Van Durme. 2019. AMR parsing as sequence-to-graph transduction. In *Proceedings of the 57th Annual Meeting of the Association for Computational Linguistics*, pages 80–94, Florence, Italy. Association for Computational Linguistics.

Embedding-based Scientific Literature Discovery in a Text Editor Application

Onur Gökçe, Jonathan Prada, Nikola I. Nikolov, Nianlong Gu, Richard H.R. Hahnloser
Institute of Neuroinformatics, University of Zurich and ETH Zurich, Switzerland
`{onur, johny, niniko, nianlong, rich}@ini.ethz.ch`

Abstract

Each claim in a research paper requires all relevant prior knowledge to be discovered, assimilated, and appropriately cited. However, despite the availability of powerful search engines and sophisticated text editing software, discovering relevant papers and integrating the knowledge into a manuscript remain complex tasks associated with high cognitive load. To define comprehensive search queries requires strong motivation from authors, irrespective of their familiarity with the research field. Moreover, switching between independent applications for literature discovery, bibliography management, reading papers, and writing text burdens authors further and interrupts their creative process. Here, we present a web application that combines text editing and literature discovery in an interactive user interface. The application is equipped with a search engine that couples Boolean keyword filtering with nearest neighbor search over text embeddings, providing a discovery experience tuned to an author's manuscript and his interests. Our application aims to take a step towards more enjoyable and effortless academic writing.

The demo of the application[1] and a short video tutorial[2] are available online.

1 Introduction

Writing is a complex problem-solving task that burdens authors with a high cognitive load (Hayes, 2012), which especially applies to inexperienced researchers (Shah et al., 2009). The typical workflow of composing an academic manuscript (be it a proposal, report, or paper) is an iterative process of conceptualizing ideas, formulating search queries, browsing search results, reading papers, eventu-

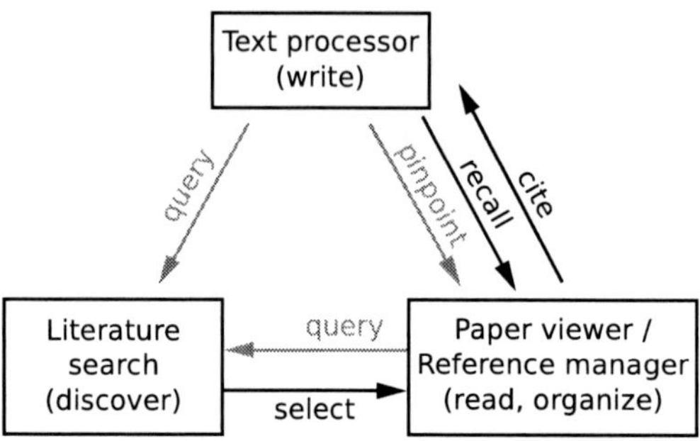

Figure 1: The typical workflow of scientific writing is largely based on independent software tools (text processor, reference manager, literature search engine, and paper viewer) that draw on diverse cognitive processes (recalling and citing articles, as well as searching, retrieving, and reading articles, black). Our web application focuses on assisting authors in literature discovery and in pinpointing relevant text passages in a paper (red).

ally followed by assimilating and integrating the discovered knowledge.

The current toolbox of scientific writing consists of text editors, search engines, reference managers, and paper viewers. These components are typically independent applications with limited interactivity. Consequently, authors are forced to navigate through diverse user interfaces repeatedly and need to link different parts of their workflow manually. We believe that there is a need for technology that makes literature discovery a seamless extension of the writing experience (Figure 1).

Implicitly, each scientific statement requires an in-depth search for supporting or conflicting findings in the literature. Accordingly, authors must retain a strong motivation to iterate through many combinations of search terms even when the apparent gain from the search becomes sub-optimal (Azzopardi et al., 2018). In addition, the keywords intended for traditional search engines can be in-

---

[1] `https://SciEditorDemo2020.herokuapp.com/`
[2] `https://youtu.be/pkdVU60IcRc`

Proceedings of the 58th Annual Meeting of the Association for Computational Linguistics, pages 320–326
July 5 - July 10, 2020. ©2020 Association for Computational Linguistics

trinsically biased because authors seek confirmation (Nickerson, 1998) or because of gaps in their knowledge (Athukorala et al., 2013). The use of synonymous terminology, such as with the names of species in botany (Rivera et al., 2014) or field-specific nomenclature (Hodges, 2008), further complicates formulating comprehensive search queries. Last but not least, the exponential increase in the number of scientific publications (Larsen and von Ins, 2010) makes it increasingly difficult to keep track of the literature and to incorporate new findings into one's work.

Such challenges call for novel tools to alleviate the obstacles faced by authors. We, therefore, set out to design a workflow that simplifies the exploration of the scientific literature by making use of advances in natural language processing (NLP). We introduce a web application for writing scientific text with integrated literature discovery, paper reading, and bibliography management capabilities.

Our application allows authors to retrieve papers that are similar to their manuscript (or to some of its parts) by utilizing text embeddings (Section 3.2). In addition, the authors can confine the scope of retrieved papers to specific interests by applying keyword-based Boolean filters (Section 3.1). Finally, to guide the authors in skim reading, similar sentences can be automatically highlighted in the retrieved papers. With these features, we aim to make the processes of literature discovery and scientific writing more efficient and enjoyable.

2 Related Work

2.1 Platforms for Literature Search, Discovery, and Reference Management

Currently, there are many independent applications for searching for and sharing of publications (e.g., Google Scholar, Pubmed, Web of Science, Meta, ResearchGate, and Iris.AI), for managing bibliography (e.g., Mendeley, Readcube, Paperpile, EndNote, and F1000), and for processing text (e.g., Microsoft Word, Google Docs, Overleaf, Dropbox Paper, and Sciflow). However, end-to-end applications that combine text editing with NLP-powered interactive literature discovery are scarce. Traditionally, text processors can interact with external software to search for content, to manage references, or to improve writing style via plug-ins, but such interactions are typically limited.

A recent application, Raxter.io, provides a single interface for document writing and literature searching. Although Raxter.io allows fine-tuning of document-based search queries, its methods are not fully disclosed, and it neither supports flexible keyword definitions nor the automatic highlighting of relevant passages. Raxter.io also does not display the full body of papers unless the users manually import them.

2.2 Methods for Literature Discovery

Traditional search engines use a bag-of-words model with a frequency-based ranking function such as BM25 (Robertson, 2009) to retrieve documents that match a query of one or more search terms. Obtaining useful search results requires well-formulated search queries (Aula, 2003), which can be a challenging task during exploratory search (Belkin, 2000) and constitutes a cognitive load (Gwizdka, 2010) that our application aims to ease.

Document similarity search methods (Wan et al., 2008), by contrast, use entire documents as the search queries, circumventing the need to define keywords for the search. State-of-the-art methods for retrieving similar documents rely on text embeddings (Conneau et al., 2018; Adi et al., 2016; Le and Mikolov, 2014) and on efficient approximate nearest neighbor search algorithms (Johnson et al., 2017). However, embedding-based search methods seem rather inflexible in refining searches, because it is unclear how to steer search results in a particular direction without painstakingly having to modify the query document.

Both keyword- and embedding-based search methods provide unique advantages, but there have not been many attempts at combining these methods to overcome their respective limitations.

3 Literature Discovery

The pipeline for literature discovery in our application consists of two steps (Figure 2). First, the search engine retrieves a subset of the papers from our database that match a user-defined keyword-based filter. Second, the search engine ranks the filtered papers according to their similarity to the manuscript using document embeddings. We describe each of the two steps in detail below. Our database contains 2.7M papers from the Pubmed Central Open-Access subset (PMC-OA)[3].

---

[3]https://www.ncbi.nlm.nih.gov/pmc/tools/openftlist/

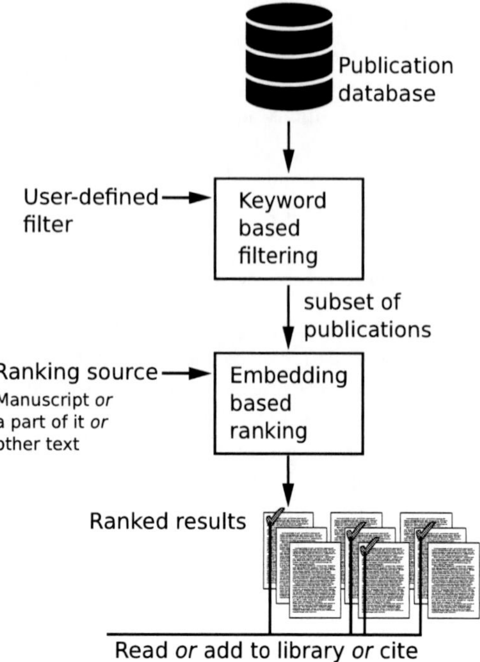

Figure 2: Overview of the literature discovery pipeline in our application. The search engine first filters our database for papers that match a set of user-defined keywords, and then ranks the filtered results according to their embedding-based proximity to a ranking source, such as an entire user manuscript. The top-ranked papers are presented to the user who can then save, cite, or read them, with the possibility of highlighting the most relevant sentences.

3.1 Keyword-based Filtering

An embedding-based search might return many papers that are similar to the manuscript but are of limited interest to the author. For example, authors of a medical manuscript on *lung cancer* may seek similar treatments in the literature for another organ, but embedding-based ranking might retrieve papers only on lung cancer. The keyword-based filter can, in such cases, be used to restrict the ranking operation either to the papers mentioning that *other organ* or to papers that do not mention *lung*. Thus, filtering allows an author to focus the nearest neighbor search on the target keywords or on their absence.

The filtering operation uses an inverted index of all unigrams in the database after the removal of stop words and word stemming (snowball) using the NLTK library[4]. The resulting index has a dictionary size of 9.61M unigrams and requires $\sim$4

[4]https://www.nltk.org/

GB of memory.

3.2 Embedding-based Ranking

The ranking operation uses the document embeddings of the papers in our database. Given a *ranking source* such as a paragraph or the entire manuscript, "embedding-based ranking" sorts the papers returned by the keyword-based filter according to their cosine distance to the embedding of the ranking source. In other words, embedding-based ranking performs a brute-force nearest neighbor search on a subset of papers. The embedding of the ranking source is computed on demand whenever a search is performed.

As the document embedding model, we use Sent2Vec (Pagliardini et al., 2018) because of its simplicity, speed, and good performance on various benchmark datasets (Pagliardini et al., 2018; Nikolov and Hahnloser, 2019). The model has 400 dimensions and is trained on the PMC-OA corpus using a unigram vocabulary of $\sim$0.75M terms. After the training, we pre-compute the embeddings of all papers in our database and keep them in memory, which requires $\sim$4 GB.

To test the performance of our model, we performed experiments on a simple text retrieval task. The goal of this task was to retrieve the full body of a parent paper given its abstract as the search query. We randomly sampled 10000 abstracts from the database and retrieved the 20 most similar papers for each abstract. As an evaluation metric, we counted the fraction of retrievals in which the parent paper appeared on top or among the top 20 results. Our model retrieved the correct parent paper as the top search result in 83.1% of the trials, compared to 71.0% when using a Sent2Vec model trained on Wikipedia (Pagliardini et al., 2018). Furthermore, the parent paper was among the top 20 retrievals in 95.1% of cases when using our model, compared to 87.0% for the Wikipedia Sent2Vec model. The higher retrieval performance of our model in this task likely arises from its training on a domain-specific corpus that contains rare words and terminologies (Roy et al., 2017; Blagec et al., 2019). This suggests that the model would need to be retrained at regular intervals, particularly when papers from other domains are added to the database.

We have not systematically analyzed the retrieval performance when the query is formed by merely a part of the manuscript such as a block of a few sentences (Gong et al., 2018; De Boom et al., 2015). We leave a detailed exploration of the effects of the query length on performance to future work.

3.3 Scalability of Literature Discovery

Although fast and efficient approximate nearest neighbor methods exist for retrieving the K nearest neighbors of a query vector, such schemes apply to ranking only, but not to the joint filtering and ranking steps (when nearest neighbors are sought among a subset of embeddings from the database). For this reason, in our search engine, there is no simple alternative to brute force search. Nevertheless, we find that retrieval is sufficiently fast, largely because the filtering step reduces the number of neighbors that need to be ranked. In future work, we will explore optimizations of the search engine, such as using approximate hashing techniques (Datar et al., 2004; Norouzi et al., 2012).

4   User Interface and Workflow

The user interface (UI) consists of **(1)** a *text editor* that provides basic functionality for drafting a manuscript, such as loading saving documents, formatting text, and inserting LaTeX equations, code snippets, or bullet points (Figure 3a, left), and **(2)** a *literature explorer* encompassing multiple components, which can be accessed on their respective tabs (Figure 3a, right):

- *Discover* for performing searches and browsing the search results to discover relevant literature

- *My Library* for managing the user bibliography and for citing papers in the manuscript

- *Read* for paper viewing and for actions that facilitate literature exploration, such as discovering similar papers to the one being viewed and highlighting the sentences in the paper that are similar to the selected text in the manuscript (Figure 3b, right)

A search can be initiated without keyword filters by clicking the "Similar papers to the manuscript" button located above the text editor. As a result, the 1000 most similar papers are listed in the *Discover* tab with their metadata (title, authors, journal, publication year, and abstract).

A more granular search can be performed by selecting a section (e.g., sentences, paragraphs) from the manuscript, which reveals a hovering menu over the selected text (visible in Figure 3b). Clicking on the magnifying glass icon on this menu performs a search using the selected text as the ranking source and consequently returns the papers similar to the selected text.

To steer discovery towards a particular set of terms, the user can define a keyword-based Boolean filter using the format `term1 term2|term3 !term4` to confine the results to those papers that contain *term1* and (*term2* or *term3*), but not *term4*.

Clicking on a search result displays the content of the paper in the *Read* tab. In this tab, the user finds additional actions above the viewed paper to interact with it.

If, after viewing the paper, the user finds it interesting, then pressing the "Add to Library" button saves the paper in the user bibliography, which can be viewed under the *My Library* tab. Alternatively, the "Cite" button places a reference to the paper at the current cursor position in the text editor and adds the paper to the user bibliography. Inserted references in the manuscript are links, and clicking on them conveniently opens the respective paper in the *Read* tab. Deleting the link removes the reference from the manuscript.

To facilitate the exploration of the literature further, the *Read* tab contains additional functions: "Discover similar papers" performs a search using the viewed paper as the ranking source. If a filter is already present in the *Discover* tab, then the search results are filtered accordingly. The "Highlight" button highlights the 20 sentences in the viewed paper that are most similar to the ranking source, i.e., similar to the query of the last search performed on the application. Alternatively, the user can select a part of the manuscript and press the marker icon on the revealed hovering menu (Figure 3b) to highlight the sentences that are most similar to the selection. The highlighting feature computes the embedding of each sentence in the viewed paper to assess similarity. The "Find Text" field uses the web-browser's built-in *find* functionality to match the value of the field with the viewed paper.

The *My Library* tab lists all the papers in the user bibliography. Ticking the "Cited content only" box filters this list to show only the papers cited in the manuscript. The user can press the "Cite" button next to a paper to insert a reference to the paper at the cursor position in the text editor. The user can also add papers to the library manually by entering

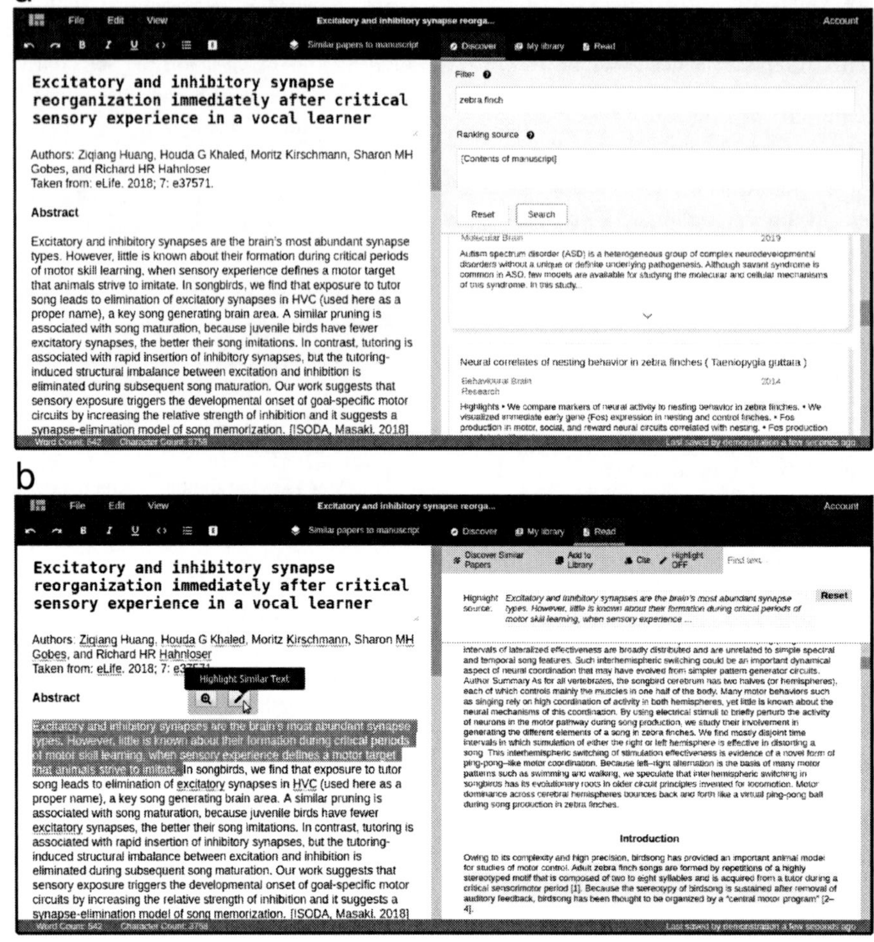

Figure 3: The user interface of the application. a) the *Discover* tab lists the retrieved papers that are similar to the manuscript. b) the *Read* tab allows users to view papers and to highlight the sentences that are similar to the selected text in the manuscript.

the digital object identifier of the paper in the form that appears upon pressing the "Manual entry" button. Items under *My Library* can be removed by clicking on the "Remove" button next to the item.

5   Conclusion

We have described an application that aims to reduce the manual workload involved in exploring the scientific literature. Our application combines the processes of reading papers and of writing scientific manuscripts into a single user interface and links them using NLP algorithms.

In future work, we will focus on expanding the database to include additional domains and article sources. We will work on augmenting the workflow with automated tasks, such as suggesting references as the author writes a manuscript, or notifying users about the latest publications relevant to their work. We will also seek to improve discovery performance by testing more recent text embedding methods (e.g., BERT (Devlin et al., 2018)) and by optimizing the search for different input text lengths, such as a whole document, a paragraph, or even a single sentence.

Finally, we are aware that keyword-based Boolean filtering might be prone to the same biases and challenges inherent in the traditional search queries, as discussed above. We will investigate whether query expansion techniques (Azad and Deepak, 2019) could mitigate this issue by suggesting or automatically appending semantically related keywords to the Boolean filters.

Acknowledgements

We acknowledge support from the Swiss National Science Foundation (grant 31003A_156976). We also thank the anonymous reviewers for their useful comments.

References

Yossi Adi, Einat Kermany, Yonatan Belinkov, Ofer Lavi, and Yoav Goldberg. 2016. Fine-grained analysis of sentence embeddings using auxiliary prediction tasks. arXiv:1608.04207. Version 3.

Kumaripaba Athukorala, Eve Hoggan, Anu Lehtiö, Tuukka Ruotsalo, and Giulio Jacucci. 2013. Information-seeking behaviors of computer scientists: Challenges for electronic literature search tools. In *Proceedings of the American Society for Information Science and Technology*, pages 1–11.

Anne Aula. 2003. Query formulation in web information search. In *Proceedings of the IADIS International Conference on WWW/Internet (ICWI 2003)*, pages 403–410.

Hiteshwar Kumar Azad and Akshay Deepak. 2019. Query expansion techniques for information retrieval: A survey. *Information Processing & Management*, 56(5):1698–1735.

Leif Azzopardi, Paul Thomas, and Nick Craswell. 2018. Measuring the utility of search engine result pages. In *The 41st International ACM SIGIR Conference on Research & Development in Information Retrieval - SIGIR '18*, pages 605–614.

Nicolas J. Belkin. 2000. Helping people find what they don't know. *Communications of the ACM*, 43(8):58–61.

Kathrin Blagec, Hong Xu, Asan Agibetov, and Matthias Samwald. 2019. Neural sentence embedding models for semantic similarity estimation in the biomedical domain. *BMC bioinformatics*, 20(1):178.

Alexis Conneau, German Kruszewski, Guillaume Lample, Loïc Barrault, and Marco Baroni. 2018. What you can cram into a single vector: Probing sentence embeddings for linguistic properties. arXiv:1805.01070. Version 2.

Mayur Datar, Nicole Immorlica, Piotr Indyk, and Vahab S. Mirrokni. 2004. Locality-sensitive hashing scheme based on p-stable distributions. page 253.

Cedric De Boom, Steven Van Canneyt, Steven Bohez, Thomas Demeester, and Bart Dhoedt. 2015. Learning semantic similarity for very short texts. In *2015 IEEE International Conference on Data Mining Workshop (ICDMW)*, pages 1229–1234.

Jacob Devlin, Ming-Wei Chang, Kenton Lee, and Kristina Toutanova. 2018. BERT: Pre-training of deep bidirectional transformers for language understanding. arXiv:1810.04805. Version 2.

Hongyu Gong, Tarek Sakakini, Suma Bhat, and JinJun Xiong. 2018. Document similarity for texts of varying lengths via hidden topics. In *Proceedings of the 56th Annual Meeting of the Association for Computational Linguistics (Volume 1: Long Papers)*, pages 2341–2351.

Jacek Gwizdka. 2010. Distribution of cognitive load in web search. *Journal of the American Society for Information Science and Technology*, 61(11):2167–2187.

John R. Hayes. 2012. Modeling and remodeling writing. *Written Communication*, 29(3):369–388.

Karen E Hodges. 2008. Defining the problem: terminology and progress in ecology. *Frontiers in Ecology and the Environment*, 6(1):35–42.

Jeff Johnson, Matthijs Douze, and Hervé Jégou. 2017. Billion-scale similarity search with GPUs. arXiv:1702.08734. Version 1.

Peder Olesen Larsen and Markus von Ins. 2010. The rate of growth in scientific publication and the decline in coverage provided by science citation index. *Scientometrics*, 84(3):575–603.

Quoc Le and Tomas Mikolov. 2014. Distributed representations of sentences and documents. In *International conference on machine learning*, pages 1188–1196.

Raymond S. Nickerson. 1998. Confirmation bias: A ubiquitous phenomenon in many guises. *Review of General Psychology*, 2(2):175–220.

Nikola I Nikolov and Richard H R Hahnloser. 2019. Large-scale hierarchical alignment for data-driven text rewriting. In *Proceedings of Recent Advances in Natural Language Processing*, pages 844–853.

M. Norouzi, A. Punjani, and D. J. Fleet. 2012. Fast search in hamming space with multi-index hashing. pages 3108–3115.

Matteo Pagliardini, Prakhar Gupta, and Martin Jaggi. 2018. Unsupervised learning of sentence embeddings using compositional n-gram features. In *Proceedings of the 2018 Conference of the North American Chapter of the Association for Computational Linguistics: Human Language Technologies (Volume 1: Long Papers*, pages 528–540.

Diego Rivera, Robert Allkin, Concepción Obón, Francisco Alcaraz, Rob Verpoorte, and Michael Heinrich. 2014. What is in a name? the need for accurate scientific nomenclature for plants. *Journal of Ethnopharmacology*, 152(3):393–402.

Stephen Robertson. 2009. The probabilistic relevance framework: BM25 and beyond. *Foundations and Trends in Information Retrieval*, 3(4):333–389.

Arpita Roy, Youngja Park, and Shimei Pan. 2017. Learning domain-specific word embeddings from sparse cybersecurity texts. arXiv:1709.07470. Version 1.

Jatin Shah, Anand Shah, and Ricardo Pietrobon. 2009. Scientific writing of novice researchers: what difficulties and encouragements do they encounter? *Academic Medicine*, 84(4):511–6.

Xiaojun Wan, Jianwu Yang, and Jianguo Xiao. 2008. Towards a unified approach to document similarity search using manifold-ranking of blocks. *Information Processing & Management*, 44(3):1032–1048.

MMPE: A Multi-Modal Interface Using Handwriting, Touch Reordering, and Speech Commands for Post-Editing Machine Translation

Nico Herbig[1], Santanu Pal[1,2], Tim Düwel[1], Kalliopi Meladaki[1], Mahsa Monshizadeh[2],
Vladislav Hnatovskiy[1], Antonio Krüger[1], Josef van Genabith[1,2]

[1]German Research Center for Artificial Intelligence (DFKI),
Saarland Informatics Campus, Germany
[2]Department of Language Science and Technology,
Saarland University, Germany
{firstname.lastname}@dfki.de
{firstname.lastname}@uni-saarland.de

Abstract

The shift from traditional translation to post-editing (PE) of machine-translated (MT) text can save time and reduce errors, but it also affects the design of translation interfaces, as the task changes from mainly generating text to correcting errors within otherwise helpful translation proposals. Since this paradigm shift offers potential for modalities other than mouse and keyboard, we present MMPE, the first prototype to combine traditional input modes with pen, touch, and speech modalities for PE of MT. Users can directly cross out or hand-write new text, drag and drop words for reordering, or use spoken commands to update the text in place. All text manipulations are logged in an easily interpretable format to simplify subsequent translation process research. The results of an evaluation with professional translators suggest that pen and touch interaction are suitable for deletion and reordering tasks, while speech and multi-modal combinations of select & speech are considered suitable for replacements and insertions. Overall, experiment participants were enthusiastic about the new modalities and saw them as useful extensions to mouse & keyboard, but not as a complete substitute.

1 Introduction & Related Work

As machine translation (MT) has been making substantial improvements in recent years[1], more and more professional translators are integrating this technology into their translation workflows (Zaretskaya et al., 2016; Zaretskaya and Seghiri, 2018). The process of using a pre-translated text as a basis and improving it to create the final translation is called post-editing (PE). While translation memory (TM) is still often valued higher than MT (Moorkens and O'Brien, 2017), a recent study

by Vela et al. (2019) shows that professional translators chose PE of MT over PE of TM and translation from scratch in 80% of the cases. Regarding the time savings achieved through PE, Zampieri and Vela (2014) find that PE was on average 28% faster for technical translations, Toral et al. (2018) report productivity gains of 36% when using modern neural MT, and Aranberri et al. (2014) show that PE increases translation throughput for both professionals and lay users. Furthermore, it has been shown that PE not only leads to reduced time but also reduces errors (Green et al., 2013).

Switching from traditional translation to PE results in major changes in translation workflows (Zaretskaya and Seghiri, 2018), including the interaction pattern (Carl et al., 2010), yielding a significantly reduced amount of mouse and keyboard events (Green et al., 2013). This requires thorough investigation in terms of interface design, since the task changes from mostly text production to comparing and adapting MT and TM proposals, or put differently, from control to supervision.

While most computer-aided translation (CAT) tools focus on traditional translation and incorporate only mouse & keyboard, previous research investigated other input modalities: automatic speech recognition (ASR) for dictating translations has already been explored in the 90s (Dymetman et al., 1994; Brousseau et al., 1995) and the more recent investigation of ASR for PE (Martinez et al., 2014) even argues that a combination with typing could boost productivity. Mesa-Lao (2014) finds that PE trainees have a positive attitude towards speech input and would consider adopting it, and Zapata et al. (2017) found that ASR for PE was faster than ASR for translation from scratch. Due to these benefits, commercial CAT tools like memoQ and MateCat are also beginning to integrate ASR.

The CASMACAT tool (Alabau et al., 2013) allows the user to input text by writing with e-pens in

---

[1]WMT 2019 translation task: http://matrix.statmt.org/, accessed 07. Jan 2020

Proceedings of the 58th Annual Meeting of the Association for Computational Linguistics, pages 327–334
July 5 - July 10, 2020. ©2020 Association for Computational Linguistics

a special area. A vision paper (Alabau and Casacuberta, 2012) proposes to instead use e-pens for PE sentences with few errors in place and provides examples of symbols that could be used for this. Studies on mobile PE via touch and speech (O'Brien et al., 2014; Torres-Hostench et al., 2017) show that participants especially liked reordering words through touch drag and drop, and preferred voice when translating from scratch, but used the iPhone keyboard for small changes. Teixeira et al. (2019) also explore a combination of touch and speech; however, their touch input received poor feedback since (a) their tile view (where each word is a tile that can be dragged around) made reading more complicated, and (b) touch insertions were rather complex to achieve within their implementation. In contrast, dictation functionality was shown to be quite good and even preferred to mouse and keyboard by half of the participants. The results of an elicitation study by Herbig et al. (2019a) indicate that pen, touch, and speech interaction should be combined with mouse and keyboard to improve PE of MT. In contrast, other modalities like eye tracking or gestures were seen as less promising.

This paper presents MMPE, the first translation environment combining standard mouse & keyboard input with touch, pen, and speech interactions for PE of MT. It allows users to directly cross out or hand-write new text, drag and drop words for reordering, or use spoken commands to update the text in place. All text manipulations are logged in an easily interpretable format (e.g., *replaceWord* with the old and new word) to facilitate translation process research. The results of a study with 11 professional translators show that participants are enthusiastic about having these alternatives, and suggest that pen and touch are well suited for deletion and reordering operations, whereas speech and multi-modal interaction are suitable for insertions and replacements.

2 The MMPE Prototype

This section presents the MMPE prototype (see Figure 1), which combines pen, touch, and speech input with a traditional mouse and keyboard approach for PE of MT. The prototype is designed for professional translators in an office setting. A video demonstration is available at `https://youtu.be/tkJ9OWmDd0s`.

2.1 Apparatus

On the software side, we decided to use Angular[2] for the frontend, and node.js[3] for the backend.

The frontend, including all of the newly implemented modalities for text editing, is what the system currently focuses on. While this Angular frontend could be used in a browser on any device, we initially design for the following hardware to optimally support the implemented interactions: we use a large tiltable touch & pen screen (see Figure 1a), namely the Wacom Cintiq Pro 32 inch display. Together with the Flex Arm, this screen can be moved up in the air to work in a standing position, or it can be tilted and moved flat on the table (similar to how users use a tablet), thereby supporting better pen and touch interaction (as requested in Herbig et al. (2019a)). To avoid limitations in ASR through a potentially bad microphone, we further use the Sennheiser PC 8 Headset for speech input. Last, mouse and keyboard are provided.

Since it is not the focus of this work, the backend is kept rather minimal: it allows saving and loading of projects (including the MT) from JSON files, can store log files, etc. Here, the project files simply contain an array of segments with source, target, as well as any MT or TM proposal that should initially be shown for PE.

2.2 Overall Layout

Figure 1d shows our implemented horizontal source-target layout, where each segment's status (unedited, edited, confirmed) is visualized between source and target. On the far right, support tools are offered as requested in Herbig et al. (2019a): (1) the unedited MT output, to which the user can revert his editing using a button, and (2) a corpus combined with a dictionary: when entering a word or clicking/touching a word in the source view on the left, the Linguee[4] website is queried to show the word in context and display its primary and alternative translations. The top of the interface shows a toolbar where users can enable or disable speech recognition as well as spell checking, save and load projects, or navigate to another project.

The current segment is enlarged, thereby offering space for handwritten input and allowing the user to view a lot of context while still seeing the current segment in a comfortable manner (Herbig

---

[2]https://angular.io/, accessed 07. Jan 2020
[3]https://nodejs.org/en/, accessed 07. Jan 2020
[4]https://www.linguee.com/, accessed 07. Jan 2020

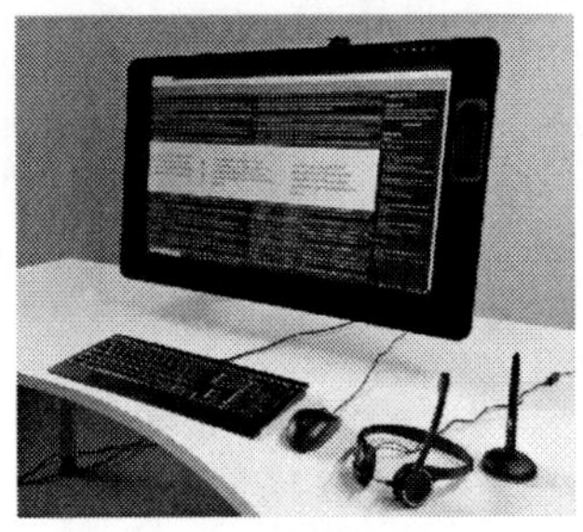

(a) Apparatus.

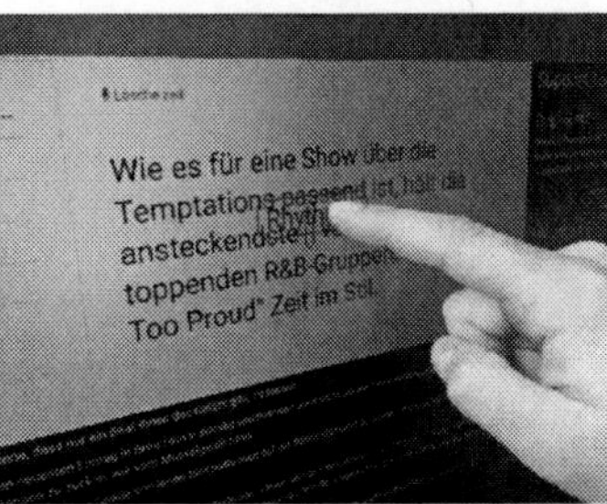

(b) Handwriting on left target view.

(c) Touch reordering on right target view.

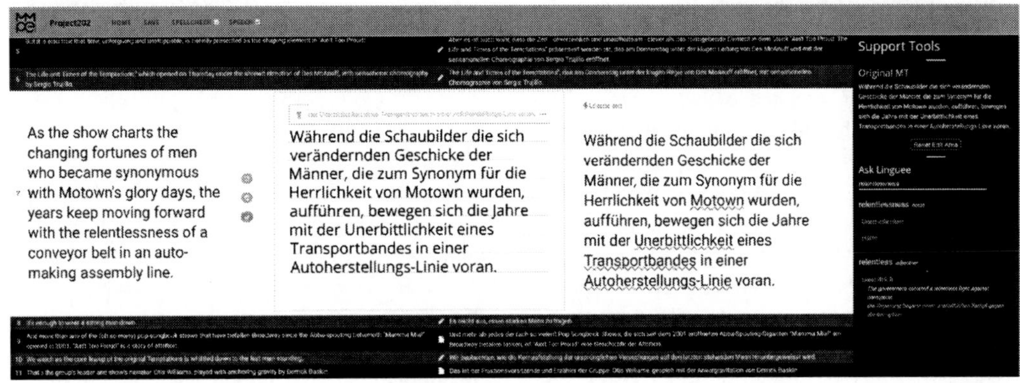

(d) Screenshot of the interface.

Figure 1: Overview of the MMPE prototype.

et al. (2019a)). The view for the current segment is further divided into the source segment (left) and two editing planes for the target, one for handwriting and drawing gestures (middle), and one for touch deletion & reordering, as well as standard mouse and keyboard input (right). Both initially show the MT proposal, and synchronize on changes to either one. The reason for having two editing fields instead of only one is that some interactions are overloaded, e.g., a touch drag can be interpreted as both hand-writing (middle) and reordering (right). Undo and redo functionality for all modalities, as well as confirming segments, are also implemented through buttons between the source and target texts, and can further be triggered through hotkeys. The target text is spell-checked, as a lack of this feature was criticized in Teixeira et al. (2019).

2.3 Left Target View: Handwriting

For handwriting recognition (see Figure 1b), we use the MyScript Interactive Ink SDK[5]. Apart from merely recognizing the written input, it offers gestures[6] like strike-through or scribble for deletions, breaking a word into two (draw line from top to bottom), and joining words (draw line from bottom to top). For inserting words, one can directly write into empty space, or create such space first by breaking the line (draw a long line from top to bottom), and hand-writing the word then. All changes are immediately interpreted, i.e., striking through a word deletes it immediately instead of showing it in a struck-through visualization. While it is not necessary to convert text from the handwritten appearance into computer font, the user can do so using a small button at the top of the editor. The editor further shows the recognized handwritten text immediately at the very top of the drawing view in a small gray font, where alternatives for the current recognition are offered when clicking on a recognized word. Since all changes from this drawing view are immediately synchronized into the right-hand view, the user can also see the recognized text there. Apart from using the pen, the user can use his/her finger or the mouse on the left-hand editing view for hand-writing.

---

[5]https://developer.myscript.com/, accessed 07. Jan 2020

[6]https://developer.myscript.com/docs/concepts/editing-gestures/, accessed 07. Jan 2020

2.4 Right Target View: Touch Reordering, Mouse & Keyboard

On the right-hand editing view, the user can delete words by simply double-tapping them with pen/finger touch, or reorder them through a simple drag and drop procedure (see Figure 1c). This procedure visualizes the picked-up word as well as the current drop position through a placeholder element. Spaces between words and punctuation marks are automatically fixed, i.e., double spaces at the pickup position and missing spaces at the drop position are corrected. This reordering functionality is strongly related to Teixeira et al. (2019); however, only the currently dragged word is temporarily visualized as a tile to offer better readability. Furthermore, the cursor can be placed between words using a single tap, allowing the user to combine touch input with e.g., the speech or keyboard modalities (see below). Naturally, the user can also edit and navigate using mouse and keyboard, where all common shortcuts work as expected from other software (e.g., ctrl+arrow keys or ctrl+c).

2.5 Speech Input

To minimize lag during speech recognition, we use a streaming approach, sending the recorded audio to IBM Watson servers to receive a transcription, which is then interpreted in a command-based fashion. Thus, our speech module not only handles dictations as in Teixeira et al. (2019) but can correct mistakes in place.

The transcription itself is visualized at the top of the right target view (see Figure 1c). As commands, the user has the option to *"insert"*, *"delete"*, *"replace"*, and *"reorder"* words or subphrases. To specify the position if it is ambiguous, one can define anchors as in *"after"*/*"before"*/*"between"*, or define the occurrence of the token (*"first"*/*"second"*/*"last"*). A full example is *"insert A after second B"*, where A and B can be words or subphrases. In contrast to the other modalities, character-level commands are not supported, so instead of deleting an ending, one should replace the word. Again, spaces between words and punctuation marks are automatically fixed upon changes. For the German language, nouns are automatically capitalized using the list of nouns from Wiktionary[7].

2.6 Multi-modal Combinations

Last, the user can use a multi-modal combination, i.e., pen/touch/mouse combined with speech. For this, a target word/position first needs to be specified by placing the cursor on or next to a word using the pen, finger touch, or the mouse/keyboard; alternatively, the word can be long-pressed with pen/touch. Afterwards, the user can use a voice command like *"delete"*, *"insert A"*, *"move after/before A/between A and B"*, or *"replace by A"* without needing to specify the position/word, thereby making the commands less complex.

2.7 Logging

We implemented extensive logging functionality: on the one hand, we log the concrete keystrokes, touched pixel coordinates, etc.; on the other hand, all UI interactions (like *segmentChange* or *undo/redo/confirm*) are stored, allowing us to analyze the translator's use of MMPE.

Most importantly, however, we also log all text manipulations on a higher level to simplify text editing analysis: for *insertions*, we log whether a single or multiple words were inserted, and add the actual words and their positions as well as the segment's content before and after the insertion to the log entry. *Deletions* are logged analogously, and for *reorderings*, we add the old and the new position of the moved words to the log entry. Last, for *replacements*, we log whether only a part of a word was replaced (i.e., changing the word form), whether the whole word was replaced (i.e., correcting the lexical choice), or whether a group of words was replaced. In all cases, the words before and after the change, as well as their positions and the overall segment text are specified in the log entry.

Furthermore, all log entries contain the modality that was used for the interaction, e.g., Speech or Pen, thereby allowing the analysis of which modality was used for which editing operation. All log entries with their timestamps are created within the Angular client and sent to the node.js server for storage in a JSON file.

3 Evaluation

We evaluated the prototype with 11 professional translators[8]. Since our participants were German

---

[8]The study has been approved by the university's ethical review board, and participants were paid for their time. The data and analysis scripts can be found at `https://mmpe.dfki.de/data/ACL2020/`.

[7]https://en.wiktionary.org/wiki/Category:German_noun_forms, accessed 07. Jan 2020

natives, we chose a EN-DE translation task to avoid ASR recognition errors occurring in non-native commands (Dragsted et al., 2011). In the following, "modalities" refers to Touch (T), Pen (P), Speech (S), Mouse & Keyboard (MK), and Multi-Modal combinations (MM, see Section 2.6), while "operations" refers to Insertions, Deletions, Replacements, and Reorderings. More details on the evaluation are presented in Herbig et al. (2020).

3.1 Method

The study took approximately 2 hours per participant and involved three separate stages. First, participants filled in a questionnaire capturing demographics as well as information on CAT usage. In stage two, participants received an explanation of all of the prototype's features and then had 10–15 minutes to explore the prototype on their own and become familiar with the interface. Finally, stage three included the main experiment, which is a guided test of all implemented features combined with Likert scales and interviews, as described in detail below.

The main part tests each of the 5 modalities for each of our 4 operations in a structured way. For this, we prepared four sentences for each operation by manually introducing errors into the reference sentences from the WMT news test set 2018. Thus, overall each participant had to correct 4 segments per operation (4) using each modality (5), which results in $4 \times 4 \times 5 = 80$ segments. Within the four sentences per operation, we tried to capture slightly different cases, like deleting single words or a group of words. The prototype was adapted for this controlled task such that it displays a popup when selecting a segment, visualizing the necessary correction to apply as well as the modality to use. The reason why we provided the correction to apply was to ensure a consistent editing behavior across all participants, thereby making the following measurements comparable: each modality had to be rated for each operation on 7-point Likert scales assessing whether the modality is a good fit, whether it is easy to use, and whether it is a good alternative to MK. Furthermore, participants had to order the modalities from best to worst for each operation. Last, we captured their comments in an interview after each operation and measured the times required to fix the introduced errors. In the end, a final unstructured interview to capture high-level feedback on the interface was conducted.

3.2 Results & Discussion

Figure 2 depicts the results of the 3 Likert scales of the 5 modalities for the 4 tasks. The participants' orderings of modalities for the operations were mostly in line with these ratings, as we will discuss in the next sections.

According to subjective ratings, modality ordering, and comments, *P(en)* is among the best modalities for deletions and reordering. However, other modalities are superior for insertions and replacements, where P was seen as suitable only for short modifications, and to be avoided for more extended changes. In terms of timings, P was also among the fastest for deletions and reorderings, and among the slowest for insertions. What is interesting, however, is that P was significantly faster than S and MM for replacements (by 6 and 7 seconds on average) even though it was rated lower. Participants also commented very enthusiastically about pen reordering and deletions, as they would nicely resemble manual copy-editing. The main concern for hand-writing was the need to think about and to create space before actually writing.

Results for *T(ouch)* were similarly good for deletions and reorderings, but it was considered worse for insertions and replacements. Furthermore, and as we expected due to its precision, pen was preferred to finger touch by most participants. However, in terms of timings, the two did not differ significantly, apart from replace operations (where pen was faster). Even for replacements, where T was rated as the worst modality, it actually was (non-significantly) faster than S and MM.

S(peech) and *M(ulti)-M(odal)* PE were considered the worst and were also the slowest modalities for reordering and deletions. For insertions and replacements, however, these two modalities were rated and ordered 2nd (after MK) and in particular much better than P and T. Timing analysis agrees for insertions, being 2nd after MK; for replacements, however, S and MM were the slowest even though the ratings put them ahead of P and T. Insertions are the only operation where MM was (non-significantly) faster than S, since the position did not have to be verbally specified. Even though participants were concerned regarding formulating commands while mentally processing text, they considered S and MM especially interesting for adding longer text. The main advantage of MM would be that one has to speak less, albeit at the cost of doing two things at once.

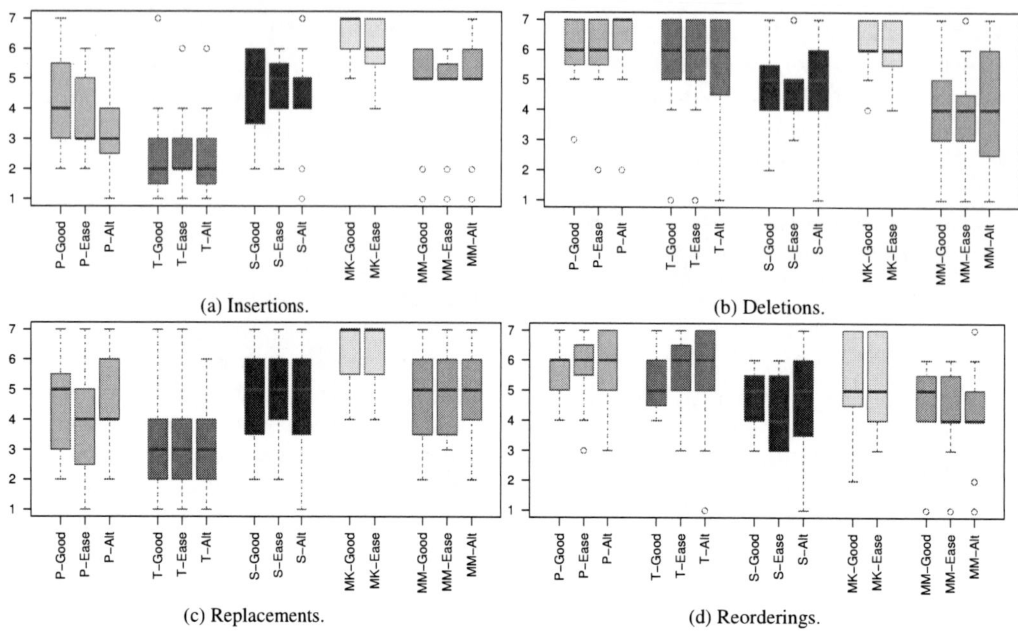

Figure 2: Subjective ratings of the five modalities for the four operations on the 7-point Likert scales for goodness, ease of use, and whether it is a good alternative to MK.

M(ouse) & K(eyboard) received the best scores for insertions and replacements, where it was also the fastest. Furthermore, it got good ratings for deletions and reorderings. For deletions, MK was comparably fast to P, T, and S. For reordering, however, it was slower than P and T. Some participants commented negatively on MK, stating that it only works well because of "years of expertise", and being "unintuitive" especially for reordering.

Overall, many participants provided very positive feedback on this first prototype combining pen, touch, speech, and multi-modal combinations for PE MT, encouraging us to continue. They especially highlighted that it was nice to have the option to switch between modalities. Furthermore, several promising ideas for improving the prototype were proposed, e.g., to visualize whitespaces.

4 Conclusion

While more and more professional translators are switching to the use of PE to increase productivity and reduce errors, current CAT interfaces still heavily focus on traditional mouse and keyboard input. This paper therefore presents MMPE, a CAT prototype combining pen, touch, speech, and multi-modal interaction together with common mouse and keyboard input possibilities. Users can directly cross out or hand-write new text, drag and drop words for reordering, or use spoken commands to update the text in place. Our study with professional translators shows a high level of interest and enthusiasm about using these new modalities. For deletions and reorderings, pen and touch both received high subjective ratings, with pen being even better than mouse & keyboard. For insertions and replacements, speech and multi-modal interaction were seen as suitable interaction modes; however, mouse & keyboard were still favored and faster.

As a next step, we will improve the prototype based on the participants' valuable feedback. Furthermore, an eye tracker will be integrated into the prototype that can be used in combination with speech for cursor placement, thereby simplifying multi-modal PE. Last, we will investigate whether using the different modalities has an impact on cognitive load during PE (Herbig et al., 2019b).

Acknowledgments

This research was funded in part by the German Research Foundation (DFG) under grant number GE 2819/2-1 (project MMPE). We thank AMPLEXOR (https://www.amplexor.com) for their excellent support in providing access to professional human translators for our experiments.

References

Vicent Alabau, Ragnar Bonk, Christian Buck, Michael Carl, Francisco Casacuberta, Mercedes García-Martínez, Jesús González, Philipp Koehn, Luis Leiva, Bartolomé Mesa-Lao, et al. 2013. CASMACAT: An open source workbench for advanced computer aided translation. *The Prague Bulletin of Mathematical Linguistics*, 100:101–112.

Vicent Alabau and Francisco Casacuberta. 2012. Study of electronic pen commands for interactive-predictive machine translation. In *Proceedings of the International Workshop on Expertise in Translation and Post-Editing – Research and Application, Copenhagen, Denmark*, pages 17–18.

Nora Aranberri, Gorka Labaka, A Diaz de Ilarraza, and Kepa Sarasola. 2014. Comparison of post-editing productivity between professional translators and lay users. In *Proceeding of AMTA Third Workshop on Post-editing Technology and Practice*, pages 20–33.

Julie Brousseau, Caroline Drouin, George Foster, Pierre Isabelle, Roland Kuhn, Yves Normandin, and Pierre Plamondon. 1995. French speech recognition in an automatic dictation system for translators: The TransTalk project. In *Proceedings of Eurospeech Fourth European Conference on Speech Communication and Technology*, pages 193–196.

Michael Carl, Martin Jensen, and Kay Kristian. 2010. Long distance revisions in drafting and post-editing. *CICLing Special Issue on Natural Language Processing and its Applications*, pages 193–204.

Barbara Dragsted, Inger Margrethe Mees, and Inge Gorm Hansen. 2011. Speaking your translation: Students' first encounter with speech recognition technology. *Translation & Interpreting*, 3(1):10–43.

Marc Dymetman, Julie Brousseau, George Foster, Pierre Isabelle, Yves Normandin, and Pierre Plamondon. 1994. Towards an automatic dictation system for translators: The TransTalk project. In *Proceedings of the ICSLP International Conference on Spoken Language Processing*.

Spence Green, Jeffrey Heer, and Christopher D Manning. 2013. The efficacy of human post-editing for language translation. In *Proceedings of the SIGCHI Conference on Human Factors in Computing Systems*, pages 439–448. ACM.

Nico Herbig, Tim Düwel, Santanu Pal, Kalliopi Meladaki, Mahsa Monshizadeh, Antonio Krüger, and Josef van Genabith. 2020. MMPE: A multimodal interface for post-editing machine translation. In *Proceedings of the 58th Annual Meeting of the Association for Computational Linguistics*. Association for Computational Linguistics.

Nico Herbig, Santanu Pal, Josef van Genabith, and Antonio Krüger. 2019a. Multi-modal approaches for post-editing machine translation. In *Proceedings of the 2019 CHI Conference on Human Factors in Computing Systems*, page 231. ACM.

Nico Herbig, Santanu Pal, Mihaela Vela, Antonio Krüger, and Josef Genabith. 2019b. Multi-modal indicators for estimating perceived cognitive load in post-editing of machine translation. *Machine Translation*, 33(1-2):91–115.

Mercedes Garcia Martinez, Karan Singla, Aniruddha Tammewar, Bartolomé Mesa-Lao, Ankita Thakur, MA Anusuya, Banglore Srinivas, and Michael Carl. 2014. SEECAT: ASR & eye-tracking enabled computer assisted translation. In *The 17th Annual Conference of the European Association for Machine Translation*, pages 81–88. European Association for Machine Translation.

Bartolomé Mesa-Lao. 2014. Speech-enabled computer-aided translation: A satisfaction survey with post-editor trainees. In *Proceedings of the EACL 2014 Workshop on Humans and Computer-assisted Translation*, pages 99–103.

Joss Moorkens and Sharon O'Brien. 2017. Assessing user interface needs of post-editors of machine translation. In *Human Issues in Translation Technology*, pages 127–148. Routledge.

Sharon O'Brien, Joss Moorkens, and Joris Vreeke. 2014. Kanjingo – a mobile app for post-editing. In *Proceedings of the 17th Annual Conference of the European Association for Machine Translation*.

Carlos S.C. Teixeira, Joss Moorkens, Daniel Turner, Joris Vreeke, and Andy Way. 2019. Creating a multimodal translation tool and testing machine translation integration using touch and voice. *Informatics*, 6.

Antonio Toral, Martijn Wieling, and Andy Way. 2018. Post-editing effort of a novel with statistical and neural machine translation. *Frontiers in Digital Humanities*, 5:9.

Olga Torres-Hostench, Joss Moorkens, Sharon O'Brien, Joris Vreeke, et al. 2017. Testing interaction with a mobile MT post-editing app. *Translation & Interpreting*, 9(2):138.

Mihaela Vela, Santanu Pal, Marcos Zampieri, Sudip Kumar Naskar, and Josef van Genabith. 2019. Improving CAT tools in the translation workflow: New approaches and evaluation. In *Proceedings of Machine Translation Summit XVII Volume 2: Translator, Project and User Tracks*, pages 8–15.

Marcos Zampieri and Mihaela Vela. 2014. Quantifying the influence of MT output in the translators' performance: A case study in technical translation. In *Proceedings of the EACL 2014 Workshop on Humans and Computer-assisted Translation*, pages 93–98.

Julián Zapata, Sheila Castilho, and Joss Moorkens. 2017. Translation dictation vs. post-editing with cloud-based voice recognition: A pilot experiment. *Proceedings of MT Summit XVI*, 2.

Anna Zaretskaya and Míriam Seghiri. 2018. *User Perspective on Translation Tools: Findings of a User Survey*. Ph.D. thesis, University of Malaga.

Anna Zaretskaya, Mihaela Vela, Gloria Corpas Pastor, and Miriam Seghiri. 2016. Comparing post-editing difficulty of different machine translation errors in Spanish and German translations from English. *International Journal of Language and Linguistics*, 3(3):91–100.

Torch-Struct:
Deep Structured Prediction Library

Alexander M. Rush
Cornell Tech
Department of Computer Science
`arush@cornell.edu`

Abstract

The literature on structured prediction for NLP describes a rich collection of distributions and algorithms over sequences, segmentations, alignments, and trees; however, these algorithms are difficult to utilize in deep learning frameworks. We introduce Torch-Struct, a library for structured prediction designed to take advantage of and integrate with vectorized, auto-differentiation based frameworks. Torch-Struct includes a broad collection of probabilistic structures accessed through a simple and flexible distribution-based API that connects to any deep learning model. The library utilizes batched, vectorized operations and exploits auto-differentiation to produce readable, fast, and testable code. Internally, we also include a number of general-purpose optimizations to provide cross-algorithm efficiency. Experiments show significant performance gains over fast baselines. Case studies demonstrate the benefits of the library. Torch-Struct is available at `https://github.com/harvardnlp/pytorch-struct`.

1 Introduction

Structured prediction is an area of machine learning focusing on representations of spaces with combinatorial structure, as well as algorithms for inference and parameter estimation over these structures. Core methods include both tractable exact approaches like dynamic programming and spanning tree algorithms as well as heuristic techniques such linear programming relaxations and greedy search.

Structured prediction has played a key role in the history of natural language processing. Example methods include techniques for sequence labeling and segmentation (Lafferty et al., 2001; Sarawagi and Cohen, 2005), discriminative dependency and constituency parsing (Finkel et al., 2008; McDonald et al., 2005), unsupervised learning for

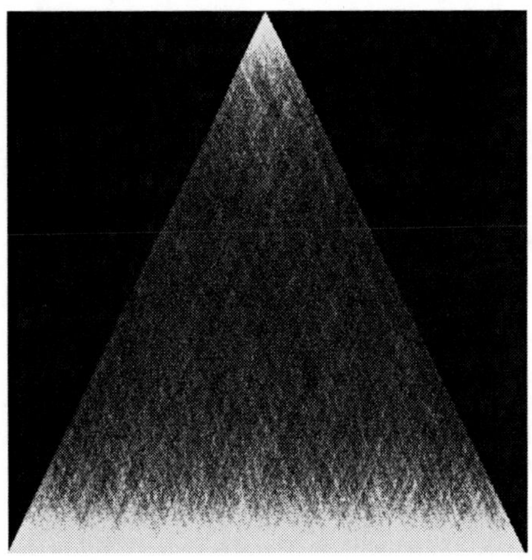

Figure 1: Distribution of binary trees over an 1000-token sequence. Coloring shows the marginal probabilities of every span. Torch-Struct is an optimized collection of common CRF distributions used in NLP that is designed to integrate with deep learning frameworks.

labeling and alignment (Vogel et al., 1996; Goldwater and Griffiths, 2007), approximate translation decoding with beam search (Tillmann and Ney, 2003), among many others.

In recent years, research into deep structured prediction has studied how these approaches can be integrated with neural networks and pretrained models. One line of work has utilized structured prediction as the final layer for deep models (Collobert et al., 2011; Durrett and Klein, 2015). Another has incorporated structured prediction within deep learning models, exploring novel models for latent-structure learning, unsupervised learning, or model control (Johnson et al., 2016; Yogatama et al., 2016; Wiseman et al., 2018). We aspire to make both of these use-cases as easy to use as standard neural networks.

The practical challenge of employing structured

Proceedings of the 58th Annual Meeting of the Association for Computational Linguistics, pages 335–342
July 5 - July 10, 2020. ©2020 Association for Computational Linguistics

Name	Structure ($\mathcal{Z}$)	Parts ($\mathcal{P}$)	Algorithm ($A(\ell)$)	LoC	T/S	Sample Reference
Linear-Chain, HMM	Labeled Chain	Edges (NC^2)	Forward-Backward	20	390k	(Lafferty et al., 2001)
Factorial-HMM	Labeled Chains	Trans. (LC^2) Obs. (NC^L)	Factorial F-B	20	25k	(Ghahramani and Jordan, 1996)
Alignment	Alignment	Match (NM) Skips ($2NM$)	DTW, CTC	50	13k	(Needleman and Wunsch, 1970)
Semi-Markov	Seg. Labels	Edge(NKC^2)	Segmental F-B	30	87k	(Baum and Petrie, 1966) (Sarawagi and Cohen, 2005)
Context-Free	Labeled Tree	CF Rules (G) Term. (CN)	I-O CKY	70	37k	(Kasami, 1966)
Simple CKY	Labeled Tree	Splits (CN^2)	0-th order CKY	30	118k	(Kasami, 1966)
Dependency	Proj. Tree	Arcs (N^2)	Eisner Alg	40	28k	(Eisner, 2000)
Dep (NP)	Non-Proj. Tree	Arcs (N^2)	Matrix-Tree Chiu-Liu (MAP)	40	1.1m	(Koo et al., 2007) (McDonald et al., 2005)
Auto-Regressive	Sequence	Prefix (C^N)	Greedy Search, Beam Search	60	-	(Tillmann and Ney, 2003)

Table 1: Models and algorithms implemented in Torch-Struct. Notation is developed in Section 5. *Parts* are described in terms of sequence lengths N, M, label size C, segment length K, and layers / grammar size L, G. Lines of code (*LoC*) is from the log-partition ($A(\ell)$) implementation. *T/S* is the tokens per second of a batched computation, computed with batch 32, $N = 25, C = 20, K = 5, L = 3$ (K80 GPU run on Google Colab).

prediction is that many required algorithms are difficult to implement efficiently and correctly. Most projects reimplement custom versions of standard algorithms or focus particularly on a single well-defined model class. This research style makes it difficult to combine and try out new approaches, a problem that has compounded with the complexity of research in deep structured prediction.

With this challenge in mind, we introduce Torch-Struct with three specific contributions:

- *Modularity*: models are represented as distributions with a standard flexible API integrated into a deep learning framework.

- *Completeness*: a broad array of classical algorithms are implemented and new models can easily be added.

- *Efficiency*: implementations target computational/memory efficiency for GPUs and the backend includes extensions for optimization.

In this system description, we first motivate the approach taken by the library, then present a technical description of the methods used, and finally present several example use cases.

2 Related Work

Several software libraries target structured prediction. Optimization tools, such as SVM-struct (Joachims, 2008), focus on parameter estimation. Model libraries, such as CRFSuite (Okazaki, 2007), CRF++ (Kudo, 2005), or NCRF++(Yang and Zhang, 2018), implement inference for a fixed set of popular models, usually linear-chain CRFs. General-purpose inference libraries, such as PyStruct (Müller and Behnke, 2014) or TurboParser (Martins et al., 2010), utilize external solvers for (primarily MAP) inference such as integer linear programming solvers and ADMM. Probabilistic programming languages, for example languages that integrate with deep learning such as Pyro (Bingham et al., 2019), allow for specification and inference over some discrete domains. Most ambitiously, inference libraries such as Dyna (Eisner et al., 2004) allow for declarative specifications of dynamic programming algorithms to support inference for generic algorithms. Torch-Struct takes a different approach and integrates a library of optimized structured distributions into a vectorized deep learning system. We begin by motivating this approach with a case study.

3 Motivating Case Study

While structured prediction is traditionally presented at the output layer, recent applications have deployed structured models broadly within neural networks (Johnson et al., 2016; Kim et al., 2017; Yogatama et al., 2016, inter alia). Torch-Struct aims to encourage this general use case.

To illustrate, we consider a latent tree model. ListOps (Nangia and Bowman, 2018) is a dataset of mathematical functions. Each input/output pair consists of a prefix expression x and its result y, e.g.

$$x = [\,\text{MAX}\ 2\ 9\ [\,\text{MIN}\ 4\ 7\,]\ 0\,]\ \ y = 9$$

Models such as a flat RNN will fail to capture the hierarchical structure of this task. However, if a model can induce an explicit latent z, the parse tree of the expression, then the task is easy to learn by a tree-RNN model $p(y|x, z)$ (Yogatama et al., 2016; Havrylov et al., 2019).

Let us briefly summarize a latent-tree RL model for this task. The objective is to maximize the probability of the correct prediction under the expectation of a prior tree model, $p(z|x; \phi)$,

$$Obj = \mathbb{E}_{z \sim p(z|x;\phi)}[\log p(y \mid z, x)]$$

Computing the expectation is intractable so policy gradient is used. First a tree is sampled $\tilde{z} \sim p(z|x; \phi)$, then the gradient with respect to ϕ is approximated as,

$$\frac{\partial}{\partial \phi} Obj \approx (\log p(y \mid \tilde{z}, x) - b)(\frac{\partial}{\partial \phi} p(z|x; \phi))$$

where b is a variance reduction baseline. A common choice is the self-critical baseline (Rennie et al., 2017),

$$b = \log p(y \mid z^*, x) \text{ with } z^* = \arg\max_z p(z|x; \phi)$$

Finally an entropy regularization term is added to the objective encourage exploration of different trees, $Obj + \lambda \mathbb{H}(p(z \mid x; \phi))$.

Even in this brief overview, we can see how complex a latent structured learning problem can be. To compute these terms, we need 5 different properties of the structured prior model $p(z \mid x; \phi)$:

Sampling Policy gradient, $\tilde{z} \sim p(z \mid x; \phi)$

Density Score policy samples, $p(z \mid x; \phi)$

Gradient Backpropagation, $\frac{\partial}{\partial \phi} p(z \mid x; \phi)$

Argmax Self-critical, $\arg\max_z p(z \mid x; \phi)$

Entropy Objective regularizer, $\mathbb{H}(p(z \mid x; \phi))$

For structured models, each of these terms is non-trivial to compute. A goal of Torch-Struct is to make it seamless to deploy structured models for these complex settings.

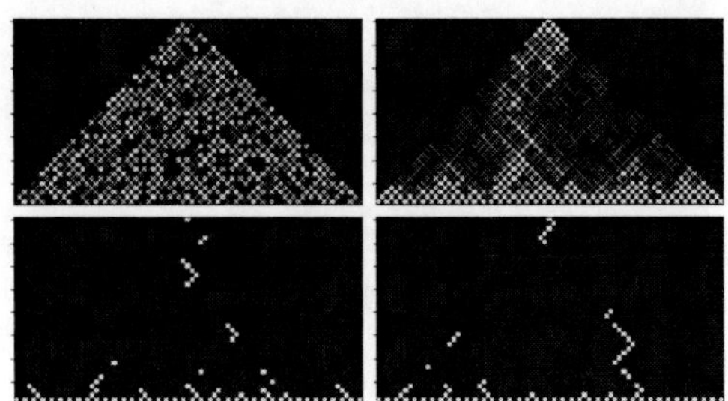

Figure 2: Latent Tree CRF example where each cell represents a span (i, j). Torch-Struct can be used to compute many different properties of a structured distribution. (a) Log-potentials ℓ for each part/span. (b) Marginals for $\text{CRF}(\ell)$ computed by backpropagation. (c) A single argmax tree $\arg\max_z \text{CRF}(z; \ell)$. (d) A single sampled tree $z \sim \text{CRF}(\ell)$.

4 Library Design

The library design of Torch-Struct follows the distributions API used by both TensorFlow and Py-Torch (Dillon et al., 2017). For each structured model in the library, we define a conditional random field (CRF) distribution object. From a user's standpoint, this object provides all necessary distributional properties. Given log-potentials ℓ output from a deep network, the user can request samples $z \sim \text{CRF}(\ell)$, probabilities $\text{CRF}(z; \ell)$, modes $\arg\max_z \text{CRF}(\ell)$, or other distributional properties such as $\mathbb{H}(\text{CRF}(\ell))$. The library is agnostic to how these are utilized, and when possible, they allow for backpropagation to update the input network. The same distributional object can be used for standard output prediction as for more complex operations like attention or reinforcement learning.

Figure 2 demonstrates this API for a binary tree CRF over an ordered sequence, such as $p(z \mid x; \phi)$ from the previous section. The distribution takes in log-potentials ℓ which score each possible span in the input. The distribution converts these to probabilities of a specific tree. This distribution can be queried for predicting over the set of trees, sampling a tree for model structure, or even computing entropy over all trees.

Table 1 shows all of the structures and distributions implemented in Torch-Struct. While each is internally implemented using different specialized algorithms and optimizations, from the user's perspective they all utilize the same external distributional API, and pass a generic set of distributional tests.[1] This approach hides the internal complexity

---

[1]The test suite for each distribution enumerates over all

of the inference procedure, while giving the user full access to the model.

5 Technical Approach

5.1 Conditional Random Fields

We now describe the technical approach underlying the library. To establish notation, first consider the implementation of a softmax categorical distribution, $\mathrm{CAT}(\ell)$, with one-hot categories z with $z_i = 1$ from a set $\mathcal{Z}$ and probabilities given by the softmax over logits ℓ,

$$\mathrm{CAT}(z; \ell) = \frac{\exp(z \cdot \ell)}{\sum_{z' \in \mathcal{Z}} \exp(z' \cdot \ell)} = \frac{\exp \ell_i}{\sum_{j=1}^{K} \exp \ell_j}$$

Define the log-partition as $A(\ell) = \mathrm{LSE}(\ell)$, i.e. log of the denominator, where LSE is the log-sum-exp operator. Computing probabilities or sampling from this distribution, requires enumerating $\mathcal{Z}$ to compute the log-partition A. A useful identity is that derivatives of A yield category probabilities,

$$p(z_i = 1) = \frac{\exp \ell_i}{\sum_{j=1}^{n} \exp \ell_j} = \frac{\partial}{\partial \ell_i} A(\ell)$$

Other distributional properties can be similarly extracted from variants of the log-partition. For instance, define $A^*(\ell) = \log \max_{j=1}^{K} \exp \ell_j$ then[2]: $\mathbb{I}(z_i^* = 1) = \frac{\partial}{\partial \ell_i} A^*(\ell)$.

Conditional random fields, $\mathrm{CRF}(\ell)$, extend the softmax to combinatorial spaces where $\mathcal{Z}$ is exponentially sized. Each z, is now represented as a binary vector over polynomial-sized set of *parts*, $\mathcal{P}$, i.e. $\mathcal{Z} \subset \{0,1\}^{|\mathcal{P}|}$. Similarly log-potentials are now defined over parts $\ell \in \mathbb{R}^{|\mathcal{P}|}$. For instance, in Figure 2 each span is a part and the ℓ vector is shown in the top-left figure. Define the probability of a structure z as,

$$\mathrm{CRF}(z; \ell) = \frac{\exp z \cdot \ell}{\sum_{z'} \exp z' \cdot \ell} = \frac{\exp \sum_p \ell_p z_p}{\sum_{z'} \exp \sum_p \ell_p z_p'}$$

Computing probabilities or sampling from this distribution, requires computing the log-partition term A. In general, computing this term is now intractable, however for many core algorithms in NLP there are exist efficient combinatorial algorithms for this term (a list of examples is given in Table 1).

---

structures to ensure that properties hold. While this is intractable for large spaces, it can be done for small sets and was extremely useful for development.

[2]This is a subgradient identity, but that deep learning libraries like PyTorch generally default to this value.

Name	Ops ($\oplus, \otimes$)	Backprop	Gradients
Log	LSE, $+$	Δ	$p(z_p = 1)$
Max	max, $+$	Δ	$\arg\max_z$
K-Max	$k\max, +$	Δ	K-Argmax
Sample	LSE, $+$	$\sim$	$z \sim \mathrm{CRF}(\ell)$
K-Sample	LSE, $+$	$\sim$	K-Samples
Count	$\sum, \times$		
Entropy ($\mathbb{H}$)	See (Li and Eisner, 2009)		
Exp.	See (Li and Eisner, 2009)		
Sparsemax	See (Mensch and Blondel, 2018)		

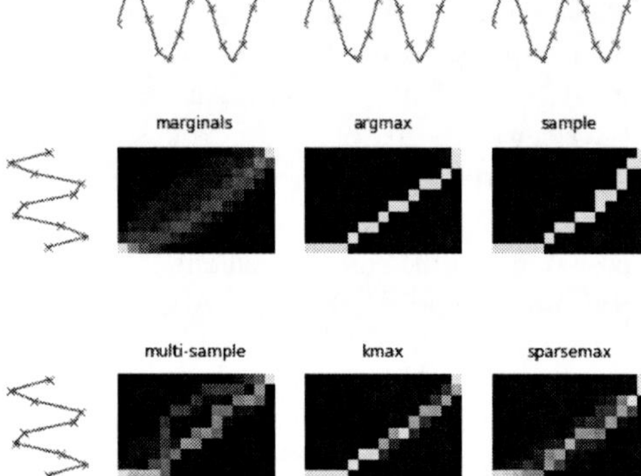

Table 2: (Top) Semirings implemented in Torch-Struct. *Backprop/Gradients* gives overridden backpropagation computation and value computed by this combination. (Bot) Example of gradients from different semirings on sequence alignment with dynamic time warping.

Derivatives of the log-partition again provide useful distributional properties. For instance, the marginal probabilities of parts are given by,

$$p(z_p = 1) = \frac{\exp \sum_{z:z_p=1} z \cdot \ell}{\sum_{z'} \exp z' \cdot \ell} = \frac{\partial}{\partial \ell_p} A(\ell)$$

Similarly derivatives of A^* correspond to whether a part appears in the argmax structure, $\mathbb{I}(z_p^* = 1) = \frac{\partial}{\partial \ell_p} A^*(\ell)$.

While these gradient identities are well-known (Eisner, 2016), they are not commonly deployed in practice. Computing CRF properties is typically done through two-step specialized algorithms, such as forward-backward, inside-outside, or similar variants such as viterbi-backpointers (Jurafsky and Martin, 2014). Common wisdom is that these approaches are more efficient implementations.

However, we observe that recent engineering of faster gradient computation for deep learning has made gradient-based calculations competitive with hand-written calculations. In our experiments, we found that using these identities with autodifferentiation was often faster, and much simpler, than custom two-pass approaches. Torch-Struct is thus designed around using gradients for distributional computations.

5.2 Dynamic Programming and Semirings

Torch-Struct is a collection of generic algorithms for CRF inference. Each CRF distribution object, $\mathrm{CRF}(\ell)$, is constructed by providing $\ell \in \mathbb{R}^{|\mathcal{P}|}$ where the parts $\mathcal{P}$ are specific to the type of distribution. Internally, each distribution is implemented through a single function for computing the log-partition function $A(\ell)$. From this function, the library uses autodifferentiation and the identities from the previous section, to define a complete distribution object. The core models implemented by the library are shown in Table 1.

To make the approach concrete, we consider the example of the simplest structured model, a linear-chain CRF $p(z_1, z_2, z_3 \mid x)$.

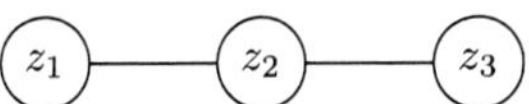

The model has C labels per node with a length N utilizing a first-order linear-chain (Markov) model. This model has $N - 1 \times C \times C$ parts corresponding to edges in the chain, and thus $\ell \in \mathbb{R}^{N-1 \times C \times C}$ log-potentials. The log-partition function $A(\ell)$ factors into two reduce computations,

$$
\begin{aligned}
A(\ell) &= \log \sum_{c_3, c_2} \exp \ell_{2,c_2,c_3} \sum_{c_1} \exp \ell_{1,c_1,c_2} \\
&= \mathrm{LSE}_{c_3,c_2}[\ell_{2,c_2,c_3} + [\mathrm{LSE}_{c_1} \ell_{1,c_1,c_2}]]
\end{aligned}
$$

Computing this function left-to-right using dynamic programming yields the standard *forward* algorithm for computing the log-partition of sequence models. As we have seen, the gradient with respect to ℓ produces marginals for each part, i.e. the probability of a specific labeled edge.

We can further extend the same function to support generic *semiring* dynamic programming (Goodman, 1999). A semiring is defined by a pair $(\oplus, \otimes)$ with commutative $\oplus$, distribution, and appropriate identities.

$$
A(\ell) = \bigoplus_{c_3,c_2}[\ell_{2,c_2,c_3} \otimes [\bigoplus_{c_1} \ell_{1,c_1,c_2}]]
$$

The log-partition utilizes $\oplus, \otimes = (\mathrm{LSE}, +)$, but we can substitute alternatives. For instance, utilizing the log-max semiring $(\max, +)$ in the forward algorithm yields the max score. As we have

seen, its gradient with respect to ℓ is the argmax sequence, negating the need for a separate argmax (Viterbi) algorithm. Some distributional properties cannot be computed directly through gradient identities but still use a forward-backward style compute structure. For instance, sampling requires first computing the log-partition term and then sampling each part, (forward filtering / backward sampling). We can compute this value by overriding each backpropagation operation for the $\oplus$ to instead compute a sample.

Table 2 shows the set of semirings and backpropagation steps for computing different terms of interest. We note that many of the terms necessary in the case-study can be computed with variant semirings, negating the need for specialized algorithms.

6 Optimizations

Torch-Struct aims for computational and memory efficiency. Implemented naively, dynamic programming algorithms in Python are prohibitively slow. As such Torch-Struct provides key primitives to help batch and vectorize these algorithms to take advantage of GPU computation and to minimize the overhead of backpropagating through chart-based dynamic programmming. We discuss three optimizations: a) Parallel Scan, b) Vectorization, and c) Semiring Matrix Multiplications. Figure 3 shows the impact of these optimizations on the core algorithms.

Parallel Scan Inference The commutative properties of semiring algorithms allow flexibility in the order in which we compute $A(\ell)$. Typical implementations of dynamic programming algorithms are serial in the length of the sequence. On parallel hardware, an appealing approach is a parallel scan ordering (Särkkä and García-Fernández, 2019), typically used for computing prefix sums. To compute, $A(\ell)$ in this manner we first pad the sequence length N out to the nearest power of two, and then compute a balanced parallel tree over the parts, shown in Figure 4. Concretely each node layer would compute a semiring matrix multiplication, e.g. $\bigoplus_c \ell_{n,\cdot,c} \otimes \ell_{n+1,c,\cdot}$. Under this approach, assuming enough parallel cores, we only need $O(\log N)$ steps in Python and can use parallel operations for the rest. Similar parallel approach can also be used for computing sequence alignment and semi-Markov models.

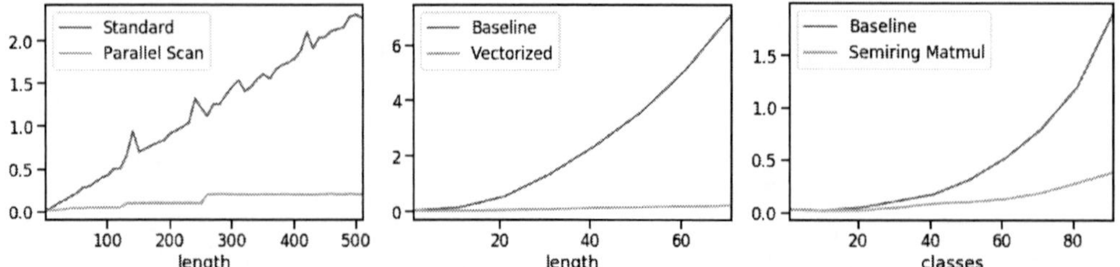

Figure 3: Speed impact of optimizations. Time is given in seconds for 10 runs with batch 16. (a) Speed of a linear-chain forward with 20 classes for lengths up to 500. Compares left-to-right ordering to parallel scan. (b) Speed of CKY inside with lengths up to 80. Compares inner loop versus vectorization. (c) Speed of linear-chain forward of length 20 with up to 100 classes. Compares broadcast-reduction versus CUDA semiring kernel. (Baseline memory is exhausted after 100 classes.)

Vectorization Computational complexity is even more of an issue for algorithms that cannot easily be parallelized. For example, parsing algorithms the generalize CKY are common in NLP. The CKY algorithm has a bottleneck that it must compute each width from 1 through N in serial; however internally each one of these steps can be vectorized. Assuming we have computed all inside spans of width less than d, computing the inside span of width d requires computing for all i,

$$C[i, i + d] = \bigoplus_{j=i}^{i+d-1} C[i, j] \otimes C[j + 1, i + d]$$

In order to vectorize this loop over i, j, we need to reindex the chart. Instead of using a single chart C, we split it into two parts: one right-facing $C_r[i, d] = C[i, i + d]$ and one left facing, $C_l[i+d, N-d] = C[i, i+d]$. After this reindexing, the update can be written.

$$C_r[i, d] = \bigoplus_{j=1}^{j-1} C_r[i, j] \otimes C_l[i + d, N - d + j]$$

Unlike the original, this formula can easily be computed as a vectorized semiring dot product. This allows use to compute $C_r[\cdot, d]$ in one operation. Variants of this same approach can be used for many more complex dynamic programs.

Semiring Matrix Operations The two previous optimizations reduce most of the cost to semiring matrix multiplication. In the specific case of the $(\sum, \times)$ semiring these can be computed very efficiently using matrix multiplication, which is highly-tuned on GPU hardware. However, this semiring is not particularly useful and prone to underflow. For

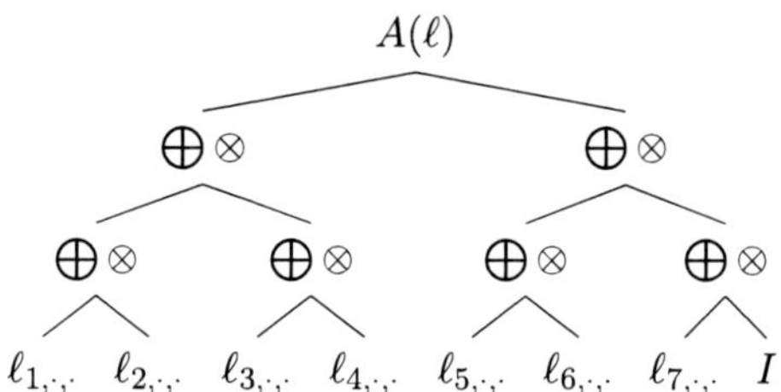

Figure 4: Parallel scan implementation of the linear-chain CRF inference algorithm (parallel forward). Here $\bigoplus \otimes$ represents a semiring matrix operation and I is padding to produce a balanced tree.

other semirings, such as log and max, these operations are either slow or very memory inefficient. For instance, for matrices T and U of sized $N \times M$ and $M \times O$, we can broadcast with $\otimes$ to a tensor of size $N \times M \times O$ and then reduce dim M by $\bigoplus$ at a huge memory cost.

To avoid this issue, we implement custom CUDA kernels targeting fast and memory efficient tensor operations. For log, this corresponds to computing,

$$V_{m,o} = \log \sum_n \exp(T_{m,n} + U_{n,o} - q) + q$$

where $q = \max_n T_{m,n} + U_{n,o}$. To optimize this operation on GPU we utilize the TVM language (Chen et al., 2018) to layout the CUDA loops and tune it to hardware. This produces much faster operations, although still less efficient that matrix multiplication which is heavily customized to hardware.

7 Conclusion and Future Work

We present Torch-Struct, a library for deep structured prediction. The library achieves modularity through its adoption of a generic distributional

API, completeness by utilizing CRFs and semirings to make it easy to add new algorithms, and efficiency through core optimizations to vectorize important dynamic programming steps. In addition to the problems discussed so far, TorchStruct also includes several other example implementations including supervised dependency parsing with BERT, unsupervised tagging, structured attention, and connectionist temporal classification (CTC) for speech. Code demonstrates that the model is able to replicate standard deep learning results, although we focus here on the fidelity and implementation approach of the core library. The full library is available at `https://github.com/harvardnlp/pytorch-struct`.

In the future, we hope to support research and production applications employing structured models. We also believe the library provides a strong foundation for building generic tools for interpretablity, control, and visualization through its probabilistic API. Finally, we hope to explore further optimizations to make core algorithms competitive with highly-optimized neural network components. These approaches provide a benchmark for improving autodifferentiation systems and extending their functionality to higher-order properties.

Acknowledgements

We thank Yoon Kim, Xiang Lisa Li, Sebastian Gehrmann, Yuntian Deng, and Justin Chiu for discussion and feedback on the project. The project was supported by NSF CAREER 1845664, NSF 1901030, and research awards by Sony and AWS.

References

Leonard E Baum and Ted Petrie. 1966. Statistical inference for probabilistic functions of finite state markov chains. *The annals of mathematical statistics*, 37(6):1554–1563.

Eli Bingham, Jonathan P Chen, Martin Jankowiak, Fritz Obermeyer, Neeraj Pradhan, Theofanis Karaletsos, Rohit Singh, Paul Szerlip, Paul Horsfall, and Noah D Goodman. 2019. Pyro: Deep universal probabilistic programming. *The Journal of Machine Learning Research*, 20(1):973–978.

Tianqi Chen, Thierry Moreau, Ziheng Jiang, Haichen Shen, Eddie Yan, Leyuan Wang, Yuwei Hu, Luis Ceze, Carlos Guestrin, and Arvind Krishnamurthy. 2018. Tvm: end-to-end optimization stack for deep learning. *arXiv preprint arXiv:1802.04799*.

Ronan Collobert, Jason Weston, Léon Bottou, Michael Karlen, Koray Kavukcuoglu, and Pavel Kuksa.

2011. Natural language processing (almost) from scratch. *Journal of machine learning research*, 12(Aug):2493–2537.

Joshua V Dillon, Ian Langmore, Dustin Tran, Eugene Brevdo, Srinivas Vasudevan, Dave Moore, Brian Patton, Alex Alemi, Matt Hoffman, and Rif A Saurous. 2017. Tensorflow distributions. *arXiv preprint arXiv:1711.10604*.

Greg Durrett and Dan Klein. 2015. Neural crf parsing. *arXiv preprint arXiv:1507.03641*.

Jason Eisner. 2000. Bilexical grammars and their cubic-time parsing algorithms. In *Advances in probabilistic and other parsing technologies*, pages 29–61. Springer.

Jason Eisner. 2016. Inside-outside and forward-backward algorithms are just backprop (tutorial paper). In *Proceedings of the Workshop on Structured Prediction for NLP*, pages 1–17.

Jason Eisner, Eric Goldlust, and Noah A Smith. 2004. Dyna: A declarative language for implementing dynamic programs. In *Proceedings of the ACL 2004 on Interactive poster and demonstration sessions*, pages 32–es.

Jenny Rose Finkel, Alex Kleeman, and Christopher D Manning. 2008. Efficient, feature-based, conditional random field parsing. In *Proceedings of ACL-08: HLT*, pages 959–967.

Zoubin Ghahramani and Michael I Jordan. 1996. Factorial hidden markov models. In *Advances in Neural Information Processing Systems*, pages 472–478.

Sharon Goldwater and Tom Griffiths. 2007. A fully bayesian approach to unsupervised part-of-speech tagging. In *Proceedings of the 45th annual meeting of the association of computational linguistics*, pages 744–751.

Joshua Goodman. 1999. Semiring parsing. *Computational Linguistics*, 25(4):573–605.

Serhii Havrylov, Germán Kruszewski, and Armand Joulin. 2019. Cooperative learning of disjoint syntax and semantics. *arXiv preprint arXiv:1902.09393*.

Thorsten Joachims. 2008. Svmstruct: Support vector machine for complex outputs.

Matthew J Johnson, David K Duvenaud, Alex Wiltschko, Ryan P Adams, and Sandeep R Datta. 2016. Composing graphical models with neural networks for structured representations and fast inference. In *Advances in neural information processing systems*, pages 2946–2954.

Dan Jurafsky and James H Martin. 2014. Speech and language processing. vol. 3.

Tadao Kasami. 1966. An efficient recognition and syntax-analysis algorithm for context-free languages. *Coordinated Science Laboratory Report no. R-257*.

Yoon Kim, Carl Denton, Luong Hoang, and Alexander M. Rush. 2017. Structured attention networks. *CoRR*, abs/1702.00887.

Terry Koo, Amir Globerson, Xavier Carreras Pérez, and Michael Collins. 2007. Structured prediction models via the matrix-tree theorem. In *Joint Conference on Empirical Methods in Natural Language Processing and Computational Natural Language Learning (EMNLP-CoNLL)*, pages 141–150.

Taku Kudo. 2005. Crf++: Yet another crf toolkit. *http://crfpp. sourceforge. net/*.

John Lafferty, Andrew McCallum, and Fernando CN Pereira. 2001. Conditional random fields: Probabilistic models for segmenting and labeling sequence data.

Zhifei Li and Jason Eisner. 2009. First-and second-order expectation semirings with applications to minimum-risk training on translation forests. In *Proceedings of the 2009 Conference on Empirical Methods in Natural Language Processing: Volume 1-Volume 1*, pages 40–51. Association for Computational Linguistics.

André FT Martins, Noah A Smith, Eric P Xing, Pedro MQ Aguiar, and Mário AT Figueiredo. 2010. Turbo parsers: Dependency parsing by approximate variational inference. In *Proceedings of the 2010 Conference on Empirical Methods in Natural Language Processing*, pages 34–44. Association for Computational Linguistics.

Ryan McDonald, Fernando Pereira, Kiril Ribarov, and Jan Hajič. 2005. Non-projective dependency parsing using spanning tree algorithms. In *Proceedings of the conference on Human Language Technology and Empirical Methods in Natural Language Processing*, pages 523–530. Association for Computational Linguistics.

Arthur Mensch and Mathieu Blondel. 2018. Differentiable dynamic programming for structured prediction and attention. *arXiv preprint arXiv:1802.03676*.

Andreas C Müller and Sven Behnke. 2014. Pystruct: learning structured prediction in python. *The Journal of Machine Learning Research*, 15(1):2055–2060.

Nikita Nangia and Samuel R Bowman. 2018. Listops: A diagnostic dataset for latent tree learning. *arXiv preprint arXiv:1804.06028*.

Saul B Needleman and Christian D Wunsch. 1970. A general method applicable to the search for similarities in the amino acid sequence of two proteins. *Journal of molecular biology*, 48(3):443–453.

Naoaki Okazaki. 2007. Crfsuite: a fast implementation of conditional random fields (crfs).

Steven J Rennie, Etienne Marcheret, Youssef Mroueh, Jerret Ross, and Vaibhava Goel. 2017. Self-critical sequence training for image captioning. In *Proceedings of the IEEE Conference on Computer Vision and Pattern Recognition*, pages 7008–7024.

Sunita Sarawagi and William W Cohen. 2005. Semi-markov conditional random fields for information extraction. In *Advances in neural information processing systems*, pages 1185–1192.

Simo Särkkä and Ángel F García-Fernández. 2019. Temporal parallelization of bayesian filters and smoothers. *arXiv preprint arXiv:1905.13002*.

Christoph Tillmann and Hermann Ney. 2003. Word reordering and a dynamic programming beam search algorithm for statistical machine translation. *Computational linguistics*, 29(1):97–133.

Stephan Vogel, Hermann Ney, and Christoph Tillmann. 1996. Hmm-based word alignment in statistical translation. In *Proceedings of the 16th conference on Computational linguistics-Volume 2*, pages 836–841. Association for Computational Linguistics.

Sam Wiseman, Stuart M Shieber, and Alexander M Rush. 2018. Learning neural templates for text generation. *arXiv preprint arXiv:1808.10122*.

Jie Yang and Yue Zhang. 2018. Ncrf++: An open-source neural sequence labeling toolkit. In *Proceedings of the 56th Annual Meeting of the Association for Computational Linguistics*.

Dani Yogatama, Phil Blunsom, Chris Dyer, Edward Grefenstette, and Wang Ling. 2016. Learning to compose words into sentences with reinforcement learning. *arXiv preprint arXiv:1611.09100*.

Conversation Learner – A Machine Teaching Tool for Building Dialog Managers for Task-Oriented Dialog Systems

†Swadheen Shukla*   †Lars Liden*   †Shahin Shayandeh*   ‡Eslam Kamal
†Jinchao Li   †Matt Mazzola   †Thomas Park   †Baolin Peng   †Jianfeng Gao

†Microsoft Research AI
‡Microsoft Corporation

{swads,laliden,shahins,eskam,jincli,mattm,thpar,bapeng,jfgao}@microsoft.com

Abstract

Traditionally, industry solutions for building a task-oriented dialog system have relied on helping dialog authors define rule-based dialog managers, represented as dialog flows. While dialog flows are intuitively interpretable and good for simple scenarios, they fall short of performance in terms of the flexibility needed to handle complex dialogs. On the other hand, purely machine-learned models can handle complex dialogs, but they are considered to be black boxes and require large amounts of training data. In this demonstration, we showcase *Conversation Learner*, a machine teaching tool for building dialog managers. It combines the best of both approaches by enabling dialog authors to create a dialog flow using familiar tools, converting the dialog flow into a parametric model (e.g., neural networks), and allowing dialog authors to improve the dialog manager (i.e., the parametric model) over time by leveraging user-system dialog logs as training data through a machine teaching interface.

1 Introduction

The proliferation of messaging applications and hardware devices with personal assistants has spurred the imagination of many in the technology industry to create task-oriented dialog systems that help users complete a wide range of tasks through natural language conversations. Tasks include customer support, IT helpdesk, information retrieval, appointment booking, etc. The wide variety of tasks has created the need for a flexible task-oriented dialog system development platform that can support many different use cases, while remaining simple for developers to use and maintain.

A task-oriented dialog system is typically built as a combination of three discrete systems, performing language understanding (for identifying user intent and extracting associated information), dialog management (for guiding users towards task completion), and language generation (for converting agent actions to natural-language system responses). The Dialog Manager (DM) contains two sub-systems: the Dialog State Tracker (DST) for keeping track of the current dialog state, and the Dialog Policy (DP) for determining the next action to be taken in a given dialog instance. The DP relies on the internal state provided by DST to select an action, which can be a response to the user, or some operation on the back-end database (DB). In this paper, we present a novel approach to building dialog managers (DMs).

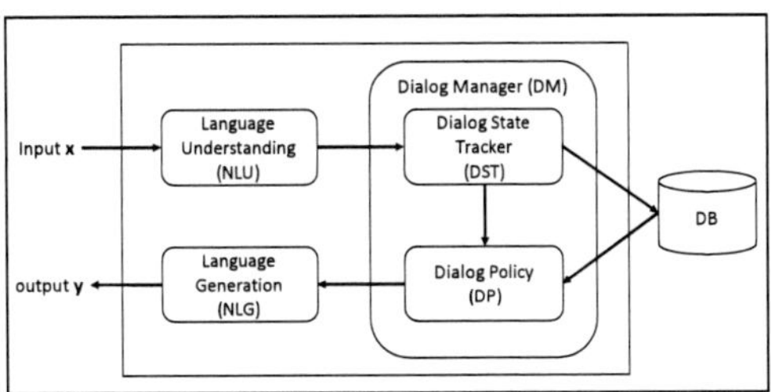

Figure 1: An architecture for a task-oriented dialog system.

In a typical industrial implementation of a task-oriented dialog system, the DM is expressed as a *dialog flow*, which is often a finite state machine, with nodes representing dialog activities (system actions) and edges representing conditions (dialog states that represent the previous user-system interactions). Since a dialog flow can be viewed as a set of *rules* that specify the flow between dialog states, it may also be called a *rule-based DM*.

There has been an increasing need for tools to help dialog authors[1] develop and maintain rule-

---

[1]In this paper, "author" may refer to developers, business owners, or domain experts who define and maintain the conversational aspects of a task-oriented dialog system.

*Equal contribution.

Proceedings of the 58th Annual Meeting of the Association for Computational Linguistics, pages 343–349
July 5 - July 10, 2020. ©2020 Association for Computational Linguistics

based DMs. These tools are often implemented as drag-and-drop WYSIWYG tools that allow users to specify and visualize all the details of the dialog flow. They often have deep integration with popular Integrated Development Environments (IDEs) as editing frontends. Examples of rule-based or partially rule-based DMs include Microsoft's Power Virtual Agents (PVA) [2] and Bot Framework (BF) Composer [3], Google's Dialog Flow [4], IBM's Watson Assistant [5], Facebook's Wit.ai [6] and Amazon's Lex [7]. It should be noted that most of these tools have some built-in machine-learned NLU capabilities, i.e. intent classification and entity detection, that can be leveraged to trigger different rule-based dialog flows, e.g. asking appropriate questions based on missing slots from the dialog state.

However, a rule-based DM suffers from two major problems. First, these systems can have difficulty handling complex dialogs. Second, updating a rule-based DM to handle unexpected user responses and off-track conversations is often difficult due to the rigid structure of the dialog flow, the long-tail (sparseness) of user-system dialogs, and the complexity in jumping to unrelated parts of the flow.

In end-to-end approaches proposed recently (Madotto et al., 2018; Lei et al., 2018), the DM is implemented as a neural network model that is trained directly on text transcripts of dialogs. Gao et al. (2019) presents a survey of recent approaches. One benefit provided by using a neural network model is that the network infers a latent representation of dialog state, eliminating the need for explicitly specifying dialog states. Neural-based DMs has been an area of active development for the research community as well as in industry; PyDial (Ultes et al., 2017), ParlAI (Miller et al., 2017), Plato (Papangelis et al., 2020), Rasa (Bocklisch et al., 2017), DeepPavlov (Burtsev et al., 2018), and ConvLab (Lee et al., 2019) are a few examples. However, these machine-learned neural DMs are often viewed as black boxes from which dialog authors have difficulty interpreting why individual use cases succeed or fail. Further, these approaches often lack a general mechanism for accepting task-specific knowledge and constraints, thus requiring a large number of validated dialog transcripts for training. Collection and curation of this type of corpus is often infeasible.

This paper presents Conversation Learner, a machine *teaching* tool for building DMs, which combines the strengths of both rule-based and machine-learned approaches. Conversation Learner is based on Hybrid Code Networks (HCNs) (Williams et al., 2017) and the *machine teaching* discipline (Simard et al., 2017). Conversation Learner allows dialog authors to (1) import a dialog flow developed using popular dialog composers, (2) convert the dialog flow to an HCN-based DM, (3) continuously improve the HCN-based DM by reviewing user-system dialog logs and providing updates via a machine teaching UI, and (4) convert the (revised) HCN-based DM back into a dialog flow for further editing and verification.

Section 2 describes the architecture and main components of Conversation Learner. Section 3 demonstrates Conversation Learner features. Section 4 presents a case study of using Conversation Learner as the DM of a text-based customer support dialog system.

2 Conversation Learner

Development of any DM follows an iterative process of generation, testing, and revision. Conversation Learner follows a three-stage DM development process:

1. Dialog authors develop a rule-based DM (dialog flow) using a dialog composer.

2. The DM is imported into a HCN dialog system. Users (or human subjects recruited for system fine-tuning) interact with the system and generate user-system dialog logs.

3. Dialog authors revise the DM by selecting representative failed dialogs from the logs and teaching the system to complete these dialogs successfully. Run regression testing. Return to step 2.

This development process is illustrated in Figure 2 (Bottom). The overall architecture of Conversation Learner is shown in Figure 2 (Top). It consists of four components: (1) a DM converter that converts a dialog flow between rule-based and HCN-based DM representations; (2) an HCN-based DM engine; (3) a machine teaching module

---

[2]https://powervirtualagents.microsoft.com/

[3]https://github.com/microsoft/BotFramework-Composer

[4]https://dialogflow.com/

[5]https://www.ibm.com/watson/

[6]https://wit.ai/

[7]https://aws.amazon.com/lex/

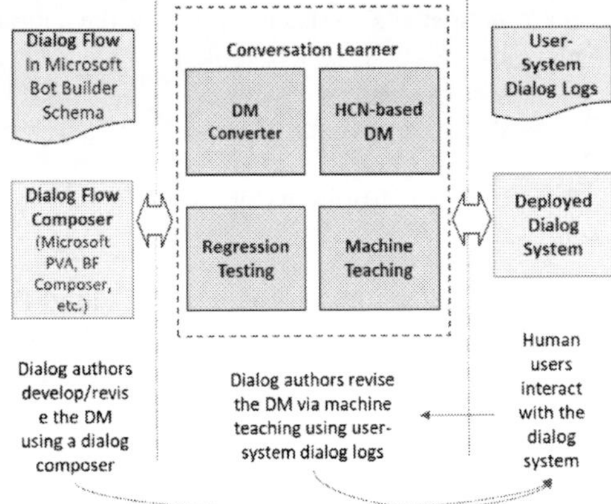

Figure 2: The architecture of Conversation Learner (Top) and the development of DMs using Conversation Learner (Bottom).

that allows dialog authors to revise the HCN-based DM; and (4) an evaluation module that allows side-by-side comparison of the dialogs generated by different DMs. We describe each component in detail below.

2.1 HCN-based DM

The Conversation Learner HCN consists of a set of task-specific action templates, an entity module, a set of action masks, and a Recurrent Neural Network (RNN). Each action template can be a textual communicative action, rich card, or an API call. The entity module detects entity mentions in user utterances, grounds the entity mentions (e.g., by mapping an entity mention to a specific row in a dataset), and performs entity substitution in a selected action template to produce a fully-formed action (e.g., by mapping the template "the weather of [city]?" to "the weather of Seattle?"

Each action mask represents an "if-then" rule that determines the set of valid actions for some conditions (i.e., particular dialog states or user inputs).

The RNN maintains dialog states and selects system actions. For each turn in a training dialog, a combination of features, including the user utterance embedding, its bag of words vector, and the set of extracted entities are concatenated to form a feature vector that is passed to the RNN, specifically a Long Short Term Memory (LSTM) network. The RNN computes a hidden state vector, which is retained for the next timestep. Next, a softmax activation layer is used to calculate a probability distribution over the available system action tem-

plates. An action mask is then applied, and the result is normalized to select the highest-probability action as the best response for the current turn.

The HCN can be trained on a collection of user-system dialogs. For each system response in a dialog, the action template is labeled. The training of HCN takes two steps. First, all unique action templates are imported into the HCN. Then, the RNN, which maps states to action templates, is optimized for minimizing the categorical cross-entropy on training data. More specifically, each dialog forms one minibatch, and updates of the RNN are done via non-truncated back-propagation through time.

Readers are referred to Williams et al. (2017) for a detailed description of HCN. It should be noted that CL leverages the same network architecture as HCN with enhancements and modifications to generate context features from training samples.

2.2 DM converter

The DM converter converts a rule-based DM, developed using a dialog composer, to an HCN-based DM, which can then be improved via training dialogs and machine teaching.

Given a dialog flow, the DM converter automatically generates a set of training dialogs that represent the dialog flow. This process is done by performing an exhaustive set of walks over the dialog flow and generating training dialog instances for each walk. Rules that determine transitions in the dialog flow are represented as action masks in the HCN. The HCN is trained on the generated training dialogs as described in Section 2.1.

The DM converter can also convert a revised HCN-based DM back to a dialog flow by aggregating the individual training dialogs back into a graph for further editing and verification using a dialog composer.

2.3 Machine Teaching

The HCN-based DM can be improved via machine teaching (Simard et al., 2017). "Machine teaching" is an active learning paradigm that focuses on leveraging the knowledge and expertise of domain experts as "teachers". This paradigm puts a strong emphasis on tools and techniques that enable teachers - particularly non-data scientists and non-machine-learning experts - to visualize data, find potential problems, and provide corrections or additional training inputs in order to improve the system's performance.

For Conversation Learner, we developed a UI for visualizing and editing logged user-system dialogs that had failed to complete their tasks successfully. The teacher does not need to revise the DM directly (e.g., via writing code or by modifying dialog structure in a hierarchical composer tool). The teacher simply corrects cases where the dialog system responded poorly or incorrectly.

The teacher can make three types of corrections: (1) correct entity detection and grounding errors; (2) correct state-to-action mapping; or (3) create a new action template.

In cases where a large number of logged dialogs exists, we use active learning to provide a ranking of the candidate dialogs most likely to benefit from machine teaching intervention.

Our empirical tests show that machine teaching requires considerably fewer training samples than traditional machine learning approaches to improve system performance. We commonly observe significant improvements in DM performance by providing a dozen or fewer teaching examples.

There are three main reasons the HCN + machine teaching combination is so effective. First, dialog authors are generally subject matter experts who can make well-informed decisions about which actions the DM should perform in individual situations. If the DM has to automatically learn an action policy from logs, a large corpus of data is required. Second, the HCN allows dialog authors to explicitly encode domain-specific knowledge as action templates (bot activities or responses) and action masks (when a given response should be disallowed) without learning. Third, we can use intelligent filtering to select the most impactful failed dialogs for teachers to review.

2.4 Regression Testing

To effectively compare the performance of various dialog systems using different DMs, we developed a regression testing module. The module replays user utterances from transcripts of existing conversations against the DMs being tested; each DM then provides response action(s) for each turn. The module displays side-by-side comparisons of the resulting conversations from each DM, up to the point where the DM responses diverge. Human judges then rate the conversations as "left better", "right better" or "same".

At the end of the rating session, a report is generated showing the performance of conversational flow amongst the DMs, as rated by the human judges.

3 System Demonstration

The system demonstration consists of the following steps:

1. The dialog author creates a rule-based DM using a dialog composer tool. We showcase the usage of Microsoft Power Virtual Agent system for this step.

2. The rule-based DM is exported to a common representation, e.g. Microsoft's '.dialog' schema[8].

3. The dialog flow is then imported into the Conversation Learner system. The import process involves traversing the dialog flow and creating dialog transcript instances for each traversal.

4. The generated dialog transcripts are run through both the rule-based system and Conversation Learner to demonstrate the improvement in dialog-handling flexibility provided by Conversation Learner's machine-learned DM.

5. For transcripts containing failures to complete the user's desired task, we demonstrate the machine teaching UI used to 'correct' errors and generate new training examples for revising the DM.

4 Case Study

To evaluate Conversation Learner's performance, we used dialog transcripts from Microsoft's text-based customer support system[9]. This customer support system uses a sophisticated rule-based DM to handle various customer support scenarios. It was created and is regularly updated by domain experts. We chose to use transcripts of actual user-system dialogs in order to measure the performance of the DMs in a realistic setting.

The customer support system consists of hundreds of "topics" out of which we selected three: "language settings", "installing or changing fonts",

---

[8] `https://github.com/microsoft/ botbuilder-dotnet/blob/master/schemas/ sdk.schema`

[9] These transcripts were scrubbed of any personally identifiable information.

Turn	Dialog
1	usr: How to reduce font size agt: How can I help you with fonts today?
2	usr: Adjust font size agt: Would you like to change the font size in an app or the size of text on your screen?
3	usr: Change size of text on screen agt: Change the size of text in Windows 10 using Display settings or use Magnifier. <Link to solution>
4	agt: Did that solve your problem? usr: Yes
5	agt: Great! Glad that helped.

Table 1: A sample human-agent dialog from the customer support logs

and "sign in problems". Table 1 shows an example of a user-system dialog for "change font" topic. Figure 3 shows the representation of a specific topic's dialog flow in the Microsoft Power Virtual Agents *dialog composer*. We exported the dialog flow graph of the support system from this system, then followed the process described in Section 2.2 to train our machine-learned HCN-based DM. Figure 4 shows an example of a generated train dialog.

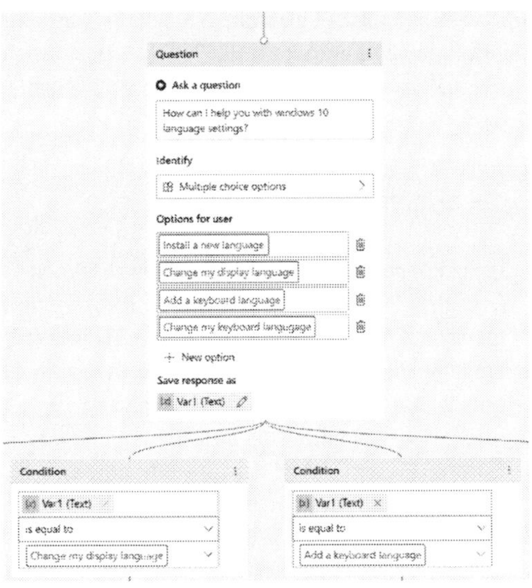

Figure 3: An example of a rule-based dialog defined in the Microsoft Power Virtual Agents system

After generating the HCN-based DM, we ran the set of dialog transcripts against both rule-based and HCN-based DMs. For the majority of conversations, users followed the expected flow, so the HCN-based DM produced the same results as the rule-based DM. For those that differed, we used human judges to do a blind qualitative evaluation of the conversations and choose the conversation

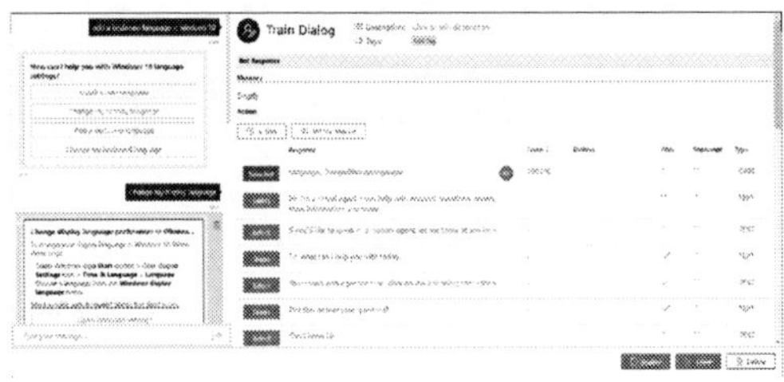

Figure 4: An example train dialog generated by traversing the different paths of a dialog tree (left), and DM actions generated from the tree (right)

that provided the best task-completion result.

User Rating	# of Convs.	%
CL is same	2749	91.63%
CL is better	136	4.53%
CL is worse	115	3.83%
Overall variation		0.7% (better)

Table 2: Initial results of human evaluation of 3000 dialogs against Conversation Learner (CL) and a rule-based dialog system.

As shown in Table 2, the HCN-based DM provided better results for many transcripts, but there was an almost equal number of dialogs where the rule-based DM was rated better. The rule-based DM may perform better in cases where specialized hard-coded logic was added to handle issues such as input normalization or rewriting.

An example dialog comparison is shown in Figures 5 and 6. As seen in Figure 6, the HCN-based DM handles cases where the user utterance does not match a known phrase, better than the rules-based system. The HCN is also able to handle unexpected transitions between dialog nodes.

In a rule-based system, updating the DM to handle unexpected user responses and off-track conversations is much harder due to the rigid structure of the dialog flow graph, the long-tail nature of user-system dialog transcripts (a large number of sparse examples), and complexity in transitioning between unrelated parts of the dialog flow.

Next, we demonstrate that the performance of the HCN DM can be substantially improved by adding just 3 to 5 teaching examples via the machine teaching UI presented in Section 2.3. For this experiment, we chose dialog transcripts that contained common patterns of conversational problems, like users switching context, repeating themselves or asking follow-up questions, and corrected

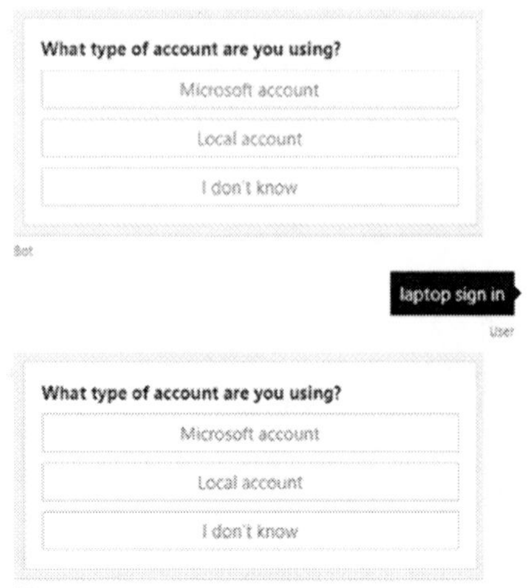

Figure 5: A sample dialog from a rule-based system. Notice that the system just repeats its previous question (as a rule) since it did not understand the user reply.

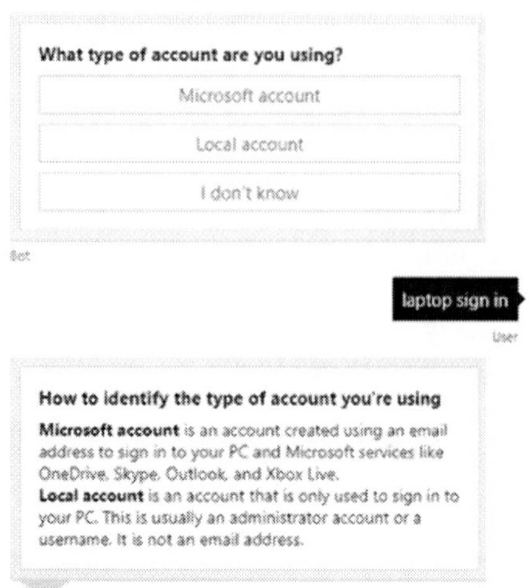

Figure 6: Same dialog as Figure 5 in Conversation Learner. Notice that the user response is accurately generalized to one of the available options when possible.

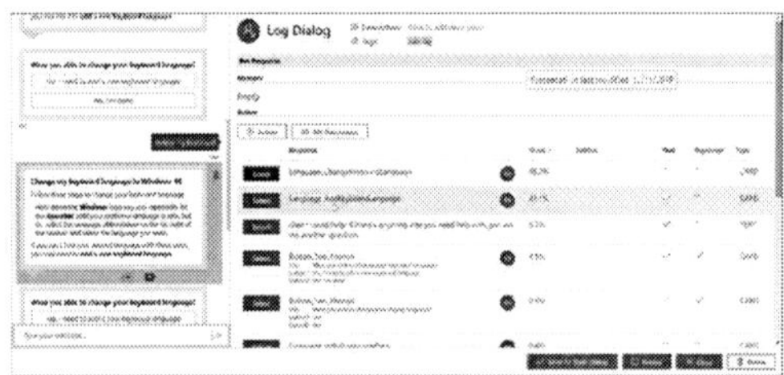

Figure 7: Machine Teaching UI for *correcting* dialogs to revise DM.

the dialog policy by creating or selecting the appropriate system action to resolve the problem. Once these additional examples are added, as illustrated in Figure 7 the HCN-based DM's performance improvement over the rule-based DM nearly tripled, from 4.53% to 13.8%.

User Rating	# of Convs.	%
CL is same	2562	85.4%
CL is better	414	13.8%
CL is worse	24	0.81%
Overall variation		12.99% (better)

Table 3: Results of human evaluation of 3000 dialogs after improving Conversation Learner (CL) model with machine teaching.

As shown in Table 3, minimal intervention from a dialog author by providing a small number of corrections to problematic user-system dialog logs can have a significant impact on the performance of the DM. As new users interact with the system and new transcripts are generated, the dialog author can continuously improve the HCN DM's performance by making corrections and adding new training data.

5 Conclusion

In this paper, we presented *Conversation Learner*, a machine teaching tool for building dialog policy managers. We have shown that the CL HCN-based DM can be bootstrapped from a rule-based DM preserving the same behavior expected from the rule-based system. Using the CL machine teaching UI, the dialog author can provide corrections to the logged user-system dialogs and further improve the CL's DM performance. We demonstrated this through a case study based on dialog transcripts from Microsoft's text-based customer support system where the gains were approximately 13%.

We are planning to extend this work by looking into following problems: 1) Investigating effectiveness of different ranking algorithms for log correction recommendation, 2) Optimizing number of training samples and action masks generated from the rule-based DM, and 3) Improving predictions of HCN-based DM by looking into alternative network architectures.

References

Tom Bocklisch, Joey Faulkner, Nick Pawlowski, and Alan Nichol. 2017. Rasa: Open source language understanding and dialogue management. *CoRR*, abs/1712.05181.

Mikhail Burtsev, Alexander Seliverstov, Rafael Airapetyan, Mikhail Arkhipov, Dilyara Baymurzina, Nickolay Bushkov, Olga Gureenkova, Taras Khakhulin, Yuri Kuratov, Denis Kuznetsov, Alexey Litinsky, Varvara Logacheva, Alexey Lymar, Valentin Malykh, Maxim Petrov, Vadim Polulyakh, Leonid Pugachev, Alexey Sorokin, Maria Vikhreva, and Marat Zaynutdinov. 2018. DeepPavlov: Open-source library for dialogue systems. In *Proceedings of ACL 2018, System Demonstrations*, pages 122–127, Melbourne, Australia. Association for Computational Linguistics.

Jianfeng Gao, Michel Galley, and Lihong Li. 2019. Neural approaches to conversational ai. *Foundations and Trends® in Information Retrieval*, 13(2-3):127–298.

Sungjin Lee, Qi Zhu, Ryuichi Takanobu, Xiang Li, Yaoqin Zhang, Zheng Zhang, Jinchao Li, Baolin Peng, Xiujun Li, Minlie Huang, and Jianfeng Gao. 2019. Convlab: Multi-domain end-to-end dialog system platform. *CoRR*, abs/1904.08637.

Wenqiang Lei, Xisen Jin, Min-Yen Kan, Zhaochun Ren, Xiangnan He, and Dawei Yin. 2018. Sequicity: Simplifying task-oriented dialogue systems with single sequence-to-sequence architectures. In *Proceedings of the 56th Annual Meeting of the Association for Computational Linguistics (Volume 1: Long Papers)*, pages 1437–1447, Melbourne, Australia. Association for Computational Linguistics.

Andrea Madotto, Chien-Sheng Wu, and Pascale Fung. 2018. Mem2Seq: Effectively incorporating knowledge bases into end-to-end task-oriented dialog systems. In *Proceedings of the 56th Annual Meeting of the Association for Computational Linguistics (Volume 1: Long Papers)*, pages 1468–1478, Melbourne, Australia. Association for Computational Linguistics.

Alexander H. Miller, Will Feng, Adam Fisch, Jiasen Lu, Dhruv Batra, Antoine Bordes, Devi Parikh, and Jason Weston. 2017. Parlai: A dialog research software platform. *CoRR*, abs/1705.06476.

Alexandros Papangelis, Mahdi Namazifar, Chandra Khatri, Yi-Chia Wang, Piero Molino, and Gokhan Tur. 2020. Plato dialogue system: A flexible conversational ai research platform.

Patrice Y. Simard, Saleema Amershi, David Maxwell Chickering, Alicia Edelman Pelton, Soroush Ghorashi, Christopher Meek, Gonzalo Ramos, Jina Suh, Johan Verwey, Mo Wang, and John Wernsing. 2017. Machine teaching: A new paradigm for building machine learning systems. *CoRR*, abs/1707.06742.

Stefan Ultes, Lina M. Rojas Barahona, Pei-Hao Su, David Vandyke, Dongho Kim, Iñigo Casanueva, Paweł Budzianowski, Nikola Mrkšić, Tsung-Hsien Wen, Milica Gasic, and Steve Young. 2017. PyDial: A Multi-domain Statistical Dialogue System Toolkit. In *Proceedings of ACL 2017, System Demonstrations*, pages 73–78, Vancouver, Canada. Association for Computational Linguistics.

Jason D. Williams, Kavosh Asadi, and Geoffrey Zweig. 2017. Hybrid code networks: practical and efficient end-to-end dialog control with supervised and reinforcement learning. *CoRR*, abs/1702.03274.

NSTM: Real-Time Query-Driven News Overview Composition at Bloomberg

Joshua Bambrick[1], Minjie Xu[1], Andy Almonte[1], Igor Malioutov[1],
Guim Perarnau[1], Vittorio Selo[1], Iat Chong Chan[2, *]

[1]Bloomberg, London, United Kingdom
[2]OakNorth, London, United Kingdom

[1]{jbambrick7,mxu161,aalmonte2,imalioutov,gperarnau,vselo}@bloomberg.net
[2]iat.chan@oaknorth.com

Abstract

Millions of news articles from hundreds of thousands of sources around the globe appear in news aggregators every day. Consuming such a volume of news presents an almost insurmountable challenge. For example, a reader searching on Bloomberg's system for news about the U.K. would find 10,000 articles on a typical day. Apple Inc., the world's most journalistically covered company, garners around 1,800 news articles a day.

We realized that a new kind of summarization engine was needed, one that would condense large volumes of news into short, easy to absorb points. The system would filter out noise and duplicates to identify and summarize key news about companies, countries or markets.

When given a user query, Bloomberg's solution, Key News Themes (or NSTM), leverages state-of-the-art semantic clustering techniques and novel summarization methods to produce comprehensive, yet concise, digests to dramatically simplify the news consumption process.

NSTM is available to hundreds of thousands of readers around the world and serves thousands of requests daily with sub-second latency. At ACL 2020, we will present a demo of NSTM.

1 Introduction

In many domains, finding contextually-important news as fast as possible is a key goal. With millions of articles published around the globe each day, quickly finding relevant and actionable news can mean the difference between success and failure.

When provided with a search query, a traditional system returns links to articles sorted by relevance. However, users typically encounter (near) duplicate or overlapping articles, making it hard to quickly identify key events and easy to miss less-reported stories. Moreover, news headlines are frequently sensational, opaque, or verbose, forcing readers to open and read individual articles.

For illustration, imagine an analyst sees the price of Amazon.com stock drop and wants to know why. With a traditional system, they would search for news on the company and wade through many stories (307 in this case[1]), often with duplicate information or unhelpful headlines, to slowly build up a full picture of what the key events were.

By contrast, using *NSTM (Key News Themes)*, this same analyst can search for 'Amazon.com', over a given time horizon, and promptly receive a concise and comprehensive overview of the news, as shown in Fig. 1. We tackle the challenges involved with consuming vast quantities of news by leveraging modern techniques to semantically cluster stories, as well as innovative summarization methods to extract succinct, informational summaries for each cluster. A handful of *key stories* are then selected from each cluster. We define a (story cluster, summary, key stories) triple as one *theme* and an ordered list of themes as an *overview*.

NSTM works at web scale but responds to arbitrary user queries with sub-second latency. It is deployed to hundreds of thousands of users around the globe and serves thousands of requests per day.

2 Design Goals

We focus on the scenario where a news search query can render many matching news articles, from tens up to hundreds of thousands. The task is to create a succinct overview of the results to help our users to easily grasp the gist of them without combing through the individual articles.

Since the matching articles often cover various aspects and events, NSTM must first cluster related stories to form a clear separation among them.

Furthermore, the system must extract a concise

---

*Order reflects writing contributions; M.X., I.C.C., and J.B. designed and developed a prototype of the system; All implemented the production system; A.A. managed the project. I.C.C. worked on the project while employed by Bloomberg.

[1]The corresponding overview can be found in Appendix C.

Proceedings of the 58th Annual Meeting of the Association for Computational Linguistics, pages 350–361
July 5 - July 10, 2020. ©2020 Association for Computational Linguistics

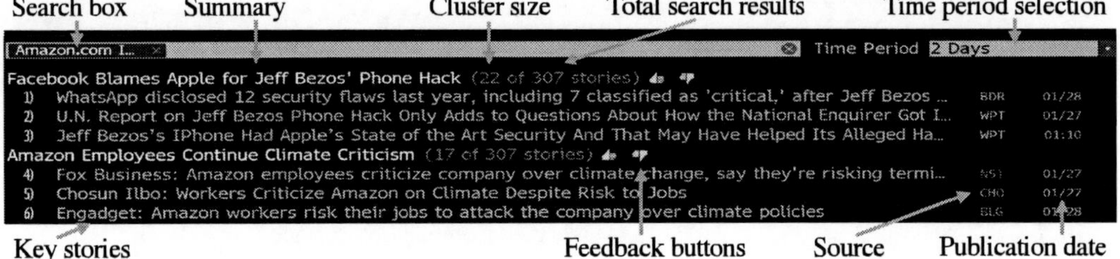

Figure 1: A query-based UI for NSTM showing two themes. The un-cropped screenshot is in Appendix C.

(up to 50 characters, or roughly 6 tokens) summary for each cluster. It needs to be short enough to be understandable to humans with a single glance, but also rich enough to retain critical details from a minimal 'who-does-what' stub, so the most popular noun phrase or entity alone will not suffice. Such conciseness also helps when screen space is limited (for context-driven applications or mobile devices).

From each cluster, NSTM must surface a few key stories to provide a sample of its contents. The clusters themselves should also be ranked to highlight the most important few in limited screen space.

Finally, the system must be fast. It may only take up to a few seconds for the slowest queries.

Main technical challenges: **1)** There is no public dataset corresponding to this overview composition problem with all the requirements set above, so we were required to either define new (sub-)tasks and collect new annotations, or select techniques by intuition, implement them, and iterate on feedback; **2)** Generating summaries which are simultaneously accurate, informational, fluent, and highly concise necessitates careful and innovative choices of summarization techniques; **3)** Supporting arbitrary user searches in real-time places significant performance requirements on the system whilst also setting a high bar for its robustness.

3 Related Work

A comparable system is Google News' 'Full Coverage' feature[2], which groups stories from different sources, akin to our clustering approach. However, it doesn't offer summarization and its clustered view is unavailable for arbitrary search queries.

SUMMA (Liepins et al., 2017) is another comparable system which integrates a variety of NLP components and provides support for numerous media and languages, to simultaneously monitor several media broadcasts. SUMMA applies the online clustering algorithm by Aggarwal and Yu (2006) and the extractive summarization algorithm by Almeida and Martins (2013). In contrast to NSTM, SUMMA focuses on scenarios with continuous multimedia and multilingual data streams and produces much longer summaries.

4 Approach

4.1 Architecture

The functionality of NSTM can be formulated as: given a search query, generate a ranked list (*overview*) of the key *themes*, or (news cluster, summary, key stories) triples, that concisely represent the most important matching news events.

Fig. 2 depicts the system's architecture. The *story ingestion service* processes millions of published news stories each day, stores them in a search index, and applies online clustering to them. When a search query is submitted via a user interface (①️ in the diagram), the *overview composition service* retrieves matching stories and their associated online cluster IDs from the search index (②️). The system then further clusters the retrieved online clusters into the final clusters, each corresponding to one theme (③️). For each such cluster, the system extracts a concise summary and a handful of key stories to reflect the cluster's contents (④️). This creates a set of themes, which NSTM ranks to create the final overview. Lastly, the system caches the overview for a limited time to support future reuse (⑤️) before returning it to the UI (⑥️).

4.2 News Search

The first step in the NSTM pipeline is to retrieve relevant news stories (①️ in Fig. 2), for which we leverage a customized in-house news search engine based on Apache Solr.[3] This supports searches based on keywords, metadata (such as news source

---

[2]https://www.blog.google/products/news/new-google-news-ai-meets-human-intelligence/

[3]http://lucene.apache.org/solr/

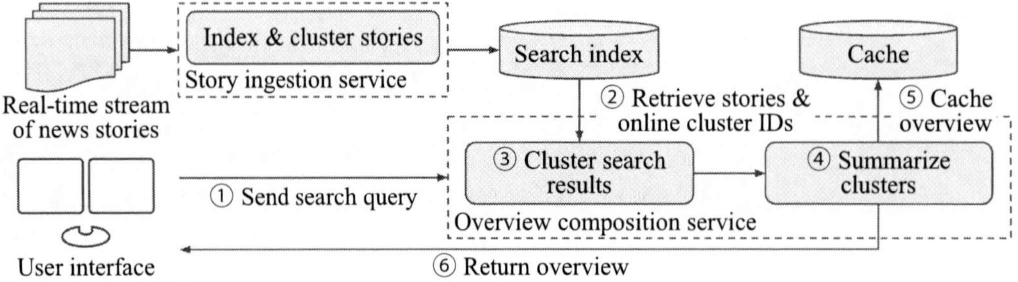

Figure 2: The architecture of NSTM. The digits indicate the order of execution whenever a new request is made.

and time of ingestion), and tags generated during ingestion (such as topics, regions, securities, and people). For example, TOPIC:ECOM AND NOT COMPANY:AMZN[4] will retrieve all news about 'E-commerce' but exclude Amazon.com.

NSTM uses Solr's *facet* functionality to surface the largest k online clusters (detailed in Sec. 4.3.2) in the search results, before returning n stories from each. This tiered approach offers better coverage and scalability than direct story retrieval.

4.3 Clustering

4.3.1 News Embedding and Similarity

At the core of any clustering system is a similarity metric. In NSTM, we define the similarity between two articles as the cosine similarity between their embeddings as computed by NVDM (Miao et al., 2016), i.e., $\tau(d_1, d_2) = 0.5(\cos(\mathbf{z}_1, \mathbf{z}_2)+1)$, where $\mathbf{z} \in R^n$ denotes the NVDM embedding.

Our choice is motivated by two observations: **1)** The generative model of NVDM is based on bag-of-words (BoW) and $P(w|\mathbf{z}) = \sigma(W^\top \mathbf{z})$ where σ is the softmax function, $W \in R^{n \times V}$ is the word embedding matrix in the decoder and V is the size of the vocabulary. This resembles the latent topic structure popularized by LDA (Blei et al., 2003) which has proven effective in capturing textual semantics. Additionally, the use of cosine similarities is naturally motivated by the fact that the generative model is directly defined by the dot-product between the story embedding (z) and a shared vocabulary embedding (W). **2)** NVDM's Variational Autoencoder (VAE) (Kingma and Welling, 2014; Rezende et al., 2014) framework makes the inference procedure much simpler than LDA and it also supports decoder customizations. For example, it allows us to easily integrate the idea of introducing

a learnable common background word distribution into the generative model (Arora et al., 2017).

We trained the model on an internal corpus of 1.85M news articles, using a vocabulary of size about 200k and a latent dimension n of 128.

4.3.2 Clustering Stages

We divide clustering into two stages in the pipeline, **1)** online incremental clustering at story ingestion time, and **2)** hierarchical agglomerative clustering (HAC) at query time (③ in Fig. 2). The former is used to produce query-agnostic *online clusters* at a relatively low cost to handle the daily influx of millions of news stories. These clusters reduce the computational cost at query time. However, due to its online nature, over-fragmentation, among other quality issues, occurs in the resulting clusters. This necessitates further refinement at query time when an offline HAC step is performed on top of the retrieved online clusters. A similar, but more complicated, design was adopted in Vadrevu et al. (2011) for clustering real-time news search results.

At both stages, we compute the cluster embedding $\mathbf{z}_c \in R^n$ as the mean of all the story embeddings therein, and evaluate similarities between clusters (individual stories are taken as singleton clusters) using the metric τ defined in Sec. 4.3.1.

For online clustering, we apply an in-house implementation which uses a distributed pool of workers to reduce latency and increase throughput. It merges each incoming story with the closest cluster if the similarity is within a parameterized threshold and otherwise creates a new singleton cluster.

For HAC, we apply fastcluster[5] (Müllner, 2013) to construct the dendrogram. We use complete linkage to encourage more congruent clusters and then form flat clusters by cutting the dendrogram at the same (height) threshold. To further

---

[4]This is Bloomberg's internal news search query syntax, which maps closely to the final query submitted to Solr.

[5]https://www.jstatsoft.org/article/view/v053i09

reduce fragmentation where similar clusters are left un-clustered, we apply HAC twice recursively.

To find a reasonable similarity threshold, we manually annotated just over 1k pairs of news articles. Each annotator indicated whether they would expect to see the articles grouped together or not in an overview. We then selected the threshold which achieved the highest F_1 score on this binary classification task, which was 0.86.

4.4 Summary Extraction

Clustering search results (Vadrevu et al., 2011) is a meaningful step towards creating a useful overview. With NSTM, we push this one step further by additionally generating a concise, yet still human-readable, summary for each cluster (④ in Fig. 2).

Due to the unique style of the summary explained in Sec. 2, the scarcity of training data makes it hard to train an end-to-end seq2seq (Sutskever et al., 2014) model, as is typical for abstractive summarization. Also, this technique would only offer limited control over the output. Hence, we opt for an extractive method, leveraging OpenIE (Banko et al., 2007) and a BERT-based (Devlin et al., 2019) sentence compressor (both illustrated in Fig. 3) to surface a pool of sub-sentence-level candidate summaries from the headline and the body, which are then scored by a ranker.

4.4.1 OpenIE-based Tuple Extraction

Open Domain Information Extraction (OpenIE) presents an unsupervised approach to extract summary candidates from an input sentence.

First, we construct a dependency parse tree of the sentence, using a model based on Kiperwasser and Goldberg (2016) (① in Fig. 3).

From this tree, we extract predicate-argument n-tuples using an adapted reimplementation of Pred-Patt (White et al., 2016) (②). The tuples represent nested proto-semantic parses of the sentence, and typically correspond to well-formed phrases. This method applies rules cast over Universal Dependencies (Nivre et al., 2016) so syntactic patterns are unlexicalized and language-neutral.

We then prune these tuples (③), applying rules which reduce the arguments to their syntactic heads, while heuristics keep named entities and multi-word expressions intact. We recursively intersect the resulting tuples to create more tuples.

Finally, to render summary candidates, we create a titlecased surface form of each tuple (④).

4.4.2 BERT-based Sentence Compression

In addition to the rule-based OpenIE system, we apply a Transfer Learning-based solution, using a novel in-house dataset specific to our sub-task. In particular, we model candidate summary extraction as a 'sentence compression' task (Filippova et al., 2015), where each story is split into sentences and tokens are classified as *keep* or *delete* to make each sentence shorter, while retaining the key message.

We oversaw the manual annotation of a dataset which maps sentences to compressed equivalents that correspond to summaries. When presented with a news story, annotators selected one sentence and deleted words to create a high quality summary. This rendered 10k annotations which we randomly partitioned into train (80%) and test (20%) sets.

The task is formulated as sequence tagging, whereby each sub-token (① in Fig. 3), defined using the BERT vocabulary, is classified as *keep* or *delete* (②). We implement this using a feedforward layer on top of a Bloomberg-internal pre-trained neural network, akin to the uncased English BERT-Base model, applying an adapted implementation.

To create a compression, we stitch sub-tokens labelled *keep* together (③). Lastly, we use postprocessing rules to improve formatting (④), such as titlecasing and fixing partial-entity deletion (where only some sub-tokens of a token/entity are deleted).

4.4.3 Summary Candidate Ranking

Tuple generation and sentence compression provide a pool of summary candidates for individual news stories. These are further aggregated across stories within a cluster to form the final pool. To identify the best summary for the cluster, we trained a sequence-pair model $s_\theta(a, c)$ to score each candidate c given an article a. Such article-level scores for a candidate are computed against all the stories in a cluster and then aggregated (e.g., averaged) to produce the final cluster-level scores, which we use for ranking.

For this purpose, we collected an in-house annotated dataset. We sampled a few thousand news articles and generated 33k summary candidates from them using OpenIE,[6]. Then we asked internal annotators to label each as *Great*, *Acceptable* or *Terrible* were it to be used as a summary for the article, considering both readability and informativeness.

From this dataset, we constructed about 48k pairwise samples $(c, c')|a$ where c is labelled more

---

[6] At this time, we hadn't considered sentence compression.

Automaker ST is investing $2B in electric vehicles (EVs), atoning for the 2018 scandal

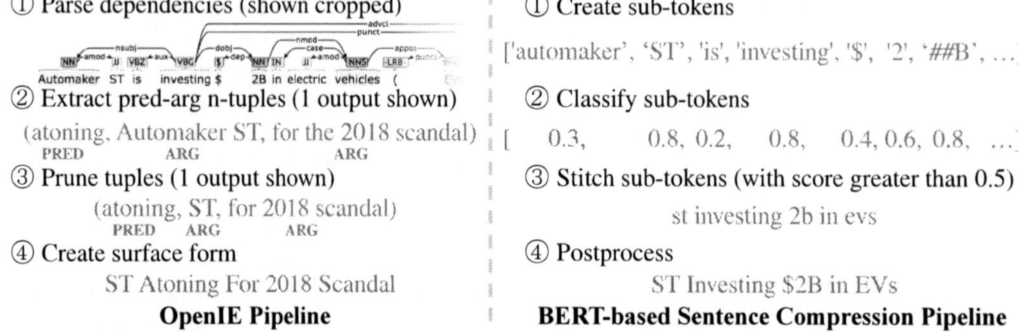

Figure 3: Illustrations of the symbolic OpenIE (left) and neural sentence compression (right) candidate extraction pipelines. We apply both, to render a diverse pool of candidate summaries, and use a ranker to select the best.

favorably than c' for a given common article a, and the model $s_\theta(a, c)$ was then trained to match such preferences using pairwise margin loss, i.e., $\max(0, 1 - s_\theta(a, c) + s_\theta(a, c'))$.

We considered a few models, including a parameter-free baseline which scores candidate-article pairs as the dot-product of their NVDM (Sec. 4.3.1) embeddings, i.e., $s = z_a^\top z_c$. We also considered this model's bilinear extension $s = z_a^\top W z_c$ where W is the learnable weight matrix. Lastly, we tried neural network models, such as DecAtt (Parikh et al., 2016). We evaluated these models on a held-out test set with metrics such as pairwise ranking accuracy and NDCG. We opted to productionize the baseline model, since it was the simplest and performed on par with the others.[7]

Because NVDM uses a bag-of-words model, this ranker ignores syntax entirely. We believe that its empirical success owes to both the well-formedness of the majority of the candidates and the averaging effect that amplifies the 'signal-noise ratio' when the scores are averaged over the cluster.

Empirically, this approach tends to surface 'informational' summaries, in contrast to headlines which are often 'sensational'. We posit that this is because high-ranked summaries must also be representative of story bodies, not just headlines.

4.4.4 Combining Summary Candidates

OpenIE and sentence compression offer distinct ways to extract candidates, and we experimented with each as the sole source of summary candidates in our pipeline. On the basis of ROUGE

scores (Lin and Hovy, 2003; Lin, 2004) (details in Appendix B), the latter provides superior results.

However, in a production system which informs business decisions, we must consider factors which aren't readily captured by metrics which compare generated and 'gold' outputs. For example, changing a single word can reverse the meaning of a summary, with only a small change in such scores. Hence, we consider a range of pros and cons.

The sentence compression method is supervised and is trained to produce summaries which can take advantage of news-specific grammatical styles. However, the OpenIE system is much faster and offers greater interpretability and controllability.

Since the neural and symbolic systems provide different advantages, we apply both. This renders a diverse pool of candidate summaries from which the ranker's task is to select the best. At the pooling stage we also impose a length constraint of 50 characters and exclude any longer candidates.

4.5 Key Story Selection

As a sample from the full story cluster, NSTM selects an ordered list of *key stories* which are deemed to be *representative*. We select these using a heuristic based on intuition and client feedback.

Our approach is to re-cluster all stories in the cluster using HAC (see Sec. 4.3.2), to create a parameterized number of sub-clusters. For each sub-cluster, we select the story that has maximum average similarity τ (as per Sec. 4.3.1) to the other sub-cluster stories. This strategy is intended to select stories which represent each cluster's diversity.

We sort the key stories by sub-cluster size and time of ingestion, in that order of precedence.

---

[7]E.g., with NDCG$_5$, the (untrained) NVDM dot-product yields 0.61, while the bilinear model and DecAtt yield 0.64.

354

4.6 Theme Ranking

We have described how (story cluster, summary, key stories) triples, or *themes*, are created. However, some themes are considered to be more *important* than others since they are more useful to readers. It is tricky to define this concept concretely but we apply proxy metrics in order to estimate an importance *score* for each theme. We rank themes by this score and, in order to save screen space, return only the top few ('key') themes as an *overview*.

The main factor considered in the importance score is the size of the story cluster – the larger the cluster, the larger the score. This heuristic corresponds to the observation that more important themes tend to be reported on more frequently. Additionally, we consider the entropy of the news sources in the cluster, which corresponds to the observation that more important themes are reported on by a larger number of publishers and reduces the impact of a source publishing duplicate stories.

4.7 Caching

Since many user requests are the same or use similar data, caching is useful to minimize response times. When NSTM receives a request, it checks whether there is a corresponding overview in the cache, and immediately returns it if so. 99.6% of requests hit the cache and 99% of requests are handled within $215ms$.[8] In the event of a cache miss, NSTM responds in a median time of $723ms$.[9]

We apply two mechanisms to ensure cache freshness. Firstly, we preemptively invoke NSTM using requests that are likely to be queried by users (e.g., most read topics) and re-compose them from scratch at fixed intervals (e.g., every 30 min). Once computed, they are cached. The second mechanism is user-driven: every time a user requests an overview which is not cached, it will be created and added to the cache. The system will subsequently preemptively invoke NSTM using this request for a fixed period of time (e.g., 24 hours).

5 Demonstration

NSTM was deployed to our clients in 2019. Using the UI depicted in Fig. 1, users can find overviews for customized queries to help support their work. From this screen, the user can enter a search query using any combination of Boolean logic with tag- or keyword-based terms. They may also alter the

---

[8]Computed for all requests over a 90-day period.

[9]Computed for the top 50 searches over a 7-day period.

	Summary	Size
1	Facebook to Settle Recognition Privacy Lawsuit	90
2	Facebook Warns Revenue Growth Slowing	79
3	Facebook Stock Drops 7% Despite Earnings Beat	70
4	Facebook to Remove Coronavirus Misinformation	49
5	Mark Zuckerberg to Launch WhatsApp Payments	19

Table 1: Ranked theme summaries and cluster sizes for 'Facebook' (1,176 matching stories) from 31 Jan. 2020.

	Summary	Size
1	Britain to Leave the EU	459
2	Bank of England Would Keep Interest Rate Unchanged	141
3	Sturgeon Demands Scottish Independence Vote	71
4	Pompeo in UK for Trade Talks	45
5	Boris Johnson Hails 'Beginning' on Brexit Day	63

Table 2: Ranked theme summaries and cluster sizes for 'U.K.' (13,858 matching stories) from 31 Jan. 2020.

period that the overview is calculated over (this UI offers 1 hour, 8 hour, 1 day, and 2 day options).

This interface also allows users to provide feedback via the 'thumb' icons or plain-text comments. Of several hundred per-overview feedback submissions, over three quarters have been positive.

Tables 1 and 2 show example theme summaries generated for the queries 'Facebook' and 'U.K.'. Note that the summaries are quite different from what has previously been studied by the NLP community (in terms of brevity and grammatical style) and that they accurately represent distinct events.

In addition to user-driven settings, NSTM can be used to supplement context-driven applications. One example, demonstrated in Appendix D, uses themes provided by NSTM to help explain why companies or topics are 'trending'.

6 Conclusion

We presented NSTM, a novel and production-ready system that composes concise and human-readable news overviews given arbitrary user search queries.

NSTM is the first of its kind; it is query-driven, it offers unique news overviews which leverage clustering and succinct summarization, and it has been released to hundreds of thousands of users.

We also demonstrated effective adoption of modern NLP techniques and advances in the design and implementation of the system, which we believe will be of interest to the community.

There are many open questions which we intend to research, such as whether autoregressivity in neural sentence compression can be exploited and how to compose themes over longer time periods.

References

Charu C Aggarwal and Philip S Yu. 2006. A framework for clustering massive text and categorical data streams. In *Proceedings of the 2006 SIAM International Conference on Data Mining*, pages 479–483. SIAM.

Miguel Almeida and André Martins. 2013. Fast and robust compressive summarization with dual decomposition and multi-task learning. In *Proceedings of the 51st Annual Meeting of the Association for Computational Linguistics (Volume 1: Long Papers)*, pages 196–206, Sofia, Bulgaria. Association for Computational Linguistics.

Sanjeev Arora, Yingyu Liang, and Tengyu Ma. 2017. A simple but tough-to-beat baseline for sentence embeddings. In *Proceedings of the 5th International Conference on Learning Representations*, ICLR'17. OpenReview.net.

Michele Banko, Michael J. Cafarella, Stephen Soderland, Matt Broadhead, and Oren Etzioni. 2007. Open information extraction from the web. In *Proceedings of the 20th International Joint Conference on Artifical Intelligence*, IJCAI'07, page 2670–2676, San Francisco, CA, USA. Morgan Kaufmann Publishers Inc.

David M. Blei, Andrew Y. Ng, and Michael I. Jordan. 2003. Latent dirichlet allocation. *J. Mach. Learn. Res.*, 3:993–1022.

Jacob Devlin, Ming-Wei Chang, Kenton Lee, and Kristina Toutanova. 2019. BERT: Pre-training of deep bidirectional transformers for language understanding. In *Proceedings of the 2019 Conference of the North American Chapter of the Association for Computational Linguistics: Human Language Technologies, Volume 1 (Long and Short Papers)*, pages 4171–4186, Minneapolis, Minnesota. Association for Computational Linguistics.

Katja Filippova, Enrique Alfonseca, Carlos A. Colmenares, Lukasz Kaiser, and Oriol Vinyals. 2015. Sentence compression by deletion with LSTMs. In *Proceedings of the 2015 Conference on Empirical Methods in Natural Language Processing*, pages 360–368, Lisbon, Portugal. Association for Computational Linguistics.

Diederik P. Kingma and Max Welling. 2014. Auto-encoding variational bayes. In *2nd International Conference on Learning Representations, ICLR 2014, Banff, AB, Canada, April 14-16, 2014, Conference Track Proceedings*.

Eliyahu Kiperwasser and Yoav Goldberg. 2016. Simple and accurate dependency parsing using bidirectional LSTM feature representations. *Transactions of the Association for Computational Linguistics*, 4:313–327.

Renars Liepins, Ulrich Germann, Guntis Barzdins, Alexandra Birch, Steve Renals, Susanne Weber, Peggy van der Kreeft, Hervé Bourlard, João Prieto, Ondřej Klejch, Peter Bell, Alexandros Lazaridis, Alfonso Mendes, Sebastian Riedel, Mariana S. C. Almeida, Pedro Balage, Shay B. Cohen, Tomasz Dwojak, Philip N. Garner, Andreas Giefer, Marcin Junczys-Dowmunt, Hina Imran, David Nogueira, Ahmed Ali, Sebastião Miranda, Andrei Popescu-Belis, Lesly Miculicich Werlen, Nikos Papasarantopoulos, Abiola Obamuyide, Clive Jones, Fahim Dalvi, Andreas Vlachos, Yang Wang, Sibo Tong, Rico Sennrich, Nikolaos Pappas, Shashi Narayan, Marco Damonte, Nadir Durrani, Sameer Khurana, Ahmed Abdelali, Hassan Sajjad, Stephan Vogel, David Sheppey, Chris Hernon, and Jeff Mitchell. 2017. The SUMMA platform prototype. In *Proceedings of the Software Demonstrations of the 15th Conference of the European Chapter of the Association for Computational Linguistics*, pages 116–119, Valencia, Spain. Association for Computational Linguistics.

Chin-Yew Lin. 2004. ROUGE: A package for automatic evaluation of summaries. In *Text Summarization Branches Out*, pages 74–81, Barcelona, Spain. Association for Computational Linguistics.

Chin-Yew Lin and Eduard Hovy. 2003. Automatic evaluation of summaries using n-gram co-occurrence statistics. In *Proceedings of the 2003 Human Language Technology Conference of the North American Chapter of the Association for Computational Linguistics*, pages 150–157.

Yishu Miao, Lei Yu, and Phil Blunsom. 2016. Neural variational inference for text processing. In *Proceedings of the 33rd International Conference on International Conference on Machine Learning - Volume 48*, ICML'16, pages 1727–1736. JMLR.org.

Daniel Müllner. 2013. fastcluster: Fast hierarchical, agglomerative clustering routines for R and Python. *Journal of Statistical Software, Articles*, 53(9):1–18.

Joakim Nivre, Marie-Catherine De Marneffe, Filip Ginter, Yoav Goldberg, Jan Hajic, Christopher D Manning, Ryan McDonald, Slav Petrov, Sampo Pyysalo, Natalia Silveira, et al. 2016. Universal dependencies v1: A multilingual treebank collection. In *Proceedings of the Tenth International Conference on Language Resources and Evaluation (LREC'16)*, pages 1659–1666.

Ankur Parikh, Oscar Täckström, Dipanjan Das, and Jakob Uszkoreit. 2016. A decomposable attention model for natural language inference. In *Proceedings of the 2016 Conference on Empirical Methods in Natural Language Processing*, pages 2249–2255, Austin, Texas. Association for Computational Linguistics.

Danilo Jimenez Rezende, Shakir Mohamed, and Daan Wierstra. 2014. Stochastic backpropagation and approximate inference in deep generative models. In *Proceedings of the 31th International Conference on Machine Learning, ICML 2014, Beijing, China, 21-26 June 2014*, pages 1278–1286.

Ilya Sutskever, Oriol Vinyals, and Quoc V. Le. 2014.
Sequence to sequence learning with neural networks.
In *Advances in Neural Information Processing Systems 27: Annual Conference on Neural Information Processing Systems 2014, December 8-13 2014, Montreal, Quebec, Canada*, pages 3104–3112.

Srinivas Vadrevu, Choon Hui Teo, Suju Rajan, Kunal Punera, Byron Dom, Alexander J. Smola, Yi Chang, and Zhaohui Zheng. 2011. Scalable clustering of news search results. In *Proceedings of the Fourth ACM International Conference on Web Search and Data Mining*, WSDM'11, pages 675–684, New York, NY, USA. ACM.

Aaron Steven White, Drew Reisinger, Keisuke Sakaguchi, Tim Vieira, Sheng Zhang, Rachel Rudinger, Kyle Rawlins, and Benjamin Van Durme. 2016. Universal Decompositional Semantics on Universal Dependencies. In *Proceedings of the 2016 Conference on Empirical Methods in Natural Language Processing*, pages 1713–1723, Austin, Texas. Association for Computational Linguistics.

A   Acknowledgements

This has been a multi-year project, involving contributions from many people at different stages.

In particular, we thank Miles Osborne, Marco Ponza, Amanda Stent, Mohamed Yahya, Christoph Teichmann, Prabhanjan Kambadur, Umut Topkara, Ted Merz, Sam Brody, and Adrian Benton for reviewing and commenting on the manuscript; We further thank Adela Quinones, Shaun Waters, Mark Dimont, Ted Merz and other colleagues from the News Product group for helping to shape the vision of the system; We also thank José Abarca and his team for developing the user interface; We thank Hady Elsahar for helping to improve summary ranking during his internship; Finally, we thank all colleagues (especially those in the Global Data department) who helped to produce high quality in-house annotations and all others who contributed valuable thoughts and time into this work.

B   End-To-End Evaluation

We evaluate the end-to-end NSTM system when using the OpenIE (Sec. 4.4.1) and the BERT-based sentence compression (Sec. 4.4.2) algorithms as the sole source of candidate summaries. We also conducted one experiment where both were used to create a shared pool of candidates (as per Sec. 4.4.4).

We test the system end-to-end using the manually-annotated Single Document Summarization (SDS) test set described in Sec. 4.4.2. To implement SDS, our experimental setup assumes that only one story was returned by a search request (as per Sec. 4.2). We evaluate the output from each system with ROUGE (Lin and Hovy, 2003; Lin, 2004)[10]. The results are presented in Table 3.

Metric	OpenIE	BSC	Both
ROUGE-1 F_1	0.831	0.863	0.851
ROUGE-2 F_1	0.609	0.701	0.667
ROUGE-3 F_1	0.530	0.640	0.599
ROUGE-4 F_1	0.492	0.603	0.562
ROUGE-L F_1	0.621	0.706	0.670

Table 3: ROUGE scores for the Single-Document Summarization task in the end-to-end system, when using OpenIE, BERT-based sentence compression (BSC) and both to construct the pool of candidate summaries.

---

[10]https://github.com/google/seq2seq/blob/master/seq2seq/metrics/rouge.py

C Screenshots of A Query-Driven User Interface

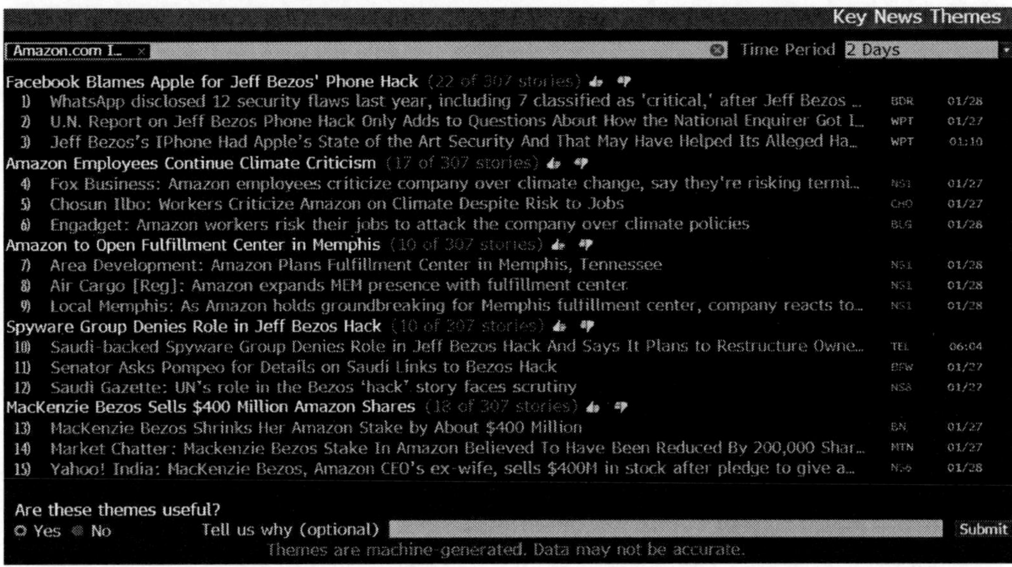

Figure 4: Screenshot (taken on 29 January 2020) of a query-driven interface for NSTM showing the overview for the company 'Amazon.com'.

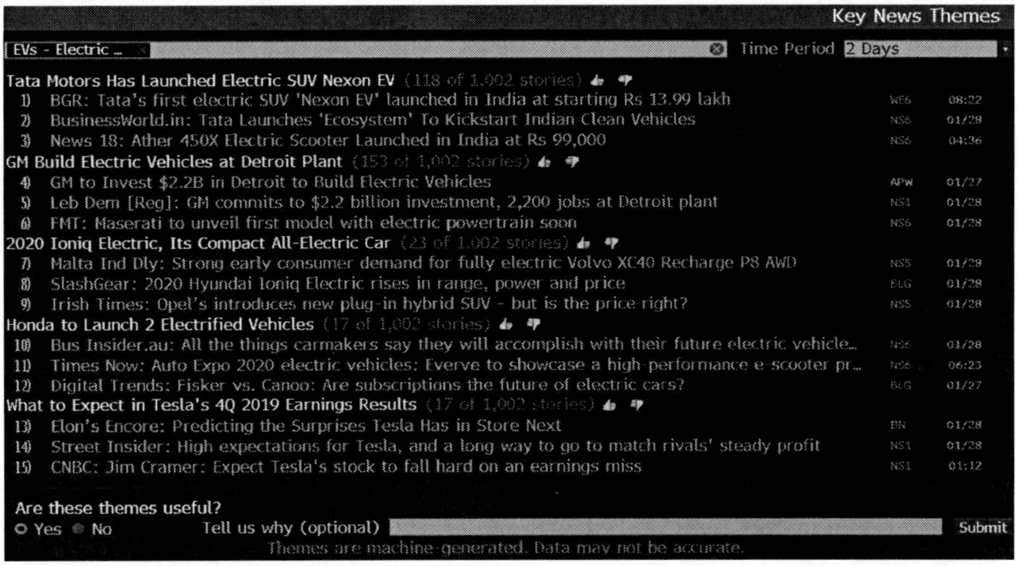

Figure 5: Screenshot (taken on 29 January 2020) of a query-driven interface for NSTM showing the overview for the topic 'Electric Vehicles'.

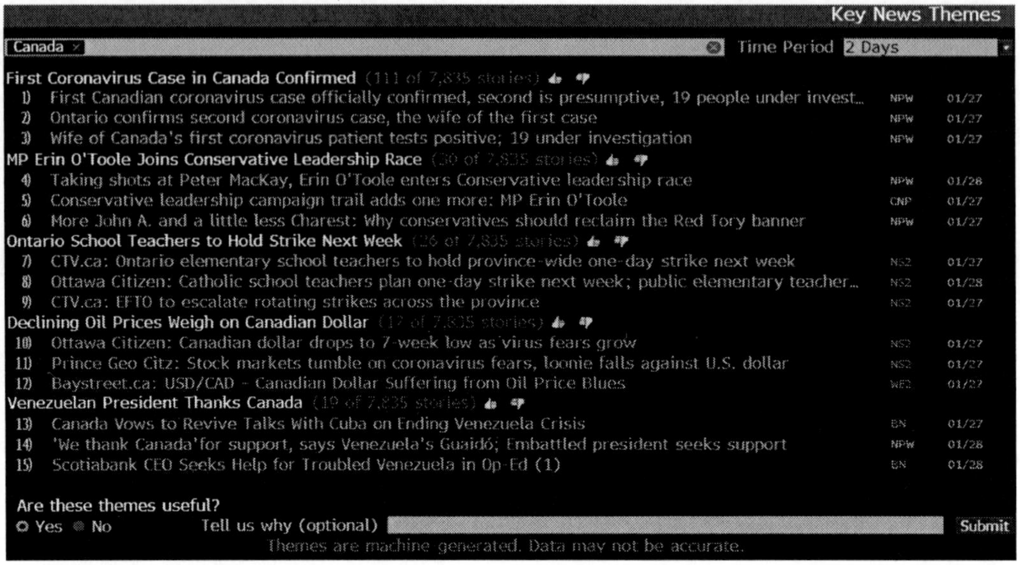

Figure 6: Screenshot (taken on 29 January 2020) of a query-driven interface for NSTM showing the overview for the region 'Canada'.

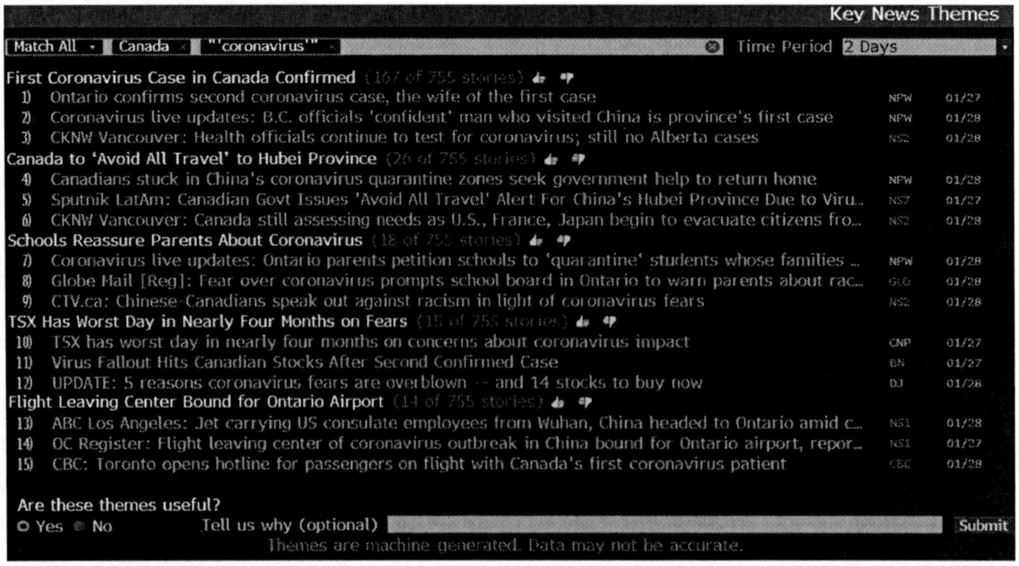

Figure 7: Screenshot (taken on 29 January 2020) of a query-driven interface for NSTM showing the overview for a complex query, including a keyword.

Settings ▾   News Trends

Companies   Security List   Topics   Region Worldwide ▾   Trend Period 1 Day ▾

News Reader Activity   News Sentiment   Twitter Sentiment   News Volume   Twitter Volume   Social Velocity

Largest Increase   Largest Total

Security	Δ Act.	↓ GN	Δ Price	Δ AVAT	News Summary
1) General Electric Co			+10.44%	+662.40%	GE Beats Profit, Cash Flow Estimates on Aviation
2) AT&T Inc			-2.46%	+121.37%	HBO Max Squeezes AT&T Revenue
3) Intelsat SA			-22.10%	+921.85%	U.S. Senate Proposal Limit C-Band Payout
4) Advanced Micro Devi...			-7.98%	+254.18%	AMD Revenue Forecast Disappoints
5) Apple Inc			+2.26%	+108.73%	Record Apple Q1 2020 Revenue and Profit Apple
6) Starbucks Corp			-3.06%	+89.65%	Starbucks Closed Half Stores in China Coronavirus
7) Tesla Inc			+0.67%	-25.75%	Tesla Earnings Are Coming
8) Deutsche Bank AG			+1.65%	-6.28%	Deutsche Bank Delays Raises to Fixed Pay
9) LVMH Moet Hennessy ...			-1.19%	+37.84%	Luxury Group LVMH Posts Record Sales
10) Walt Disney Co/The			-1.22%	-3.20%	Loki Marvel in Disney+ Series
11) Goldman Sachs Grou...			-0.46%	+42.35%	Term YORK The Goldman Sachs Group, Inc.
12) Anthem Inc			-5.24%	+304.44%	Insurer Anthem Misses 4Q Earnings Forecasts
13) McDonald's Corp			+2.69%	+154.75%	McDonald's Quarterly Sales Growth, Profit
14) American Airlines Gr...			+2.14%	-4.24%	American Airlines Suspending Flights to China
15) L Brands Inc			+13.35%	+1.27k%	Talks to Sell the Victoria's Secret Brand
16) JPMorgan Chase & Co			+0.67%	-35.11%	JPMorgan Keeps Bonuses Flat for Bankers, Traders
17) Credit Suisse Group ...			+0.75%	-26.61%	Credit Suisse Shed U.S. Private Bank With Eye
18) Novartis AG			+1.26%	+71.34%	Novartis Delivered Sales Growth
19) Mastercard Inc			-0.19%	+57.71%	Mastercard Earnings, Revenue Beat in Q4
20) Boeing Co/The			+2.77%	+264.12%	Boeing Posts Loss Since 1997 Max Costs Skyrocket

Figure 8: Screenshot (taken on 29 January 2020) of a context-driven application of NSTM. In the 'Security' column are the companies that have seen the largest increase in news readership over the last day. Each entry in the 'News Summary' column is the summary of the top theme provided by NSTM for the adjacent company.

Figure 9: Screenshot (taken on 29 January 2020) of a context-driven application of NSTM. In the 'News Topic' column are the topics that have seen the largest volume of news readership over the past 8 hours. Each entry in the 'News Summary' column is the summary of the top theme provided by NSTM for the adjacent topic.

SUPP.AI: Finding Evidence for Supplement-Drug Interactions

Lucy Lu Wang, Oyvind Tafjord, Arman Cohan, Sarthak Jain, Sam Skjonsberg,
Carissa Schoenick, Nick Botner, Waleed Ammar
Allen Institute for AI
Seattle, WA 98103
{lucyw, oyvindt, armanc, sarthakj, sams, carissas, nickb, waleeda}@allenai.org

Abstract

Dietary supplements are used by a large portion of the population, but information on their pharmacologic interactions is incomplete. To address this challenge, we present SUPP.AI, an application for browsing evidence of supplement-drug interactions (SDIs) extracted from the biomedical literature. We train a model to automatically extract supplement information and identify such interactions from the scientific literature. To address the lack of labeled data for SDI identification, we use labels of the closely related task of identifying drug-drug interactions (DDIs) for supervision. We fine-tune the contextualized word representations of the RoBERTa language model using labeled DDI data, and apply the fine-tuned model to identify supplement interactions. We extract 195k evidence sentences from 22M articles (P=0.82, R=0.58, F1=0.68) for 60k interactions. We create the SUPP.AI application for users to search evidence sentences extracted by our model. SUPP.AI is an attempt to close the information gap on dietary supplements by making up-to-date evidence on SDIs more discoverable for researchers, clinicians, and consumers.

1 Introduction

More than half of US adults use dietary supplements (Kantor et al., 2016). Supplements include vitamins, minerals, enzymes, and other herbal and animal products. Supplements and pharmaceutical drugs, when taken together, can cause adverse interactions (Sprouse and van Breemen, 2016; Asher et al., 2017; Ronis et al., 2018). Some studies describe the prevalence of supplement-drug interactions (SDIs) in the hospital setting (Levy et al., 2016, 2017a,b) or among groups such as patients with cancer (Alsanad et al., 2014), cardiac disease (Karny-Rahkovich et al., 2015), HIV/AIDS (Jalloh et al., 2017), or Alzheimer's disease (Spence

et al., 2017). However, these studies largely rely on manual curation of the literature, and are slow and expensive to produce and update. It is also difficult to aggregate their results, and researchers, clinicians, and consumers can lack appropriate up-to-date information to make informed decisions about supplement use.

A resource that provides experimental evidence for SDIs could serve as a good intermediary tool, allowing experts to quickly access information and translate it for healthcare providers and consumers. Such a tool could ease the bottleneck of manual curation by directing researcher attention to the most pertinent and novel interactions appearing in recent trials and case reports. Our goal is to create such a resource using state-of-the-art methods in NLP and IE, and allow users to better identify appropriate uses of supplements as well as risks for SDIs.

Automated approaches have been used to extract drug-drug interactions (DDIs) from literature and other documents (Tari et al., 2010; Percha et al., 2011; Segura-Bedmar et al., 2011; Kim et al., 2014; Zhang et al., 2016; Noor et al., 2017; Lim et al., 2018), complementing broadly-used but primarily manual methods (Grizzle et al., 2019). We expand upon this work to automatically extract evidence for SDIs, as well as supplement-supplement interactions (SSIs), from a large corpus of 22M biomedical and clinical texts derived from Semantic Scholar.[1] We leverage labeled datasets for DDI identification for supervision, and train a model that transfers to the related task of identifying supplement interactions. We surface the resulting evidence on SUPP.AI for browsing and search.

To summarize, our contributions are:

1. A model for identifying SDI/SSI evidence

2. A dataset of 195k evidence sentences supporting supplement interactions, publicly accessi-

---

[1] https://www.semanticscholar.org/

362

Proceedings of the 58th Annual Meeting of the Association for Computational Linguistics, pages 362–371
July 5 - July 10, 2020. ©2020 Association for Computational Linguistics

ble for download or via a web API, and

3. SUPP.AI, an application for browsing and searching the extracted evidence.

2 Supplement interaction browser

Information on supplement interactions have immediate implications on public health, which can only be realized by making the data easily accessible to any interested researcher, clinician or consumer. We note that many medical providers in developing countries do not have subscriptions to clinical databases such as TRC[2] and UpToDate,[3] and may lack an easy way to identify possible supplement interactions before prescribing drugs to their patients. To fill this gap, we develop SUPP.AI (available at https://supp.ai/), an application for browsing evidence of supplement interactions extracted from clinical and biomedical literature. SUPP.AI allows users to:

- Search for supplements or drugs,
- Search through potential interactions,
- Browse evidence sentences with supplement and drug entities highlighted,
- Navigate links to source papers

We design SUPP.AI to be a rapid way for users to access and search extracted SDI and SSI evidence. Our goal for this application is to provide a high quality, broadly-sourced, up-to-date, and easily accessible platform for searching through SDI and SSI evidence, while providing sufficient information for users to judge the quality of each piece of evidence. In Section 3, we describe the NLP pipeline used to extract evidence from scientific papers. Below, we describe the user interface and data features of SUPP.AI.

2.1 User interface

Besides the main search page seen by users when they first navigate to the site, SUPP.AI consists of two other types of pages: entity and interaction pages. Entity pages provide information about one supplement or drug, and a list of potential interacting entities, sorted by quantity of evidence. We provide information such as synonyms, drug trade names, and definitions about each entity upon hover over or expansion. Interaction pages display

all discovered pieces of evidence supporting an interaction between a pair of entities. The evidence is sorted by additional features extracted from source papers, such as the level of evidence and recency, discussed in Section 2.2.

Figure 1 shows the interface, with results for the ginkgo supplement. Results on the entity page (*left*) list 140 possible interactions to entities such as Warfarin and Nitric Oxide. When a result is selected, the interaction page is displayed (*right*), showing evidence sentences supporting the interaction along with metadata and links to each source paper. Spans linked to supplement and drug entities in evidence sentences are highlighted. To see more context or detail about the interaction, the user can navigate to the source paper to continue reading.

2.2 Supporting data for search

We extract additional paper metadata as a way to judge evidence quality. From Semantic Scholar, we retrieve the paper title, authors, publication venue, and year of publication. Medical Subject Headings (MeSH) tags associated with each paper are used to determine whether its results are derived from clinical trials, case reports, or animal studies. We also attempt to identify the retraction status of each paper, again using MeSH tags. Evidence sentences are ordered and presented based on associated paper metadata, prioritizing non-retracted studies, clinical trials, human studies, and recency (year of publication).

Using the RxNorm relationship *has_tradename* via the Unified Medical Language System (UMLS) Metathesaurus (Bodenreider, 2004), we derive trade names associated with drug ingredients, e.g. *Prozac* and *Sarafem* are trade names of the ingredient *fluoxetine*. Trade drugs are associated with active drug ingredients and indexed for search. Users can query a trade name rather than an active ingredient and be directed to the relevant interactions.

2.3 Data & API

Data on the site are periodically updated as new papers are incorporated into the Semantic Scholar corpus. Snapshots of the data are available for download at https://api.semanticscholar.org/supp/. Live data on the site, which is updated more frequently, can be accessed through our search API, documented at https://supp.ai/docs/api. Additionally, we provide training data, evaluation data, and the curated drug/supplement identifier lists (discussed in Section 3) used to

---

[2]https://naturalmedicines.therapeuticresearch.com/
[3]https://www.uptodate.com/

Figure 1: Top results for interactions with Ginkgo (*left*), and top evidence sentences for the SDI between Ginkgo and Warfarin (*right*). Source paper metadata are given below each evidence sentence.

produce the dataset of interactions at `https://github.com/allenai/sdi-detection`. We encourage others to reuse our data and model to improve information availability around supplement interactions and safety.

3 Methods

An overview of our NLP pipeline is given in Figure 2. We first retrieve Medline-indexed articles using the Semantic Scholar API,[4] and pre-process the text to generate candidate evidence sentences (Section 3.1). We then use our DDI-detection model, a neural network classifier based on BERT (Devlin et al., 2018) and fine-tuned on labeled DDI data from Ayvaz et al. (2015) (Section 3.2), to classify sentences for the existence of an interaction. Sentences classified as positive by our model are collated and surfaced on `SUPP.AI` (Section 2).

3.1 Generating candidate evidence

Approximately 22M Medline-indexed articles are downloaded using the Semantic Scholar API. The scispaCy library (Neumann et al., 2019) is used to perform sentence tokenization, NER, and entity linking over all paper abstracts. Entity mentions are linked to Concept Unique Identifiers (CUIs) from the UMLS Metathesaurus. An example sentence from Vaes and Hendeles (2000) is shown with linked entity mentions:

```
Hemorrhage and tendencies were noted in
   C0019080
four cases with ginkgo use and in three
     C0868928      C0330205
```

---

[4] https://api.semanticscholar.org/

```
cases with garlic; in none of these
C0868928      C0017102
cases were patients receiving warfarin.
C0868928      C0030705            C0043031
```

Of these linked entities, we preserve entities on a list of curated supplements and drugs (entities in blue). We generate these curated lists in a semi-automatic fashion, by querying the children of UMLS supplement and drug classes and performing fuzzy name matching to known supplements or drugs crawled from the web. We also perform clustering of similar entities to reduce redundancy in the final dataset, e.g., combining several variants of Vitamin D together into a single entity. Details on identifier curation and clustering are given in Appendix A.

We retain all sentences containing at least two entity mentions. For each sentence, we generate candidate evidence as each combination of two entity spans from that sentence.

3.2 DDI-detection model

We train a DDI-detection model to predict whether a given candidate sentence provides evidence of an interaction between two drug entities. Our DDI-detection model uses pre-trained BERT models (Bidirectional Encoder Representations from Transformers) (Devlin et al., 2018) to encode input sequences. These models have been shown to be effective at domain transfer, and are able to achieve high performance using small amounts of task-specific annotated data. In particular, we use the large version of the pre-trained RoBERTa model, a further-optimized BERT model, that has approximately 340M parameters (Liu et al., 2019).

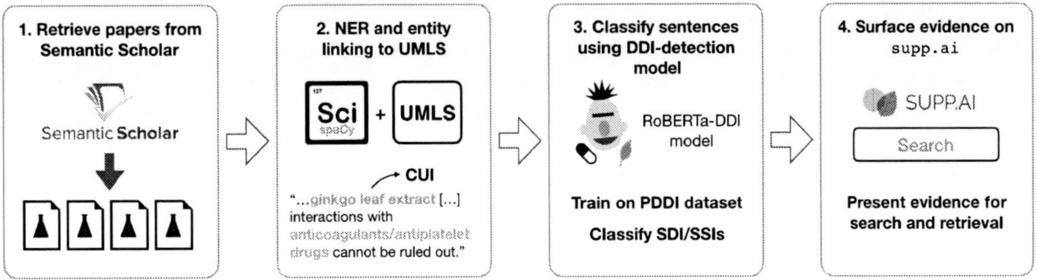

Figure 2: Pipeline for identifying sentences containing evidence of SDIs and SSIs.

We fine-tune the pre-trained embeddings of the RoBERTa language model using labeled data for DDI classification, and we call the resulting model RoBERTa-DDI.

Input layer: The input layer consists of the sequence of byte-pair encoding word pieces (Radford et al., 2019) in a sentence. We replace entity mention spans with the special tokens `[Arg1]` and `[Arg2]`. This helps generalization by preventing the model from memorizing entity pairs with positive interactions in the training set. For example:

```
[CLS] Combination [Arg1] may also
decrease the plasma concentration of
[Arg2]. [SEP]
```

where `[Arg1]` and `[Arg2]` replace the spans "hormonal contraceptives" and "acetaminophen" respectively. We add special tokens `[CLS]` and `[SEP]` at the beginning and end of each sentence to leverage their representations learned in pretraining. At prediction time, candidate sentences are masked similarly and fed to the trained model.

Model architecture: As the name implies, RoBERTa-DDI uses the pre-trained RoBERTa representations (Liu et al., 2019) to encode input sequences. We refer readers to Liu et al. (2019), Devlin et al. (2018), and Vaswani et al. (2017) for more details on BERT and transformer architecture. For the RoBERTa-DDI model, we add a dropout layer followed by one feedforward (output) layer with a softmax non-linearity, which takes the representation of the `[CLS]` token at the top transformer layer as input and outputs probabilities for labels $\{0, 1\}$, where 1 indicates an interaction.

Model training: Due to similarities between DDIs and SDIs/SSIs, we hypothesize that a classifier trained to identify DDI evidence should perform well in identifying SDI and SSI evidence. We therefore take advantage of existing labeled data

for categorizing DDIs to fine-tune the model. We use pre-trained weights distributed by the authors of Liu et al. (2019), and further fine-tune the model parameters (as well as parameters of the output layer) using labeled DDI data from the Merged-PDDI dataset (Ayvaz et al., 2015).

In particular, we use training data from the DDI-2013 (Segura-Bedmar et al., 2013) and NLM-DailyMed (Stan et al., 2014) datasets, as they are relatively large and contain evidence sentences with annotated drug mention spans. The DDI-2013 dataset consists of sentences extracted from Drug-Bank and Medline; the NLM-DailyMed dataset draws sentences from cardiovascular drug product labels retrieved from DailyMed. Both datasets contain multi-class labels for different types of interactions. We distinguish between detection, a binary classification problem where the goal is to determine whether an interaction exists or not, and multi-class classification, where the goal is to determine the type of interaction. In this work, we focus on detection, but provide results for a variant of our model trained on classification that obtains SOTA performance compared to prior work.

For detection, we collapse labels corresponding to all interaction types (e.g., mechanism, advise, effect, etc.) into binary labels of 0 and 1, where 0 means no interaction, and 1 means an interaction of some type exists. Collapsing the positive labels is necessary for training one DDI-detection model on both the DDI-2013 and NLM-DailyMed datasets, since the two datasets are annotated with inconsistent interaction types. We preserve the train/test splits used in Ayvaz et al. (2015), and create a development set from the training set for iteration on model design and tuning.

A sentence from the training data can contain multiple drug entities. For training, we generate pairwise combinations of drug mention spans in each sentence. We note that many sentences are seen multiple times by our model with different labeled spans. Due to combinatorial explosion, and to prevent our model from learning excessively from a few instances containing lots of entity mentions, we restrict the training data to sentences containing less than or equal to 100 pairwise entity combinations. Table 1 shows the resulting data splits for the two datasets.

Dataset	Train	Dev.	Test	Label=1
DDI-2013	18362	2069	5688	17.2%
NLM-DailyMed	11372	1255	927	22.7%

Table 1: DDI training data split.

Our training hyperparameters follow those presented by Liu et al. (2019) (learning rate = 1e-5; 4 epochs). No additional hyperparameter tuning is performed.

4   Results & evaluation

Of the 22M articles we retrieve, around 4.6M abstracts contain candidate sentences. After initial filtering, 33.0M candidate sentences containing supplement entity mentions are classified by RoBERTa-DDI. Around 625k (1.9%) of these sentences are classified as positive for an interaction. We perform entity normalization across positive sentences based on CUI clusters, and perform additional ad hoc filtering of evidence to eliminate incorrectly detected spans resulting from poor NER and linking, such as the span "retina" linking to Vitamin A (C0040845). The resulting 195k sentences contain mentions of 2044 unique supplements and 2772 unique drugs, and provide evidence sentences for 60k interactions sourced from 133k papers.

Comparisons of model variants on DDI classification and detection (including SOTA results on both tasks) are given in Appendix B. To evaluate the transferability of DDI detection to the related task of SDI/SSI detection, we use a test set consisting of 500 sentences annotated for the presence or absence of a supplement interaction. To obtain a balanced test set despite the rare presence of a positive interaction, we sample half the instances from the set of sentences labeled as positive by a previous variant of our model based on fine-tuning BERT-large, and the other half from those labeled as negative. After manual annotation, 40% of the sampled instances were positive for an interaction. Annotation was performed by two authors without seeing model predictions, with an inter-annotator agreement of 94%. This test set was used for final evaluation, and never for model development or tuning. Table 2 shows the performance of RoBERTa-DDI on the DDI and supplement test sets. Performance on the SDI test set has precision 0.82, recall 0.58, and F1-score 0.68. Although there is performance degradation during transfer, the precision of detection remains high at 0.82.

Decrease in recall can be attributed to a larger percentage of positive instances in the SDI test set (roughly 40%, compared to 20% in the DDI training data). Another factor is the presence of incorrectly labeled entity spans in the supplements test set due to NER/linking errors. To better understand this second source of errors, we attempt to evaluate the performance of the scispaCy entity linker. Processing each sentence from the two DDI training sets using scispaCy, we determine that only 80% of drug entities from DDI-2013 and 76% from NLM-DailyMed are recognized and linked. The likelihood of supplement entities being successfully linked is likely lower, due to sparse training data for supplement NER and linking. These numbers provide an estimate of the global ceiling on recall for our model. In future work, we aim to explore ways to improve NER and linking and assess their impact on the results of SDI detection. SDI/SSI sentences in our output set can also be labeled by biomedical expert annotators and used to further tune the model for SDI/SSI detection.

Evaluation set	Prec.	Rec.	F1
Drugs (DDI-2013)	0.90	0.87	0.88
Drugs (NLM-DailyMed)	0.83	0.85	0.84
Supplements-500	0.82	0.58	0.68

Table 2: The RoBERTa-DDI model (trained on drug-drug interaction labels) is evaluated on two DDI evaluation sets (first two rows) and our supplement interaction evaluation set (last row).

5   Discussion

Information describing the safety and efficacy of dietary supplements can be difficult to find. The inability to locate evidence of SDIs can challenge clinician ability to advise patients and cause risks for consumers of dietary supplements. It is our hope that extracting evidence for SDIs/SSIs from a large corpus of scientific literature and making the evidence available through an easily accessible search interface can offset some of these risks.

This work demonstrates how NLP techniques can be extraordinarily useful for extracting information and relationships specific to an application domain in healthcare. Re-purposing existing labeled data from related domains (that would be expensive to generate in a new domain) can be a way to derive maximum utility from curation efforts. Continuing, we look to investigate fine-grained interaction types, and provide better classification of the level of evidence provided by each sentence or document towards a particular SDI or SSI. We also aim to leverage similar techniques for identifying evidence of indications, contraindications, and side effects of dietary supplements from the biomedical and clinical literature, and make these discoverable on `SUPP.AI`.

5.1 Related Work

Consumer-facing websites such as the NIH Office of Dietary Supplements[5] or WebMD[6] provide facts about common supplements, but this information can be incomplete and may not support researcher or clinician needs. TRC Natural Medicines[7] and UpToDate[8], two dedicated clinical resources, contain high-quality, curated evidence, but may not be broadly accessible due to their subscription format. Drug databases like DrugBank (Wishart et al., 2018), RxNorm (Nelson et al., 2011), and the National Drug File Reference Terminology (NDFRT) (Simonaitis and Schadow, 2010) contain only partial coverage of supplement terminology (Manohar et al., 2015b), and primarily focus on aggregating drug information.

Several prior studies have experimented with extracting safety information of supplements and supplement interactions from various forms of text. Zhang et al. (2015) employ machine learning techniques to filter supplement interaction relationships in SemMedDB, a database of relationships extracted from Medline articles. Jiang et al. (2017) develop a model for identifying adverse effects related to dietary supplements as reported by consumers on Twitter, and discover 191 adverse effects pertaining to 4 dietary supplements. Fan et al. (2016) and Fan and Zhang (2018) analyze unstructured clinical notes to predict whether a patient started, continued or discontinued a dietary supplement, which can be useful as a building block

for identifying adverse effects in clinical notes (as attempted by the same authors in Fan et al. (2017) for the drug warfarin). Wang et al. (2017) proposes using topic models to analyze the adverse effects of dietary supplements as mentioned in the Dietary Supplement Label Database, and finds that Latent Dirichlet Allocation models (Blei et al., 2003) can be used to group dietary supplements with similar adverse effects based on their labels. As far as we know, there are no other studies investigating the task of sentence-level identification of SDI/SSI evidence from the scientific literature. No previous work has investigated the utility of using labeled DDI data for transfer learning to SDI/SSI identification.

5.2 Limitations

There are several limitations of this work. First, we distinguish between supplements and drugs. Both supplements and drugs are pharmacologic entities, with their separate classification more attributable to marketing and social pressures rather than functional differences. However, due to this somewhat arbitrary distinction, supplement entities are not well represented in databases of pharmaceutical entities, and less information is publicly available on their interactions. We also use UMLS CUIs as a way of identifying supplement and drug entities. The lack of a standardized terminology to describe dietary supplements is discussed in Manohar et al. (2015a) and Wang et al. (2016), which estimate UMLS coverage of these terms to be between 14-54%. This limitation prevents us from identifying many supplement entities. Lastly, our dependence on NLP-pipeline tools sets a performance ceiling due to unsolved problems in NER and linking. Although scispaCy is performant and detects a large number of relevant entities, our evaluations show that many supplement and drug entities are missed. A system such as MetaMapLite (Demner-Fushman et al., 2017) has higher recall, but performance is slow and there are practical challenges to using it to process large numbers of documents.

Conclusion

Insufficient regulation in the supplement space introduces dangers for the many users of these supplements. Claims of interactions are difficult to validate without links to source evidence. We create an NLP pipeline to detect SDI/SSI evidence from scientific literature, leveraging UMLS identifiers, scispaCy for NER and entity linking, BERT-based

---

[5] https://ods.od.nih.gov/

[6] https://www.webmd.com/vitamins/index

[7] https://naturalmedicines.therapeuticresearch.com/

[8] https://www.uptodate.com/

language models for classification, and labeled data from a related domain for training. We use this pipeline to extract evidence from 22M biomedical and clinical articles with high precision. The extracted SDI/SSI evidence are made search-able through a public web interface, SUPP.AI, where we integrate additional metadata about source papers to help users make decisions about the reliability of evidence. Our dataset and web interface can be leveraged by researchers, clinicians, and curious individuals to increase understanding about supplement interactions. We hope to encourage additional research to improve the safety and benefits of dietary supplements for their consumers.

Acknowledgments

We would like to thank Oren Etzioni for his indispensable feedback and support of this project. We thank Amandalynne Paullada for contributing to an earlier prototype, and we thank Asma Ben Abacha, Pieter Cohen, Taha Kass-Hout, Beth Ranker, Lia Schmitz, Heidi Tafjord, and our users for helpful comments on improving SUPP.AI.

References

Saud M. Alsanad, Elizabeth M. Williamson, and Rachel L. Howard. 2014. Cancer patients at risk of herb/food supplement-drug interactions: a systematic review. *Phytotherapy research: PTR*, 28(12):1749–1755.

Gary N. Asher, Amanda H. Corbett, and Roy L. Hawke. 2017. Common Herbal Dietary Supplement-Drug Interactions. *American Family Physician*, 96(2):101–107.

Serkan Ayvaz, John Horn, Oktie Hassanzadeh, Qian Zhu, Johann Stan, Nicholas P. Tatonetti, Santiago Vilar, Mathias Brochhausen, Matthias Samwald, Majid Rastegar-Mojarad, Michel Dumontier, and Richard D. Boyce. 2015. Toward a complete dataset of drug-drug interaction information from publicly available sources. *Journal of Biomedical Informatics*, 55:206–217.

David M. Blei, Andrew Y. Ng, and Michael I. Jordan. 2003. Latent dirichlet allocation. *J. Mach. Learn. Res.*, 3:993–1022.

Olivier Bodenreider. 2004. The unified medical language system (umls): integrating biomedical terminology. *Nucleic acids research*, 32 Database issue:D267–70.

Geeticka Chauhan, Matthew B. A. McDermott, and Peter Szolovits. 2019. Reflex: Flexible framework for relation extraction in multiple domains. In *BioNLP@ACL*.

Dina Demner-Fushman, Willie J. Rogers, and Alan R. Aronson. 2017. Metamap lite: an evaluation of a new java implementation of metamap. *Journal of the American Medical Informatics Association : JAMIA*, 24:841–844.

Jacob Devlin, Ming-Wei Chang, Kenton Lee, and Kristina Toutanova. 2018. Bert: Pre-training of deep bidirectional transformers for language understanding. *ArXiv*, abs/1810.04805.

Yadan Fan, Terrence Adam, Reed McEwan, Serguei V. S. Pakhomov, Genevieve B. Melton, and Rui Zhang. 2017. Detecting signals of interactions between warfarin and dietary supplements in electronic health records. In *MedInfo*.

Yadan Fan, Lu He, and Rui Zhang. 2016. Classification of use status for dietary supplements in clinical notes. *2016 IEEE International Conference on Bioinformatics and Biomedicine (BIBM)*, pages 1054–1061.

Yadan Fan and Rui Zhang. 2018. Using natural language processing methods to classify use status of dietary supplements in clinical notes. In *BMC Medical Informatics and Decision Making*.

Amy J. Grizzle, John Horn, Carol Collins, Jodi Schneider, Daniel C. Malone, Britney Stottlemyer, and Richard David Boyce. 2019. Identifying Common Methods Used by Drug Interaction Experts for Finding Evidence About Potential Drug-Drug Interactions: Web-Based Survey. *Journal of Medical Internet Research*, 21(1):e11182.

Mohamed A. Jalloh, Philip J. Gregory, Darren Hein, Zara Risoldi Cochrane, and Aleah Rodriguez. 2017. Dietary supplement interactions with antiretrovirals: a systematic review. *International journal of STD & AIDS*, 28(1):4–15.

Keyuan Jiang, Yongbing Tang, G. Elliott Cook, and Michael M. Madden. 2017. Discovering potential effects of dietary supplements from twitter data. In *Proceedings of the 2017 International Conference on Digital Health*, pages 119–126.

Elizabeth D. Kantor, Colin D. Rehm, Mengmeng Du, Emily White, and Edward L. Giovannucci. 2016. Trends in Dietary Supplement Use Among US Adults From 1999-2012. *JAMA*, 316(14):1464–1474.

Orith Karny-Rahkovich, Alex Blatt, Gabby Atalya Elbaz-Greener, Tomer Ziv-Baran, Ahuva Golik, and Matityahu Berkovitch. 2015. Dietary supplement consumption among cardiac patients admitted to internal medicine and cardiac wards. *Cardiology Journal*, 22(5):510–518.

Sun Kim, Haibin Liu, Lana Yeganova, and W. John Wilbur. 2014. Extracting drug-drug interactions from literature using a rich feature-based linear kernel approach. *Journal of biomedical informatics*, 55:23–30.

Jinhyuk Lee, Wonjin Yoon, Sungdong Kim, Donghyeon Kim, Sunkyu Kim, Chan Ho So, and Jaewoo Kang. 2019. Biobert: a pre-trained biomedical language representation model for biomedical text mining. *Bioinformatics*.

Ilana Levy, Samuel Attias, Eran Ben Arye, Lee Goldstein, and Elad Schiff. 2016. Interactions between dietary supplements in hospitalized patients. *Internal and Emergency Medicine*, 11(7):917–927.

Ilana Levy, Samuel Attias, Eran Ben-Arye, Lee Goldstein, and Elad Schiff. 2017a. Adverse events associated with interactions with dietary and herbal supplements among inpatients. *British Journal of Clinical Pharmacology*, 83(4):836–845.

Ilana Levy, Samuel Attias, Eran Ben-Arye, Lee Goldstein, and Elad Schiff. 2017b. Potential drug interactions with dietary and herbal supplements during hospitalization. *Internal and Emergency Medicine*, 12(3):301–310.

Sangrak Lim, Kyubum Lee, and Jaewoo Kang. 2018. Drug drug interaction extraction from the literature using a recursive neural network. volume 13, page e0190926.

Yinhan Liu, Myle Ott, Naman Goyal, Jingfei Du, Mandar Joshi, Danqi Chen, Omer Levy, Mike Lewis, Luke Zettlemoyer, and Veselin Stoyanov. 2019. Roberta: A robustly optimized bert pretraining approach. *ArXiv*, abs/1907.11692.

Nivedha Manohar, Terrance J. Adam, Serguei V. Pakhomov, Genevieve B. Melton, and Rui Zhang. 2015a. Evaluation of Herbal and Dietary Supplement Resource Term Coverage. *Studies in Health Technology and Informatics*, 216:785–789.

Nivedha Manohar, Terrence Adam, Serguei V. S. Pakhomov, Genevieve B. Melton, and Rui Zhang. 2015b. Evaluation of herbal and dietary supplement resource term coverage. *Studies in health technology and informatics*, 216:785–9.

Stuart J. Nelson, Kelly Zeng, John Kilbourne, Tammy Powell, and Robin Moore. 2011. Normalized names for clinical drugs: Rxnorm at 6 years. *Journal of the American Medical Informatics Association : JAMIA*, 18:441–8.

Mark Neumann, Daniel King, Iz Beltagy, and Waleed Ammar. 2019. Scispacy: Fast and robust models for biomedical natural language processing. *ArXiv*, abs/1902.07669.

Adeeb Noor, Abdullah Assiri, Serkan Ayvaz, Connor Clark, and Michel Dumontier. 2017. Drug-drug interaction discovery and demystification using Semantic Web technologies. *Journal of the American Medical Informatics Association: JAMIA*, 24(3):556–564.

Yifan Peng, Shankai Yan, and Zhiyong Lu. 2019. Transfer learning in biomedical natural language processing: An evaluation of bert and elmo on ten benchmarking datasets. *ArXiv*, abs/1906.05474.

Bethany Percha, Yael Garten, and Russ B. Altman. 2011. Discovery and explanation of drug-drug interactions via text mining. *Pacific Symposium on Biocomputing. Pacific Symposium on Biocomputing*, pages 410–21.

Alec Radford, Jeffrey Wu, Rewon Child, David Luan, Dario Amodei, and Ilya Sutskever. 2019. Language models are unsupervised multitask learners.

Martin J. J. Ronis, Kim B. Pedersen, and James Watt. 2018. Adverse Effects of Nutraceuticals and Dietary Supplements. *Annual Review of Pharmacology and Toxicology*, 58:583–601.

Sunil Kumar Sahu and Ashish Anand. 2017. Drug-drug interaction extraction from biomedical text using long short term memory network. *Journal of biomedical informatics*, 86:15–24.

Isabel Segura-Bedmar, Paloma Martínez, and María Herrero-Zazo. 2013. Semeval-2013 task 9 : Extraction of drug-drug interactions from biomedical texts (ddiextraction 2013). In *SemEval@NAACL-HLT*.

Isabel Segura-Bedmar, Paloma Martínez, and César de Pablo-Sánchez. 2011. A linguistic rule-based approach to extract drug-drug interactions from pharmacological documents. *BMC bioinformatics*, 12 Suppl 2:S1.

Linas Simonaitis and Gunther Schadow. 2010. Querying the national drug file reference terminology (ndfrt) to assign drugs to decision support categories. *Studies in health technology and informatics*, 160 Pt 2:1095–9.

Justin Spence, Monica Chintapenta, Hyanggi Irene Kwon, and Amie Taggart Blaszczyk. 2017. A Brief Review of Three Common Supplements Used in Alzheimer's Disease. *The Consultant Pharmacist: The Journal of the American Society of Consultant Pharmacists*, 32(7):412–414.

Alyssa A. Sprouse and Richard B. van Breemen. 2016. Pharmacokinetic Interactions between Drugs and Botanical Dietary Supplements. *Drug Metabolism and Disposition: The Biological Fate of Chemicals*, 44(2):162–171.

Johann Stan, Dina Demner-Fushman, Kin Wah Fung, Sonya E. Shooshan, Laritza Rodriguez, and Olivier Bodenreider. 2014. Title : A supervised machine learning framework for the extraction of drug-drug interactions from structured product labels.

Luis Tari, Saadat Anwar, Shanshan Liang, James Cai, and Chitta Baral. 2010. Discovering drug–drug interactions: a text-mining and reasoning approach based on properties of drug metabolism. volume 26, page i547–i553.

Luc Paul Frank Vaes and Leslie Hendeles. 2000. Interactions of warfarin with garlic, ginger, ginkgo, or ginseng: nature of the evidence. *The Annals of pharmacotherapy*, 34:1478–82.

Ashish Vaswani, Noam Shazeer, Niki Parmar, Jakob Uszkoreit, Llion Jones, Aidan N. Gomez, Lukasz Kaiser, and Illia Polosukhin. 2017. Attention is all you need. In *NIPS*.

Yefeng Wang, Terrence J. Adam, and Rui Zhang. 2016. Term Coverage of Dietary Supplements Ingredients in Product Labels. *AMIA Annual Symposium proceedings*, 2016:2053–2061.

Yefeng Wang, Divya R. Gunashekar, Terrence Adam, and Rui Zhang. 2017. Mining adverse events of dietary supplements from product labels by topic modeling. In *MedInfo*.

David S. Wishart, Yannick D. Feunang, An C. Guo, Elvis J. Lo, Ana Marcu, Jason R. Grant, Tanvir Sajed, Daniel Johnson, Carin Li, Zinat Sayeeda, Nazanin Assempour, Ithayavani Iynkkaran, Yifeng Liu, Adam Maciejewski, Nicola Gale, Alex Wilson, Lucy Chin, Ryan Cummings, Diana Le, Allison Pon, Craig Knox, and Michael Wilson. 2018. DrugBank 5.0: a major update to the DrugBank database for 2018. *Nucleic Acids Research*, 46(D1):D1074–D1082.

Rui Zhang, Terrance J. Adam, Gyorgy Simon, Michael J. Cairelli, Thomas C. Rindflesch, Serguei V. S. Pakhomov, and Genevieve B. Melton. 2015. Mining biomedical literature to explore interactions between cancer drugs and dietary supplements. In *AMIA Joint Summits on Translational Science proceedings. AMIA Joint Summits on Translational Science*.

Yaoyun Zhang, Heng-Yi Wu, Jun Xu, Jingqi Wang, Ergin Soysal, Lang Li, and Hongwei Xu. 2016. Leveraging syntactic and semantic graph kernels to extract pharmacokinetic drug drug interactions from biomedical literature. volume 10, page 67.

Yijia Zhang, Wei Zheng, Hongfei Lin, Jian Wang, Zhihao Yang, and Michel Dumontier. 2018. Drug–drug interaction extraction via hierarchical rnns on sequence and shortest dependency paths. In *Bioinformatics*.

Wei Zheng, Hongfei Lin, Ling Luo, Zhehuan Zhao, Zhengguang Li, Yijia Zhang, Zhihao Yang, and Jian Wang. 2017. An attention-based effective neural model for drug-drug interactions extraction. In *BMC Bioinformatics*.

A   Supplement and drug identifiers

We generate lists of supplement and drug entities based on UMLS Concept Unique Identifiers (CUIs) using a semi-automated method. For supplements, we identify NCI thesaurus (NCIT) concepts

Test dataset	Num. pairwise instances	RoBERTa-DDI (Trained on DDI-2013 and NLM-DailyMed)	RoBERTa-DDI (Trained on DDI-2013 only)
DDI-2013 (All)	5688	0.88	0.89
DDI-2013 (DrugBank)	5251	0.89	0.90
DDI-2013 (Medline)	437	0.73	0.77
NLM-DailyMed	927	0.84	0.70
All	6615	0.87	0.85

Table 3: F1-scores of RoBERTa-DDI trained using different training data. Test data contains all pairwise combinations of entities in test sentences.

such as "Dietary Supplement" (NCIT: C1505, CUI: C0242295), "Vascular Plant" (NCIT: C14336, CUI: C0682475), and "Antioxidant" (NCIT: C275, CUI: C0003402) as likely parents of supplement terms. We recursively extract child entities of these parent classes from UMLS, deriving an initial list of supplements. To improve recall, we extract supplement names from the TRC Natural Medicines database,[9] perform fuzzy string matching to entities in UMLS, and add any identified CUIs to our list of supplements. The list is manually reviewed to remove non-supplement entities, those for which we could not identify any marketed supplement or medicinal uses. Following curation, we retain 2139 unique supplement entities.

Similarly, we generate a corresponding list of drug CUIs from parent entity "Pharmacologic Substance" (NCIT: C1909, CUI: C1254351) and any UMLS entity with a DrugBank identifier. Fuzzy name matching between drugs on drugs.com[10] and UMLS entities is used to identify drugs and experimental chemicals missed through UMLS search alone. Due to the significantly larger number of drugs compared to supplements, manual curation of this list is impractical at this time. This process generates a list of 15252 unique drug CUIs. Any entity that is identified as both a supplement and a drug is categorized exclusively as a supplement for the purposes of this work.

Similar supplement and drug entities are merged, such as those with overlapping names, e.g., entities corresponding to UMLS C0006675, C0006726, C0596235, and C3540037 all describe variants of Calcium and are merged under the supplement entity C3540037 ("Calcium Supplement"). The

---

[9] https://naturalmedicines.therapeuticresearch.com/
[10] https://drugs.com/

Model	Reference	F1 (classification)	F1 (detection)
Bi-LSTM (w/ max and attentive pooling)	Sahu and Anand (2017)	0.69 (macro-F1)	-
Hierarchical Bi-LSTM + Attention + dependency path	Zhang et al. (2018)	0.73 (unspecified)	-
Bi-LSTM (w/ attention and negative instance filtering)	Zheng et al. (2017)	0.77 (unspecified)	0.84
BioBERT embeddings	Chauhan et al. (2019)	0.72 (macro-F1)	0.87
BERT-large embeddings fine-tuned on DDI-2013	Peng et al. (2019)	0.79 (micro-F1)	-
RoBERTa-DDI fine-tuned on DDI-2013	-	0.82 (micro-F1)	0.89

Table 4: Baseline models for DDI detection and reported performance on the DDI-2013 test set. Results are shown for classification (5-way classification) and detection (binary classification).

canonical CUI representing a cluster is selected manually. Drug, supplement, and canonical mappings are provided in our data repository.

B DDI model performance

We train RoBERTa-DDI on a combination of DDI-2013 and NLM-DailyMed training data. In Table 3, we report the F1-scores of model variants on the test data. We show the performance of the final variant of RoBERTa-DDI (trained on both DDI-2013 and NLM-DailyMed) as well as a variant trained only on DDI-2013 training data (last column), which performs best on the DDI-2013 test set, but suffers when tested on NLM-DailyMed. We also further break down performance on the DrugBank and Medline sub-corpora within DDI-2013.

The DDI-2013 dataset is used as a benchmark dataset for DDI detection and classification, and is part of the BLUE benchmark suite (Peng et al., 2019). RoBERTa-DDI outperforms recently-reported SOTA performance on DDI detection in the DDI-2013 dataset using BioBERT (Lee et al., 2019) (F1 = 0.87) (Chauhan et al., 2019). Peng et al. (2019) also report SOTA performance on the DDI-2013 classification task, achieving 0.79 micro-F1 using a tuned BERT-large model. For comparison, we show the results of RoBERTa-DDI trained on DDI-2013 multi-class classification, which achieves 0.82 micro-F1 on DDI-2013 classification. We provide previously reported SOTA performance metrics on DDI-2013 in Table 4. We note that because the interaction classes are unbalanced in the DDI-2013 dataset, reported classification micro- and macro-F1-scores in previous work are not directly comparable.

The inclusion of the NLM-DailyMed corpus increases training data diversity and should improve generalization for the task of detecting SDI/SSI evidence. Thus, although RoBERTa-DDI trained on

DDI-2013 has the highest performance on the DDI-2013 test set, RoBERTa-DDI trained over all training data performs the best overall, and we use this model variant to classify evidence for SUPP.AI.

LEAN-LIFE: A Label-Efficient Annotation Framework
Towards Learning from Explanation

Dong-Ho Lee[1]* Rahul Khanna[1]* Bill Yuchen Lin[1] Seyeon Lee[1] Qinyuan Ye[1]
Elizabeth Boschee[2] Leonardo Neves[3] Xiang Ren[1,2]
[1]Department of Computer Science, University of Southern California
[2]Information Science Institute, University of Southern California   [3]Snap Inc.
{dongho.lee,rahulkha,yuchen.lin,seyeonle,qinyuany}@usc.edu,
boschee@isi.edu, lneves@snap.com, xiangren@usc.edu

Abstract

Successfully training a deep neural network demands a huge corpus of labeled data. However, each label only provides limited information to learn from and collecting the requisite number of labels involves massive human effort. In this work, we introduce LEAN-LIFE[1], a web-based, Label-Efficient AnnotatioN framework for sequence labeling and classification tasks, with an easy-to-use UI that not only allows an annotator to provide the needed labels for a task, but also enables LearnIng From Explanations for each labeling decision. Such explanations enable us to generate useful additional labeled data from unlabeled instances, bolstering the pool of available training data. On three popular NLP tasks (named entity recognition, relation extraction, sentiment analysis), we find that using this enhanced supervision allows our models to surpass competitive baseline F1 scores by more than 5-10 percentage points, while using 2X times fewer labeled instances. Our framework is the first to utilize this enhanced supervision technique and does so for three important tasks—thus providing improved annotation recommendations to users and an ability to build datasets of *(data, label, explanation)* triples instead of the regular *(data, label)* pair.

1   Introduction

Deep neural networks have achieved state-of-the-art performance on a wide range of sequence labeling and classification tasks such as named entity recognition (NER) (Lample et al., 2016; Ma and Hovy, 2016), relation extraction (RE) (Zeng et al., 2015; Zhang et al., 2017; Ye et al., 2019), and sentiment analysis (SA) (Wang et al., 2016). However, they only yield such performance levels

---

*Both authors contributed equally.

[1]The source code is publicly available at `http://inklab.usc.edu/leanlife/`.

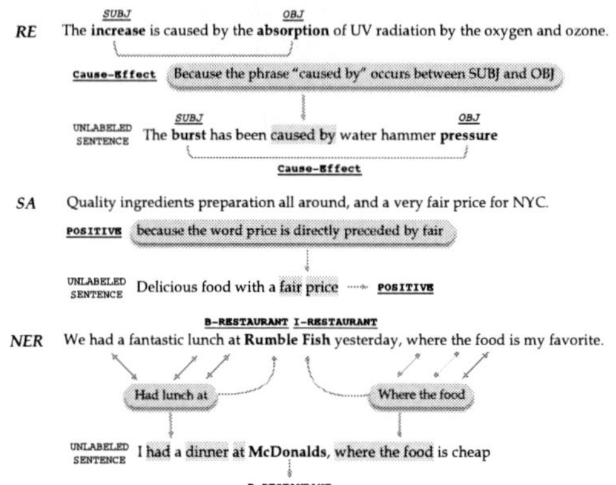

Figure 1: **Leveraging Labeling Explanations: 1) RE**: the explanation *"the phrase 'caused by' occurs between SUBJ and OBJ"* can aid in weakly labeling unlabeled instances like *"The burst has been caused by water hammer pressure"* with the label *"cause-effect"*; **2) NER**: Trigger spans near the labeled restaurant such as *"had lunch at"* and *"where the food"* can aid in weakly labeling unlabeled instances like *"I had a dinner at McDonalds, where the food is cheap"*.

in supervised learning scenarios, and in particular when human-annotated data is abundant. As we seek to apply NLP models to larger variety of domains, such as product reviews (Luo et al., 2018), social media messages (Lin et al., 2017), while reducing human annotation efforts, better annotation frameworks with label-efficient learning techniques are crucial to our progress.

Annotation frameworks have been explored by several previous works (Stenetorp et al., 2012; Bontcheva et al., 2014; Morton and LaCivita, 2003; de Castilho et al., 2016; Yang et al., 2018a). These existing open-source sequence annotation tools mainly focus on optimizing user-friendly user interfaces, such as providing shortcut key functionality to allow for faster tagging. The frameworks also attempt to provide annotation recommendation to reduce human annotation ef-

Proceedings of the 58th Annual Meeting of the Association for Computational Linguistics, pages 372–379
July 5 - July 10, 2020. ©2020 Association for Computational Linguistics

forts. However, these recommendations are provided by a pre-trained model or via dictionary look-ups. This methodology of providing recommendations often proves to be unhelpful when little annotated data exists for pre-training, as is usually the case for natural language tasks being applied to domain-specific or user-provided corpora.

To resolve this issue, AlpacaTag, an annotation framework for sequence labeling (Lin et al., 2019) attempts to provide annotation recommendations from a learned sequence labeling model that is incrementally updated by batches of incoming human annotations. Its model training follows an active learning strategy (Shen et al., 2017), which is shown to be a label-efficient, thus it attempts to minimize human annotation efforts. AlpacaTag selects the most informative batches of documents for humans to annotate and thus achieves a more cost-effective way of using human efforts. While active learning allows the model to achieve higher performance earlier in the learning process, model performance could be improved if additional supervision existed. It is imperative that provided annotation recommendations be as accurate as possible, as inaccurate annotation recommendations from the framework can push users towards generating noisy data, hindering instead of aiding the model training process.

Our effort to prevent this problem is centered around allowing annotators to provide additional supervision by capturing labeling explanations, while still taking advantage of the cost-effectiveness of active learning. Specifically, as shown in Fig. 1, we allow annotators to provide explanations for their decisions in natural language or by selecting *triggers*—nearby phrases that provide helpful context for their decisions. These enhanced annotations allow for model training over both user-provided labels, as well as weakly labeled data created by parsing explanations into high precision labeling rules. We therefore make attempts to ameliorate the erroneous recommendation problem by a performance-boosting training strategy that incorporates both labeled and unlabeled data.

Our work is also similar to recent attempts that exploit explanations for an improved training process (Srivastava et al., 2017; Hancock et al., 2018; Zhou et al., 2020; Wang* et al., 2020), but with two main differences. First, we embed this improved process in a practical application and sec-

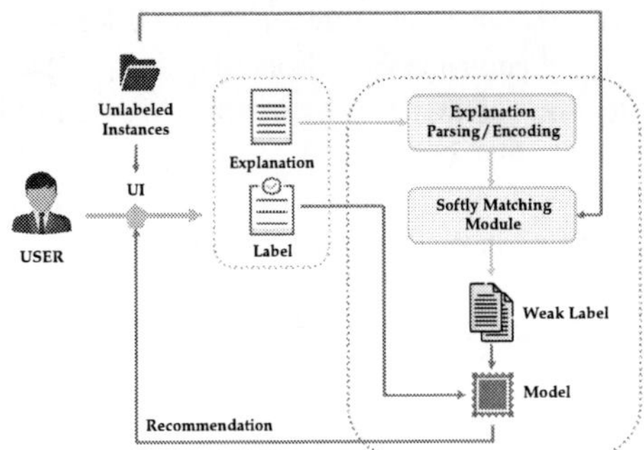

Figure 2: **System Architecture**.

ond, we design task specific architectures to incorporate the now captured explanations into training.

To the best of our knowledge, there is no existing open-source, easy-to-use, recommendation-providing, online-learning annotation framework that can also capture explanations. LEAN-LIFE is the first framework to capture and leverage explanations for improved model training and performance, while still inheriting the advantages of existing tools. We summarize our contributions as:

• **Improved Model Training:** Our recommendation models use a performance improving training process that leverages explanations to weakly label unlabeled instances. Our models improve on competitive baseline F-1 scores by more than 5-10 percentage points, while using 2X less data.

• **Multiple Supported Tasks:** Our framework supports both sequence labeling (as in NER) and sequence classification (as in RE, SA).

• **Explanation Dataset Creation:** We make it easy to build a new type of dataset, one that consists of triples of: text, labels and labeling explanations. The exporting of this captured data is available in two common data formats, CSV and JSON.

2 System Overview

As shown in Fig. 2, our framework consists of two main components, a user-friendly web-UI that can capture labels and explanations for labeling decisions, and a weak supervision framework that parses explanations for the creation of weakly labeled data. The framework then uses this weakly labeled data in conjunction with user-provided labels to train models for improved annotation recommendations. Our UI shows annotators unlabeled instances (can be sampled using active learning), along with annotation recommendations in an effort to reduce annotation costs. We use PyTorch to build our models and implement an API for communication between the web-UI and our weak supervision framework. The learned parameters of our framework are updated in an online fashion, thus improving in near real time. We will first touch on the annotation UI (§3) and then go into our weak supervision framework (§4).

3 UI for Capturing Human Explanation

The emphasis of our front-end design is to simplify the capture of both label and explanation for each labeling decision, while reducing annotation effort via accessible annotation recommendation. Our framework supports two forms of explanations, *Triggers* and *Natural Language*. A Trigger is a group of words in the sentence being annotated that aided the annotator's labeling decision, while Natural Language is a written explanation of the labeling decision. This section presents first the UI for capturing triggers (§3.1) and then the UI for capturing natural language explanations (§3.2).

3.1 Capturing Triggers

Fig. 3 illustrates how our framework can capture both a named entity (NE) label and triggers for the sentence "We had a fantastic lunch at Rumble Fish yesterday where the food is my favorite". The user is first presented with a piece of text to annotate (Annotating Section), the available labels that may be applied to sub-sequences (spans) of text (in the blue header) and recommendations of what spans of text should be considered as NE mentions (Named Entity Recommendation Section). The user may choose to select a span of text to label, or they may click on one of the recommended spans below (Fig. 2a). If the user clicks on a recommended span, a small pop-up displaying the available labels appear with the recommended label circled in red (Fig. 2a). Once the user selects a label for a span of text by either clicking on the desired label button or via a predefined shortcut key (ex: for Restaurant the shortcut key is **r**), a pop-up appears (Fig. 2b), asking the user to select helpful spans (triggers) from the text that provide useful context in deciding the label for the NEM—multiple triggers may be selected. The user may cancel their decision to label a span of text with a label by clicking the *x* button in the pop-up, but if the user wants to proceed and has selected at least one trigger, they finish the labeling by hitting done. Then, their label is visualized in the Annotating Section by highlighting the NEM.

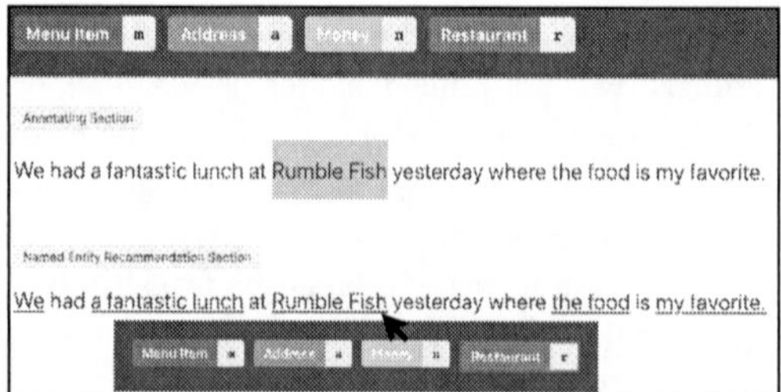

(a) the labels appear in the header, followed by an annotating section; tagging suggestions are shown as underlined spans at the bottom of the page. A user may hover over a tagging suggestion or select a span in order to apply a label to a substring.

(b) after clicking a label to assign to a text span, a pop up appears asking the user to explain their decision by selecting nearby "trigger" text spans.

Figure 3: The workflow to annotate a NE label and trigger span. ("Rumble Fish" as Restaurant).

3.2 Capturing Natural Language

Fig. 4 illustrates how for the sentence "Tahawwur Hussain Rana who was born in Pakistan but is a Canadian citizen" our framework can capture both a relation label between NEs and the subsequent natural language explanation. First, the user is tasked to find the NEs in the sentence. After labeling at least two non-consecutive spans of text as NEs, the user may check off the boxes that appear above the labeled NEs. Once two boxes have been checked off, the labels in the blue header are replaced with the labels for relations. The click-order of the checked boxes is displayed and is considered the order of the relation. Also, we display a recommend label to the user in the header section with a circle (Fig. 2a). After clicking on a label, a pop-up appears asking the user to indicate semantic and syntactic reasons as to why the labeling decision is true. Since the natural language explanations are assumed to be made up of predefined predicates, as the user types we incrementally provide predicates to aid the construction of an explanation (Fig. 2b). In this way, we nudge users towards writing explanations the semantic parser is able to break down, allowing our framework to extract a useful logical form from the explanation.

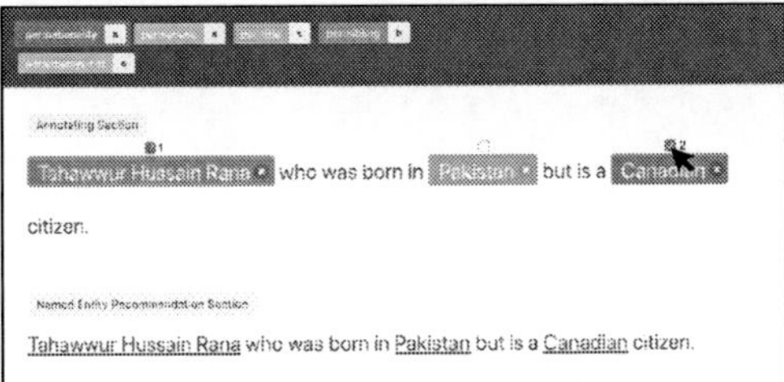

(a) After two NEs have been checked off, the relation labels replace the entity labels in the header; a suggested relation label is again circled in red.

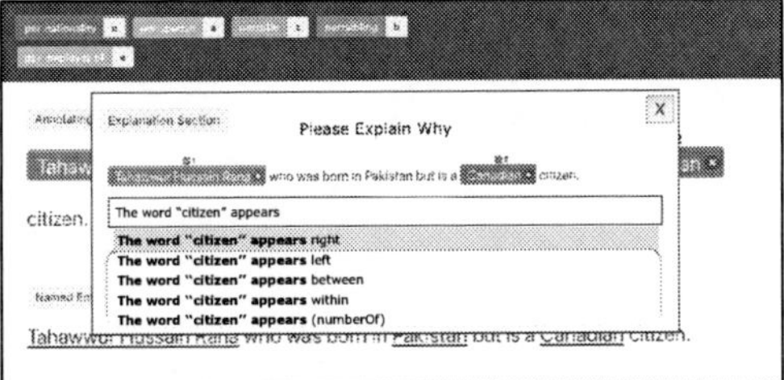

(b) After selecting a label for a relation, a pop up will ask the user to explain their decision in natural language. As the reasons must be parsed for understanding, suggested parsable predicates are shown to lead users to parsable explanations.

Figure 4: The workflow to annotate a relation label and NL explanation. ("per:nationality" as a relation label between "Tahawwur Hussain Rana" and "Canadian").

4 LEAN-LIFE Framework

Our Weak Supervision Framework is composed of two main components, a weak labeling module that parses explanations to create labeling rules and a downstream model. The framework parses user-provided explanations to generate weakly labeled data and then trains the appropriate downstream model with this augmented training data. Our weak labeling module supports both explanation formats provided to the annotator in the UI—triggers and natural language. This section first introduces how the module utilizes triggers (§4.1) and then presents how the module deals with natural language(§4.2).

4.1 Input: Trigger

When a trigger is inputted into the system, we generate weak labels for our training data via soft-matching between trigger representations and unlabeled sentences (Lin et al., 2020). Each sentence may contain one or more triggers, but each trigger is associated with only one label. Our framework jointly learns a mapping between triggers and their label using a linear layer with a soft-max output

and a log-likelihood loss, as well as the semantic similarity between the triggers and their associated sentences using contrastive loss—we weigh both objectives equally. Through this joint learning, our trigger representations can capture label knowledge as well as semantic information. We use these representations to improve model training by generating weakly labeled data via soft matching on the unlabeled sentences. More specifically, for each unlabeled sentence, we first calculate the semantic similarity between the sentence and all collected triggers and then filter out all triggers where the similarity distance is larger than our fixed threshold. We then generate a trigger-aware sentence encoding for each threshold-passing trigger and feed these encodings into a downstream classifier for label inference. Finally, we conduct majority vote over outputted label sequences to finalize our weak labels for the unlabeled sentence. In this manner we are able to train over more data, where a good portion of it is weakly labeled.

4.2 Input: Natural Language

When natural language is inputted into the system, our module grows training data via soft-matching between logical forms parsed from natural language explanations and unlabeled sentences. The module follows the Neural Execution Tree framework of (Wang* et al., 2020) when dealing with natural language. First, the explanation is parsed into a logical form by a semantic parser. Previous works have suggested using similar logical forms to improve model training by strict matching on the pool of unlabeled sentences to generate additional labeled data. However, (Wang* et al., 2020) proposes an improved model training paradigm, which relaxes this strict matching constraint, subsequently improving weak labeling coverage and allowing for a larger pool of unlabeled data to be used for model training. Our module does assume each NL explanation can be broken down into a logical form composed of clauses consisting of predicates from four categories—hence the auto-suggest feature in the UI. At weak labeling, the module scores how likely a given unlabeled sentence fits each clause and then constructs an aggregate score representing the match between the logical form and the unlabeled sentence. If the final score is above configurable thresholds, we weakly label the sentence with the appropriate label.

As shown in Fig. 5, the scoring portion of our

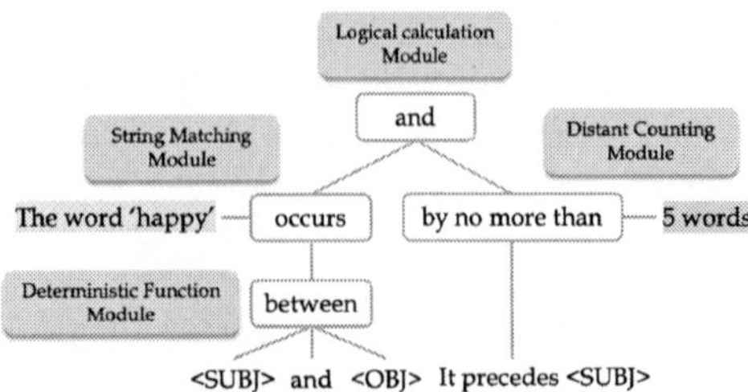

Figure 5: Weakly labeling module for exploiting natural language explanation. the keyword is 'happy'

module has four parts: *String Matching Module, Distant Counting Module, Deterministic Function Module*, and the *Logical Calculation Module*. The first three modules are responsible for evaluating if different clauses in the logical form are applicable for the given unlabeled sentence, while the *Logical Calculation Module's* job is to aggregate scores between the various clauses. The *String Matching Module* returns a sequence of scores $[s_1, s_2, ..., s_n]$ indicating the similarity between each token w_i and the keyword q—"happy" in Fig. 5. Our *Distant Counting Module* aims to relax the distance constraint stated in the explanation, ex: "by no more than 5 words". If the position of keyword q strictly satisfies the constraint, the score is set to 1, otherwise the score decreases as the constraint is less satisfied. Finally, the *Deterministic Function Module* deals with deterministic predicates like "LEFT", "BETWEEN", which can only be exactly matched in terms of the keyword q. Scores are the aggregated by the *Logical Calculation Module* to output a final relevancy score.

5 Experiments

We conduct extensive experiments investigating label efficiency to prove the effectiveness of our annotation models. We found that using natural language explanations for RE and SA, and trigger explanations for NER provided the best results. For the downstream model portion of our weak supervision framework, we use common supervised method for each task: (1-RE) BLSTM+ATT (Bahdanau et al., 2015) adds an attention layer onto LSTM to encode an sequence. (2-SA) ATAE-LSTM (Wang et al., 2016) combines the aspect term information into both the embedding layer and attention layer to help the model concentrate on different parts of a sentence.

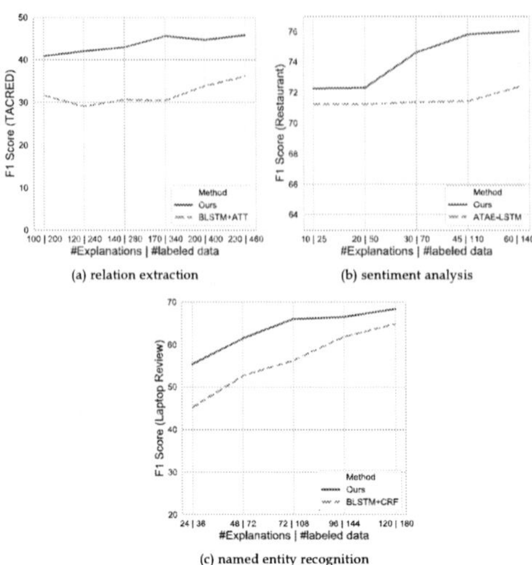

Figure 6: **Label Efficiency**. We choose commonly-used supervised baselines for comparison.

(3-NER) BLSTM+CRF (Ma and Hovy, 2016) encodes character sequences into a vector and concatenates the vector with pre-trained word embeddings to feed into word-level BLSTM. Then, it applies a CRF layer to predict sequence labels. Then we compare these methods as baselines.

Tasks and Datasets We test our implementation on three tasks: RE, SA, NER. We use TACRED (Zhang et al., 2017) for RE, Restaurant review from SemEval 2014 Task 4 for SA, and Laptop reviews (Pontiki et al., 2016) for NER.

Label Efficiency We claim that when starting with little to no labeled data, it is more effective to ask annotators to provide a label and an explanation for the label, than to just request a label. To support this claim, we conduct experiments to demonstrate the label efficiency of our explanation-leveraging-model. We found that the time for labeling one instance plus providing an explanation takes 2X times more time than just simply providing a label. Given this annotation time observation, we compare the performance between our improved training process and the traditional label-only training process by holding annotation time constant between the two trials. This means we expose the label-only supervised model to the appropriate multiple of labeled instances that the label-and-explanation supervised model is shown Fig. 6. Each marker on the x-axis of the plots indicate a certain interval of annotation time, which is represented by the number of label+explanations our augmented model training paradigm is given vs. how many labels the traditional label-only model training is shown. We use the F-1 metric to compare the performances. As shown in Fig. 6, we see that our model not only is more time and label efficient than the label-only training process, but it also outperforms the label-only training process. Given these results, we believe it is worth to request a user to provide both a label and an explanation for the label. Not only does the improvement in performance justify the extra time required to provide the explanation, but we also can achieve higher performance with fewer datapoints / less annotation time.

6 Related Works

Leveraging natural language explanations for additional supervision has been explored by many works. (Srivastava et al., 2017) first demonstrated the idea of using natural language explanations for weak labeling by jointly training a task-specific semantic parser and label classifier to generate weak labels. This method is limited though, as the parser is too tightly coupled to the already labeled data, thus their weak learning framework is not able to build a much larger dataset than the one it already has. To address this issue, (Hancock et al., 2018) proposed a weak supervision framework that utilizes a more practical rule-based semantic parser. The parser constructs a logical form for an explanation that is then used as a labeling function—this resulted in a significant increase of the training set. Another effort can be found in (Camburu et al., 2018) work to extend the Stanford Natural Language Inference dataset with natural language explanations—this extension was done for the important textual entailment recognition task. They demonstrate the usefulness of explanations as an additional training signal for learning more comprehensive sentence representations. Even earlier (Andreas et al., 2016) explored breaking down natural language explanation into linguistic sub-structures for learning collections of neural modules which can be assembled into neural networks. Our framework is very related to the above weak supervision methods via explanation.

Another approach to weak supervision is attempting to transfer knowledge from a related source to the target domain corpus (Lin and Lu, 2018; Lan et al., 2020). Shang et al. (2018) and Yang et al. (2018) proposed using a domain-specific dictionary for matching on the unannotated target corpus. Both efforts employ Partial CRFs (Liu et al., 2014) which assign all possible labels to unlabeled words and maximize the total probability. This approach addresses the incomplete annotation problem, but heavily relies on a domain-specific seed dictionary.

7 Conclusion

In this paper, we propose an open-source web-based annotation framework LEAN-LIFE that not only allows an annotator to provide the needed labels for a task, but can also capture explanation for each labeling decision. Such explanations enable a significant improvement in model training while only doubling per instance annotation time. This increase in per instance annotation time is greatly outweighed by the benefits in model training, especially in a low resource settings, as proven by our experiments. This is an important consideration for any annotation framework, as the quicker the framework is able to train annotation recommendation models to reach high performance, the sooner the user receives useful annotation recommendations, which in turn cut down on the annotation time required per instance.

Better training methods also allow us to fight the potential generation of noisy data due to inaccurate annotation recommendations. We hope that our work on LEAN-LIFE will allow for researches and practitioners alike to more easily obtain useful labeled datasets and models for the various NLP tasks they face.

Acknowledgements

This research is based upon work supported in part by the Office of the Director of National Intelligence (ODNI), Intelligence Advanced Research Projects Activity (IARPA), via Contract No. 2019-19051600007, NSF SMA 18-29268, and Snap research gift. The views and conclusions contained herein are those of the authors and should not be interpreted as necessarily representing the official policies, either expressed or implied, of ODNI, IARPA, or the U.S. Government. We would like to thank all the collaborators in USC INK research lab for their constructive feedback on the work.

References

Jacob Andreas, Marcus Rohrbach, Trevor Darrell, and Dan Klein. 2016. Neural module networks. In *Proceedings of the IEEE Conference on Computer Vision and Pattern Recognition*, pages 39–48.

Dzmitry Bahdanau, Kyunghyun Cho, and Yoshua Bengio. 2015. Neural machine translation by jointly learning to align and translate. In *3rd International Conference on Learning Representations*.

Kalina Bontcheva, Ian Roberts, Leon Derczynski, and Dominic Rout. 2014. The gate crowdsourcing plugin: Crowdsourcing annotated corpora made easy. In *Proc. of EACL*, pages 97–100. Association for Computational Linguistics.

Oana-Maria Camburu, Tim Rocktäschel, Thomas Lukasiewicz, and Phil Blunsom. 2018. e-snli: Natural language inference with natural language explanations. In *Advances in Neural Information Processing Systems 31*, pages 9539–9549. Curran Associates, Inc.

Richard Eckart de Castilho, Eva Mujdricza-Maydt, Seid Muhie Yimam, Silvana Hartmann, Iryna Gurevych, Anette Frank, and Chris Biemann. 2016. A web-based tool for the integrated annotation of semantic and syntactic structures. In *LT4DH@COLING*, pages 76–84. The COLING 2016 Organizing Committee.

Braden Hancock, Paroma Varma, Stephanie Wang, Martin Bringmann, Percy Liang, and Christopher Ré. 2018. Training classifiers with natural language explanations. In *Proceedings of the 56th Annual Meeting of the Association for Computational Linguistics (Volume 1: Long Papers)*, pages 1884–1895, Melbourne, Australia. Association for Computational Linguistics.

Guillaume Lample, Miguel Ballesteros, Sandeep Subramanian, Kazuya Kawakami, and Chris Dyer. 2016. Neural architectures for named entity recognition. In *Proc. of NAACL-HLT*, pages 260–270. Association for Computational Linguistics.

Ouyu Lan, Xiao Huang, Bill Yuchen Lin, He Jiang, Liyuan Liu, and Xiang Ren. 2020. Learning to contextually aggregate multi-source supervision for sequence labeling. In *Proceedings of Association for Computational Linguistics*.

Bill Y. Lin, Frank Xu, Zhiyi Luo, and Kenny Zhu. 2017. Multi-channel BiLSTM-CRF model for emerging named entity recognition in social media. In *Proceedings of the 3rd Workshop on Noisy User-generated Text*, pages 160–165, Copenhagen, Denmark. Association for Computational Linguistics.

Bill Yuchen Lin, Dong-Ho Lee, Ming Shen, Ryan Moreno, Xiao Huang, Prashant Shiralkar, and Xiang Ren. 2020. Triggerner: Learning with entity triggers as explanations for named entity recognition. In *Proceedings of Association for Computational Linguistics*.

Bill Yuchen Lin, Dong-Ho Lee, Frank F. Xu, Ouyu Lan, and Xiang Ren. 2019. AlpacaTag: An active learning-based crowd annotation framework for sequence tagging. In *Proceedings of the 57th Annual Meeting of the Association for Computational Linguistics: System Demonstrations*, pages 58–63, Florence, Italy. Association for Computational Linguistics.

Bill Yuchen Lin and Wei Lu. 2018. Neural adaptation layers for cross-domain named entity recognition. In *Proceedings of the 2018 Conference on Empirical Methods in Natural Language Processing*, pages 2012–2022, Brussels, Belgium. Association for Computational Linguistics.

Yijia Liu, Yue Zhang, Wanxiang Che, Ting Liu, and Fan Wu. 2014. Domain adaptation for CRF-based Chinese word segmentation using free annotations. In *Proceedings of the 2014 Conference on Empirical Methods in Natural Language Processing (EMNLP)*, pages 864–874, Doha, Qatar. Association for Computational Linguistics.

Zhiyi Luo, Shanshan Huang, Frank F. Xu, Bill Yuchen Lin, Hanyuan Shi, and Kenny Zhu. 2018. ExtRA: Extracting prominent review aspects from customer feedback. In *Proceedings of the 2018 Conference on Empirical Methods in Natural Language Processing*, pages 3477–3486, Brussels, Belgium. Association for Computational Linguistics.

Xuezhe Ma and Eduard Hovy. 2016. End-to-end sequence labeling via bi-directional LSTM-CNNs-CRF. In *Proceedings of the 54th Annual Meeting of the Association for Computational Linguistics (Volume 1: Long Papers)*, pages 1064–1074, Berlin, Germany. Association for Computational Linguistics.

Thomas Morton and Jeremy LaCivita. 2003. WordFreak: An open tool for linguistic annotation. In *Companion Volume of the Proceedings of HLT-NAACL 2003 - Demonstrations*, pages 17–18.

Maria Pontiki, Dimitris Galanis, Haris Papageorgiou, Ion Androutsopoulos, Suresh Manandhar, Mohammad AL-Smadi, Mahmoud Al-Ayyoub, Yanyan Zhao, Bing Qin, Orphée De Clercq, Véronique Hoste, Marianna Apidianaki, Xavier Tannier, Natalia Loukachevitch, Evgeniy Kotelnikov, Nuria Bel, Salud María Jiménez-Zafra, and Gülşen Eryiğit. 2016. SemEval-2016 task 5: Aspect based sentiment analysis. In *Proceedings of the 10th International Workshop on Semantic Evaluation (SemEval-2016)*, pages 19–30, San Diego, California. Association for Computational Linguistics.

Jingbo Shang, Liyuan Liu, Xiaotao Gu, Xiang Ren, Teng Ren, and Jiawei Han. 2018. Learning named entity tagger using domain-specific dictionary. In *Proceedings of the 2018 Conference on Empirical Methods in Natural Language Processing*, pages 2054–2064, Brussels, Belgium. Association for Computational Linguistics.

Yanyao Shen, Hyokun Yun, Zachary Lipton, Yakov Kronrod, and Animashree Anandkumar. 2017. Deep active learning for named entity recognition. In *Proceedings of the 2nd Workshop on Representation Learning for NLP*, pages 252–256, Vancouver, Canada. Association for Computational Linguistics.

Shashank Srivastava, Igor Labutov, and Tom Mitchell. 2017. Joint concept learning and semantic parsing from natural language explanations. In *Proceedings of the 2017 Conference on Empirical Methods in Natural Language Processing*, pages 1527–1536, Copenhagen, Denmark. Association for Computational Linguistics.

Pontus Stenetorp, Sampo Pyysalo, Goran Topić, Tomoko Ohta, Sophia Ananiadou, and Jun'ichi Tsujii. 2012. brat: a web-based tool for NLP-assisted text annotation. In *Proceedings of the Demonstrations at the 13th Conference of the European Chapter of the Association for Computational Linguistics*, pages 102–107, Avignon, France. Association for Computational Linguistics.

Yequan Wang, Minlie Huang, Xiaoyan Zhu, and Li Zhao. 2016. Attention-based LSTM for aspect-level sentiment classification. In *Proceedings of the 2016 Conference on Empirical Methods in Natural Language Processing*, pages 606–615, Austin, Texas. Association for Computational Linguistics.

Ziqi Wang*, Yujia Qin*, Wenxuan Zhou, Jun Yan, Qinyuan Ye, Leonardo Neves, Zhiyuan Liu, and Xiang Ren. 2020. Learning from explanations with neural execution tree. In *International Conference on Learning Representations*.

Jie Yang, Yue Zhang, Linwei Li, and Xingxuan Li. 2018a. YEDDA: A lightweight collaborative text span annotation tool. In *Proceedings of ACL 2018, System Demonstrations*, pages 31–36, Melbourne, Australia. Association for Computational Linguistics.

Yaosheng Yang, Wenliang Chen, Zhenghua Li, Zhengqiu He, and Min Zhang. 2018b. Distantly supervised NER with partial annotation learning and reinforcement learning. In *Proceedings of the 27th International Conference on Computational Linguistics*, pages 2159–2169, Santa Fe, New Mexico, USA. Association for Computational Linguistics.

Qinyuan Ye, Liyuan Liu, Maosen Zhang, and Xiang Ren. 2019. Looking beyond label noise: Shifted label distribution matters in distantly supervised relation extraction. In *Proceedings of the 2019 Conference on Empirical Methods in Natural Language Processing and the 9th International Joint Conference on Natural Language Processing (EMNLP-IJCNLP)*, pages 3841–3850, Hong Kong, China. Association for Computational Linguistics.

Daojian Zeng, Kang Liu, Yubo Chen, and Jun Zhao. 2015. Distant supervision for relation extraction via piecewise convolutional neural networks. In *Proceedings of the 2015 Conference on Empirical Methods in Natural Language Processing*, pages 1753–1762, Lisbon, Portugal. Association for Computational Linguistics.

Yuhao Zhang, Victor Zhong, Danqi Chen, Gabor Angeli, and Christopher D. Manning. 2017. Position-aware attention and supervised data improve slot filling. In *Proceedings of the 2017 Conference on Empirical Methods in Natural Language Processing*, pages 35–45, Copenhagen, Denmark. Association for Computational Linguistics.

Wenxuan Zhou, Hongtao Lin, Bill Yuchen Lin, Ziqi Wang, Junyi Du, Leonardo Neves, and Xiang Ren. 2020. Nero: A neural rule grounding framework for label-efficient relation extraction. *The Web Conference*.

What's The Latest? A Question-driven News Chatbot

Philippe Laban
UC Berkeley
phillab@berkeley.edu

John Canny
UC Berkeley
canny@berkeley.edu

Marti A. Hearst
UC Berkeley
hearst@berkeley.edu

Abstract

This work describes an automatic news chatbot that draws content from a diverse set of news articles and creates conversations with a user about the news. Key components of the system include the automatic organization of news articles into topical chatrooms, integration of automatically generated questions into the conversation, and a novel method for choosing which questions to present which avoids repetitive suggestions. We describe the algorithmic framework and present the results of a usability study that shows that news readers using the system successfully engage in multi-turn conversations about specific news stories.

1 Introduction

Chatbots offer the ability for interactive information access, which could be of great value in the news domain. As a user reads through news content, interaction could enable them to ask clarifying questions and go in depth on selected subjects. Current news chatbots have minimal capabilities, with content hand-crafted by members of news organizations, and cannot accept free-form questions.

To address this need, we design a new approach to interacting with large news collections. We designed, built, and evaluated a fully automated news chatbot that bases its content on a stream of news articles from a diverse set of English news sources. This in itself is a novel contribution.

Our second contribution is with respect to the scoping of the chatbot conversation. The system organizes the news articles into chatrooms, each revolving around a *story*, which is a set of automatically grouped news articles about a topic (e.g., articles related to Brexit).

The third contribution is a method to keep track of the state of the conversation to avoid repetition of information. For each news story, we first generate

a set of essential questions and link each question with content that answers it. The motivating idea is: *two pieces of content are redundant if they answer the same questions.* As the user reads content, the system tracks which questions are answered (directly or indirectly) with the content read so far, and which remain unanswered. We evaluate the system through a usability study.

The remainder of this paper is structured as follows. Section 2 describes the system and the content sources, Section 3 describes the algorithm for keeping track of the conversation state, Section 4 provides the results of a usability study evaluation and Section 5 presents relevant prior work.

The system is publicly available at `https://newslens.berkeley.edu/` and a demonstration video is available at this link: `https://www.youtube.com/watch?v=eze9hpEPUgo`.

2 System Description

This section describes the components of the chatbot: the content source, the user interface, the supported user actions and the computed system answers. Appendix A lists library and data resources used in the system.

2.1 Content Sources

We form the content for the chatbot from a set of news sources. We have collected an average of 2,000 news articles per day from 20 international news sources starting in 2010. The news articles are clustered into *stories*: groups of news articles about a similar evolving topic, and each story is automatically named (Laban and Hearst, 2017). Some of the top stories at the time of writing are shown in Figure 1(a).

2.2 User Interface

The chatbot supports information-seeking: the user is seeking information and the system delivers in-

Proceedings of the 58th Annual Meeting of the Association for Computational Linguistics, pages 380–387
July 5 - July 10, 2020. ©2020 Association for Computational Linguistics

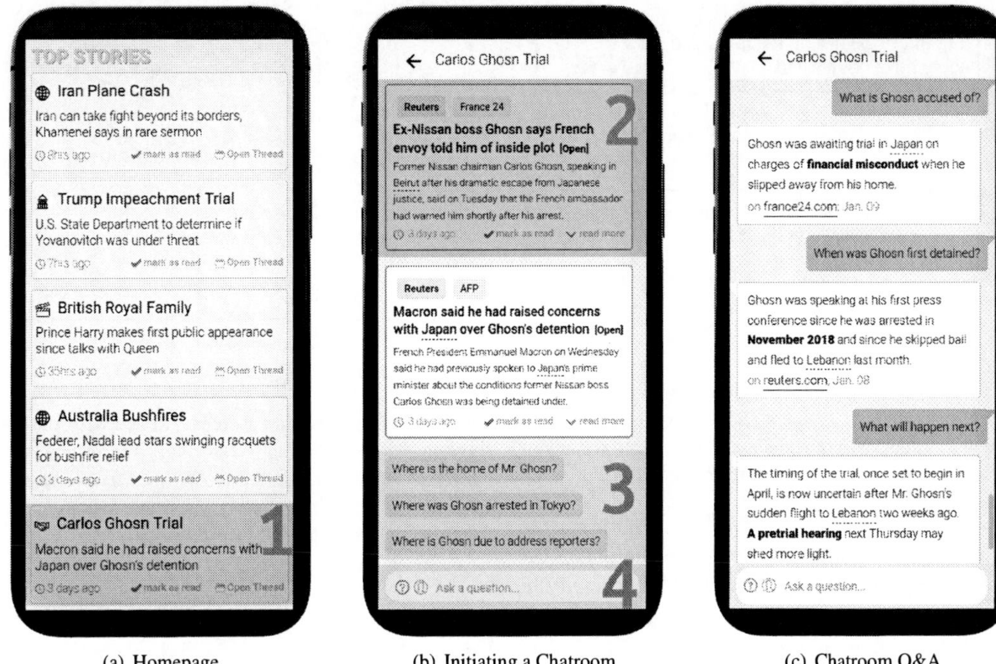

(a) Homepage   (b) Initiating a Chatroom   (c) Chatroom Q&A

Figure 1: **Screenshots of the news chatbot** (a) Homepage lists most recently active chatrooms (Zone 1 is an example chatroom) (b) Newly opened chatroom: Zone 2 is an event message, Zone 3 the Question Recommendation module, and Zone 4 a text input for user-initiated questions. Event messages are created via abstractive summarization. (c) Conversation continuation with Q&A examples. Sentences shown are extracted from original articles, whose sources are shown. Answers to questions are bolded.

formation in the form of news content.

The homepage (Figure 1(a)) lists the most active stories, and a user can select a story to enter its respective chatroom (Figure 1(b)). The separation into story-specific rooms achieves two objectives: (1) clarity to the user, as the chatrooms allow the user to exit and enter chatrooms to come back to conversations, and (2) limiting the scope of each dialogue is helpful from both a usability and a technical standpoint, as it helps reduce ambiguity and search scope. For example, answering a question like: "What is the total cost to insurers so far?" is easier when knowing the scope is the Australia Fires, compared to all of news.

Articles in a story are grouped into events, corresponding to an action that occurred in a particular time and place. For each event, the system forms an *event message* by combining the event's news article headlines generated by an abstractive summarizer model (Laban et al., 2020).

Zone 2 in Figure 1(b) gives an example of an event message. The event messages form a chronological timeline in the story.

Because of the difference in respective roles, we expect user messages to be shorter than system responses, which we aim to be around 30 words.

2.3 User Actions

During the conversation, the user can choose among different kinds of actions.

Explore the event timeline. A chatroom conversation starts with the system showing the two most recent event messages of the story (Figure 1(b)). These messages give minimal context to the user necessary to start a conversation. When the event timeline holds more than two events, a "See previous events" button is added at the top of the conversation, allowing the user to go further back in the event timeline of the story.

Clarify a concept. The user can ask a clarification question regarding a person or organization (e.g., Who is Dennis Muilenburg?), a place (e.g., Where is Lebanon?) or an acronym (e.g., What does NATO stand for?). For a predetermined list of questions, the system will see if an appropriate Wikipedia entry exists, and will respond with the

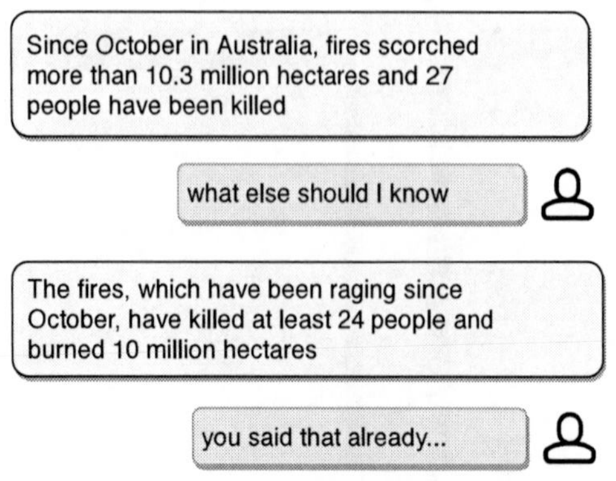

Figure 2: **Example of repetition from the system.** Repeating facts with different language is undesirable in a news chatbot. We introduce a novel question tracking method that attempts to minimize repetition.

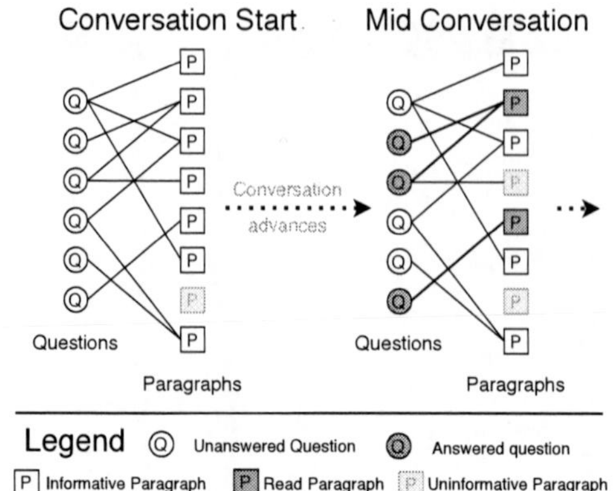

Figure 3: **Conversation state is tracked with the P/Q graph.** As the conversation advances, the system keeps track of answered questions. Any paragraph that does not answer a new question is discarded. Questions that are not answered yet are recommended.

first two paragraphs of the Wikipedia page. For geographical entities, the system additionally responds with a geographic map when possible.

Ask an open-ended question. A text box (Zone 4 in Figure 1(b)) can be used to ask any free-form question about the story. A Q&A system described in Section 3 attempts to find the answer in any paragraph of any news article of the story. If the Q&A system reaches a confidence level about at least one paragraph containing an answer to the question, the chatbot system answers the question using one of the paragraphs. In the system reply the Q&A selected answer is bolded. Figure 1(c) shows several Q&A exchanges.

Select a recommended question. A list of three questions generated by the algorithm described in Section 3 is suggested to the user at the bottom of the conversation (Zone 3 in Figure 1(b)). Clicking on a recommended questions corresponds to asking the question in free-form. However, because recommended questions are known in advance, we pre-compute their answers to minimize user waiting times.

3   Conversation State

One key problem in dialogue systems is that of keeping track of conveyed information, and avoiding repetition in system replies (see example in Figure 2). This problem is amplified in the news setting, where different news organizations cover content redundantly.

We propose a solution that takes advantage of a Question and Answer (Q&A) system. As noted above, the motivating idea is that two pieces of content are redundant if they answer the same questions. In the example of Figure 2, both system messages answer the same set of questions, namely: "When did the fires start?", "How many people have died?" and "How many hectares have burned?", and can therefore be considered redundant.

Our procedure to track the knowledge state of a news conversation consists of the following steps: (1) generate candidate questions spanning the knowledge in the story, (2) build a graph connecting paragraphs with questions they answer, (3) during a conversation, use the graph to track what questions have been answered already, and avoid using paragraphs that do not answer new questions.

Question Candidate Generation. We fine-tune a GPT2 language model (Radford et al., 2019) on the task of question generation using the SQuAD 2.0 dataset (Rajpurkar et al., 2018). At training, the model reads a paragraph from the training set, and learns to generate a question associated with the paragraph. For each paragraph in each article of the story (the paragraph set), we use beam search to generate K candidate questions. In our experience, using a large beam size (K=20) is important, as one paragraph can yield several valid questions. Beam search enforces exploration, with the first step of beam search often containing several interrogative words (what, where...).

For a given paragraph, we reduce the set of questions by deduplicating questions that are lexically close (differ by at most 2 words), and removing questions that are too long (>12 words) or too short ($<$5 words).

Building the P/Q graph. We train a standard Q&A model, a Roberta model (Liu et al., 2019) finetuned on SQuAD 2.0 (Rajpurkar et al., 2018), and use this model to build a paragraph / question bipartite graph (P/Q graph). In the P/Q graph, we connect any paragraph (P node), with a question (Q node), if the Q&A model is confident that paragraph P answers question Q. An example bipartite graph obtained is illustrated in Figure 3, with the question set on the left, the paragraph set on the right, and edges between them representing model confidence about the answer.

Because we used a large beam-size when generating the questions, we perform a pruning step on the questions set. Our pruning procedure is based on the realization that two questions are redundant if they connect to the same subset of paragraphs (they cover the same content). Our objective is to find the smallest set of questions that cover all paragraphs. This problem can be formulated as a standard graph theory problem known as the set cover problem, and we use a standard heuristic algorithm (Caprara et al., 1999). After pruning, we obtain a final P/Q graph, a subgraph of the original consisting only of the covering set questions.

The P/Q graph embodies interesting properties. First, the degree of a question node measures how often a question is answered by distinct paragraphs, providing a measure of the question's importance to the story. The degree of a paragraph node indicates how many distinct questions it answers, an estimate of its relevance to a potential reader. Finally, the graph can be used to measure question relatedness: if two questions have non-empty neighboring sets (i.e., some paragraphs answer both questions), they are likely to be related questions, which can be used as a way to suggest follow-up questions.

Using the P/Q graph. At the start of a conversation, no question is answered, since no paragraph has been shown to the user. Therefore, the system initializes a blank P/Q graph (left graph in Figure 3). As the system reveals paragraphs in the conversation, they are marked as *read* in the P/Q graph (shaded blue paragraphs in the right graph of Figure 3). According to our Q&A model, any question connected to a read paragraph is *answered*, so we mark all neighbors of read paragraphs as answered questions (shaded blue questions on the right graph of Figure 3). At any stage in the conversation, if a paragraph is connected to only answered questions, it is deemed *uninformative*, as it will not reveal the answer to a new question.

As the conversation moves along, more paragraphs are read, increasing the number of answered questions, which in turn, increases the number of uninformative paragraphs. We program the system to prioritize paragraphs that answer the most unanswered questions, and disregard uninformative paragraphs. We further use the P/Q graph to recommend questions to the user. We select unanswered questions and prioritize questions connected to more unread paragraphs, recommending questions three at a time.

4 Study Results

We conducted a usability study in which participants were assigned randomly to one of three configurations:

- TOPQR: the recommended questions are the most informative according to the algorithm in Section 3 (N=18),

- RANDQR: the recommended questions are randomly sampled from the questions TOPQR would not select (however, near duplicates will appear in this set) (N=16),

- NOQR: No questions are recommended, and the Question Recommendation module (Zone 3 in Figure 1(b)) is hidden (N=22).

These are contrasted in order to test (a) if showing automatically generated questions is beneficial to news readers, and (b) to assess the question tracking algorithm against a similar question recommendation method with no conversation state.

4.1 Study Setup

We used Amazon Mechanical Turk to recruit participants, restricting the task to workers in English-speaking countries having previous completed 1500 tasks (HITs) and an acceptance rate of at least 97%. Each participant was paid a flat rate of $2.50 with the study lasting a total of 15 minutes. During the study, the participants first walked through an introduction to the system, then read the news for 8 minutes, and finally completed a short survey.

During the eight minutes of news reading, participants were requested to select at least 2 stories to read from a list of the 20 most recently active

Measured Value	TOPQR	RANDQR	NOQR
# participants	18	16	22
# chatrooms opened	3.2	2.9	3.1
# msgs. / chatroom	24.9 *	15.3 *	8.1
# rec. questions asked	11.9 *	8.2 *	-
# own questions asked	1.5	1.1	2.2
# total questions asked	13.4 *	9.3 *	2.2
latency (seconds)	1.84 *	1.88 *	4.51

Table 1: **Usage statistics of the news chatbot during the usability study.** Participants either saw most informative recommended questions (TOPQR), randomly selected recommended questions (RANDQR) or no recommended questions (NOQR). $*$ signifies statistical difference with NOQR ($p < 0.05$).

Measured Value	TOPQR	RANDQR	NOQR
(1) dull ... stimulating (7)	5.28 *	5.06	4.20
(1) frustrating ... satisfying (7)	5.00 *	4.43	4.00
(1) rigid ... flexible (7)	4.71	4.66	4.14
(1) terrible ... wonderful (7)	4.79	4.69	4.20
exploring new features	5.80	5.50	5.14
learning to operate	5.40	5.25	5.06
performing task is straightforward	5.40	5.56	5.20
system reliability	5.80	5.19	5.67
system speed	6.20	5.87	5.44
rec. questions are clear	5.78 *	4.87	4.28
answers are informative	5.07 *	4.44	3.64

Table 2: **QUIS satisfaction results.** Likert values on a scale from 1 to 7, higher is better unless stated otherwise. $*$ signifies statistical difference with NOQR ($p < 0.05$).

news stories.[1] The participants were prompted to choose stories they were interested in.

The survey consisted of two sections: a satisfaction section, and a section for general free-form feedback. The satisfaction of the participants was surveyed using the standard Questionnaire for User Interaction Satisfaction (QUIS) (Norman et al., 1998). QUIS is a series of questions about the usability of the system (ease of use, learning curve, error messages clearness, etc.) answered on a 7-point Likert scale. We modify QUIS by adding two questions regarding questions and answers: "Are suggested questions clear?" and "Are answers to questions informative?" A total of fifty-six participants completed the study. We report on the usage of the system, the QUIS Satisfaction results and textual comments from the participants.

4.2 Usage statistics

We observed that participants in the QR-enabled interfaces (TOPQR and RANDQR) had longer conversations than the NOQR setting, with an average chatroom conversation length of 24.9 messages in the TOPQR setting. Even though the TOPQR setting had average conversation length longer than RANDQR, this was not statistically significant.

This increase in conversation length is mostly due to the use of recommended questions, which are convenient to click on. Indeed, users clicked on 8.2 questions on average in RANDQR and 11.9 in TOPQR. NOQR participants wrote on average 2.2 of their own questions, which was not statistically higher than TOPQR (1.5) and RANDQR (1.1), showing that seeing recommended questions

---

[1]We manually removed news stories that were predominantly about politics, to avoid heated political questions, which were not under study here.

did not prevent participants from asking their own questions.

When measuring the latency of system answers to participant questions, we observe that the average wait time in TOPQR (1.84 seconds) and RANDQR (1.88 seconds) settings is significantly lower than NOQR (4.51 seconds). This speedup is due to our ability to pre-compute answers to recommended questions, an additional benefit of the QR graph pre-computation.

4.3 QUIS Satisfaction Scores

Overall, the systems with question recommendation enabled (TOPQR and RANDQR) obtained higher average satisfaction on most measures than the NOQR setting. That said, statistical significance was only observed in 4 cases between TOPQR and NOQR, with participants judging the TOPQR interface to be more stimulating and satisfying.

Although not statistically significant, participants rated the suggested questions for TOPQR almost 1 point higher than RANDQR, providing some evidence that incorporating past viewed information into question selection is beneficial.

Participants judged the answers to be more informative in the TOPQR setting. We interpret this as evidence that the QR module helps teach users what types of questions the system can answer, enabling them to get better answers. Several NOQR participants asked "What can I ask?" or equivalent.

4.4 Qualitative Feedback

Thirty-four of the fifty-six participants opted to give general feedback via an open ended text box. We tagged the responses into major themes:

1. 19 participants (7 TOPQR, 7 RANDQR, 5 NOQR) expressed interest in the system (e.g., *I enjoyed trying this system out. I particularly liked that stories are drawn from various sources.*)

2. 11 participants (4, 3, 4) mentioned the system did not correctly reply to questions asked (e.g., *Some of the questions kind of weren't answered exactly, especially in the libya article*),

3. 10 participants (2, 3, 5) found an aspect of the interface confusing (e.g., *This system has potential, but as of right now it seems too overloaded and hard to sort through.*)

4. 6 participants (4, 2, 0) thought the questions were useful (e.g., *I especially like the questions at the bottom. Sometimes it helps to remember some basic facts or deepen your understanding*)

The most commonly mentioned limitation was Q&A related errors, a limitation we hope to mitigate as automated Q&A continues progressing.

5 Related Work

News Chatbots. Several news agencies have ventured in the space of dialogue interfaces as a way to attract new audiences. The chatbots are often manually curated for the dialogue medium and advanced NLP machinery such as a Q&A systems are not incorporated into the chatbot.

On BBC's Messenger chatbot[2], a user can enter search queries, such as "latest news" or "Brexit news" and obtain a list of latest BBC articles matching the search criteria. In the chatbot produced by Quartz[3], journalists hand-craft news stories in the form of pre-written dialogues (aka choose-your-own adventure). At each turn, the user can choose from a list of replies, deciding which track of the dialogue-article is followed. CNN[4] has also experimented with choose-your-own adventure articles, with the added ability for small talk.

Relevant Q&A datasets. NewsQA (Trischler et al., 2017) collected a dataset by having a crowd-worker read the summary of a news article and ask a follow-up question. Subsequent crowd-workers answered the question or marked it as not-answerable.

NewsQA's objective was to collect a dataset, and we focus on building a usable dialogue interface for the news with a Q&A component.

CoQA (Reddy et al., 2019) and Quac (Choi et al., 2018) are two datasets collected for questions answering in the context of a dialogue. For both datasets, two crowd-workers (a student and a teacher) have a conversation about a piece of text (hidden to the student in Quac). The student *must ask* questions of the teacher, and the teacher answers using extracts of the document. In our system, the questions asked by the user are answered automatically, introducing potential errors, and the user can choose to ask questions or not.

In this work, the focus is not on the collection of naturally occurring questions, but in putting a Q&A system in use in a news dialogue system, and observing the extent of its use.

Question Generation (QG) has become an active area for text generation. A common approach is to use a sequence to sequence model (Du et al., 2017), encoding the paragraph (or context), an optional target answer (answer-aware (Sun et al., 2018)), and decoding a paired question. This common approach focuses on the generation of a single article, from a single piece of context, often a paragraph. We argue that our framing of the QG problem as the generation of a series of questions spanning several (possibly redundant) documents is a novel task.

Krishna and Iyyer (2019) build a hierarchy of questions generated for a single document; the document is then reorganized into a "Squashed" document, where paragraphs and questions are interleaved. Because our approach is based on using multiple documents as the source, compiling all questions into a single document would be long to read, so we opt for a chatbot.

6 Discussion

During the usability study, we obtained direct and indirect feedback from our users, and we summarize limitations that could be addressed in the system.

Inability to Handle Small Talk. 4 participants attempted to have small talk with the chatbot (e.g. asking "how are you"). The system most often responded inadequately, saying it did not understand the request. Future work may include gently directing users who engage in small talk to a chit-chat-style interface.

---

[2]https://www.messenger.com/t/BBCPolitics
[3]https://www.messenger.com/t/quartznews
[4]https://www.messenger.com/t/cnn

Inaccurate Q&A system. 32% of the participants mentioned that answers are often off-track or irrelevant. This suggests that further improvements in Q&A systems are needed.

Dealing with errors. Within the current framework, errors are bound to happen, and easing the user's path to recovery could improve the user experience.

7   Conclusion

We presented a fully automated news chatbot system, which leverages an average of 2,000 news articles a day from a diverse set of sources to build chatrooms for important news stories. In each room, the system takes note of generated questions that have already been answered, to minimize repetition of information to the news reader.

A usability study reveals that when the chatbot recommends questions, news readers tend to have longer conversations, with an average of 24 messages exchanged. These conversation consist of combination of recommended and user-created questions.

Acknowledgments

We would like to thank Ruchir Baronia for early prototyping and the ACL reviewers for their helpful comments. This work was supported by a Bloomberg Data Science grant. We also gratefully acknowledge support received from an Amazon Web Services Machine Learning Research Award and an NVIDIA Corporation GPU grant.

References

Alberto Caprara, Matteo Fischetti, and Paolo Toth. 1999. A heuristic method for the set covering problem. *Operations research*, 47(5):730–743.

Eunsol Choi, He He, Mohit Iyyer, Mark Yatskar, Wentau Yih, Yejin Choi, Percy Liang, and Luke Zettlemoyer. 2018. Quac: Question answering in context. In *Proceedings of the 2018 Conference on Empirical Methods in Natural Language Processing*, pages 2174–2184.

Xinya Du, Junru Shao, and Claire Cardie. 2017. Learning to ask: Neural question generation for reading comprehension. In *Proceedings of the 55th Annual Meeting of the Association for Computational Linguistics (Volume 1: Long Papers)*, pages 1342–1352.

Kalpesh Krishna and Mohit Iyyer. 2019. Generating question-answer hierarchies. In *ACL*.

Philippe Laban and Marti A Hearst. 2017. newslens: building and visualizing long-ranging news stories. In *Proceedings of the Events and Stories in the News Workshop*, pages 1–9.

Philippe Laban, Andrew Hsi, John Canny, and Marti A Hearst. 2020. The summary loop: Learning to write abstractive summaries without examples. In *Proceedings of the 58th Annual Meeting of the Association for Computational Linguistics (Volume 1: Long Papers)*. To appear.

Yinhan Liu, Myle Ott, Naman Goyal, Jingfei Du, Mandar Joshi, Danqi Chen, Omer Levy, Mike Lewis, Luke Zettlemoyer, and Veselin Stoyanov. 2019. Roberta: A robustly optimized bert pretraining approach. *arXiv preprint arXiv:1907.11692*.

Kent L Norman, Ben Shneiderman, B Harper, and L Slaughter. 1998. Questionnaire for user interaction satisfaction. *University of Maryland (Norman, 1989) Disponível em*.

Alec Radford, Jeffrey Wu, Rewon Child, David Luan, Dario Amodei, and Ilya Sutskever. 2019. Language models are unsupervised multitask learners.

Pranav Rajpurkar, Robin Jia, and Percy Liang. 2018. Know what you don't know: Unanswerable questions for squad. In *Proceedings of the 56th Annual Meeting of the Association for Computational Linguistics (Volume 2: Short Papers)*, pages 784–789.

Siva Reddy, Danqi Chen, and Christopher D Manning. 2019. Coqa: A conversational question answering challenge. *Transactions of the Association for Computational Linguistics*, 7:249–266.

Xingwu Sun, Jing Liu, Yajuan Lyu, Wei He, Yanjun Ma, and Shi Wang. 2018. Answer-focused and position-aware neural question generation. In *Proceedings of the 2018 Conference on Empirical Methods in Natural Language Processing*, pages 3930–3939.

Adam Trischler, Tong Wang, Xingdi Yuan, Justin Harris, Alessandro Sordoni, Philip Bachman, and Kaheer Suleman. 2017. Newsqa: A machine comprehension dataset. In *Proceedings of the 2nd Workshop on Representation Learning for NLP*, pages 191–200.

A Resources Used

The libraries and data sources used in the described system are as follows:

Transformers library[5] used to train the GPT2-based Question Generation model and the Roberta-based Q&A model.

spaCy library[6] used to do named-entity extraction, phrase and keyword extraction.

Wikidata[7] for entity linking and collection of textual content of relevant Wikipedia pages used in special case questions.

MongoDB[8] and **Flask**[9] for storing and serving the content to the user.

SetCoverPy[10] for its implementation of standard set cover algorithms in Python.

List of news sources present in the dataset used by the system, in alphabetical order: Aa.com.tr, Afp.com, Aljazeera.com, Allafrica.com, Apnews.com, Bbc.co.uk, Bloomberg.com, Chicagotribune.com, Chinadaily.com.cn, Cnet.com, Cnn.com, Foxnews.com, France24.com, Independent.co.uk, Indiatimes.com, Latimes.com, Mercopress.com, Middleeasteye.net, Nytimes.com, Reuters.com, Rt.com, Techcrunch.com, Telegraph.co.uk, Theguardian.com, Washingtonpost.com

---

[5] https://github.com/huggingface/transformers
[6] https://github.com/explosion/spaCy
[7] https://www.wikidata.org/
[8] https://www.mongodb.com/
[9] https://flask.palletsprojects.com/en/1.1.x/
[10] https://github.com/guangtunbenzhu/SetCoverPy

Author Index